National Welfare Handbook

27th edition

Carolyn George
David Simmons
Djuna Thurley
Stewart Wright

Child Poverty Action Group

Published by CPAG Ltd
1-5 Bath Street, London EC1V 9PY

© CPAG Ltd 1997

A CIP record for this book is available from the British Library

ISBN 0 946744 92 0

Design by Devious Designs 0114 275 5634
Typeset by Page Bros, Norwich
Printed by Clays Ltd, Bungay, Suffolk

The authors

Carolyn George is a welfare rights worker with CPAG's Citizens' Rights Office and also works as a part-time lecturer at the University of Northumbria and as a freelance trainer.

David Simmons is a welfare rights worker with the National Association of Citizens' Advice Bureaux.

Djuna Thurley is a welfare rights worker with CPAG's Citizens' Rights Office.

Stewart Wright is a barrister in a London chambers and specialises in social security law.

Acknowledgements

We are especially grateful to Martin Barnes, Beth Lakhani, Jim McKenny, Kenny McKintyre, Susan Mitchell, David Thomas and Lynn Webster for their meticulous checking and helpful suggestions. We are also grateful to Lynn Webster and Geoff Tait for reading and commenting on the manuscript.

We would like to thank the many contributors who have come before and, in particular, those who have worked on the post-1988 versions of this *Handbook:* Martin Barnes, Sarah Campling, Rob Good, Andrew Grealey, Janet Gurney, John Hannam, Ian Hillier, Beth Lakhani, Jan Luba, Jim McKenny, Lee Ogilby-Webb, Anna Ravetz, Marcus Revell, Jim Read, Mark Rowland, Geoff Tait, Gary Vaux, Penny Waterhouse, Lynn Webster and Penny Wood.

We would also like to acknowledge the generous help given by staff at the DSS, Benefits Agency, Further Education Funding Council, Independent Tribunal Service President's Office and the Department for Employment and Education; their co-operation has been invaluable.

Thanks are also due to Frances Ellery, Deborah Lyttelton and Mary Shirley for their editorial and production work; to Paula McDiarmid for her proofreading; and to Katherine Dawson and Andrew Land for their swift and conscientious indexing.

Finally we would like to say thank you to the staff of Page Bros and Clays Ltd for keeping to a very tight schedule.

The law covered in this book was correct on 18 March 1997 and includes regulations laid up to this date.

Contents

Abbreviations used in the text

AA	Attendance allowance
AMA	Adjudicating medical authority
AO	Adjudication officer
BAMS	Benefits Agency Medical Service
CCB	Community charge benefit
CSA	Child Support Agency
CTB	Council tax benefit
DAT	Disability appeal tribunal
DLA	Disability living allowance
DSS	Department of Social Security
DWA	Disability working allowance
EC	European Community
EEA	European Economic Area
EEC	European Economic Community
ECJ	European Court of Justice
EMO	Examining medical officer
EOC	Equal Opportunities Commission
ETU	Earnings top-up
EU	European Union
FC	Family credit
GP	General practitioner
HB	Housing benefit
ICA	Invalid care allowance
IB	Incapacity benefit
IS	Income support
ITS	Industrial Tribunal Service
JSA	Jobseeker's allowance
MAT	Medical appeal tribunal
PAYE	Pay-as-you-earn
REA	Reduced earnings allowance
SDA	Severe disablement allowance
SERPS	State Earnings Related Pension Scheme
SMP	Statutory maternity pay
SSAT	Social security appeal tribunal
SSP	Statutory sick pay
UB	Unemployment benefit

Means-tested benefit rates

Income support/income-based jobseeker's allowance applicable amounts £

Personal allowances

under 18* (usual rate)	29.60
under 18* (in certain circumstances)	38.90
aged 18-24	38.90
aged 25 or over	49.15

Single parent

under 18* (usual rate)	29.60
under 18* (in certain circumstances)	38.90
aged 18 or over	49.15

Couple

both under 18*	58.70
both 18 or over	77.15

Dependent children

0 – September after 11th birthday	16.90
September after 11th birthday – September after 16th birthday	24.75
September after 16th birthday – day before 19th birthday	29.60

Dependent children with protected roles

aged 11 before 7 April 1997	24.75
aged 16 before 7 April 1997	29.60
aged 18 before 7 April 1997	38.90

For eligibility of under-18s and calculating amounts, see pp57-58

Premiums

Family premium	10.80
Family premium – lone parent rate	15.75
Disabled child	20.95

Pensioner

single	19.65
couple	29.65

Enhanced pensioner

single	21.85
couple	32.75

	£
Higher pensioner	
single	26.55
couple	38.00
Disability	
single	20.95
couple	29.90
Severe disability	
single	37.15
couple (if one qualifies)	37.15
couple (if both qualify)	74.30
Carers	13.35

Some claimants have their applicable amount calculated differently. This applies to claimants who are:

- only entitled to the urgent cases rate – see p46
- subject to a child support benefit penalty – see p110
- voluntarily unemployed – see p54
- on strike – see p58
- in residential care or nursing homes – see p84
- in hospital – see p94
- prisoners – see p98
- without accommodation – see p99.

Housing benefit applicable amounts

Personal allowances and premiums as for income support, except

single person aged 16-24	38.90
single parent under 18	38.90
family premium – lone parent rate	22.05
couple both under 18	58.70

Council tax benefit

Personal allowances and premiums as for income support, except

family premium – lone parent rate	22.05

Family credit

Adult credit	47.65
Premium for working 30 hours or more	10.55
*Child credit**	
under 11	12.05
aged 11-15	19.95
aged 16-17	24.80
aged 18	34.70
Applicable amount (ie, threshold level)	77.15

Disability working allowance   £

Adult credit

single	49.55
couple/lone parent	77.55
Premium for working 30 hours or more	10.55

Child credit**

under 11	12.05
aged 11-15	19.95
aged 16-17	24.80
aged 18	34.70

Applicable amount (ie, threshold level)

single	57.85
couple/lone parent	77.15

Social fund payments

Maternity expenses	100.00
Cold weather payment	8.50

Capital limits

Income support	8,000.00
Family credit	8,000.00

Residential accommodation (income support/housing benefit)

upper limit	16,000.00
disregarded	10,000.00
Housing benefit	16,000.00
Council tax benefit	16,000.00
Disability working allowance	16,000.00

**From 7 October 1997, rates for dependants will change from the September after their 11th and 16th birthdays.

Non-means-tested benefit rates

Earnings replacement benefits

	Claimant £pw	Adult dependant £pw	Child dependant £pw
Contribution-based jobseeker's allowance			
under 18	29.60		
under 25	38.90		
25 and over	49.15		
Short-term incapacity benefit			
lower rate	47.10	29.15	
lower rate (over pensionable age)	59.90	35.90	11.20*
higher rate	55.70	29.15	11.20*
higher rate (over pensionable age)	59.90	35.90	11.20*
Long-term incapacity benefit	62.45	37.35	11.20*
Invalidity allowance (transitional)			
higher rate	13.15		
middle rate	8.30		
lower rate	4.15		
Statutory sick pay	55.70		
Severe disablement allowance	37.75	22.40	11.20*
Age related addition –			
higher rate	13.15		
middle rate	8.30		
lower rate	4.15		
Statutory maternity pay (lower rate)	55.70		
Maternity allowance			
higher rate	55.70	29.15	
lower rate	48.35	29.15	
Invalid care allowance	37.35	22.35	11.20*

	Claimant £pw	Adult dependant £pw	Child dependant £pw
Widowed mother's allowance	62.45		11.20*
Widow's pension (55 or over)	62.45		
(45-54)	from 18.74- 58.08		

Retirement pension			
Category A	62.45	37.35	11.20*
Category B for a married woman	37.35		11.20*
Category B for a widow	62.45		11.20*
Category B for a widower	62.45		11.20*
Category C for a person not a married woman	37.35	22.35	11.20*
Category C for a married woman	22.35		11.20*
Category D	37.35		11.20*+

Benefits for the severely disabled

£pw

Attendance allowance
  higher rate 49.50
  lower rate 33.10

Disability living allowance

Care component
  Higher 49.50
  Middle 33.10
  Lower 13.15
Mobility component
  Higher 34.60
  Lower 13.15

Industrial injuries benefits

Disablement benefit - variable, up to 100%
(18 or over)   20.22-101.10

Industrial death benefit

Widow
  higher permanent rate 62.45
  lower permanent rate 18.74
Widower 62.45
Child 11.20*

Benefits for children   £pw
Child benefit
    (for only/eldest child)   11.05
    (for other child(ren)   9.00
    for only/eldest child (lone parent rate) 17.10**
Guardian's allowance   11.20*
Child's special allowance   11.20*

* These are reduced by £1.30 if you receive child benefit for an only or eldest child.
⁺ Increase for child dependant only paid with Category D pension if there is an underlying entitlement to Category A, B or C pension.
** Some lone parents can opt to claim the lower £11.05 rate – see *Rights Guide to Non-Means-Tested Benefits* 1997/98, p169.

Income tax allowances   £pa
Personal allowance   4,045
Married couple allowance   1,830
Additional personal allowance for caring for children   1,830
Blind person's allowance   1,280

National insurance contributions
gross weekly earnings
Below £62   Nil
£62-465   2% on the first £62 and
                           10% on the rest, up to £465

This is the 'contract-in' rate for Class 1 contributions. For other NI rates, see CPAG's *Rights Guide to Non-Means-Tested Benefits*, Chapter 12.

Bands of taxable income (£)   *1996/97*
Lower rate – 20%   £0-£4,100
Basic rate – 23%   £4,101-£26,100
Upper rate – 40%   over £26,100

PART ONE

Introduction

CHAPTER ONE

An introduction to means tests

This *Handbook* covers only 'means-tested' benefits. This chapter explains:

1. Which benefits are means tested (below)
2. The administration of means-tested benefits (p4)
3. How means tests work (p5)

1. WHICH BENEFITS ARE MEANS TESTED

Non-means-tested benefits are those paid with only limited considera-tion of how much money you have (your 'means' of support), provided you satisfy certain basic conditions such as being available for work, disabled or widowed. Examples of non-means-tested benefits are *contribution-based* jobseeker's allowance and incapacity benefit (which replace earnings) and child benefit and disability living allowance (which are to meet specific needs).

To be entitled to some of the earnings replacement benefits you have to have paid sufficient national insurance contributions; for some non-means-tested benefits there is a requirement that you should have lived in Great Britain for a certain length of time. For information about non-means-tested benefits, see CPAG's *Rights Guide to Non-Means-Tested Benefits* (20th edn, 1997/98, £8.95, £3 for claimants) and the *Jobseeker's Allowance Handbook* (2nd edn, 1997/98, £6.95, £2.50 for claimants), both post-free from CPAG Ltd). However, the main benefit rates are included at the front of this book.

By contrast, to be entitled to **means-tested benefits** you do not have to pay any national insurance contributions. Instead, you must satisfy certain basic conditions and your income and capital must be sufficiently low. This involves detailed investigation of your means. The ways means tests work are outlined on pp5–6.

You may be entitled to a combination of non-means-tested and means-tested benefits. For example, you might receive incapacity benefit and child benefit topped up by income support. You might also qualify for help with your rent (housing benefit) and your council tax (council tax benefit).

The **means-tested benefits** covered in this *Handbook* are:

* income support (IS) (p8);
* family credit (FC) (p184);
* disability working allowance (DWA) (p199);
* earnings top-up (ETU) (p197);
* housing benefit (HB) (p214);
* council tax benefit (CTB) (p300);
* social fund (SF) payments (pp410 and 422);
* help with National Health Service charges (p466);
* free milk and vitamins (p478);
* free school meals and other education benefits (Appendix 1);
* housing renovation grants and other local authority grants and services (Appendix 1);
* discretionary payments for disabled people (Appendix 1).

This *Handbook* does not cover *income-based* jobseeker's allowance (JSA). A summary of the basic rules is given in Chapter 4, but for detailed information about income-based JSA, see the *Jobseeker's Allowance Handbook*, 2nd edn, 1997/98.

Some benefits are administered by the Benefits Agency on behalf of the Department of Social Security (DSS) and others are administered by local authorities or other organisations.

Working and entitlement to means-tested benefits

IS is restricted to those who are not working 'full time' (see p13). FC and DWA are restricted to those who are working full time.

* **Benefits only for people not in full-time work:**
  - income support
  - income-based jobseeker's allowance
  - social fund cold weather payments, community care grants and budgeting loans
  - free school meals
* **Benefits only for people in full-time work:**
  - family credit
  - disability working allowance
  - earnings top-up
* **Benefits for people both in and out of work:**
  - housing benefit
  - council tax benefit

- social fund maternity payments, funeral payments and crisis loans
- education benefits (other than free school meals)
- housing renovation grants

2. THE ADMINISTRATION OF MEANS-TESTED BENEFITS

The administration of the various benefits described in this *Handbook* varies enormously depending on who is responsible for them.

- The Benefits Agency administers income support (IS), income-based jobseeker's allowance (JSA), family credit (FC), disability working allowance (DWA) and the social fund (SF) on behalf of the DSS. Initial claims for IS should be made and dealt with locally but most London claims are dealt with centrally by large centres in Glasgow, Belfast and Ashton-in-Makerfield. All FC claims are sent to an office in Blackpool, and DWA claims to an office in Preston.
- The Employment Service deals with claims for JSA.
- Local authorities (usually district councils outside London) administer HB, CTB and housing renovation grants.
- Local education authorities (county councils and metropolitan boroughs outside London) administer education benefits.
- The Health Benefits Division administers health benefits.
- Various other organisations deal with the other benefits covered in Appendix 1.

Standards of service

The Secretary of State sets annual performance targets for the Benefits Agency covering the time it takes to pay benefit, accuracy, customer satisfaction and financial recovery (overpayments and fraud detection). The Agency also sets internal targets after consultation with Ministers. These are included in a national *Business Plan* which is published annually. The Agency is also required to publish a national *Customer Charter*. Local offices should also produce a business plan and customer service statement, and benefit payment targets should be displayed in office waiting rooms.

3. HOW MEANS TESTS WORK

For most benefits there are complicated rules for assessing your needs and resources, and thus your entitlement. Some other benefits are payable once you have qualified for a different means-tested benefit (known as a 'passported' benefit). Other benefits are 'discretionary' and there are no set rules for deciding whether your means are sufficient or whether you should be paid.

The main non-discretionary benefits

- Income support
- Income-based jobseeker's allowance
- Family credit
- Disability working allowance
- Housing benefit
- Council tax benefit
- Health benefits (other than free milk and vitamins)
- Some housing renovation grants

It is not always necessary to consider all the benefits listed above separately because, if you qualify for IS or income-based JSA, you automatically satisfy the means test for the other benefits (excluding FC and DWA).

With the exception of FC and DWA, all the benefits have similar ways of taking account of your needs. These involve adding up personal allowances for each member of the family and then adding on extra amounts to take account of extra expenses you may have because of your circumstances (see Chapter 18).

All the benefits (including FC and DWA) also have similar ways of calculating resources to take into account both your income and your savings and other capital assets. If you have too much capital, you are not entitled to any benefit at all. If you have a lesser amount of capital, it may reduce the amount of benefit to which you are entitled because it is treated as producing an income (see Chapters 19 and 20).

Once your needs and your income have been calculated, your benefit entitlement can be worked out. In the case of IS, income-based JSA and health benefits, that is done simply by deducting your income from your needs. In the cases of HB and CTB, there are more complicated formulae which take into account the amount of your rent or council tax, as well as your other needs and your income. The higher your income, the less benefit you receive, but those with incomes substantially above

IS or income-based JSA level may receive some help. The formulae are set out in Chapters 13 and 16.

FC and DWA are also calculated on the basis of a complicated formula. It takes into account your family's size but is not intended directly to represent your needs (see pp190 and 204).

Passported benefits

Some benefits do not have their own means tests. To be entitled you simply have to be entitled to another 'passporting' benefit. These are:

Passporting benefit	Passported benefit
IS, FC, DWA, income-based JSA	SF maternity expenses payments
IS, FC, DWA, HB, CTB, income-based JSA	SF funeral expenses payments
IS, FC, DWA, income-based JSA	Health benefits
IS, income-based JSA	SF cold weather payments
IS, income-based JSA	SF community care grants and budgeting loans
IS, income-based JSA	Free school meals
IS, income-based JSA	Housing renovation grants

In the case of all SF payments, it is a further condition of entitlement that your capital is not above a certain level (see pp435, 444 and 448). For free school meals there are no other tests. If you are entitled to IS or income-based JSA, your children are entitled to free school meals.

Discretionary benefits

Where a benefit is discretionary, your means are obviously crucial in deciding whether or not to award the benefit. Social fund crisis loans, budgeting loans, community care grants and earnings top-up are paid on a discretionary basis, although certain rules also have to be followed (see Chapters 22, 23 and 24). To get a budgeting loan or community care grant, you must be entitled to IS or income-based JSA.

Where local authorities have the power to make payments for things like school uniforms, they can do it on a purely discretionary basis but often have local means tests similar to the IS means test.

PART TWO

Income support

CHAPTER TWO

The basic rules of entitlement

This chapter covers:
1. Introduction to income support and basic rules (see below)
2. Who can claim income support? (p10)
3. Full-time work (p15)
4. Studying and claiming income support (p16)
5. Presence in and temporary absence from Great Britain (p22)

I. INTRODUCTION

Income support (IS) is a benefit for people with a low income. It is not paid to unemployed people who have to be available for and actively seeking work who may be able to claim jobseeker's allowance instead (see Chapter 4 and CPAG's *Jobseeker's Allowance Handbook*, 2nd edn, 1997/98 for further details). It is not paid to people in full-time work who may be able to claim family credit (FC – see Chapter 10), earnings top-up (ETU - see Chapter 10) or disability working allowance (DWA – see Chapter 11) instead.

If you pay rent or council tax you may be entitled to housing benefit (see Chapter 12) and council tax benefit (see Chapter 16), as well as IS.

If you are entitled to IS you also qualify for:

- health service benefits such as free prescriptions (see Chapter 26); *and*
- education benefits such as free school meals (see Appendix 1).

You may also qualify for social fund payments (see Chapters 21-25).

If you or your partner start working full time (see p13) or increase your earnings and stop getting IS, you might be able to get a back-to-work benefit (see Chapter 9).

The principal conditions

You can claim IS if you satisfy the following rules:[1]

- You are at least 16. If you are at school or college, see p16–22.
- You fit into one of the groups of people who can claim IS (see p10).
- Your income is less than your applicable amount (see p24).
- Your savings and other capital are worth £8,000 or less. If you live in a residential or nursing care home, the capital limit is £16,000 (see p384). Some capital (in particular, your home) may be ignored (see Chapter 20).
- Neither you nor your partner are in full-time paid work (see p13). You can claim if you are temporarily away from full-time work – eg, you are sick.
- You are not in full-time education (although there are exceptions to this rule – see p16). If you are studying part time, see p21.
- You are not getting either income-based or contribution-based jobseeker's allowance and your partner is not getting income-based jobseeker's allowance.
- You satisfy the 'habitual residence test' (see p69) and are present in Great Britain (although there are exceptions to this rule – see p22).

There are some groups of claimants to whom special rules apply. Those rules are covered in Chapter 5.

You do not have to have paid national insurance contributions to qualify for IS.

Who you can claim for

You can claim for your 'family'. See Chapter 17 for who counts as your family. If you do not fit into one of the groups of people who can claim IS, but your partner does (see p10) s/he could be the claimant (see p122). Whichever one of you claims IS, the other should seek advice about how to protect her/his national insurance record. See the *Rights Guide to Non-Means-Tested Benefits*, 20th edn, 1997/98 for more details about national insurance credits.

How to claim

You must claim IS in writing, on form A1 (SP1 for pensioners) which you can obtain free from your local Benefits Agency office. For more detailed information about claims and how they are dealt with, see p122.

You may be able to get a crisis loan from the social fund to tide you over until your benefit is paid (see p446).

You have to make a separate claim to your local authority for housing benefit (see p265) and for council tax benefit (see p310).

2. WHO CAN CLAIM INCOME SUPPORT?

IS is a benefit for people who do not work full time (see p13). You can claim IS if you fit into one of the following groups:

Age

- You are aged 60 or more.
- On 6 October 1996, or at any time in the previous eight weeks:
  - you were aged 50–59; *and*
  - you had not been in full-time work (see p13) for 10 years; *and*
  - you had no prospect of getting full-time work; *and*
  - during the 10 years (see above) you were getting IS without having to sign on as available for and actively seeking work or would not have been required to sign on had you claimed IS.

  If you stop claiming IS for up to eight weeks you can still qualify for IS under this rule when you claim again, so long as you do not work full time during the period.

Sick and disabled people

- You are incapable of work because of illness or disability and you:
  - are receiving statutory sick pay; *or*
  - satisfy the 'own occupation' or 'all-work' test for incapacity benefit; *or*
  - are treated as incapable of work by an adjudication officer, for example because you suffer from a severe condition or have an infectious disease or are blind; *or*
  - are sick but are treated as capable of work because you are disqualified from receiving incapacity benefit due to misconduct or failure to accept treatment.

  (See *Rights Guide to Non-Means-Tested Benefits*, 20th edn, 1997/98.)

  If you have been claiming jobseeker's allowance (JSA) and are only likely to be sick for a short time, you do not necessarily have to claim IS. When you are sick for less than two weeks, you can sometimes continue to claim JSA even though you are incapable of work (see the *Jobseeker's Allowance Handbook*, 2nd edn, 1997/98 for further details).

- You are appealing a decision by the Benefits Agency not to treat you as incapable of work under the 'own occupation test' or the 'all-work' test or under the old incapacity rules that applied before 13 April 1995 (see *Rights Guide to Non-Means-Tested Benefits*, 20th edn; 1997/98 for details). You can get IS until your appeal has been decided. If you are required to satisfy the 'own occupation test' you must continue to send in medical certificates during the period of your appeal. If you are appealing about the 'all-work' test and you do not come within any of the other groups of people who can claim IS, your IS is reduced by 20 per cent of the personal allowance for a single claimant of your age (unless on 12 April 1995 you had been off sick for 28 weeks, or on invalidity benefit or severe disablement allowance, and it is the first time the test has been applied to you).[2] If you are in this situation you would be better off signing on and claiming JSA, but it might be difficult for you to persuade the Employment Service to allow you to do so. If you do sign on as available for work, say you are doing so because the Benefits Agency has said you are capable of work. Signing on should not prejudice your appeal.[3] If your appeal is successful, any reduction in the amount of your benefit, for example because you lose the disability premium (see p333), must be repaid to you.
- You are mentally or physically disabled and because of this your earnings capacity or the number of hours you can work is reduced to 75 per cent or less of that for a person without your disability in the same job.
- You are registered blind (certified blind in Scotland). If you regain your sight you continue to be treated as blind for 28 weeks after you have been taken off the register.
- You work while living in a residential care or nursing home (see p15).

Carers and people with childcare responsibilities

- You are a single parent claiming for a child under 16.
- You are a single person fostering a child under 16 through a local authority or voluntary organisation.
- You are looking after a child under 16 because their parent or the person who usually looks after them is temporarily away or ill.
- You are claiming for a child under 16 and your partner is temporarily out of the UK.
- You are pregnant and unable to work; or there are 11 weeks or less before the week your baby is due, or your baby was born not more than seven weeks ago.
- You are looking after your partner, or a child under 19 for whom you are claiming, who is temporarily ill.

- You are a carer *and*:
  - receive invalid care allowance; *or*
  - the person for whom you care either receives or has been awarded attendance allowance (AA) or the highest or middle rate care component of disability living allowance (DLA); *or*
  - the person for whom you care has claimed AA or DLA. You are entitled to IS for up to 26 weeks from the date of the claim for AA/DLA or until the claim is decided, whichever comes first.

  If you cease meeting these conditions or stop being a carer, you can continue to claim IS for a further eight weeks. After that, you will not get IS unless you fit into one of the other groups of people who can claim described in this chapter.

Pupils, students and people on training courses

- You qualify for IS while in 'relevant education' (see p17).
- You are a disabled student and you satisfy one of the conditions on p20 – definition of 'disabled student'.
- You are a student who can claim IS (see p20).
- You are under 24 and on a Youth Training course being provided by a Training and Enterprise Council (in Scotland, by a Local Enterprise Company). Youth Training is obtained via Youth Credits which have different names in different areas (see *Youthaid Guide to Training and Benefits for Young People* listed in Appendix 4).

  Trainees who are likely to qualify for IS are 16-year-olds on the lower rate training allowance, young people with a dependent child, young people whose IS includes a disability premium (see p333), young people who have to live away from home (see p45) and those aged 18 or over. They include claimants whose severe disablement allowance ceased when they started a training course but who continue to be entitled to the disability premium.[4]

  Some participants in training schemes have the legal status of employees (and are normally given contracts of employment). If you are an employee, you will not qualify for IS if you are in full-time work (see p13). You might qualify for family credit (FC), disability working allowance (DWA) or earnings top-up (ETU) instead (see pp184, 199 and 197).

Others

- You have to go to court as a JP, juror, witness or party to the proceedings.

- You have been remanded in custody, or committed in custody but only until your trial or until you have been sentenced (see p98).
- You are a refugee who is learning English in order to obtain employment. You must be on a course for more than 15 hours a week and, at the time the course started, you must have been in Britain for a year or less. You can get IS for up to nine months.
- You are a 'person from abroad' and are entitled to the urgent cases rate of IS (see p82).
- You are involved in a trade dispute or have been back to work for 15 days or less following a trade dispute (see p58).

3. FULL-TIME WORK

You cannot usually get IS if you or your partner are in full-time paid work.[5] If you are the one claiming IS, this means working 16 hours or more each week. For your partner it means 24 hours or more each week. If you both work less than this, you can still get IS. Paid lunch hours count towards the 16- or 24-hour total.[6] If you or your partner normally work over 16/24 hours or more but are off sick or on maternity leave you can claim. If you work part time and your partner works at least 16 hours but less than 24 hours each week, between you, you might choose to claim family credit (FC) disability working allowance (DWA) or earnings top-up (ETU) (see pp184, 199 and 187). However, you should seek advice before deciding whether to claim. For example, if you are paying a mortgage and can get IS to help you with your housing costs (see Chapter 3), you might be better-off on IS instead of FC, DWA or ETU.

Paid work includes work for which you expect payment. This means you expect to get payment for work you are doing now at some time in the future.[7] You must have a real likelihood of getting payment for your work, not just a hope or desire to make money. A self-employed writer who has never sold a manuscript may well be working with no real expectation of payment and thus not be treated as in full-time work even if s/he spends a lot of time writing.[8] However, if you have set up a business which is not yet making money but is likely to do so in the future – eg, an estate agency – you count as working in expectation of payment. Ultimately it depends on how viable your employment really is.[9]

Where your hours fluctuate, your weekly hours are worked out as follows:

- If you have a regular pattern of work, the average hours worked throughout each work 'cycle' is used – eg, if you regularly work three weeks on and one week off, your hours are the average over the four-week period.

If you work for part of the year only, for example, in a school or other educational establishment and your work cycle is a year, your hours will be averaged in a different way. The school holidays or similar vacations when you do no work are ignored in calculating your average hours. So if you work less than 16 hours a week during term-time only, you are eligible for IS. However, if you work 16 hours or more each week you might be entitled to FC, ETU or DWA instead (see Chapters 10 and 11).[10]

- Where there is no pattern, the average over the five weeks before your claim is used, or a different period if this would be more accurate.[11]
- If you have just started work and no pattern is yet established or your working arrangements have changed and your previous work pattern no longer applies, the number of hours or average of hours you are expected to work each week is used.[12]

Appeal if you think the average was calculated unfairly, unless you are better off claiming FC/ETU/DWA instead (see Chapters 10 and 11).

Exceptions to the 16/24 hour rule

You are treated as in full-time work and are not entitled to IS, even if you work less than 16 hours in a week (in the case of your partner, 24 hours), if:[13]

- you are off work because of a holiday. If you do not get any holiday pay you could try for a crisis loan (see p346);
- you are away from work without a good reason;
- you have ceased full-time work but have received pay in lieu of wages or in lieu of notice or holiday pay from your last job or an *ex gratia* payment in recognition of loss of employment (see p354);[14]
- you or your partner are involved in a trade dispute for seven days or less.[15]

You are not treated as in full-time work even if you work 16/24 hours or more each week if:[16]

- you are disabled and because of this:
  - your earnings are 75 per cent or less of what a person without your disability would reasonably expect to earn, working the same hours in that job, or in a comparable one;

- – your hours of work are 75 per cent or less than a person without your disability would reasonably be expected to do in that or a comparable job;
- you work at home as a childminder (see p362);
- you are on a government training scheme;
- you are working for a charity or voluntary organisation or you are a volunteer and are giving your services free (except for your expenses). Where you receive any nominal payment, even if it is below your earnings disregard, you could be counted as in full-time work. The only way round this is for the organisation to pay you for a specific number of hours a week and for you to be a volunteer for the remainder of the time (but see p380 on notional income);
- you or your partner are involved in a trade dispute and it is more than seven days since the dispute started (see p58). This will also apply for the first 15 days following your return to work after having been involved in a trade dispute;
- you can claim IS because you are caring for someone (see p12 for further information). It is only the hours spent caring that do not count as full-time work. If you do other work as well as being a carer, you must keep your hours in that job below 16/24;
- you are working while living in a residential care or nursing home, or a local authority home. This applies during temporary absences from the home too. It only covers people who are being paid at the special rates for people in homes (see pp84-94);
- you work as a part-time firefighter, auxiliary coastguard, member of the territorial or reserve forces, or at running or launching a lifeboat;
- you are performing duties as a local authority councillor;
- you are a foster parent receiving an allowance for your caring responsibilities.

Self-employed people

The full-time work rule applies to self-employed as well as employed earners. If you simply invest in a business and do not help to run it you are not treated as self-employed.[17]

A key problem for many self-employed people is that they work long hours for little financial reward, sometimes even making a loss. Nevertheless, the work is done in expectation of payment and counts as full-time work. If you are in this position and you are not entitled to FC, ETU or DWA (see Chapters 10 and 11), or it is not enough for your needs, you will need to claim IS or income-based JSA. You can only do this if you reduce your working hours to below 16 or abandon self-employment altogether. If you want to claim income-based JSA, you should seek specialist advice before pursuing this course because there are very strict sanctions if you give up work voluntarily (see the *Jobseeker's Allowance Handbook*, 2nd edn, 1997/98).

There may be a local scheme which pays you an allowance to help you set up your business. This is not considered to be 'payment' in deciding if you are in full-time paid work. However, if you work in your business for 16 hours or more each week and you reasonably expect to receive payment for the work (other than your allowance) you are treated as being in full-time work. If you work less than 16 hours a week, you should check that you still qualify for the allowance because this is usually paid to enable you to work full time.[18]

4. STUDYING AND CLAIMING INCOME SUPPORT

People in full-time education cannot usually qualify for IS, but there are some exceptions. You may be able to claim if you are studying part time (see p21). The rules of entitlement depend partly on your age and partly on your course as follows:

- You count as in 'relevant education' if you are under 19 and on a full-time non-advanced course. (See p17 to find out if you can claim IS.)
- You count as a student if:
  - you are under 19 and on a full-time advanced course (see p20 to find out if you can claim IS.);
  - you are 19 or over but under 60 and on a full-time advanced or non-advanced course. (See p20 to find out if you can claim IS.)

The rules about who can get IS are different for each of the groups above.

If you are not entitled to IS but you have a partner who is not studying, s/he could be the IS claimant instead.

Under 19 in 'relevant education'

If you are under 19 and on a full-time non-advanced course at school or college you count as being in what is known as **'relevant education'**. You usually cannot claim IS,[19] but there are exceptions (see p17).

'Non-advanced course' means a course up to and including A-levels or higher level Scottish certificate of education. Your course is full time if it lasts more than 12 hours a week including instruction, tuition, supervised study, exams, practical work and projects provided for in the curriculum, but not including homework or other unsupervised study and meal breaks.[20] While you are in 'relevant education', your parents (or anyone acting as your parents) can get child benefit for you and claim for you if they get IS or one of the other means-tested benefits (see p325).

Who can get IS while in 'relevant education'?

You can get IS while in 'relevant education' (see p16) if:[21]

- you have a child for whom you can claim (see p325);
- you are so severely disabled that you are unlikely to get a job in the next 12 months;
- you are an orphan, and have no one acting as your parent;
- you have to live away from your parents and any person acting in their place because you are estranged, or you are in physical or moral danger, or there is a serious risk to your physical or mental health, or you have left local authority care and cannot go home. The physical or moral danger does not have to be caused by your parents. Therefore a young person who is a refugee and cannot rejoin her/his parents can claim IS while at school.[22]

  A 'person acting in place of your parents' includes a local authority or voluntary organisation if you are being cared for by them, or foster parents. In the last case this is only until you leave care.[23] It would not include a person who is your sponsor under the immigration laws.[24]

  'Estrangement' implies emotional disharmony,[25] where you have no desire to have any prolonged contact with your parents or they feel similarly towards you. It is possible to be estranged even though your parents are providing some financial support or you still have some contact with them. If you are in care, it is also possible to be estranged from a local authority. If you are, then you could qualify for IS if you have to live away from local authority accommodation;[26]

- you live apart from your parents and any person acting in their place and they are unable to support you *and*:
  - are in prison; *or*
  - are unable to come to Britain because they do not have leave to enter under UK immigration laws;[27] *or*
  - are chronically sick or are mentally or physically disabled. This covers people who could get a disability premium or higher pensioner premium or have an armed forces grant for car costs because of disability or are substantially and permanently disabled;

- you are a refugee and have started a course of 15 hours or more a week to learn English in order to obtain employment during your first year in Britain. This will apply for up to nine months.

Claiming IS when you leave 'relevant education'

Once you have left 'relevant education' (see p16) you might be able to claim IS if you satisfy the rules for getting IS described in this chapter. However, you might continue to be treated as in 'relevant education' after you have stopped studying. The day on which you cease to be treated as in 'relevant education' is called the **terminal date** (see below) but your parents continue to get benefit for you until the end of that week. If you leave school before the legal school-leaving date, you are treated as having stayed on until that date. You are able to get benefit in your own right from the Monday following your terminal date. If you fit into one of the groups of people who can claim, you might get IS (see p10). If not, you might get jobseeker's allowance (if you are 16 or 17 you have to satisfy special rules, see CPAG's *Jobseeker's Allowance Handbook*, 2nd edn, 1997/98). The Monday after your terminal date is also the first day of the **child benefit extension period** (see the *Rights Guide to Non-Means-Tested Benefits*, 1997/98 edn, Chapter 10) during which, if you cannot get benefit in your own right, your parents can go on claiming child benefit and IS or other means-tested benefits for you (see p325).

Terminal dates

Time of leaving school	*Terminal date*
Christmas	First Monday in January
Easter	First Monday after Easter Monday
May/June	First Monday in September

If you return to school or college solely to take exams, you still count as in 'relevant education'. So, for example, if you leave school at Easter and return to take exams in the following term, you will not be able to claim benefit in your own right until the first Monday in September,[28] unless you are a person who can claim while in full-time 'relevant education' (see p17).

You can claim earlier if you are 19 before the appropriate terminal date[29] or if you are able to get IS while in full-time 'relevant education' (see p17) or come within one of the qualifying groups during the final vacation.

Students

If you are a full-time student, you cannot usually claim IS for the duration of your course, including vacations.[30] See p20 for exceptions to this rule. See p21 if you are studying part time.

You count as a student if:[31]

- **You are under 19 and on a full-time course of advanced education.** 'Advanced education' means degree or postgraduate level qualifications, teaching courses, HND, diplomas of higher education, HND or HNC of the Business Technology Education Council or the Scottish Vocational Education Council and all other courses above advanced GNVQ or equivalent, OND, A-levels, highers or Scottish certificate of sixth year studies. See below for what counts as a full-time course.
- **You are 19 or over but under pensionable age** (currently 60 for women and 65 for men) **and on a full-time course of study**. If your course is full time you are treated as a student regardless of the level of the course. See below for what counts as a full-time course.

Full-time courses [32]

In England and Wales your course counts as full time if:

- It is totally or partly funded by the Further Education Funding Council (FEFC) and involves more than 16 hours of **guided learning** each week.

   Courses funded by the FEFC are usually academic or vocational courses leading to a recognised qualification. The FEFC also funds basic literacy and numeracy courses, English as a second language programmes, courses which prepare you to move on to qualification-bearing courses, and courses developing independent living skills for people with learning difficulties. The FEFC does not fund leisure or general interest courses.

   'Guided learning' is not defined by the rules but the Benefits Agency says this means time which is spent in the presence of a teacher, lecturer or demonstrator as opposed to time which you spend doing homework or unsupervised private study at college.[33] Obviously, time which you spend in meal and other breaks cannot be 'guided learning', nor can time spent taking examinations. The number of guided learning hours you do each week will be set out in your learning agreement. This is signed by you and the college. The Benefits Agency will use this agreement to decide whether or not you are on a full-time course.

- It is not funded by the FEFC and is a **full-time course of study**. Whether a course counts as a full-time course depends on the college or university. Definitions are often based on local custom and practice within education authorities, or determined by the demands of course validating bodies, or by the fact that full-time courses can attract more resources. The college or university's definition is not absolutely final, but if you want to challenge it you will have to produce a good argument showing why it should not be accepted.[34] If your course is only for a few hours each week, you should argue that it is not full time. However, a course could be full time even though you only have to attend a few lectures a week.[35]

In Scotland your course counts as full time if:[36]

- It is totally or partly funded by the Secretary of State for Scotland (SOSS) at a college of further education, is not higher education *and*:
  - it involves more than 16 hours a week of classroom based or workshop based programmed learning under the guidance of a teacher; *or*
  - it involves more than 21 hours study a week, 16 hours or less of which involve classroom based or workshop based programmed learning and the rest of which involve using structured learning packages with the help of a teacher.

  The number of hours of 'learning' you do each week will be set out in a document. This is signed by you and the college. The Benefits Agency will use this document to decide whether or not you are on a full-time course.
- It is funded totally or partly by the SOSS and is a full-time course of higher education (see p19 for what counts as a full-time course of study).
- It is not funded by the SOSS and is a full-time course of study at a college of further education (see p19 for what counts as a full-time course of study).

Students who can claim IS

Even if you are a student, you can claim IS if you are:[37]

- a single parent or foster parent of a child under 16; *or*
- a student from abroad and entitled to an urgent cases payment because you are temporarily without funds (see p82); *or*
- a disabled student[38] and you satisfy one of the following conditions:
  - you qualify for the disability premium or severe disability premium (see pp333 and 338);
  - you have been incapable of work for 28 weeks (see p10). Two or more periods when you are incapable of work are joined to form a single period if they are separated by less than eight weeks;
  - you qualify for a disabled students' allowance because you are deaf.

The rules changed on 1 September 1990. If you were a disabled student on IS around that time, see p15 of the 25th edition of the *National Welfare Benefits Handbook; or*

- a couple who are both full-time students and you have a child, and it is the summer vacation; *or*
- a pensioner; *or*
- a refugee learning English (see p13); *or*
- a full-time student under the rules described on pp19–20 but were getting IS while studying part time under the rules that applied until 7 October 1996 (see *National Welfare Benefits Handbook* 1996/97 edn, pp12–16 for further details). You can continue to get IS if:
  - you were getting IS continuously from 31 July 1996 until 7 October 1996; *and*
  - you were not claiming jobseeker's allowance in the week after 7 October 1996; *and*
  - you are on the same course as you were on 31 July 1996; *and*
  - you satisfy the rules for entitlement to IS (see p9) and fit within one of the groups of people who can claim (see p10).

You can get IS until your course ends or you abandon it. You can also get IS during a break in your claim of 12 weeks or less.

Giving up your course

If you abandon your course or are dismissed from it you can claim IS from that date so long as you fit into one of the groups of people who can claim (see p10). However, you cannot claim IS if you are still pursuing your studies by, for example, taking a year out to study for and resit exams, or spending an optional year abroad as part of a language course unless you are a student who can claim IS (see above).[39] If you are not a student who can claim IS and you have to take time off due to sickness, you might be able to claim IS once you count as a 'disabled student' (see p20).

If you are on a sandwich course you count as a student even if you have been unable to find a placement.[40]

Studying part time

You can get IS while studying part time if you fit into one of the groups of people who can claim (see p10). You count as studying part time if:

- you are on a part-time course; *or*
- you are studying part time on a full-time course.[41]

To see if your course counts as full time or part time see pp16–20.

Where you are attending a modular course, whether your course is part time will depend on such things as the number of modules you are taking, the number of hours you study each week and whether the course is one which you could attend part or full time.[42]

5. PRESENCE IN AND TEMPORARY ABSENCE FROM GREAT BRITAIN

Normally you can only get IS while you are living in Great Britain (for more details, see the *Migration and Social Security Handbook*, 2nd edn, 1997). If you have recently come to this country from abroad either for the first time or because you have been living abroad, you must satisfy a 'habitual residence' test (see p69). If you do not satisfy the habitual residence test or you or your partner are a recently-arrived immigrant with restrictions on your stay, see p63.

Once you have established your right to IS, it is possible to claim during temporary absences abroad. Benefit can continue to be paid for up to either four or eight weeks. To qualify for IS while abroad you must have been entitled to IS before you left the country, not expect to be away for more than a year and continue to satisfy the other rules for getting IS described in this chapter while you are away.[43]

Under the **four-week rule** you must also fall within one of the following groups:[44]

- you are going to Northern Ireland. (If you are going there long term, you should sign on at your local office in Northern Ireland and claim IS there);
- you and your partner are both abroad and your partner qualifies for a pensioner, enhanced pensioner, higher pensioner, disability or severe disability premium;
- you are incapable of work *and*:
  - you have been continuously incapable for the previous 28 weeks and you are terminally ill or receiving the highest rate of DLA care component; *or*
  - you have been continuously incapable for 364 days.
  Two or more periods when you are incapable of work are joined together to form a single period if they are separated by less than eight weeks;
- you are incapable of work and going abroad specifically for treatment of the incapacity from an appropriately qualified person. Before you go you should check that the Benefits Agency accepts that this rule applies to you.

However, you will not satisfy the four-week rule if you are:

- in 'relevant education' (see p16);
- involved in a trade dispute, or for the first 15 days after you have returned to work following the dispute;
- receiving an urgent cases payment of IS as a 'person from abroad';
- incapable of work for less than 28 weeks or appealing a decision of the Benefits Agency not to treat you as incapable of work (see p10).

Under the **eight-week rule** you must be taking a child abroad specifically for medical, physiotherapy or similar treatment from an appropriately qualified person. The child must count as part of your family (see p325).

If you qualify for IS under the four- or eight-week rule, your benefit is normally paid to you on your return, but if you are a member of a couple you can ask for it to be paid to your partner during your absence instead. If you are not entitled to IS while abroad or you have already used up your four- or eight-week entitlement, your partner will have to make a claim in her/his own right (see p122).

If it is your partner who goes abroad, your benefit is reduced after four weeks (eight weeks if your partner is taking a child abroad for medical treatment). You are then paid as if you were a single claimant or single parent, but your joint income and capital counts.[45]

While you are temporarily out of the country, you may be entitled to housing benefit to cover your rent, and council tax benefit towards your council tax (see p214 (HB) and p300 (CTB)). If your IS stops, you must make a fresh claim for these benefits.

CHAPTER THREE

How your benefit is calculated

This chapter covers:

1. THE BASIC CALCULATION

The amount of income support (IS) you get depends on your needs – called your 'applicable amount' – and on how much income and capital you have. For the rules on income see Chapter 19, and on capital, Chapter 20.

There are three stages involved in working out your IS.

Calculate your 'applicable amount'

Your applicable amount consists of:

- **personal allowances** (see Chapter 18) for each member of your family; *plus*
- **premiums** (see Chapter 18) for any special needs; *plus*
- **housing costs**, principally for mortgage interest payments, see p25.

Your applicable amount might be reduced if you are:

- unwilling to apply for child support maintenance (see pp108-13); *or*
- not signing on as available for and actively seeking work while appealing a decision of the Benefits Agency that you are not incapable of work under the 'all-work' test (see p11) unless you fit into one of the other groups of people who can claim IS (see p10).

Calculate your income

This is the amount you have coming in each week from other benefits, part-time earnings, maintenance etc (see Chapter 19).

Deduct your income from your applicable amount

Example

Ms Hughes is a single parent aged 27 with a daughter aged 8. She has no housing costs to be covered by IS. Her applicable amount is:

£49.15	personal allowance
£16.90	personal allowance for child aged 8
£15.75	family premium (lone parent rate)
£81.80	Total

Her income is £17.10 child benefit (lone parent rate).

Her IS is £81.80 (applicable amount) minus £17.10 (income) = £64.70.

Different rules for deciding how your benefit is calculated apply to you if you are:

- in local authority residential accommodation (p92);
- in a residential care home or nursing home (p84);
- in hospital (p94);
- a prisoner (p98);
- a person without accommodation (p99);
- 16 or 17 years old (p44);
- a 'person from abroad' (p63);
- affected by a trade dispute (p58).

People who are members of, and fully maintained by, a religious order do not get any IS at all.

You may get more than your normal IS entitlement because you are receiving transitional protection (see p46).

2. HOUSING COSTS

IS can include a variety of payments for your housing costs if:[1]

- the type of housing costs can be met by IS (see p26);
- you, or someone in your family, are liable to pay the housing costs (see p26);

- the housing costs are for the home in which you normally live (see p27).

There are some situations in which you might not get help with housing costs. These are:

- for the first few weeks after you claim. You are expected to rely on mortgage protection payments or other income or savings initially (see p41);
- where you take out a loan while you are on IS or income-based JSA or during a period of 26 weeks between two claims (see p31).

There are also restrictions on the amount you can be paid if:

- your housing costs are too high (see p38);
- you increase a loan while on IS or income-based JSA (see p32).

Which housing costs can be met[2]

Your IS can include the following housing costs:

- mortgage interest payments (see p30);
- interest under a hire purchase agreement taken out to buy your home (see p30);
- interest on loans used to pay for repairs and improvements or to meet a service charge for repairs and improvements (see p34);
- 'other housing costs'
  - rent or ground rent (feu duty in Scotland) if you have a lease of more than 21 years;
  - service charges (though some are excluded – see p35);
  - rentcharge payments;
  - payments under a co-ownership scheme;
  - rent if you are a Crown tenant (minus any water charges);
  - payments for a tent and its pitch if that is your home.

You cannot get housing costs for rent (this is covered by housing benefit (HB) not IS), nor the cost of residential care or nursing home fees (these are treated differently, see p84).[3]

Are you liable to pay housing costs?[4]

If you, or your partner, are liable to pay housing costs (eg, a mortgage or long lease) you can claim help with these costs. You do not have to be legally liable.[5] However, you are not treated as liable to pay housing costs if you pay these to someone who is a member of your household (see p318 for the meaning of household).

You are treated as liable if you share the costs with other members of your household, at least one of whom is liable. In this case, you can be paid for your share,[6] as long as those you share with are not 'close relatives' of yourself or your partner and it is reasonable to treat you as sharing. ('Close relative' means a parent, parent-in-law, son, son-in-law, daughter, daughter-in-law, step-parent, stepson, stepdaughter, brother, sister or the partner of any of these. Sister or brother includes a half-sister or half-brother. An adopted child ceases to be related to her/his natural family on adoption and becomes the relative of her/his adoptive family.[7])

Even if someone else is liable to pay the housing costs, you can claim if that person is not paying and you have to meet the cost yourself in order to continue to live in your home. You must show that it is reasonable for you to pay instead of her/him – eg, where you have given up your home to live with and care for someone and s/he has now gone into a nursing home, or where you have separated from your partner.

If, under the terms of your mortgage, you are not required to pay any interest currently, you cannot receive IS for housing costs. This applies to special mortgage schemes for pensioners where the mortgage is repaid from your estate when you die rather than by regular monthly payments.[8]

If you are on strike your partner is treated as liable for housing costs to enable her/him to make a claim.[9]

Are the housing costs for the home in which you normally live?

Housing costs are paid for the home in which you or a member of your family normally live (see Chapter 17 for who counts as your family). You cannot usually be paid for any other home,[10] but if you have to make payments on two properties, see p29 for exceptions to this rule.

Your home is defined as the building, or part of the building, in which you live and any garage, garden, outbuildings, and other premises and land which it is not reasonable or practicable to sell separately.[11] If you are liable to pay the mortgage on a property but have no immediate intention of living there you cannot get help with the cost.[12]

There are special rules if:

- you have just moved into your home (see p28);
- you are away from home (see p28);
- you are liable to pay housing costs on more than one home (see p29).

Moving house[13]

If you have just moved into your home but were liable to pay housing costs before moving in, your IS can include these costs for a period of up to four weeks before your move if your delay in moving was reasonable, and you claimed IS before moving in, *and*:

• you were waiting for adaptations to be finished that meet needs you or a member of your family have because of a disability; *or*
• you became responsible for the housing costs while you were in hospital or residential care; *or*
• you were waiting for a social fund payment to help you set up home – eg, for help with removal costs or furniture and bedding. This only applies if you have a child of five or under, or you qualify for a pensioner, enhanced pensioner, higher pensioner, disability, severe disability or disabled child premium.

If the earlier IS claim you made before you moved was turned down you must claim again within four weeks of moving in to qualify. The amount for housing costs will not actually be paid until you move in.

Temporary absence from home

If you are temporarily away from home but are still entitled to IS, have not rented out your home and intend to return, your housing costs continue to be paid for a period as follows:

• 13 weeks[14] if you are unlikely to be away for longer than this (but see below);
• 52 weeks[15] if you are unlikely to be away for longer than this (or in exceptional circumstances, unlikely to be away for substantially longer than this) and you are:
  – in hospital;
  – receiving care (approved by a doctor) in the UK or abroad, as long as this is not in a residential care or nursing home;
  – receiving medical treatment or convalescing (approved by a doctor) or your partner or a dependent child is, in the UK or abroad, as long as this is not in a residential care or nursing home;
  – attending a training course away from home in the UK or abroad. Your training course counts if it is provided by or on behalf of or by arrangement with or approved by a government department, the Secretary of State, Scottish Enterprise or Highlands and Islands Enterprise;
  – in a bail hostel or in prison on remand;

- in a residential care or nursing home for short-term or respite care. However, if you are in the home for a trial period to see if you wish to move there permanently, you can only get your housing costs met for 13 weeks.[16] You must intend to return home if the accommodation is not suitable. If the home does not suit your needs you can have further trial periods in other homes, so long as you are not away from home for more than 52 weeks in total;
- providing care for someone living in the UK or abroad and this is approved by a doctor;
- caring for a child whose parent or guardian is receiving medical treatment or care (approved by a doctor) away from home;
- away from home through fear of violence (see below for what counts as violence and below if you need to claim for two homes); *or*
- a student (see p19) who is neither able to get housing costs for two homes nor is a single claimant or a lone parent who is liable to pay housing costs on one but not both of a term time and a home address (see p30).

There is no linking rule with these provisions, which means that a new period can start if you return home even for a short stay – eg, a day or a weekend.[17]

Housing costs for more than one home

If you have to pay housing costs for two homes you can get IS for both:[18]

- for up to four weeks if you have moved into a new home and cannot avoid having to pay for the other one as well;
- indefinitely if you left your home because of either domestic violence or fear of other violence in that home. See p27 for what counts as your home. So long as you left home because of the violence and are still away from home because of it, it does not matter if you were away from home for some other reason during this period – for example, because you were in prison.[19] 'Violence' means violence against you and not caused by you[20] and includes violence in your old home or from a former member of your family. Fear of a racial attack should be covered provided the attack would take place *in* the old home. You will have to show that it is reasonable for you to get payment for two homes. Thus, if you do not intend to return home or someone else is paying the mortgage, you might not get IS for both homes;
- indefinitely if you are one of a couple and you or your partner are a student (see p19) or on a training course (see p28) and living away from your home (see p30).

In all other cases you can only be paid housing costs for one home.

If you have to live in temporary accommodation while essential repairs are done to your normal home and you only have to pay for housing costs for one of the homes, your IS covers those costs.[21] This is not subject to the normal limits on temporary absence from home[22] (see p28). If you have to pay housing costs for both homes, you may be able to claim IS for both for up to four weeks (see p29). After that you are only paid for one home. This could be your normal home if you are unlikely to be away for more than 13 or 52 weeks (see p28) or your temporary home if you will be away for longer.

If you have to live away from your normal home because you are a student (see p19) **or on a training course** (see p28) IS can cover the housing costs as follows:

• if you are one of a couple and have to live apart, you can get IS for both of your homes if it is reasonable for both to be met;[23]
• if you are a single person or lone parent and are having to pay housing costs for *either* your normal home or your term-time accommodation you can get IS for the home for which you pay but not both.[24]

If neither of the above apply you may only get IS for your normal home for up to 52 weeks (see p28).[25]

If you are getting IS for your term-time accommodation and you stop living there during a vacation, you cannot get housing costs unless you are away because you are in hospital.[26]

Mortgages and loans

An amount for mortgage payments is included in your IS applicable amount under the rules described below. We use the term 'mortgage' to refer to mortgages, hire purchase agreements or loans.

It is important to remember that:

• not all loans qualify for help;
• you might not get your full housing costs met initially (see p41);
• deductions can be made if other people live in your home (see p36);
• restrictions might be made – eg, if your housing costs are too high (see p38) or if you increased your loan while on IS or income-based JSA (see p31). For circumstances in which you are allowed to increase your loan, see p32;
• your IS for housing costs only covers interest on your loan(s) and the amount you are paid is calculated in a special way (see p33);
• payment is made direct to the lender (see p140).

You are only paid where your loan qualifies. Your loan qualifies if it was:[27]

- taken out to buy the home in which you live. Loans taken out to pay for materials and labour to build your own home are covered as well as those to buy an existing property.[28] If you have bought an additional interest in the home – eg, by buying out your ex-partner's share in your home after you separated or by purchasing the freehold on a leasehold property[29] or by buying your partner's share back from a trustee in bankruptcy if s/he is bankrupt[30] or by buying out sitting tenants[31] – you can get help with this cost (although if you did this while on IS or income-based JSA you might not get help, see below).

    If all or part of your loan was taken out to pay for something other than your home (eg, to buy a car or set up a business) you cannot get help with the cost even if the loan is secured on your home (but see p43);

- taken out to repay a loan which was itself taken out in order to buy a home (see above). However, if the second loan is also for things that do not qualify for help, for example, to pay debts or to pay for a holiday, you only get help with the amount of the original loan.

Example

Mr Clay took out a new mortgage of £60,000. £45,000 was to pay off the mortgage he took out to buy his home and £15,000 was to pay off business debts. He will get help with the loan for £45,000.

Remember also that even if all of your second loan qualifies, you might not get help if you took out the loan while on IS or income-based JSA (see below).

Even where your home is used for both business and domestic purposes and neither part can be sold off separately, you can only get help with the interest payable on the loan for the part of the property where you live.[32]

If the mortgage was taken out to pay for repairs or improvements, see p34. If you have other housing costs, see p35.

Taking out loans while on IS or income-based JSA[33]

Even if your loan was taken out to buy your home you cannot get IS to help you pay the cost if you took it out during any of the following periods:[34]

- when you were on IS or income-based JSA; *or*

* when you were living as a member of the family with someone who was on IS or income-based JSA (see Chapter 17 for who counts as your family); *or*
* during a period of 26 weeks between two IS or income-based JSA claims as described above.

You can get IS for your housing costs even if one of the above applies if:

* your loan was taken out before 2 May 1994;
* your loan was taken out after 2 May 1994 but you have since stopped getting IS and income-based JSA for more than 26 weeks;[35]
* you re-mortgaged your home to pay off your original house purchase loan,[36] *or* you sold your previous home, paid off a loan which you took out to buy a home or pay for repairs or improvements, and have now taken out a new loan for a new property.[37]

    The original loan must have qualified (see p31) and you must not have taken it out during any of the periods described on pp31-2. You cannot get help with any increase in your housing costs. Thus, if your original mortgage was £30,000 and you took out a new loan for £35,000 to pay this off, you can only get IS housing costs on £30,000 of the second loan;
* you buy your home and immediately beforehand you were in rented accommodation and getting HB. However, your housing costs are restricted to the amount of HB you previously received plus any IS housing costs you were already getting.[38] Subsequent increases in the standard rate of interest or in the 'other housing costs' (see p35) you were already getting are met, and the amount you get does not later reduce if the cost goes down again;[39]
* you were only getting 'other housing costs' (see p35) paid with your IS (eg, as a Crown Tenant) and you then buy a home.[40] However, to begin with you will only get the amount you had been getting for those other costs. This amount can be increased as for those who were formerly in rented accommodation (see above);
* you have taken out, or increased, your loan to buy a home which is better suited than your former home to the needs of a disabled person.[41] The disabled person does not have to be a member of your family nor to have previously lived with you. A 'disabled person' is anybody for whom you or someone living with you is getting a disabled child, disability, enhanced pensioner or higher pensioner premium as well as other people living in your home who would get one of these premiums if they were on IS. It also includes a person who is sick, but, under the incapacity rules, is either disqualified from

receiving benefit or is treated as capable of work (see the *Rights Guide to Non-Means-Tested Benefits*, 20th edn, 1997/98 and p10);
- you have a boy and a girl aged 10 or over and you increased your loan to move to a home where they could have separate bedrooms.[42]

It seems that the rule *is* intended to apply if, following divorce or separation, you buy out your former partner's share of your home – you will not get the mortgage interest paid in relation to that share. Similarly, if you take out a loan or increase an existing loan to buy a home after separation, the rule will in principle apply. However, where couples on IS or income-based JSA separate, it can be argued that each should be entitled to housing costs up to the amount of the loan they were liable to pay when they were together.[43] So, for example, if you were liable to pay a mortgage of £50,000 when you were together, you can argue that you should each be entitled to housing costs on a mortgage of up to £50,000 when you separate.

How are my mortgage payments calculated?

Your IS does not cover the whole of your mortgage payments. You can get help with interest on the loan(s) but not with capital repayments or the cost of associated insurance premiums.[44] Thus claimants with an endowment mortgage will not get the insurance element paid.

Your lender may be prepared to accept interest-only payments for a while and it is important to discuss this with them so that you do not fall into arrears and risk losing your home. If you have to make capital repayments you may be able to increase your income by taking in lodgers (see p374 for how this affects your IS). Payments made direct to the lender by relatives, friends or a charity towards the capital repayments can also be ignored (see p373).

Your IS housing costs are worked out using the amount of your loan which qualifies (see p31) taking into account any restrictions that have been made (see pp31 and 38). A standard rate of interest is used, not what you actually have to pay.[45] IS housing costs are worked out net of tax relief provided this is deducted at source by your lender. The standard rate of interest is set by the DSS and is currently 7.2 per cent. If your repayments are higher because your lender charges a higher rate of interest you will have to meet the shortfall yourself. However, if you are paying less than 5 per cent interest (eg, under a special low-start mortgage scheme) your payments are calculated using the interest rate you pay. If the interest rate on your mortgage goes above 5 per cent, the standard rate will be used.

Your housing costs for repairs and improvements (see p34) are calculated in the same way as for mortgages.

Example

Mr and Mrs Khan have a repayment mortgage. The outstanding loan of £30,000 qualifies (see p31). Tax relief is deducted at source. They pay interest at the rate of 7.5%.

£30,000 x 85% (loan net of tax relief at 15%) x 7.2% (standard interest rate) = £1,836.00

Their weekly IS housing costs are £1,836.00 ÷ 52 = £35.31.

There can be a limit on how much interest will be paid. If your loan is for more than £100,000 you might only be paid interest on this figure (see p38). If your housing costs are lower than this but still thought to be too high they might be restricted (see p39).

Loans for repairs and improvements[46]

It is important to remember that:

* not all loans qualify for help;
* you might not get your full costs met initially (see p41);
* deductions can be made if other people live in your home (see p36);
* your IS only covers interest on your loan(s) and there is a special way the amount you can be paid is calculated (see p33).

IS will not meet the cost of repairs and improvements to the home or the cost of service charges for these (but see p35). However, if you take out a loan to pay for the repairs and improvements or the service charge (or to pay off an earlier loan taken out for this purpose) you may get help with the interest. You must use the loan for the repairs and improvements or service charge within six months (longer if this is reasonable). A bank overdraft you arrange to pay for the repairs or improvements counts as a loan.[47] You can only get help if the repairs or improvements are to maintain your current home,[48] or any part of the building in which it is contained, in a habitable condition. If this applies, you can get interest on a loan to pay for any of the following:

* provision of a bath, shower, toilet, wash basin and the necessary plumbing and hot water;
* repairs to your heating system;
* damp-proof measures;
* provision of ventilation and natural lighting;
* provision of drainage facilities;
* facilities for preparing and cooking food;
* home insulation;

- provision of electric lighting and sockets;
- storage facilities for fuel or refuse;
- repairs of unsafe structural defects;
- adaptations for a disabled person (see p32);
- providing separate bedrooms for children of different sexes aged 10 or over who are part of your family.

If your loan is also for other repairs and improvements, you will only be paid housing costs for the proportion which relates to any of the items listed above.

If your loan is for the right sort of repairs or improvements, the amount payable is calculated as for mortgages – you do not get full help when you first claim (see p41) and the standard interest rate is used (see p33). The restriction on taking out loans while on IS or income-based JSA does not apply to those taken out for repairs and improvements.

Help with 'other housing costs'

You are paid the normal weekly charge for all other housing costs covered by IS.[49] See p26 for what is covered. Where you pay your 'other housing costs' annually or irregularly, the weekly amount will be worked out by dividing what is payable for the year by 52. You might not get your full costs met initially (see p41).

If your other housing costs have been waived because you have paid for repairs or redecoration which are not your responsibility, you can still get IS for them for up to eight weeks.[50]

Service charges

A 'service' is something which is agreed and arranged on your behalf and for which you are required to pay. Thus, if you own a flat and the lessor arranges the exterior painting of the building for which you have to pay a share of the cost, your IS includes this as a service charge. Some service charges are specifically excluded (see the list of ineligible service charges listed on pp231). Some service charges only count if they relate to the provision of 'adequate accommodation' (see p230). In deciding if they do, the adjudication officer must take account of the nature of your accommodation as well as its suitability for your personal needs.[51]

House insurance paid under the terms of your lease can be a service charge, but insurance required by a building society as a condition of your mortgage is not.[52] Service charges to cover minor repairs and maintenance are covered but service charges for repairs and improvements listed on p34 are not – you must take out a loan to pay for these, and the interest on the loan can be covered by IS housing costs (see p34).

Services provided by an outside authority which you arrange yourself are not covered. Thus charges for water and sewerage paid to a water board are not met.[53]

Charges for the following items cannot be met:[54]

- fuel, where this is included in your housing costs. If there is no specific charge for fuel, set deductions are made as follows:

heating	£9.25	lighting	£0.80
hot water	£1.15	cooking	£1.15

- repairs and improvements listed on p34. You are expected to take out a loan to pay for these and can claim the interest as a housing cost (see p34);
- ineligible services listed on p231.

If you normally pay service charges annually you will have to ask if you can make weekly payments.

Calculating your total housing costs

Once you have worked out which housing costs can be met by IS you need to:

- calculate the weekly amount for each;
- add these amounts together;
- deduct any amounts for non-dependants living in your home (see below);
- deduct any restrictions being made because your housing costs are too high (see p38).

Remember that a reduced amount is paid for the early weeks of your claim (see p41).

Deductions for other people living in your home[55]

If other people normally live with you in your home but are not part of your family for benefit purposes (see p318) – they are called 'non-dependants' – a set deduction is usually made from your housing costs. Thus, if an adult son or daughter, or an elderly relative shares your home, you may need to ask her/him for a contribution towards your outgoings.

A person can only be treated as living with you if s/he shares rooms other than a bathroom, toilet or common access areas.[56] This includes people who share the use of a kitchen. A person who is separately liable to pay rent to a landlord is not counted as living with you.

When no deduction is made

No deduction is made from your housing costs if the person living with you is not treated as a 'non-dependant' (though any rent they pay to you will affect the amount of your IS, see p374). A person does not count as a non-dependant if s/he:[57]

- is liable to pay you, or your partner, in order to live in your home – eg, a sub-tenant, licensee or boarder. This also applies to other members of her/his household. The payment must be on a commercial basis. A low charge does not necessarily mean that the arrangement is not commercial, nor do you have to make a profit. An arrangement between friends can be commercial.[58] Close relatives (see p27) count as non-dependants even if they pay for their accommodation;
- is someone other than a close relative (see p27) to whom you, or your partner, are liable to make payments on a commercial basis (ie, as a sub-tenant, licensee or boarder) in order to live in her/his property. Other members of her/his household do not count as non-dependants either;
- jointly occupies your home and is a co-owner or joint tenant with you or your partner. Your joint occupier's partner is not a non-dependant. Close relatives (see p27) who jointly occupy your home are treated as non-dependants unless they had joint liability prior to 11 April 1988 or it existed on or before the date you first lived in the property (or your partner did if s/he is the joint owner/tenant). However, in this situation no non-dependant deduction is made for your close relatives (see p27);
- is employed by a charitable or voluntary organisation as a resident carer for you, or your partner, and you pay for that service (even if the charge is nominal). If the carer's partner also lives in your home s/he does not count as a non-dependant.

Even if you do have a non-dependant in your home no deduction is made if:[59]
- a deduction is already being made from your HB;
- you, or your partner, are blind or treated as blind (see p11);
- you, or your partner, get attendance allowance (or equivalent benefits paid because of injury at work or a war injury) or the care component of disability living allowance.

In addition no deduction is made for a non-dependant who is:

- staying with you but who normally lives elsewhere;
- 16 or 17 years old, or getting a Youth Training allowance;

- a full-time student. This also applies during the summer vacation as long as s/he is not working full time (see p13);
- 18–24 years old and getting IS or income-based JSA;
- not living with you at present because s/he has been in hospital for more than six weeks, or is in prison;
- a co-owner or joint tenant with you, or your partner, even if s/he is a close relative (see p27).

The amount of deductions

If you have a non-dependant living with you who is 18 or over, a fixed amount is usually deducted from your housing costs, whatever s/he pays you. If your non-dependant is working full time (see p13), the amount depends on her/his weekly gross income as follows:

Gross weekly income	*Non-dependant deduction*
£152 or more	£33
£116–151.99	£17
£78–115.99	£13
Less than £78	£ 7

In all other cases, a £7 deduction is made, but see p37 for situations when no deduction is made.

Gross income includes wages before tax and national insurance are deducted plus any other income the non-dependant has (but not attendance allowance, disability living allowance or payments from the Macfarlane Trusts, the Eileen Trust, the Fund or the Independent Living Funds).

A deduction is made for each non-dependant in your home, but if there is more than one and they include a couple only one deduction is made for the couple. In this case their joint income counts and the highest possible deduction is made.

If you are a joint owner with someone other than your partner, any deductions are shared proportionally between you and the other owner(s).

Restrictions if your housing costs are too high

If the mortgages on your home amount to more than £100,000, your housing costs might not be met in full (see p39).[60] This includes all mortgages taken out to buy your home and also any loans for repairs and improvements. The restriction is applied proportionately to each loan. If a loan was taken out to adapt your home for a disabled person (see p32), it is ignored when working out if your loans exceed the maximum. If you are getting housing costs on more than one home (see p29) you can be paid up to this limit for each.[61]

Upper limits for loans have only existed since 2 August 1993 and have changed twice since that date. The limit has been £100,000 since 10 April 1995. However:

- your limit is £125,000 if you have been entitled to IS since 11 April 1994;
- your limit is £150,000 if you have been entitled to IS since 2 August 1993;
- there is no limit if you have been entitled to IS from before 2 August 1993.

If you are uncertain about which limit applies to you, you should seek advice. If you are considering increasing your mortgage or loan, see p31.

Even if you have borrowed less than the limit, housing costs can be restricted if:[62]

- your home (excluding any part which you let) is too big for you and your family. When deciding if your home is too big, a comparison is made with other accommodation which would be suitable given the size of your household. Any non-dependants (see p36) or foster children in your home count as part of your family for this purpose. The needs of everyone in your family must be considered. For example, if a member of your family needs extra space because of a disability, or you have a child or elderly relative in care who regularly comes to stay with you, your need for a large home may be justified;
- the area in which you live is more expensive than other areas where there is accommodation suitable for your needs. An area is 'something more confined, restricted and compact than a locality or district...It might consist of...a number of roads, refer to a neighbourhood and even to a large block of flats.'[63] The area should not be chosen on too wide a basis – ie, you should not be expected to move to a completely different part of the country;
- the outgoings on your home which are met by IS housing costs (see pp30, 34 and 35) are higher than on other properties in the area which are suitable for your needs.

The capital value of your home cannot be taken into account.[64]

No restriction should be made even if suitable accommodation is available if it is not reasonable for you to look for cheaper accommodation. Account should be taken of:[65]

- the general level of housing costs in the area and whether a suitable alternative is available. This means that property must be generally available, not necessarily available to you personally;[66]
- your family circumstances – eg, your employment prospects, the age and state of health of your family members and whether the move would have a detrimental effect on a child's education if s/he would have to change schools.

These are not the only situations which count.[67] A move may not be reasonable where:

- the size of your family would make it difficult to find accommodation;
- you need to be near relatives or friends to provide (or receive) care or support;
- you have moved a number of times recently;
- it would be difficult to sell your property[68] or you have negative equity or selling would cause you financial hardship;[69]
- you have lived in your home for many years and it is now too large because you are separated or divorced, or your children have left home, or your partner has died;
- prior to your claim you were advised by the Benefits Agency that full mortgage interest would be paid;[70]
- you could not get another mortgage on a property.[71]

Even if it is reasonable for you to move, your housing costs should not be restricted for 26 weeks if you, or a member of your family, were able to meet these costs when they were first taken on. Your housing costs are not restricted for a further 26 weeks if you are trying to find cheaper accommodation. If full payment is made initially but later, following a review your housing costs are restricted, the 26-week periods begin from the date of the review.[72] Periods of 12 weeks or less when you were not getting IS or income-based JSA are included when calculating these periods. In addition, if you have only recently become one of a couple or separated from your partner and you make a new claim within 12 weeks, periods when your partner was in receipt of IS count towards the 26-week period.

You should be notified of any intention to restrict your benefit.[73]

If it is appropriate to restrict your housing costs, the amount paid is limited to what you would have to pay for a suitable alternative property. This is a subjective test – if the equity in your property was sufficient to buy a new home outright your IS housing costs could be nil.[74]

If you are left with insufficient money to pay your housing costs you may be in danger of losing your home, particularly if you are on IS for a long time. You should inform your lender and discuss with them how to resolve the situation. You should also seek independent debt advice. Ultimately, you may have to sell your home and buy somewhere cheaper but you could try and make up the shortfall by taking in a lodger (see p374) or finding a part-time job and benefiting from the earnings disregard (see pp357-59). Another way around the problem is to move out and put your house up for sale. The capital value of your house can be disregarded for a period while you take reasonable steps to sell it (see p390).[75] If you also rent it out while trying to sell, the income from any tenants can be disregarded up to the value of any mortgage outgoings which you have on the property.[76]

Reduced payment during the first weeks of your claim

Even if you are entitled to IS to cover your housing costs, these will not be paid until you have been claiming IS for a period.[77] This includes mortgages and loans (see p30), loans for repairs and improvements (see p34) and 'other housing costs' (see p35). However, you can be paid straight away if:[78]

- you or your partner are 60 or over;
- you are claiming for payments as a Crown tenant, under a co-ownership scheme or for a tent.

All other claimants get a reduced amount of help initially. How long this lasts depends on when you took out your mortgage or loan or agreed to pay 'other housing costs' and how long you have been on IS. You are expected to use mortgage protection policy payments, savings or disregarded income to meet any shortfall. If you do not have enough to pay the shortfall you should approach your lender to discuss how you can protect your home.

If you took your loan out or agreed to pay 'other housing costs' before 2 October 1995 (the Benefits Agency calls these 'existing housing costs') you get:[79]

- nothing for the first 8 weeks of your claim;
- 50 per cent of your housing costs for the next 18 weeks;
- full housing costs after 26 weeks on IS.

This 26-week waiting period can also apply if you take out a loan after 2 October 1995, provided it replaces a loan taken out before that date and is with the same lender, for the same property and for the same amount (or lower) as the earlier loan.

If you took your loan out or agreed to pay 'other housing costs' after

1 October 1995 (the Benefits Agency calls these 'new housing costs') you get:[80]

- nothing for the first 39 weeks of your claim;
- full housing costs after 39 weeks on IS.

However, if the loan replaces another loan taken out before 2 October 1995, see above.

Certain claimants are exempt from this 39-week waiting period. Instead the 26-week waiting period described above applies. This is the case if you:[81]

- are a single parent and have claimed IS because your partner has left you or died, unless you become one of a couple again;
- are claiming IS because you are a carer (see p12);
- are in prison awaiting trial or sentence;
- have been refused payments under a mortgage protection policy due to a pre-existing medical condition or because you are HIV positive.

If you have two loans or agreements to pay 'other housing costs' and one was taken out before and one after 1 October 1995, the relevant waiting periods apply to each.[82]

If you have already been entitled to IS for more than 26 or 39 weeks when you take out your loan or agreement to pay 'other housing costs' you can be paid your full housing costs straight away (but see p31 for the rules restricting housing costs if you take out or increase a loan while on IS or income-based JSA).

To help you get full housing costs earlier, you are treated as being on IS for certain weeks prior to your claim even though you were not actually receiving it. You are treated as in receipt of IS:[83]

- for any period when you were getting or were treated as entitled to income-based JSA;[84]
- during a period of 12 weeks or less between two periods when:
  - you were getting IS or income-based JSA; *or*
  - you were treated as entitled to IS or income-based JSA.
  This period is extended to 26 weeks if you were getting full housing costs but stopped getting IS because you received child support maintenance, and this has now reduced as a result of child support rule changes in April 1995 or because an interim maintenance assessment has been replaced or terminated (see the *Child Support Handbook*, 1997/ 98 edn for details);
- any period for which you are awarded IS or income-based JSA after review or an appeal;

- during the time when your partner was claiming IS or income-based JSA on her/his own, provided you make a claim for IS within 12 weeks of becoming a couple;
- during the time when your ex-partner was claiming IS or income-based JSA for you both, provided you claim IS within 12 weeks of separating;
- during the time when your partner was claiming IS or income-based JSA for you both, if you take over the claiming role;
- during the time when someone who was not your partner was claiming IS or income-based JSA for you and another dependent child or young person. You must claim within 12 weeks of this and you must be a member of another family (see p318 for who counts as your family) and be claiming for that other child;
- during periods when you stop getting IS or income-based JSA because you or your partner are doing an employment training or rehabilitation course;
- for up to 39 weeks where you were not entitled to IS because your income or capital was too high *and*.[85]
  - you have been getting contribution-based JSA, unemployment benefit, statutory sick pay or incapacity benefit (or credits for unemployment or incapacity); *or*
  - you are a lone parent or a carer (see p12) and you or someone claiming on your behalf has previously been refused IS. This does not apply if you or your partner are working full-time (see p13), or you are a student who cannot claim IS (see p19) or are temporarily absent from Great Britain and not entitled to IS (see p22).

Where you were not entitled to IS because your income was too high, you are treated as entitled for any period where you were getting payments under a mortgage protection policy. This could be longer than 39 weeks.

If you reclaim IS within 26 weeks of a previous claim during which you were getting housing costs and you have been receiving payments under an employment insurance policy which has since run out, periods when you were getting those payments are ignored in calculating the 26/39-week waiting periods. This means that you can requalify for housing costs sooner.

Transitional protection if you have been claiming since before 2 October 1995

The rules on payment of housing costs changed on 2 October 1995. Some people will qualify for a lower amount of housing costs than they did before that date. However, there are two types of transitional protection which ensure that you should be no worse off than you were under the old rules.

- You can continue to get certain types of housing costs for which, since 2 October 1995, IS can no longer be paid. These are:[86]
  - accumulated arrears of interest;
  - interest on a secured loan which was not for house purchase, taken out when you were one of a couple, where your partner had left and could not or would not pay the cost or had died;
  - interest on a loan for repairs and improvements under the pre-2 October 1995 rules.

  You can continue to get these if they were included in your housing costs before 2 October 1995, for as long as you remain on IS (or are treated as being on IS) and fulfil the qualifying conditions. See the *National Welfare Benefits Handbook*, 1995/96 edn, pp30-32 for more details on how these costs were assessed.
- If you were on IS both on and after 1 October 1995 and the amount of housing costs to which you are now entitled is less because of the new rules, you can get an extra payment to make up the loss.[87]

  This payment is called an 'add-back' and is equal to the difference between what you used to get and your new entitlement. Where you have more than one loan, the 'add-back' for each is calculated separately.

  The 'add-back' reduces if your new entitlement to housing costs increases. You will lose the 'add-back' when your new entitlement equals what you used to get under the old rules. You also lose it if you stop getting IS or income-based JSA for more than 12 weeks or if you cease to qualify for housing costs. If you lose the 'add-back' but your partner makes a claim for you within 12 weeks, s/he can continue to get the 'add-back' to which you were entitled.

3. RATES OF BENEFIT PAID TO 16/17-YEAR-OLDS

Single people and single parents

There are two levels of payment:[88]

- lower rate   £29.60
- higher rate   £38.90

You are paid at the higher rate if:[89]

- you qualify for the disability premium (see p333); *or*

- you are an orphan with no one acting as your parent (which includes foster parents, a local authority or a voluntary organisation if you are in care or are being looked after by them); *or*
- you are living away from parents and any person acting as your parent, and immediately before you were 16 you were in custody, or being looked after by a local authority who placed you with someone other than a close relative (see p27); *or*
- you are living away from parents and any person acting as your parent, and instead are living elsewhere:
  - as part of a programme of resettlement or rehabilitation under the supervision of the probation service or a local authority; *or*
  - to avoid physical or sexual abuse; *or*
  - because you need special accommodation due to mental or physical illness or handicap; *or*
- you are living in accommodation away from your parents and any person acting as your parent, they are unable to support you financially and they are:
  - in custody; *or*
  - unable to enter Great Britain because of the immigration laws; *or*
  - 'chronically sick or mentally or physically disabled' (see p17); *or*
- you have to live away from parents and any person acting as your parent, because:
  - you are estranged from them (see p17); *or*
  - you are in physical or moral danger; *or*
  - there is a serious risk to your physical or mental health.

Couples[90]

The amount paid to couples depends on your ages and whether one or both of you would be eligible for IS as a single person.

- One partner aged 18 or over and the other under   £77.15
  18 *and*
  - entitled to IS (or would be if not a member of a couple); *or*
  - entitled to income-based JSA; *or*
  - entitled to discretionary JSA on grounds of severe hardship
  (see CPAG's *Jobseeker's Allowance Handbook* 2nd edn, 1997/98 for further information about JSA).
- Both under 18 *and*   £58.70
  - both entitled to IS (or would be if not a member of a couple; *or*
  - one is responsible for a child; *or*

- the partner of the person claiming is entitled to income-based JSA; *or*
- the partner of the person claiming is entitled to discretionary JSA on grounds of severe hardship (see above).

- The claimant aged 25 or over and the other under 18 *and*
     £49.15
  - not entitled to IS (even if not a member of a couple); *and*
  - not entitled to income-based JSA; *and*
  - not entitled to discretionary JSA on grounds of severe hardship (see above).
- The claimant is 18–24 and the other under 18 *and*
     £38.90
  - not entitled to IS (even if s/he was not a member of a couple); *and*
  - not entitled to income-based JSA; *and*
  - not entitled to discretionary JSA on grounds of severe hardship (see above).
- Both under 18 and one is entitled to IS at the higher rate for under-18s.
     £38.90
- Both under 18 and one is entitled to IS at the lower rate for under-18s.
     £29.60

4. TRANSITIONAL PROTECTION

Some claimants are paid more than their basic IS entitlement because they receive an amount of transitional protection. This was created when IS replaced supplementary benefit in April 1988 and covers people who were claiming supplementary benefit immediately before 11 April 1988 and have been on IS ever since. For more details see the 19th edition of the *National Welfare Benefits Handbook*. If you do not have this we can supply a photocopy of the relevant parts. Write to CPAG, 1-5 Bath Street, London EC1V 9PY.

5. URGENT CASES PAYMENTS

Who can claim

If you do not satisfy the normal rules for IS, you may be able to get an urgent cases payment if you come within one of the following groups:[91]

- you are a 'person from abroad' and meet certain conditions (see p82);
- you are treated as possessing income which was due to be paid to you but which has not been paid (see p381). If you were due to receive a social security benefit but it has not yet been paid you will not be treated as possessing it. The income you are treated as possessing must not be readily available to you and there must be a likelihood that if you do not get a payment, you or your family will suffer hardship.[92]

Even if your partner is entitled to ordinary IS you can claim urgent cases payments instead if the amount you receive would be higher.

It is important to note that an urgent cases payment is a payment of IS and thus you are automatically eligible for other benefits (see p6).

If you do not come within these rules but have no money, you may be able to get a crisis loan from the social fund (see p446).

How much you can get

Applicable amounts

Urgent cases payments of IS are paid at a reduced rate. Your applicable amount is:

- a personal allowance for you (and your partner). It is paid at 90 per cent of the personal allowance that would have been paid had you qualified for IS in the normal way; *plus*
- full personal allowances for any children; *plus*
- premiums and housing costs or residential allowance, if any, and any 'protected sum' paid because you were a boarder prior to 10 April 1989.[93]

If you are living in a residential or nursing home and have 'preserved rights' (see p85), you receive 90 per cent of the personal allowance for you (and your partner) plus full personal allowances for any children plus the amount normally allowed for your accommodation. You get 98 per cent of the amount paid if you are in a local authority home.[94]

If your benefit is reduced because you are appealing a decision of the Benefits Agency that you are not incapable of work under the 'all-work' test and are not signing on for work in the meantime (see p11) the 20 per cent deduction is applied before the 10 per cent urgent cases reduction.[95]

Income and capital

Almost all of your income and capital is taken into account before an urgent cases payment is made.

Income

All your income counts except the following:[96]

- assumed income from capital between £3,000 and £8,000 (£10,000 and £16,000 if you live in a residential or nursing home – see p375);
- income you are treated as having if you are applying for an urgent cases payment for that reason;
- backdated payments of IS made to you once the Home Office accepts you are a refugee (see p76);
- any housing benefit (HB) and/or council tax benefit;
- any payment made to compensate you for the loss of entitlement to housing benefit supplement or HB;
- any payment from any of the Macfarlane Trusts, the Eileen Trust, the Fund, or the Independent Living Funds;
- payments made by haemophilia sufferers to their partner or children, out of money originally provided by one of the Macfarlane Trusts. If the sufferer has no partner or children, payments made to a parent, step-parent or guardian are also disregarded, but only for two years. These payments are also disregarded if the sufferer dies and the money is paid out of the estate;
- payments arising from the Macfarlane Trusts which are paid by a person to a haemophiliac partner, or to their child(ren).

Certain income is treated as capital if you get IS under the normal rules (see p389). However, if you apply for an urgent cases payment the following is treated as income:[97]

- any lump sum paid to you not more than once a year for your work as a part-time firefighter, part-time member of a lifeboat crew, auxiliary coastguard or member of the Territorial Army;
- any refund of income tax;
- holiday pay which is not payable until more than four weeks after your job ended;
- any irregular charitable or voluntary payment.

Capital[98]

Your capital is calculated in the usual way (see Chapter 20) but the following is also taken into account:

- money from the sale of your home which you intend to use to buy another;
- the liquid assets of a business (eg, cash in hand);

- arrears of the following: mobility supplement, disability living or disability working allowance, attendance allowance, IS, family credit or any concessionary payments made to compensate for non-payment of any of these benefits;
- backdated payments of IS, HB or council tax benefit made to you once the Home Office accepts you are a refugee (see p76);
- money which had been deposited with a housing association and which is now to be used to buy a home;
- up to £200 of a training bonus received after being on Training for Work;
- a refund of tax on a mortgage or loan taken out to buy, or to do repairs and/or improvements to your home.

CHAPTER FOUR

Jobseeker's allowance

This chapter covers:

1. INTRODUCTION TO JOBSEEKER'S ALLOWANCE

Jobseeker's allowance (JSA) was introduced on 7 October 1996. It replaces income support (IS) (for those who have to look for work in order to qualify for benefit) and unemployment benefit. Claims for JSA are made at local JobCentres.

This chapter gives only a summary of the main jobseeker's allowance rules. For full details, see CPAG's *Jobseeker's Allowance Handbook*, 2nd edn, 1997/98.

JSA has two elements:

* *Contribution-based* JSA can be paid for the first 26 weeks of the 'jobseeking period' (see below) if you satisfy contribution conditions.
* *Income-based* JSA can be paid during the 'jobseeking period' (see below) if you satisfy the means test (see p52). It can be paid on its own or in addition to *contribution-based* JSA.

The 'jobseeking period' is the period during which you meet the conditions of entitlement for JSA or in which you receive a hardship payment.[1]

You cannot get JSA for the first three days of the 'jobseeking period' unless you have been entitled to IS, incapacity benefit or invalid care allowance *or* you are aged 16 or 17 and are getting JSA under the 'severe hardship' rules (see the *Jobseeker's Allowance Handbook,* 2nd edn, 1997/98).[2]

Passported benefits

If you get income-based JSA, you may have a right to receive the following payments from the social fund:

- a cold weather payment (see p418)
- a funeral expenses payment (see p413)
- a maternity expenses payment (see p410)

You can also be considered for community care grants (see p434), budgeting loans (see p444) and crisis loans (see p446).

If you get income-based JSA, you automatically qualify for a number of other benefits and types of help such as free prescriptions and free school meals (see p6). The rules about these are the same as for IS (see Chapter 26 and Appendix 1).

2. INCOME-BASED JOBSEEKER'S ALLOWANCE

If you have not paid or been credited with enough national insurance contributions to get *contribution-based* JSA, you might still qualify for *income-based* JSA if your income and savings are low enough to pass the means test. If you do qualify for contribution-based JSA, you should claim income-based JSA as well if:

- you have a family and want to claim benefit for them as well as yourself;
- you need help with your housing costs (the rules are generally the same as for IS, see the *Jobseeker's Allowance Handbook,* 2nd edn, 1997/98).

You can claim income-based JSA if you satisfy the following rules:[3]

- neither you nor your partner are in full-time paid work (see p13 for what counts as full-time work);
- you satisfy the 'labour market conditions' (see p52);
- you are at least 16 but under pensionable age (60 for women and 65 for men). 16- and 17-year-olds have to satisfy special rules;
- you are not in full-time education.

The means test

The way income-based JSA is calculated is broadly the same as for IS (see Chapters 3, 18, 19 and 20). The capital limit is £8,000 (£16,000 if you live in residential care or similar accommodation, see p384).

If you are 'sanctioned', for example because you have left a job without a good reason, then your JSA can be paid at a reduced rate for a period if you qualify for a hardship payment and, sometimes, not at all (see p54). The amount you are paid can also be reduced if you are a lone parent and refuse – without a good reason – to co-operate with the Child Support Agency in seeking maintenance for your children (see p108 for the IS rules, which are the same). If you are sanctioned, you might be able to get a hardship payment (see p54).

3. THE LABOUR MARKET CONDITIONS

To get JSA, you must prove that you are genuinely looking for work. To qualify you must:

- be capable of work; *and*
- be available for work; *and*
- be actively seeking work; *and*
- have a current jobseeker's agreement with the Employment Service.

'Available for work'

You are treated as available for work if you are willing and able to take up any job immediately. In some cases you do not have to be available immediately, for example, if you have caring responsibilities or are doing voluntary work.[4] You are allowed to place restrictions on the sort of job you are prepared to take, for example, the pay you will accept (for the first six months of your claim only), the type of work you will do or where you are willing to work, so long as you can show that you still have a reasonable chance of getting a job.[5] In deciding whether you still have a reasonable chance, the Employment Service must consider such things as, for example, your skills and experience and the length of time you have been unemployed.[6] For up to 13 weeks at the beginning of your claim (your 'permitted period'), you can be allowed to concentrate your search for work on vacancies in your normal occupation.[7]

You can be **treated as available for work** in certain circumstances, for example, during short spells of sickness (a maximum of two periods of two weeks in 12 months you are unemployed) or for the week following your discharge from prison.[8]

Even if you are available for work, you will nevertheless be **treated as unavailable** if:[9]

- you are a full-time student;
- you are on temporary release from prison;
- you are receiving maternity allowance or statutory maternity pay (for further details of these benefits see the *Rights Guide to Non-Means-Tested Benefits,* 20th edn, 1997/98).

You generally must be prepared to accept any offer of employment which would involve at least 40 hours a week. You can restrict your availability to less than 40 hours a week in certain circumstances, for example, if this is reasonable in the light of your physical or mental condition.

'Actively seeking work'

You must be actively trying to find work each week in which you are unemployed. You must take such 'steps' as you can reasonably be expected to take, to have the best prospects of getting employment. Steps include applying for jobs by letter or telephone, getting information about possible jobs from employers, registered employment agencies, and advertisements in newspapers and preparing a CV.[10]

When deciding whether you have taken reasonable steps to find work the adjudication officer must take account of, for example, your skills, qualifications, any health and physical or mental limitations, the attempts you have made to find work in previous weeks, whether you are doing voluntary work, whether you are homeless, and attempts you have made to find accommodation.[11]

You can be **treated as actively seeking work** in certain weeks including:[12]

- the first and last weeks for which you claim;
- two weeks in any period of 12 months while you are away from home – eg, on holiday, in the UK. You must give the Employment Service advance notice;
- during short spells of sickness (see p10).

The jobseeker's agreement

You must enter into a jobseeker's agreement to get JSA. It must be signed both by you and an Employment Service Officer (EO).[13] The EO will not sign it unless s/he believes you qualify as available for and actively seeking work. The agreement must contain certain information, including:[14]

- the hours you are available for work each week;
- any restriction you are allowed to place on the work you are prepared to do;
- the type of job you are looking for;
- the steps you will take to actively seek work; *and*
- a statement of your rights if you and the ESO cannot agree about what should be in the agreement.

4. SANCTIONS AND HARDSHIP PAYMENTS

There are a number of situations when JSA might not be paid to you even if you would otherwise be entitled.[15] No JSA will be paid for the length of your sanction period unless you qualify for a hardship payment (see below). The length of your sanction period could be a fixed period of two or four weeks (for example, if you refuse to carry out a reasonable jobseeker's direction or lose your place on a compulsory training scheme through misconduct) or for a period from one to 26 weeks – for example, if you lose your job through misconduct or give up your job voluntarily without just cause.

If you are sanctioned and your partner could claim IS or JSA, s/he should consider claiming instead of you to preserve your entitlement in full.

Hardship payments

If you are sanctioned, during your sanction period (see above), you will not be paid *contribution-based* JSA at all. However, if you are entitled to *income-based* JSA, you might be able to get a hardship payment. To qualify for a hardship payment, you must prove that you, your partner or a member of your family (see p318 for who counts as your family) will suffer hardship if no payment is made.[16] You usually cannot get a hardship payment for the first two weeks of your sanction period. However, you can get a hardship payment straight away if, for example:

- you or your partner is pregnant and will suffer hardship if no payment is made; *or*
- you or your partner have children who will suffer hardship; *or*
- you qualify for a disability premium with your income-based JSA.

If you get a hardship payment, premiums and housing costs are paid in full, but your income-based JSA is reduced by an amount equal to 40 per cent of the personal allowance for a single claimant.[17] The reduction is the same even if you are one of a couple. A smaller reduction of 20 per cent is made where you, your partner or child is pregnant or seriously ill.

5. SHOULD YOU CLAIM JOBSEEKER'S ALLOWANCE OR INCOME SUPPORT?

Although you cannot claim JSA and income support (IS) at the same time,[18] you might be able to choose which benefit to claim. For example, you might want to claim IS instead of JSA if:

- you automatically qualify as incapable of work and are therefore exempt from the 'all-work' test, for example because you are registered blind, terminally ill or have a severe learning disability (see *Rights Guide to Non-Means-Tested Benefits*, 20th edn, 1997/98);
- you are caring for a disabled person and qualify for invalid care allowance;
- you are 60 or over; *or*
- you are a single parent of a child under 16.

If you are in this position, you should claim IS instead of JSA, together with any other benefit you may be entitled to such as incapacity benefit, severe disablement allowance or invalid care allowance. The rates of benefit are the same, but you will not have to sign on every fortnight or look for work or risk being sanctioned (see p54).

There are other situations when you can claim either JSA or IS. However, you might want to claim JSA to protect your national insurance record. You should seek advice before deciding which benefit to claim if:

- you are 16 or 17 years old and claiming benefit while you are in 'relevant education' (see p16);
- you are looking after a member of your family who is temporarily ill.

If you have a partner and you are claiming *contribution-based* JSA, you could claim *income-based* JSA to top up your income but your partner might be able to claim IS for you (see p10). If you are in this situation, you should check to see how you would be better off financially. For example, your partner should claim IS if s/he qualifies for the IS disability premium (see p333) because s/he is entitled to statutory sick pay or has been incapable of work for 196 days (if terminally ill) or 364 days (see p334-35). You cannot get the disability premium for her/him if you claim income-based JSA.

If you work part time (see p13) **and your partner works at least 16 hours but no more than 24 hours each week, between you, you might choose to claim family credit (FC), disability working allowance (DWA) or earnings top-up (ETU)** (see pp184, 199 and 197). However, you should seek advice before deciding whether to claim. For example, if you are paying a mortgage and can get income-based JSA to help you with your housing costs, you might be better off on income-based JSA instead of FC, DWA or ETU.

CHAPTER FIVE

Special rules for special groups

This chapter covers:
1. 16/17-year-olds (below)
2. People involved in a trade dispute (p58)
3. People from abroad (p63)
4. Residential and nursing care (p84)
5. People in hospital (p94)
6. Prisoners (p98)
7. People without accommodation (p99)

1. 16/17-YEAR-OLDS

If you are aged 16 or 17, you are entitled to income support (IS) in your own right if you satisfy the normal rules of entitlement.[1] You should not have your claim refused or be turned away by the Benefits Agency simply because you are aged 16 or 17.

You should note the following points, however.

- You are only entitled to IS if you fall into one of the categories of claimants eligible for IS listed on p10.[2]
- If you are in 'relevant education', you are only entitled to IS in specified circumstances (see p17)[3]. If you are in or have recently left non-advanced education and are living with someone who is 'responsible' for you, you can be included in their IS claim (see p325).
- If you are eligible for IS but are not claiming it, you may instead be eligible for income-based jobseeker's allowance (JSA).[4] It will usually be better to claim IS to avoid the requirement to be available for and actively seeking work and training and the attendant risk of benefit sanctions (see CPAG's *Jobseeker's Allowance Handbook* 1997/98 for details). If you claim IS rather than JSA, however, you will not receive national insurance credits (see CPAG's *Rights Guide to Non-Means-Tested Benefit* 1997/98 for information about credits). You are not entitled to income-based JSA, however, unless you satisfy all the conditions. You

are specifically excluded from getting JSA if you are in relevant education.

- If you are not entitled to IS, you may be entitled to income-based JSA. You must normally be registered with the Careers Service and be available for, and actively seeking, work and training. In addition, you will only be entitled to JSA in specified circumstances and sometimes for a limited period. See the special rules for 16/17-year-olds in CPAG's *Jobseeker's Allowance Handbook* 1997/98 for details.
- If you are not entitled to IS or JSA, you can claim discretionary payments of JSA if you will otherwise suffer severe hardship. See CPAG's *Jobseeker's Allowance Handbook* 1997/98; for details.
- There are two rates of IS personal allowance payable to 16 and 17-year-olds. See p44 for details.

2. PEOPLE INVOLVED IN A TRADE DISPUTE

You are not entitled to JSA for any week in which you are involved in a trade dispute although your partner may be.[5] You are entitled to IS in certain circumstances, at a reduced rate.[6]

Involvement in a trade dispute

A trade dispute is any dispute relating to an employment matter whether between employers and employees or between different groups of employees.[7] You are treated as involved in a trade dispute if:

- you are not working because of a stoppage of work due to a trade dispute at your place of work; *or*
- you otherwise withdraw your labour in furtherance of any trade dispute.[8]

Your 'place of work' means the place or premises where you work. It does not include a separate department carrying out a separate branch of work which is commonly undertaken as a separate business elsewhere.[9] It may, however, be difficult to show that separate branches of work are carried on as separate businesses, and that the separate branches are not integrated.[10]

You are not treated as involved in a trade dispute during a period of 'incapacity for work' (four or more days of incapacity) or during a maternity period (six weeks before your baby is due until the end of the seventh week after the birth).[11]

You are not treated as involved in a trade dispute at your place of work if:

- you can prove you are 'not directly interested' in the dispute - ie, you will not be affected by its outcome (this could apply if your terms and conditions will not be affected whatever the outcome, or you leave your job and will not gain anything when the dispute is resolved);[12] *or*
- during a stoppage, you are made redundant, or you become genuinely employed elsewhere, or you genuinely resume work with your employer but then leave for a reason other than the trade dispute.[13]

You are assumed to be involved in a trade dispute pending a decision by an adjudication officer as to whether you are actually so involved.[14]

You are treated as engaged in full-time work for the first seven days you or your partner stop work because of a trade dispute in the circumstances described above.[15] This means neither you, nor your partner, can claim IS during this period.[16] If there is a series of stoppages caused by the same trade dispute, the rule only applies for the first seven days of the first stoppage.[17] If you were getting IS immediately before the stoppage, the rule should not apply at all.[18]

Calculation of IS

Applicable amounts

If you are treated as involved in a trade dispute, your IS applicable amount (see p329) is calculated as follows:[19]

For a single person involved in a trade dispute:	Nil
For a couple without children where both are involved in a trade dispute:	Nil
For a couple without children where only one partner is involved in a trade dispute:	Half the personal allowance for a couple *plus* half the couple rate of any premium payable for the person not involved in the dispute, *plus* housing costs, if appropriate.
For a single parent who is involved in a trade dispute:	The normal personal allowances for the children, *plus* the family premium paid at the lone parent rate, *plus* disabled child premium, *plus* housing costs, if appropriate.

For a couple with children where only one is involved in a trade dispute:	Half the personal allowance for a couple, *plus* half the couple rate of any premium payable for the person not involved in the dispute, *plus* the normal personal allowances for the children and the family premium, *plus* disabled child premium, *plus* housing costs, if appropriate.
For a couple with children where both are involved in a trade dispute:	The normal personal allowances for children, *plus* the family premium, *plus* disabled child premium, *plus* housing costs, if appropriate.

Housing costs are payable unless all members of the family are involved in a trade dispute. Those members not involved in the dispute are treated as responsible for the costs.[20]

Actual and 'assumed' strike pay

If you, or your partner, are involved in a trade dispute, special rules apply relating to actual and 'assumed' strike pay.

First, any payments you actually receive from a trade union in excess of £26.50 a week count as income and are deducted from your IS applicable amount. Payments of up to £26.50 a week are ignored. If you and your partner are both involved in a trade dispute, only £26.50 in total is ignored.[21]

Secondly, whether or not you actually receive any payments, £26.50 is deducted from your IS. If you and your partner are both involved in a trade dispute, £26.50 is still deducted.[22] This deduction may extinguish your entitlement to any IS.

Example
Childless couple, one on strike, whose only income is £30 a week strike pay.

Applicable amount:	£38.55	(half normal amount)
less income:	£ 3.50	(strike pay *less* £26.50 disregard)
	£35.05	
less	£26.50	(assumed strike pay)
= IS payable	£ 8.55	

If their strike pay was £40, their income of £13.50 (£40 less £26.50 disregard) and their assumed strike pay of £26.50 would extinguish their entitlement to any IS.

If their strike pay was £26.50 or less, it would be disregarded and their IS would be £38.55 (applicable amount) less £26.50 assumed strike pay.

Other income and capital

Other income and capital is treated in the way described in Chapters 19 and 20 except that the following are taken into account in full as income:

- any tax refund due because of the stoppage of work;[23]
- any payment made under sections 17 or 24 of the Children Act 1989 (in Scotland, sections 12, 24 or 26 Social Work (Scotland) Act 1968);[24]
- all charitable or voluntary payments (whether regular or irregular, with no £20 disregard for regular payments) except any payment from the Macfarlane Trusts, the Eileen Trust or the Fund, or either of the Independent Living Funds;[25]
- payments of income in kind except any payment from the Macfarlane Trusts, the Eileen Trust or the Fund, or either of the Independent Living Funds;[26]
- holiday pay which is not payable until more than four weeks after your employment ends or is interrupted[27] (this counts as earnings and therefore attracts an earnings disregard – see p357);
- any advance of earnings or a loan made by your employer.[28] Where these payments are earnings, they attract an earnings disregard.

Any payments received or due because the person involved in the trade dispute is currently unemployed are also treated as income and counted in full.[29]

Benefit loans on return to work

If you return to work with the same employer, whether or not the trade dispute has ended, you can receive IS for the first 15 days back at work, in the form of a loan.[30] You are not treated as in full-time work for this period.[31] If you are a member of a couple you are not entitled to IS if your partner is in full-time work.[32] Your applicable amount is calculated according to the normal rules. Your income (including any earnings you receive from your employer) is calculated in the same way as if you were still involved in the dispute (see above) except that any income tax refunds are ignored, and there is no deduction from your benefit for assumed strike pay.

Any IS that you are awarded is paid in advance.[33] You may not get IS if you are entitled to less than £5.[34]

Repayment of the loan

Any IS paid during your first 15 days back at work can be recovered by deductions from your earnings.[35] If this is not practical (eg, because you are currently unemployed) it can be recovered directly from you.[36]

The amount deducted from your earnings is worked out by comparing your 'protected earnings' with your 'available earnings'.

Your **'protected earnings'** are an amount equal to:

* your applicable amount excluding housing costs; *plus*
* £27; *less*
* child benefit paid at basic or lone parent rate.[37]

Note: Some lone parents qualify for child benefit paid at the lone parent rate but may opt to claim basic rate child benefit. One parent benefit and child benefit were amalgamated from 7 April 1997 – see CPAG's *Rights Guide to Non-Means-Tested Benefits.*

Your **'available earnings'** are the whole of your earnings, including sick pay, after all 'lawful' deductions have been made.[38] These include tax and national insurance contributions, trade union subscriptions and any amount being deducted under a court order or, for instance, a child support deduction order. Any bonus or commission if paid on a different day is treated as paid on your next normal pay day.[39]

If your available earnings are less than £1 above your protected earnings level, there will be no deduction. If they are £1 or more above, your employer will deduct half of the difference between your protected and available earnings. If you are paid monthly, your protected earnings are multiplied by five. If your monthly available earnings are less than £5 above this level, no deduction is made. Otherwise, half the excess is deducted. If your earnings are paid daily, the amount of your protected earnings and the £1 figure is divided by five to determine the amount (if any) of the deduction. The calculation can be adjusted as appropriate where your wages are paid at other intervals.[40] If you are paid more than one lot of earnings on a pay day, your protected earnings and the £1 figure are multiplied to reflect this.[41]

A deduction notice is sent to your employer by the Benefits Agency setting out your protected earnings level and the amount of IS to be recovered.[42] If you have not actually received the IS and you can satisfy your employer that you have not, no deduction should be made.[43] Your employer *can* begin making the deductions from the first pay day after receiving the notice and *must* start doing so one month after getting it.[44] A deduction notice ceases to have effect if:

* it is cancelled or replaced; *or*
* you stop working for that employer; *or*

- your IS loan has been repaid; *or*
- 26 weeks have passed since the date of the notice.[45]

If you stop work, another deduction notice can be sent if you get another job and part of your IS loan is still outstanding.[46]

You must tell the Benefits Agency within ten days if you leave a job or start another while part of your IS loan remains unpaid.[47] If you fail to do so you can be prosecuted.[48] It is a criminal offence for your employer to fail to keep records of deductions and supply the Benefits Agency with these.[49] If your employer fails to make a deduction which should have been made from your pay, the Benefits Agency can recover the amount from your employer instead.[50]

Other benefits during a trade dispute

- You can get a social fund payment for **maternity** and **funeral expenses** (see Chapter 21) and travel expenses to visit a close relative or a member of the same household who is ill[51] (see p432).
- A crisis loan can only be awarded in cases of **disaster** (see p433) or for items needed for **cooking or space heating**.[52] Budgeting loans are not available to strikers.[53]
- Strikers and their families may be entitled to **free prescriptions, free dental treatment and free glasses** (see Chapter 26).

3. PEOPLE FROM ABROAD

Introduction

This chapter gives a brief outline of the rights of claimants designated 'persons from abroad'. For further information, you should consult JCWI's *Immigration and Nationality Law Handbook*, CPAG's *Income Related Benefits: The Legislation* and CPAG's *Migration and Social Security Handbook* (listed in Appendix 4).

Your right to IS depends on:

- your immigration status; *and*
- whether you satisfy, or are exempt from, the 'habitual residence' test (see p69).

Certain categories of claimants are classed as 'persons from abroad' under the IS regulations because of their immigration status, and are not entitled to IS under the normal rules (see p10). *All* claimants, including British citizens, who fail to satisfy the 'habitual residence' test (unless exempt), are also classed as 'persons from abroad' and are denied IS.

The IS claim forms ask whether you, or anyone you are claiming for, have come to live in the UK in the last five years. If the answer is 'yes', you are likely to be interviewed to determine whether you, or the person you are claiming for, are a 'person from abroad'. The forms also ask whether you have come to the UK under a sponsorship undertaking (see p82).

Your immigration status may not always be clear. There are close links between the Benefits Agency and the Home Office. Making a claim for IS could alert the immigration authorities to the fact that you are here unlawfully, or that you have broken your conditions of entry by claiming 'public funds' (see p65).

It is vitally important, therefore, to get specialist advice before claiming IS if you are unsure about your position. You can get advice from your local law centre, citizens advice bureau or other advice agency which deals with immigration problems. You can also get specialist advice from the Joint Council for the Welfare of Immigrants (JCWI), 115 Old Street, London EC1V 9JR (tel: 0171 251 8706). If you are a refugee or asylum-seeker, you can contact the Refugee Council, 3 Bondway, London SW8 1SJ (tel: 0171 582 9927).

The following rules apply to people claiming IS. Almost identical rules apply to people claiming income-based JSA (for who can get this, see p50). Like IS, income-based JSA can be paid at the urgent cases rate. However, to qualify for JSA at the normal or urgent cases rate you must have no conditions on your stay restricting your right to take employment. The habitual residence test is also discussed in terms of both IS and income-based JSA.

'Persons from abroad'

If you are classed as a 'person from abroad' under the IS regulations, you are not entitled to IS under the normal rules.[54] You may, however, be entitled to urgent cases payments of IS (see p22). If your partner is not a 'person from abroad', s/he can claim IS under the normal rules but will not receive any benefit for you (see p66).

You are classed as a 'person from abroad' under the IS regulations if you fall into any of the following categories.[55] The first category can apply to *any* person including a British citizen. The remaining categories apply to people who are subject to immigration control and refer to various types of immigration status.

- You are not 'habitually resident' or treated as 'habitually resident' in the UK, Republic of Ireland, Channel Islands or the Isle of Man. The 'habitual residence' test is discussed on p69.

- You have 'limited leave' to enter or remain in the UK subject to the condition or requirement that you do not have recourse to 'public funds'. The meaning and scope of this is discussed below and on p67.
- You have been allowed temporary admission to the UK (this applies to people liable to be detained).
- You are waiting for an initial decision on your immigration status.
- You have been in the UK for less than five years, subject to a sponsorship *undertaking* (see p82). **Note:** You are entitled to normal rate IS if you become a British citizen, and to urgent cases payments of IS if your sponsor dies (see p82).
- You are an asylum-seeker. **Note:** Some asylum-seekers are entitled to urgent cases payments of IS (see p77).
- You are an EU national, 'required to leave the UK' by the Secretary of State (see p75).
- You are an 'overstayer' – ie, your limited leave has expired and you have stayed on without seeking permission from the Home Office.
- You are subject to a deportation order.
- You are an illegal immigrant, *and* you have not applied to the Home Office to regularise your stay.

If you come within the last three categories you should always seek independent advice before approaching the Benefits Agency.

Limited leave and public funds

'Limited leave' means permission to enter or remain in the UK for a specified period of time, sometimes with a prohibition on working. 'Public funds' is defined in the immigration rules as IS, income-based JSA, housing benefit (HB), council tax benefit (CTB), family credit (FC), disability working allowance (DWA), disability living allowance, attendance allowance, invalid care allowance, severe disablement allowance, child benefit and housing for homeless people under the Housing Act 1985 (or equivalent in Scotland and Northern Ireland).

Most visitors, students, business and self-employed people, people with a work permit, artists, writers, people of independent means, fiancé(s) and spouses (unless they have been given indefinite leave) are given limited leave with a public funds prohibition.

Nationals from the European Economic Area (EEA) (see p72 for a list of countries) do not require leave to enter or remain in the UK, but in certain circumstances they may still be refused IS or income-based JSA as 'persons from abroad'.[56] Nationals from Cyprus do not count as 'persons from abroad'. Nor do Maltese or Turkish nationals unless they have applied for variation of their conditions of leave.[57] Turkish nationals who have worked within the European Union (EU) may, however, have special rights and should seek legal advice.

People entitled to IS under the normal rules

If you do not fall into any of the categories on pp64–65, you are entitled to IS under the normal rules.[58] In practical terms, this means you are entitled to IS if you satisfy (or are exempt from) the 'habitual residence' test (see p69) and you fall into any of the following categories:

- You are a British citizen.
- You are a British Overseas citizen with the right of re-admission to the UK.
- You have the right of abode in the UK or a certificate of patriality.
- You have 'indefinite leave' to enter or remain in the UK. This includes the situation where another person has undertaken to maintain and accommodate you, and you have been here for more than five years, or where no formal undertaking has been given (see p82).
- You have been granted refugee status, or 'exceptional leave to remain' (see p75).
- You are a national of Eire, the Channel Islands, or the Isle of Man.
- You are a national of Cyprus, Malta or Turkey. **Note:** If you are a citizen of Malta or Turkey and you are applying for your leave conditions to be varied, see p65.
- You are an EEA/EU national (but see p75).
- You are in GB and you left Montserrat after 1 November 1995 because of a volcanic eruption there.

The above groups may also be eligible for income-based JSA.

Couples and families

Entitlement to income support

The following rules apply where one or more members of your family are 'persons from abroad'.

- If you are a 'person from abroad' (see p64), you are not entitled to IS under the normal rules either for yourself, or for any members of your family.[59] You may be entitled to urgent cases payments of IS (see p82).
- If your partner is not a 'person from abroad' but you are, s/he can claim IS but will not receive any benefit for you or any other family member who is a 'person from abroad'.[60] Full housing costs are payable.[61] You are still treated as a couple for IS purposes (see p319), so your joint resources are taken into account.

- Couples where both partners are not 'persons from abroad' and single parents who are not 'persons from abroad', can claim IS for children who are.[62] But claimants who are 'persons from abroad' cannot claim benefit for children even if the children are *not* 'persons from abroad'.[63]
- Foreign fiancé(s) and spouses who are admitted for settlement on the condition that they can maintain and accommodate themselves, count as 'persons from abroad' and are not entitled to IS until they are granted indefinite leave to remain in the UK.[64] A foreign spouse is granted a 12-month probationary period of leave following either the date of her/his entry to the UK or the date of marriage in the UK. Before the 12 months expires s/he should apply for indefinite leave to remain.

The above rules also apply to income-based JSA.

Implications of claiming public funds

If you claim IS but do not receive benefit for your partner because s/he is a 'person from abroad' s/he may not be treated as having recourse to public funds. However, you should get advice first before claiming any public funds benefit (see p65), if your partner or child is a 'person from abroad'.

From November 1996, a 'person from abroad' may have a condition stamped in her/his passport that s/he should not have recourse to public funds. Arguably, even if s/he does not claim benefit but her/his British or settled partner does, s/he indirectly has recourse to public funds. Where this happens s/he will be in breach of her/his immigration conditions and may have her/his leave curtailed, or even be deported. It is unclear whether a 'person from abroad' *should* be treated as having recourse to public funds if the amount of benefit received by the British or settled partner is unaltered by the presence in the family of a 'person from abroad'. Until now it has been policy to treat such 'persons from abroad' as *not* having recourse to public funds. Benefit paid to a British or settled person would be unaltered by the presence in the household of a person from abroad in the following circumstances:

- **IS/income-based JSA:** benefit is paid at the single person rate where a partner is a 'person from abroad' (see p66);
- **FC/DWA:** benefit is paid at the same rate whether there is a single person or a couple (see p190 and 204);
- **HB/CTB:** where maximum benefit is payable anyway – eg, because the claimant receives IS/income-based JSA, see p248 and 303;

- **attendance allowance/disability living allowance:** benefit is paid for the individual only. (For details see CPAG's *Migration and Social Security Handbook*.)

If policy changes and a person is treated as having recourse to public funds even though s/he benefits only indirectly as explained above, s/he might then be regarded as being in breach of the immigration rules and have her/his leave curtailed or be deported. Check future editions of CPAG's *Welfare Rights Bulletin* for what happens in practice. Whether or not policy changes, it would probably not be wise for the British/settled person to claim a benefit (ie HB/CTB) where the benefit payable would go up to take account of the person from abroad in the family. Although the person who is the 'person from abroad' has not made the claim, her/his presence will have increased the amount of public funds payable.

Where a person is admitted subject to a requirement *only* not to have recourse to public funds (no stamp in passport), the person will not be in breach of any immigration conditions if her/his partner claims. However, any person who benefits indirectly from a claim could still lose her/his right to stay or have her/his application for permanent leave refused.

Thus, a claim by the settled partner at the time when the foreign spouse is applying for indefinite leave could result at best in a delay in granting indefinite leave, at worst the foreign spouse could lose the right to stay altogether.

You will also need to get advice before claiming IS or any other public funds benefit (see p65) if your spouse or fiancé(e) is applying for entry clearance (obtaining permission abroad to come to the UK). In general, a claim for public funds is an indication that the settled partner is not in a position to maintain the other member of the couple and a claim may thus jeopardise the application.

Note: Some people who count as 'persons from abroad' for IS and income-based JSA may be *treated* as having a right of residence in Great Britain and be able to claim non-contributory non-means-tested benefits (see CPAG's *Rights Guide to Non-Means-Tested Benefits* 1997/98), and FC and DWA (see p85 and 200). A person who is a 'person from abroad' for IS and income-based JSA may qualify for child benefit (see CPAG's *Migration and Social Security Handbook*).

One partner abroad

If your partner is abroad but intends to come to the UK and you have lived together as a couple abroad, you may not be entitled to IS because you and your partner may be treated as members of the same household (see p318).

If you or your partner go abroad temporarily, you may be entitled to continue to claim IS as a couple for four or eight weeks (see p22). After four or eight weeks, if you qualify for benefit you will be paid as a single person or single parent.[65] However, if your partner is abroad temporarily, you may still be treated as a couple for IS purposes, which means that your joint income and capital will be taken into account.[66] See p323 for details of when you do and do not count as a couple for IS purposes. If your partner is abroad permanently, you can claim IS as a single person or parent.

The habitual residence test

The habitual residence test applies to IS, income-based JSA, HB and CTB.

You are not entitled to IS or income-based JSA under the normal rules unless you are habitually resident or are treated as habitually resident in the UK, Republic of Ireland, the Channel Islands or the Isle of Man. You are classed as a 'person from abroad' (see p63).[67]

The habitual residence test is applied to claimants (but not partners or dependants), including British citizens. The following people, however, are automatically treated as habitually resident in the UK and are therefore exempt from the test:

- EEA citizens who are classed as 'workers', or have the right to reside in the UK under specified EC legislation. See p73 for details.
- Recognised refugees or people who have been granted 'exceptional leave to remain' in the UK (see p75).[68]
- People in GB who left Montserrat after 1 November 1995 because of a volcanic eruption there.

If you were entitled to IS on 31 July 1994, you do not have to satisfy the habitual residence test unless you make a new claim after that date.[69] Completing a new claim form on a change of circumstances where IS is already in payment should not count as a new claim. Swapping claimants, however, does (see p123).

The meaning of 'habitually resident'

The term 'habitually resident' is not defined in the IS or JSA regulations. In ordinary, everyday language, your 'habitual residence' is the place which has become your normal home. How is this to be determined, however, when you move from one place to another?

Although there has been a certain amount of caselaw on the meaning of 'habitual residence', the concept remains complex and imprecise. The 'habitual residence test' is therefore open to highly subjective and inconsistent decision-making by adjudication officers (AOs). Particular groups tend to be targeted for detailed investigation, including European nationals and people (especially from ethnic minority communities) who spend lengthy periods overseas.

The concept of 'habitual residence' occurs in EU law relating to migrant workers[70] but the DSS appears now to have accepted that this interpretation is not applicable to IS claimants.

Two social security commissioner decisions[71] which considered the meaning of 'habitual residence' in the context of IS, are now the basis for DSS guidance[72] and have established the following principles:[73]

• The term 'habitual residence' must be given its ordinary and natural meaning. There is no absolute definition or list of factors which determines a person's habitual residence. Each case must be considered on its merits, taking into account all the relevant circumstances and the facts of the case.

• You must have a 'settled intention' to reside in a country – ie, to make your home there for a temporary or permanent period.

• You must be actually resident for 'an appreciable period of time' before you become 'habitually resident'. What counts as an appreciable period of time depends on the facts of each case. There is no minimum period but habitual residence cannot be acquired in a day. When deciding what is an appreciable period, it is appropriate to take account of family law cases on child abduction – for this purpose habitual residence may be established in one month.[74] Previous visits to prepare for settled residence, can form part of the required period of residence. The question in each individual case is whether in all the circumstances, including the settledness of a person's intentions, residence has continued for a sufficient period to make it habitual.

  In the first decision the commissioner suggested that a citizen of the UK, of whatever ethnic origin, having lived abroad and without any ties overseas could expect to become habitually resident after three months. The second commissioner advised AOs not to rely on this example. In spite of this, there is a tendency for local offices to treat three months as an unofficial minimum – this is wrong.[75]

• Factors that are important are the length, continuity and general nature of actual residence rather than your intentions.

• The 'viability' of your residence may be one relevant factor but whereas one commissioner held that living arrangements dependent on public funds, including IS, were not viable,[76] the other firmly stated that there was no condition that only residence without recourse to public funds counted towards the required 'appreciable period'.[77]

- You can retain your habitual residence in a country despite periods of temporary absence and you can be habitually resident in more than one country, or none.

These principles will also apply to income-based JSA.

Tactics

- Since the habitual residence test operates as an exclusion from IS and income-based JSA, the onus of proof lies with the Benefits Agency to establish that you are *not* habitually resident.[78] It is vital, nevertheless, that you produce as much evidence as possible to show that you *are* habitually resident, taking into account the above points on the meaning of the term. You should prepare your case thoroughly before attending a Benefits Agency interview or a social security appeal tribunal (SSAT).

- If you fail the test, you may be able to satisfy it at a later date, particularly if there is a change in your circumstances, or simply through the passage of time. Repeated claims for IS or income-based JSA can highlight your determination to remain in the UK, as well as the unfairness of the test. Some local offices are refusing to accept repeat claims if there is an appeal pending. This is wrong – the local office should accept the claim and make a decision.

- If you are refused IS or income-based JSA because of the habitual residence test, you can request a review, or appeal to an SSAT. You can ask for an expedited hearing of your appeal if you are suffering hardship (see p156). Always ask for an oral hearing, so that you can explain your circumstances in person. The tribunal must apply the test from the date of claim to the date of your appeal hearing.[79]

- If you have no money to live on because you have failed the habitual residence test, you could:
  - apply to the Benefits Agency for an 'extra-statutory payment'. The most effective way of doing this is to ask your MP to put your case in writing to the Secretary of State for Social Security;
  - apply to your local social services department for financial assistance if you have children. If you do not have children then you can ask your local authority to pay you under the National Assistance Act if you face destitution (see asylum-seekers, p81);
  - apply for a social fund crisis loan. Although you have to be able to repay a loan, if you are likely to be counted as habitually resident in the near future then you will qualify for benefit and you can argue that the DSS should, therefore, consider granting you a loan.

- The legality of the habitual residence test has been challenged, so far unsuccessfully,[80] but there may be further challenges. See future editions of CPAG's *Welfare Rights Bulletin* for latest developments.

Current challenges will decide whether:

- the more flexible ordinary residence criteria should be adopted for deciding habitual residence (see CPAG's *Rights Guide to Non-Means-Tested Benefits* 1997/98);
- habitual residence can start on the first day of your residence;
- the viability test is legitimate;[81]
- EEA nationals can use periods of working in the EEA (apart from the UK) to count towards satisfying the appreciable period of time. To do this they will have to cite EEC Regulation 1408/71 which attempts to co-ordinate the provision of social security for migrant workers within the EC.[82] (See CPAG's *Migration and Social Security Handbook*.)

European Economic Area citizens

If you are a national of the EEA (see below for countries covered), you and your dependants have rights under European Community (EC) and UK law to enter and reside in the UK.[83] You also have the right to claim IS or income-based JSA under the normal rules.[84]

You are not entitled to IS or income-based JSA, however, unless you satisfy or are treated as satisfying the 'habitual residence' test (see p73). Certain categories of EEA nationals are automatically treated as habitually resident in the UK (see below).

In certain circumstances, claiming IS or income-based JSA can undermine your right of residence in the UK and result in the Secretary of State 'requiring you to leave'. Although action to remove you is very unlikely, your benefit may stop (see p75). (If you are from Iceland or Norway you cannot be required to leave.)

EC law is particularly complex and can only be covered briefly here. If you are unsure about your rights, always seek specialist advice (see Appendix 3 for sources of further information and advice).

Who is an EEA national?

You are an EEA national if you are a citizen of one of the following countries:

- the Member States of the EU – ie, Austria, Belgium, Denmark, Finland, France, Germany, Greece, Italy, Luxembourg, Netherlands, Portugal, Republic of Ireland, Spain, Sweden, UK;

- two Member States of the European Free Trade Association – Iceland and Norway.

Those treated as 'habitually resident'

In order to qualify for IS or income-based JSA, you must normally satisfy the 'habitual residence' test (see p69). You are, however, automatically treated as habitually resident in the UK if you are:[85]

- a worker for the purposes of EEC Regulations 1612/68 or 1251/70 (see below); *or*
- a person with the right to reside in the UK under EEC Directives 68/360 or 73/148 (see p74).

Your spouse, dependent children under 21 and other dependent relatives are also treated as habitually resident.[86]

If you are a British citizen, you can only be an EU 'worker' or person with the right to reside in the UK under the above provisions, if you are returning after working in another EEA country.[87]

In most circumstances a person classed as a worker (see below) will have to claim income-based JSA, not IS. Note that some groups classed as workers will have ceased or be unable to work and will be claiming IS, not income-based JSA.

'Workers'

The term 'worker' is not defined in EC legislation. Its meaning is far from clear and is the subject of complex and sometimes contradictory caselaw. It should be given a broad interpretation, however, and includes many people who are not actually working.[88]

You should be covered if you fall into any of the following categories.

- You are working in the UK, whether full- or part-time. Any genuine and effective work should count, so long as it is not so irregular and limited that it is a purely marginal or ancillary activity.[89]
- You have worked in the UK but have become involuntarily unemployed or temporarily incapable of work.[90]
- You have worked in the UK, have become involuntarily unemployed and must take on occupational retraining to compete in the job market.[91]
- You have voluntarily given up work in the UK to take up vocational training linked to your previous job.[92] A person who gives up work voluntarily or involuntarily but then immediately signs on as available for work may also keep the status of a worker.[93] The DSS guidance[94] does not reflect the commissioner's finding.

- You have been temporarily laid off and are seeking to return to work with the same employer in the UK.[95]
- You have ceased to work in the UK because of permanent incapacity, *and*
  - you have resided continuously in the UK for at least two years; *or*
  - your spouse is (or was before marrying you) British; *or*
  - your incapacity resulted from an industrial injury or disease which entitles you to benefit (eg, incapacity benefit, industrial injuries benefits).[96]
- You have retired on or after pensionable age; *and*
  - you have resided continuously in the UK for at least three years and were employed in the UK for at least 12 months immediately before retiring; *or*
  - your spouse is (or was before marrying you) British.[97]

Work-seekers

If you are looking for work in the UK but have not worked here before, the Benefits Agency will almost certainly not treat you as a 'worker' and you will not be exempt from the habitual residence test.[98] EU and domestic caselaw has found that if you have come to the UK to seek work, you are not a 'worker' for the purposes of EEC Regulation 1612/68.[99] This applies even if you have previously worked in another Member State,[100] although you may be able to argue otherwise in terms of the wording of the benefit regulations. If you are not classed as a worker, you may be able to cite EEC Regulation 1408/71 to help you satisfy the habitual residence test (see p69). If you are refused benefit because you are a work-seeker, you should seek specialist advice to appeal (see p156). Work-seekers who have not worked in the UK are excluded from the provision of EEC Regulation 1251/70.

Right to reside in the UK

The following categories of people and their families have the right to reside in the UK under EEC Directives 68/360 and 73/148:

- 'Workers' (see p73).[101] Work-seekers are not covered.[102]
- Self-employed people or providers of services on a commercial basis.[103]
- Recipients of commercial services (this could include financially independent tourists, business travellers and people paying for private education or health care).[104]

Your right to reside in the UK is confirmed by the granting of a residence permit but the lack of a permit does not negate that right.[105]

You may lose the right of residence if you leave the UK for more than six months unless it is for military service.

'Requirement to leave' the UK

If you are an EU national (see p72), claiming IS or income-based JSA can, in certain circumstances, result in you receiving a letter from the Home Office stating that you are no longer lawfully resident in the UK and that you should make arrangements to leave. The power of the Secretary of State to issue such letters has been upheld by the courts.[106]Although the power to remove you exists under UK immigration law,[107] it is rarely used and you cannot be deported simply because you have claimed benefit.[108]

Notification that you should leave the UK is likely if:

- You have been claiming benefit while seeking work for more than six months. The Home Office argue that you are no longer a 'worker' exercising Community rights in these circumstances. The European Court of Justice has upheld the Government's right to impose such a time limit on work-seekers, with the proviso that if you can show you have 'genuine chances' of finding work, you retain your right of residence.[109]
- You have claimed benefit when your right to reside in the UK is subject to the condition that you are self-supporting.[110] This condition applies to students, pensioners and others who are not covered by EEC Directives 68/360 and 73/148 (see p74).

The IS and income-based JSA regulations state that if you are an EU national who is 'required to leave' the UK by the Secretary of State, you are no longer entitled to benefit.[111] The Court of Appeal has held that this applies to people who have received the Home Office letters referred to above.[112] An appeal to the House of Lords is pending (see future editions of CPAG's *Welfare Rights Bulletin* for latest developments).

Refugees and people with 'exceptional leave to remain'

Refugees

The UK is a signatory to the 1951 United Nations Convention on the Status of Refugees which gives refugees certain rights of asylum in a foreign country, including the right to public relief and assistance. A refugee is defined under the convention as someone who is unable or unwilling to return to his own country because of a '...well founded fear of persecution for reasons of race, religion, nationality, membership of a particular social group or political opinion...'

If the Home Office accept that you are a refugee, you and your family are entitled to remain in the UK and claim IS or income-based JSA under the normal rules from the date you are recorded as a refugee by the Secretary of State.[113] You do not have to satisfy the 'habitual residence' test (see p69).[114]

You, or your partner, can also claim backdated urgent cases payments of IS for any period following the first refusal of your asylum claim (if you claimed asylum 'on arrival in the UK' – see p78), or the date of your asylum claim (if you claimed asylum other than 'on arrival in the UK'). You cannot, however, get IS for any period prior to 5 February 1996 and you must submit your claim for backdated payments within 28 days of being notified that you have been accepted as a refugee.[115] (The normal rules about good cause for backdating benefit do not apply.) You cannot get backdated IS urgent cases payments for any week in which you were receiving contribution-based JSA, even if your IS urgent cases applicable amount is higher than the JSA you received, unless the member of the couple who did not qualify for JSA makes the claim for IS urgent cases.[116] Only IS, and not income-based JSA, can be backdated when you are granted refugee status.

'Exceptional leave to remain'

In some circumstances, the Home Office will not accept that you are a refugee but will grant you 'exceptional leave to remain' in the UK on humanitarian grounds (your family will not normally be allowed to join you until you have been in the UK for four years). Some people from Somalia and Iraq have recently been granted 'exceptional leave to remain' because it was temporarily unsafe to return to their countries.

Some people are granted exceptional leave for reasons other than applying for asylum. Initially exceptional leave may be given for a year but it does not count as limited leave. A person applying for an extension of their exceptional leave, provided they applied before the original leave had expired continues to be treated as a person with exceptional leave.

If you are granted 'exceptional leave to remain' in the UK, you are entitled to claim IS or income-based JSA under the normal rules. You do not have to satisfy the 'habitual residence' test (see p69).[117]

Asylum-seekers

Immigration issues

Option to claim jobseeker's allowance

You are treated as an asylum-seeker while you are applying for refugee status[118] (see p75). You are generally given temporary leave to enter or remain in the UK while your application for asylum is being considered. If your application for asylum is refused, you have the right of appeal. It can take several months and sometimes two or three years before your application for asylum is finally decided, although the Government has now introduced quicker procedures and curtailed appeal rights for many asylum-seekers.

Under immigration law, asylum-seekers are not disallowed from claiming 'public funds' (see p65), but under the social security rules governing entitlement to public funds benefits only a minority of asylum-seekers now qualify. As an asylum-seeker you can apply to the Home Office for permission to work after six months. You cannot claim income-based JSA until you have permission to work.[119]

If you have been in Great Britain for some time you may satisfy the contribution conditions for JSA. If you need to claim a means-tested benefit as well you will have to claim income-based JSA rather than IS, unless your partner claims IS instead.[120]

In most circumstances even after you have this permission to work, and you sign on and use the services of the JobCentre, you should still continue to claim IS urgent cases payments rather than urgent cases income-based JSA. This is because you will not then be required to satisfy the rules relating to availability for/actively seeking work and having a current jobseeker's agreement.

Restrictions on benefit entitlement

The Government introduced sweeping restrictions to the rights of asylum-seekers to claim benefits from 5 February 1996.[121] Previously, asylum-seekers were entitled to claim urgent cases payments of IS and other benefits until their applications for asylum were finally decided. Under the new rules, most asylum-seekers were excluded from all entitlement to IS and most other non-contributory benefits.

The rules were widely criticised as unjust and contrary to international conventions. A legal challenge was successfully mounted and some of the new rules were declared invalid by the Court of Appeal in June 1996[122] (see p79 for how the court case affected entitlement). One of the Judges commented that '... the Regulations necessarily contemplate for some a life so destitute that to my mind no civilised nation can tolerate it'. Despite this, the Government re-introduced the rules by Act of Parliament and thus in a valid form, with effect from 24 July 1996.[123]

Entitlement to IS

If you are an asylum-seeker, you are not entitled to IS under the normal rules because you are classed as a 'person from abroad' (see p64).[124] You are entitled to urgent cases payments of IS (see p82) if you fall into one of the following categories (you may be entitled to backdated payments if you are subsequently accepted as a refugee - see p76):

(a)   You applied for asylum 'on arrival in the UK'[125]

- Your application for asylum must be officially recorded.
- The phrase 'on arrival in the UK' (see p80) is not defined in the regulations. It is probably intended to mean 'at the port of entry' and DSS guidance says it means 'before clearing immigration control'.[126] Arguably, it could also include those who apply immediately or very soon after entry. The Benefits Agency are unlikely to accept this argument, so you will need to appeal to an SSAT (see p156).
- You must have arrived from a country other than the Irish Republic, the Channel Islands or the Isle of Man and you must not be 're-entering' the UK. You may not qualify, therefore, if you spent time in Eire immediately before arriving in the UK, or you were recently in the UK as a visitor and you return as an asylum-seeker.
- You are entitled to urgent cases payments of IS until you receive a decision on your asylum application.[127] You are not entitled to IS pending an appeal against an asylum decision, unless the decision was determined before 5 February 1996 and an appeal was pending on that date or was submitted within the time limits specified in the immigration rules.[128] What counts as the date on which an asylum claim is determined is not defined in immigration law (see date of decision, p79).
- If you claimed IS at any time before 5 February 1996, see (c) below.

(b)   You apply for asylum following a special declaration by the Secretary of State[129]

- The declaration is to the effect that your country is subject to such a fundamental change of circumstances, you would not normally be ordered to return there by the Secretary of State. You must be a national of the country concerned. Stateless people are not covered.

- You must submit your application for asylum within the three months following the date of the declaration. Your application must be officially recorded.
- You are entitled to urgent cases payments of IS until you receive a decision on your asylum application.[130] For what counts as the date on which a decision is made see below.

(c) You were entitled to IS as an asylum-seeker before 5 February 1996[131]

- All asylum-seekers were eligible for urgent cases payments of IS prior to 5 February 1996. If you were entitled to IS before that date, your entitlement continues until you receive a decision on your asylum application. You are not entitled to IS pending an appeal against an asylum decision, unless the decision was determined before 5 February 1996, and an appeal was pending on that date or was submitted within the time limits specified in the immigration rules.[132]
- You should be covered if you were entitled to IS at any time before 5 February 1996. The regulations do not say that you have to be entitled on or immediately before 5 February (contrary to DSS advice[133]).
- You may be able to backdate your entitlement to come within this provision by requesting a review or appealing (see pp131 and 158).
- Any members of your family (see p318) on 5 February 1996 are also covered, allowing them to claim IS if, for example, they separate from you or reach the age of 16, or if you 'swap' claimants (see p123).[134]

Note: Entitlement from 5 February to 24 July 1996

Although the above rules only came into effect on 24 July 1996 (when the Asylum and Immigration Act nullified the June 1996 court case), transitional protection was only extended to asylum-seekers entitled to IS before 5 February 1996 (see (c) above). As a result those first claiming IS between 5 February and 24 July, lost their entitlement from the latter date unless they satisfied the new rules. A legal challenge on this point was unsuccessful but an appeal is pending[135] (see future editions of CPAG's *Welfare Rights Bulletin* for latest developments). It is not possible to claim backdated IS solely for the period 5 February to 24 July by submitting a late claim or review (unless you are subsequently accepted as a refugee – see p75).[136]

Date of decision refusing asylum

You cease to be an asylum-seeker entitled to IS if this decision was made on 5 February 1996 or later. However, the date of determination could be one of several dates. The date of determination is not defined in immigration law. The DSS has treated the date of determination as:

- the date of the actual decision;
- the date on which the asylum-seeker is notified of the decision.

It could also be the date of the letter in which reasons for refusal are given. The right of appeal against a refusal of asylum status runs from the date the asylum-seeker is notified of the decision which may be months after the initial decision. The Benefits Agency now interprets the determination date as the date of the initial decision, which is why asylum-seekers may learn of the refusal first from the DSS when benefit is withdrawn.

Asylum-seekers who were notified that their asylum application had failed soon after 5 February 1996 should consider requesting a review of the withdrawal of benefit on the grounds that the decision refusing asylum was actually taken earlier. For details about reviews and backdating see p131.

On arrival in the UK

The Benefits Agency has accepted that a person who is 'prevented' from claiming asylum because, eg, there is no interpreter available, can be treated as applying on arrival if s/he does so as soon as an interpreter is present.[137] This suggests that the Benefits Agency accepts that a person claims 'on arrival' if s/he does so as soon as is reasonably possible.

Documentation

There are often problems in providing acceptable evidence of identification and status when you claim IS as an asylum-seeker if you have come to the UK without the usual travel and identity documents, or with false documentation.

- If you apply for asylum 'on arrival in the UK' (see above), you should be issued with a 'standard acknowledgement letter' (SAL1). You should also be given a form IS96 confirming you have been granted 'temporary admission' to the UK. These documents should be accepted by the Benefits Agency as proof of your identity and status.
- If you apply for asylum after entry to the UK, you will be given a GEN32 form calling you for interview. You should subsequently be given a standard acknowledgement letter (SAL2) which should be accepted by the Benefits Agency as proof of your identity and status.
- If you do not have an SAL, the Benefits Agency can contact the Home Office by telephone for confirmation of your status. The Benefits Agency should be willing to interview you to establish identity and should take account of relevant correspondence concerning your application for asylum produced by a lawyer or advice agency. If you

cannot produce evidence of your identity, you may have to produce an affidavit sworn before a solicitor.

- An SAL issued before 12 October 1995 was not numbered so as to indicate whether it was issued at the port of entry or after entry.

People not entitled to IS

There are few options for asylum-seekers who are not entitled to IS.

- You should ask your MP to take up your case with the Secretary of State for Social Security and request an extra-statutory payment (see p139). (A large number of queries about lack of access to benefits and the hardship caused may influence MPs to change the law.)
- You are entitled to apply for a crisis loan from the social fund to alleviate the consequences of a disaster (see p447). The *Social Fund Guide* stresses that a person from abroad who is not entitled to IS is not excluded from a crisis loan and that '...particular attention should be given to the clothing needs of asylum-seekers...'[138] The problem is that you must be able to show you are likely to be able to repay the loan.
- You will lose access to some passported benefits. You can however get health benefits on grounds of low income (see p466).
- If you have children, you should approach your social services department for help under the Children Act 1989. It has a duty to safeguard the welfare of children in need by providing services which could include accommodation, food, heat and, exceptionally, cash payments (but not for ongoing circumstances).[139]
- The Court of Appeal has held that destitute asylum-seekers are entitled to assistance from local authorities under s21 of the National Assistance Act 1948.[140] Section 21 covers the provision of accommodation, including board and other associated services and amenities. Some local authorities are making weekly payments to asylum-seekers who are not entitled to benefit as well as providing accommodation. There is no reason why people facing destitution because they have failed the 'habitual residence test' should also not be covered by s21.
- For advice on charitable sources of help, contact the Refugee Council (see Appendix 3). Local churches and other religious centres may also be able to help.

Sponsorship undertakings

Most people subject to immigration control are admitted to the UK on the condition that they can maintain and accommodate themselves. A relative or friend in the UK can act as a sponsor to help satisfy this condition.

In some cases, sponsors are required to give a written undertaking under the terms of the Immigration Act 1971 (normally on a special Home Office form – RON 112), that they will provide maintenance and accommodation. Such undertakings are not always required, and it is not government policy to request undertakings from spouses whose partners and/or children are joining them from abroad. (Another member of the family or friend could be required to sign an undertaking for them.) Voluntary declarations of sponsorship which are commonly used to support applications to enter the UK are *not* undertakings – this distinction is often not understood by the DSS.

If you have been in the UK subject to a mandatory sponsorship undertaking for less than five years, you are not entitled to IS under the normal rules unless you become a British citizen.[141] After five years, you are entitled to IS under the normal rules. The five years runs either from your date of entry into the UK, or the date the undertaking was given, whichever was later.[142] You are entitled to urgent cases payments of IS during the five-year period if your sponsor dies.[143]

If you were entitled to IS before 5 February 1996 as a person subject to a mandatory sponsorship undertaking, the above rules do not apply to you.[144] You remain entitled to IS.

If you are paid benefit as a sponsored immigrant and your sponsor did sign an undertaking the Benefits Agency can recover the amount of benefit paid to you from your sponsor.[145] It has been government policy not to enforce this power if your sponsor cannot afford to pay. If the undertaking was given before 23 May 1980, the Benefits Agency does *not* have the power to recover any money from the sponsor.[146]

Urgent cases payments

If you are not entitled to IS under the normal rules because you are classed as a 'person from abroad' (see p64), you are entitled to urgent cases payments of IS if any of the following circumstances apply to you:

• You have 'limited leave' to remain in the UK on the condition that you do not have recourse to 'public funds', but you are temporarily without money. You are entitled to urgent cases payments of IS for a maximum of 42 days if:

- you have supported yourself without recourse to public funds during your limited leave; *and*
- you are temporarily without funds because remittances from abroad have been disrupted; *and*
- there is a reasonable expectation that your supply of funds will be resumed.[147]
- You are an asylum-seeker and you satisfy the rules set out on pp77-80.[148]
- You have been in the UK subject to a sponsorship undertaking for less than five years and your sponsor has died (see p82).[149]

Note:

- Urgent cases payments of IS are less than normal IS. Your personal allowance is 10 per cent less and there are modified rules relating to income and capital. Asylum-seekers are not eligible to claim non-contributory benefits including disability living allowance and attendance allowance. They will, therefore, not be able to qualify for the disability-related premiums except where an adult establishes incapacity for work for a period of a year. See p46 for full details of urgent cases payments and CPAG's *Rights Guide to Non-Means-Tested Benefits* 1997/98 edn.
- You do not have to satisfy the 'habitual residence' test to receive urgent cases payments.
- Urgent cases payments are payments of IS and therefore act as a 'passport' to other benefits – eg, social fund and health benefits.
- Urgent cases payments count as 'public funds' under the immigration rules (see p65). Asylum-seekers and people subject to mandatory sponsorship undertakings are not normally prohibited from claiming public funds, however, while a claim for a short period from people with limited leave is unlikely to affect their immigration status. If in doubt, seek advice (see Appendix 3).
- As an asylum-seeker you may be allowed to work after six months. If you are looking for work you can opt to claim income-based JSA at the urgent cases rate but it will generally be simpler to continue to claim IS urgent cases. If you qualify for contribution-based JSA you will have to claim the urgent cases rate of income-based JSA and not IS.

4. RESIDENTIAL AND NURSING CARE

This section covers:

- IS for people with 'preserved rights' (p85)
- IS for people without 'preserved rights' in independent homes (p90)
- IS for people in local authority homes (p92)
- Local authority funding and charges for residential and nursing care (p93)

Residential or nursing care in this section means:

- local authority care homes (see p92); *and*
- independent (ie, private or voluntary sector) residential care or nursing homes (see below and p90).

If you go into residential or nursing care, you are entitled to IS if you satisfy the normal rules, but your 'applicable amount' is usually calculated differently. There are also more generous capital rules, including an upper limit of £16,000 (see p385 for details).

The Government's community care reforms introduced a new funding structure for residential care from 1 April 1993.[150] Under the previous system, people entering independent residential care or nursing homes were entitled to claim special higher rates of IS to help pay their fees. Most people who have remained in independent homes since 31 March 1993 have 'preserved rights' to continue to claim these special rates of IS (see p85).

If you enter independent care for the first time after 31 March 1993 you do not have 'preserved rights'. You can still claim IS, but only at the normal rates plus a 'residential allowance' (see p90). If you need more public funding to pay for a place in an independent home you must apply to your local authority social services department (see p91).

If you are in a local authority home, you do not have 'preserved rights'. Your IS applicable amount is worked out differently to that for people in independent care (see p92).

If you are in a local authority home or a local authority is funding your place in an independent home, any IS you are entitled to will be clawed back in weekly charges, together with most other income you have. See p93 for details.

People with preserved rights

Who has preserved rights?[151]

You have preserved rights to claim special higher rates of IS if you were living in most types of independent residential care or nursing homes (see p88) on 31 March 1993 and:

- you were getting IS at the special higher rates; *or*
- you were not getting IS because you were able to afford to pay for the home yourself; *or*
- one of the above would have applied but for the fact that you were absent from the home for:
  - up to 4 weeks if you were a temporary resident;
  - up to 13 weeks if you were a permanent resident;
  - up to 52 weeks if you were in hospital.

You are covered if the home you were living in was a residential care or nursing home, as defined on p90. Complex rules apply if you were living in a home with less than four residents or provided by a close relative or the Abbeyfield Society.[152] You should seek specialist advice if this applies to you. In certain circumstances, you will also have preserved rights if your partner had them.[153]

Losing preserved rights[154]

You will lose your preserved rights if you are absent from an independent home for:

- more than 4 weeks if you are a temporary resident;
- more than 13 weeks if you are a permanent resident;
- more than 52 weeks if you are in hospital.

Note: You do not lose your preserved rights if you move from one independent home to another, as long as any gap does not exceed the above periods.

Calculation of IS

If you have preserved rights, your IS applicable amount consists of an amount for personal expenses and an accommodation allowance to cover all or part of the charge made by the home. You are not entitled to any premiums. If you are a member of a couple see p323. Attendance allowance and disability living allowance are taken into account as income when calculating your IS.[155]

Personal expenses[156]

These are as follows:

Single claimant	£14.10
Couple	£28.20
Dependent child aged 18+	£14.10
16-17	£ 9.80
11-15	£ 8.45
0-10	£ 5.80

Accommodation allowance

The amount you receive will cover the weekly charge for your accommodation including meals and services where these are provided, but only up to a maximum level (see below).[157]

If you have to pay for some meals separately, your accommodation allowance will include for each person, either an amount to cover the actual cost of the meals if they can be provided by the home, *or*, if not,[158]

- £1.10 for breakfast
- £1.55 for lunch
- £1.55 for dinner

unless your meals taken outside the home cost less.

If you pay additional charges for heating, attendance needs, extra baths, laundry or a special diet you follow for medical reasons, these will be included in the accommodation allowance, so long as they are provided by the home and not by an outside agency.[159] You will not get the cost of these meals and/or extra services met in full if your accommodation charge plus the cost of meals or extra services is more than the maximum (see below).

If you receive housing benefit towards part of your accommodation charge this will be deducted from that charge and reduce your IS accordingly.[160]

Maximum accommodation allowances[161]

Your accommodation charge (including any charges for additional services and meals) will usually only be met up to a maximum level. This maximum varies depending on the type of home you are in and the type of care you receive.[162] You may find that the amount payable does not fully cover your home fees.

If you are in a residential care home the maximum varies according to the type of care the home is registered to provide, or if the home is not registered, according to the type of care you receive.[163] The type of care depends on the health conditions and/or age of the residents – see the table on p88 for details. If more than one category could apply to you, the amount you get is decided as follows:[164]

- where the home is registered to provide the type of care you get, you will receive the amount that is allowed for that type of care;
- if the care you receive is different from the type the home is registered to provide, you will receive the allowance for the lower or lowest of the categories of care which the home is registered to provide;
- in any other case you will receive the amount most consistent with the care you receive.

If you are in a nursing home the maximum varies according to the type of care you actually receive. The type of care depends on your health conditions and/or age - see the table on p88 for details. If more than one category could apply to you, you receive the amount most consistent with the care you receive.[165] You could, for example, get the 'terminal illness' rate if that is the level of care you receive even though you are not, in fact, terminally ill.[166]

Some homes may be registered both as a residential care and a nursing home. In these cases your maximum accommodation allowance will be decided according to whether you are receiving residential or nursing care.

The tables below list the maximum amounts payable in residential care and nursing homes. The following definitions apply to the categories of health conditions noted in the tables:

'Mental disorder' is defined as 'mental illness, arrested or incomplete development of mind, psychopathic disorder, and any other disorder or disability of mind'.[167]

'Mental handicap' is defined as 'a state of arrested or incomplete development of mind which includes impairment of intelligence and social functioning'.[168] 'Senility' is not mental handicap but can amount to a mental disorder.[169]

'Disablement' is defined as meaning that you are 'blind, deaf or dumb or substantially and permanently handicapped by illness, injury or congenital deformity or any other disability prescribed by the Secretary of State'.[170]

'Very dependent elderly' means you are over pension age and *either*:

- registered or certified as blind; *or*
- entitled to attendance allowance or disability living allowance care component at the highest rate (even if it is not payable because you have not met the qualifying period); *or*
- getting war or industrial injury constant attendance allowance.[171]

Residential care homes

Health condition/age	Maximum payable
Old age	£208
Past or present mental disorder but excluding mental handicap	£220
Past or present drug or alcohol dependence	£20
Mental handicap	£250
Physical disablement if under pension age, or, if over pension age, claimant had become disabled before reaching 60 (65 if a man)	£285
Physical disablement (over pension age and not disabled before reaching 60 (woman) or (65 man)	£208
Very dependent elderly (see definition above)	£240
Any other condition	£208

The above amounts are increased by £41 a week for homes in the Greater London area (see p90 for definition).

Nursing homes

Health condition/age	Maximum payable
Past or present mental disorder but excluding mental handicap	£312
Mental handicap	£318
Past or present drug or alcohol dependence	£312
Physical disablement, if under pension age, or if over pension age, claimant had become disabled before reaching 60 (65 if a man)	£352
Over pension age and had become physically disabled after reaching 60 (65 if a man)	£311
Terminal illness	£311
Any other condition (including elderly)	£311

The above amounts are increased by £46 a week for homes in the Greater London area (see p90 for definition).

Getting more than the maximum

You can get more than the maximum if:

- you have lived in the same accommodation for over 12 months and could afford it without IS when you moved in. You will get your full accommodation charge for up to 13 weeks after you claim IS[172] if you are trying to move but need time to find suitable alternative accommodation. Income which is normally disregarded for IS may be taken into account during the 13 weeks.[173] The 13-week concession does not apply if you are being accommodated by the local authority because you are homeless or under the authority's duty to promote the welfare of children; *or*
- you have been living in a residential care or nursing home since 28 April 1985 and your accommodation allowance under the present rules is lower than what you received then plus £10. (For further details on this see the 22nd edition of the *Handbook*, p78.)[174]

Money from other sources

If your IS does not meet your accommodation fees, you will have to try to obtain the balance from other sources. Money from charities or relatives which is used to pay fees is ignored for IS purposes.[175] Your local authority can only provide 'topping-up' finance in restricted circumstances. They are only responsible for providing funding if:[176]

- you lose your preserved rights (see p85); *or*
- you were under pension age on 31 March 1993; *or*
- you are over pension age, have been evicted from a residential care home and need to move to another residential care home (not a nursing home), which is owned or managed by a different person.

When the special rates are not payable

You will not receive the special rates of IS if:[177]

- your home is run by a 'close relative' (see p27) or your residency is not a commercial one; *or*
- you are away on holiday for up to 13 weeks; *or*
- you entered the home to take advantage of the special rates; *or*
- you are aged 16-18 inclusive and are in care – unless you are liable to pay for the accommodation yourself other than to a local authority.

Temporary absences

If you go into hospital, see p96.

If you have to pay a retaining fee to keep your home while you are temporarily absent from it, up to 80 per cent of your accommodation allowance is payable to cover it (in addition to any other IS you are entitled to) for up to four weeks, or 52 weeks if you have been in hospital for more than six weeks or you are in a local authority home.[178] Commissioners disagree about your entitlement to a retaining fee if you are temporarily away from your usual care home and are temporarily living in another independent residential care home.[179]

People without preserved rights in independent homes

If you do not have 'preserved rights', you are not entitled to the special higher rates of IS. This applies to everybody first entering an independent care or nursing home after 31 March 1993.

You are still entitled to claim IS if you satisfy the normal rules. Your applicable amount is calculated in the normal way – ie, personal allowances plus premiums (see p329).You are also, in most cases, entitled to a 'residential allowance' to help pay your home fees (see below). If you are a member of a couple, see p323. If you go into hospital, see p97.

If you go into an independent home for a temporary period (either for respite care or a trial period) and you have housing costs in your own home, see p28. If you go into an independent home permanently you cannot be paid housing costs on your former home or claim housing benefit to cover your residential care fees.[180]

Residential allowance[181]

You are entitled to a residential allowance of £56 a week (£62 if a home is in the Greater London area – see below) if you are living in an independent residential care or nursing home (see below). You must be 16 or over, receiving personal care and not have 'preserved rights' (see p85). Your accommodation must be provided on a commercial basis.

- Greater London includes parts of Essex (Chigwell, Dagenham and Waltham Cross), Hertfordshire (Elstree, Ridge, Shenley, South Mimms, South Broxbourne) and Surrey (Spelthorne and part of Elmbridge).[182]
- You are counted as living in an independent residential care home if the home is:[183]
    - registered or deemed to be registered under the Registered Homes Act 1984 or the Social Work (Scotland) Act 1968 (homes which provide board and personal care are now required to be registered); *or*

– run by a body established by Royal Charter or Act of Parliament (other than a local authority) and provides board and personal care.

If you live in other unregistered accommodation, you will not be entitled to a residential allowance but you will be able to claim housing benefit (see p214).

• You are counted as living in an independent nursing home if the home is:[184]
    – registered as a nursing home under the Registered Homes Act 1984 or the Nursing Homes Registration (Scotland) Act 1938 or the Mental Health (Scotland) Act 1984; *or*
    – run by a body established by Royal Charter or special Act of Parliament.

A hospice does not count as a nursing home.[185]

The residential allowance stops after three weeks' absence from your home (six weeks if you are in hospital - separate periods in hospital are linked if they are less than 28 days apart).[186]

Effects of local authority funding

If you cannot afford or can no longer afford to pay for a place in an independent home, you can apply to your local authority for funding (see p93). You will have to use most of your income, including your IS to pay local authority charges.

If you are funded by the local authority you may find that your IS goes down after four weeks. This is because your attendance allowance (AA) or disability living allowance (DLA) (care component) will stop and you will therefore lose entitlement to the severe disability premium (and sometimes the higher pensioner premium) – see p338.[187] In some circumstances (eg, when you have a property for sale), you may be better off not receiving funding from your local authority, so that you can retain entitlement to AA/DLA and the severe disability premium.

If you are receiving local authority funding, charitable or voluntary payments used to top up the funding to pay for a more expensive home are disregarded as income for IS purposes.[188] If you are not receiving local authority funding, charitable or voluntary payments towards the home fees are disregarded up to a maximum of the difference between your applicable amount (less the amounts listed as personal expenses on p86) and the home fees.[189]

People in local authority homes

If you are permanently in a local authority home, your IS applicable amount is worked out in a special way. You do not have 'preserved rights' (see p85) and you are not entitled to a 'residential allowance' (see p90). You will get less IS than if you were in an independent home. You will also always lose your AA/DLA care component after four weeks. You will have to use your IS to pay local authority charges (see p93).

What counts as a local authority home

For IS purposes, you are counted as living in a local authority home if:[190]

- the home is owned or managed by a local authority; *and*
- the accommodation is provided under sections 21 and 24 of Part III of the National Assistance Act 1948 or sections 13B and 59 of the Social Work (Scotland) Act 1968 or section 7 of the Mental Health (Scotland) Act 1984; *and*
- board is provided (but if you buy and pay for food when you want – eg, in a café or canteen on the premises, this does not count as board – this will apply to many local authority hostels, the residents of which can claim ordinary rate IS and housing benefit); *and*
- you are not a person who is under 18 and in the care of a local authority in Scotland.

If you are living in a home which transferred from the local authority to the independent sector after 11 August 1991 while you were there, you will still be treated as living in a local authority home for IS purposes.[191]

IS entitlement

If you or your partner are in a local authority home, your IS applicable amount is worked out as follows:[192]

- **If you are a single person** your applicable amount is a set figure of £62.45 a week (no premiums are payable). If you are temporarily in the home, you can continue to get housing costs on your normal home (see p28).
- **If you are a single parent** your applicable amount is a set figure of £62.45 a week. If you are temporarily in the home, you can continue to get IS for your children (see Chapter 17), the family premium or family premium lone parent rate plus IS housing costs (see p26).
- **If you are one of a couple:**
  - if you or your partner are temporarily in the home you are still treated as a couple for IS. Your applicable amount will be £62.45 for

the partner in the home plus the normal allowance (including premiums) for a single person for the other partner;
 – if you or your partner have permanently moved into a home, you are no longer treated as a couple for IS. The partner in the home will have an applicable amount of £62.45 a week. The other partner must claim IS separately as a single person or parent;
 – if you are both in a home, you will each have an applicable amount of £62.45. If you are temporary residents, you can continue to get IS housing costs for your normal home (see p28).
 • If your child is living with you in a home you can claim the normal child allowance for her/him.
 • If you go into hospital, see p96.

Local authority funding and charges for residential care

Funding

If you cannot afford to pay for a place in a home and you do not have 'preserved rights' (see p85 for exceptions), you can apply for funding from your local authority social services department. This may happen if you are going into a home for the first time, or you are already in a home and your capital falls below £16,000 (see p385). If social services assess you as needing residential or nursing care, they must provide and fund a suitable placement for you.[193] This could either be in a local authority home or an independent home, in which case the local authority must contract to pay the full fees to the provider. There are no legal maximum rates of funding but the local authority is not obliged to pay more than is necessary to provide a placement which is suitable for your needs.

Charges

If you are in a local authority home or being funded by a local authority in an independent home, you will have to pay a weekly accommodation charge to the authority.[194] The charge is means-tested and the charging rules are laid down in national regulations.[195] They are based on the IS regulations but there are important differences. Guidance on the regulations is set out in the *Charging for Residential Accommodation Guide* issued by the Department of Health.
 The main features of the charging rules are:

 • If you have more than £16,000 capital, you must pay a charge equal to the full cost of your placement. Property is treated as for IS (see p389), but:

   – property up for sale is not disregarded;
   – property occupied by anyone can be disregarded;
   – the share of a jointly owned property is valued differently.

Notional capital rules are similar to the IS rules (see p397). If you cannot afford to pay your charge because your capital is tied up in a property, the local authority can place a legal charge on the property and collect the debt when it is sold.[196]

- If you have less than £16,000 capital, your charge will be:
  – your total weekly income (including IS and tariff income from capital over £10,000 (see p385) but excluding most income disregarded under the IS rules); *less*
  – a personal allowance of at least £14.10 a week (ie, you must be left with a least this amount after paying your charge).

You cannot be charged more than the full fees for the home.

- Unlike the IS rules, only *your* income and capital counts – *not* your partner's. Joint savings are divided in half.
- The local authority can impose a standard reasonable charge for temporary placements of up to eight weeks.[197] If you have housing costs on your normal home, see p26.

5. PEOPLE IN HOSPITAL

If you, your partner or child goes into hospital, your IS is usually reduced after a specified period. Other benefits (eg, incapacity benefit, retirement pension) may also be reduced, which means you may still be entitled to some IS or you might even qualify for IS for the first time.

   The reductions apply if a person is receiving free in-patient treatment in a hospital or similar institution under NHS legislation.[198] People paying fees for their maintenance, other than under specified legislation, will not be exempt.[199] People in nursing homes funded by health authorities or health boards may also be caught by the rules.[200]

Housing costs

IS housing costs (see p27) are payable for your normal home for up to 52 weeks while you are in hospital, providing you are unlikely to be away for substantially longer than 52 weeks.[201] Someone else may be able to get IS housing costs no longer paid to you (see p26).

Single people in hospital

After four weeks any attendance allowance (AA) or disability living allowance (DLA) you receive stops and you therefore lose your severe disability premium[202] (carers lose their carer's premium eight weeks after their invalid care allowance stops[203]).

After six weeks your IS applicable amount is reduced to £15.60[204] plus any housing costs.

After 52 weeks your applicable amount is reduced to £12.50.[205] You can be paid less than this if:[206]

- you are unable to look after your own affairs (eg, mentally ill or senile) and another person has been appointed to act on your behalf; *and*
- the IS is paid to the hospital at the request of the appointee, or to the hospital as the appointee; *and*
- a doctor who is treating you certifies that you cannot make use of all or part of your benefit, and that it cannot be used on your behalf.

This rule could leave you without any income at all, though your relatives and the hospital staff should be consulted about how much you should receive. Your appointee could refuse to allow the Benefits Agency to pay the hospital direct. S/he could receive payments on your behalf instead to make sure you get the money.

Single parents in hospital

After four weeks any AA/DLA you receive stops and you therefore lose your severe disability premium[207] (carers lose their carer's premium eight weeks after their invalid care allowance stops[208]).

After six weeks your IS applicable amount is reduced to £15.60 *plus* your children's personal allowances, *plus* the family and disabled child premiums,[209] *plus* housing costs.

After 52 weeks you will lose your housing costs. You will also be treated as a single person (see p325) once you are likely to be in hospital for substantially longer than 52 weeks.[210] If your child is also in hospital, see below.

Note: the family premium is paid at a higher rate for lone parents (see p333).

Couples

After four weeks if one of you is in hospital, that partner will lose her/his AA/DLA. If both of you are in hospital, you will both lose your AA/DLA. In either case, you can continue to get the severe disability premium, but only at the single person rate.[211] Carers lose their carer's premium eight weeks after their invalid care allowance stops.[212]

After six weeks if one of you is in hospital, your IS applicable amount is reduced by £12.50. This also applies if both of you are in hospital but only one of you has been there for over six weeks. If both of you are in hospital for over six weeks your applicable amount is £31.20 personal allowance for you both, *plus* personal allowances for your children and family and disabled child premiums (if applicable), *plus* housing costs.[213]

After 52 weeks if one or both of you are in hospital, you will count as single people once one of you is likely to be in hospital for substantially longer than 52 weeks.[214]

If only one of you is in hospital, that person's applicable amount will be £12.50 and the other person must claim separately as a single claimant or lone parent. If both of you are in hospital and have no children, you will each have an applicable amount of £12.50.[215] If both of you are in hospital and you have children, one of you is treated as responsible for the children and has an applicable amount of £15.60 *plus* the children's personal allowances, disabled child premiums (if applicable) and the family premium.[216] The other partner has an applicable amount of £12.50.[217]

If a child is also in hospital, see below.

Children in hospital

If your child goes into hospital, your IS stays the same for 12 weeks. After that the personal allowance you receive for the child reduces to £12.50.[218] Any premiums you receive in relation to the child remain in payment. Even if your child loses the care component of DLA because s/he has been in hospital for over 12 weeks, you still get a disabled child premium, as long as s/he continues to be treated as a member of your family (see p325).[219]

The rule about adjustment to IS for a child in hospital applies equally where parent(s) and child are in hospital.[220]

People in residential care or nursing homes

Up to six weeks in hospital

- **If you have 'preserved rights'** (see p85) and you go into hospital for six weeks or less you will still get your personal allowance and your accommodation allowance as long as you still have to pay the charge for the home – or a reduced allowance if the charge is reduced.[221] If you are single, do not have to pay the charge, and are unlikely to return to the home, you will get IS as a hospital patient (see p94). If you are

likely to return but do not have to pay the charge, you will get your personal allowance as a home resident (see p86), *plus* meals allowance, if any.[222]
- **If you do not have preserved rights,** you will continue to receive your usual IS, including the residential allowance, for the first six weeks in hospital.[223] If you are a single claimant who is permanently resident in a local authority home, however, you are only entitled to an applicable amount of £14.10.[224]

After six weeks in hospital

- **If you have preserved rights** (see p86) your personal allowance is £15.60 (£31.20 if your partner is also in hospital). You can also get an amount to cover a retaining fee for the home or IS housing costs (see p89). If a member of your family remains in the home you are entitled to your normal accommodation allowance (less your meals allowance) taking into account any reduction in the charge. Children in hospital for a longer period than 12 weeks have a personal allowance of £12.50.[225]
- **If you do not have preserved rights** your IS is reduced in accordance with the rules explained on pp94-95. If you are a single claimant who is permanently in a local authority home, your applicable amount remains £14.10.[226]

Patients detained under the Mental Health Act

Single people detained under the Mental Health Act 1983 (in Scotland, Mental Health (Scotland) Act 1984), who were in prison immediately before their detention have an applicable amount of £12.50.[227]

Going in and out of hospital

- The date your IS applicable amount reduces depends on whether your IS is paid in advance or arrears.[228] If you are paid in arrears, the reduction takes place from the first day of the benefit week in which you have been in hospital for six weeks (not counting the day of admission). If your IS is paid in advance, the reduction takes effect from the first day of the benefit week which coincides with, or follows, the date when you have been in hospital for six weeks. In the first case you could *lose* up to six days' full benefit; in the second you could *gain* up to six days' full benefit.
- Separate stays in hospital less than 28 days apart are added together in calculating the length of time you have been in hospital.[229]

- If you or a member of your family stop being a patient for any period of less than a week you should be paid your full IS for the days you are at home.[230]
- Your entitlement on the days you enter and leave hospital is unclear. It may be possible to argue that the days on which you enter or leave hospital are not days in hospital because you do not spend 24 hours in hospital on those days and the rules imply that your benefit should change on the day on which you leave hospital. Social security commissioners do not agree on how to interpret the law.[231] DSS guidance says the day you enter hospital does not count as a day in hospital but the day you leave does.[232] If you lose out because you are treated as a patient on these days you should seek advice.

6. PRISONERS

If you are a prisoner (see below), you are not entitled to any IS, apart from housing costs (see p25), which are only payable while you are detained in custody, awaiting trial or sentence.[233] You will also not be entitled to jobseeker's allowance (JSA) (see CPAG's *Jobseeker's Allowance Handbook* 1997/98). Your partner can claim IS/JSA as a single person or lone parent while you are a prisoner.[234] If your dependent child becomes a prisoner, you cannot get IS for her/him.[235] If you have no other children you will no longer qualify for the family premium or family premium lone parent rate (you will no longer count as a lone parent and may have to claim income-based JSA instead of IS).

You count as a prisoner if you are detained in custody awaiting trial or sentence, are serving a custodial sentence or are on temporary release.[236] You do *not* count as a prisoner if you are released on licence or parole or you are remanded in a bail or probation hostel.[237] If you are in a bail or probation hostel away from your partner, you may still be counted as a couple for IS purposes because you would count as a couple who are temporarily separated but intend to be reunited (see p324).[238]

Other sources of help

- Housing benefit and council tax benefit are payable for up to 52 weeks if you are remanded in custody or a bail hostel pending trial or sentence; or up to 13 weeks if you are serving a custodial sentence (see p217).
- Somebody caring for you while you are on temporary release can claim a community care grant for living expenses (see p436). The Prison

Department can make a payment for your home leave if your family is not getting IS, but cannot afford to support you. It can also pay for board and lodging during a period of temporary release if you are homeless.

- Help with the cost of visiting a close relative in prison comes from the Home Office. For this purpose, 'close relative' means husband, wife (including an established unmarried partner), brother, sister, parent and child. Adopted and fostered children and adoptive and foster parents are included. If the close relative is too ill, or too young, to travel alone, the fares of an escort can also be paid. It is normal policy to cover the travel costs (including an overnight stay and meals allowance where necessary), of up to 26 visits in a 12-month period if you are receiving IS or family credit. If your income is low but above IS level, the Home Office may pay part of the cost. Your income is assessed in the same way as for health benefits (see p466). You apply for help with the cost of visits on form F2022 obtainable from your local Benefits Agency office, or from the Assisted Prison Visits Unit, PO Box 2152, Birmingham B15 1SD, tel: 0121 626 2797. There is no right of appeal against a refusal by the Home Office of fares or a warrant for a visit but you could take up the matter with your MP.
- When you are released from prison, you may receive a discharge grant, which is treated as capital for IS purposes.[239] If you need help with the cost of basic essentials (eg, clothing, furniture, rent in advance), you may be able to get a social fund payment (see p422).

7. PEOPLE WITHOUT ACCOMMODATION

You are entitled to the normal IS personal allowances (see p330) for you and your partner, but you cannot get an allowance for a child dependant or any premiums for yourself, your partner or children.[240] If you are known in an area, you should get your IS by giro, payment card or order book in the normal way, but if you are 'likely to move on or mis-spend your money' you may be required to collect your benefit on a daily or part-week basis.[241] If you become homeless and have no money, you may initially need a crisis loan (see p446).

'Accommodation' is not defined in the legislation. The *Adjudication Officers' Guide* describes it as, 'An effective shelter from the elements which is capable of being heated; and in which occupants can sit, lie, cook and eat; and which is reasonably suited for continuous occupation.'[242] People in tents, etc may therefore not be 'without accommodation' and could get premiums.

The Benefits Agency may decide you have an unsettled way of life and refer you to a voluntary project centre as an alternative. This should only be done with your consent and if a place is available. Income support should not be refused or delayed if you are unwilling to take the 'advice' being offered, or are not interested in being resettled.[243]

It may be argued that if you are forced to live on the streets that this is a threat to your health and that the local authority has a duty to provide accommodation for you under the National Assistance Act.[244]

CHAPTER SIX

Maintenance payments

This chapter is divided as follows:

1. Lone parents (below)
2. Liability to maintain (p103)
3. The child support scheme (p105)
4. The effect of maintenance on income support (p113)

This chapter deals with the liability of a person to maintain others and the effect any maintenance payments have on income support (IS). Some of the provisions affect sponsors who have signed undertakings to maintain people from abroad; the implications for them are dealt with on p82.

If you are claiming income-based jobseeker's allowance (JSA), see the *Jobseeker's Allowance Handbook*, 2nd edn, 1997/98.

The rules about maintenance for children under the Child Support Act 1991 are included where they affect your right to, or the amount of, your benefit. For further information about the child support scheme, see CPAG's *Child Support Handbook*.

Payments of maintenance for yourself could be on a voluntary basis, or under a court order. Detailed advice about maintenance orders is beyond the scope of this *Handbook* and you should see a solicitor. If you are receiving IS you can apply for legal aid for court proceedings. In addition, you can get free advice from a solicitor under the Green Form scheme.

If you have been getting child maintenance (see p178) and you or your partner start working full time (see p13) or increase your earnings and stop getting IS, you might be able to get a child maintenance bonus (see p177).

1. LONE PARENTS

While you are claiming for a child under 16, you fit into one of the groups of people who can claim IS (see p10). If you satisfy the other rules of entitlement described in Chapter 2, you might be able to claim.

As a single parent or someone looking after a child on your own, you are likely to be able to claim child benefit at the lone parent rate for your oldest child (£17.10 a week). It is not necessary to be a parent of the child. For full details, see CPAG's *Rights Guide to Non-Means-Tested Benefits*. By claiming the lone parent rate of child benefit you might be taken off IS. If you are not on IS you will not get free school meals or access to the social fund. If you are currently claiming child benefit you do not have to claim the lone parent rate. See the *Rights Guide to Non-Means-Tested Benefits* for further details.

If you claim IS within three months of the birth of a child, claim a maternity expenses payment from the social fund (see p410).

You are entitled to maintenance payments for your child(ren) whether or not you were married and possibly for yourself if you were married. You are required to apply for child maintenance if you claim IS income-based jobseeker's allowance (JSA), family credit (FC) or disability working allowance (DWA), unless exempt (see p106), and the money you get affects your benefit (see p114).

Young mothers

If you are under 16, you cannot claim IS but can claim child benefit and also health benefits (see p466). If your parents (or someone else) are entitled to include you in their family (see p325), they can also include your baby in their family for the purpose of a claim for IS or other means-tested benefits and they can claim a maternity payment from the social fund (see p410) if they are entitled to IS, income-based JSA, FC or DWA.

If you are 16 or over, you can claim IS if you fit into one of the groups of people who can claim (see p10) and satisfy the other rules of entitlement described in Chapter 2. If you are still in relevant education, see p16.

You can get maintenance for your child from the father, and will be required to apply for it if you are claiming IS/income-based JSA/FC/DWA in your own right unless you are exempt (see p106).

Claiming after a relationship breakdown

If your marriage or other relationship breaks down you can claim benefit in your own right as a single person or lone parent. If you both remain living under the same roof but live separate lives, you can make separate claims for IS (and other means-tested benefits) and should not be treated as a married or cohabiting couple, provided that you keep separate households (see p319). You may be entitled to maintenance for yourself from your ex-partner and this affects the amount of your benefit (see p113). You must apply for maintenance for your children if you are on IS/income-based JSA/FC/DWA unless you are exempt (see p106) and this also affects the amount of your benefit (see p114).

2. LIABILITY TO MAINTAIN

Your spouse is liable to maintain you and your children for as long as IS is being paid to you.[1] Your ex-spouse is not liable to maintain you after you are divorced (unless s/he sponsored you when you came from abroad, see p82). Nor is s/he liable to maintain children over 16 who are independent or any children over the age of 19.

A sponsor who has given an undertaking to support a person from abroad financially is also liable to maintain that person (see p82).

A parent who does not live with the person who is looking after her/his child(ren) is expected to pay child maintenance on a regular basis to that person. If you are the parent looking after the child(ren) and claiming IS/income-based JSA/FC/DWA you are required to apply for this maintenance unless exempt (see p106). However, you can refuse to apply for maintenance and have your benefit paid at a reduced rate (see p108).

Separation due to care needs

Sometimes a couple are forced to live apart because one of them needs care or treatment. If your spouse is in hospital, or in a residential or nursing home you may be assessed and paid as separate individuals for benefit purposes (see p323). However, you still remain liable to support your spouse and you may be asked to make a financial contribution towards her/his care if you are able.

Amount of maintenance

The Child Support Agency's formula for calculating child support maintenance is a rigid one and there is little scope for disputing the assessment unless the calculation is based on incorrect information. However, departures from the formula are allowed in certain circumstances, for example, where you or an absent parent have a disabled child or where an absent parent's travel costs to see your children are expensive or if a parent's life style is more extravagant than the income s/he has declared allows. See the *Child Support Handbook* for an explanation of the formula and details of the departure rules.

There is more flexibility about how much your spouse is required to pay for you and s/he can negotiate with the Benefits Agency to pay an amount s/he can afford given her/his outgoings. As a starting point for negotiations, the Benefits Agency compares her/his net income with the total of:[2]

- the IS personal allowances and premiums s/he would qualify for if entitled to IS;
- household expenses including rent, mortgage and council tax (excluding arrears);
- 15 per cent of her/his net wage (to cover expenses for work); *and*
- the balance of any other expenses exceeding the 15 per cent margin that are considered essential.

If s/he has a new partner, two calculations are performed – one as if s/he was single and the other using joint incomes. The lower figure is used as the basis for negotiation.

If the Benefits Agency feels that your spouse is not paying enough it has the right to take her/him to court (see below).

Enforcing a claimant's maintenance order

If there is already an order in favour of, or for the benefit of, you or your children, the Secretary of State may do anything which you could do to enforce or vary the order.[3] This is no longer necessary for children where the Child Support Agency has taken over cases with previous court orders (see p105).

Furthermore, if the Secretary of State notifies the relevant court officer that s/he wishes to be informed of any application by either the claimant or the liable relative to vary the order, enforce it or have any arrears remitted, s/he will be given that information and is entitled to take part in the proceedings.[4] Nevertheless, any maintenance which then has to be paid is paid to you (unless diverted – see below).

Collection by the Benefits Agency

If maintenance is payable through a magistrates' court (including orders made in the county court or High Court but registered in the magistrates' court) and it is paid irregularly, it can be paid to the Benefits Agency when it does arrive.[5] In return, the Benefits Agency gives you an order book for the amount of IS you would receive if no maintenance was being paid. The Benefits Agency does not usually accept this sort of arrangement unless payments have actually been missed, but may if you have a good reason for wanting it done and you explain why.

The Child Support Agency may collect other types of maintenance at the same time as child support.[6]

An order for the Secretary of State

The Secretary of State can take proceedings against anyone who has a liability to pay maintenance for an ex-partner or child (see p103). The application is heard in a magistrates' court.[7] Since 5 April 1993, the courts have not had the power to make new orders for maintenance for children, other than consent orders.[8]

The court is entitled to refuse an order if you have been guilty of adultery, cruelty or desertion.[9] The fact that there was an agreement that you would not ask for maintenance is not a bar to an order being made,[10] although all the circumstances must be taken into account.[11]

Prosecution

As a last resort your spouse can be prosecuted if IS is paid as a result of her/his persistently refusing or neglecting to maintain you or your children. You can even be prosecuted for failing to maintain yourself! This is uncommon. Although the power remains in respect of children, it is very unlikely to be used given that child maintenance is now being dealt with by the Child Support Agency (see below).

In either case, the maximum penalty is three months' imprisonment or a fine of £2,500 or both.[12] If you are charged with such an offence, see a solicitor. Legal aid may be available to help meet the cost.

3. THE CHILD SUPPORT SCHEME

Maintenance for children is dealt with by the Child Support Agency and is called child support maintenance. If you are getting maintenance for a child under a voluntary agreement or court order, this can continue until the Child Support Agency takes on your case. If you want to apply for child maintenance and have not been approached by the Child Support Agency, you can request a maintenance application form.

Some IS claimants were sent maintenance application forms but did not make an application. If you have not had any communication from the Child Support Agency other than a routine reminder, your case will have been deferred. The Child Support Agency began dealing with the remaining deferred cases in November 1996.

If you make a new or repeat claim for IS/income-based JSA/FC/DWA, you must apply to the Child Support Agency for a maintenance assessment unless exempt (see p106). Failure to do so could affect the amount of benefit you receive (see below).

Any maintenance you receive counts as income when calculating your benefit. However, the processing of your benefit claim by the Benefits Agency should not be held up by the Child Support Agency.

The Child Support Agency assessment overrides any previous maintenance agreement, including a court order. The courts now have only limited powers to make maintenance orders for children – see the *Child Support Handbook* for full details of the child support scheme.

The requirement to co-operate

If you are claiming IS, JSA, FC or DWA the Secretary of State may require you to apply for child support maintenance from your child's other parent where you are living apart and you have care of your child for at least part of the week[13] (see the *Child Support Handbook* for details of shared care situations). Although the Secretary of State has the discretion not to do so, you are generally required to apply. S/he must consider the welfare of any children involved.[14] You can be exempt from applying where you or your child would be put at risk of suffering **harm or undue distress** if you gave your authorisation for child maintenance to be pursued (see p107). The child support officer will decide if your reasons are sufficient to justify this exemption. If your reasons are not accepted, your benefit could be paid at a reduced rate (see p108).

This requirement applies not only to lone parents, but also to couples where one of the children in the family has a parent who is living elsewhere. It even applies if you are not receiving a personal allowance for the child.[15] The requirement does not apply where a child lives with neither parent. In this case, an application for child maintenance from the person looking after the child is voluntary.

Providing authorisation

Unless you have sent the Child Support Agency details of a risk of harm or undue distress (see p107), if you claim IS/income-based JSA/FC/DWA you are asked to complete a child support maintenance application form. If you sign the form, you are giving your authorisation to the Child Support Agency to pursue child maintenance. Without your signature, the Child Support Agency cannot take any action to pursue maintenance. **Do not sign the maintenance application form unless you are sure that you want to apply for child support maintenance.**

If you are looking after children who have different parents, see the *Child Support Handbook*.

If you sign the maintenance application form and later find that you or your children are at risk of harm or undue distress (see p107) as a result of the maintenance assessment, you can ask the Child Support Agency to stop pursuing maintenance.[16]

The Child Support Agency will go through the same procedure as if you had refused to co-operate at the beginning. If the child support officer decides you are no longer required to co-operate, the Child Support Agency must stop pursuing the maintenance. Otherwise, the Child Support Agency continues to act on the original authorisation and pursues the maintenance. You do not have the option of having your benefit reduced (see p110) at this stage. You may want to contact your MP for support.

Providing information

Unless you or your children would be at risk of harm or undue distress (see below), as well as providing authorisation you must provide information and evidence to enable the Child Support Agency to trace the absent parent and to assess and collect child support maintenance.[17]

See the *Child Support Handbook* for details of what the Child Support Agency can expect you to provide.

Harm or undue distress

You do not have to provide authorisation or information if doing so would put you or your child at risk of harm or undue distress.

When you claim IS you are asked on the claim form if you or your child(ren) would be put at risk of suffering harm or undue distress if you were required to pursue maintenance. If you think this applies to you, you should say so and give details of your situation. This will be followed up by the Child Support Agency. See the *Child Support Handbook* for further details.

Harm or undue distress is not defined, so if you believe that you or any of the children living with you would be at risk of harm or distress if you applied for child maintenance, you should explain to the Child Support Agency why this is so. The exemption certainly covers situations where there is a possibility of violence or where there has been rape, sexual abuse, threats or other harassment.[18] There does not need to have been a history of actual violence. A child support officer decides if a fear of violence is reasonably held.

There will be many other situations in which you would find it distressing to pursue maintenance – eg, where you have not had any contact with the other parent for many years, you had a clean-break divorce, the other parent is threatening to contest who the child lives with, you chose to have the child against the father's wishes, or you believe it would threaten the arrangement between the other parent and the children.

Each case is decided on its merits. Your word should be accepted without any supporting evidence unless you contradict yourself or the child support officer thinks the information is improbable,[19] for example, where you have named a celebrity as the father of your child.

It will take the Child Support Agency many weeks to decide whether you are exempt. It is important not to sign a maintenance application form in the meantime. See below for the procedure the Child Support Agency must follow if you refuse to co-operate.

Refusal to co-operate with the Child Support Agency

If you refuse to authorise the Child Support Agency to seek maintenance for your child(ren) or to provide information to help them assess maintenance liability, your benefit (IS, income-based JSA, FC or DWA) may be paid at a reduced rate.[20] However, your benefit claim must still be processed by the Benefits Agency. You do not need to withdraw your benefit claim to avoid child support maintenance being pursued. If you do not want to apply for child support maintenance, do not sign the maintenance application form (see p106).

You should be notified in writing whether or not you have been exempted from the requirement to provide the necessary authorisation or information (see pp106 and 107). If you are still required to co-operate, you will be warned in writing that your benefit could be reduced unless you do so.[21] You must respond within two weeks, giving your reasons why you think you or your children would suffer harm or undue distress (see p107) if you were required to co-operate. You can use this time to get supporting letters – eg, from friends and relatives, your doctor, child's school, or other helpful organisations – if you wish. If you do submit further information, the Secretary of State should let you know whether there are now reasonable grounds for believing there is a risk of harm or undue distress. If s/he is still not satisfied, your case will be referred to the area manager who is a child support officer. S/he will write to you asking you either to provide the authorisation or information requested, or to explain why you have not done so. You are given 14 days in which to respond.[22] Even at this stage, you should not sign the maintenance application form if you believe you should be exempt, because you do not have a right of appeal until the end of the procedure. See the *Child Support Handbook* for more details about the procedure.

The rules about the procedure the Child Support Agency must follow if you refuse to co-operate changed on 7 October 1996. If you failed to co-operate before that date, the old rules still apply.[23] See the *Child Support Handbook* 1996/97 edn, pp101–12.

In order to avoid a benefit penalty (see p110) it is important that you explain the harm or undue distress which could arise if you authorise the Child Support Agency to pursue maintenance and make it clear that this is why you do not wish to co-operate. You do not have to reply in writing – a telephone call is acceptable.[24] Nor do you have to provide evidence to prove that you would be under threat. Your word should be accepted,[25] though it is always useful to point to specific examples of problems which have occurred in the past or reasons why you believe they might occur in the future, to help illustrate what effect your co-operation might have. If there are reasonable grounds for believing that you or your child would suffer harm or undue distress were authorisation to be given, no further action is taken and you are advised of this.[26]

If the child support officer does not accept that there is any risk s/he can decide that your IS/income-based JSA/FC/DWA should be paid at a reduced rate. S/he makes what is known as a 'reduced benefit direction' or 'benefit penalty' (see p110). When deciding whether to issue a reduced benefit direction, the child support officer must consider whether the welfare of any child involved would be adversely affected, for example, because of her/his age or state of health or her/his parent's.[27]

A reduced benefit direction cannot be issued where:[28]

- IS or income-based JSA is paid to you or your partner which includes a disabled child premium, a disability premium or a higher pensioner premium (this applies even if it is your partner who has the disability);
- the disabled child premium or the disability premium is included in your exempt income for child support maintenance purposes (see the *Child Support Handbook* for details) if you are in receipt of FC/DWA (this does not recognise your partner's disability).

Right of appeal

You have a right of appeal to an independent child support appeal tribunal against a reduced benefit direction.[29] You must appeal within 28 days of the decision being sent to you, although a late appeal will be accepted if you have special reasons.[30] The special reasons do not have to relate to your own personal circumstances or actions. They could include things like the amount of money involved or how strong your case is. The reduced benefit direction will be imposed in the meantime, unless you decide to co-operate by providing the authorisation or information after it is issued.

The benefit penalty

The adjudication officer at the Benefits Agency must follow a reduced benefit direction issued by a child support officer. Your benefit should be paid in full until a direction is issued but will then be adjusted. A current award of FC/DWA can be changed if a reduced benefit direction is issued, cancelled or suspended (see p196).

Benefit can be reduced even if your benefit does not include an amount for the child(ren) for whom maintenance is being claimed.[31] However, no reduction is made if you are in hospital, a residential care or nursing home, or a local authority residential home.[32]

If a reduction is being made to your FC or DWA and you then go on to IS or income-based JSA, the deduction continues to be made.[33]

Only one reduction can be made from your benefit even if you refuse to co-operate in seeking maintenance for children from different relationships.[34] However, if another child is born or joins your household the question of giving authorisation and information in relation to that additional child arises, and a second reduced benefit direction could be issued if you again fail to co-operate. If a second direction is made, the original one ceases even if it would otherwise run for several more months.[35] See below for how long your benefit can be paid at a reduced rate in this situation.

The amount of the reduction and how long it lasts

The reduction lasts for three years and is currently £19.66 a week.[36] This period begins on the first day of the second benefit week after the adjudication officer has reviewed and revised your claim.[37] If the reduction takes your benefit to below 10 pence (IS or income-based JSA) or 50 pence (FC or DWA), a lower deduction is made so that you are left with this minimum amount of benefit.[38] When benefit rates are increased in April the amount of the reduction also increases. For IS, this happens straightaway but with FC or DWA it is adjusted when your claim is next renewed.[39] At the end of the three-year period, if you still refuse to co-operate, your benefit can be paid at this reduced rate for a further three years.

If a second reduced benefit direction is made against you because you refuse to co-operate in relation to an additional child, the original direction lapses and the reduction under the new direction lasts for a fresh three years.[40] For example, you may have already had your benefit reduced for seven months under the original direction for your first child and, although this ends early, you are penalised for a further three years under the new one after refusing to provide authorisation in respect of your new baby's absent parent.

The rules about the amount of the reduction and how long it lasts changed on 7 October 1996. If your reduced benefit direction began before that date, the old rules still apply.[41] You cannot get more than one reduced benefit direction for the same children. See the *Child Support Handbook* 1996/97 edn, pp112-14.

When a benefit penalty ends early

Normally a reduced benefit direction lasts for three years (see p110). However, it will end earlier if you decide to provide the authorisation or information requested by the Child Support Agency.[42] It can also be terminated on review (see p112).

The benefit penalty is also suspended or withdrawn where:

- you stop getting IS/income-based JSA/FC/DWA.[43] If you reclaim one of these benefits within 52 weeks, the benefit penalty is reinstated for the remainder of the three year period. You must be given 14 days notice of this. If your new claim is more than 52 weeks after you last received IS/income-based JSA/FC/DWA the direction is no longer valid. However, the requirement to co-operate still applies and you will be asked to complete a maintenance application form. A new direction could be made, though it should only run for the balance of the three years which was not used up on the previous claim;
- the child(ren) cease(s) to be eligible for maintenance because they are over 16 and have left non-advanced education, or are 19 or over. If they become eligible again (eg, because they return to full-time education) the penalty can be resumed;[44]
- you stop living with and caring for the child(ren). The benefit reduction can be reinstated if you resume your role as carer;[45]
- you are paid IS at a special rate because you are in hospital, a residential care or nursing home or a local authority residential home (see Chapter 5). Initially the direction is suspended, but if you stay there for more than 52 weeks it ceases completely;[46]
- your child(ren) (if in Scotland) or their absent parent successfully apply to the Child Support Agency for a maintenance assessment.[47]

Both you and the Benefits Agency adjudication officer should be notified if a reduced benefit direction ceases, and given an explanation.[48]

A direction can also be cancelled if it was made in error, or not ended earlier due to an error (in this case the money will be repaid).[49] This can include situations where the child support officer did not accept your explanation why you or your children were at risk of harm or undue distress (see p107) but now does.

Where a reduction under a second reduced benefit direction (see p110) ends early, the first direction may be resurrected if you have not co-operated in relation to that absent parent. In this case the reduction is for the balance of the three-year period remaining, after taking account of how long your benefit has been reduced under both directions.[50]

The rules about what happens when a second reduced benefit direction ends early changed on 7 October 1996. If your earlier reduced benefit direction was made before 7 October 1996, the old rules still apply, even if the second direction was made after that date.[51] See the *Child Support Handbook* 1996/97 edn, p114.

Reviewing a reduced benefit direction

A reduced benefit direction must be reviewed if you, or someone on your behalf, provides additional reasons explaining why:

- you failed to co-operate with the Child Support Agency (see p106);
- you are no longer obliged to co-operate (see p106);
- the child(ren)'s welfare is likely to be put in jeopardy by the continuing existence of a direction.[52]

The review is done by a child support officer (but not the one who made the direction). S/he may decide to end the direction from the date that the reasons were supplied. You should be given a full written decision and informed of your rights of appeal if the direction is not withdrawn.

Deductions from the absent parent's IS

Deductions of £5 a week can be made from an absent parent's IS as a contribution towards the maintenance of her/his child(ren).[53] This does not apply if the absent parent:[54]

- is aged under 18;
- qualifies for a family premium or has day-to-day care of any child (see the *Child Support Handbook* for details of 'day-to-day care');
- receives incapacity benefit, maternity allowance, statutory sick pay or maternity pay, severe disablement allowance, attendance allowance, disability living or working allowances, invalid care allowance, industrial injuries disablement benefit, a war pension or a payment from either of the Independent Living Funds. If this benefit is not paid solely because of overlapping rules, or an inadequate contribution record, s/he is still exempt from deductions.

If you are an absent parent on IS and have children from two or more different relationships, only one deduction can be made and the £5 is apportioned between the people who care for the child(ren).[55]

If you think that the decision to make deductions from your IS is wrong, you can apply in writing to the Child Support Agency for a review. You should try to show that the decision was given in ignorance of relevant facts, was based on a mistake about the facts or was wrong in law. A different child support officer will review the decision. If you still do not agree with the decision you can appeal to a child support appeal tribunal but must do this within 28 days.[56] If your circumstances change you can also apply for a review.

If you are not exempt from the deductions, the Child Support Agency sends a notification to the Benefits Agency. This request for deductions to be made is binding on the adjudication officer of the Benefits Agency, unless other deductions are being made from IS which take precedence (see p146). Deductions for child support maintenance cannot be made from any benefit other than IS or jobseeker's allowance, unless sickness/incapacity benefit, severe disablement allowance or retirement pension are paid in the same girocheque or order book as IS. If you are an absent parent who is not exempt from the deductions but disagree that the Benefits Agency can make the deductions because other deductions have a higher priority, you have a right of appeal to a social security appeal tribunal (see Chapter 8).

4. THE EFFECT OF MAINTENANCE ON INCOME SUPPORT

Child support payments count in full when calculating IS. Other payments made by liable relatives (see below) are treated as maintenance and are also taken into account when working out your benefit.

Liable relatives

For this purpose the following are 'liable relatives':[57]

- a husband or wife. This includes one from whom you are separated or divorced;
- a parent of a child or young person under 19 for whom you are claiming (this could include a step-parent);
- a parent of a young person under 19 who is claiming IS in her/his own right (this could include a step-parent);
- a person who has been living with and maintaining a child or young person under 19 or maintaining a young person under 19 who is claiming IS in her/his own right and can therefore reasonably be treated as her/his father;

- if you are a 'person from abroad', a sponsor who has given an undertaking to support you financially (see p82).

There are special rules about how payments to you or to someone else on your behalf by a liable relative are taken into account (see p115).

It is important to note that not all liable relatives whose payments affect IS are legally 'liable to maintain' claimants so as to enable the Secretary of State to obtain maintenance from them (see p105).

If you are entitled to payments under a court order you can either get regular periodical payments for yourself, or a lump sum to be paid in one go or by instalments. If you are receiving IS, it is not usually a good idea to have a lump sum instead of periodical payments because most lump sums are treated as income at a sufficiently high level to disqualify you from benefit altogether even if they are for amounts well below the usual capital limit (see p384). However, some lump sums are treated as capital and are not affected by this rule (see p118).

If you are on FC/DWA, see p368.

Child support maintenance

All payments of child support maintenance are treated as income and are taken fully into account on a weekly basis.[58] Where payments are made monthly, multiply by 12 and divide by 52 to obtain a weekly amount. Where regular payments are made at intervals other than each week or month, the payments are spread over the period, including any part week. It is the actual payments made, and not the amount due under the Child Support Agency assessment, which are taken into account in this way.[59]

The Benefits Agency should not calculate IS on the assumption that maintenance payments due under the Child Support Agency assessment will be made where this has not been happening. For example, a parent who would be floated off IS if payments due under the assessment were made can continue to receive IS if the child maintenance is not received. There have been some delays in obtaining increased or reinstated IS. If this is a problem, seek advice.

Collection and enforcement

Child maintenance can be paid to the Child Support Agency rather than direct to you as the carer, if the Secretary of State agrees.[60] If you want this to happen, ask the Child Support Agency. You can request this on the maintenance application form or at a later date. This is useful where maintenance payments are likely to be irregular or unreliable, or where you do not want to be located by the other party. If the Child Support Agency is collecting the payments for you, enforcement action should begin automatically when a payment is missed. Where payment should be made direct to you, it is up to you to contact the Child Support Agency and the Benefits Agency when a maintenance payment does not arrive.

If you are on IS and your child(ren)'s absent parent is making payments to the Child Support Agency, your child support maintenance is paid in the same order book/girocheque as your IS. The Child Support Agency retains the payments made by the absent parent. If the Agency does not receive your child support maintenance payment, you can still cash the full amount of IS.

Arrears at the beginning of the child support assessment

There are always arrears accrued by the time the assessment is made. Usually these arrears will be paid to, and retained by, the Child Support Agency if you are on IS. However, if the payment is made to you, the IS which has been overpaid to you can be recovered by the Benefits Agency.[61]

Arrears due during a claim

The Child Support Agency is responsible for collecting arrears of child support maintenance if you are on IS. The Agency retains an amount of arrears equal to any IS you were paid because the maintenance was not paid when it was due.[62]

Arrears paid for a period before the claim

A payment due before the IS claim but paid late during the claim is treated as paid in the week in which it was due.[63] Therefore only child support maintenance both due for and received in the weeks of the claim can be taken into account by the Benefits Agency.

Payments of other maintenance

If a liable relative (see p113) makes payments to you which are not child support maintenance (see p105) these are dealt with in a special way.[64] For the rules about child support maintenance, see p114.

Payments by liable relatives are treated as income and are taken fully into account to reduce your IS except:[65]

- payments in kind (unless you or your partner is involved in a trade dispute) (see p58);
- boarding school fees (but see p345);
- any payment to, or for, a child or young person who does not count as a member of your household (see p326);
- payments made after the liable relative has died;

- any payments arising from disposing of property after divorce or separation (which would normally be capital – see p119);
- payments made to someone else for the benefit of you or a member of your family, or made to you or a member of your family for someone else (such as mortgage capital payments), provided that it is reasonable to ignore the payment and it is not used for food, ordinary clothing or footwear, fuel, your eligible rent (see p227), eligible council tax (see p302), or those housing costs that are met through IS. It is well worth appealing in a case where a payment is not ignored on this ground because a tribunal may take a different view as to what is reasonable;
- money from a liable relative which has already been taken into account under a previous claim, or which has already been recovered out of overpaid IS; and amounts which have been used up before a decision is made (provided that the money has not been spent in order to increase or become entitled to IS).[66]

See also, lump sums treated as capital (p118) and treated as income (p120).

Periodical payments

Payments made by liable relatives which are periodical payments are:[67]

- any payment made, or due to be made, regularly, whether voluntarily or under a court order or other formal agreement;
- any other small payment no higher than your weekly IS;
- any payment made instead of one or more regular payments due under an agreement (whether formal or voluntary), either as payment in advance or arrears. This does not include any arrears due before the beginning of your entitlement to IS.

Periodical payments which are received on time are each spread over a period equal to the interval between them – ie, monthly payments are spread over a month. They are multiplied by 12 and divided by 52 to produce a weekly income figure.[68]

Arrears of periodical payments due during your claim

When a payment arrives during a claim and it includes a lump sum for arrears (or in advance), the payment is spread over a period calculated by dividing it by the weekly amount of maintenance you should have received.[69]

Example

You should receive £80 a month. It is not paid for three months and then you receive £200.

£80 a month is treated as producing a weekly income of:

$$\frac{£80 \times 12}{52} = £18.46$$

The £200 is taken into account for:

$$\frac{200}{18.46} = 10.83 \text{ weeks}$$

You are therefore assumed to have an income of £18.45 for the next ten weeks and six days. The maintenance payments due to you are still two weeks and one day in arrears (£40).

If a payment is specifically identified as being arrears for a particular period, it will, in practice, often be taken into account for a forward period from the week after you inform the Benefits Agency about it. However, it ought to be attributed to the past period which it was intended to cover, unless it is 'more practicable' to choose a later week.[70] In this case the Secretary of State can recover the full amount of extra benefit paid to you while maintenance was not being received.[71] (This can still be done when you receive a payment after your claim ends which is for arrears of maintenance that should have been paid while you were still claiming.) If the amount of benefit you were receiving then and are receiving now are both greater than the weekly amount of maintenance, it does not matter whether the adjudication officer spreads the payment over the period when payment should have been made or forwards from a date after the payment was received.

However, for some people it does make a difference and you should argue for the payment to be spread over whichever period is more advantageous to you. This will depend on the amount of IS you would otherwise receive, the amount of the payment and whether any other periodical payments are being made.

Example

You should have been receiving maintenance at the rate of £25 a week but eight weeks are missed and you have to claim IS at the rate of £15 a week to top up your part-time earnings. You reduce the number of hours you are working and your entitlement to IS then increases to £30 a week. You then receive a payment of arrears of maintenance which includes £200 to make up the missing eight weeks from before your IS was increased. However, you do not receive any further maintenance payments.

If that payment were taken into account at the rate of £25 a week for eight weeks from the date it was made, you would lose all £200. However, if it were attributed to the period when the maintenance ought to have been paid in the first place, you would lose only £120 (£15 × 8) because that is all the benefit you were paid then. If you can pay £120 to the Benefits Agency, you have a very good argument that it is not 'more practicable' to spread the payment forwards rather than over the past period. You should appeal if it is not accepted.

On the other hand, if you started to receive regular maintenance payments from the date the arrears were received, you would be better off having the payment of arrears spread forwards. This is because the new maintenance payments would reduce your IS to £5 a week so that taking the arrears into account for eight weeks would cost you only £40 (£5 × 8).

Arrears of periodical payments due before your claim

If the arrears are for a period before your claim they are not treated as a periodical payment.[72] Adjudication officers tend to treat the payment from a liable relative as income rather than capital except to the extent that you have already spent it. This means that they spread it over a future period (see p120). But you should argue that the regulations do not exclude arrears from the definition of periodical payments just to have them brought back into the calculation as other liable relative payments. The regulations exclude arrears from the liable relative provisions altogether. Such payments are to be treated as capital (or as disregarded income if you are receiving current periodical payments). Any other interpretation is unfair and gives the Secretary of State an unwarranted windfall at your expense.[73] It is also contrary to the rule for arrears of child support maintenance (see p115).

Lump sums treated as capital

If you receive a lump sum from a liable relative (see p113), it is better if it can be treated as capital rather than income if it would not take your capital over £8,000 (£16,000 if you live in a residential or nursing home – see p344). (If it is more than £8,000/£16,000, you will not receive any benefit whether it is treated as capital or income, although you might be able to reclaim sooner if it were capital.)

However, only the following lump sums from liable relatives can be treated as capital:[74]

- any payment arising from a 'disposition of property' (see below) in consequence of your separation, divorce, etc;
- any gifts not exceeding £250 in any period of 52 weeks (and not so regular as to amount to periodical payments);
- any payment in kind (unless you or your partner is involved in a trade dispute – see p58);
- any payment made to someone else for the benefit of you or a member of your family (such as special tuition fees), or paid to you or a member of your family to pay to someone else, which it is unreasonable to take into account – you can appeal to a tribunal which may take a different view from the adjudication officer about what is reasonable;
- any boarding school fees (but see p345);
- any payment to, or for, a child or young person who has left your household;
- any payment which you have used before the adjudication officer makes her/his decision provided that you did not use it for the purpose of gaining entitlement to IS – it should not be taken into account if you have used it to clear debts such as your solicitor's bill;
- any other payment if the liable relative is already making periodical payments equal to:
  - your IS if the payments include payments for you;
  - your child's applicable amount and any family premium if the payments are only for a child.
  If the periodical payments stop or fall below that level, what is left of the lump sum is taken into account as income (see p120).[75]

'Disposition of property'

It is vital to distinguish between payments arising from a disposition of property and those that are not. 'Property' is not confined to houses and land, but includes any asset such as the contents of your former home or a building society account. There is a 'disposition' when those contents are divided up or your former partner buys out your interest.[76] Therefore, any lump sum which is paid in settlement of a claim to a share in any property is treated as capital. It is only those lump sums which are paid instead of income which are liable to be treated as income.[77] It is important to take this into account in any negotiations with your former partner and you should make sure your solicitor knows about this rule.

It is best if any court order is drawn up so as to record that any lump sum is in settlement of a claim to an interest in property. However, this is not essential and the Benefits Agency should accept a letter from your solicitor explaining why a lump sum was asked for and agreed.

Note that the proceeds of sale of your former home may be disregarded altogether for a period of time (see p391). Other capital, such as the home itself and its contents, may also be disregarded (see p390). There is therefore an advantage, while you are on benefit, to ask for a greater share of the home and accept less in the way of capital or income which would be taken into account to reduce your benefit.

Lump sums treated as income

Lump sums which are neither treated as capital (see p118) nor periodical payments (see p116) are treated as income and are spread over a period so as to disqualify you (or your child) from IS for as long as possible.

If you are not also receiving periodical payments, the lump sum is treated as producing a weekly income equal to:[78]

- if the lump sum is for you or for you and any children, your IS plus £2;
- if the lump sum is just for a child or children, the personal allowance for you and each child for whom you get maintenance, any disabled child premium or family premium, and any carer's premium if it is paid because you are caring for a disabled child for whom you receive maintenance. However, if your IS entitlement plus £2 would be less than this amount (eg, because you had other income), the lower amount is used. This means that the lump sum disqualifies you from IS for a longer period.

If you are receiving periodical payments (see p116), the income is calculated as being the difference between the periodical payment and:[79]

- the amount of IS plus £2 which would be paid if you did not get the periodical payment when it is paid for you alone or you and your children;
- the child's personal allowance plus family premium if the periodical payment is just for a child.

If the periodical payments are varied or stop, the calculation is done again taking the balance of the lump sum into account.[80]

The lump sum is treated as producing that weekly income for a period beginning on the first day of the benefit week in which the payment is received and lasting for a number of weeks calculated by dividing the amount of the payment by the weekly income. For example, if you receive a lump sum of £2,000 which the above rules treat as producing a weekly income of £50, your IS is reduced by £50 for 40 weeks. The period can start in a later week if that is more practical.[81]

If you are disqualified, and your circumstances change so that your entitlement to IS would be higher, or the benefit rates are altered, ask the Benefits Agency to recalculate the period of your disqualification using the new figures.

Arrears of periodical payments due before your claim are often treated as being a lump sum so as to disqualify you from benefit. However, you should argue that that is wrong (see p118).

CHAPTER SEVEN

Claims, reviews and getting paid

This chapter is about how income support (IS) is administered. It covers:

1. Claims (below)
2. Decisions and reviews (p129)
3. Payments of benefit (p135)
4. Overpayments and fraud (p146)
5. Complaints about administration (p154)

I. CLAIMS

As a claimant you deal with your local branch office and this is where your claim should go. You can obtain leaflets and information there and ask a benefit adviser to give advice and help with claims. S/he has access to your computerised records.

London claimants have their claims dealt with by social security centres set up to deal with work which does not require face-to-face contact with the public. There are three centres, in Glasgow, Belfast and Ashton-in-Makerfield. Although the benefit centres decide your claim, you should still use your branch office to make initial claims or if you have any queries about your claim.

How to make a claim

You need a national insurance number so that your claim can be computerised. If you do not have one you may experience some delay because your claim is dealt with manually. You can get one by applying to the Contributions Agency. You need to provide evidence of your identity.

If you are a single person, a single parent or one of a lesbian or gay couple, you claim on your own behalf. If you are a heterosexual couple you must choose which one of you will claim for you both (see p319). However, if you are a member of a couple claiming backdated IS after one of you is awarded refugee status (see p76), the claim must be made by the refugee.[1] Where you have a choice about who can claim and you cannot agree, the Secretary of State decides.[2] You can change which partner claims, provided the partner previously claiming is agreeable.[3]

It can be worth swapping who claims, for example, if:

- it would entitle you to a disability premium (see p333);
- one of you is about to go abroad or otherwise lose entitlement – eg, become a student;
- one of you fits into one of the groups of people who can claim IS but not the other (see p10). However, you should both seek advice about how to protect your national insurance record;
- one of you is working less than 16 hours a week and the other is working between 16 and 24 hours a week (see p13 for what counts as working full time).

But if you get transitional protection because you used to get supplementary benefit, you lose this if you swap.

You might be able to choose whether to claim IS or income-based jobseeker's allowance. See p55 for further information.

The Secretary of State can authorise an **'appointee'** to act on your behalf if you cannot claim for yourself – eg, you are mentally ill or suffering from senile dementia.[4] If this happens, the appointee takes on all your responsibilities as a claimant. Normally this would only apply from the date the appointment is agreed, but if someone acts on your behalf before becoming your official appointee her/his actions can be validated in retrospect by her/his appointment.[5] Someone can become an appointee by applying in writing to the Benefits Agency. S/he must be over 18.

If you are an appointee for a claimant who dies, you must re-apply for appointee status in order to settle any outstanding benefit matters.[6] An executor under a will can also pursue an outstanding claim or appeal on behalf of a deceased claimant even if the decision was made before the formal grant of probate.[7]

The claim form

A claim for IS must be in writing and normally on the appropriate form,[8] which is free of charge.[9] Get form SP1 (for pensioners) or A1 (other claimants) from your local Benefits Agency office, or by filling in the tear-off slip in leaflet IS1 available from your local post office. The form tells you the address to which it must be sent. If you get the form by telephoning or writing to the Benefits Agency office, your claim will generally count as having been made when you asked for the form.

If you just write a letter, or send in the wrong form, the Benefits

Agency will send you an IS form. Similarly, if you do not fill in the IS form properly it will return it to you. If you get it back to the Benefits Agency correctly filled in within a month, you count as having claimed on the date it got your first letter or form. The Secretary of State can extend this one-month period if s/he thinks it reasonable[10] – eg, because you were ill. See p126 for more information about the date of your claim. If you want to withdraw or amend your claim, notify the Benefits Agency office before it makes its decision.[11]

Note: The rules about claiming and the information you must provide are due to change in October 1997. See p125 for further details.

Information to support your claim

If you have a mortgage, form MI12 will be given to you with your IS claim form. Give this to your lender, who will provide details about your mortgage and return the form to the Benefits Agency.

Your lender is also required to notify the Benefits Agency of any changes to the amount you owe or the interest payable during your claim. If you have this information you must also advise the Benefits Agency just in case your lender fails to do so.

You can be asked to supply any other 'certificates, documents, information or evidence' considered relevant to your claim or to an issue arising from your claim – eg, birth certificate, rent book, or bank statement. If you or your partner are 60 or over you must provide details of any personal pension scheme or retirement annuity contract which you have taken out. Your pension fundholder may also be asked to give details of your pension rights.[12]

In some cases the Benefits Agency may refuse to accept evidence that you are who you say you are. Many travellers and Irish claimants find that the evidence they provide is simply not accepted as genuine – eg, there is suspicion about the validity of birth certificates. Asylum-seekers and Black people may also face hostility and mistrust when claiming. Where, for example, you have had to use forged papers to flee from persecution, the Benefits Agency often assumes you are making a fraudulent claim. Sometimes evidence is required even though there are good reasons why it is not available – eg, a national insurance number. It is important to try to provide any evidence to support your claim. If you are asked to provide information which you do not have, ask what other evidence would be accepted. Press the Benefits Agency to be clear about what is required and why, and complain if you feel that any requests for information are unreasonable (see p154). You may also wish to approach your local race equality council if you feel that you have been racially discriminated against.

If you do not provide the information, the adjudication officer must decide your claim within a reasonable length of time, on the basis of the details s/he already has.[13] If it is not possible to accurately assess your housing costs or your entitlement to severe disability premium the adjudication officer can exclude these from your IS until they can be calculated.[14] If you think the Benefits Agency is delaying a decision unreasonably, see p131. If the adjudication officer decides against you, you should appeal, but remember to try and find some evidence to support your claim if you are to succeed at the tribunal.[15]

New rules from October 1997

The rules about claiming and the information you must provide when you claim are due to change. From 6 October 1997, it will be your responsibility to produce information and evidence to verify your IS claim. CPAG's *Welfare Rights Bulletin* will provide an update later in the year. The main rules are:

- All claims for IS will have to be made on a fully completed claim form and any proof required by the Benefits Agency provided at the same time. The date of claim will be the date these are received in the benefit office *or* the date a claimant or someone on her/his behalf first contacts a benefit office (eg, by telephone or letter) if a fully completed form and any proof required are provided within one month. If a claimant provides the required proof more than one month after her/his initial contact with the benefit office, the date of claim will be the date the proof is delivered unless the rules on backdating benefit described on p127 apply.
- Some claimants will be exempt from these rules. They should give notice that they are unable to complete the form as soon as possible (the Benefits Agency says within one month of initial contact, see above) and show that:
  - the form could not be completed or the required proof obtained because of a physical, mental, learning or communication difficulty and it is not 'reasonably practicable' for someone to complete the form or get the proof on their behalf; *or*
  - the required proof does not exist; *or*
  - the required proof could not be obtained without serious risk of physical or mental harm to the claimant and it is not 'reasonably practicable' to get it in another way; *or*
  - the required proof could only be obtained from a third party and it is not 'reasonably practicable' to get it from her/him; *or*

– the Secretary of State thinks sufficient proof has been provided to show that the claimant is not entitled to the benefit claimed, so it would be inappropriate to require further proof.

Changes of circumstance after you claim

You may be on benefit for quite a long time, during which your circumstances may change. You must inform the benefit office, in writing, of any change which might affect the amount of, or your right to, benefit.[16] Keep a copy of the letter you send reporting such changes. The Benefits Agency can accept notification by some other method (ie, by telephone), but this is not always acted on so it is best to do it in writing.

If you fail to report a change and, as a result, you receive too much benefit, the Benefits Agency may take steps to recover the overpayment (see p147) or even treat this as fraud (see p153).

The date of your claim

Your claim is usually treated as made on the day it reaches the Benefits Agency office.[17] This applies even if it is a day on which the office is closed.[18] If your claim is sent by post it should be accepted as having been delivered unless it is proved not to have been. However, you will have to persuade the adjudication officer that you did post it.[19]

Note: From October 1997, the rules about the date of your claim will be much stricter. You will usually have to submit a fully completed claim form, including all the proof required, within one month of your intitial contact with the Benefits Agency. See p125 for further details.

You can claim up to three months before you qualify,[20] thus giving the Benefits Agency time to ensure you receive benefit as soon as you are entitled. This can be useful if you know you are going to qualify – eg, you are due to come out of hospital or a care home. Otherwise, you must usually claim on the first day you want benefit to start (but see below for information about when your claim can be backdated).[21] However, if you are claiming backdated IS because you have been awarded refugee status, see p76.

If you claim family credit (FC) or disability working allowance (DWA) when you should have claimed IS, your claim can be treated as made on the day you claimed FC or DWA. This is the case if you were refused FC or DWA because neither you nor your partner are in full-time work (see p13) and you claim IS within 14 days of the decision refusing your claim.[22] You can ask for your claim to start on a later date, for example, where you have just finished work and have earnings that will be taken into account for a certain period of time (see p354).

Backdating claims

If you claim IS late, your claim can be backdated:

- for up to one month if the Secretary of State decides there are good administrative reasons (see below);
- for up to three months if you can show that it was not reasonable to expect you to claim before you did and your delay was for one of the specified reasons on p128.

If you want your claim to be backdated you must ask for this to happen or the Benefits Agency will not consider it.[23]

If you are claiming backdated IS after you are awarded refugee status these rules do not apply (see p76).[24]

Note: The rules about backdating of claims changed on 7 April 1997. If you claimed backdated IS before that date, the old, more favourable, rules apply (see pp126-27 of the *National Welfare Benefits Handbook*, 1996/97 edn).

Good administrative reasons

The Secretary of State can accept your claim up to one month late if s/he thinks there are good administrative reasons, but only if one of the following applies:[25]

- your claim is late because the office where you are supposed to claim was closed and there were no other arrangements for claims to be made;
- you could not get to the Benefit Office due to difficulties with the type of transport you normally use and there was no reasonable alternative;
- there were adverse postal conditions, for example, bad weather or a postal strike;
- you stopped getting another benefit but were not informed until after your entitlement ceased so you could not claim IS in time;
- you claimed IS in your own right within one month of separating from your partner;
- a close relative of yours died in the month before your claim. Close relative in these circumstances means your partner, parent, son, daughter, brother or sister.

Backdating for other specified reasons

Your claim can be backdated for up to three months if you can show that it was not reasonable to expect you to claim earlier than you did for one of the following specified reasons:[26]

- you have learning, language or literacy difficulties *or* are deaf or blind *or* were sick or disabled *or* were caring for someone who is sick or disabled *or* were dealing with a domestic emergency which affected you *and* it was not 'reasonably practicable' for you to get help to make your claim from anyone else;
- you were given information by an officer of the Department of Social Security or the Department for Education and Employment and as a result thought you were not entitled to benefit;
- you were given advice in writing by a CAB or other advice worker, a solicitor or other professional adviser (eg, an accountant), a doctor or a local authority and as a result thought you were not entitled to benefit;
- you or your partner were given written information about your income or capital by your employer or former employer or a bank or building society and as a result you thought you were not entitled to benefit;
- you could not get to the office because of bad weather.

The rules on backdating are very strict. If you are claiming IS late, it is important to explain why. Provide evidence or information that backs this up, for example, a copy of the letter from your adviser or information from your employer which misled you (see above). If you have been misled, misinformed or insufficiently informed by an officer of the DSS, explain how and when this happened and where possible, give the name and a description of the officer concerned. Where relevant, you should explain why there is no one else who could help you make your claim.

Even if you satisfy the rules described above, IS cannot be paid for more than three months before the date on which you actually claim.[27] You may be paid less than three months' arrears if you claim because of a new interpretation of the law[28].

Note: The rules about backdating of claims changed on 7 April 1997. If you claimed backdated IS before that date, you might be able to get up to 12 months' arrears (see pp126-27 of the *National Welfare Benefits Handbook*, 1996/97 edn).

If you are prevented from receiving benefit because your claim was more than three months late due to an error on the part of the Benefits Agency, you should try to persuade the Benefits Agency to meet its moral obligation and make an *ex gratia* payment or extra-statutory payment to you, as compensation (see p139). To do this, simply write to your Benefits Agency office and ask. The intervention of an MP or the Ombudsman (see p155) may help in these circumstances.

If a person has been formally appointed by a court or the Secretary of State to act on your behalf, your appointee must show that it was not reasonable to expect her/him to claim sooner than s/he did for one of the reasons listed above.[29] If someone is informally acting on your behalf, you must show this. You must also show that it was reasonable for you to delegate responsibility for your claim and that you took care to supervise the person helping you.[30]

2. DECISIONS AND REVIEWS

It is important to know who makes the decision on any particular question in your claim because that determines how you challenge it if you disagree.

Most decisions are made by an adjudication officer at the Benefits Agency office where you claimed IS.[31]

An adjudication officer at the Child Benefit Centre may advise:

- whether you are in 'relevant education' (see p16).

While an adjudication officer elsewhere is being consulted on your case, it will be assumed s/he has decided against you and IS will be refused in the meantime.[32]

Decisions made by the Secretary of State are:

- whether to accept a claim made other than on the approved form;
- whether a claim for one benefit can be treated instead of, or in addition to, a claim for another benefit;[33]
- whether to demand recovery of an overpayment, and the amount of weekly deductions (subject to the maximum, see p151);
- whether to suspend benefit pending determination of a question on review or appeal;
- whether to take action against people who are liable to maintain claimants (see p105);
- whether to appoint a person as an appointee;
- who should be the claimant when a couple are unable to decide;
- whether to issue or replace giros and order books and how IS should be paid;
- whether to pay an interim payment;
- whether a school or college is a 'recognised educational establishment';
- circumstances in which a claim is to be treated as withdrawn.

You should be notified in writing of the decision on your claim unless the decision is to pay you in cash, or your benefit is being stopped and it is reasonable not to give you a written decision.[34] Sometimes a decision is unclear or difficult to understand. To get an explanation, write to the appropriate office within three months of that decision,[35] or seek independent advice. If you appeal against an adjudication officer's decision (see Chapter 8) the papers you receive will give the full background to the decision.

You should automatically receive a letter showing how your benefit has been worked out.[36] You can ask for a more detailed breakdown. Check the details on this form.

Contacting benefit offices

Writing to your office is nearly always the best way to have your case dealt with. It ensures there is a permanent record of what you said and enables you to cover all the relevant points clearly. Always put your name, address, the date and your national insurance number at the top of your letter. If possible, make a copy of it. You should also keep all letters and forms sent to you. Such a record may help you or your adviser to work out later whether any decision can be challenged.

The *Customer Charter* states that the Agency will reply to all letters within ten working days (seven days if it is a letter of complaint). If you are sent a partial reply you should be told how long it will be before your letter can be fully answered. The person writing to you should give their name and telephone number.

If there is a delay in getting a reply, you can telephone to find out why, but it may be better to write a short reminder and only telephone if you still receive no response.

Nevertheless, on occasion, **telephoning your benefit office** may be necessary. If you are a London claimant, try your branch office first. If you have to ring the centre in Belfast, Glasgow or Ashton-in-Makerfield, you are only charged the local rate. Be ready to give your surname and national insurance number. Try to get the name, title and telephone extension number of the person you speak to as this may be useful in the future. Make a brief note of what is said, together with the date. If the information is important, follow up the telephone call with a letter confirming what the Benefits Agency said so that any misunderstanding can be cleared up. Offices are usually reluctant to write merely to confirm a telephone conversation.

Visiting your office enables you to have a detailed conversation with an officer. However, check the opening times first. An appointment can usually be arranged by telephone. You should expect the receptionist to see you within 10 minutes. However, at busy times you should not have to wait more than 30 minutes. Be prepared to wait longer if you need to see someone else. The receptionist should tell you how long it is likely to take. If you want a private interview, this should be provided. Staff you see will wear name badges.

Take any documents with you which may be relevant otherwise you may be asked to make a second visit to provide the additional information. Again, follow up any important meeting with a letter confirming the points you or the Benefits Agency have made or ask the office to confirm in writing any advice to you. It is a good idea to take a friend or relative with you, not only for moral support, but also as a witness to what is said.

If you cannot get to the office, for example because of your age, health or a disability, an officer may be able to make a **home visit** if your case cannot be dealt with by telephone. Ask if you need a visit. If you are refused and are not satisfied with the explanation, ask to speak to a supervisor or the customer care manager.

If you are a London claimant, you can go to your local branch office to discuss your claim. The staff will contact the social security centre in Belfast, Glasgow or Ashton-in-Makerfield if necessary.

Delays

It is very unlikely that you will get an immediate decision on your claim because the facts need to be checked and your benefit calculated. However, an adjudication officer should decide a claim for IS within 14 days 'so far as practicable'.[37]

If you have been waiting more than 14 days for a decision, contact the benefit office. First, check that your claim has been received. If it has not, let the office have a copy of your claim or fill out a new form and refer them to the claim form you sent in earlier.

If your claim has been received but not dealt with, ask for an explanation. If you are not satisfied with the explanation for the delay, make a complaint (see p154). Benefits Agency offices have a *Customer Charter* which sets time limits for dealing with claims and you can refer to this. The national *Customer Charter* has a target claim clearance time for IS of five working days, which sets a minimum standard for all local offices.

In addition to taking the steps already described, you should ask the office to make interim payments to you while you wait for the decision (see p136). You may also be able to obtain a crisis loan (see p446).

Reviews

An adjudication officer can review a decision of an adjudication officer, social security appeal tribunal (SSAT), or social security commissioner if there are grounds (see p132). This can be done even if the original decision was made a long time ago.

You can ask for a review or the adjudication officer may decide that one is necessary. The person who wants the review is the one who has to show there are grounds (see below). It is best to ask for a review in writing giving the reasons why you think one should take place. Claims for benefit or questions you ask about your entitlement can be treated as requests for a review.[38]

Following a review, the original decision may be changed either to increase *or* decrease the amount of your IS *or* remove entitlement to benefit altogether. You should seek advice before you seek a review if you are concerned about what could happen in your case. If a review decision does not give you all that you wanted, you can try to make a late appeal against the original decision[39] (but see p158).

Awards of IS are made for an indefinite period. If you cease to satisfy the conditions of entitlement, the decision awarding you benefit must be reviewed if one of the grounds for review applies (see below).[40] This is the case even where the amount of benefit to which you are entitled is simply reduced or increased, for example, where you are claiming IS because you are sick but you then recover and have to claim on the basis that you are a single parent.

A decision may only be reviewed if:[41]

- **There was a mistake about the facts of your case or it was made in ignorance of relevant facts**. If a decision is reviewed on this ground, the review decision takes effect from the beginning of the period covered by the original decision. If it is in your favour, you receive arrears (see p133 for how much you can be paid). If not you may have been overpaid and the adjudication officer decides whether or not to recover the overpayment (see p146).
- The original decision was made by an adjudication officer (not a tribunal or commissioner) and was **legally wrong**.
- **Your circumstances have changed since the original decision** or it is anticipated that they will do so. A decision can only be reviewed on this basis if you are currently entitled to benefit and your situation changes. If you were correctly refused IS in the past and your circumstances are now different, you must make a fresh claim.[42] An amendment to the law counts as a change of circumstances, but a decision of a court or commissioner that the law has been wrongly interpreted does not.[43] A new medical opinion is not a change of circumstances,[44] but a medical opinion following an examination might give evidence of such a change.[45] Some situations never count as a change of circumstance: the repayment of a student loan; and your absence from a nursing or residential care home for less than a week.[46]

  If a decision is reviewed on this ground, the review decision takes effect from the first day of the week in which the change occurs if you

are paid in arrears, or the week following the change if you are paid in advance (unless the change occurs on the first day of your benefit week in which case it is that day).[47]
• The original decision on your claim was based on a **Secretary of State's decision** which has itself now been changed.

An adjudication officer might review but still not change the decision. Alternatively, s/he might decide that there are no grounds for a review. In either case, you can appeal against the decision (see p156). This can be useful if you did not appeal against the original decision in time and cannot make a late appeal (see p158). Where the adjudication officer says there are no grounds for a review, you must show why there are, as well as give your reasons for disputing the review decision. In an appeal the tribunal must identify which decision is to be reviewed, establish whether there are grounds for review and from what date, and then check if the limitations on backdating restrict the arrears which can be paid (see below).[48]

Although in an appeal the tribunal is usually considering whether the adjudication officer had grounds to review a decision, it is possible for them to review a decision themselves if new facts of which the adjudication officer was unaware but which give grounds for review, come to light during the hearing.[49] It is not necessary for them to adjourn the hearing and refer the matter back to the adjudication officer, though they may choose to do this instead.

A review can be a quicker and simpler way of getting a decision changed than an appeal. It can also be a way of getting round the three-month time limit for appeals (see p156).

Payment of arrears of benefit on review

If the adjudication officer agrees to change the decision, you can usually get arrears of benefit going back one month before the date you requested a review, or if you did not request a review, from the date the review took place.[50] It is important to make it clear that you want payment for the past period.

Note: The rules about payment of arrears of benefit changed on 7 April 1997. If you requested a review before that date, the old, more favourable, rules apply (see pp131-33 of the *National Welfare Benefits Handbook*, 1996/97 edn).

You can get more than one month's backdating if[51] the ground for review was that the decision was wrong in law because the adjudication officer overlooked or misinterpreted part of an Act, Order, regulation, or decision of a commissioner or court when deciding your claim.

You can get more than one month's backdating if[52] the ground for review was ignorance of, or mistake about, the facts (see p132) and you can show that the decision is being changed because:

- there is specific evidence which the adjudication officer (or SSAT) who originally decided the claim had, but which they failed to take into account even though it was relevant. This applies even if the evidence does not conclusively prove your entitlement. So long as it raised a strong possibility that you were entitled, it should have been taken into account;[53]
- there is documentary or other written evidence of your entitlement which the DSS, DHSS or Department of Employment had, but failed to give to the adjudication officer (SSAT or commissioner), at the time of the earlier decision;
- new evidence has come to light which did not exist earlier and could not have been obtained. This will only apply if you provide this evidence as soon as possible after it is available to you;
- you want your IS to be reviewed because you have become entitled to another benefit and arrears of that benefit are payable for more than one month.[54] This provision helps you if you did not get certain premiums paid with your IS because of delays in assessing another benefit – eg, where a DLA claim took 18 months to be decided and you have missed out on the severe disability premium for this period. You can only ask for a review if you have claimed IS. It is therefore important to claim IS while you are waiting to hear about your claim for another benefit. If you wait to claim IS until you hear, you can only get if you satisfy the backdating rules on p127.

If you are trying to get arrears going back several years, it may be difficult to identify the grounds for review, particularly where the Benefits Agency has destroyed old papers relating to your claim. The onus is on you to show that your claim should be reviewed and you cannot simply rely on the Benefits Agency's lack of evidence.[55]

You may get less than one month's backdating if your entitlement is reviewed following a new interpretation of the law by a social security commissioner or court. In this case you get arrears back to the date of the decision by the commissioner or court.[56] This is what is known as the 'anti-test case rule'. See the *Rights Guide to Non-Means-Tested Benefits* for more information. This rule only applies if you ask for a review on the grounds that the decision in your case was found to be legally wrong by the decision of the commissioner or court in the test case (and not for some other reason) (see p132). In addition, you must have asked for the review after the test case decision.[57] You can avoid the anti-test case rule by applying for a late appeal rather than a review (but see p158). You can do this even if a review has taken place but has not given you all the arrears you are claiming.[58]

If you were underpaid benefit because of a clear error by the DSS/ Benefits Agency you could apply for compensation as well as getting arrears owed to you (see p139).

3. PAYMENTS OF BENEFIT

The Secretary of State decides how benefit is paid to you.[59] You are paid by giro, benefit order book, or directly into a bank or building society account.[60] It may be possible to be paid cash in certain circumstances.[61] The Government intends to introduce benefit payment cards in the near future.

Once you have been awarded benefit you must cash the payment within a year of it being due.[62] This period can be extended if you can show good cause for the delay.[63] However, an order book is only valid for three months and a giro for one month. If you do not cash them within this period you will have to try to get a replacement.

If you are entitled to less than 10 pence a week you are not paid IS at all, unless you are receiving another social security benefit which can be paid with IS. If you are entitled to less than £1 a week the Secretary of State can decide to pay you quarterly in arrears.[64] If your IS includes a fraction of a penny it is rounded up to a full penny if it is more than a half penny. Otherwise the fraction is ignored.[65]

You are paid in advance if you are:[66]

- receiving retirement pension; *or*
- over pension age (60 for a woman, 65 for a man) and not receiving incapacity benefit, or severe disablement allowance nor involved in a trade dispute (unless you were receiving IS immediately before the dispute began); *or*
- receiving widows' benefits (but only if you are not providing or required to provide medical evidence of incapacity for work); *or*
- returning to work after a trade dispute.

If you are paid in advance, your entitlement begins on the first pay day of any other social security benefit to which you are entitled (or would be entitled if you had sufficient contributions) following the date of your claim for IS. For example, retirement pension is paid on a Monday. If you claim IS on a Wednesday you are entitled to IS in advance from the following Monday. But if you claim on a Monday you get it from that day.

You are paid in arrears if you are not in one of the above groups.[67] Your entitlement to IS starts from the date of your claim (see p126).[68]

Once your entitlement has been worked out, the Secretary of State decides how often and on which day of the week you are paid[69] unless you are entitled to incapacity benefit; severe disablement allowance; retirement pension; or widows' benefits. If you are entitled to one of these (or would be if you satisfied the contribution conditions), you are paid IS on the same day of the week as that other benefit and at the same intervals.[70] If you are incapable of work and not getting incapacity benefit you are paid fortnightly in arrears.

Interim payments

If payment of your IS is delayed you may be in urgent need of money. If this is the case, you can ask for what are known as 'interim payments'.

An interim payment can be made where it seems that you are or may be entitled to IS and where:[71]

- you have claimed IS but not in the correct way (eg, you have filled in the wrong form, or filled in the right form incorrectly or incompletely) and you cannot put in a correct claim immediately (eg, because the Benefits Agency office is closed); *or*
- you have claimed IS correctly, but it is not possible for the claim or for a review or appeal which relates to it to be dealt with immediately;
- you have been awarded benefit, but it is not possible to pay you immediately other than by means of an interim payment.

However, if your claim is being appealed, an interim payment can only be made if the Secretary of State thinks you are entitled to some benefit. This rule might be invalid in a case involving EC law. If you think this applies to you, you should seek advice.

The decision whether or not to award an interim payment is the Secretary of State's and therefore you cannot appeal to a tribunal if you are refused, though it may be possible to apply for judicial review (see p172). If you are refused an interim payment, contact your MP and see Chapter 24 for whether you can get a crisis loan. You could also try using the emergency service (see p139).

An interim payment can be deducted from any later payment of IS and if it is more than your actual entitlement, the overpayment can be recovered.[72] You should be notified of this in advance, unless the payment is made because you have not received child support maintenance. In this case, any overpayment is recovered from the arrears of maintenance rather than your benefit.

Suspension and withholding of payments

The Secretary of State can order payment of your IS to be *suspended* if:

- **a question has arisen about your entitlement to benefit.**[73] In this case, all or part of the benefit due to you is suspended pending a review or appeal of the decision about your entitlement. For example, if you are being paid IS but it is thought that you are in full-time work, your benefit may be suspended while information is gathered about the true situation;
- **it looks as though your IS award should be revised;**[74]
- **you are awarded benefit on appeal but the Benefits Agency wants to appeal against that decision.**[75] If this happens, your award can only be suspended for three months after the adjudication officer receives the decision while they consider an appeal to the Social Security Commissioner or courts. If the Benefits Agency decides to appeal, it must notify you in writing within the three months. You will then not be paid until your case is resolved;
- **you are due to be paid arrears of a benefit but you may also have been overpaid.**[76] Your arrears may be withheld in whole or in part while the possible overpayment is investigated.

The Benefits Agency used to suspend your benefit if it was appealing (or considering an appeal) to the courts about someone else's claim, and the issue under appeal affected your claim. However, this rule was found to be unlawful.[77] If your benefit has been suspended in this way you should ask the Benefits Agency to start paying your benefit immediately and to give you what has been withheld so far. You should be given what was withheld even if the appeal about someone else's claim has already been decided. Even if the decision was negative, you should be paid up to the date of that decision. If the Benefits Agency refuses to pay, you should seek advice. Where a tribunal, a commissioner or a court has awarded you benefit, the Benefits Agency can only suspend your benefit if it appeals your case (see above).[78]

The decision to suspend benefit is made by the Secretary of State and you cannot appeal against it to a tribunal. Your only remedy is judicial review (see p172). You must negotiate to get your benefit reinstated and/or request an interim payment. You should try to persuade the Secretary of State that it is unreasonable to suspend payment of your benefit, particularly if hardship is caused.

Your benefit can be *withheld* if:[79]

- **you fail to provide information in support of your claim** within 28 days of being asked;
- **you do not send in sick notes;**
- there are **doubts about where you are living**.

If you later fulfil these requirements you can be paid any benefit that has been withheld, but you must normally apply within 12 months.[80]

Lost and missing payments

If you lose a giro or order book after you have received it, report the loss immediately to the benefit office by telephone or personal visit and confirm the loss in writing, requesting a replacement at the same time. If your giro is lost or stolen before you have had a chance to cash it, the Secretary of State has a duty to replace it. This applies even if the giro is subsequently cashed by someone else,[81] though you will need to satisfy the Benefits Agency that it was not you who cashed it. You should also report the matter to the police, and note the investigating officer's name and number.

If the benefit office refuses to issue a replacement, or takes too long considering your request, you can take legal action to get the benefit due to you. You cannot appeal to a tribunal if a payment goes missing, but you can sue the Secretary of State in the county court.[82] This can take time, so you may wish to claim a crisis loan to tide you over (see p446).

Before taking legal action you should write to the local Benefits Agency office requesting it to replace the giro within a reasonable time – eg, seven days. Explain that court action will be taken if it does not respond. Keep a copy of the letter.

If the Benefits Agency does not replace your giro or order book, you need to begin proceedings in the local county court. The forms to do this are available from the county court. Complete these and return them to the court. You have to pay a court fee, calculated as a percentage of your unpaid giro. The fee is refundable if you win. The Benefits Agency is allowed time to respond to your summons, but you will almost certainly find that the local Benefits Agency office will replace your giro without the need to proceed to a court hearing. Your court fee is repaid separately by the Benefits Agency Solicitors (see Appendix 2 for address), and you should not withdraw the summons until you have received both a replacement giro and your court fee. If the Benefits Agency refuses to pay benefit for a future period covered by a lost order book, you can take court action in the High Court (see p172).

Emergencies

If you have lost all your money or there has been a similar crisis, it is possible to get help at any time.

Any local police station should have a contact number for Benefits Agency staff on call outside normal office hours. In London there is a special Benefits Agency office open in the evenings and at weekends for emergencies. It is Keyworth House, Keyworth Street, London SE1 (tel: 0171 401 9692 or, during the day, 0171 620 1456).

There will also be a duty social worker who can be contacted via your local social services department or council, or via the police.

Compensation payments

In line with the Benefits Agency's *Customer Charter*, you should expect prompt, courteous and efficient service from staff dealing with your claim. If you are dissatisfied with the way your claim has been administered you can seek compensation. The Benefits Agency uses a circular, *Financial Redress for Maladministration*, to help it decide when and how much compensation should be paid.

Benefits Agency errors

Sometimes the Benefits Agency makes mistakes about the amount of your benefit. Also, you might be given incorrect advice or information by the Benefits Agency which means you claim late. Where possible it corrects the mistake by carrying out a review and awarding you the correct benefit (see p131) or by backdating your claim (see p127).

If the procedures for review or backdating do not apply or do not properly compensate you for the effects of the mistake that has occurred, you may claim compensation (known as an *ex gratia* payment). You should ask for a payment equal to the money you have lost, but you could also ask for additional amounts to cover interest on arrears, extra expenses you had to pay out, and to compensate you for any hardship or distress suffered owing to the mistake. Payments are discretionary, so you should stress the Benefits Agency error and the fact that you have suffered as a consequence of official negligence, in order to ensure payment. If your loss was as a clear result of incorrect advice or negligence on the part of the Benefits Agency, you may be able to bring a court action for damages. You will need the help of an advice agency or solicitor to do this.

Delays by the Benefits Agency

Benefits Agency offices have target times for dealing with claims, but they are not always able to meet these. If there is a long delay in assessing your entitlement, you are entitled to compensation if:[83]

- a significant reason for the delay was Benefits Agency error; *and*
- the amount of benefit involved was more than £100; *and*
- the delay in payment was more than two months (IS), six months (family credit) or one month (disability working allowance); *and;*
- any compensation would be £10 or more.

You are not automatically awarded compensation although the Benefits Agency should automatically consider whether it should be paid where you are owed arrears of benefit. However, you should still write to your local Benefits Agency office and ask. If you do not get a sympathetic response you could ask your MP to write on your behalf, or to take up your case with the Social Security Minister.

Payments to other people

Payment is usually made direct to you but there are some circumstances in which payments can be made to other people or organisations on your behalf.

- If you are unable to manage your own money, your benefit is paid to a person appointed to act on your behalf (see p123).[84]
- If it is in the interests of you, your partner or your children, the Secretary of State can pay your benefit to someone else.[85] For example, if you are neglecting your children even though benefit is being paid for them, it might be paid to another person to help look after them. If your partner is refusing to support you, all or part of her/his benefit can be paid to you.

Mortgage direct payments

When you first claim IS you may not receive help with your housing costs (see p25) and you must meet these costs from other income – eg, a mortgage protection policy. Once you qualify for help with housing costs the amount for mortgage interest is paid direct to your lender for each complete week that you are on benefit.[86] The only exceptions to this are where your lender is not covered by, or has opted out of, the mortgage payments scheme.[87] The Benefits Agency should tell you if this applies and you must pay your own mortgage.

Payments to cover your mortgage interest are made to your lender. Your housing costs are deducted from your total IS entitlement and you get the balance.[88] You have to make up any difference between what the Benefits Agency pays to your lender and the amount you owe them. This could include such things as non-dependant deductions or a restriction due to excessive housing costs. If you get incapacity benefit, severe disablement allowance or retirement pension paid on the same giro/order book as your IS, deductions can be made from these benefits too. If you do not have enough benefit to meet the full cost, all but 10 pence of your benefit is paid over and you must pay the rest yourself.[89]

Payments are made four-weekly in arrears[90] even if your payments are due on a calendar month basis, so you may appear to be in arrears even though your full mortgage is being met. You might need to explain this to your lender. If the Benefits Agency deducts your housing costs from your IS but fails to pay these to your lender in time and as a result you have to pay interest on arrears that build up or you lose your home, you should seek advice. You might be able to claim compensation.[91]

If you have more than one type of housing cost, deductions for non-dependants (see p36) and certain restrictions for excessive housing costs are apportioned using a formula (see p145).[92]

If you are in mortgage arrears, no amount towards the arrears can be deducted from your benefit if your lender is covered by the mortgage payments scheme (see p140). If you are in this situation, you should seek financial advice. If you are in arrears of other housing costs, see p142.

Other direct deductions

Amounts can also be deducted from your IS for other housing costs, fuel, water charges, the recovery of social fund loans (see p451), council tax arrears, community charge arrears, child maintenance (see p112), fines and overpayments (see p151).[93]

Deductions are made at the Benefits Agency office before you receive your regular benefit payment. If you want to have deductions made to help you clear any arrears or debts, ask at the Benefits Agency office dealing with your IS claim. If you disagree with a decision about deductions, you can appeal (see p156).

When can direct deductions be made?[94]

Rent arrears[95] **(and any inclusive water, fuel and service charges)**
If you are in arrears with your rent while on benefit, an amount can be deducted from your IS and paid direct to your landlord.

'Rent arrears' do not include the amount of any non-dependant deductions (see p254), but can cover any water charges or service charges payable with your rent and not met by housing benefit. Fuel charges included in your rent cannot be covered by direct deductions if they change more than twice a year.

To qualify for direct deductions your rent arrears must amount to at least four times your full weekly rent. If you have not paid your full rent for more than eight weeks, direct deductions can be made automatically if your landlord asks the Benefits Agency to make them.[96] If your arrears relate to a shorter period, deductions can only be made if it is in the 'overriding interests' of your family to do so.[97] In either case the adjudication officer must be satisfied that you are in rent arrears. Even if you are, you can ask her/him not to make direct deductions, for example, where you are claiming compensation from your landlord because of the state of repair of your home.[98] Once your arrears are paid off, direct payments can continue for any fuel and water charges inclusive in your rent.[99]

Housing costs[100]

Mortgage payments are usually paid direct to your lender (see p140). If this applies to you (or would if your lender had not opted out of the scheme) then the deductions under this provision will only cover payments for other types of housing costs.[101]

If your current IS includes money for such housing costs and you are in debt for these costs (excluding payments for a tent and ground rent/ feu duty unless paid with your service charges[102]), deductions can be made from your benefit both to clear the debt and to meet current payments. Deductions are made if it would be 'in the interests' of you or your family to do so.

You can only qualify for direct deductions if you owe more than half of the annual total of the relevant housing cost. This condition can be waived if it is in the 'overriding interests' of you or your family that deductions start as soon as possible – eg, repossession of your home is imminent.[103]

In the case of mortgage payments, you must have paid less than eight weeks' worth of full payments in the last 12 weeks. The amount of mortgage interest taken into account is the amount after deductions for non-dependants (see p36).

Residential accommodation charges[104]

If you receive IS, the amount you are paid may cover charges for your accommodation if you live in a residential care or nursing home, or local authority residential accommodation (see p84).

These charges can be met by direct deductions from your benefit if you have failed to budget for the charges from your benefit and it is in your interest that deductions should be made. Even if these conditions do not apply direct payments can be made if you are in a home run by a voluntary organisation for alcoholics or drug addicts.

Water charges[105]
If you get into debt with charges for water and sewerage, direct deductions might be made – 'debt' includes any disconnection, reconnection and legal charges. If you pay your landlord for water with your rent, deductions are made under the arrangements for rent arrears (see p141).[106]

Deductions can be made if you failed to budget and it is in the interests of your family to make deductions.[107] If you get into debt with water charges you should consider making an agreement for direct deductions because the water authority can cut off your water supply if you do not meet your debts and current charges. If you are in debt to two water companies you can only have a deduction for arrears made to one of them at a time. Your debts for water charges should be cleared before your debts for sewerage costs, but the amount paid for current consumption can include both water and sewerage charges.[108]

Fuel debts[109]
If you are in debt, an amount can be deducted from your benefit each week and paid over to the fuel board in instalments – usually once a quarter. This is known as 'fuel direct'. In return, the fuel board agrees not to disconnect you. Deductions can be made where:[110]

- the amount you owe is £49.15 or more (including reconnection/disconnection charges if you have been disconnected); *and*
- you continue to need the fuel supply; *and*
- it is in your interest to have deductions made.

The amount deducted for current consumption is whatever is necessary to meet your current weekly fuel costs. This is adjusted if the cost increases or decreases and deductions for current payments can be continued after the debt has been cleared.[111]

Council tax and community charge arrears[112]
Deductions can be made from IS if the local authority gets a liability order from a magistrates' court (in Scotland, a summary warrant or decree from a sheriff's court) and applies to the Benefits Agency for recovery to be made in this way. For community charge purposes, if they want to recover arrears from both partners in a couple the order must be against both of them. Deductions can be made for arrears and any unpaid costs or penalties imposed. Deductions cannot be made for council tax arrears while community charge deductions are being made.

Hostel payments[113]

If you (or your partner) live in a hostel *and* you have claimed housing benefit (HB) to meet your accommodation costs *and* your payments to the hostel cover fuel, meals, water charges, laundry and/or cleaning of your room, part of your benefit can be paid direct to the hostel for these items. You do not have to be in arrears for this to apply. These costs are all items which cannot be covered by HB (see p228) and which you must meet from your IS. Fuel costs are not paid direct if the charge varies according to actual consumption, unless the charge is altered less than three times a year.

Fines, costs and compensation orders[114]

Magistrates' courts (any court in Scotland) can apply to the Benefits Agency for a fine, costs or compensation order to be deducted from your IS. Only one court application can be dealt with at a time – if a second application is made it is not dealt with until the first debt is paid.

Deductions can only be made if you are over 18, on IS, and you have defaulted on payments. Payments continue until the debt is paid off, or your IS ceases or is too low to cover the repayments.

Maintenance for children

Deductions can be made from an absent parent's IS as a contribution towards the maintenance of her/his child(ren)[115] (see p112).

How much can be deducted?

Deductions are made to pay off the debt, or current weekly costs or both.[116]

Type of arrears	*Deduction for arrears*	*Deduction for ongoing cost*
Mortgage direct payments*	Nil	Current weekly cost
Housing costs*	£2.50 each housing debt (maximum of £7.50 payable)	Current weekly cost
Rent arrears	£2.50	Nil (met by HB)
Fuel	£2.50 each fuel debt (maximum of £5.00 payable)	Estimated amount of current consumption
Water charges	£2.50	Estimated costs (adjusted every 26 weeks)

Council tax	£2.50	Nil (met by council tax benefit)
Community charge	£2.50 (single person) £3.90 (couple)	Not applicable
Fines	Nil	£2.50
Child maintenance	Nil	£5.00
Residential accommodation charges	Nil	The accommodation allowance (for those in local authority homes). All but £14.10 of your IS (for those in private or voluntary homes).
Hostel charges	Nil	Weekly amount assessed by local authority.

* If you have more than one type of housing cost and these are not met in full because of a restriction on the amount which can be covered (see p38), or a non-dependant deduction (see p36) the direct payment to meet current weekly costs is reduced as follows:[117] Multiply the amount of the restriction and/or deduction by the amount of the item of housing costs to be paid direct and then divide by the amount of total housing costs. This ensures that such reductions are shared proportionately between different items of housing costs

---

If you have debts for several items, the amount deducted is the ongoing cost for each item (see above) plus arrears. The total that can be deducted for all your arrears (excluding community charge arrears) plus a contribution towards child maintenance (if you have to make one) is £7.50 a week.[118] If deductions of £5 are being made for items of a higher priority than child maintenance (see p146), half of the child maintenance deduction will be made, ie £2.50.

In the case of fuel, rent arrears, water charges and housing costs arrears (see p142), if the combined cost of deductions for arrears and current consumption is more than 25 per cent of your total applicable amount – see p24 – the deductions cannot be made without your consent.[119]

Deductions are made from your IS and from any incapacity benefit, retirement pension or severe disablement allowance paid with it in the same giro or order book.[120] You must be left with at least 10 pence. Council tax and community charge arrears can be deducted from IS only.[121]

Priority between debts

If you have more debts or charges than can be met within the limits for direct deductions, they are paid in the following order of priority:[122]

1st other IS housing costs
2nd rent arrears (and related charges)
3rd fuel charges
4th water charges
5th council tax and community charge arrears
6th unpaid fines, costs and compensation orders
7th payments for maintenance of children

If you owe both gas and electricity, the Benefits Agency chooses which one to pay first, depending on your circumstances. If you have been overpaid benefit or given a social fund loan, you may have to repay these too by having deductions from your IS.[123] You should argue that these deductions should take a lower priority. If you have arrears for both council tax and community charge, only one application can be dealt with at a time and the earliest debt should be dealt with first.[124]

4. OVERPAYMENTS AND FRAUD

Duplication of payments

Sometimes you receive too much IS because money which is owing to you does not arrive on time. For example, if you claim child benefit but it is not paid for several weeks, your IS continues at the full rate while you are not actually receiving child benefit. However, if child benefit had been promptly paid, your IS would have been paid at a lower rate.

When you get your arrears, you must repay the IS which you would not have received if the other income had been paid on time.[125] The rule applies to all types of income which affect the amount of your IS, including other social security benefits and to arrears of child support maintenance paid to you for the period from your application to the date it is assessed by the Child Support Agency. It also applies to benefits paid by other EC States.[126] You always have to pay the money back, even though it was not your fault that the income was paid late.

Mortgage interest paid direct to a lender

Any overpayment of mortgage interest which is paid direct to your lender (see p140) must be sent back to the Benefits Agency by that lender if it arose because:[127]

- there was a reduction in the amount of your outstanding loan, the standard interest rate (see p33) or the mortgage interest rate, and your IS entitlement therefore reduced but the Benefits Agency did not adjust your mortgage direct payments; *or*
- you ceased to be entitled to IS, but only if the Benefits Agency asks for repayment within four weeks of you going off benefit.

In the former case your mortgage account should simply be corrected, but where you come off IS and interest is recovered, you will be in arrears unless you have started to make payments yourself.

Rather than ask your lender to return what was overpaid, the Benefits Agency often simply stops sending your lender your ongoing housing costs until they have recovered the overpayment. However, the Benefits Agency should not do this if you are put into arrears as a result.[128] If you are put into arrears, you should seek advice.

Other overpayments

For all other overpayments, repayment can only be required if you have misrepresented or failed to disclose a material fact and too much benefit has been paid as a result[129] (but see p152). You may have to repay even if you innocently misrepresented your situation or you failed to tell the local office certain facts because you did not understand how the benefit scheme works.

If you have been (or are being) overpaid, your benefit entitlement must be reviewed.[130] If the adjudication officer does not conduct a proper review before asking you to repay any money, the decision that you have been overpaid is invalid and you can avoid having to repay.[131] However, it is likely that your entitlement will then be reviewed correctly and benefit may then be recoverable (see p131). Pending this review, some or all of your current benefit can be suspended (see p137).

Prior to 24 July 1996, an overpayment could only be recovered if the adjudication officer made a decision to recover it at the same time as s/he reviewed your entitlement to benefit.[132] However, in practice, most decisions about recovering overpayments were made after benefit entitlement had been reviewed. In this circumstance, no overpayment could be recovered. If you think this might apply to you, you should seek advice.

If you do not agree that you owe the Benefits Agency money for example because it has not reviewed your claim properly or you dispute the amount, you can appeal (see p156). Do not pay back any of the money until your appeal has been decided, as they may keep any money you voluntarily repay, even if you later win your case![133]

When can overpayments be recovered?

For all three of the following questions, the burden of proving the case lies with the adjudication officer.

Did you fail to disclose or misrepresent a material fact?

The first thing to check is whether you have been accused of failing to disclose or of misrepresenting a material fact.

Failure to disclose occurs where you do not give the Benefits Agency relevant information – eg, you forget to tell them your circumstances have changed. Misrepresentation occurs where you have given the Benefits Agency information which is inaccurate – eg, you gave an incorrect answer to a specific question on the claim form.

Failure to disclose

- You cannot be said to have failed to disclose a fact you did not know about (because of, for example, your mental incapacity).
- It must be reasonable to have expected you to notify the office of the particular facts. It is irrelevant that you did not personally realise the need to tell the Benefits Agency these facts – the test is whether a reasonable person would have realised that disclosure was required.[134]
- You cannot assume that changes in your social security benefits, paid by one section of the Benefits Agency, are known to the other sections. You should give the IS section any information which might affect your IS.[135]
- It is not necessary for you to show that you told the office in writing about your situation. It will do just as well if you give the information over the telephone, or in an office interview, either verbally or by presenting the relevant documents.[136]
- If you filled in a form while giving information, a tribunal should look at what you said in the form, but also consider whether you gave the necessary information in another way.[137] A claimant who fails to fill in a form correctly, but who gives the relevant information in the wrong place, has disclosed the material facts.[138]
- If there is no record of a verbal statement a claimant only has a case to answer once the adjudication officer has shown, 'on the balance of probabilities', that there would be a record of the conversation at the local office if it had taken place. In order to do this, the adjudication officer must give a tribunal information on:[139]

- the instructions which should have applied for recording and attaching information to the claimant's file;
- whether there were the appropriate administrative arrangements to enable these instructions to be carried out;
- to what extent *in practice* these instructions are, or are not, carried out.

Where there is no record of what happened, other than the claimant's own statement, the Benefits Agency will be unable to prove that there has been a recoverable overpayment.[140]

- You need not report a change direct to the Benefits Agency if you give the information in another way which might reasonably be expected to reach the relevant local office – eg, you tell the pensions section and ask them to inform the IS section too. However, if you realise or should have realised that the information has not reached the IS section, you are under an obligation to take further steps to inform them.[141] A short time may elapse before you can reasonably be expected to realise that the original information has not been acted on.[142]

Misrepresentation

- This can be completely innocent[143] – eg, where you did not know that your partner's earnings had changed. You would not be guilty of misrepresentation if you add the phrase 'not to my knowledge' to your statement.[144]
- It must relate to your current claim. If you have declared a fact on a previous claim but inadvertently give incorrect information on a later claim, you have to repay. The Benefits Agency are not required to check back for you.[145] However, if what you say on your claim form is obviously incorrect and the adjudication officer does not check this out, the overpayment will be due to DSS error not your misrepresentation. For example, if you say you pay ground rent and are a freeholder, the adjudication officer should recognise that this must be incorrect and check before paying.[146]
- If you are incapable of managing your affairs but nevertheless sign a claim form which is incorrectly completed, you cannot later argue that you were not capable of making a true representation of your circumstances to avoid recovery.[147]

Most overpayments arise due to a failure to disclose and it is easier to challenge such a decision than to show that you did not misrepresent. Because of this the Benefits Agency relies on general statements which you have signed to argue that a failure to disclose can later become a misrepresentation.

This can occur in two situations:[148]

- when you sign the claim form for IS. The form ends with a statement: 'I declare that the information I have given is correct and complete'. If you gave correct answers but left out relevant information because you were unaware of it, the information is incomplete and you have failed to disclose. You can argue that signing the declaration does not convert this into a misrepresentation as the declaration means 'complete insofar as I have knowledge of the material facts';[149]
- when you cash a giro or an order book. Each time you do this you are signing a declaration that you have reported any facts which could affect the amount of your IS. If you knew a fact but failed to declare it (eg, where you start getting incapacity benefit but did not tell the Benefits Agency your circumstances changed) you are misrepresenting your circumstances each time you sign the declaration, and the overpayment is recoverable due to *both* your original 'failure to disclose' *and* the later misrepresentation.

However, if you did not declare a fact because you were unaware of it, signing the declaration does not amount to a misrepresentation because all you are declaring is that you have correctly disclosed those facts *which were known to you*.

If you were told by the Benefits Agency that certain facts are irrelevant to your claim, then signing the declaration cannot be a misrepresentation if you fail to disclose those facts.[150]

Did an overpayment result?

Even if you admit that there is information you failed to give the Benefits Agency or that you did misrepresent your circumstances, you can still argue that this was not the cause of the overpayment and it therefore should not be recovered. If the Benefits Agency have been given the correct information to decide your claim by someone else, but fail to act upon it, you could argue that any overpayment did not arise because of your failure.[151]

How much is repayable?

It is always worth checking how the overpayment has been calculated as you may be asked to repay too much by mistake. Do not be afraid to ask the office for more information if you need it.

The amount of the overpayment is the difference between what was paid and what should have been paid.[152] The Benefits Agency works out the latter using the information that you originally gave the office, plus any facts which you misrepresented or did not disclose.[153] The adjudication officer must also consider whether you have also been underpaid for a past period, but you cannot offset this against the overpayment if additional facts are needed to prove the under-payment.[154] However, if your claim contained enough information to alert the adjudication officer to a potential need, and s/he did not investigate this fully, you can argue that an offset should be made. It does not matter if the overpayment was for a different period, so long as there was sufficient information to alert the adjudication officer to your need for extra benefit.[155]

If other facts come to light which suggest that you have also been underpaid you can ask the Benefits Agency to review your claim. It could then withhold any arrears owed to you to reduce the overpayment.[156]

If you were overpaid because you had too much capital, the overpayment is calculated taking account of the fact that, had you received no benefit, you would have had to use your capital to meet everyday expenses. For each 13-week period, the Benefits Agency assumes that your capital is reduced by the amount of overpaid benefit.[157] This is known as the 'diminishing capital rule' and it can help to reduce the period of the overpayment.

Recovery of overpayments

If an overpayment must be repaid, it can be done through deductions from any national insurance benefit, family credit (FC), disability working allowance, income-based JSA or IS, but no deduction can be made from guardian's allowance, child benefit, HB, or council tax benefit.[158]

If the overpayment occurred because you were paid another social security benefit late (see p146), the Benefits Agency normally deducts any overpaid IS from the arrears owing to you.[159] However, if it omits to do so you must still repay even if you have spent the money.

Other overpayments can also be recovered from arrears you are owed, except arrears where benefit has previously been suspended.[160]

When it comes to your current weekly benefit, the following are the maximum amounts which can be deducted:[161]

- £10 if you have admitted fraud or been found guilty of fraud; *or*
- £7.50 in any other case.

If you have any earnings subject to the £5, £10 or £15 disregard (see p357), or charitable income subject to a disregard (see p373) or benefit subject to a disregard (see p367), the deduction may be increased by half this amount.[162] Remember, the above are maximum amounts. The Benefits Agency might be persuaded to deduct less, especially if you have other direct deductions made from your benefit. As long as a couple are married or living together as husband and wife (see p319), the amount of overpaid benefit can be recovered from either partner's IS or FC.[163] If your appointee misrepresents your circumstances, or fails to disclose something on your behalf, it is you who has to repay any overpayment, not the appointee as s/he is simply acting on your behalf.[164]

The money can be recovered from a claimant's estate if s/he dies.[165]

The Secretary of State's discretion

It is important to note that a tribunal cannot 'write off' part of the overpayment even if there are mitigating circumstances. It can only decide if it is recoverable and, if so, how much is repayable. In a case where you acted in all innocence and hardship is likely to be caused, the best tactic is to apply to the Secretary of State who has the discretion to decide whether or not to recover the overpayment. You can do this by writing to the local office where an adjudication officer makes a decision on behalf of the Secretary of State. It is sometimes more effective to write direct to the Secretary of State at the House of Commons. Although s/he does not deal with your case personally, it can ensure that local staff take your case seriously if they are asked to investigate by the Secretary of State. In either case you may wish to involve your MP. If you have been underpaid in the past but cannot now get arrears, ask the Secretary of State to reduce the amount to be recovered by this sum if s/he will not write it off altogether.

Recovery using common law

In the drive to recoup money lost through overpayments the Benefits Agency is increasingly using other powers to get money back. If an overpayment made to you is not recoverable under the social security rules described above, the Benefits Agency may try to recover under what is known as the 'common law'. In such cases there is no right of appeal as this is not an adjudication officer's decision. There is some doubt about the validity of such recovery given that there is a clear legal code for social security which defines when payments are and are not recoverable. Nevertheless, court action is commonly threatened and has sometimes been pursued. If this happens to you, contact a local advice agency as soon as possible for help in challenging the decision.

Fraud

There is a lot of concern currently among government ministers and DSS officials about fraudulent benefit claims. As a result, a lot of resources are being put into fraud investigations and the number of prosecutions has risen. The Government intends to introduce new, stricter rules this year. See p291 for further details.

Fraud involves a deliberate intention to obtain benefit to which you are not entitled. Thus, if you deliberately fail to let the Benefits Agency know that you have extra money coming in which reduces your right to benefit, you are guilty of fraud. Other cases are less clear cut: for example, you may be suspected of living with someone as husband and wife and fail to declare this. However, this may not be because of any fraudulent intent, but rather because you are not sure how the relationship will develop and whether it will last in the longer term. You may not even have realised that you had to claim as a couple rather than as separate individuals in such situations (see p319). Nevertheless, your claim could come under scrutiny by a fraud officer and any irregularities will be checked out.

The definition of fraud and the way in which it is investigated is broadly the same for all means-tested benefits, and a fuller explanation of this and what to do if you are under investigation can be found on p289. The footnotes to that section contain IS references where these differ. Your benefit can be suspended while your claim is being investigated (see p137). However, you cannot have your benefit withdrawn solely because of fraud; only if the investigation reveals that you are no longer entitled. If your benefit is suspended, you should push for a decision to be made as speedily as possible, or for your benefit to be reinstated while the investigation is completed if this is likely to take some time.

If your benefit is stopped, you can do three things:

- **make a fresh claim for benefit**. Benefit should be paid regardless of what the situation was in the past if your circumstances are now different – eg, you were working full time, but have now stopped;
- **appeal to a tribunal** (see p156) against any alleged overpayment. If you dispute that you have claimed fraudulently, you should argue that there has been no overpayment. If you accept that you have been overpaid, you can still check the calculation of the overpayment – adjudication officers often forget the normal rules about earnings disregards, etc, when calculating the figure. It is best to appeal before any criminal proceedings have been decided;
- **apply for a social fund payment** (see p446, Crisis loans) **or an interim payment** (see p136).

Being under suspicion of fraud is very distressing and it can be difficult to re-establish your entitlement once your claim is under investigation. Fraud officers often take your papers away from the section which normally deals with your claim and it can sometimes be difficult to find out what is happening or to persuade other Benefits Agency staff to reinstate payments. Remember that a fraud officer cannot make a decision on your entitlement. S/he can only provide the adjudication officer with evidence that you are no longer entitled. If a fraud officer tries to make you give up your order book or persuade you not to claim, you should insist on a proper decision from an adjudication officer. Never withdraw your claim unless you know you are not entitled to benefit.

Some claimants have found the attitude and behaviour of fraud officers to be intimidating. While such officers are clearly required to check any irregularities on your claim, they should not threaten you or force you to do or say anything with which you do not agree. If you feel you are under undue pressure, you should ask for the interview to be terminated and complain about the manner of the investigation.

Although a fraud investigator cannot make a decision on your claim, s/he can decide whether or not to prosecute you. See p289 for further details. Remember that you can be required to repay any overpayment as well as being prosecuted.

5. COMPLAINTS ABOUT ADMINISTRATION

The procedures for appeal and review allow you to challenge decisions about your benefit (including the refusal of benefit). If you want to make a complaint simply about the way in which your benefit claim was handled there are other procedures you can follow. The things you might want to complain about could include:

- delay in dealing with your claim;
- poor administration in the benefit office (eg, they keep losing your papers, or you can never get through on the telephone);
- the behaviour of members of staff. Most benefit staff do a good job and try to be helpful, but you should certainly complain about staff rudeness or any sexist or racist remarks.

You should check your local office *Customer Charter* which sets out the standards and level of service which you can expect. The Benefits Agency produces a leaflet, *Tell us about it*, which explains your rights and contains a form which you can use to explain your complaint. You might also wish to seek compensation (see p139).

Complaining to the Benefits Agency

The Benefits Agency suggests that as a first step you should speak to the person who dealt with you. If they cannot help or you would prefer to speak to someone else, contact the supervisor or assistant manager. If you are still dissatisfied, you can contact the customer services manager of your branch office. S/he will investigate your complaint and should respond to your complaint within seven days. If this does not solve the problem you should write to the manager of your district office with details of the complaint. Keep a copy of your letter. If you are still unhappy, you can ask for independent consideration of your complaint. The Benefits Agency has said it hopes to arrange an independent service to look into complaints in all offices by June 1997. You may also wish to write a letter for the personal attention of the Chief Executive of the Benefits Agency (for address, see Appendix 2).

Complaining to your MP

If you are not satisfied with the reply from the officers to whom you have written, the next step is to take up the matter with your MP.

Most MPs have 'surgeries' in their areas where they meet constituents to discuss problems. You can get the details from your local library or citizens advice bureau. You can either go to the surgery or write to your MP with details of your complaint.

Your MP will probably want to write to the benefit authorities for an explanation of what has happened. If you or s/he are not satisfied with the reply, the next stage is to complain to the Ombudsman, via your MP.

The Parliamentary Commissioner for Administration (commonly called the 'Parliamentary Ombudsman' – see Appendix 2) investigates complaints made by MPs against government departments. The Ombudsman's office will send you a leaflet providing further information. Many of the complaints are about benefits. If s/he investigates your case, your MP will be sent a full report. If the Ombudsman finds you were badly treated, s/he will recommend an apology and possibly compensation.

CHAPTER EIGHT

Appeals

This chapter covers:

1. APPEALING TO SOCIAL SECURITY APPEAL TRIBUNALS

You can appeal to an independent social security appeal tribunal (SSAT) against any decision taken by an adjudication officer. Decisions made by the Secretary of State cannot be appealed (see p129). You should try to persuade the Secretary of State to change her/his decision as your only legal remedy is to apply to the High Court for judicial review (see p172).

Sometimes, an adjudication officer will refuse to make a decision on your claim on the grounds that you have not provided all the information required to decide your claim (see p124). If an adjudication officer does this, it effectively prevents you having the right to appeal. An adjudication officer must make a decision on every claim, even those where, having allowed a reasonable amount of time, the information demanded by the Benefits Agency has not been provided.[1] You can then appeal and it is up to the tribunal to decide whether the decision is correct.

How to appeal

Before challenging a decision, it is useful to know why it was decided against you. You have a right to a written statement of reasons if you apply for it within three months of being given the decision in writing.[2] Ask for this as soon as possible because you only have three months in which to appeal and the time limit for appealing is very strict. On receiving the statement of reasons, if there are grounds for a review, you may decide it is worth asking for a review of the decision rather than appealing straightaway (see p131). In any case, if you appeal an adjudication officer will look at the decision again (see p159).

You must appeal in writing and normally on the appropriate form. If you do not use the appropriate form, the chairperson of a tribunal can accept your appeal so long as it is in writing and includes all the information required (see below).[3] There is no guarantee of this, so use the form wherever possible. The appeal form is contained in leaflet NI246, *How to appeal,* which is available at Benefits Agency offices. The completed form should be sent or delivered to the Benefits Agency office that made the decision with which you disagree.

If you want the tribunal to deal with your appeal quickly, make this plain on your appeal form, explaining why. You could also telephone the clerk to the tribunal at the Independent Tribunal Service (see Appendix 2) to check that your appeal has been received and to ask her/him to deal with the matter quickly.

Information you must provide when you appeal

When you appeal you must provide the following information:[4]

- the benefit you are appealing about, for example, income support or family credit;
- the date the Benefits Agency sent you the decision with which you disagree. You can find this date on the letter notifying you of the decision;
- a summary of your arguments for saying the decision was wrong. You should not simply say you think the decision was wrong, but explain why.

Examples

'The Benefits Agency says I have been overpaid income support because I failed to disclose that my wife had started working part time, but I wrote to them as soon as she started work and told them what her take-home pay would be.' 'The decision is that I should not get income support for my son because he left school in June. This decision is wrong because my son decided to stay on at school and do his 'A' levels.'

It might also be helpful to include information and evidence which supports your appeal because an adjudication officer looks at the decision again and might review it (see p159).

Your appeal, including all the information above, must arrive within the three months beginning with the date the written decision was sent to you.[5] It is very important that you provide all the information within the time limit. Your appeal is not treated as made until you do.[6] If you do not include all the information on your appeal form, the chair of or clerk to the tribunal can make what is known as a 'direction' requiring you to provide the information you left out within a certain period of time.[7] The chairperson or clerk to a tribunal can give you extra time beyond the three-month time limit to provide the information required,[8] but there is no guarantee that s/he will do so. In any case, s/he can only give you a maximum of 14 more days. If you do not provide the information within the time limit, you will have to ask the chairperson of a tribunal to accept a late appeal (see below). However, it is extremely difficult to get a chairperson to do this so it is better that you provide all the information in time. If you have sent your appeal form but the chairperson or clerk only asks for extra information after the time limit has expired, the DSS have said it is their intention that your appeal should be allowed under the late appeal rules (see below).

Late appeals

The chairperson of an appeal tribunal can only accept a late appeal if:[9]

- your appeal is likely to succeed; *and*
- it is in the 'interests of justice' (see below).

Even if you meet the two conditions above, a late appeal cannot be accepted if it is more than six years since the decision you want to appeal against was made.[10]

In addition to the information you must provide on your appeal form (see p157) you must explain why your appeal is late (see below).[11]

It is only considered to be in the 'interests of justice' to allow a late appeal if:[12]

- there are special reasons which are 'wholly exceptional' and relate to the history and facts of your case; *and*
- the special reasons are sufficiently strong to give you a reasonable excuse for your delay in appealing; *and*
- the special reasons have existed since your deadline for appealing expired (see p156).

The longer you have delayed in appealing, the more compelling the special reasons have to be.

When deciding if there are special reasons, the chairperson cannot take account of the fact that:[13]

- a court or a commissioner has interpreted the law in a different way than previously understood and applied;
- you (or your adviser) misunderstood or were unaware of the relevant law, including the time limits for appealing.

You must be notified of the chairperson's decision as soon as practicable, and must be sent written reasons for it if you ask for these in writing within three months.[14]

You cannot appeal against the refusal of the chairperson to hear a late appeal,[15] but you can ask the chairperson to look at her/his decision again, or you may be able to apply to the High Court for judicial review if the decision is clearly unreasonable (see p172). However it is often simpler to ask for a review of the adjudication officer's original decision instead of making a late appeal, so long as there are grounds for review and this would give you everything to which you were entitled (see p131).

What happens after you appeal

An adjudication officer will look at the decision you are appealing about again and might change the decision, for example, on the basis of any facts, information or evidence that you provided with your appeal form. However, if you do not get everything you think you are entitled to, your appeal must still go ahead.[16]

After your appeal is received at the local office, you should receive an acknowledgement (form AT38) from the clerk of the Independent Tribunal Service, together with a questionnaire (form AR4) asking you whether you want an oral hearing (see p162) and if so, when you are available to attend. You are also sent a leaflet containing information about appeals and how to find someone to represent you at the hearing if this would be helpful.

If you want an **oral hearing**, you must tell the clerk to the tribunal.[17] You must return the questionnaire within 14 days (the chairperson of or clerk to a tribunal could give you more or fewer days than this).[18] The clerk also asks the adjudication officer if s/he wants an oral hearing. If neither of you opt for an oral hearing, the tribunal will make its decision by looking at what you said on your appeal form, any evidence or other information you provided to support your appeal, and the adjudication officer's submission (see below). This is what is known as a 'paper hearing'.

You should consider carefully whether to opt for an oral or a paper hearing. You may feel that you would rather not attend an oral hearing, for example, because you are worried about speaking for yourself or would have difficulties getting there. However, you are more likely to succeed if you attend an oral hearing, particularly where there is an argument about the facts of your case. If you attend an oral hearing, you can explain your side of the story to the tribunal. You may want to seek advice before you decide what to do. Consider whether you need representation (see Appendix 3). If you take someone with you to an oral hearing your chances of winning are much higher. You can take a friend, relative, adviser or representative with you[19] – you can have more than one person if the chairperson of the tribunal agrees.[20]

If you opt for a paper hearing, think about what other information and evidence you can get to support your appeal, and send it to the tribunal. You must send this to the clerk to the tribunal within 10 days of being sent the adjudication officer's submission about your appeal (see below). See pp166-68 for information about sorting out the facts and checking the law and the case law that applies in your case.

Even if neither you nor the adjudication officer want an oral hearing, the chairperson of the tribunal might decide that one should take place.[21] This could happen if the chairperson feels an oral hearing is necessary to help the tribunal make its decision.

The Benefits Agency prepares a detailed explanation of the reasons for its decision (known as the adjudication officer's submission) and this is sent to you on form AT2. This should be sent to you as soon as it is received by the Independent Tribunal Service, usually six to eight weeks after you appeal. If you opted for an oral hearing you are normally also told when and where the hearing will be. Your oral hearing should take place within one month of receiving the adjudication officer's submission. See p162 for information about how much notice you must be given.

If you opted for a paper hearing, but now that you have seen the adjudication officer's submission you want an oral hearing after all, you may be able to change your mind. You must tell the clerk to the tribunal before the tribunal makes its decision.

The chairperson or clerk to the tribunal might issue 'directions' requiring you or the adjudication officer to provide further information or documents.[22] A chairperson can require you or the adjudication officer to provide information or documents that are needed to help the tribunal make its decision. You can also ask the chairperson to require an adjudication officer to provide these.

The chairperson or the clerk can require you to:

- provide information, where your appeal form is incomplete (see p157);
- reply to the letter asking you about when you are available for a hearing (see p159).

If you are required to provide any information or documents, it is important that you do so. If you do not, the chairperson can:[23]

- strike out your appeal (see below);
- decide to hear your appeal straightaway, but only if:
  - you have not explained why you have not provided what has been required; *and*
  - the tribunal has sufficient information to make its decision.

This might happen, for example, where your appeal was adjourned for you to get evidence, but you have not done so after a considerable period of time. You must still be asked whether you want an oral hearing (see p159) and if you do, must be given proper notice (see p162).

A chairperson can also decide your appeal should be heard straightaway if s/he thinks you have no chance of winning, for example, where you have claimed income support but you are 15 years old or where you have claimed family credit but have no children.[24] You must be offered an oral hearing and be given proper notice as above.

You might find that your case is not dealt with if there is a test case pending which deals with the same issues as your appeal. You can insist that your case is dealt with but it might then be adjourned (but see p164).

When can a chairperson strike out your appeal?

A chairperson can strike out your appeal for 'want of prosecution' if you do not appear to be pursuing it. This might happen where you fail to provide information or documents that have been required by a chairperson or clerk (see above) or to tell the clerk when you can attend a hearing (see above).[25] This cancels your appeal.

You must be notified if this is being considered and given a reasonable amount of time to explain why you think your appeal should not be struck out. You do not have to be given notice where your address is not known or cannot be found out easily. If the chairperson is satisfied with your explanation and decides not to strike out your appeal, s/he might decide to hear your case straightaway (see above), or to give instructions to speed your appeal along.

If a chairperson strikes out your appeal, you have three months to ask for it to be reinstated.[26] It will be reinstated if you did not receive notice that your appeal might be struck out (see above) unless no notice was sent to you because your address was not known or could not have been found out easily.

Withdrawing an appeal[27]

If you change your mind about appealing, you can withdraw your appeal. You must apply in writing to the clerk to the tribunal. S/he must allow you to withdraw your appeal unless the adjudication officer has already notified her/him that s/he is opposed to this. However, once the appeal tribunal hearing has begun, you can only withdraw your appeal with the consent of the chairperson and provided the tribunal has not yet made a decision. Once an appeal has been withdrawn it cannot be reinstated, but if you decide that you want to go ahead after all, you could try to make a late appeal against the adjudication officer's original decision (but see p158).[28]

The oral hearing

You have a right to at least seven days' notice of the oral hearing unless you agree to less notice than this. If you have not been given the correct notice, the tribunal can only go ahead if you agree.[29] If you give up your right to notice the tribunal can go ahead with the hearing even if you are not there.[30]

If the hearing date is inconvenient or you want more time to prepare your case, you can ask for it to be **postponed**. You must apply in writing to the clerk to the tribunal, saying why you want your case to be postponed. You should do this as soon as you decide that you want a postponement.[31] The Independent Tribunal Service is very keen to avoid postponements, so you should ring before the hearing is due to take place to check if this has been agreed. If you do not attend and have not asked for a postponement, the tribunal can hear the case without you, and you are less likely to succeed.[32] However, they should not go ahead if you have advised them that you cannot attend and have asked for another hearing date, especially if you have a good reason for not attending.[33]

A social security appeal tribunal is heard in public unless you request a private hearing, or the chairperson thinks it should be in private. In practice, it is extremely rare for members of the public to turn up. However, the rule does mean that you could sit in on the case before your own.[34]

The tribunal members

A tribunal usually consists of three people. There is a **chairperson**, who is a lawyer, and two **'wing members'**, who sit on either side of the chairperson. They are supposed to be people who have knowledge or experience of conditions in your area, and who are representative of people living or working there. Wherever possible, at least one member of the tribunal should be the same sex as you.[35]

Tribunals can sit with only one wing member, but only if you agree. In this case, the chairperson has the casting vote.[36]

The chairperson has to record the tribunal's decision, and a statement of its findings on the relevant facts of the case and the reasons for its decision (see p164). S/he makes a note of what is said by you, your representative, the adjudication officer and any witnesses.

The standards of tribunals are the responsibility of the President of the Independent Tribunal Service (ITS). The ITS is divided into regions, with a chairperson for each region who recruits and trains tribunal members. The President issues circulars to guide tribunals on how they should conduct themselves. If you have a complaint about a tribunal member, or the way a hearing was conducted, write to your regional chairperson or the President (see Appendix 2 for addresses).

Other people present at the oral hearing

The **clerk to the tribunal** is there in an administrative capacity – eg, to pay expenses. You, your representative, an interpreter if needed and any witnesses may be able to get travel expenses paid. You can also claim for meals, loss of earnings and childcare costs.[37] The clerk should not express any views on the case.

The **presenting officer** represents the adjudication officer. S/he explains the reasons for the decision you are appealing about, but is not there to defend the Benefits Agency's decision at all costs. S/he may provide information which helps your case.

Procedure at the oral hearing

When the tribunal is ready to hear your case, you are taken in with the presenting officer.

There are no strict rules of procedure. The chairperson should start by introducing the members of the tribunal and everyone else who is present. The presenting officer then summarises the adjudication officer's written submission and you are asked to explain your reasons for disagreeing with it. Alternatively, you may be asked to explain your position first. You can call any witnesses and can ask questions of the presenting officer, and the tribunal members ask questions of you both.

Your case may be adjourned unfinished to be heard on another day because, for instance, more evidence is required. Failure to adjourn to allow you to get relevant evidence is an error of law and you can appeal to the commissioner to get the decision overturned (see p168).[38] A tribunal might adjourn your case if there is a test case pending which deals with the same issues as your appeal.[39] If this happens, you should ask them to hear your appeal based on the law as it currently stands rather than waiting for the result of the test case.

If your case is adjourned the new tribunal must rehear your case from the beginning unless it has the same three members as before or you agree to it being heard by two members of the previous tribunal without the third.[40]

You can appeal against a decision to adjourn your appeal though it will often be quicker to press for a fresh hearing.[41]

The tribunal decision

Usually you are told of the tribunal's decision at the hearing and you are given a decision notice confirming it. The decision notice includes a summary of the tribunal's reasons for its decision. If it is not given at the hearing or you opted for a paper hearing, the decision notice is sent to you later by the clerk. You must also be informed of:[42]

• your right to request a full decision (see below);
• the conditions for appealing to the commissioner (see p168).

A chairperson might decide to give you a full decision at the hearing or to send one to you later on.[43] If not, you have a right to request one but **must** do this within 21 days of being sent or given the decision notice (see above). If you lose your appeal and want to appeal to the commissioner (see p168) you **must** have a full decision. You should ask for one as soon as possible.

A full decision must include the tribunal's reasons for its decision and the relevant findings of fact. If the decision is not unanimous, the full decision must give the reasons why a tribunal member disagreed with the decision.[44]

If you have won, the Benefits Agency ought to carry out the tribunal's decision straightaway. They can do this on the basis of the decision notice (see above). However, they have three months in which to appeal against the tribunal's decision to a social security commissioner. If considering an appeal, you will not be paid while they decide what to do. If they decide to appeal, you will not be paid until the commissioner hears the case.[45] If you are left without any money, you might be able to apply for an interim payment (see p136), or get a crisis loan (see p446).

What if you disagree with the tribunal's decision?

A tribunal's decision is final. However:

- It can be reviewed in the normal way, for example where your circumstances have changed since the decision was made or new facts have come to light (see p131). However, where the tribunal made a mistake about the law you must appeal (see below).
- You or the adjudication officer can appeal to the Social Security Commissioners (see p168).
- It can be 'set aside', which means cancelling the decision and hearing the case again. A tribunal can only do this if it thinks it is just and:[46]

  - you, your representative or the presenting officer did not receive the appeal papers, or did not receive them in sufficient time before the hearing; *or*
  - you, your representative or the presenting officer were not present at the hearing. However, if you or the presenting officer chose not to attend it may not be just to set the decision aside. If you did not ask for an oral hearing (see p159) the decision cannot be set aside for this reason unless it would clearly be in the 'interests of justice' (see below); *or*
  - 'the interests of justice so require'. This applies where there has been a 'procedural irregularity'.[47] A failure to produce sufficient evidence at the hearing is not a 'procedural irregularity'.

  An adjudication officer may also ask for a decision to be set aside.
  You must apply for the decision to be set aside within three months of the decision being sent to you. A late application is only accepted if there are special reasons. The special reasons do not have to relate to your own personal circumstances or actions. They could include the amount of money involved or how strong your case is. Applications are normally decided without a hearing, so make sure you give a full explanation of your reasons when you apply.[48] You cannot appeal against a refusal to set aside, but you may be able to apply for judicial review (see p172).
  If a decision is wrongly set aside, any subsequent rehearing is invalid. The second tribunal could thus refuse to rehear the case if there was no power to set aside the previous decision.[49]

- If the written decision contains an accidental error this can be corrected by the tribunal.[50]

2. HOW TO PREPARE AN APPEAL

Your case may concern a dispute about the facts or the law, or both. Always try, if possible, to link the facts of your case and your arguments to the rules laid down in the benefit regulations.

Sorting out the facts

The tribunal has to decide your appeal on the evidence given by you and the Benefits Agency. Check through the appeal papers carefully to work out where there are disagreements between you. This will help you decide what evidence you need to win your case. Evidence consists of what you (and any witnesses) actually say at the hearing and any documents which you produce to support your case. Written evidence would include letters of support, medical reports, wage slips, bank statements, birth certificates and anything else which helps to prove the facts. If, for example, the Benefits Agency say that you failed to disclose an increase in your earnings and you have been overpaid, you could explain to the tribunal how and when you told them, but you may also be able to produce a copy of the letter which you sent informing them of the change. If you want to give any evidence or information to the tribunal, you should send it to the clerk to the tribunal at least five days before your oral hearing. Otherwise, the tribunal might decide to adjourn your case (see p164).

Proving your case with additional evidence is useful but not essential. A tribunal cannot dismiss your verbal evidence without a proper explanation of why it has done so.[51]

The presenting officer puts the adjudication officer's case at the tribunal but is very rarely the person who actually made the decision in your case. The presenting officer's submissions are not evidence,[52] nor are comments made by another adjudication officer if s/he did not decide your claim.[53] The presenting officer can report what other people have said. This is called hearsay evidence. Tribunals can accept hearsay evidence but they should carefully weigh up its value as proof, given that the person who originally made the statement is not present at the hearing. Most evidence relied on by adjudication officers is written and you can point out that you have not had the opportunity of questioning the witnesses. You are not entitled to insist on the presence of any particular witness,[54] but you should argue that the tribunal should not place any weight on the written evidence of, say, an interviewing officer if you are disputing the interview.

Both you and the Benefits Agency can ask witnesses to come and give information to support your case. Chairpersons do have the power to refuse to hear witnesses who are not relevant, but they should always be fair to claimants and generally allow witnesses to speak, even if it looks as if they may have nothing useful to say.[55]

A tribunal hearing is a complete rehearing of your case, so fresh facts and arguments can be put by either side.[56]

Checking the law

The adjudication officer often gets the law wrong so it is worth checking the benefit rules to see if they have been correctly applied in your case. This *Handbook* explains what the law says and the footnotes give you the legal references if you want to look them up for yourself. The adjudication officer will also have quoted certain parts of the law which support her/his decision and you should check these. It is quite common for the adjudication officer to quote a large number of commissioners' decisions (see below), but these are not always of direct relevance to your appeal so check them carefully. Also, check to see if you can find others which help your case.

The law consists of Acts of Parliament and regulations. You can ask to see the law concerning income support, disability working allowance and family credit at the local Benefits Agency office. It should be available for public inspection at all reasonable hours and without payment.[57]

Benefit laws are collected together in a large looseleaf book called the *Law Relating to Social Security*. It is in several volumes and is known as the 'Blue Book'. It is kept up-to-date with regular supplements. You can look at a copy of the 'Blue Book' at your nearest major library as well as at the Benefits Agency.

Most of the law you need is contained in CPAG's *Income Related Benefits: The Legislation* edited by John Mesher and Penny Wood. As well as giving the law it gives explanations of what each bit means and tells you about relevant case law (see below). Tribunal members have this textbook.

Law relating to benefit is complicated and the staff who administer benefits are issued with guidance manuals and circulars. The *Adjudication Officers' Guide* covers benefits administered by the Benefits Agency. It is written by the Chief Adjudication Officer, who is responsible for advising local adjudication officers about the law.[58] The adjudicating authorities are bound by the regulations but not by the guidance.

Case law is made by the Social Security Commissioners who are part of the appeal system.[59] Rulings they make about the meaning of benefit law are binding and must be applied in similar cases by adjudication officers and tribunals. The most important commissioners' decisions are published by HMSO and are called 'reported decisions'. They are prefixed by the letter 'R'. Thus, R(IS) 1/90 was the first commissioner's decision on IS to be reported in 1990. IS decisions are reported as R(IS), disability working allowance as R(DWA) and family credit as R(FC). Sometimes you will be referred to supplementary benefit decisions which are R(SB), and to decisions on other benefits. Only the most important decisions are reported. Decisions which are not reported are prefixed by the letter 'C', and the year is written out in full – eg, CIS/13/1989. Some unreported decisions are 'starred' by the commissioner because, for example, they deal with an important issue or deal with an aspect of benefit law for the first time. Unreported decisions are available for £1 each from the Office of the Social Security Commissioners (see Appendix 2 for address).

This *Handbook* gives references to commissioners' decisions and you can keep up-to-date with the latest commissioners' decisions by reading CPAG's bi-monthly *Welfare Rights Bulletin*. The main library in your area may have copies of reported commissioners' decisions or you can ask to see them at any Benefits Agency office.

If you want to refer to an unreported commissioner's decision, it is best to circulate it to the SSAT and Benefits Agency in advance. If this is not possible, take copies for them to the hearing. Sometimes commissioners' decisions conflict. If so, the tribunal must follow a reported decision in preference to an unreported one, and a Tribunal of Commissioners' decision to that of a single commissioner.[60] Starred unreported decisions are generally given more weight than unstarred ones. If there is a decision on the same point by the High Court on judicial review, the Court of Appeal or the House of Lords, it must be followed in preference to a commissioner's decision.

3. APPEALING TO THE SOCIAL SECURITY COMMISSIONER

Both you and the Benefits Agency have a further right of appeal to a Social Security Commissioner, but only if the tribunal has made an error of law.[61]

There is an error of law if:[62]

- the tribunal got the law wrong – eg, it misunderstood the particular benefit regulation concerned;
- there is no evidence to support the tribunal's decision;
- the facts found by the tribunal are such that, had it acted reasonably, and interpreted the law correctly, it could not have made the decision it did. This argument would be used where the facts are inconsistent

with the decision – eg, a tribunal finds that a man and a woman live in separate households, but decides they are living together as husband and wife;

• there is a breach of the rules of natural justice. This is where the procedure followed by the tribunal leads to unfairness (eg, you are not allowed to call witnesses to support you or the tribunal refuses a postponement, even though you cannot attend for a good reason and have told it so), and the result is that you lost without having a chance to put your case properly;

• the tribunal does not give proper findings of fact or provide adequate reasons for its decision (see p164). The tribunal must not simply say what its decision was. It must put down sufficient reasons so that you can see why, on the evidence, it reached the conclusion it did. It can rely on the adjudication officer's summary of the facts, but only if these are not in dispute and s/he has covered all relevant issues.[63] If the facts are not agreed the tribunal must explain which version it prefers and why.

How to appeal

You must first obtain leave to appeal.[64] This means that you have to show that there has possibly been an error of law and that you have the beginnings of a case.

If you wish to appeal, you must have the tribunal's full decision (see p164). You should first apply to the chairperson of the tribunal.[65] You must do this by writing to the clerk of the tribunal at the regional office within three months of being sent the full decision of the tribunal.[66] You must include a copy of the full decision (see p164) with your appeal.

If the chairperson refuses leave to appeal, you may make a fresh application direct to a commissioner. You must do this within 42 days, beginning on the day after the date on the notification that leave has been refused by the tribunal chairperson.[67] You must include a copy of the full decision (see p164) with your appeal.

If you miss the time limit, you may still apply for leave to appeal but any application must be made direct to a commissioner who will give you leave only if there are special reasons for the delay.[68] The special reasons do not have to relate to your own personal circumstances or actions. They could include things like the amount of money involved or how strong your case is. Delays by the post office (but not other courier firms) in delivering your appeal can be disregarded, so long as your application was prepaid and properly addressed.

Once you have been given leave to appeal, you have six weeks in which to send in notice of the appeal itself.[69] You are sent a form on

which to do this. The time may, again, be extended for special reasons.
You may have been told that your notice of application for leave has
been treated as a notice of appeal, in which case you do not have to send
in another.[70]

The written procedure

Adjudication officers at the Office of the Chief Adjudication Officer (see
Appendix 2 for address) deal with the Benefits Agency's side of the case.
A bundle of documents is prepared by that office and sent to the
commissioners' office where it is added to any submissions from you.
The commissioners' office then sends copies of the bundle, including the
adjudication officer's submission, to you.

You are given 30 days in which to reply to the submission of the
adjudication officer, although the commissioner may extend the time
limit. There is a right of reply, if required, within 30 days.[71] If you have
nothing to add and do not want to reply at any stage, tell the
commissioners' office. A commissioner has the power to strike out an
appeal that appears to have been abandoned, although you can apply for
it to be reinstated.[72]

When the commissioner has all the written submissions, s/he decides
whether or not there should be an oral hearing of the appeal. If you ask
for an oral hearing, the commissioner will hold one unless s/he feels that
the case can be dealt with properly without one.[73] Occasionally, the
commissioner decides to hold an oral hearing even if you have not asked
for one.

If there is no oral hearing, the commissioner reaches a decision on the
basis of written submissions and other documents.

Because of the length of time you usually have to wait before your case
is dealt with, you should consider making a fresh claim for benefit if, for
example, your circumstances change.

The hearing

If there is an oral hearing, it will be at the commissioners' offices in
London, Edinburgh or Belfast, or at the law courts in Cardiff, Leeds or
Liverpool. You are told the date in good time and your fares are paid in
advance if you want to attend. At least half a day is set aside for each
case. Usually, one commissioner hears your case. However, if there is a
'question of law of special difficulty', the hearing may be before a tribunal
of three commissioners,[74] but the procedure is the same.

The hearing is more formal than those before social security appeal
tribunals but the commissioner will let you say everything you want to.
Commissioners usually intervene a lot and ask questions so you need to

be prepared to argue your case without your script. A full set of commissioners' decisions and the 'Blue Books' (see p167) are available for your use. The adjudication officer is usually represented by a lawyer, so you should consider trying to obtain representation as well. The commissioner may exclude members of the public if intimate personal or financial circumstances, or matters of public security are involved.[75] This is not usually necessary because it is rare for anyone not involved in the case to attend.

The decision

The decision is always given in writing[76] – often at some length – and it may be a few weeks before it is sent to you.

After a successful appeal, the case is often sent back to a differently constituted social security appeal tribunal with directions as to how the tribunal should go about reconsidering the issues.[77] However, if the commissioner feels that the record of the decision of the original tribunal contains all the material facts, or s/he feels that it is 'expedient' to make findings on any extra factual issues necessary to the decisions, the commissioner makes the final decision.[78] It is unusual for a commissioner not to send a case back to a tribunal if there is a dispute about facts not determined by the original tribunal, unless all the evidence points in one direction.[79]

A commissioner may correct or set aside her/his decision in the same way as a tribunal (see p165).[80]

In certain circumstances, an adjudication officer may review a commissioner's decision (see p131).

4. APPEALING TO THE COURTS

You may appeal against a decision of a commissioner to the Court of Appeal (in Scotland, the Court of Session) but only if the commissioner has made an error of law (see p168) and you must first obtain leave to appeal.[81] If you want to appeal you should seek help from a solicitor, but first check that you qualify for legal aid to cover the costs.

The application for leave to appeal must first be made to a commissioner, in writing, within three months of the date when you were sent the commissioner's decision. The commissioner may extend the time limit if s/he thinks fit.[82] If you do not apply to the commissioner within the time limit and the commissioner refuses to extend it, the Court of Appeal (or Court of Session) cannot hear your appeal and you can only proceed by applying to the High Court (in Scotland, the Court of Session) for judicial review of the refusal to extend the time allowed for the appeal (see below).[83]

Applications to a commissioner for leave to appeal are almost invariably considered without an oral hearing. If the commissioner refuses, you can apply to the court for leave.[84] Your notice of application should be lodged with the Civil Appeals Office within six weeks of notification of the commissioner's refusal being sent to you.[85] The court may extend the time but you must explain the reasons for your delay and file an affidavit in support of an application for an extension of time.[86] Generally, the Court of Appeal considers your application without an oral hearing. If leave is refused, you may renew your application in open court within seven days. Similarly, if leave is granted, the Chief Adjudication Officer or the Secretary of State has seven days in which to ask for an oral hearing.[87]

If leave to appeal is granted by a commissioner or the Court of Appeal you must serve a notice of appeal on the relevant parties. There are strict time limits for doing this.[88] The solicitor to the Benefits Agency will accept service on behalf of the Chief Adjudication Officer (see Appendix 2 for address).

You cannot appeal to the Court of Appeal against the refusal of a commissioner to grant leave to appeal against a decision of a tribunal, but you can apply to the High Court for judicial review of such a refusal (see below).[89]

The procedures in Scotland are similar.

The Chief Adjudication Officer or the Secretary of State has the same rights of appeal as you.

Applying for judicial review

Occasionally it is possible to challenge the Benefits Agency by going to court for a judicial review. You will need the services of a solicitor, law centre or legal advice centre.

You can apply for judicial review of a decision made by the Secretary of State or of a tribunal chairperson or a social security commissioner who refuses to grant you leave to appeal. However, this procedure cannot usually be used if you have an independent right of appeal, such as against the decision of an adjudication officer or a social security appeal tribunal.

Meeting the cost of going to court

Legal aid is available for cases in the Court of Appeal, the High Court and the Court of Session and you should certainly seek legal advice and representation (see Appendix 3). In the past, the legal aid authorities have taken the view that an application to a commissioner for leave to appeal to the Court of Appeal cannot be covered by legal aid. However, it is arguable that such an application is a step 'preliminary to' proceedings in the Court of Appeal and is thus work for which legal aid is available.[90]

PART THREE

Back to work benefits, family credit and disability working allowance

CHAPTER NINE

Back to work benefits

This chapter covers:

1. Back to work bonus (below)
2. Child maintenance bonus (p177)
3. Extended payments of housing benefit and council tax benefit (p183)

If you or your partner start working full time or increase your earnings and stop claiming income support (IS) or income-based jobseeker's allowance (JSA) as a result, you might be able to claim a back to work bonus (see below) or a child maintenance bonus (see p177). You might also be able to claim an extended payment of housing benefit and council tax benefit (see p183). You might also be able to claim benefit to top up your pay. If you have children, this is family credit or if you do not, earnings top-up (see Chapter 10). If you have a disability this is disability working allowance (see Chapter 11).

I. BACK TO WORK BONUS

The back to work bonus was introduced on 7 October 1996. It is a tax free lump sum of up to £1,000 which you can accumulate by working part time while you are receiving jobseeker's allowance (JSA) or income support (IS). It is paid when you return to full-time work (16 or more hours a week) or when your earnings increase so that you are no longer entitled to JSA or IS.

Both *contribution-based* JSA and *income-based* JSA can qualify you for a bonus. JSA and IS are called 'qualifying benefits'. No other benefit will qualify you for the bonus.

How do you qualify for a bonus?

The detailed rules about back to work bonus are beyond the scope of this *Handbook*. For further details see Chapter 12 of CPAG's *Jobseeker's Allowance Handbook*, 2nd edn, 1997/98.

The following is a *summary* of the main qualifying conditions.
To qualify for a back to work bonus:[1]

- You must have been entitled to JSA or IS for at least 91 days. This is called the **waiting period.** The 91-day period does not have to be continuous. Separate periods adding up to 91 days will count, if the breaks in between are 12 weeks or less. Days when you are entitled to JSA or IS but during which you are not actually paid can count.
- After the waiting period, you must remain entitled to JSA or IS and you or your partner must have earnings from employment which are taken into account by the Benefits Agency to reduce your JSA or IS. Earnings that are disregarded (see p357) do not count for the back to work bonus.
- You or your partner must satisfy the **work condition.** The work condition for back to work bonus purposes is that you or your partner are no longer entitled to JSA or IS because:
  - you work for 16 hours or more a week; *or*
  - your partner (if you are entitled to income-based JSA or IS) works for 24 hours or more a week; *or*
  - your earnings (or the combined earnings of you and your partner) increase to a level at which you are no longer entitled to JSA or IS.
- You must usually claim the bonus within 12 weeks of JSA or IS stopping or within 12 weeks of the end of a period of training which followed a period when you were entitled to JSA or IS.

There are special rules for couples who get together or separate while claiming JSA or IS and for partners of people who die while claiming JSA or IS.

You can qualify for the bonus if your earnings are from self-employment.

A back to work bonus is treated as capital, but disregarded for 52 weeks for family credit, disability working allowance, housing benefit and council tax benefit purposes.

2. CHILD MAINTENANCE BONUS

If you have been getting child maintenance, you can be paid a child maintenance bonus of up to £1,000 if you or your partner return to work or increase your hours or your pay and, as a result, your entitlement to IS or income-based JSA ceases. See p178 to find out how much you can get.

Child maintenance includes:[2]

- child support maintenance (see p105);
- maintenance paid to you for your child(ren) by voluntary agreement or under a court order;
- maintenance being deducted from the benefit of an absent parent (see p112) who is liable to maintain your child(ren) see p103).

You can get a child maintenance bonus if:[3]

- you or your partner's entitlement to IS or income-based JSA ceases because one of you:
  - takes up a new job or returns to work (but not if you return to work for the same employer at the same place of work following a trade dispute[4]); *or*
  - increases your weekly hours of work; *or*
  - has an increase in earnings.
  This is what is known as the 'work condition' for child maintenance bonus purposes.
  You can get a child maintenance bonus even if your entitlement to IS or income-based JSA ceases for another reason, for example where your child maintenance or other income increases, so long as you meet the work condition within 14 days of last getting benefit.
- You or your partner start or resume work or increase your pay or hours (see above) prior to the day before:
  - your 60th birthday, if you are coming off IS; *or*
  - you reach pensionable age (currently 60 for women and 65 for men), if you are coming off income-based JSA.

  Special rules apply if you do not satisfy the work condition before those ages (see p182):
- You have been getting child maintenance (see above) during a period when you or your partner were on IS or income-based JSA (your 'bonus period' – see below);
- you claim within the time limit (see p181).

The bonus period

You accumulate a child maintenance bonus during any period from 7 April 1997 when:[5]

- you or your partner were entitled or treated as entitled to IS or income-based JSA (unless you were getting an urgent cases payment because you were treated as having income which had not been paid – see p47), whether or not it is paid;

- you are getting child maintenance (see p178) for a child who lives with you but whose other parent does not. Your child still counts as living with you if s/he is away temporarily but not for more than 12 weeks. You count as getting child maintenance if it is being collected by the Child Support Agency or Benefits Agency on your behalf (see pp104 and 114), even if they retain the payments *or* it is being taken into account as income in working out how much IS or income-based JSA you can get (see p114).

When you or your partner stop claiming IS or income-based JSA due to work (see p178) the Benefits Agency looks at how much child maintenance (see p178) you were paid during your bonus period to calculate how much child maintenance bonus you can get (see below).

If you stop meeting the conditions for building up a child maintenance bonus but are not entitled to claim one, you do not necessarily lose out. The bonus period that ended can link to a second bonus period.

Two bonus periods link to count as one if they are separated by not more than 12 weeks *or* one of the following periods:[6]

- while you are getting maternity allowance; *or*
- of not more than two years throughout which you were getting incapacity benefit, severe disablement allowance or invalid care allowance.

Example

Beth stopped getting IS but could not claim a child maintenance bonus as she was not working (see p178). Three weeks later she started getting IS again. When she takes up full-time work, the Benefits Agency should look at the child maintenance that she was paid during both bonus periods when they calculate her child maintenance bonus.

Although bonus periods can link, it is best to claim your child maintenance bonus as soon as you satisfy the work condition (see p178) – for example, if you are uncertain how long your job will last. See p182 for information about how and when you must claim.

A person's bonus period ends if s/he dies. See p182 for further information about what happens when a person with the care of a child dies.

How much child maintenance bonus can you get?

To calculate your child maintenance bonus, the Benefits Agency looks at how much child maintenance (see p178) you were paid or were meant to be paid during your 'bonus period' (see p178). Your child maintenance bonus is the lower of the following amounts:[7]

- £5, for every week where you were meant to be paid at least £5 child maintenance (see p178) *plus* for each week you were meant to be paid less than £5, the amount due; *or*
- the actual amount of child maintenance (see p178) you were paid. If it is not clear how much maintenance is being paid for your child(ren) because you are also getting it for yourself, £5 is taken into account as child maintenance (or all of what you are paid if this is less than £5).[8] Any child maintenance you get above what has been taken into account as income in working out your IS (see p114) or income-based JSA or what has been collected on your behalf by the Benefits Agency (see p104) is not included; *or*
- £1,000.

Examples

Avni's ex-husband Sanjay agreed to pay £20 child maintenance a week. He did so during her bonus period of 250 weeks. Her bonus is the lower of:

$$£5 \times 250 = £1,250 \text{ } or$$
$$£20 \times 250 = £5,000 \text{ } or$$
$$£1,000$$

Avni will get a child maintenance bonus of £1,000.

Sarah's ex-husband Phil was meant to pay £20 child maintenance a week during her bonus period of 100 weeks. During that time Phil actually paid her £4 a week. Her bonus is the lower of:

$$£5 \times 100 \text{ weeks} = £500 \text{ } or$$
$$£4 \times 100 \text{ weeks} = £400 \text{ } or$$
$$£1,000$$

Sarah will get a child maintenance bonus of £400.

Lynn's former partner Robert was meant to pay £12 child maintenance a week during her bonus period of 50 weeks. He actually paid £6 a week. She will get the lower of:

$$£5 \times 50 = £250 \text{ } or$$
$$£6 \times 50 = £300 \text{ } or$$
$$£1,000$$

Lynn will get a child maintenance bonus of £250.

While you are on IS or income-based JSA, the Secretary of State can send estimates of how much child maintenance bonus you might be paid were you to take up work.[9] The DSS intend to do this every six months.

If your child maintenance bonus would be less than £5, you are not paid at all.[10]

Claims

A claim for child maintenance bonus must be in writing and on the appropriate form.[11] You should return the form to the office where you or your partner claimed IS or income-based JSA.

If you are one of a couple, you should claim the child maintenance bonus if you are the one caring for a child for whom child maintenance is paid.[12] If both you and your partner care for children for whom child maintenance is paid, you can both qualify for a child maintenance bonus. In this case, each of you must claim. If you separate, you count as entitled to IS or income-based JSA on days when your former partner was claiming for you to help you qualify.[13]

You can claim in the week before the week in which you or your partner's entitlement to IS or income-based JSA ceases. This is useful, for example, where you know you or your partner are returning to work. Otherwise, you must claim within the time limits as follows:[14]

- no later than 28 days after you or your partner stop getting IS or income-based JSA; or
- where you are claiming because you stopped getting IS/income-based JSA 12 weeks before you reached aged 60/pensionable age (see p182), no later than 28 days after you reach that age; or
- where you only have one child and s/he dies, within 12 months of the date of her/his death. You or your partner must have been entitled to IS or income-based JSA throughout the period from the date of the death until you claim.

Your claim is usually treated as made on the date it is received by the benefit office.[15] Your claim can be backdated if you can show that throughout the period between the date by which you should have claimed, and the date you actually claimed, you had 'good cause' for failing to claim.[16] However, your claim can never be backdated more than six months. See p299 for what counts as 'good cause' for a late claim.

If you do not provide sufficient information and evidence to support your claim or complete the form properly, you will be asked to do so, usually within one month.[17] You can be given longer than this if the Secretary of State thinks it is reasonable. It is important that you reply in time. If you do not complete the form properly, you might not get a child maintenance bonus unless you can show that you have 'good cause' for claiming late (see p181).

You can ask for your claim to be amended or withdrawn.[18] You must do this in writing before a decision is made about your claim.

Special rules if you reach aged 60 or retire

You can get a child maintenance bonus without having to make a claim even if you do not satisfy the work condition (see p178) if you:[19]

- turn 60 and on the day before you or your partner were entitled to IS; *or*
- reach pensionable age (60 for women and 65 for men) and on the day before you or your partner were entitled to income-based JSA; *or*
- stop getting income-based JSA after your 60th birthday but before you reach pensionable age and you become entitled to IS within 12 weeks or during any of the periods that link bonus periods listed on p179.

You can get a child maintenance bonus even if you do not satisfy the work condition, but you have to make a claim (see p181) if:[20]

- you or your partner's entitlement to IS ceases in the 12 weeks before your 60th birthday or to income-based JSA ceases in the 12 weeks before you reach pensionable age.

Your bonus period ends when you are paid a child maintenance bonus. You cannot get another one.[21]

Death of the person with care of the child

If someone who has been getting child maintenance dies, the child maintenance bonus s/he has already accumulated can be paid to an appointee (see below) or can help the person who takes over the care of her/his child(ren) get a higher child maintenance bonus (see p179).

Payment to an appointee

If a person satisfies all of the conditions of entitlement to a child maintenance bonus described on p178 but does not claim and s/he dies within 28 days of her/his entitlement to IS or income-based JSA ceasing, the Secretary of State can appoint someone to claim a child maintenance bonus in her/his place.[22] You must apply to be an appointee within six months of the date of death and claim the child maintenance bonus, in writing, within six months of the date you are appointed. The Secretary of State can accept an application for appointment or a claim up to 12 months after the date of death in exceptional circumstances. However, if the time limit for one is extended, the other is shortened by the same amount of time. Any time between the date you apply to be an appointee and the date you are appointed is ignored.

Payment to a new carer

If you take over the care of someone's child(ren) when s/he dies, you might be able to claim any child maintenance bonus accumulated at the date of her/his death or within 12 weeks of that date. Unless you have already accumulated bonus for the same weeks, her/his bonus period (see p178) must be treated as part yours if:[23]

- on the date the person died, s/he or her/his partner was entitled to IS or income-based JSA or had been within the 12 weeks before the death;
- you are her/his close relative (see p27);
- you or your partner were entitled to IS or income-based JSA on the date of her/his death or within 12 weeks of when s/he was last entitled to those benefits.

3. EXTENDED PAYMENTS OF HOUSING BENEFIT AND COUNCIL TAX BENEFIT

You might be able to claim an extended payment of housing benefit (HB) and council tax benefit (CTB) for four weeks if you or your partner start working full time or increase your earnings. If this is the case, you can get HB and CTB at the same rate you were getting when you were claiming IS or income-based JSA. There are very strict time limits for claiming. See p250 for further details.

CHAPTER TEN

Family credit

This chapter covers all the rules about family credit and gives an outline of the new benefit, earnings top-up. It contains:

1. Introduction (below)
2. The basic rules (p185)
3. The amount of benefit (p190)
4. Special rules for special groups (p192)
5. Claims and getting paid (p192)
6. Challenging a family credit decision (p197)
7. Earnings top-up (p197)

1. INTRODUCTION

Family credit (FC) is a tax-free benefit for low-paid workers with children. It tops up your wages if you are in full-time work (see p186). If you have a disability, you should consider claiming disability working allowance (DWA) instead as this may give you more money than FC (see p199). Part-time workers should claim income support (IS) instead of FC.

If you pay rent and/or council tax you may get housing benefit (HB) (see p214) and/or council tax benefit (CTB) (see p300) as well, but your FC counts as income for these benefits. If you receive FC you will not have to pay for certain health service benefits such as prescriptions (see Chapter 26), or certain discretionary education benefits (but you will not get free school meals), or certain help from social services provided for children or young people in need (see Appendix 1). You may also qualify for social fund payments for maternity or funeral expenses and crisis loans (see Chapters 21 and 24), and you can qualify for a discretionary grant from the local authority towards the cost of certain home improvements or for insulating your home (see Appendix 1).

Family credit is a weekly payment which normally continues at the same rate for 26 weeks, regardless of any changes in your circumstances (see p196).

You qualify for FC if:

- your income is low enough. This depends on your circumstances (see Chapter 19);
- your savings and capital are not worth over £8,000 (see Chapter 20);
- you are in Great Britain (see below);
- you, or your partner (if you have one), normally work full time (ie, for 16 hours or more a week) (see p186);
- you have at least one dependent child (see p189);
- you have made a proper claim (see p192);
- neither you nor your partner are getting DWA instead (see p189).

You can claim for your 'family' (see Chapter 17).

You must claim in writing on the form in leaflet FC1 which you can get from your local post office or Benefits Agency office. For more details about claims, see p192.

2. THE BASIC RULES

Residence in Great Britain

The residence rules are explained in more detail in CPAG's *Migration and Social Security Handbook*.

To be entitled to FC you must be in Great Britain.[1] This means England, Scotland and Wales. You can be treated as being in Great Britain if:[2]

- you are present and ordinarily resident in Great Britain; *and*
- your right to reside in Great Britain is not subject to any limitation or condition (but see p186); *and*
- your partner (if any) is ordinarily resident in the United Kingdom (UK) (but see below); *and*
- at least part of your earnings (or your partner's earnings) are derived from full-time work in the UK; *and*
- your earnings (or those of your partner) do not come wholly from paid work done outside the UK.

You are ordinarily resident here if you normally live in Great Britain (or, if relevant, the UK).[3] This means that the residence here has been adopted voluntarily and for settled purposes, although not necessarily with the intention of remaining indefinitely or for more than a limited period.[4] The United Kingdom includes Northern Ireland as well as Great

Britain. If you and your partner used to live together abroad but you now live in this country and s/he lives abroad, s/he is counted as your 'partner' for social security purposes if you intend to resume living together.[5] The fact that s/he is not ordinarily resident in the UK would therefore disentitle you. The position is the same if your partner was living with you in this country but is now living abroad – if you intend to resume living together s/he is still regarded as your 'partner'. Again, the fact that s/he is not ordinarily resident in the UK would therefore disentitle you.[6]

You cannot be treated as being in Great Britain during any period you or your partner are entitled to FC or DWA in Northern Ireland.[7]

There is no requirement that a child for whom you are responsible and who is a member of your household (see p318) should be present in Great Britain.[8]

Even if you are resident in Great Britain you will not be entitled to FC if your right to be here is subject to any limitation or condition[9] (eg, if you have been granted leave to remain in Great Britain for six months as a visitor). This rule will not apply to you if:[10]

- you are a refugee;
- you are a person who has been granted exceptional leave to remain in the UK;
- you, or a member of your family, is a national of a State which is a signatory to the Agreement on the European Economic Area (the 'Oporto Agreement') – this includes all EU nationals;
- you are lawfully working in Great Britain and you, or a member of your family, is a national of a State which the European Community has an agreement with concerning equal treatment of workers;
- you were getting FC before 5 February 1996 (it will apply if subsequently there is a relevant change of circumstances – see p196). The Benefits Agency's view is that this exception no longer applies when you make a new claim for FC (ie, after the award which was current on 5 February 1996 expired). This may well be wrong. If this happens to you, ask an adviser to contact CPAG.

For more details, see the *Migration and Social Security Handbook.*

Full-time work

To be entitled to FC, you, or your partner (if any), must be 'engaged and normally engaged in remunerative work'.[11] Work includes self-employment and can also include people who work from home (eg, childminders, writers or some carers) if they are paid[12] or expect to be paid. If you have been getting a Business Start-Up Allowance, the work you do will not count as 'remunerative work' unless you are receiving (or have a realistic expectation of receiving) payment from other sources.[13] You may still be treated as in 'remunerative work' where you are employed but receive no earnings but are only paid in kind (eg, free accommodation[14] or free produce for farmworkers[15]). Note that payments in kind are generally not treated as 'earnings' (see p350) but as other income which may be disregarded (see p379).

Unless you are claiming FC on account of any other work you do, you will *not* be treated as in work if you are:

- on a scheme for which a training allowance is paid;[16] *or*
- on a course of education as a student;[17] *or*
- a volunteer or working for a charitable or voluntary organisation and only your expenses are paid;[18] *or*
- a carer paid by the health or local authority, or a voluntary organisation, for looking after someone who is not normally a member of your household.[19]

You are entitled if you:[20]

- work for not less than 16 hours, or, if your hours fluctuate, 16 hours on average, a week; *and*
- are employed at the date of claim; *and*
- are paid, or expect to be paid. Any expectation of payment must be realistic – a mere hope or desire that you will be paid is not enough to make your work count as 'remunerative' work.[21]

In addition[22] you must:

- actually work for 16 hours or more in either the week in which you claim or one of the two preceding weeks; *or*
- be expected by your employers (or yourself if you are self-employed) to work for 16 hours or more in the week after the week you claim (this applies if you have just started work); *or*
- if you are on holiday from work but are expected to (or, if you are self-employed, you expect to) work 16 hours or more in the week after you return. You are not treated as on holiday if you are off sick or on maternity leave.[23]

The work must be your normal work and you must be likely to continue in that job for at least five weeks after your claim.[24] What is 'normal' depends on your individual circumstances,[25] for example, the likely future pattern of work, the past pattern and all other relevant circumstances.[26] If you have only just started work, but are likely to continue working, this should be sufficient to enable you to qualify.[27]

If you do not do at least 16 hours' work in one of the three relevant weeks, your claim will be disallowed (unless you are starting or resuming work after a holiday and thus covered because you are expected to work more than 16 hours). This applies even if the reason you have not been working the necessary hours is because of sickness,[28] maternity leave, suspension, short-time working, lay-off or because you are only on call.[29] However, you should be treated as working if you are on duty and required to be available during a part of the day and/or night – eg, if you are a warden in sheltered housing.

In calculating your hours, include all the hours you actually work for which you are paid. If you routinely need to work over your contractual hours, these extra hours can also count even if you are not paid for them.[30] Lunch-breaks (and for DWA, paid time off to attend a hospital or clinic in relation to your disability) should be included in the total if they are paid.[31] Your total hours can be made up from more than one job but, where you are claiming as a couple, you may not add your partner's hours to your own.[32] If you are self-employed, you can count not only the hours spent on services for which you are paid, but also other time which is essential to your business – eg, preparation time.[33]

If you are employed and you have not got a normal pattern of working hours (because you have just started a new job, or just changed your hours, or just returned to work after a break of more than four weeks – 13 for DWA), you qualify if it is expected that you will work 16 or more hours on average each week.[34] If you are self-employed and have not yet worked for five weeks (or your hours have gone up to 16 or more over the past five weeks), take the average hours that you expect to work.[35]

Otherwise hours are calculated by looking at your normal cycle of work and assessing your weekly hours. If you always work the same number of hours a week this is straightforward. If your work pattern is different – eg, you work one week on and one week off – your hours are averaged out. Periods when you do not normally work (eg, the 'week off') are included when working out the average but other absences (eg, for sickness) are not.[36]

If you have no recognisable cycle of work, the average over the five-week period immediately before the week in which you claim is used, or over another period if this would more accurately reflect your average working hours.[37]

If you have a recognisable cycle of work of one year, including school or similar holidays during which you do not work, in calculating your average number of hours you should ignore those holidays and also any other periods when you do not have to work.[38]

If you are unsure about whether you are working for 16 hours or more at the time of your claim, you should make a further claim in a week when you are more certain that you are working for 16 hours or more. This is because it may take the Benefits Agency a long time to send you a decision on the first claim and, if the first claim is refused because you were working for less than 16 hours a week, any second claim will only run from the date it is made unless you meet one of the qualifying reasons for having the claim backdated (see p127).

Family credit or income support?

Sometimes it is difficult to show that you normally work at least 16 hours a week and the distinction between FC and IS is not absolute. For example, you may fail to qualify for IS because you are found to be in full-time work, yet still fail to qualify for FC because the work is held not to be the work you normally do. You may also be refused both FC and IS because adjudication officers at the local Benefits Agency office and the Family Credit Unit interpret the rules, on the same facts, differently. If this happens, appeal against both decisions and ask for them to be heard together so a tribunal can decide which benefit is appropriate. In the meantime you could apply for interim payments. Note, however, that you will only be eligible for an interim payment when you are appealing if it is clear that you are entitled to some benefit, and even then you may get turned down (see p136).

You will fall within *both* schemes if you have a partner and s/he works for 16 hours or more a week but less than 24 hours a week.[39] Alternatively, if you are a childminder working for 16 hours or more a week, you are not treated as in full-time work for the purposes of IS, and so may be entitled to claim either IS or FC/DWA. In either case you will have to choose which benefit to claim. If you have to pay housing costs (see p25), in most cases it will be better to claim IS.

Responsibility for a child

To get FC, you or your partner must be responsible for at least one child who is a member of your household.[40] You do not have to be their parent. (For when you are responsible for a child, see p325.)

Overlap with disability working allowance

You cannot get FC if you or your partner have been awarded DWA. This does not apply if:

- your DWA is due to expire within six weeks of the date you claim FC; *and*
- you fulfil all the other conditions of entitlement to FC; *and*
- you are claiming FC for the period immediately after your DWA ends.[41]

In all other cases, you have to wait until your DWA award comes to an end before claiming FC (see p193).

Check whether you are better off claiming FC or DWA (see p203).

3. THE AMOUNT OF BENEFIT

Your FC is calculated by taking account of the number and ages of your children, the income and capital you and your family possess and the amount of hours you and/or your partner work.

To work out FC, first of all calculate the **maximum FC** for your family (see below). Then compare your income (see Chapter 19) with a set figure of £77.15 (called the applicable amount).[42]

Maximum family credit

The maximum family credit is made up of an adult credit and a credit for each child.[43] The current rates are:[44]

Credit for adult (single parent or couple)	£47.65
Credit for adult working 30 hours or more a week	£10.55
Credit for child aged	
0–10	£12.05
11–15	£19.95
16–17*	£24.80
18*	£34.70
Additional partners in a polygamous marriage	
under 18*	£24.80
18 or over*	£34.70

* From 7 October 1997 there will be just one rate of credit for 16/18-year-olds, and for additional partners in a polygamous marriage. This is £24.80.

Example of maximum FC
For a couple and three children aged 5, 7 and 13 the maximum is:
£47.65	for the couple
£24.10	for the two children under 11
£19.95	for the eldest child
£91.70	is the total maximum FC for this family

You do not receive a credit for any child who:[45]

- has more than £3,000 capital (savings etc) of their own (see p385); *or*
- has a higher weekly income (other than disregarded income or that from maintenance) than the appropriate credit for a child of that age; *or*
- has been in hospital or residential accommodation because of illness or disability for 52 weeks before the date of claim (see p327).

Note: New rules will apply in respect of credits for children on claims for FC made on or after 7 October 1997. The new rules are:[46]

- a child will not be treated as being aged 11 or 16 until the first Tuesday in September following her/his 11th or 16th birthday; *and*
- only one credit will apply in respect of a child aged between 16 and 18, (until 7 October there is a higher credit for 18-year-olds).

Note that you get the extra credit immediately for a child who reaches 11, 16 or 18 on or before 6 October 1997.[47]

Your maximum FC will include an extra £10.55 a week if you and/or your partner work for 30 hours or more a week.[48] The way your hours are calculated is the same as for those working 16 hours or more[49] (see p188).

The family credit calculation

You now compare your income (see Chapter 19) with the applicable amount. If your income is the same as or below the applicable amount you receive maximum FC. If your income exceeds the applicable amount, your maximum FC is reduced by 70 per cent of the difference.[50]

Example of income higher than applicable amount
Shahida has a partner and two children aged 3 and 5. Her partner works 30 hours a week and the total family income taken into account for the purposes of FC is £107.60. The maximum FC in her case is £82.30 (£47.65 for the couple, £12.05 for each child and £10.55 because her partner works 30 hours a week).
Her income exceeds the applicable amount by £30.45 (£107.60 less £77.15); 70 per cent of the excess is £21.32.
Maximum FC   £82.30
less   £21.31 (70% of excess)
equals   £60.99 weekly FC
Shahida will therefore receive £60.99 each week in FC.

Any fractions produced at the end of the FC calculation are rounded up to a penny if they are a half-penny or more, and are ignored if less than a half-penny.[51]

The minimum amount of FC that will be paid is 50 pence a week.[52]

Your FC can be reduced if you fail to apply for child support maintenance (see p110).

Note: Some childcare costs can be deducted when working out your income (see p362).

4. SPECIAL RULES FOR SPECIAL GROUPS

People from abroad

Most people from abroad can no longer claim FC because of the residence conditions (see p185).

People involved in a trade dispute

If you are involved in a trade dispute, you can still claim FC but your normal weekly earnings are taken as those prior to the dispute[53] and so do not reflect your actual income during the dispute. Also, you, or your partner, would have to have worked in one of the three weeks around the date of your claim (see p187), or else you would need to argue that, in spite of the dispute, your employer is still expecting you to work in the following week. If you are already getting FC when you become involved in a trade dispute you continue to receive it at the same rate for the rest of the 26 weeks of your award.[54]

Since there are no other special rules under FC for the assessment of your income and capital if you or your partner are involved in a trade dispute, the normal rules apply.

5. CLAIMS AND GETTING PAID

Claims

There is an FC Helpline which can give advice about FC. The number is 01253 500050 and it is open 7.30 am – 6.30 pm Monday to Friday.

Your claim should be on form FC1. For couples, the claim must be made by the female partner unless the Secretary of State decides that it is reasonable to accept a claim from the male partner.[55] The claim is usually considered to have been made on the day it reaches the Family Credit

Unit (see Appendix 2 for address).[56] However, if you get the claim form by contacting your local Benefits Agency office, the Family Credit Unit or JobCentre, your claim will count as having been made on the day your request for the claim form was received in the office, as long as you get the claim form back to the Family Credit Unit within one month of requesting it.[57]

If you do not use the right form or if you fill it in incorrectly, the date of your first attempt to claim will still count provided you correct it within one month of being asked to do so. This time limit can be extended.[58] If you are just starting work after being unemployed you can ask a claimant adviser at the JobCentre to give you the form. Alternatively you can get it from your local Benefits Agency. Both will help you fill it in and, in either case, your claim is likely to be dealt with more speedily as the JobCentre/Benefits Agency should mark the FC1 to ensure that you get a quick decision. If you prefer, you can get the form from a post office or your local advice centre (see Appendix 3).

If you claim income support (IS) or jobseeker's allowance (JSA) when you should have claimed FC, your claim for FC can be treated as made on the day you claimed IS or JSA. This will apply if you have been refused IS or JSA because you, or your partner (if any), are in full-time work (see p13), and you claim FC within 14 days of the decision refusing your claim for IS/JSA.[59] You can ask for the FC claim to start on a later date – eg, if your wages are about to go down.

A claim for FC can be backdated for a maximum of three months. The rules on backdating are the same as for IS (see pp127-29), except that in relation to backdating for up to one month for *good administrative reasons* (see p127):

- the fact that you claimed FC within one month of your entitlement to IS or JSA stopping is an *additional* qualifying reason;[60] *and*
- the fact that the claim was made within one month of separating from your partner is *not* a qualifying reason.

If you have made a claim but then your circumstances change (eg, your income suddenly drops), you can amend or withdraw your claim. But you must act quickly. Your letter must arrive before the adjudication officer has decided your claim.[61]

If you are renewing your claim[62] after a period on FC you should be reminded that it is about to run out and invited to re-apply. You can put in your renewal claim up to 28 days before the current award expires or within 14 days of it running out. Your renewal claim then follows on immediately from your previous award. If you are changing from disability working allowance (DWA) to FC you can make your claim up to 42 days before your DWA award expires or 14 days afterwards and FC is then paid from the date the DWA ends.

When to claim

It is worth thinking carefully about when you should claim, bearing in mind:

- Awards of FC run from a Tuesday so you should try to get your claim to the Benefits Agency on a Tuesday or on the Monday before. If your claim arrives on a Wednesday, your entitlement will not start until the following Tuesday and you lose benefit for that week.[63]
- Make sure your claim is made during a week in which you are eligible to claim (see p187).
- If you are thinking about making a claim in late February or March it might be to your advantage to consider delaying the claim until April. This is because the amounts for FC are uprated in April. You will need to work out whether it is worth losing three or four weeks' FC in order to receive the higher rate for the next 26 weeks. However, if you claim no more than 28 days before benefits are increased and you do not qualify for FC at the old rates but would under the new ones, you can be treated as entitled and paid from the date the increases take effect.[64] In all other cases, even if you are not entitled on the date your claim is made, provided you would be entitled for the period beginning within three days of that date, your claim will be treated as if it had been made from the later date.[65]
- A claim for DWA can be treated as a claim for FC.[66] If you are refused DWA, you could ask for this to happen and thus have FC paid from the date of your DWA claim. If you are entitled to both you must choose which one to claim *before* a decision is made. Once you have been awarded FC you cannot change to DWA until 26 weeks have elapsed and *vice versa*.
- Consider whether your family circumstances are about to change in a way which might affect your FC. For example, if you are about to take a drop in income or have another child, it might be worth delaying your claim.
- As renewal claims will be determined as if they were made on the first day after your previous award expires, they will not normally take into account any changes of circumstances occurring within the 14-day renewal period (see p193). If any such changes would be likely to result in an increase in your new award (eg, your partner's unemployment benefit is about to end), you should consider foregoing your entitlement for this 14 days and either submit a fresh claim after the

14 days have passed, or else state in your renewal claim that you wish it to be treated as a fresh claim instead. The adjudication officer has a duty to treat your new application in the way you indicate.[67]

Send off your claim form even if you cannot complete all the details. You can send missing details or documents on later. Keep a copy of your claim in case queries arise.

How your claim is dealt with

When your claim is received by the Family Credit Unit, the information you have provided is checked and verification can be obtained from your employer about your wages or salary.[68] You should ask your employer to reply promptly. If you have claimed through a claimant adviser or local Benefits Agency, your wages are checked by telephone which speeds up your claim. On a renewal claim, if you are still working for the same employer, the Benefits Agency may accept your wage slips as evidence of your earnings and not contact your employer again.

Then your claim is referred to an adjudication officer for decision. The law requires that all claims should be dealt with within 14 days 'so far as practicable'.[69] However, from April 1996 the intention has been to process most new claims within five days.[70]

Delays and complaints

If you suffer delays, or wish to complain about how your claim has been dealt with, see pp139 and 154. The advice given there applies equally to FC.

Family credit decisions – getting paid

You are given the decision concerning your claim in writing. The letter from the Family Credit Unit should give the reasons for the decision and tell you about your right to appeal.[71] You are paid by order book or into an account (including your partner's account), whichever you have requested. If your weekly FC is £4 or less, you will usually be paid in a lump sum covering the whole 26-week period,[72] but if it is less than 50 pence a week, FC will not be paid at all.[73]

Payments will start from the first Tuesday of the week after your claim is treated as made. Payments by order book are made weekly in arrears.[74] If you have asked to be paid by direct credit transfer,[75] these payments should be credited to your account every seven days in arrears.

If your order book is lost or stolen or your FC is suspended, the rules are the same as for IS (see p138). There are similar rules for when your FC can be suspended (see p137).

Change of circumstances

If your circumstances change during the 26 weeks, this does not usually affect the amount you are paid.[76] However:

- if a child or young person leaves your household while FC is being paid and IS, DWA or FC is awarded to them or for them in a different household, your FC stops from the first day of any overlap;[77]
- if a child for whom you are responsible (see p325) ceases full-time education (see p16), and if there are no other children for whom you are responsible and who are in full-time education, your award of FC will be reviewed and you will stop getting benefit. Your FC will stop on the date the child turns 16 or the date s/he ceases full-time education, whichever is the later;[78]
- if a claimant dies during the 26-week period, FC stops if s/he was single. If s/he was one of a couple (see p319), the partner is paid the rest of the award provided that s/he was the partner when FC was claimed;[79]
- if you are later notified that FC or DWA has been awarded to you for a period beginning before your existing award, and the new award overlaps with any period of your existing award, your existing award will be terminated from the date you are notified of this, so that the new award can take its place (this may happen as a result of the time taken to complete a review of or an appeal against an earlier claim or because a later claim is backdated);[80]
- if you fail to comply with the requirement to apply for child support maintenance and a reduced benefit direction is issued (see p110), the amount of your FC is adjusted during your current award. This also applies where the reduced benefit direction ceases, is cancelled or suspended, or reinstated after a suspension.

Where your earnings are estimated and it transpires that the estimate was wrong, this does not amount to a change of circumstances and your benefit cannot be reviewed.[81] However, if you appeal against the amount of FC your award might be revised to take account of your actual earnings.

Overpayments and fraud

The rules on overpayments and fraud are the same as for IS (see p146). The IS rules limiting the maximum amount that can be recovered from your weekly benefit[82] do not apply to FC, but you should argue for realistic repayments.

6. CHALLENGING A FAMILY CREDIT DECISION

You can apply for a review of an FC decision, or appeal against it, see p131 and Chapter 8. The advice given there in relation to IS applies equally to FC, except that reviews on the grounds of a change of circumstance are very limited in relation to FC (see p196).

When an FC decision is reviewed, payment of arrears is not restricted *unless* the review was because of ignorance of, or a mistake about, the facts, and you were aware of (or should have been aware of) these facts but you failed to tell the Benefits Agency. In this case you can only get up to one month's arrears.[83]

7. EARNINGS TOP-UP

From October 1996, a new benefit, earnings top-up (ETU), has been introduced on a pilot basis in eight areas. Earnings top-up is similar to FC, but it is available to people in low-paid work who do *not* have dependent children.

In four of the areas, ETU is paid at a **lower rate** (Scheme A), and in the other four at a **higher rate** (Scheme B).

The Scheme A areas are:
- Newcastle-upon-Tyne;
- Castleford and Pontefract, Wakefield and Dewesbury, and Barnsley;
- Southend; *and*
- Bangor and Caernarfon, Conway and Colwyn, Denbigh, Dolgellau and Barmouth, Holyhead, Shotton, Flint and Rhyl, and Wrexham.

The Scheme B areas are:
- Sunderland;
- Doncaster;
- Bournemouth; *and*
- Perth and Crieff, Dumbarton, and Stirling.

The pilot scheme is intended to run for three years. The details are contained in the scheme rules, not regulations.

The calculation for ETU is very similar to that for FC. The maximum amount you will receive if you work less than 30 hours a week is as follows:

	Single under 25	*Single 25+*	*Couple*
Scheme A (lower)	£23–£35	£28–£75	£47–£65
Scheme B (higher)	£23–£35	£28–£75	£57–£70

CHAPTER ELEVEN

Disability working allowance

This chapter deals with the rules about disability working allowance. It covers:

1. INTRODUCTION

Disability working allowance (DWA) is a tax-free benefit for low-paid workers with a disability. It tops up your wages if you are in full-time work (see p200). Part-time workers can claim income support (IS) instead. If you are in low-paid work but do not have a disability you could claim family credit (FC) if you have children (see Chapter 10). If you pay rent and/or council tax you may get housing benefit (HB) (see p214) and/ or council tax benefit (CTB) (see p300) as well, but your DWA counts as income for these benefits. Receipt of DWA helps you to qualify for a disability premium with IS/HB/CTB.[1] In addition, if you receive DWA you do not have to pay for health service benefits such as prescriptions (see Chapter 26), or certain discretionary education benefits (but you will not get free school meals), or certain help from social services provided for children or young people in need (see Appendix 1). You may also qualify for social fund payments for maternity or funeral expenses and crisis loans (see Chapters 21 and 24), and you can qualify for a discretionary grant from the local authority towards the cost of certain home improvements or for insulating your home (see Appendix 1).

Disability working allowance is a weekly payment which normally continues at the same rate for 26 weeks regardless of changes in your circumstances (see p209). If your earnings are too low to pay national insurance you will get a credit for each week on DWA.[2]

Who can claim

You qualify for DWA if:

- you are 16 or over;
- your income is low enough. This depends on your circumstances (see Chapter 19);
- your savings and capital are not worth more than £16,000 (see Chapter 20);
- you are in Great Britain (see below);
- you normally work full time – ie, for 16 hours or more a week (see below);
- you have a physical or mental disability which puts you at a disadvantage in getting a job (see p201);
- you are, or have recently been, getting a sickness or disability benefit (see p202);
- you have made a proper claim (see p206);
- neither you nor your partner (if any) are getting FC instead (see p203).

Who you claim for

You claim for your 'family' (see Chapter 17). For more details about claims, see p206.

If you become sick while on DWA

There are special rules to protect your entitlement to the incapacity benefits which you were claiming before you took up work (see p192).

2. THE BASIC RULES

Residence in Great Britain[3]

The rules are the same as for FC[4] (see p185).

Full-time work

The rules are the same as for FC (see p186).

The disability and disadvantage test

To qualify for DWA you must have a physical or mental disability which puts you at a disadvantage in getting a job.[5] If you are claiming for the first time, or after a period of two years when you were not getting DWA, you simply have to sign a declaration that this applies to you. This will be accepted *unless* the information given on your claim form is contradictory, *or* the adjudication officer has other evidence which indicates that you do not fulfil that condition.[6] For all other claims, you fulfil this condition if one of the following applies:[7]

- you are paid one of the following benefits (or a Northern Ireland equivalent) – but see below:
  - the higher or middle rate care component or the higher rate mobility component of the disability living allowance;
  - attendance allowance;
  - industrial disablement benefit or a war pension, where you are at least 80 per cent disabled;
  - mobility supplement;
- you have an invalid 'trike' or similar vehicle (but see below);
- you were paid severe disablement allowance (or a Northern Ireland equivalent) for at least one day in the eight weeks prior to your 'initial claim'. Initial claim means your first successful claim for DWA, or a new claim where you have not been getting DWA during the last two years;
- you cannot keep your balance without holding on to something when standing;
- you cannot walk 100 metres on level ground without stopping or suffering severe pain. You are expected to use a walking aid (eg, crutches, a stick, a frame or an artificial limb) if you normally do so;
- you cannot use your hands behind your back (as you would when putting on a jacket or tucking your shirt in);
- you cannot extend your hands forwards in order to shake hands with someone without difficulty;
- you cannot put your hands up to your head without difficulty (as when putting on a hat);
- you cannot, with one hand, pick up a coin of 2.5cm diameter because of a lack of manual dexterity;
- you cannot pick up a full one-litre jug and pour from it into a cup without difficulty;
- you cannot turn either of your hands sideways through 180 degrees;
- you are registered blind or partially sighted;

- you cannot read 16-point print from more than 20 cm distance, even when wearing your normal glasses, if any;
- you cannot hear a telephone ring when in the same room, even with your hearing aid, if any;
- you cannot hear someone talking in a loud voice when the room is quiet and they are only two metres away from you, even with your hearing aid, if any;
- people who know you well have difficulty understanding what you say;
- you have difficulty understanding a person you know well;
- you lose consciousness during a fit, or go into a coma at least once a year during working hours;
- you are mentally ill and are receiving regular medical treatment;
- you are often confused or forgetful due to mental disability;
- you cannot do simple addition and subtraction;
- you hit people, or damage property or cannot socialise because of your mental disability;
- you cannot manage an eight-hour working day or a five-day week because of your medical condition or because you suffer from severe pain;
- following illness or accident you are undergoing rehabilitation. You can only use this condition to qualify on an initial claim (see p201).

If you fulfil the disability test for DWA because you are paid one of the specified benefits, or have an invalid trike, you will nevertheless be refused DWA if there is evidence that none of the other disability conditions are fulfilled.[8]

Receipt of a sickness or disability benefit

To qualify for DWA you must also be, or have been, receiving a sickness or disability benefit.[9] You are entitled if, *when you claim*, you are receiving:

- disability living allowance;
- attendance allowance;
- an increase of your industrial disablement benefit or war pension for attendance needs;
- a corresponding benefit from Northern Ireland.

Alternatively, you qualify if, *for at least one day in the eight weeks prior to your claim*, you were getting:

- the higher rate of short-term incapacity benefit or long-term incapacity benefit (or invalidity benefit[10]) or severe disablement allowance;
- IS, income-based jobseeker's allowance (JSA), HB or CTB, if your applicable amount included the disability or higher pensioner (on the

ground of disability) premium either for yourself or your partner (see pp333 and 336);
- a corresponding benefit from Northern Ireland.

You also meet this condition if you have an invalid trike or similar vehicle when you claim.

Similarly, you will also qualify if, for at least one day in the eight weeks prior to your claim you were on a 'training for work' course, and within the eight weeks before your first day of training you were getting either the higher rate of short-term or long-term incapacity benefit (or invalidity benefit), or severe disablement allowance (or a corresponding benefit from Northern Ireland). A 'training for work' course means one under the Employment and Training Act 1973 or, in Scotland, the Enterprise and New Towns (Scotland) Act 1990, or one you attend for at least 16 hours a week and the main purpose of which is to teach occupational or vocational skills.[11]

If you are renewing your DWA claim within eight weeks of a previous award running out, you are deemed to be receiving the appropriate award of incapacity benefit (or invalidity benefit), severe disablement allowance or a disability or higher pensioner premium paid with IS, HB or CTB (or a Northern Ireland equivalent) where your previous award was made on this basis.[12]

Entitlement to family credit

You are not entitled to DWA if, when you claim, you (or your partner) are entitled to FC.[13] However, this does not apply if:[14]

- your FC claim runs out within 28 days of your DWA claim;
- you are otherwise entitled to DWA;
- your DWA claim is for the period immediately after your FC runs out.

Check whether you are better off claiming FC or DWA. Disability working allowance is usually paid at a higher rate and entitles you to a disability premium for HB/CTB (see p333).

3. THE AMOUNT OF BENEFIT

To work out DWA, first of all calculate your maximum DWA (see below). Then compare your income (see Chapter 19) with your applicable amount which is a set figure of:

£57.85 (single claimants)

or £77.15 (couples or single parents)

If your income is less than your applicable amount you receive maximum DWA. If it is more, you get the maximum DWA minus 70 per cent of the difference between your income and the applicable amount.[15]

Your DWA can be reduced if you fail to apply for child support maintenance (see p110).

Note: As with FC (see p362), childcare costs can sometimes be deducted from your income.

Maximum DWA

This is made up of allowances for each member of your family (see p318). These are as follows:[16]

single claimant	£49.55
couple/lone parent	£77.55
credit for adult working 30 hours or more a week	£10.55
child aged:	
0-10	£12.05
11-15	£19.95
16-17*	£24.80
18*	£34.70
disabled child allowance (if applicable)	£20.95
additional partners in a polygamous marriage:	
under 18*	£24.80
18 or over*	£34.70

* From 7 October 1997, there will be just one rate of credit for 16/18-year-olds, and for additional partners in a polygamous marriage. This is £24.80.

The conditions of entitlement to the disabled child allowance are similar to those for the IS/HB/CTB disabled child premium (see p333), but there is no capital condition.[17]

Note that the age allowance for a child (as distinct from the disabled child allowance) is not payable for a child who has:

- capital of over £3,000 (see p385); *or*
- weekly income (excluding maintenance or disregarded income) which is greater than their allowance; *or*

- been in hospital or local authority residential accommodation for the 52 weeks prior to your claim because of physical or mental illness/ disability.

Note: New rules will apply in respect of the age allowances for children on claims for DWA made on or after 7 October 1997. The new rules are:[18]

- a child will not be treated as being aged 11 or 16 until the first Tuesday in September following her/his 11th or 16th birthday; *and*
- only one age allowance will apply in respect of a child aged between 16 and 18.

Note that you can get the extra allowance immediately for a child who reaches 11, 16 or 18 on or before 6 October 1997.[19]

As for FC, your maximum DWA will be increased by an extra £10.55 a week if you and/or your partner work for 30 hours or more a week.[20] The way your hours are calculated is the same as for FC[21] (see p188).

Calculating DWA

Work out your income (see Chapter 19), and compare this to your applicable amount.

Example
Winston is 19 and single. He works 35 hours a week. His income for DWA is £65. He has no savings.

His maximum DWA is £60.10 (single person's allowance of £49.55 and £10.55 because of the number of hours he works).

His income exceeds the applicable amount of £57.85 by £7.15. Thus his maximum DWA is reduced by £5.01 (70 per cent of £7.15) and he is paid £55.09 a week (£60.10 less £5.01).

If his income had been at or below £57.85 he would have received the maximum DWA.

---

4. SPECIAL RULES FOR SPECIAL GROUPS

The rules for people from abroad are the same as for FC (see p192). The rules for people involved in a trade dispute are similar to those for FC (see p192). Earnings for set periods immediately prior to the trade dispute (or periods of short-term working) are normally used to calculate your normal weekly earnings.[22]

5. CLAIMS AND GETTING PAID

Claims

You claim DWA using the claim pack[23] which you can get from the Benefits Agency, a post office or JobCentre.

If you prefer, you can ring the Benefits Enquiry Line free of charge on 0800 882200. Benefits Agency staff will discuss your claim and complete the appropriate forms for you. These are sent to you to sign and post.

Do not delay sending in the DWA1 just because you do not yet have your payslips or a completed form EEF 200 from your employer (this form confirms your hours/earnings if you have not yet worked for nine weeks) – these can be sent later.

If you are one of a couple the disabled partner should claim. If both of you are disabled you can choose who should be the claimant, but if you cannot agree the Secretary of State decides for you.[24]

If you do not use the proper form or fill it in incorrectly and then return the corrected form within one month of being asked to do so, the date of your first claim counts. This period can be extended if you have a good reason but it is best to act promptly.[25] If you want to amend or withdraw your claim, write to the Benefits Agency immediately. Your letter must arrive before the adjudication officer has decided your claim.[26]

If you claim FC, this can be treated as a claim for DWA if you would be better off.[27] However, you must let both the FC and DWA Units know that you want them to do this *before* your FC claim is assessed.

Your claim is normally treated as made on the date it is received at the DWA Unit.[28]

However, if you got the claim pack by contacting your local Benefits Agency office, the DWA Unit or JobCentre, your claim will count as having been made on the day your request for the claim pack was received in the office, as long as you get the claim pack back to the DWA Unit within one month of requesting it.[29] Also, if you start work on a Monday or Tuesday and claim DWA in the same week your claim is treated as made on the Tuesday of that week.[30]

If you claim IS or income-based JSA when you should have claimed DWA, your claim for DWA can be treated as made on the day you claimed IS or income-based JSA. This will apply if you have been refused IS or JSA because you, or your partner (if any), are in full-time work (see p13), and you claim DWA within 14 days of the decision refusing your claim for IS/income-based JSA.[31] You can ask for the DWA claim to start on a later date – eg, if your wages are about to go down.

Your claim for DWA will also be treated as having been made on an earlier date if:[32]

- you had made an earlier claim for DWA which had been refused because at the time of the claim you were not, or had not been, receiving one of the relevant sickness or disability benefits (see p202); *and*
- at the time of the earlier claim for DWA you had made a claim for one of the relevant sickness or disability benefits but the claim had not been decided; *and*
- after being refused DWA, the claim for one of the relevant sickness or disability benefits is decided in your favour; *and*
- you make a further claim for DWA within three months of the decision awarding you one of the relevant sickness or disability benefits.

In these circumstances, the further claim for DWA will be treated as having been made on either the date of your earlier claim for DWA or the date from which you are awarded the relevant sickness or disability benefit, whichever is the later.[33]

Note: This rule will not apply to you if you qualify for DWA through having been on a 'training for work' course[34] (see p203). It will also not apply if the second claim for DWA is made within three months of you being turned down on the first claim for DWA.[35] In this circumstance, the second claim is treated as a review request,[36] though your claim date is still treated as that of your later claim.[37]

A claim can be backdated for up to three months. The rules on backdating are the same as for IS (see pp127-29), except that, in relation to backdating (for up to one month) for *good administrative reasons* (see p127), the fact that the claim was made within one month of separating from your partner is not a qualifying reason.[38]

Renewal claims

If you are currently getting DWA, you should be sent a claim form eight weeks before your payments end. You can reclaim from six weeks before your award runs out and up to two weeks afterwards. It is usually best to claim as early as possible to ensure that your payments are not interrupted. On your renewal claim you have to fill in a fresh DWA1 and you will also be sent form DWA2 which asks you questions about the extent of your disability and how it affects you.

If you are currently getting FC, you can claim DWA up to four weeks before your FC expires or two weeks afterwards.[39]

For practical advice on when to claim DWA, see p194 as the rules for FC are the same.

How your claim is dealt with

When your claim is received, the information in it is checked to see if further details are needed. If so, you are asked to provide extra information or documents. You are obliged to provide this if requested and should do so *within a month*.[40] If there is a good reason this time limit can be extended, but if you reply quickly your DWA will be paid sooner. The Benefits Agency can also approach your employer for confirmation of your earnings and s/he must reply.[41]

Your claim is then passed to an adjudication officer for decision, and this should be made within 14 days if possible.[42]

If this is your first claim for DWA or you are reclaiming after two years of not getting DWA, it is usually accepted that your disability puts you at a disadvantage in getting a job if you say it does on form DWA1.[43] You do not have to fill in form DWA2 to prove this unless there is other evidence to suggest that you do not qualify, in which case the adjudication officer will ask you to do so. In all other cases, the adjudication officer considers your answers to the disability questions to decide if you qualify. The DWA2 form asks you to give the names of two health professionals who know about your disability and the adjudication officer may contact them to confirm your answers to the questions. S/he can also ask for advice from DSS doctors about your condition and how it is likely to affect you but s/he must make the decision.[44]

If necessary you can be asked to go for a medical, though this is unlikely.[45] You should be sent a written decision and informed that you can appeal if you disagree with it.[46]

Delays and complaints

If you suffer delays, or wish to complain about how your claim has been dealt with, see pp139 and 154. The advice given there applies equally to DWA.

Payment of benefit

Disability working allowance is normally paid on a Tuesday. If you claim on a different day of the week you are paid from the following Tuesday[47] (but see p206 if you have just started a job). If you are currently getting DWA or FC and you reclaim within the time limits (see p207) you are paid from the day after your last award runs out.[48] If you claim up to 28 days before the annual benefit increases (which happen each April) and you are not entitled at the old benefit rates, you can be paid from the date the new ones come in.[49]

If you are awarded DWA it is paid for 26 weeks.[50] You are paid by an order book or, if you wish and the Secretary of State agrees, into an account (including your partner's account),[51] whichever you have requested. Benefit is paid a week in arrears (by order book) or four-weekly in arrears (into a bank). If your weekly DWA is £4 or less, you will usually be paid in a lump sum covering the whole 26-week period, but if it is less than 50 pence it will not be paid at all.[52]

Payment is usually made to the claimant but it can be paid to a partner instead.[53] You could apply to the Benefits Agency for this to happen if it is more convenient, but it is the Secretary of State's decision so there is no right of appeal if this is refused. If there is a delay in assessing your DWA, you can claim an interim payment (see p136).

If your order book is lost or stolen or your DWA is suspended, the rules are the same as for IS (see p138). There are similar rules about when your DWA can be suspended (see p137).

Change of circumstances

If your circumstances change during the 26 weeks, this does not usually affect the amount you are paid.[54] However, entitlement ceases if:

- your DWA includes an amount for a child or young person (see p325), but s/he is no longer a member of your household and someone else is claiming for her/him as a dependant in their DWA/FC/IS;[55]
- the claimant dies. However, if there is a surviving partner and s/he is included in the claim, DWA continues to be paid for the remainder of the 26 weeks;[56]
- you fail to comply with the requirement to apply for child support maintenance and a reduced benefit direction is issued (see p110), the amount of your DWA is adjusted during your current award. This also applies where the reduced benefit direction ceases, is cancelled or suspended, or reinstated after a suspension;
- you are later notified that DWA or FC has been awarded to you for a period beginning before your existing award, and the new award overlaps with any period of your existing award, your existing award will be terminated from the date you are notified of this, so that the new award can take its place (this may happen as a result of the time it takes to complete a review of or appeal against an earlier claim or because a later claim is backdated).[57]

Overpayments and fraud

The rules on overpayments and fraud are the same as for IS[58] (see p146) except that the maximum rate of recovery does not apply to DWA. Nevertheless, you should argue for realistic repayments.

6. CHALLENGING A DWA DECISION

You can apply for a review of a DWA decision, or appeal against it, see p131 and Chapter 8. The advice there in relation to IS applies equally to DWA, except for the following differences:

• Your appeal may be heard by a disability appeal tribunal if any question about your disability arises, rather than a social security appeal tribunal. One of the members of the disability appeal tribunal has to be a doctor.
• Reviews on the grounds of a change of circumstances are very limited in relation to DWA (see p209).
• You cannot appeal against an initial decision. First you have to write and ask for a review. If the request for review is made within three months of receiving the decision, but the review is unsuccessful, you can then appeal against that decision.

If your review request is outside the three-month time limit the decision can only be reviewed if:[59]

• there was a mistake about or ignorance of a fact which is relevant to your claim;
• you have claimed in advance and been awarded DWA, but then do not fulfil the conditions on the date it is due to be paid. The review is to stop payment being made;
• the adjudication officer got the law wrong;
• there has been one of the changes of circumstances set out on p209.

If you were refused DWA, and made a further claim within three months of the decision, and are then awarded DWA, you are paid from the date you made the further claim.[60]

If you were awarded DWA and apply for a review within three months about the amount of the award, the general rule that reviews take effect from the beginning of an award should operate. However, only up to one month's arrears of DWA can be paid if:

• you apply for a review within three months or because there was a mistake about, or ignorance of, relevant facts; *and*
• the review arises because you provide some information which you knew (or should have known) but did not previously give to the Benefits Agency; *and*

- the review leads to a new award of DWA or an increase in the amount you are getting.

The month runs from the date you first provided the information.[61] Note the way this rule is phrased; it applies to a new award of DWA, as well as an increased award.

The rules for getting more than one month's arrears are the same as for IS (see p133).

7. GIVING UP WORK BECAUSE OF SICKNESS OR DISABILITY

If you have to stop working and you are sick, there are special rules to ensure that you can go back on to the benefit which you were claiming for your incapacity before you took a job and claimed DWA. The rules differ depending on whether you are temporarily off sick or stop work altogether.

Temporary sickness

You should claim statutory sick pay from your employer (unless you were getting sickness/invalidity/incapacity benefit or severe disablement allowance within the last eight weeks, in which case you go back on to that benefit). You continue to get your DWA and you may also be entitled to claim IS, HB and CTB if your income is low enough (see Chapters 2, 12 and 16 respectively).

Giving up work

If you give up work or training for work through ill-health and have been claiming invalidity/incapacity benefit or severe disablement allowance within the last two years, you can go straight back on to that benefit from your first day of sickness.[62] This is because days on DWA count as days of incapacity for work (and also as days when you were disabled for severe disablement allowance purposes) and your two periods of sickness are linked together. As well as any basic incapacity benefit/severe disablement allowance you get increases for your partner or child (if any) under the rules which applied on your last claim.[63] You must show that you are now incapable of work. If you have been working for some time, your incapacity may be questioned by the adjudication officer. Make it clear that you have had to give up work due to ill-health or disability when you reclaim.

Periods when you have been on DWA do not in themselves help you to get the disability premium, higher pensioner premium or the severe disability premium with IS/HB/CTB. You must requalify for these in the normal way (see pp333, 336 and 338).

If your job ends after the two-year period but you are nevertheless incapable of work, claim incapacity benefit when you stop working. With the introduction of incapacity benefit on 13 April 1995, the Government brought in special rules to give some protection to people who had been on DWA. The rules are very complicated, but the stated intention is to enable incapacity benefit, for a period, to be paid at a protected rate in certain circumstances when you have been getting DWA and then give up work because of sickness.[64]

If you give up work for reasons other than sickness or disability you should claim jobseeker's allowance instead. If you qualify you can also claim IS/HB/CTB (see Chapters 2, 12 and 16 respectively).

For details about claiming incapacity and severe disablement allowance, see the *Rights Guide to Non-Means-Tested Benefits*, 20th edn, 1997/98. For detailed information about JSA, see the *Jobseeker's Allowance Handbook*, 2nd edn, 1997/98.

PART FOUR

Housing benefit and council tax benefit

CHAPTER TWELVE

The basic rules

This chapter covers:
1. Introduction (below)
2. 'Eligible rent' (p227)
3 Rent restrictions (p232)

1. INTRODUCTION

Housing benefit (HB) is paid to people who have a low income and who pay rent. It is paid whether or not the claimant is available for or in full-time work and may be paid as well as other social security benefits, or just by itself. HB is paid by local authorities, although it is a national scheme and the rules are mainly determined by DSS regulations.

Who can claim?

You can claim HB if the following conditions are satisfied:[1]

- Your income is low enough. How low it has to be depends on your circumstances (see p247).
- Your savings and other capital are not worth more than £16,000 (see Chapter 20).
- You or your partner are liable, or treated as liable, to pay rent for accommodation (see p215). 'Rent' includes many payments not usually regarded as rent such as licensee payments, payments for bed and breakfast and hostels. It does not matter if you are in arrears, or if you have paid your rent in advance.
- You normally occupy that accommodation as your home (see p216), or are only temporarily absent from it (see p217).
- You are not excluded under the rules explained on p220.

The amount of HB you receive depends on a number of factors. The full calculation is explained on p248.

Also note that:

- HB is non-taxable and is not dependent on you having paid national insurance contributions;
- unlike income support (IS), there is no lower age limit for claiming HB.

Who you claim for

You claim for your 'family' (see Chapter 17).

Liability to pay rent

To get HB, you must normally be either the person who is liable to pay the rent, or the partner of the person who is liable. Your liability does not have to be legally binding. If your former partner is liable to make the payments on your home but is not doing so and you have to pay rent in order to remain living there the local authority must treat you as liable even if you are not legally liable.[2] It does not matter whether or not the landlord is prepared to transfer the tenancy to you or wants to evict you. Some local authorities may refuse to accept your HB claim in this situation because they allow their own interests as landlords to override their duties under the HB scheme. This is wrong. You should point out that the eligibility rules for HB and for transferring council tenancies are quite separate.

Where you have taken over paying the rent but are not the former partner of the liable person, the council has the discretion to treat you as liable if it considers that it is reasonable to do so.[3] If it refuses to exercise this discretion in your favour, request a review (see pp291-95).

Some people who are legally liable for rent are treated as though they are not liable with the result that they are not entitled to HB (see p220).

Joint liability

If you are a married or unmarried couple (see p319) and are jointly liable for the rent, only one of you can claim HB (see p265).[4]

If you are one of two or more single people who jointly occupy a home and have joint liability for the rent, you can all make separate claims for HB on your share (except in any case where the local authority thinks the joint tenancy has been 'contrived', see p220-21). The local authority apportions the eligible rent between you by considering:

- the number of jointly liable persons in the property; *and*
- the proportion of the rent actually paid by each liable person; *and*

- any other relevant factors – such as the number of rooms occupied by each jointly liable person and whether any formal or informal agreement exists between you regarding the use and occupation of the home.[5]

Where the rent includes any ineligible service charges etc., these will be apportioned between you on the same basis as the rent.[6] Note that the HB rules are different from those which apply in apportioning joint council tax liability for CTB purposes (see p302).

If only one of you is responsible for the rent, s/he is treated as the tenant and the other(s) as a non-dependant(s) (see p252).

The definition of 'unmarried couple' does not apply to lesbian or gay couples. You are regarded as two single people.

Special circumstances

If you have already paid your rent in advance before claiming HB, you can still claim HB towards it.[7]

If your landlord allows you a rent-free period as compensation for undertaking reasonable repairs or re-decoration which s/he would otherwise have had to carry out, you can still get HB. This only applies where you have actually carried out the work and then only for a maximum of eight benefit weeks in respect of any one rent-free period.[8] As you cease to be entitled to HB once a rent-free period has lasted more than eight benefit weeks, you should arrange with your landlord to schedule the work in periods of eight weeks or less separated by at least one complete benefit week where you resume paying rent.

Occupying accommodation as your home

Housing benefit can only be paid for accommodation which you normally occupy as your home.[9]

Where you or your family have more than one home, benefit is only payable on the accommodation regarded as your main home – except in certain circumstances listed below. This rule cannot be used to exclude from entitlement people who have set up home in the UK but whose family, who are no longer or who have never been, part of their household, remain living abroad[10] (but see habitual residence test – p223).

If your family is so large that the local authority have housed you in two separate dwellings, you are treated as occupying both and eligible for HB on both.[11] This does not apply if you rent two separate properties in the private rented sector.

Temporary absences from home

If you are temporarily absent from your home, have not rented it out and intend to return, you can continue to get HB as follows:

- for up to13 weeks if you are unlikely to be away for longer than this (but see below);[12]
- for up to 52 weeks if you are unlikely to be away for longer (or in exceptional circumstances, unlikely to be away for substantially longer) *and*:[13]
  - you are a remand prisoner held in custody pending trial or sentencing (including where you are in a bail hostel);
  - you are a hospital in-patient;
  - you or a dependent are undergoing medical treatment or medically approved convalescence in the UK or abroad;
  - you are providing, or receiving, 'medically approved' (ie, certified by a medical practitioner) care in the UK or abroad;
  - you are caring for a child whose parent or guardian is away from home receiving medically approved care or medical treatment;
  - you are undertaking a training course in the UK or abroad which is provided by, or on behalf of, or approved by a government department, the Secretary of State, Scottish Enterprise or Highlands and Islands Enterprise;
  - you are in residential accommodation. If you have entered this for a trial period to see if it is suitable and intend to return home if it is not, you are entitled to HB for up to 13 weeks. The 13-week period commences from the date you enter residential accommodation, provided your total period of absence does not exceed 52 weeks;
  - you are absent from home through fear of violence and are not liable for rent at your temporary address (if you are liable, see p218);
  - certain students who are eligible for HB (see pp260 and 218).

A new period of absence starts if you return home for even a short stay (DSS guidance states that a stay of at least 24 hours may be enough).[14] This does not apply, however, if you are a prisoner on temporary leave.[15]

Students and trainees

If you are either a single person or single parent who is an eligible student (see p260) or a trainee on a government training course, and living away from home during your course, you are treated as follows:

- If you are only liable for payments (including mortgage interest) at one address, then that is treated as your home, regardless of the proportion of time you actually live there. This would apply, for example, if you rent accommodation during term-time but return to live with your parents in the vacations.[16]

- If you are liable for payments at both addresses, you are only allowed to claim for the accommodation which is your main home.[17] If you are absent from that home, you may be entitled to HB for up to 52 weeks under the temporary absence rules (see p217).

If one member of a couple is an eligible student or trainee, and the couple unavoidably have to occupy separate homes and it is reasonable that HB should be paid in respect of both, the claimant is entitled to HB on both homes.[18]

Fear of violence

If you have left your previous home, and remain absent from it, through fear of, or actual violence in that home, or from a former member of your family outside the home, your HB entitlement will depend on your circumstances. 'Violence' can cover any violence that could take place within or at the home, even though it may originate from outside it – eg, racial violence.

- If you have gone to live somewhere else on a temporary basis where you are also liable to pay rent (eg, in a women's refuge) and you intend to return to occupy your former home – the local authority can continue to pay you HB on your former home as well as on your current home for up to 52 weeks if it thinks it is reasonable to do so.[19]
- If you have gone to live somewhere else on a temporary basis where you are not liable to pay rent (eg, with a close relative) and you intend to return to occupy your former home – the local authority can continue to pay you HB on your former home for up to 52 weeks under the normal temporary absence rules (see p217).
- If you have moved into a new home but remain unavoidably liable for the rent on your old home for a period after you have moved – the local authority can continue to pay you HB on your old home for up to four weeks after you moved out.[20] If you are liable for rent on your new home, you will also be able to get HB for this from the time you move in.[21]
- If you are absent from your home and are unavoidably liable to pay rent on that home, the local authority must pay you HB on your former home for up to four weeks after you moved out. This applies regardless of whether you are liable for rent on your new home and regardless of whether you intend to return.[22]

Temporary accommodation during repair work

If you move into temporary accommodation so that essential repairs can be carried out on your normal home and you are liable for payments on either (but not both) dwellings, you are treated as occupying, as your 'home', the accommodation on which you are liable to make payments.[23] If you are a private tenant you should not be liable for payments on your normal home while you are unable to live there. It is common practice for many local authorities not to make any charge for the temporary accommodation, but to continue to levy the rent on the home address. In this case, you are treated as still occupying your normal home and remain eligible for HB in respect of it. Where you do have a liability for both your normal and temporary homes, you are only regarded as occupying (and thus eligible for HB on) the one you normally occupy.

Moving house

If you have moved into new accommodation and are unavoidably liable to pay rent on both your old and new homes, you receive HB for both homes for up to four weeks. Under this rule, you only get HB on both homes if you have actually moved in.[24]

If you are not liable for rent on your old home (with one exception – see p220) you can claim HB on your new home for a period of up to four weeks before moving in, although you will not be paid until after the move.[25] To qualify for this retrospective HB you must have:

- moved into your new home;
- been liable to make payments on your new home before moving in;
- claimed HB before moving in and either, your claim was not decided until after you moved in, or it was refused (because you had not yet moved in) and you made a second claim within four weeks of moving in.

Furthermore, the delay in moving into your new home must have been reasonable and *either*:

- a member of your family is aged 5 or under, or your applicable amount includes one of the pensioner or disability premiums, and your move was delayed while the Benefits Agency decided on a claim for a social fund payment for a need connected with the move – eg, removal expenses or a household item or furniture; *or*
- the delay was necessary in order to adapt your new home to the disability needs of either you or a family member; *or*
- you became liable to make payments on your new home while you were a hospital patient or in residential accommodation.

If this rule applies and the delay was because you were waiting for disability adaptations, you can get HB on both homes for up to four weeks.[26] If the delay was for one of the other reasons, you can only get HB on the new home before you move in if you were not liable for rent on your old one.[27]

Who cannot claim

You cannot get HB if either:

- you fall into one of the groups of people who are treated as not liable for rent; *or*
- the payments you make are not eligible rent for HB (see p220).

People treated as not liable for rent

You are not entitled to HB if you fall into one of the groups of people who, even though they have to pay rent, are treated as though they are not liable to do so. This applies if:

- you are a full-time student[28] – with a few exceptions (see Chapter 14);
- you are a 'person from abroad' (see p220);[29]
- you pay rent to someone you live with *and*:
  - either it is not a commercial arrangement; *or*
  - s/he is a close relative (see p271).[30]

  You are regarded as living with your landlord if you share some accommodation with her/him other than a bathroom, toilet or hall/passageway. However, you can argue that you do not live with your landlord unless you also share living arrangements such as cooking and financial arrangements.

  DSS guidance suggests that local authorities should not assume you do not have a commercial arrangement just because you pay below a market rent or because the landlord does not rent for purely financial reasons, so long as s/he covers her/his expenses;[31]
- you have made an agreement to pay rent in order to take advantage of the HB scheme. This rule cannot be used if you have been liable to pay rent for the accommodation at any time during the eight weeks before you made the agreement.[32]

  Many local authorities assume that if you are living in accommodation owned by a friend or relative your rent liability must have been created to take advantage of the HB scheme. This assumption should always be challenged on review. Just because you are related to your landlord does not make a tenancy contrived! It may be useful to show that you were paying rent prior to claiming HB, or that the relative was renting the property to someone else previously. You could also explain that s/he needs to charge rent to cover outgoings on the property and that it was done for sound financial reasons, not just because HB was available to meet the rent. The High Court has criticised the argument that a tenancy must be contrived if you could not afford to live there without getting HB, since it could be said that this would disqualify all HB claimants! Instead, the local authority should consider all the circumstances – eg, your means, circumstances and intentions and those of your landlord. It should consider what would happen if HB was not paid – eg, you might be evicted;[33]

- you became jointly liable to pay rent within eight weeks of having been a non-dependant of one of the other joint occupiers, unless you can satisfy the local authority that the change in arrangements was not made to take advantage of the HB scheme;[34]
- you are a member of, and are fully maintained by, a religious order;[35]
- you are living in a residential care or nursing home[36] (but see p227).

Payments which are not eligible rent

You cannot get HB if the payments you make for your accommodation do not count as 'eligible rent'. This applies where:

- you are provided with residential accommodation by a local authority and it is either registered under the Registered Homes Act 1984 or owned or managed by the local authority and the charge includes meals.[37] Even if meals are not provided you cannot get HB for your accommodation costs if you were in the home on 31 March 1993 and excluded from HB at that time;[38]
- you own your accommodation or have a lease of more than 21 years – unless you are a 'shared owner' (ie, buying part of your house or flat and renting the rest), in which case you can get HB on the part you rent.[39] You are treated as the owner of the property if you have the right to sell it – even though you may not be able to do this without the consent of other joint owners;[40]
- you are getting income support (IS) and housing costs are included in your IS applicable amount (see p25).[41] If you are now getting your housing costs met through IS but were previously getting HB for the same accommodation, your HB continues for your first four weeks on IS. This is deducted from your IS so you do not get any extra benefit; it is merely an administrative arrangement to help with the transfer of housing costs from HB to IS;[42]
- you are a Crown tenant. There is a separate scheme for some Crown tenants, check with the Crown Agent;[43]

- you make payments under a co-ownership scheme under which you will receive a payment related to the value of the accommodation when you leave;[44]
- you make payments under a hire purchase (for, say, the purchase of a mobile home), credit sale or a conditional sale agreement except to the extent that it is in respect of land.[45]

Person(s) from abroad

'Person(s) from abroad' is a legal term rather than a literal description of the claimant. If you are classed as a person from abroad, you are not entitled to HB. The term applies to some foreign nationals but also to British nationals who fail the habitual residence test.

Local authorities have been advised to add questions to their claim forms asking about your nationality and whether you have come to this country in the last five years. Some local authorities substitute two years for five years (see p224). Detailed guidance has been issued to them to decide if you are a person from abroad, but there will sometimes be liaison between them and the Immigration and Nationality Department to check your immigration status. You should be advised if they are intending to do this. There will also be liaison between the local authority and the Benefits Agency if you are claiming IS as well, and information which you give to one department could be passed to the other.[46]

You may be interviewed to check out whether you are entitled to claim and you will certainly be asked to produce proof of your identity and immigration status. You do not have to produce your passport, but you will need some other way of verifying your status. If you do not have this, the local authority should interview you and make a decision on the balance of probabilities.

If you are a couple and your partner is not classed as a person from abroad, s/he can claim for you both and you are paid the full amount for a couple. However, in some cases your immigration status could be jeopardised by your partner's claim for HB, as it counts as 'public funds' under the Immigration Rules (see p65). If you are here subject to the condition that you should not have recourse to public funds, you should seek independent immigration advice before your partner claims HB. See p67 for more information – it may not be wise for your partner to claim.

If you are a married or unmarried couple and both of you are persons from abroad, you will not be entitled to HB.

If you are unsure about how a claim for HB might affect your right to remain in the UK, you should get independent advice about this before making a claim. If you subsequently discover that you can claim with no problems, you should ask for your benefit to be backdated on the grounds you have 'good cause for a late claim' (see p268).

You are classed as a **person from abroad** if you do not satisfy either

- the immigration status test (see below); *or*
- the habitual residence test (see below).

The immigration status test

You are **not classed as a person from abroad** under the immigration status test if:

- you are an **asylum-seeker** and satisfy certain conditions (see p224);
- you are a **sponsored immigrant** and satisfy certain conditions;
- you are in receipt of **IS/income-based jobseeker's allowance (JSA)**;
- you are in GB and left **Monserrat** after 1 November 1995 because of the effects of a volcanic eruption.[47]

You are classed as a person from abroad because of your immigration status if you do not fall into one of the above groups *and*;

- you have limited leave to enter or remain in the UK subject to the requirement that you have no recourse to public funds[48] but this does not apply if:[49]
  - either you are a national of the European Economic Area (EEA) (see p72 for a list of countries), Malta, Turkey or Cyprus; *or*
  - your funds from abroad have been temporarily disrupted and there is a reasonable expectation that they will resume (provided you have not been without funds for more than 42 days in one period of limited leave);
- you were given limited leave to enter or remain in the UK and have overstayed the period of your leave;[50]
- you are subject to a deportation order unless your removal has been deferred in writing by the Secretary of State;[51]
- you are an illegal entrant unless you have the Secretary of State's written consent to stay;[52]
- you are an EEA national who has been required to leave by the Secretary of State (see p75);[53]
- you are an asylum-seeker in certain circumstances (see p224);
- you are a sponsored immigrant in certain circumstances (see p224).

The habitual residence test

You are also classed as a person from abroad if you are **not habitually resident and are not treated as habitually resident** in the UK.[54] The DSS recommended that the test be applied to any claimant who has been resident here for under five years.[55] Some local authorities have decided to follow the advice of the Social Security Advisory Committee and apply the test only to those claimants resident for less than two years.[56]

You are not classed as a person from abroad under the habitual residence test if you are actually habitually resident or are treated as habitually resident. You are treated as habitually resident if you are:[57]

- an **asylum-seeker** and satisfy certain conditions;
- a **sponsored immigrant** and satisfy certain conditions;
- in receipt of **IS/income-based JSA**;
- you are in GB and left **Monserrat** after 1 November 1995 because of the effects of a volcanic eruption;
- you are an EEA worker or from an EEA State or have a right to reside in the UK;
- you are a refugee;
- you have exceptional leave to remain;
- your funds from abroad have been temporarily disrupted and there is a reasonable expectation that they will resume (provided you have not been without funds for more than 42 days in one period of limited leave);
- you are subject to a deportation order but your deportation has been deferred in writing by the Secretary of State;
- you are an illegal entrant who has the Secretary of State's written consent to stay.

People with sponsorship undertakings

If you were given leave to enter the UK subject to a sponsorship undertaking, you are entitled to HB if either:[58]

- you have been resident in the UK for at least five years; *or*
- the person who gave the undertaking has died; *or*
- you were entitled to or were receiving HB before 5 February 1996.[59]

For more about sponsorship undertakings and benefit see p82.

Asylum-seekers

If you are an asylum-seeker, you are entitled to HB if either:

- you applied for asylum on arrival in the UK (for the meaning of this see pp78-80); *or*
- you applied for asylum within the three months following a declaration by the Secretary of State that your country is subject to such a fundamental change of circumstances that you would not normally be ordered to return there;[60] *or*

- you were entitled to HB as an asylum-seeker before 5 February 1996.[61] In this case you remain entitled until you receive a decision on your application. You are not entitled pending an appeal unless the decision was made before 5 February 1996.[62]

For more about asylum seekers, see p77.

Retrospective entitlement to housing benefit/ council tax benefit if you are granted refugee status

If you are notified that you have been granted refugee status, you do not count as a person from abroad and can therefore claim HB/council tax benefit (CTB) from that date. If, while you were seeking asylum, you were not entitled to HB/CTB because you were classed as a person from abroad, you may be entitled to a retrospective award of HB/CTB for that past period.

Claims

You must make a claim for retrospective HB/CTB within 28 days of the date you are notified by the Secretary of State that you have been recorded as a refugee.[63] You must claim within the time limit as a late claim cannot be backdated.[64] If you have lived in more than one local authority area, you should make your claim to the local authority in whose area you last lived before being granted refugee status.[65]

Date of claim

Your HB/CTB claim will be treated as made on either:[66]

- *if you applied for asylum on arrival* in the UK, from the date your application was first refused or 5 February 1996, whichever is later; *or*
- *if you applied for asylum other than on arrival* in the UK (see p 78), the date of your asylum application or 5 February 1996, whichever is later.

HB/CTB can be paid for whole or part of the period from the date the claim is treated as made until the date you were notified of your refugee status.[67] Any HB/CTB which has already been paid to you or any partner of yours over this period is deducted from your award.[68]

Example

Meral applied for asylum on arrival in the UK in December 1995. She was paid HB until March 1996, when her asylum application was refused. In October 1996, she started living as a couple with Barry who has since been claiming HB for both of them. In April 1997, she is granted refugee status. She claims HB immediately.

Meral is entitled to retrospective HB from the March 1996 (when her asylum application was refused) until April 1997 when she was granted refugee status. However, the award is reduced by the amount of HB paid to her partner for both of them from October 1996 onwards.

How your claim is assessed

You must provide any evidence and information you have or could reasonably get which the local authority may reasonably require to determine your entitlement.[69] The authority can ask for information from your landlord, from the person you paid rent to, from any person who paid the rent on your behalf or from another local authority.[70]

You must notify the local authority of any changes of circumstances which might be relevant to your HB/CTB entitlement over the period for which you are claiming.[71] Where you are unable to provide the necessary evidence, the local authority must determine your claim on the basis of the information you have been able to provide.[72]

Payment of benefit

Once the local authority decides you are entitled to retrospective HB/CTB, they must make payment within 14 days.[73] Any outstanding council tax liability for the period covered by the award is paid off before any remaining CTB is paid to you. If your rent has not been paid, part or all of your HB award can be paid direct to the landlord. If your landlord was a local authority, any eligible rent owing to them is deducted from your award and only the balance paid to you.[74] Otherwise, HB can be paid to your landlord where the local authority considers it reasonable to do so.[75] The landlord must show that you have not paid your rent for part or all of the period of your award and the local authority must give you an opportunity to give reasons why payment should not be made to the landlord.

Residential care or nursing homes

Payments for residential care and nursing homes are usually not covered by HB.[76]

If you are provided with accommodation by a local authority see p221. If you live in a private or voluntary home you can claim if:

- you were entitled to, or became entitled to HB, before 30 October 1990.[77] This protection lasts for life;
- you lived there prior to 1 April 1993 and were either in full-time work, or making payments on a commercial basis in a home run by a close relative, or living in a home for less than four people. This protection applies until you leave the home (apart from temporary absences) or if you cease to qualify for HB;[78]
- you live in a Royal Charter or Act of Parliament residential home (eg, Salvation Army establishments). You can claim either IS or HB to cover your accommodation costs. This does not apply if you are in a nursing home;
- you live in a small home which is not required to be registered under the Registered Homes Act 1984 – eg, some adult placement or supported lodging schemes.

If you are entitled to HB while in a residential care or nursing home, the tariff income and capital rules differ from the normal ones – see p385.

2. 'ELIGIBLE RENT'

Your 'eligible rent' is the amount of your rent which is taken into account for the purpose of calculating your housing benefit (HB). It may be less than the actual amount that you pay because it might not include all payments.

Your eligible rent is your contractual rent, minus:

- any ineligible charges (see p228); *and minus*
- any amount above the level to which your rent is restricted under the rent restriction rules (see p282).

Students may find their eligible rent further reduced by the student rent deduction (see p263).

If you are jointly liable you can claim HB on your 'share' (see p215).

What counts as 'eligible rent'

The following charges are eligible rent for HB purposes:[79]

- Rent you pay in respect of a tenancy.
- Payments you make in respect of a licence or other permission to occupy premises.
- Mesne profits (in Scotland, violent profits) which include payments made if you remain in occupation when a tenancy has been ended.
- Other payments for use and occupation of premises.
- Payments of eligible service charges (see p230) required as a condition of occupation.
- Rent, including mooring charges for a houseboat.
- Site rent for a caravan or mobile home (but not a tent, although that might be met through IS – see p25).
- Rent paid on a garage or land (unless used for business purposes). Either you must be making a reasonable effort to end your liability for it, or you must have been unable to rent your home without it.[80]
- Contributions made by a resident of a charity's almshouse.
- Payments made under a rental purchase agreement under which the purchase price is paid in more than one instalment and you will not finally own your home until all, or an agreed part of, the purchase price has been paid.
- In Scotland, payments in respect of croft land.

Parts of your rent which are not eligible

You may find that your HB is less than your contractual rent because ineligible charges are deducted. Ineligible charges include:

- Most fuel charges (see below).
- Some service charges (see p231).
- Charges for meals (see p231).
- Water rates.[81]
- Payments for any part of your accommodation which is used exclusively for business purposes.[82]
- Rent supplements charged to clear your rent arrears.[83]
- Any amount above the level to which your rent is restricted under the rent restriction rules (see pp232-46).[84]

Fuel charges

As a rule of thumb, if the charge is specified this amount is deducted from your rent. If the charge is not specified, a fixed amount is deducted.

- If your fuel charge is specified on your rent book or is readily identifiable from your agreement with your landlord – the full amount of the charge is deducted in arriving at your eligible rent.[85] Where your fuel charge is specified but the local authority considers it to be unrealistically low in relation to the fuel provided, the charge is treated as unspecified and a flat-rate deduction made instead (see below).

This is also the case where your total fuel charge is specified but contains an unknown amount for communal areas. If you are a council tenant, the regulations assume your fuel charges are always specified or readily identifiable since the local authority is also your landlord.[86]

- If your fuel charge is not readily identifiable – a flat-rate deduction is made for fuel.[87] The flat-rate fuel deductions are:

(a) Where you and your family occupy more than one room:
  – for heating (other than hot water)   £9.25
  – for hot water   £1.15
  – for lighting   £0.80
  – for cooking   £1.15

(b) Where you and your family occupy one room only:
  – for heating alone, or heating combined with either hot water or lighting or both   £5.60
  – for cooking   £1.15

These amounts are added together where fuel is supplied for more than one purpose. If you are a joint tenant, all the deductions are apportioned according to your share of the rent.[88]

Where flat-rate fuel deductions have been made in calculating your HB, the local authority must notify you about this and explain that if you can produce evidence from which the actual or approximate amount of your fuel charge can be estimated, the flat-rate deductions may be varied accordingly.[89] However, there is no point in providing such evidence unless it is likely to show that your charge is less than the flat-rate deductions – eg, where you live in a small bedsit.

Guidance suggests that the lower deduction for one room only should apply where you occupy one room exclusively – even if you share other rooms (such as a bathroom or kitchen, or communal lounge in a hotel).[90] You should also argue for the lower level of deductions to be made where you are forced to live in one room because the other room(s) in your accommodation are, in practice, unfit to live in – eg, because of severe mould/dampness etc).

Fuel for communal areas

If you pay a service charge for the use of fuel in communal areas, and that charge is separately identified from any other charge for fuel used within your accommodation, it may be included as part of your eligible rent.[91] Communal areas include access areas like halls and passageways, but not rooms in common use except those in sheltered accommodation – eg, a shared TV lounge or dining-room etc.[92] If you pay a charge for the provision of a heating system (eg, regular boiler maintenance etc), this is also eligible where the amount is separately identified from any other fuel charge you pay.[93]

Service charges

Most service charges are covered by HB, but only if payment is a condition of occupying the accommodation rather than an optional extra.[94] Some service charges are specifically excluded (see p231).

The following services are eligible for HB:

- Services for the provision of adequate accommodation including general management costs, gardens, children's play areas, lifts, entry phones, communal telephone costs, portering, rubbish removal, TV and radio relay (only relay for ordinary UK channels is covered – not satellite dishes or decoders. Cable TV is also excluded unless it is the only practicable way of providing you with ordinary domestic channels).[95]
- Laundry facilities (eg, a laundry room in an apartment block), but not charges for the provision of personal laundry.[96]
- Furniture and household equipment, but not if there is an agreement that the furniture will eventually become yours.[97]
- Cleaning of communal areas.[98]
- Cleaning within your own accommodation, but only if no one living in the household is able to do it.[99]
- Emergency alarm systems in accommodation designed or adapted for elderly, sick or disabled people, or which is otherwise suitable for them taking into account factors such as size, heating system or other facilities. In all other cases, emergency alarms are ineligible.[100]
- Counselling and support services, but only to the extent that they are necessary for the provision of adequate accommodation, or are provided by someone (whether a landlord or her/his employee) who spends the majority of time during which s/he provides services, providing services which are eligible.[101]

If the local authority regards any of the above charges as excessive it will estimate a reasonable amount given the cost of comparable services.[102]

The following services are not eligible for HB:[103]

- food including prepared meals (see below);
- sports facilities;
- TV rental and licence fees (but see p230);
- transport;
- personal laundry service;
- medical expenses;
- nursing and personal care;
- counselling and other support services (but see p230);
- any other charge not connected with the provision of adequate accommodation and not specifically included in the list of eligible charges above.

Any ineligible service charge must be deducted in full from your rent. Where the ineligible charge is specified, this amount is deducted. Authorities have the power to substitute their own estimate where they consider the amount is unreasonably low.[104] Where the amount is not specified in your rent agreement, the local authority estimates how much is fairly attributable to the service, given the cost of comparable services.[105] Where a HB claim is referred to the rent officer, s/he will provide a valuation for certain services (see p236).

Charges for meals

Where your housing costs include an amount for meals, the local authority makes set deductions.[106] These always apply, regardless of the actual cost of your meals.[107]

Where at least three meals a day are provided:
- for the claimant and each additional member of the family aged 16 (see p232) or over — £17.55
- for each additional member of the family aged under 16 — £ 8.85

Where breakfast only is provided:
- for the claimant and each additional member of the family, regardless of age — £ 2.10

In all other cases (part-board):
- for the claimant and each additional member of the family aged 16 or over — £11.65
- for each additional member of the family aged under 16 — £ 5.85

For these purposes, a person is treated as having attained the age of 16 on the first Monday in September following her/his 16th birthday.

The standard deductions are made for everyone who has meals paid for by you – including meals for someone who is not part of your 'family' – eg, a non-dependant.[108]

3. RENT RESTRICTIONS

The amount of your eligible rent may be restricted if the local authority decide that either your rent is too high or accommodation too large. If you live in a deregulated private tenancy new rules for deciding whether your rent should be restricted came into force on 2 January 1996 (the 'local reference rent' rules). The rules in force before January 1996 continue to apply to certain claimants who are exempt from the local reference rent rules. Where the local reference rent rules do apply and you are a single claimant aged under 25 you may find your rent restricted to the level of the 'single room rent' by the rules which came into force on 7 October 1996.

Further restrictions come into force in October 1997 affecting claims subject to the local reference rent rules (see pp238 and 239.)

If the local reference rent rules apply, your eligible rent is restricted to the level of the 'maximum rent' (see p238). If the pre-January rules apply, your eligible rent may be restricted to an amount the local authority considers appropriate (see p243).

Summary of local authority rent restriction procedure

The procedure for restricting rent can be summarised as follows:

Step 1: The local authority refers your claim to the rent officer unless you have an excluded tenancy (see p233).
Step 2: The rent officer makes determinations as to the level of rent and size of your accommodation (see p233).
Step 3: The local authority decides whether you are exempt from the local reference rent rules (see p236).
Step 4: If you are not exempt, the local reference rent rules apply. The local authority calculates your maximum rent on the basis of the rent officer determinations. If your rent is restricted the local authority may use its discretion to pay extra (see p240). The local authority checks to see whether there should be a delay before any restriction is imposed (see p239).

Step 5: If you are exempt from the local reference rent rules, the local authority decides whether to restrict your rent using the rules in force pre-January 1996 (see p248). The local authority checks to see whether there should be a delay before any restriction is imposed (see p248).

Excluded tenancies (Step 1 – see p232)

Following a claim for HB, the local authority must make a reference to the rent officer unless your tenancy is an 'excluded tenancy'.[109] Excluded tenancies are:[110]

- a regulated tenancy (that is a tenancy entered into before 15 January 1989 or, in Scotland, 2 January 1989);
- a Home Office bail hostel or probation hostel;
- a housing action trust tenancy;
- a former local authority or new town letting which has been transferred to a new owner, unless there has been a rent increase since the transfer, and the local authority considers your accommodation is unreasonably large or expensive;
- a registered housing association letting, unless the local authority considers your accommodation to be unreasonably large or expensive.

If your tenancy is excluded, the local authority can use their general power to decrease your eligible rent (see p241) to an amount it considers 'appropriate'. It should have evidence and objective justification to do so and must exercise its discretion properly. You can ask for a review (see p291).

Rent officer determinations (Step 2 – see p232)

If your tenancy is not excluded (see above), the local authority refers it to the rent officer.[111] The rent officer may make a number of determinations about your rent making comparison with other private sector rents in the locality. These determinations are valid for 12 months. However, a tenancy can be referred back to the rent officer within this period, for example, if there is a change in the terms of the tenancy, the composition of the household, the condition of the property or if a child reaches the age of 10 or 16.[112] This means that a determination made for a previous tenant may be valid for your claim. If you are not given details of the rent officer's determinations, consider asking for a written statement of reasons (see p292).

The rent officer may make determinations relevant to your specific property (the significantly high rent, size-related rent and exceptionally high rent) as well as determinations which indicate the average rents for specific types of accommodation in the locality (the local reference rent and single room rents).

Significantly high rent determination

If your rent is significantly higher than that paid for similar tenancies and dwellings, the rent officer determines an amount your landlord might reasonably have got for your tenancy.[113]

Size-related rent determination

If your accommodation is larger than you are allowed under the size criteria, the rent officer determines an amount your landlord might reasonably have got for a similar tenancy of an appropriate size. [114]

The size criteria

One bedroom, or room suitable for living in, is allowed for each of the following occupiers (each occupier coming only into the first category for which they are eligible):[115]

- a married or unmarried couple;
- a person who is not a child (ie, aged 16 or over);
- two children of the same sex;
- two children under 10;
- a child.

In addition, you are allowed the following number of rooms suitable for living in:

Number of occupiers	Number of rooms
less than 4	1
4-6	2
7 or more	3

A person counts as an 'occupier' if the local authority includes them on the form they use to refer your tenancy to the rent officer.[116] You may be able to argue that, for example, a child who comes to stay regularly, although not a member of your family, is an occupier and should be included on the form so that their needs can be taken into account.

If any of the rooms in your home are not suitable for living in (for example, because of their size, condition or lack of ventilation) you should argue that they should be ignored.

Exceptionally high rent determination

If your rent or the lowest of the determinations made so far is exceptionally high, the rent officer determines the highest amount which your landlord might reasonably have got for an assured tenancy of an appropriate size.[117]

Single room rent

The rent officer only provides a single room rent figure if you are a 'young individual' (see p239). S/he does not notify the local authority of the amount of the single room rent unless it is lower than your rent or the lowest of the determinations made so far.[118]

The single room rent is the midpoint of 'reasonable market rents' for accommodation in which the tenant has exclusive use of one room only and other than that only shares (or has no) kitchen, shares a toilet and makes no payment for board or attendance.[119]

(**Note:** *The Government has announced that they intend to extend the single room rent to single claimants aged 25–59 from October 1997* – see p239.)

Local reference rent

The local reference rent is the midpoint of 'reasonable market rents' for assured tenancies of an appropriate size (under the size criteria).[120] It is only provided if your rent or the lowest of the rent officer determinations (excluding the single room rent) exceeds it.

Example 1
Tina lives in a one-bedroom flat. It has a separate living room. Her rent is £60 a week. The rent officer decides that, although the accommodation is an appropriate size, the rent is too high for the tenancy and so notifies the local authority of the following:

Significantly high rent determination	£55
Local reference rent	£50

Example 2
Paul and Sarah share a two-bedroom flat which has a living room and a dining room. They pay £75 rent a week. The rent officer decides that the accommodation is too big and the rent too high for the property, so notifies the local authority of the following:

Significantly high rent determination	£65
Size-related rent determination	£60
Local reference rent	£50

Example 3
Carl has a two-bedroom flat with two living rooms. He pays £90 a week rent. The rent officer decides that, not only is the flat too big but the rent is too high. S/he also thinks that the rent is exceptionally high. The local authority is notified of the following:

Significantly high rent determination	£80
Size-related rent determination	£70
Exceptionally high rent determination	£75
Local reference rent	£50

Service charges in rent officer determinations

Rent officer determinations do not include charges for medical expenses, nursing, personal care or ineligible counselling and support.[121] The significantly high, size-related and local reference rent figures include charges for fuel, meals and water if these are included in your contractual rent.[122] If the determinations include other ineligible charges, the rent officer will provide a valuation of these services.[123] The exceptionally high rent determination only includes charges for fuel and meals where the rent officer specifies this.[124] The local reference rent (see p235) excludes ineligible charges apart from fuel, meals and water.[125] The single room rent does not include any services[126] (except that fuel and water charges will be deducted from the single room rent for 25-29-year-olds – see p239).

Notification

The rent officer notifies the local authority of her/his determinations within five working days or 25 if s/he intends to visit.[127]

Exemption from the local reference rent rules (Step 3 – see p231)

The local authority must decide whether you are exempt from the local reference rent rules. You are exempt if you are either an exempt claimant or live in exempt accommodation.[128]

You are an **exempt claimant** if:

• you have been continuously entitled to and in receipt of HB since 1 January 1996. Breaks in your claim of up to four weeks are ignored.[129] Remember that you may be able to get your claim backdated; *and*

- you continue to occupy the same property as your home (except where you are forced to move because fire, flood or natural catastrophe makes it uninhabitable).

If you are thinking of making any changes to your claim, you should check that you will not lose your exemption by so doing. This would happen, for example, if you moved (including moving rooms within the same house) or if your partner took over the claim (but see below).

An exemption can be **transferred** to a new claimant in some limited circumstances. You are an exempt claimant if:

- you claim HB because an exempt claimant dies and you are a member of the former claimant's family, or any relative occupying the same accommodation without a separate right to do so. You must continue to occupy the same property and make your claim within four weeks of the death. If you can get your claim backdated to within the four weeks, you may be able to argue that the exemption should be transferred to you (see p268);
- you claim HB because your partner (who was exempt) has been detained in custody and is not entitled to HB under the temporary absence rules. You must continue to occupy the same property and must make your claim within four weeks of the imprisonment;
- you claim HB because your former partner (who was exempt) has left the dwelling and you are no longer living together as husband and wife. You must continue to occupy the same property and claim within four weeks of the date they left.

You live in **exempt accommodation** if:

- you live in hostel accommodation for people without a fixed way of life which is funded by the Resettlement Agency;[130]
- you live in accommodation provided by a housing association, non-metropolitan county council, registered charity or voluntary organisation where care, support or supervision is provided either by your landlord or, on her/his behalf, by someone else.[131] These terms are not defined in law and are open to review. It may be possible to argue that your accommodation is provided by one of the relevant organisations even if they are not actually your landlord.

If you are exempt, the local authority has to decide whether to restrict your rent using the pre-January 1996 rules (see p248).

The local authority determines the maximum rent (Step 4 – see p232)

If you are not exempt, the local reference rent rules apply and the local authority calculates your 'maximum rent' on the basis of the rent officer's determinations.

Definitions[132]
- The *reckonable rent* is your contractual rent minus ineligible charges apart from fuel, meals and water.
- The *relevant rent* is the lowest of the significantly high, size related and exceptionally high rent determinations minus ineligible charges apart from fuel, meals and water.
- The *appropriate rent* is the lowest of the reckonable and relevant rents. (This is a local authority term, not one found in regulations.)
- The *maximum rent* is the figure to which your eligible rent is restricted after the calculation has been done.

The calculation

To calculate your maximum rent, the local authority identify your appropriate rent (see above). It then compares the appropriate rent with the local reference rent (see p235).

If your appropriate rent is less than the local reference rent, the maximum rent is the appropriate rent.

If the appropriate rent is higher than the local reference rent, the maximum rent is the local reference rent plus half the difference between the local reference rent and appropriate rent (subject to a maximum of twice the local reference rent).[133]

(Any amount for fuel, meals and water is deducted at the final stage.[134])

Your HB will be restricted to the level of the maximum rent although the local authority can use their discretion to pay extra HB (see p240). There may also be a delay before the restriction is imposed (see p239).

From October 1997, HB will only be paid up to the level of the local reference rent. However, if you are getting HB which includes the 50 per cent top up outlined above, you remain eligible for the 50 per cent top up in certain circumstances. This will apply if you remain continuously entitled to and in receipt of HB for the same dwelling and you are:

- aged under 60 but are not a 'single claimant' or a young individual; *or*
- aged 60 or over.

The single room rent is to be extended to apply to single people aged 25-29. It will apply to you if you are not exempt from the local reference rent rules, are classed as a 'single claimant' and make or renew a claim or move after 5 October 1997. You do not count as a 'single claimant' if you are a housing association tenant, have the severe disability premium, or have a non-dependant living with you. See CPAG's *Welfare Rights Bulletin* for further details.

Under 25s

You are a 'young individual' if you are a single claimant (not a single parent) under the age of 25 who is neither a housing association tenant nor a care leaver under the age of 22.[135] If you are a young individual and subject to the local reference rent rules (see p236), the single room rent (see p235) applies. If your maximum rent calculated as described above is lower than the single room rent, then that maximum rent figure will apply. Otherwise, your maximum rent will be the single room rent.[136] (NB The local authority may use their discretion to pay more (see p240).) There may be a delay before the restriction is imposed (see below).

See CPAG's *Welfare Rights Bulletin* for updates.

Renegotiating your rent

Once the maximum rent figure has been calculated, your HB will continue to be paid at this level for the rest of the benefit period unless you negotiate a level below that of the maximum rent, in which case you get HB up to the level to which you have renegotiated.[137] (The same applies if you renegotiate your rent following a pre-tenancy determination.[138])

If the landlord increases your rent, you can ask for a discretionary payment to cover the increase (see p240).

Delay in applying rent restrictions

If a member of your family or a relative who occupied the same dwelling without a separate right to do so, dies, then either no restriction applies for 12 months from the date of death or any maximum rent which applied at the time of death continues to do so for the 12 months.[139]

If you, or a family member or relative (as above), could meet the payments when you took the tenancy on, no restriction can be made for 13 weeks provided you did not receive HB in the preceding 52 weeks.[140]

Discretion to increase entitlement

If the local authority restricts your eligible rent for HB purposes you should ask it to exercise its discretion to increase your eligible rent.[141] You must be entitled to some HB on the basis of the maximum rent figure.

You will also have to show that unless the maximum eligible rent is increased, you, or a member of your family, will suffer 'exceptional hardship'. This is not defined but should be given its ordinary everyday meaning. If in doubt, apply. The amount of the discretionary payment cannot take your HB entitlement to a level higher than that to which you would be entitled had no rent restriction taken place. (Note that if the rent officer has attributed too much of your rent to ineligible service charges (see p236), the local authority can substitute a lower figure in deciding the level up to which discretionary payments can be made.)

Local authorities have been issued with guidance providing a list of factors which they may want to consider when deciding whether there is exceptional hardship.[142] The guidance is not exhaustive nor binding – every claim should be considered on its merits.

The factors the local authority may take into account include:

- Is there a risk of eviction if the shortfall in the rent is not met? The local authority may consider other outgoings you have which may make it harder for you to meet the shortfall.
- Do you have any assets or disregarded income which might be used to meet the shortfall? If you do have savings or disregarded income, it does not automatically follow that it is reasonable for them to be used to meet any shortfall. It may be for example, that you have other priority expenses or debts, or that your savings are small and would soon be exhausted.
- Is it possible for you to negotiate with the landlord for a reduction in your rent? The local authority should not assume that it is reasonable or possible for you to negotiate with your landlord. However, a statement from your landlord that your rent cannot be reduced may improve your chances of getting a payment.
- Do you, or a member of your family, suffer from any health problems? If you do, this may affect your ability to find cheaper alternative accommodation. The shortfall in HB may lead to a deterioration in your health or the health of a member of your family.

Your local authority may use local guidance to reflect local needs and priorities but this should not conflict with the national guidance. It may be helpful to see any local guidance before making an application or, if unsuccessful, applying for review. The total amount of discretionary spending under this provision will be strictly cash-limited and only partly funded through central government subsidy.

If a decision is made to make a discretionary payment, the award will last for the length of the benefit period unless there is a relevant change in your circumstances. The local authority can set the benefit for a short period if it anticipates a change of circumstances and can review your award in the light of budgetary or other considerations.

It is possible for you to be awarded a discretionary payment as outlined above in addition to an exceptional circumstances payment (see p256).[143] It is probably best to ask for both types of payment in the same letter.

Discretion to decrease entitlement

In addition to the powers to restrict your eligible rent, outlined above, the local authority also has the power to reduce the amount of your eligible rent if it considers that the figure imposed under the rent officer procedures is too high.[144] The local authority has to exercise this power properly and should be challenged by way of review if you do not consider that it has done so.

This discretion does not apply to cases exempt from the local reference rent rules (see p236),[145] but can be applied in cases excluded from referral to the rent officer (see p233) – for example, where you are over occupying.

Pre-tenancy determinations

If you are thinking of renting accommodation privately you can apply to the local authority for a pre-tenancy determination (PTD).[146] This will tell you what rent figure will be used to calculate your HB. You can apply if you are already receiving HB and your tenancy is due for renewal. You can also apply if you are already renting accommodation privately and think you are going to have to claim HB in the near future – eg, because of a drop in your income.

If you wish to apply for a PTD you obtain a form from your local authority. You will need to complete it and ask your prospective landlord to sign it. You then return it to the local authority. It must then be forwarded to the rent officer within three days of receipt.[147] The rent officer will then send you, the prospective landlord and the local authority the rent figures which s/he has decided within five working days unless they need more details from the local authority.[148]

If you rent the property these will be the figures used to calculate your HB. The PTD is valid in respect of the individual property for 12 months from the date it is made unless the terms of the tenancy agreement are changed, or your family composition changes. You may, therefore, find that your request for a PTD is returned by the local authority to you, because someone else has applied, within the last 12 months, for a PTD on the same property and with the same family composition as yours. Their PTD is binding on you.

You cannot appeal against a PTD unless you accept the tenancy and claim HB in which case you can request a review and ask that the rent officer looks at it again.

If you subsequently negotiate a lower rent with your landlord – see p239.

Review

You have the right, under the standard HB review procedures (see p291), to challenge a restriction in your eligible rent. However, because of the way that maximum rent is calculated, the scope for review is limited. Your review request could relate to, either:

- the rent officer determinations; *or*
- a local authority decision either to refuse to use its discretion to increase the amount of benefit payable so that the full amount of your eligible rent is met.

If your request relates to the **rent officer** figures, the local authority must pass any representations you make or evidence you supply to the rent officer within seven days. While it is not easy to challenge rent officers because they have access to a large database with information of rents in the area, it may be possible in some circumstances. If, for example, the rent officer has said your rent is significantly high, you may be able to get them to reconsider by providing evidence of similar tenancies where tenants who are not on HB are paying the same rent as you. The rent officer must get the advice of one or two other rent officers and notify the local authority of their decision within 20 working days.

The rent officer can reduce your maximum rent if you request a review so you need carefully to consider your position before so doing. You could end up with less HB as a result. If, as a result of redetermination by the rent officer the maximum rent is increased, the increase applies from the date of the original determination – ie, you are awarded any arrears of HB which result from it. If the maximum rent is reduced it does not apply retrospectively and does not mean that you will have been overpaid.[149]

If your review request relates to a decision on discretionary payments, put forward any arguments that will help to satisfy the authority that you will suffer exceptional hardship if extra payments are not made. Even if they are satisfied of this, they will not be able to make the payments if the budget would be exceeded. If you are asking for a further review (see p293), the review board can only review determinations the local authority have made, so make sure you have already asked for discretionary payments to be considered at an earlier stage.

The pre-January 1996 rules (Step 5 – see p232)

If you are exempt from the local reference rent rules (see p236), the local authority uses the pre-January 1996 rules in deciding whether to restrict your eligible rent.

If the local authority decides to impose a rent restriction in your case, you should insist on a full explanation. If you believe that the local authority has failed to apply all the proper tests or has been influenced by irrelevant facts, you should ask for a review.

The various steps which local authorities must take are as follows:

- The local authority considers whether your rent or accommodation is unreasonable (see below).
- If your rent or accommodation is unreasonable, the local authority must consider whether you are in a protected group.
- If you are in a protected group, the local authority cannot restrict your rent unless there is suitable alternative accommodation available to you and it is reasonable to expect you to move.
- If your rent or accommodation is unreasonable and either you are not in a protected group, or you are, but there is cheaper suitable alternative accommodation for you to move to, the local authority can restrict to an appropriate level (see p245).
- The local authority considers whether there should be a delay before the restriction applies.

Is your rent or accommodation unreasonable?

The local authority can only consider your rent or accommodation unreasonable if either of the following apply:[150]

- your accommodation is larger than is reasonably needed for you and anyone who also occupies the accommodation (including non-dependants and sub-tenants) – taking account of suitable alternative accommodation occupied by other households of the same size; *or*
- your rent is unreasonably high compared with that for suitable alternative accommodation elsewhere. Rent includes, among other things, any service charges or licence fees you have to pay.[151] The local authority is not bound by the rent officer figures. Although they may have regard to them, their decision should be made on the above criteria which are different from the rent officer's criteria.

Is your home too large?

The needs of everyone living in your accommodation must be considered. For example, you might need additional space because someone has a disability, or they live elsewhere but regularly come to visit you. You should also argue that it is reasonable to remain in a home where you have lived for many years but which is now larger than you need.

Is it too expensive?

It is not sufficient for the local authority to show that cheaper alternative accommodation exists. It must also be 'suitable' for you personally,[152] – eg, if you currently have security of tenure, any suitable alternative accommodation should have the same. Like should be compared with like – eg, if you have a private sector tenancy, no comparison should be made with local authority or housing association rents.

The Court of Appeal has said that comparisons should only be made with suitable alternative accommodation which forms part of an 'active housing market'. This means that the accommodation must currently be available for rent, although not necessarily to the claimant.[153] Local authorities should also not 'make comparisons with other parts of the country where accommodation costs differ widely from those which apply locally'.[154]

It is not enough for the local authority to argue that your rent is merely higher than that for suitable alternative accommodation. It must be 'unreasonably' higher. In making this comparison, the local authority must consider the full spectrum of rents which could be paid for such accommodation and not just the cheapest.[155]

Are you in a protected group?

If the local authority has decided that your rent is unreasonable, it must then consider whether you are in a protected group.[156] You are in a protected group if you, any member of your family (see p318) or a relative who occupies the same accommodation without a separate right to do so:

- is aged 60 or over; *or*
- satisfies any of the tests of being incapable of work for social security purposes (see p10); *or*
- has a child or young person living with them for whom they are responsible (see p325).

If you are in a protected group, then the local authority must go on to consider whether cheaper suitable alternative accommodation is available and whether it is reasonable to expect you to move.[157]

Is there cheaper suitable alternative accommodation?

If a local authority considers that suitable alternative accommodation is available, it does not need to refer to specific properties, but must have sufficient evidence to demonstrate the existence of an 'active housing market' in accommodation of a suitable type, rent and location for you.[158] It is not sufficient to say that, in general, there are a lot of cheaper properties available locally.[159] Accommodation should not be regarded as available if, in practice, there is little or no possibility of the claimant being able to obtain it – eg, because it could only be obtained on payment of a large deposit.[160] You should insist on being told exactly what accommodation is being referred to, why it is considered 'suitable' for you and those who live with you, and on what evidence it is considered to actually be available to you.

Is it reasonable to expect you to move?

The regulations compel local authorities to consider the adverse effects of a move on your job and on the education of any child or young person living with you.[161] The authority can also take account of any other relevant factors. You should press the local authority to consider other relevant factors. If they refuse to do so, you should request a review.

If your rent or accommodation is unreasonable and either:
– you are not in a protected group; *or*
– you are in a protected group but there is cheaper suitable alternative accommodation available and it is reasonable to expect you to move; the local authority must restrict your eligible rent to whatever it considers appropriate. It must take into account your individual circumstances and the cost of suitable alternative accommodation elsewhere.

Although the local authority should not be unduly influenced by the amount of subsidy payable it could take this into account when deciding on a reasonable level of eligible rent. The reduction cannot reduce the eligible rent below that payable for suitable alternative accommodation.[162]

Should there be a delay before a restriction is applied?

No restriction can be made within 12 months of the death of a member of your family or a relative who occupied the same accommodation without a separate right to do so.[163] If you, a family member or relative (as above) could meet the payments when you took on the tenancy, no restriction applies for 13 weeks providing you were not in receipt of HB in the preceding 52 weeks.[164]

Rent Increases

If your rent is assessed under the local reference rent rules – see p239. If the pre-January rules apply, and your rent is increased, the local authority has the power not to increase your HB by the full amount if it decides that:

- the increase is unreasonably high compared with the increases in suitable alternative accommodation;
- the increase is unreasonable because a previous increase has occurred within the preceding 12 months.[165]

Where the local authority considers a rent increase to have been unreasonable, it may either refuse to meet all of that increase or only so much of it as it considers appropriate. If your rent has been increased for the second time in under 12 months but is still below the market level for suitable alternative accommodation, or the increase reflects improvements made to your accommodation, you should press for the full amount to be allowed.[166] If the local authority refuses, you should ask for a review (see p291).

CHAPTER THIRTEEN

The amount of benefit

This chapter covers:

1. The basic calculation (below)
2. Extended payments of HB/CTB (p250)
3. Deductions for non-dependants (p252)
4. Extra benefit in exceptional circumstances (p256)
5. People in hospital (p256)
6. Transitional payments (p257)

1. THE BASIC CALCULATION

How your benefit is worked out

This depends on:

- your 'applicable amount' (see Chapter 18);
- your 'eligible rent' (see p227);
- whether any deductions are to be made for non-dependants (see p252);
- your income (see Chapter 19).

The most housing benefit (HB) you can get is called your 'maximum housing benefit'. This is your 'eligible rent' less any deductions for non-dependants.[1] In some exceptional cases you can get extra HB (see p256).

Because entitlement to income support (IS) or income-based jobseeker's allowance (JSA) acts as an automatic passport to maximum HB (once you have made a claim for HB), the local authority does not need to work out applicable amounts, income or capital[2]. However, if you are not on IS or income-based JSA, you do need to work them out (see below).

No HB is payable if the amount would be less than 50 pence a week.[3] A local authority may round any figure used in working out your entitlement to the nearest penny (a half-penny is rounded upwards). The steps below will help you to calculate HB.

If you are on IS/income-based JSA
- Work out your **maximum HB.** This is your eligible rent minus any non-dependant deductions.
- If you are on IS/income-based JSA, you are entitled to maximum HB.

If you are not on IS/income-based JSA
- Check that your capital is not too high (see Chapter 20).
- Work out your **maximum HB.** This is your eligible rent minus any non-dependant deductions.
- Work out your applicable amount (see Chapter 18).
- Work out your income (see Chapter 19 but also p263 if you are a student).
- **If your income is less than or equal to your applicable amount,** you are entitled to maximum HB.
- **If your income is greater than your applicable amount,** work out the difference. The amount of HB you are entitled to is maximum HB minus 65 per cent of the difference between your income and applicable amount.

Example I

Mr and Mrs Feinstein and their adult son live together in a flat. Mrs Feintein is the sole tenant and pays rent of £65 a week, which includes all their fuel. Mr Feinstein receives income-based JSA for himself and his wife while they are looking for work. Their son earns £110 a week gross. Mr Feinstein claims HB.

His eligible rent is £53.65 a week (ie, £65 – £12.35 deducted because of the fuel charges – see p228).

His son counts as a non-dependant and the appropriate deduction for him is £13 a week (see p252).

Therefore, his maximum HB is £39.65 a week (£52.65 – £13). Because he receives income-based JSA, his HB is £39.65 a week. The amount is lower than his actual rent because his fuel charge is not covered by HB and because his son is expected to make a contribution to the rent.

Example 2
Mrs Feinstein then finds a job for which she is paid £120 a week after deductions of tax and national insurance contributions. There is no occupational pension scheme. Her husband ceases to be entitled to income-based JSA because she now works full-time and he makes a new claim for HB.

Mr Feinstein's maximum HB is still £39.65 a week.

His applicable amount is £77.15 (the standard rate for a couple – see p331).

His income is £110 a week (because £10 of his wife's earnings is disregarded – see p359).

The difference between his income and his applicable amount is therefore £32.85 a week.

65 per cent of £32.85 a week is £21.35 a week.

Mr Feinstein's HB is therefore £39.65 – £21.35 = £18.30 a week.

If you come off IS/income-based JSA because of starting work or increasing your income from work, you may be entitled to an extended payment of the same amount of HB you were getting while on IS/income-based JSA for a further four weeks (see p250).

Calculating a weekly amount of HB

Entitlement to HB is always paid for a specific benefit week, a period of seven consecutive days beginning with a Monday and ending on a Sunday.[4] If you pay rent at different intervals (eg, monthly) the amount has to be converted to a weekly figure before HB can be calculated.[5]

If the rent period is not a whole number of weeks, you divide the figure by the number of days in the period. This 'daily rent' is then multiplied by seven to give the equivalent weekly figure to be used in the calculation.[6]

Rent-free periods

If you have a regular rent-free period (eg, you pay rent on a 48-week rent year) you get no HB during your rent-free period. Your applicable amount, weekly income, non-dependant deductions, the set deductions for meals and fuel charges and the minimum amount payable (but not your eligible rent) are adjusted.[7] The rules for doing this are:

- Where your rent is paid weekly or in a whole multiple of weeks, you should multiply the figures to be converted by 52 (or 53 as appropriate) to give the annual amounts. Then divide by the number of weeks in the year in which you actually pay rent. So, for a 48-week

rent year, all the figures would need to be multiplied by 52 and the result divided by 48.[8]
- Where your rent is paid on some other basis, you should multiply all the figures to be converted by 365 (or 366 as appropriate) and divide the result by the number of days in the rent year for which rent is actually payable. So, if you pay rent every calendar month except December (31 days), all the figures would need to be multiplied by 365 and the result divided by 334 (365 – 31).[9]

This rule does not apply if your landlord has temporarily waived the rent in return for you doing repairs, see p216.

2. EXTENDED PAYMENTS OF HOUSING BENEFIT/COUNCIL TAX BENEFIT

If you are on **income support** (IS)/income-based jobseeker's allowance (JSA) and your entitlement ends because you start work or increase your hours of or income from work, you may be entitled to an extended payment of housing benefit (HB)/council tax benefit (CTB). This means that for four weeks you continue to receive the same amount of HB/CTB as you did in your last week of entitlement to IS/income-based JSA.

You are entitled to an extended payment of HB/CTB if[10]:

- you were entitled to and in receipt of IS/income-based JSA and your entitlement ended because you or your partner started work (including self employed work) or increased your earnings from or hours of work; *and*
- before your IS/income-based JSA entitlement ceased you were:
  - available for and actively seeking work;
  - or your applicable amount included the family premium (lone parent rate) or if you were a carer, the carer premium;
  - or you were on a Government training scheme and getting a training allowance; *and*
- you had been continuously entitled to and in receipt of either IS or JSA or both for 26 weeks for any combination of the above reasons; *and*
- you expect the work (or increase) to last for five weeks or more; *and*
- your liability for rent will continue for at least four weeks; *and*
- if you were getting IS, you are under 60. (It does not matter if your partner is over 60, even if it is they who are starting work.); *and*

- you make a claim within eight days of the day your entitlement to IS/income-based JSA ceased (see below).

Claims for extended payments

You can claim extended payments from the Benefits Agency, Employment Service or local authority. You must claim on the approved form, properly completed, within eight days of the day your entitlement to IS/income-based JSA ceased[11]. A claim for an extended payment cannot be backdated. If you fail to claim in time because of incorrect advice from a member of staff from the Benefits Agency or Employment Service, you should complain and request compensation. Your HB claim is fast tracked if, as well as claiming an extended payment within eight days, you claim standard in-work HB within 15 days of IS/income-based JSA ceasing.[12]

The amount of the extended payment

If you continue to live in the same property, the weekly amount of your extended payment is the actual HB payable in your last full week of your IS/income-based JSA claim[13]. (Ignore rent free weeks.) This means that if extra HB was in payment for exceptional hardship (see p240) it continues to be paid for the extended payment period. If you move house (other than into local authority accommodation), you continue to get the weekly amount of HB payable on your old home[14]. No account is taken of changes in circumstances over the extended payment period such as non-dependants, rent increases, increases in income, rent free weeks.

The only change of circumstances which affects the amount of your extended payment is where you move to local authority accommodation. In this case, the amount of the extended payment is the eligible rent at your new address minus any non-dependant deductions which applied at the old address. This is the only change of circumstances which affects the amount of an extended payment.

The weekly amount of your extended payment of CTB is the amount of CTB you got in the last week before your entitlement to IS/income-based JSA ceased. If you move, you get the maximum CTB applicable to your new address minus any non-dependant deductions which applied at your old address.[15]

In-work claims for benefit

An extended payment is a payment of HB/CTB, so if you make a claim for standard in-work HB/CTB within four weeks of the end of the extended payment period, your HB/CTB entitlement will be continuous.[16] This will mean, for example, that if you are exempt from the local reference rent rules, you should continue to be exempt unless you move home (see p236). In some cases, your entitlement to standard, in-work HB/CTB might be more than the amount on top of your extended payment. This could happen where, for example, your rent increases or a non-dependant with a high income moves out. In this case HB/CTB can be paid up to the level of your standard, in-work HB/CTB entitlement.[17]

Benefit on two homes

Even if you get an extended payment, you may still qualify for HB on two homes (see p219).[18]

3. DEDUCTIONS FOR NON-DEPENDANTS

If someone normally lives you (see p253) on a non-commercial basis but is not part of your family for benefit purposes, they are called non-dependants[19]. They are assumed to contribute towards your rent whether they do so or not and a set deduction is made from your housing benefit (HB). You should consider asking them to reimburse you at least the amount of the deduction.

The following people who live with you do not count as non-dependants[20]:

- a child or young person living with you who is not a member of your household (see p326);
- someone who jointly occupies your home and is either is a co-owner or jointly liable with you or your partner to make payments in respect of occupying it; *unless*
  - they live with the person to whom they are liable to make payments and either that person is a close relative or the agreement is not on a commercial basis; *or*
  - the local authority considers that their liability to make payments was contrived to take advantage of the HB scheme (see p259); *or*
- someone who is liable to pay rent on a commercial basis to you or your partner unless they are a close relative or the local authority considers their liability to be contrived (see p253);
- any person, or a member of their household, to whom you or your partner are liable to pay rent on a commercial basis unless they are a close relative or the local authority considers your liability to be contrived (see p253);

- someone who is employed by a charitable or voluntary organisation as a resident carer for you or your partner and you pay for the service.

A non-dependant is only regarded as living with you if s/he is not separately liable for her/his own housing costs and s/he shares some accommodation with you apart from a bathroom, lavatory, or a communal area such as a hall, passageway or a room in common use in sheltered accommodation.[21] For example, where part of your home has been converted to include a self-contained 'granny-flat', the person occupying it would not be a non-dependant even though s/he may share your bathroom and toilet. It may be possible to argue that a person cannot be considered to be 'residing with' you unless s/he also shares living arrangements, such as cooking and paying the bills, as well as accommodation. Before advancing this argument it is important to check that you will be better off, because income from non-dependants is ignored but income from other people may be taken into account (see p374).

Arrangement contrived to take advantage of the housing benefit scheme

If the local authority thinks that a person's liability for rent was created to take advantage of the HB scheme, that person counts as a non-dependant.

This applies where:

- a person's liability appears to the local authority to be contrived to take advantage of the HB scheme, unless they were otherwise liable to pay rent in the previous eight weeks;
- a joint occupier was a non-dependant in the previous eight weeks unless the local authority is satisfied that the change in arrangements was not made to take advantage of the HB scheme.

Deductions from your eligible rent

When no deduction is made

- No non-dependant deductions are made if either you or your partner are registered blind or have regained your eyesight within the last 28 weeks, or receive attendance allowance, constant attendance allowance, or the care component of the disability living allowance.[22]
- No deduction is made in respect of any non-dependant who is:[23]
  - currently staying in your household but whose normal home is elsewhere;
  - receiving a youth training allowance;

- a full-time student during her/his period of study, unless it is the summer vacation and s/he is in full-time work;
- in hospital for more than six weeks;
- in prison;
- under 18 years old;[24]
- aged under 25 and receiving IS/income-based JSA.[25]

The amount of deductions

You should try to provide information to show which deduction applies. If you cannot, ask the local authority to consider their circumstances – eg, are they doing a job which is normally very low-paid.

Unless you or your non-dependant(s) are exempt, a deduction is made from your eligible rent for every non-dependant living in your household except in the case of a non-dependant couple – see below. These are:[26]

Circumstances of the non-dependant	*Deduction*
Aged 18 or over and in full-time work with a weekly gross income of:	
– £250 or more	£39.00
– £200–£249.99	£36.00
– £152–£199.99	£33.00
– £116–£151.99	£17.00
– £78–£115.99	£13.00
All others (for whom a deduction is made)	£ 7.00

Full-time work is paid employment of 16 hours or more each week.[27] In averaging the number of hours worked, any recognised holidays or leave are ignored. The local authority also ignores any absences from work which, in its opinion, are without good cause.[28] Where the number of hours worked fluctuates, the average is taken.[29] However, where a person is on IS/income-based JSA for more than three days in any benefit week, they are not treated as being in full-time work for that week.[30]

Generally, non-dependants on training schemes are not regarded as being in full-time work. If they are aged 18/24 and were on IS/income-based JSA prior to the training scheme, no deduction should be made.[31]

A non-dependant who is on sick or maternity leave is not in full-time work, even if the employer is making up the non-dependant's full wages.[32]

The earnings amounts are gross figures – ie, in the case of wages the amount before any deductions. They relate to the total income of the non-dependant (apart from attendance allowance, constant attendance allowance, disability living allowance and payments from any of the Macfarlane Trusts, the Eileen Trust, the Fund and the Independent Living Funds[33]), and not just income from employment.

The earnings bands only apply to non-dependants in full-time work. A non-dependant who works less than 16 hours will not attract the higher levels of deduction even if their weekly gross income exceeds £78.

The DSS guidance stresses that local authorities are not expected to investigate the income of non-dependants in every case.[34]

Non-dependant couples

Only one deduction is made for a married or unmarried couple (or the members of a polygamous marriage) who are non-dependants. Where the individual circumstances of each partner are different, the highest deduction is made.[35] For the purpose of deciding which earnings band applies (see p254), their joint income counts, even if only one of them is in full-time work.[36]

Non-dependants of joint occupiers

Where joint occupiers share a non-dependant, the deduction is divided between them. This should be done taking into account the proportion of housing costs paid by each one. But no apportionment should be made between the members of a couple.[37] Where the person is a non-dependant of only one of the joint occupiers, the full deduction will be made from that person's benefit only.

Income and capital of a non-dependant

Normally, the income and capital of any non-dependant is completely ignored when assessing your HB entitlement,[38] except for deciding which non-dependant deduction applies. However, if:

- you are not on IS/income-based JSA, *and*
- the income and capital of the non-dependant are both greater than yours, *and*
- the local authority is satisfied you have made an arrangement with the non-dependant to take advantage of the HB scheme,

your benefit entitlement is assessed on the basis of the non-dependant's income and capital rather than your own.[39] Any income and capital normally treated as belonging to you is completely ignored, but the rest of the calculation proceeds as normal.[40]

If this applies to you, seek a review of the decision (see p291).

4. EXTRA BENEFIT IN EXCEPTIONAL CIRCUMSTANCES

If the local authority considers your circumstances to be 'exceptional', it can pay you extra housing benefit (HB) over and above your normal entitlement.[41] This is in addition to the discretion the local authority has to increase HB where exceptional hardship would be caused by the local reference rent restriction rules (see p240). The meaning of the term 'exceptional circumstances' is not defined, and you should argue for it to be used wherever hardship would otherwise arise. Your circumstances do not have to be unique to count as exceptional.[42]

It is your individual circumstances which count and this power should not be used to pay extra benefit on the basis of predefined conditions. In any case where additional HB is paid, it can either be paid on a weekly basis for as long as the exceptional circumstances warrant it, or can be made as a 'one-off award'.

You will not be considered for any additional HB unless you specifically ask for it. Make sure you give clear reasons why you need the additional help. If you are refused, you should ask for a review.

The overall limit is your eligible rent[43] (see p227). The local authority cannot use this power unless you are entitled to receive HB during the period of payment of the extra benefit. The power can only be used to pay HB in addition to, and not as a substitute for, normal entitlement.[44]

The local authority also has the power to pay extra HB/CTB to people getting either a war disablement pension or a war widow's pension including similar pensions paid by non-UK governments, by disregarding all of them as income, rather than just disregarding £10.[45] If the authority uses this power it must apply the income disregard to all people in receipt of these benefits.

5. PEOPLE IN HOSPITAL

If you remain entitled to income support (IS)/income-based jobseeker's allowance (JSA) while in hospital you will receive maximum housing benefit (HB), provided you continue to satisfy the temporary absence rules (see p217). If you or your partner go into hospital and you cease to be entitled to IS/income-based JSA your HB is affected as follows:

• up to six weeks – there is no change to your HB;
• after six weeks – benefit is reduced for adults in hospital.

If you are likely to be in hospital for more than 52 weeks you will not be entitled to HB under the temporary absence rules. If someone remains living in your home, they will need to make the claim for HB.

There are no reductions to your benefit if a dependent child goes into hospital.

After six weeks in hospital

* Single claimant – your applicable amount is reduced to £15.60.[46]
* Single parent – your applicable amount is reduced to £15.60 personal allowance plus any children's personal allowances, plus any family premium (including the lone parent rate where applicable) and disabled child premiums.[47]
* Couple with one adult in hospital – your applicable amount is reduced by £12.50.[48]
* Couple with both adults in hospital – your applicable amount is reduced to £31.20 personal allowance for you both, plus any children's personal allowances, plus any family and disabled child premiums.[49]
* Partners of polygamous marriages where not all partners have been in hospital for six weeks. Your applicable amount is reduced by £12.50 for each adult in hospital for over six weeks.[50]
* Partners of polygamous marriages where all adults are in hospital. Your applicable amount reduces to £15.60 for each partner, plus any allowances for children, plus any family or disabled child premiums.[51]

The six weeks are calculated by adding together any separate stays in hospital less than 28 days apart.[52] The reduction takes effect from the beginning of the benefit week (see p272) after you have been in hospital for six weeks.

6. TRANSITIONAL PAYMENTS

In April 1988, HB was changed. Some people who were worse off under the new scheme were made payments to compensate for their losses. For information on how payments were originally calculated, see the 19th edition of the *Handbook*, p209.

CHAPTER FOURTEEN

Special rules for students

This chapter covers:

Most full-time students cannot claim housing benefit (HB) during their course, including all the vacation periods falling within it. Students who remain eligible for HB are subject to additional rules. There are special rules for the treatment of students' income (see p263). For students and council tax benefit (CTB), see Chapter 16.

1. GENERAL RULES

Who counts as a student

A student is someone attending a course of study at an educational establishment.[1] This covers any full-time, part-time or sandwich course, either advanced or non-advanced, whether or not you get a grant for attending it. The term educational establishment is not defined in law, but DSS guidance suggests it should include private as well as state-funded institutions. You are treated as a student until either the last day of the course or until you abandon it or are dismissed from it. 'Last day of the course' means the date on which the last day of the final academic year is officially scheduled to fall and not the date you actually leave if you do so just before then.[2]

Full-time students

You are a 'full-time student' if you are on a full-time course (including a sandwich course).[3] The rules for deciding whether your course is full or part time depend on whether it is funded by the Further Education Funding Council (FEFC).

If your course is not funded by the FEFC, the local authority is expected to decide whether your course is full time by looking at the nature of the course you are attending and, if in doubt, by consulting the educational establishment involved. Local authorities are advised that student grants are normally only payable for full-time courses. If you get a grant, and especially if the level of your grant seems appropriate to a full-time course, the local authority will probably decide to treat you as a full-time student.[4] If you disagree with a decision made by the local authority, you should request a review (see p291).

If your course is funded by the FEFC, then whether it is classed as full or part time depends on the number of guided learning hours it involves. (In Scotland the reference is to classroom or workshop based programmed learning under the guidance of teaching staff.) Guided learning hours include lectures, tutorials and supervised study but exclude unsupervised study, home work and meal breaks. Your college can provide a document showing the number of such hours your course involves.[5] Your course is full time if it involves:

- more than 16 guided learning hours; *or*
- in Scotland, more than 16 hours classroom or workshop based programmed learning under the guidance of teaching staff; *or*
- in Scotland, more than 21 hours a week, made up of 16 hours classroom or workshop based learning and additional hours using structured learning packages.

Transitional protection

If you were entitled to HB on 31 July 1996 while on an FEFC-funded course, you may be able to continue to get HB even if your course would now be defined as full time. Provided you satisfy the other conditions of entitlement, you can continue to get HB if:[6]

- you continue to attend the same course; *and*
- you have been continuously entitled to HB since 31 July 1996 (periods of up to 12 weeks during which you are not entitled after 7 October 1996 are ignored).

The period of study

If you are eligible for HB, the amount of your entitlement depends on whether that week falls either inside or outside a period of study.

Your period of study[7] is:

(a) where your course is for one year or less – the period from the first to the last day of the course; *or*

(b) where your course is for more than one year and a grant is paid, or would be paid, on the basis of you studying throughout the year (as in many post-graduate courses) – the period from the first day of the course until the day before the next year of the course. In the final year the period of study ends with the last day of your final academic term; *or*

(c) in any other case (ie, in most cases), where your course is for more than one year – from the first day of each academic year until the day before the start of the recognised summer vacation. In the final year the period of study ends with the last day of your final academic term.

In deciding whether or not your grant has been assessed on the basis of you studying throughout the whole year (as in (b) above), the local authority should ignore supplements to your grant (eg, dependants' allowances) which are paid for the full year, regardless of the length of the course.

Your period of study includes periods of practical experience outside the educational establishment for students on sandwich courses.[8]

Your HB entitlement is calculated differently during the period of study than outside it. For example, the student rent deduction only applies during the period of study (see p263). (See also p369 for treatment of grant income.) You may find, therefore, that your HB entitlement is higher during the summer vacation and that you need to make a new claim or check that your entitlement is reviewed at that time.

2. STUDENTS WHO ARE ELIGIBLE

Part-time students can claim housing benefit (HB). Full-time students are not normally entitled to HB, but there are a number of exceptions. You can claim if:[9]

* you are on income support (IS)/income-based jobseeker's allowance (JSA);
* you are under 19 and not following a course of higher education. Higher education includes degree courses, teachers' training, HND, HNC, post-graduate courses;
* you and your partner are both full-time students and have a dependent child or young person;
* you are a lone parent who satisfies the conditions for the family premium (lone parent rate);

- you are a lone foster parent where the child has been formally placed with you by a local authority or voluntary agency;
- you meet the conditions for the disability premium, or would do if you were not disqualified from incapacity benefit (see p10); *or*
- you have been incapable of work for 28 weeks (see p10). Two or more periods when you are incapable are joined to form a single period if they are separated by less than eight weeks; *or*
- you meet the conditions for the severe disability premium; *or*
- were getting IS immediately before 1 September 1990 as a disabled student on the grounds that you would be unable to get a job within a reasonable period of time compared to other students unless you have stopped getting IS for a continuous period of 18 months or more; *or*
- claimed HB/IS after 1 September 1990 and for any period in the 18 months before you claimed HB/IS, were getting IS as a disabled student in both advanced or non-advanced education unless you have stopped getting IS for a continuous period of 18 months or more; *or*
- satisfy the conditions for a grant supplement in the form of a disabled student's allowance award because of deafness;
- you are a pensioner who satisfies the conditions for one of the pensioner premiums.

Partners who are not themselves ineligible as students can claim HB.[10]

3. STUDENTS WHO ARE INELIGIBLE

Full-time students

Full-time students are not entitled to housing benefit (HB), except for the exceptions noted above.

Being away from your term-time accommodation

If you are a full-time student who is eligible for HB (see p260) and your main reason for occupying your home is to enable you to attend your course, you cannot get HB on that home for any full week of absence falling outside the period of study.[11]

This rule does not apply if:

- you are away from home because you are in hospital;[12]
- the main reason for occupying your home is not to enable you to attend your course but for some other purpose – for example, to provide a home for your children or for yourself if you do not have a normal home elsewhere;[13] *or*

• you are a non-student partner.

In these cases, any absences are dealt with under the temporary absence rules (see p217).

Accommodation rented from an educational establishment

If you rent your accommodation from your educational establishment you are not eligible to claim HB during your period of study (see p259).[14]

This only applies where you pay rent to the same educational establishment as the one you attend for your studies. It does not apply where your educational establishment itself rents the accommodation from a third party, unless this is on a long lease or where the third party is an education authority providing the accommodation as part of its functions.[15]

However, the local authority can still apply this rule if it decides that your educational establishment has arranged for your accommodation to be provided by a person or body other than itself in order to take advantage of the HB scheme.[16]

If you and your partner jointly occupy accommodation rented from your educational establishment, and your partner is not a student, the restriction also applies to her/him if s/he is the claimant.[17]

Regardless of any restrictions which may apply during your period of study, you can claim HB if you continue to rent your accommodation from your educational establishment outside that period.[18]

Living in different accommodation during term-time

The rules about claiming HB for two homes are explained on p218.

If you are a member of a couple and receive HB for two homes, the assessment of HB for each home is based on your joint income, your couple's applicable amount and, in both cases, the rent deduction (see p263) and corresponding income 'disregard' is applied.

4. STUDENTS FROM OVERSEAS

Most overseas students cannot claim housing benefit (HB) because they are persons from abroad (see p222). Even if you are entitled, a successful claim for HB could affect your right to stay in this country and it is best to get immigration advice before making a claim.

Partners of ineligible overseas students

Where you are not eligible, but there are no restrictions on your partner, either as a student or as a person from abroad, s/he may be able to claim instead.[19] However, if s/he receives HB and you are a person from abroad (see p222) this may affect your right to remain in the UK under the immigration rules because a claim by one partner is a claim for both (see p222).

5. CALCULATING STUDENTS' BENEFIT

If you or your partner get income support (IS) or a training allowance, none of the rules below apply to you.

If you do not get IS but you and/or your partner are eligible for housing benefit (HB), your entitlement is calculated in the same way as for other non-IS claimants (see p248), apart from the extra rules below.

Assessing your rent – the student rent deduction

If you are a full-time student, your weekly eligible rent (see p227) is, in most cases, reduced during your period of study by:

- £25.20 if you are attending a course in London; *or*
- £17.45 if you are studying elsewhere.[20]

The level of deduction depends on the area where you study rather than where you live. When it applies, it is made every week during your period of study (see p259), even where a grant is not paid or is paid for term-time only. It does not apply outside your period of study.

In any week in which your eligible rent is reduced, your income is reduced by the same amount. The overall effect of this is that you get less HB.

The rent deduction applies equally where it is the claimant's partner who is a full-time student,[21] but only one rent deduction and income disregard should be made where both partners are full-time students.

When the student rent deduction does not apply

The student deduction is not made if:[22]

- you are on IS or income-based JSA;
- you or your partner receive a training allowance for your own maintenance or for that of your child;
- you are a student on a sandwich course during any period of work experience (industrial, professional or commercial);

- your income for HB purposes is less than the sum of your applicable amount and the amount of the rent deduction, and one of the following also applies:
  - you are a single parent and your applicable amount includes the family premium (lone parent rate); *or*
  - the disability premium applies (or would apply if you were not disqualified from incapacity benefit); *or*
  - you have been incapable of work (or treated as incapable) for a continuous 28-week period (including separate periods eight weeks or less apart); *or*
  - you have a partner and only one of you is a full-time student.

If none of these apply to you and the deductions result in hardship, you should ask the authority to make a discretionary addition to your HB, see p256. The authority will not be able to increase your HB above the eligible rent figure calculated under the main rules (see p227) – for students this means your eligible rent before the student rent deduction has been applied.[23]

6. PAYMENTS

Students are covered by all the normal rules on the administration and payment of housing benefit (HB). However, there are two provisions which can apply specifically to students.

First, the local authority has the discretion to decide how long your benefit period should last. For most students, there are two benefit periods a year – one during the period of study, and the other during the long summer vacation (see p259).

Secondly, the local authority may decide to pay a rent allowance once each term except that students have the same right as other claimants to insist on fortnightly payments if their entitlement is more than £2 a week (see p273).

CHAPTER FIFTEEN

Claims, payments and reviews

This chapter covers:

1. CLAIMS

Who can make a claim

If you are a single person (including a single parent or a member of a gay or lesbian couple), you make a claim for housing benefit (HB) on your own behalf.

If you are a member of a couple, or a partner in a polygamous marriage, you can decide between you who should claim. The choice of claimant will not normally affect the level of HB you receive (but see pp262 and 235 for some important exceptions). In particular, if you are exempt from the local reference rent rules and are considering changing the claim into your partner's name, you should check whether doing so could result in you losing your exemption and becoming subject to the harsher rent restriction rules (see p236). If you cannot agree who should be the claimant, the local authority can decide for you.[1]

If a person is either temporarily or permanently unable to manage her/his own affairs, the local authority must accept a claim made by someone formally appointed to act legally on that person's behalf – eg, someone appointed with power of attorney, a receiver appointed by the Court of Protection, or, in Scotland, a tutor, curator or other guardian administering the person's estate.[2]

Otherwise the local authority can decide to make someone over 18 an appointee who can act on the claimant's behalf.[3] For the purpose of the claim, an appointee has the responsibility of exercising all rights and duties as though s/he were the claimant.[4] You can write in to ask to be an appointee, and can resign after giving four weeks' notice. The local authority may terminate any appointment at any time.[5]

How to make a claim

All claims must be made in writing in a way which is 'sufficient in the circumstances', and accompanied by the information necessary to assess your claim.[6] Claim forms are available from your local authority – but if you are claiming income support (IS) or income-based JSA you will find special shortened HB and council tax benefit (CTB) claim forms (NHB1) in your IS/income-based JSA claim form.[7]

DSS guidance suggests that a letter stating that you wish to claim could be regarded as an acceptable alternative to a claim form.[8] Where a claim by letter is not accepted as sufficient, you will be sent an official claim form to fill in. If you return this within four weeks (or longer at the local authority's discretion), it is treated as if it had been received on the date of your original claim.[9] Similarly, if you do not complete the claim form properly but return it properly completed within four weeks (or longer, if the local authority allows more time), it is treated as though it was received on the date of your original claim.[10]

Send your claim form immediately, as other information and evidence can be sent later (see p267).

You cannot claim by telephone. However, if you telephone to ask for a claim form, ask on the form to have your claim backdated to the date of your phone call (or longer, if appropriate) because you have good cause for a late claim (see p268).

You may amend or withdraw your claim in writing at any time before it has been assessed. Amendments must be made in writing and are treated as though they were part of your original claim.[11] A notice to withdraw your claim takes effect from the day it is received.[12]

Usually, you claim HB and CTB together but in Scotland some claimants have to make separate claims for HB and CTB. This is because District Councils are responsible for HB and Regional Councils are responsible for CTB. In most cases, however, District Councils agree to operate the CTB scheme for Regional Councils on an agency basis so that only one claim is necessary.

Where to make your claim

Unless you are claiming IS/income-based JSA as well, you should always return your claim to the address on the form.[13]

If you are claiming IS/income-based JSA, you can either send your claim to your Benefits Agency office or to the local authority.[14] If you claim IS/income-based JSA and send your HB/CTB claim to the Benefits Agency, it must be forwarded by them to the local authority within two working days of either the date your IS/income-based JSA claim was assessed, or the date your HB/CTB claim was received, whichever is later, or as soon as reasonably practicable after that.[15] If you know there are significant delays at your local Benefits Agency office, it may be wise to send your HB/CTB form directly to the local authority. If you do this the local authority will want to verify your entitlement to IS/income-based JSA before assessing your HB. This may speed up your HB/CTB claim.

Information to support your claim

Your application for HB should be accompanied by all the information and evidence needed to assess your claim, but you should not delay your claim just because you do not have all the evidence ready to send.[16] You must supply any information requested in connection with your claim within four weeks – or longer if the local authority thinks you need more time.[17] If you fail, without good reason, to provide information which it is reasonable for them to request, the local authority does not have to process your claim.[18] Contact them as soon as possible with the information requested and ask them to extend the four-week period, if you need more time. You do not need to declare receipt of payments, either for yourself or for a non-dependant, from any of the Macfarlane Trusts, the Eileen Trust, the Fund, nor income in kind.[19]

Your date of claim

Your date of claim is important because it affects the date from which your HB begins (see p272). Usually, your claim is treated as made on the day it reaches the local authority.[20] The only exceptions are if:

- you have successfully claimed IS/income-based JSA and your HB claim reached the Benefits Agency within four weeks of your IS/income-based JSA claim – your HB claim is treated as having been made on the first day of entitlement to IS/income-based JSA (including the three waiting days for JSA);[21]

- you have unsuccessfully claimed IS/income-based JSA. Your HB claim is treated as having been made on the day it reached either the Benefits Agency or the local authority, whichever is earlier;[22]
- you have made an advance claim (see below);
- you are on IS/income-based JSA and have just become liable to pay rent. If your HB claim form reaches the authority or Benefits Agency office within four weeks of you becoming liable, the HB claim is treated as being made on the date that you first became liable.[23]

Your HB normally starts from the Monday after the date of your claim.[24] This is called your date of entitlement (see p272).

Backdating a claim

If you failed to claim, you can make a late claim and receive backdated HB, if you can prove you have continuous good cause for your failure throughout the whole time for which you want to claim.[25] Any backdated HB is calculated on both your circumstances and the HB rules which applied over the backdating period.

What amounts to 'good cause' is not spelled out in the HB regulations (see p299).

If you think you may be entitled to benefit for an earlier period you should claim as soon as possible. This is because HB cannot be backdated for more than 52 weeks before the date of your request for backdating (which may be after the date of your original claim for HB), so you lose any unclaimed HB in respect of an earlier period.[26] Where your request for backdating was made before 1 April 1996, you are not subject to the 52-week limit on backdating and should press for payment for as long a period as you can show good cause.[27] If you claimed late because you were given wrong information, or misled by the local authority, you should press for an ex gratia payment as compensation. In addition, you should ask for additional HB on the grounds of exceptional circumstances (see p256). If you received HB but were underpaid more than 52 weeks ago (see Reviews, p291), you could ask for an *ex-gratia* payment or extra benefit in exceptional circumstances (see p256).

Advance claims

There are two situations where advance claims can be made.

- If you become liable for rent for the first time but cannot move in until after your liability begins, it is important that you claim HB as soon as you are liable. This is because, once you have moved in, you may be

able to receive HB for up to four weeks prior to moving in (providing you satisfy the conditions set out on p219).[28]
- If you are not entitled to HB now, but will become entitled within 13 weeks of claiming, the local authority can treat your claim as having been made in the benefit week immediately before you are first entitled.[29] If this happens, you do not need to make a further claim later on.

Making a further claim when your HB runs out

Your HB is paid to you for a period up to 60 weeks, after which you have to re-apply. The length of this benefit period (see p272) depends on the circumstances of your case[30] and you must be told how long it will last.[31] If you make a repeat claim not more than 13 weeks before, and not less than four weeks after, your current benefit period ends, your new benefit period starts immediately your old one finishes.[32] If you have been granted benefit for more than 16 weeks and you have not made a further claim within eight weeks of the end of your existing benefit period, the local authority must send you an application form and remind you to reclaim.[33]

If you are on IS or income-based JSA or your applicable amount includes the disability, severe disability or higher pensioner premium and you have not made a repeat claim by the last week of your benefit period, the local authority can extend that benefit period by four weeks. DSS guidance says this is to allow them time to issue a reminder or make a home visit if appropriate.[34]

Except where you are moving from IS to income-based JSA or vice versa, if your entitlement to IS/income-based JSA ends you will have to re-apply for HB (see p278).[35] A repeat claim form must be sent to you and, providing you return this within four weeks of the end of your previous benefit period, your new benefit period follows on without a break.[36]

If your partner or former partner was the original claimant but you are now making an HB claim for the same accommodation costs, the DSS guidance suggests that your claim will be treated as a repeat claim.[37]

If your date of claim has been backdated your benefit period begins in the benefit week in which your claim was actually received.[38]

2. DECISIONS

Delays

The local authority must make a decision on your claim, tell you in writing what the decision is, and pay you any housing benefit (HB) you are entitled to within 14 days, or, if that is not reasonably practicable, as soon as possible after that.[39] The local authority is under no duty to deal with your claim if:

- your claim was not accepted because you did not claim on an official form, or your form was not properly filled in and you did not re-submit it within four weeks of being asked to do so (see p266); *or*
- you failed to provide information needed to assess your claim within four weeks of being asked to do so (see p267); *or*
- you have told the local authority you have withdrawn your claim (see p266); *or*
- you have reclaimed benefit more than 13 weeks before the end of your current benefit period (see p269).[40]

In practice, many local authorities take considerably longer than 14 days to deal with claims. If you consider the delay is unreasonable you should write to the HB manager and threaten a formal complaint of 'maladministration' to the Ombudsman (see p298), unless you are paid within 14 days. Send a copy of the letter to your ward councillor and to the councillor who chairs the council committee responsible for HB. If this does not produce results, or if the delay is causing you severe hardship, you should consider court action.

If you are a private tenant and have not received your rent allowance within 14 days of your claim, you can get a payment on account (see p274).

Notification of the decision

Who should be notified

The following should be notified because they are 'persons affected' by the decision:[41]

- the claimant;
- an appointee (see p265);
- your landlord or agent in relation to a decision whether or not to make direct payment to that landlord/agent (see p275);
- the benefit authority;

- any person, including a landlord, from whom the benefit authority decides to recover a recoverable overpayment.

Only a 'person affected' can request reasons for a decision, apply for review or apply for a decision to be set aside, and these must be signed personally by them.[42]

Information a notification should contain

The local authority must include in its notification a minimum amount of information.[43] In addition, it may also include other relevant information.[44]

All notifications must tell you:

- of your right to ask for a further written explanation of the decision, how you can do this, and the time limit for doing so[45] (see p292); *and*
- of your right to ask for the decision to be reviewed, how you can do this, and the time limit for doing so[46] (see p292).

Other information that must be provided varies with the particular circumstances of your case. All the following should be included where relevant:[47]

- the normal weekly amount of HB you are entitled to;
- your weekly eligible rent;
- the amount of any notional fuel deductions, why they have been made, and that they can be varied if you can provide evidence of the actual amount involved;
- the amount and category of any non-dependant deductions;
- if you are a private tenant, the day your HB will be paid and whether payment will be made weekly, monthly etc;
- the date on which your entitlement starts and how long it will last (your benefit period);
- if you are not receiving income support (IS)/income-based jobseeker's allowance (JSA), how your applicable amount is calculated;
- if you are not receiving IS/income-based JSA, how your income has been assessed;
- if your level of HB is less than the minimum amount payable, that this is the reason why you have no entitlement;
- if your claim was successful, your duty to notify the local authority of any changes in circumstances which might affect your entitlement and what kinds of changes should be reported;
- if your claim was unsuccessful, a statement explaining exactly why you are not entitled;

- if it has been decided to pay your rent allowance direct to your landlord, information saying how much is to be paid to your landlord and when payments will start;
- if the income and capital of a non-dependant has been used instead of yours to calculate your HB (see p255), additional information saying that this has happened and why.

Local authorities have also been recommended to tell you, in non-IS cases, if they think you are likely to be entitled to IS.[48]

3. PAYMENT OF BENEFIT

When your entitlement starts

In most cases your entitlement to housing benefit (HB) starts in the benefit week following your date of claim.[49] A benefit week is a period of seven days running from Monday to Sunday.[50]

However, if you claim in the same week in which you become liable for rent, your HB entitlement starts in that benefit week.[51] This means that:

- if your rent is due weekly or at intervals of a multiple of a week, your HB starts at the beginning of the week in which liability starts – ie, you receive a full week's benefit for that first week, even if your tenancy did not start until part-way through that week;[52]
- if your rent is due at other intervals your HB starts on the same day your liability actually begins.[53]

When your entitlement ends

Your **benefit period** is the length of time for which your HB is paid before you need to re-apply.[54] Local authorities have discretion as to the length of benefit period they set, up to a maximum of 60 weeks. The benefit period may end early (see **When changes in circumstances take effect,** p278).

If your entitlement to HB ends because you have stopped claiming income support (IS)/income-based jobseeker's allowance (JSA) due to starting work or increasing your hours of or income from work, you may be entitled to an extended payment of HB for four weeks (see p250).

How your benefit is paid

If your landlord is the housing authority responsible for the payment of

HB, you receive HB in the form of a reduction in your rent. This is called a rent rebate.[55]

If you are a private tenant, you receive HB in the form of a rent allowance which is usually paid to you[56] although, in some cases, it may be paid direct to your landlord or to someone acting on your behalf (see p275).

Although rent allowances are normally paid in the form of a cheque or giro, the local authority has the discretion to pay you by whatever method it chooses but, in doing so, it must have regard to your 'reasonable needs and convenience'.[57] It should not insist on payment into a bank account if you do not already have a bank or giro account, nor make you collect it if it involves a difficult journey.[58] If it does, you should ask for a review (see p292) and complain to your local councillor (see p298). If that has no effect, ask your MP to take the matter up with the local authority, and also complain to the Ombudsman (see p298).

HB is paid in arrears (but see below if you or your partner have been getting HB since 6 October 1996). **Payments of HB which are made to you** are made at intervals of a week, two weeks, four weeks or a month, depending on when your rent is normally due. It can also be paid at longer intervals if you agree.[59]

If your rent allowance is less than £1 a week, the local authority can choose to pay your benefit up to six months in arrears.[60]

You can insist on two-weekly payments if your rent allowance is more than £2 a week unless HB in paid direct to your landlord (see below).[61] The local authority can pay your rent allowance weekly either to avoid an overpayment or where you are liable to pay rent weekly and it is in your interests for HB to be paid weekly.[62]

Payments made direct to your landlord are made four weekly or monthly in arrears (but see below if you or your partner have been getting HB since 6 October 1996). If HB is also paid to your landlord for other tenants, the first payment for you can be made at a shorter interval so that your payments are brought into line with the cycle of payments for the other tenants.[63]

The rules for when payments of HB are made changed on 7 October 1996. HB is now paid in arrears while payments direct to a landlord are made four-weekly or monthly in arrears (as above). However, there is some transitional protection if:[64]

- you have been continuously entitled to and in receipt of HB on the same property since 6 October 1996; *or*
- your partner was continuously entitled to and in receipt of HB since 6 October 1996, but has died and you make a new claim within four weeks of the death.

If this applies to you:

- payments of HB are generally made two weeks before the end of the period they are paid for (so payments for two weeks are made in advance and payments for four weeks midway through the period); *and*
- payments to your landlord can be made at intervals other than four weeks or a month.[65]

Interim payments on account

Local authorities are required to deal with your claim and pay your HB within 14 days as far as possible.[66] If you are a private tenant and the local authority has not been able to assess your HB within this period, you should receive a payment on account while your claim is being sorted out.[67] The local authority should automatically do this.

Some local authorities treat these interim payments as though they are discretionary. However, the law says the local authority must pay you an amount which it considers reasonable, given what it knows about your circumstances, and DSS guidance reminds them of their duty to pay.[68]

Interim payments can only be refused if it is clear that you will not be entitled or the reason for the delay is that they have asked you for information or evidence in support of your claim and you failed, without good cause, to provide it (see p267).[69] If the delay has been caused by a third party (eg, the rent officer, your bank or employer) this does not affect your right to an interim payment. If your local authority has not made a payment on account, you should complain. You could also argue that it is guilty of maladministration and apply to the Ombudsman (see p298).

If the local authority makes a payment on account, it should notify you of the amount and that it can recover any overpayment which occurs if your actual HB entitlement is different from the interim amount.[70]

If your interim payment is less than your true entitlement, your future HB can be adjusted to take account of the under or overpayment.[71]

Lost and missing cheques and giros

The law says nothing about the replacement of lost or missing giros, as it is seen as an administrative matter. If the local authority refuses to replace a payment which has never arrived, you can either try appealing on the basis that the authority has not paid you[72] or threaten to sue them in the county court. The process is the same as for the Benefits Agency (see p138).

Payment of your benefit to someone else

Sometimes payment may be made to a third party.

Payment to a claimant's personal representative

Where an appointee, or some other person legally empowered to act for you, has claimed HB on your behalf, that person can also receive the payments[73] (see p265).

If you are able to claim HB for yourself, you can still nominate an agent to receive, or collect it for you. To do this you must make a written request to the local authority. Anyone you nominate must be aged 18 or over.[74]

If a claimant dies, any unpaid HB may be paid to their personal representative or, where there is none, to their next of kin aged 16 or over. For payment to be made, a written application must be received by the local authority within 12 months of the claimant's death. However, the time limit can be extended at the local authority's discretion.[75] Where HB was being paid to the landlord prior to the claimant's death, the local authority can pay any outstanding HB to clear remaining rent due.

Payment direct to a landlord

The local authority must pay your HB including payments on account[76] directly to the landlord (or the person you pay rent to) if:

- you or your partner are on IS/JSA and the Benefits Agency has decided to pay part of your benefit to your landlord for arrears (see p141 and the *Jobseeker's Allowance Handbook*);[77] *or*
- you have rent arrears equivalent to eight weeks' rent or more, unless the local authority considers it to be in your overriding interest not to make direct payments[78] – in which case, your HB is withheld (see p276). Once your arrears have been reduced to less than eight weeks' rent, compulsory direct payments will stop. The local authority can then choose to continue direct payments on a discretionary basis if it considers it to be in your best interests to do so (see below).

The local authority may pay your HB directly to the landlord (or person you pay rent to):[79]

- if you have requested or agreed to direct payments; *or*
- without your agreement, if it decides that direct payments are in the best interests of yourself and your family; *or*
- without your agreement, if you have left the address for which you were getting HB and there are rent arrears. In this case, direct

payments of any unpaid HB due in respect of that accommodation can be made, up to the total of the outstanding arrears.

The local authority needs to be advised of the above circumstances, and your landlord could contact them about this.[80]

If you are granted refugee status and receive a retrospective award of HB, part or all of that award can be paid direct to the landlord (see p225).[81]

If you have just claimed HB, and the local authority thinks you have not already paid your rent and it would be in the interests of the 'efficient administration' of HB, they may make the first cheque payable to the landlord although they will send it to you.[82]

If the local authority implements direct payments, both you and your landlord should be notified accordingly. If it is not in your interests to have HB paid directly to your landlord (eg, because you are deliberately withholding rent to force your landlord to carry out repairs) it is worth trying to persuade the authority to withhold it rather than paying it to your landlord where there are more than eight weeks' arrears. Landlords can sometimes place authorities under pressure to pay them direct and the authority may not use this alternative option as a result.

Withholding benefit

Your rent allowance must be withheld if you have rent arrears equivalent to eight weeks' rent or more but the local authority has decided it is in your overriding interest not to make direct payments to your landlord[83] (see p275).

HB should not be withheld if either you pay off your arrears or can satisfy the local authority that you will pay off your arrears once you have received your payments.[84]

If the local authority subsequently decides it is no longer in your overriding interest not to pay your landlord, the HB withheld must be paid direct to your landlord unless your arrears have been reduced to less than eight weeks' rent (see p275).

Your rent allowance may be withheld in the following circumstances:

- if the authority believes you are not paying your rent regularly to your landlord, payment may be withheld[85] until either you pay off your rent arrears or satisfy the local authority that you will pay off your rent arrears once you have received the amount withheld;[86]
- if the rent officer (see p233) gives seven days notice but you deny her/ him entry to your home, the local authority can withhold your HB for as long as you continue to deny entry. If it is your landlord who denies entry, any HB that would have been paid direct to the landlord may be withheld;[87]

- if a query has arisen about your entitlement to, or the payment of, your HB, payment is withheld pending a review of your entitlement (see p291);[88]
- any payment of arrears may be withheld if the local authority thinks you may have been overpaid and that the overpayment is recoverable[89] (see p282);
- if the authority has evidence:
  - which has not been considered by an adjudication officer (AO); *and*
  - which raises a reasonable doubt as to the amount of your income and capital for IS/income-based JSA purposes; *and*
  - which consequently raises a question as to your HB entitlement,
  it can withhold payment until the AO has determined your IS/income-based JSA entitlement and the local authority has renewed your HB.[90]

4. CHANGES IN YOUR CIRCUMSTANCES

Duty to report changes of circumstances

From the moment you claim housing benefit (HB), you have a duty to let the local authority know in writing of any changes in your circumstances which you might reasonably know are likely to affect your HB in any way. If you do not, you may be overpaid HB and might have to pay it back, or you may be underpaid HB. If your benefit is paid to someone else on your behalf, the duty to report any relevant changes extends to her/him as well.[91] The local authority must tell you about the changes you have to report.[92] (See p291 for details of the Fraud Bill.)

You must always report the following changes, in writing, to the local authority:[93]

- any change to your rent if you are a private tenant;
- when entitlement to income support (IS)/income-based jobseeker's allowance (JSA) ends. You should not assume that the Benefits Agency will do this on your behalf. Make sure that you make a fresh claim for HB if you are still on a low income after coming off IS/income-based JSA;
- any change in the number of, or circumstances of, any non-dependants that may affect the level of deductions made to your benefit (see p252).

If you do not receive IS/income-based JSA you must also report:

- any change in family income or capital;

- any change in the number of boarders or sub-tenants or in the payments made by them;
- any change in your status (eg, marriage, cohabitation, separation or divorce).

Other changes

Whether or not you get IS/income-based JSA, there may be other changes which the local authority requires you to report, depending on the particular circumstances of your case. The need to report these additional changes must be drawn to your attention at the time you are notified of your HB entitlement.[94] This is important because you only have a duty to report changes which you 'might reasonably be expected to know' might affect your HB.[95]

You do not have to report:[96]

- any changes in your rent if you are a local authority tenant;
- changes in the ages of members of your family, or of non-dependants, unless the change results in a young person ceasing to be a member of the family.[97]

It is important that you should remember to report any changes to the right department. Your duty to notify changes is to the HB department not to the local authority as a whole.[98]

When changes in circumstances take effect

If you have made an application for HB and reported a change of circumstances before the local authority has assessed your claim, your application is assessed on the basis of the revised information you have provided.

If a change of circumstances takes place within your benefit period, the local authority must establish the date on which that change actually occurred.[99] Where you have ceased to be entitled to some other social security benefit, the date the change occurred must always be taken as the day after your last day of entitlement to that benefit.[100]

In most cases, the change takes effect from the start of the benefit week after the one in which the change actually occurred.[101] This means that, on whatever day of the week the change actually occurs, the change is implemented as from the following Monday. This includes cases where IS/income-based JSA stops and HB ends, apart from the exceptions listed below.

- If IS/income-based JSA ends because another benefit becomes payable, the HB benefit period ends at the end of the benefit week in which the payment of IS/income-based JSA ceases. (**NB** The benefit period does not end if you move from IS to income-based JSA or vice versa.[102])

- Where IS/income-based JSA ends in any other case, the HB benefit period ends at the end of the benefit week in which IS/income-based JSA entitlement ceases (ie, the normal rule applies).[103]
- Where a child or young person reaches the age of 11 or 16, the personal allowance in respect of them (see p330) increases from the first Monday in September following the 11th or 16th birthday.[104]
- A change in rent is taken into account in the benefit week in which it actually occurs. If you pay your rent weekly, or in a multiple of weeks, the change is taken into account for the whole of the week in which it occurs. This means that the change takes effect on the Monday, though your rent may not have changed until, say, the Thursday, of that week. If you pay rent monthly, the change is taken into account on the day it actually occurs.[105]
- A change in your income solely due to a change in tax and national insurance contributions can be disregarded for up to 30 weeks (see p349).[106]
- A change in the HB regulations takes effect from the date the amendment occurs.[107] The annual uprating of other social security benefits, provided it takes place between 1 and 15 April, takes effect from the first Monday in April if you pay rent weekly (or in multiples of weeks). If you pay at other intervals it counts from 1 April.
- A payment of income (or arrears of income) for a past period is taken into account from the date it would have been taken into account had it been paid on time (see p278).[108] Your past entitlement thus falls to be reviewed and any resulting overpayment may be recoverable (see p282).

If you receive arrears of a social security benefit relating to a period before 6 March 1995, they are taken into account for a forward period from the date the award is actually made.[109] Any lump sum in respect of arrears counts as capital. If arrears of a social security benefit relate to a period after 6 March 1995, DSS guidance says that those arrears should be taken into account from the date they would have been taken into account had they been paid on time.[110] However, you should argue that this is wrong because arrears of benefit are capital not income (they would need to be income for the guidance to be right).[111]

If two or more changes occurring in the same benefit week would, according to the above rules, normally take effect in different benefit weeks, they are treated as taking effect in the same benefit week in which they occur. They take effect from the beginning of that benefit week (unless one of the changes relates to monthly rent, in which case all the changes take effect on the same day as the rent changes).[112] If you pay rent weekly (or in multiples of weeks) and the annual uprating occurs at the same time as another change (excluding a change to your rent or the HB Regulations) they all count from the first Monday in April.[113]

Reassessment of your benefit

The local authority may deal with your change of circumstances by ending your benefit period early and inviting you to reclaim so that your entitlement can be completely reassessed.[114] This always happens if you have ceased to be entitled to IS/income-based JSA[115] (unless you have moved from IS to income-based JSA or vice versa).[116] Otherwise, the local authority reviews your existing entitlement and either increases or reduces your existing HB, as appropriate.[117] A review is likely to cause less disruption to your benefit payments than a fresh claim, so you may wish to ask for them to consider this option, particularly if your circumstances change quite frequently. Local authorities rarely use this option and may need to be persuaded to do so.

5. OVERPAYMENTS

If the information you give the local authority is wrong, or if you do not report a change in your circumstances (see p277), you could end up being paid too much housing benefit (HB). You could also be overpaid as a result of an official error or delay which is not your fault. Not all overpayments are legally recoverable although local authorities sometimes recover them illegally.

What is an overpayment

An overpayment is any amount of HB which has been paid to you but to which the local authority decides (either when they make the initial decision on your claim or on review) that you were not entitled under the regulations.[118] A 'payment' includes both a direct payment of benefit to you or your landlord and also HB credited on your rent account.[119] The local authority must have actually paid you some HB to which you were not entitled for an overpayment to have taken place.

Dealing with overpayments

Local authorities should take the following steps in an overpayment case:

Step 1 Establish the cause, or causes, of the overpayment (see below).

Step 2 Determine whether any of the overpayment is legally recoverable by the local authority under the regulations (see p282).

Step 3 Decide, where the overpayment is legally recoverable, whether or not recovery should be sought (see p284).

Step 4 Work out the amount of the overpayment and the period over which it occurred (see p284).

Step 5 Decide from whom recovery should be made, by what method and at what rate (see p286).

Step 6 Notify you of all the above decisions regarding the overpayment and give you an opportunity to request further information or a review (see p283).

The cause of the overpayment

The reason why any overpayment has taken place determines whether, and from whom, it is legally recoverable.

An overpayment may arise for a number of reasons.[120] These are:

- Claimant error or fraud if you or someone acting on your behalf (eg, an appointee) are responsible for the overpayment taking place. You may have caused the overpayment innocently or fraudulently.
- Official error if the overpayment is due to a mistake made whether in the form of something done or not done, by the local authority, Benefits Agency or the Employment Service acting on behalf of the Benefits Agency. However, if you or someone acting on your behalf (eg, an appointee), or someone to whom the payment was made (eg, an agent or landlord), contributed to the overpayment it is classified as a claimant error.
- 'Payment on account' if a private tenant has received an interim payment which is subsequently found to exceed her/his actual benefit entitlement (see p274).
- Other errors including overpayments caused by a third party such as your landlord or employer, or which may not be anyone's fault.

An overpayment may have more than one cause, in which case the local authority must separately identify the amount of the overpayment which has arisen as a result of each particular cause. For example, if you delay notifying the local authority of a change in circumstances for three weeks and then the local authority subsequently fails to take any action for a further two weeks, two kinds of overpayment have taken place – a 'claimant error' overpayment for the first three weeks and an 'official error' overpayment for the last two weeks.

Overpayments which are recoverable

Most overpayments, including all HB 'payments on account' (see p274), are legally recoverable, which means that the local authority can make you pay them back. However, you do not have to pay back an overpayment if:[121]

- it was due to an official error (see p281); *and*
- it was paid for a past period; *and*
- you or someone acting on your behalf (eg, an appointee) or someone to whom the payment was made (eg, an agent or landlord), could not have reasonably been expected to know that an overpayment was being made at the time that the payment was notified or received.

This rule does not apply where HB has been credited to your rent account for a future period. In this case, the forward award of HB can be withdrawn even if it arose due to official error. Benefit paid after the date your claim is reviewed is recoverable.

Where too much HB has been credited to your account for a past period you could argue that the overpayment cannot be recovered if you have not been notified of the credit.[122] If you are a private tenant you should argue that if official errors lead to the wrong payments being directly credited to your bank/giro account or that of your appointee, agent or landlord, the past overpayment is not recoverable unless you were notified of the payment.

For the overpayment to be recoverable, the local authority only needs to show that either you, *or* the person acting on your behalf, *or* the person HB was paid to caused or contributed to the overpayment and that only one of you could reasonably have been expected to know that HB was being overpaid.[123]

The extent to which you can reasonably be expected to realise that an overpayment is being made to you depends on the extent to which the local authority has advised you about the scheme or your duties and obligations, particularly about your duty to notify changes of circumstances. It depends not on what you know, but on what you could have known at the time of the payment or the notification.

If, for example, you declared your full capital but the local authority took the wrong amount into account, you could argue that you could not reasonably have known that you were being overpaid because of the complexity of the tariff income rules, which makes it hard for a claimant to understand how their capital has been assessed. On the other hand if you have declared an increase in income and your HB was not reduced it may be harder to argue that you could not have known that you were being overpaid, because the local authority may say that you should have expected a consequent decrease in your HB. However, the local authority is not entitled to simply assume that because you knew your HB was wrong you must have known you were being overpaid (some changes of circumstances may increase your HB and lead to you being underpaid). Remember that the local authority must show, not just that you could have reasonably been expected to know that you might have been overpaid, but that you were overpaid.[124] You should always argue that as a claimant, you cannot be expected to know the intricacies of the HB legislation and that unless it was glaringly obvious that a change of circumstances would reduce your HB you should be given the benefit of the doubt.

Notification of overpayments

If the local authority decides that a recoverable overpayment has occurred, it must write to the person from whom recovery is being sought (within 14 days, if possible) and notify them accordingly.[125] This notification must state:[126]

- the fact that there is an overpayment which is legally recoverable;
- the reason why there is a recoverable overpayment;
- the amount of the recoverable overpayment;
- how the amount of the overpayment was calculated;
- the benefit weeks to which the overpayment relates;
- if recovery is to be made from future benefit, how much the deduction will be;
- that you have a right to ask for a further written explanation of any of the decisions the local authority has made regarding the overpayment, how you can do this and the time limit for doing so;
- that you have a right to ask the local authority to reconsider any of the decisions it has made regarding the overpayment, how you can do this and the time limit for doing so.

It may also include any other relevant matters.

If you write and ask the local authority for a more detailed written explanation of any of the decisions it has made regarding the overpayment, it must send you this within 14 days or, if this is not reasonably practicable, as soon as possible after that.[127] Notifications provided by many local authorities have been either inadequate or non-existent. Such authorities are in breach of their statutory duties. If your local authority does not give proper notification, you should write and point out that the decision to recover the overpayment is not valid until you are given proper notification. No recovery should be sought until after you have been notified and have had a chance to discuss your case or apply for a review.[128]

Recovering overpayments

Any overpayment of a 'payment on account' must be recovered by the local authority in every case[129] (see p274). All other recoverable overpayments may be recovered at the local authority's discretion.[130] Some recover all recoverable overpayments and others only recover those caused by claimant error.

Nevertheless, local authorities have a legal duty to exercise their judgement on whether or not to make a recovery on the merits of each and every individual case. While they may have general policy guidelines on how to approach the issue in a consistent manner, these must not be so rigid as to effectively decide the outcome of each case in advance. A policy of always recovering recoverable overpayments would, therefore, amount to an unlawful 'fettering' of the local authority's discretion which could be challenged by judicial review.

If you have been overpaid and this was either not your fault or the result of a genuine mistake or oversight on your part, you should ask the local authority not to recover the overpayment, especially if recovery causes you hardship. If the local authority still insists on proceeding with recovery action, you should ask for a review. The rules allow you to ask for a review on the recovery method and the rate of recovery.[131] This is not the same as IS rules where you cannot appeal these decisions. DSS guidance says that a decision to recover a recoverable overpayment is not open to review.[132] You should request a review and argue that this is wrong. A decision to recover is a 'determination' under the HB Regulations and therefore open to review.[133] Furthermore, the review board has the same power to exercise discretion as the local authority.[134] If the overpayment was caused by someone else, you could suggest that recovery is made from her/him (but see p286). You may be asked to repay an irrecoverable overpayment on a voluntary basis. You are under no legal obligation to do so.

The amount of overpayment which is recoverable

The authority should distinguish between those overpayments it regards as recoverable and those it does not. Complications can arise where some of the overpayment is caused by claimant error and some by official error. You should also check that the authority has offset certain payments against the overpayment. These are:

• Any part of the overpayment which is not recoverable.

- Any amount to which you were properly entitled during the period to which the overpayment relates.[135]
- If you have been getting a rent rebate over the overpayment period and, for some reason, have paid more into your rent account than you should have paid according to your original (incorrect) benefit assessment, any overpayment arising over that period may be reduced by the amount of the excess payment. The authority will probably not apply this rule where the extra rent is to repay your rent arrears.[136]
- A recoverable overpayment has occurred because your capital has been incorrectly assessed – eg, because the local authority made a mistake, was misled, or not told, about how much capital you or your family have. If this overpayment is for a period of more than 13 benefit weeks, the local authority applies the 'diminishing capital rule' when calculating the amount of the overpayment.[137]

The logic behind the diminishing capital rule is that, had your unassessed capital been taken into account in the first place, and your HB consequently reduced or withdrawn, you would have drawn on your capital in order to help meet your housing costs. The rule works in the following way:[138]

- The amount overpaid during the overpayment period is first calculated in the normal way.
- At the end of the first 13 benefit weeks the claimant's assessed capital is reduced by the amount of the overpaid HB which occurred over that period.
- This reduced capital is then used to recalculate the claimant's entitlement, and hence, overpayment, from the beginning of the 14th benefit week onwards.
- This procedure is then repeated for each subsequent block of 13 weeks until either the claimant's capital is reduced to below £3,000 (so it has no effect on entitlement) or there are less than 14 weeks left before the end of the overpayment period.

The reduction in capital only takes place at the end of each complete block of 13 weeks in the overpayment period. This means the rule has no effect until the beginning of the 14th week of the overpayment period. It also means that capital cannot be regarded as reducing over any period of less than 13 weeks.[139]

If you are making voluntary repayments following an official error, make sure the local authority has taken the diminishing capital rule into account when calculating the amount of the overpayment. The diminishing capital rule is only relevant for calculating overpayments. Your current entitlement is based on your actual capital.

Recovery action

There are special rules that lay down who a local authority can recover an overpayment from and how they can recover it. There are no rules about the rate of recovery. You can challenge any decisions they take in recovering an overpayment from you (see p292).

From whom the overpayment is recovered

An overpayment can be recovered from:[140]

- you (or your partner where you were members of the same household both at the time the overpayment was made and while it is being recovered);
- the person to whom the payment was made;
- where the overpayment was the result of a misrepresentation or failure to disclose a material fact, from the person who misrepresented or failed to disclose. (This means that an overpayment could be recovered from the landlord, for example, even where they did not actually receive the payment.)

If HB was paid direct to your landlord but is subsequently recovered from her/him because you were not in fact entitled to that HB, new regulations which came into force in April 1997 say that this will put you in rent arrears. However, there is an argument that regulations cannot do that and that your landlord simply has a debt that s/he can recover from you. You will still owe the money, but the landlord will not be able to obtain possession of your home for its non-payment. If you find yourself in this position, you should get advice.[141]

In the event of the death of the person from whom recovery is being sought, local authorities may consider recovering any outstanding overpayment from that person's estate.[142]

How the overpayment is recovered

The local authority can recover an overpayment of HB:

- by deductions from the HB entitlement of any of the people from whom recovery can be made (see p287); *or*
- where it is unable to do so by requesting the Secretary of State to make deductions from other social security benefits (see p287); *or*
- by any other lawful method of recovery (see p288).

Recovery from HB

If your landlord has been overpaid HB for another tenant, the local authority cannot recover this from your HB. [143] (But see p291 for details of the Fraud Bill.) If deductions are made from your ongoing HB entitlement, you will have to make up the amount so that your rent liability is met in full. Otherwise, you will fall into rent arrears. Overpayments arising as a result of a 'payment on account' (see p274) can only be recovered through deductions from HB, unless you no longer have any current entitlement.[144]

Recovery through the Benefits Agency

The local authority can ask the Benefits Agency to recover the overpayment by making deductions from most other social security benefits if:

- a recoverable overpayment has been made as a result of a misrepresentation or failure to disclose a material fact by, or on behalf of, the claimant or some other person to whom HB has been paid; *and*
- the local authority is unable to recover that overpayment from any HB entitlement; *and*
- the person who misrepresented or failed to disclose is receiving at least one of the relevant benefits (see below) at a sufficiently high rate for deductions to be made.[145]

Deductions cannot be made from child benefit or guardian's allowance and, arguably, incapacity benefit because they are not benefits under the Social Security Act 1975. The amount that can be deducted from income support (IS)/income-based jobseeker's allowance (JSA) is unspecified. You should make representations to the Benefits Agency if deductions cause hardship.

Overpayments of HB cannot be recovered by deductions from council tax benefit (CTB) (and vice versa).[146] If deductions stop because the person ceases to be entitled to that social security benefit, or entitlement drops below the minimum for deductions, the Benefits Agency notifies the local authority which, once again, becomes responsible for any further recovery action.

Other methods of recovery

An overpayment can also be recovered by the local authority asking for payment in a lump sum. As a last resort, the local authority can recover the money you owe through the county court if it thinks you could afford to make repayments.[147] You have six weeks to ask for a review of the decision that the overpayment is recoverable (see p292). This should be borne in mind when local authorities are deciding when to start proceedings. A local authority is not entitled to issue court proceedings for recovery if it has not followed the correct procedure for deciding that there has been a recoverable overpayment. If they do take court action, you can raise any procedural failings as a defence. The correct procedure has not been followed if, for example, the local authority has not issued the correct notification (see p283).[148]

If a local authority recovers overpaid HB by adjusting its own rent account, the overpayment should be separately identified and you should be informed that the amount being recovered does not represent rent arrears. Local authorities are reminded in guidance from the DSS that overpayments of HB in respect of their own tenants are not rent arrears and should not be treated as such.[149]

How much is recovered

A local authority can decide how much of a recoverable overpayment it will actually recover. It can ask for the whole amount at once or recover it by instalments.

If you are not on IS/income-based JSA but your income is below or not much above your IS/income-based JSA level, you should argue for the same weekly maximum (see p151) to apply. You should also ask the local authority to take into account any other debts or financial commitments or health problems you may have.[150] Complain if the rate of recovery is causing you hardship.

You should check that the methods used by the authority and the rates of recovery are consistent between groups of claimants. For example, council tenants should not be required to repay overpayments in a lump sum (ie, the whole overpayment is debited to their account) where private tenants can repay by instalment – ie, by weekly deductions made to their HB. If this is happening, you should ask for a review.

6. FRAUD

What is fraud?

You are guilty of fraud if, in order to get housing benefit (HB) (or more HB), you deliberately make false statements or use false documents or information.[151] A deliberate failure to report a change of circumstances may constitute fraud.[152]

If a mistake arose through genuine error or oversight, you cannot be prosecuted for fraud and you should make sure that you do not say or sign anything which could give the local authority the opportunity to accuse you of fraud. (See p291 for details of the Fraud Bill.)

Remember that there is a difference between overpayment and fraud and the local authority should distinguish clearly between your current entitlement, any past overpayments and deliberate fraud. Make sure that the following steps have been followed:

- Establish the facts. Ask what information they have on your claim and correct any inaccuracies. If they are relying on anonymous allegations against you, insist that they tell you who is making these so that you can comment. Check whether they have proof that you have committed fraud and whether their information is reliable. While the authority is establishing the facts they can withhold your HB (see p276).
- Re-assess entitlement. Any new information might not lead to a change in your HB, but your entitlement could go down or even end. You can ask for a review of your entitlement if you disagree (see p292).
- Calculate any overpayment. This should be dealt with under the normal rules (see p284).
- Decide whether fraud has been committed. If the authority considers that your actions were deliberate and that you have gained HB to which you were not entitled as a result they could prosecute you. The power to prosecute is in addition to the right to recover any overpayment.

What happens if you are accused of fraud?

If you are asked to attend an interview, get advice and/or take a friend or adviser with you. Fraud staff are very aware of the need to make savings by identifying cases where HB is being wrongly paid and sometimes claimants complain of being pressured into making statements that are not accurate. If you feel this is happening to you, make sure you do not agree to anything which is not true and ask for the interview to be terminated if necessary. If you feel that the behaviour of the interviewing officer was inappropriate, you should complain.

It can be very threatening to be suddenly accused of fraud and the important thing is to try to remain calm, listen to the allegations against you and then explain the true position. You do not have to say anything if you do not want to, but remember that if there is any doubt as to your entitlement, your HB could be suspended while further enquiries are made (see p277).

Fraud staff have the power to do interviews under caution. If this happens they should advise you of your right to silence. They should explain that it may harm your defence if you do not mention when questioned something you later rely on in court and that they will be taking a formal record of the interview which could be used as evidence in a court hearing.[153] If you are interviewed under caution, try to make notes of what was said immediately afterwards. Prosecutions often take some time and it is easy to forget what was said, particularly if you were feeling flustered.

Do not forget that fraud officers can ask about other benefits too if they think you are fraudulently claiming more than one. Local authorities can investigate any allegations that you are living with someone as husband and wife, even if you are also getting IS/income-based JSA.[154]

Prosecution[155]

If the local authority feels that it has strong enough evidence against you, it can prosecute you for fraud. This is normally done within three months of sufficient evidence being obtained to justify a prosecution, or within 12 months of the offence being committed. You should seek advice if this happens and ideally get a solicitor to represent you in court. If you lose you face a fine of up to £2,000, or up to three months' imprisonment, or both. Remember that you may also have to repay any overpaid HB on top of this.

You will not always be prosecuted even if you have committed fraud. The decision to prosecute takes account of a number of factors – eg, the amount of money involved, the reliability of the evidence against you, whether you have been guilty of fraud in the past, any social factors and your physical or mental condition, whether you voluntarily confessed, and whether there was any maladministration of your case or any shortcomings in the way the investigation was handled.[156]

A prosecution should not jeopardise any future claims for HB so long as you are legitimately entitled. However, you may face difficulties in getting your claim assessed promptly because, for example, the local authority decides to check out your circumstances especially thoroughly given your past conviction. You should complain if it takes an unreasonable amount of time to decide your claim.

The Fraud Bill

The Fraud Bill was going through Parliament at the time this book went to press. See CPAG's *Welfare Rights Bulletin* for further details.

The main features of the bill for the purposes of HB are:

- Local authorities are to have the power to require certain information from landlords and agents (for example about property they own or manage in the UK).
- The penalties for fraud are to be increased.
- It will be an offence to fail to notify (or 'knowingly cause another person to fail to notify') a relevant change of circumstances without 'reasonable excuse'.
- Local authorities and the Secretary of State will have the power to offer payment of a penalty as an alternative to prosecution if a recoverable overpayment has been made and they consider that there are grounds for instituting proceedings against you. The penalty will be 30 per cent of the amount of the overpayment.
- Local authorities will have the power to recover overpayments made to a landlord for one tenant from HB paid to them for another tenant.

7. REVIEWS

A review is the process by which a local authority or the housing benefit review board (see p293) looks again at a decision and decides whether it should be altered. Such a review may be in your favour or may reduce the amount of benefit you receive.

If you wish to challenge a decision, you can do so only by asking for a review.

Local authority reviews

The local authority can review any of its own decisions, and those of the review board, at any time if:

- there has been a change of circumstances (see p277); *or*
- it is satisfied the decision was made in ignorance of, or based on a mistake as to, some material fact. In the case of a review board decision, this must be shown by fresh evidence that was not available

to the board (and which could not have been put before the board at the time); *or*

- in the case of a local authority decision only, it is satisfied that it was based on a mistake as to the law. However, local authorities cannot decide that a regulation is invalid because the Secretary of State exceeded his powers in making it.[157]

If a decision is amended on a review initiated by a local authority, this counts as a fresh decision requiring notification in the normal way, so you can ask for yet another review (see below) if it is unfavourable to you.[158]

Your right to a review

You can also ask for a review of any decision (including a local authority review decision) simply on the ground that you disagree with it. The right to a review also applies to other people affected by the decision (see p270).[159] Such an application must be received by the local authority within six weeks of the decision being notified to you,[160] although the local authority can allow a late application if there are special reasons.[161] The local authority must tell you of your right to apply for a review every time you are notified of a decision.[162] If it fails to do so, that will be a special reason for allowing a late application. An application for an extension must be made in writing, and, if it is refused, the local authority's decision is final[163] (although, in an exceptional case, it might be challenged by judicial review – see p297).

If you want a written explanation from the local authority (see pp270-71) so that you can state your case more effectively, the period between your request reaching the local authority and the explanation being posted to you is ignored when calculating the six-week limit.[164] It is often worth asking the local authority for a written explanation before formally requesting a review, because the law is complicated and you will then know the basis on which the decision was taken. However, if the reasons for the decision are clear or your situation is urgent, you should not delay asking for a review. You can ask for a further written explanation at any time.[165]

There is no time limit laid down within which the authority must carry out the review. Some local authorities have a policy of carrying out the review within 14 days of receiving a request for a review.

You must be notified in writing of the outcome of the review. The information given to you following the review must conform to the normal rules about the notification of decisions (see p270). It must also inform you of your right to ask for a further review by a review board (see below).[166]

If a decision is altered on review, the revised decision takes effect from the date of the original decision.[167] However, if the review results in an increase in your housing benefit (HB), arrears cannot normally be paid for more than 52 weeks before the date the local authority first received your request for the review. The only exception is where the local authority has reversed a decision not to backdate your claim under the 'good cause for a late claim' provisions – in which case any arrears may be paid for up to 52 weeks before the date your request for backdating was made[168] (see p268).

The housing benefit review board

A hearing before a review board is the nearest thing there is to an independent appeal for HB cases. Although review boards are not really independent, they must act as if they are. The review board is made up of local authority councillors.

Applying for a hearing

If you have exercised your right to a review (see p291), and remain dissatisfied with the local authority's decision, you can write and ask for a further review. It is this 'further review' that is carried out by a housing benefit review board.

When you apply, you must give your reasons. These need not be detailed or technical as long as it is clear what it is you disagree with. The request for the further review must reach the local authority within 28 days of the notification of the internal review being posted to you.[169] The review board may extend the deadline if there are special reasons for doing so. An application for an extension must be made to the chair of the review board in writing, and, if it is refused, the review board's decision is final (although, in an exceptional case, it might be challenged by judicial review – see p297).[170]

The hearing

A hearing before a review board should take place within six weeks of your request reaching the local authority or, if that is not reasonably practicable, as soon as possible after that.[171] Some authorities make claimants wait months for a review board hearing. If this has happened in your case, write and threaten to make a complaint of maladministration to the Ombudsman (see p298). However, if you are challenging a decision to restrict your eligible rent (see p232) and the local authority has asked the rent officer to reconsider your case as a result, the review board may decide to defer your hearing pending the outcome.[172]

You must be given at least ten days' notice of the time of the hearing and the place where it will be held, otherwise you have the right to insist on another date being set.[173] If you have been given adequate notice but would like the hearing to be postponed, or if you wish to withdraw your request for a hearing altogether, you must write to the review board chairperson who decides whether the hearing should still proceed.[174]

The review board consists of at least three local authority councillors (or members of the New Town Corporation, Development Board for Rural Wales or Scottish Special Housing Association) one of whom acts as chairperson.[175] But if there are only two members of the board present when you attend, the hearing can go ahead provided all parties consent.[176] DSS guidance suggests that the board should not consist of anyone who has had a previous involvement in your case.[177] If the issue to be considered by the review board affects your claim for HB and/or council tax benefit (CTB) and/or community charge benefit (eg, the assessment of your income), the same review board can consider your claim for any combination of all three benefits at the same time, provided everyone concerned in the case agrees.[178]

The board chairperson decides how the hearing should be conducted.[179] You also have the right to attend the hearing and to present your case, call witnesses and question the local authority's witnesses. You can be accompanied to the hearing or be represented. During the hearing your representative has the same rights as you in presenting your case.[180] The local authority should pay your travelling expenses and those of one other person who accompanies or represents you, also any other person affected (eg, called as witnesses).[181] The tactics for presenting a case before the review board are similar to those for social security appeal tribunals (see p166).

The review board has the right to ask people to give evidence, but it cannot compel anyone to appear before them who does not wish to.[182] If you fail to attend a hearing, the review board can proceed in your absence.[183] If you were unable to attend through circumstances beyond your control, and the review board has given an unfavourable decision, you may be able to have the decision 'set aside' (see p296).

If the review board decides to adjourn a hearing and the case is subsequently heard by a board composed of any different members, the second board should hear your whole case again.[184]

The decision

After hearing your case, the review board either confirms or alters the decision of the local authority.[185] If the board is not unanimous, a majority decision is taken. If there is an even number of members, the chairperson has a second or casting vote if necessary.[186] The chairperson must record the board's decision and its finding on any material question of fact.[187]

In arriving at its decision, the review board is bound only by the law and not by any local authority or DSS policy. It may exercise any discretion open to the local authority under the regulations.[188] It is bound by decisions on HB in the High Court, the Court of Appeal, the House of Lords and the European Court of Justice. Decisions in these courts on other benefits or related issues may be persuasive. It is not bound by any of its own previous decisions, nor by any of the decisions made by SSATs or Social Security Commissioners on similar cases and issues in other areas of the social security system, although it can take them into account. In particular, it should be slow to disagree with a commissioner's decision as commissioners are judges with considerable experience of this sort of law.

A copy of the decision must be sent to you within seven days or, if that is not practicable, as soon as possible after that, together with the reasons for the decision and the board's findings of fact.[189] These should give a clear explanation of why you have won or lost.[190] If the review board has altered the local authority's decision in any way, the local authority must implement the board's decision with effect from the date the original decision was made.[191]

If the board has awarded additional HB, arrears may only be paid for up to 52 weeks before the date on which the local authority completed its initial internal review. The only exception is where the review board have overturned a previous local authority decision not to backdate a claim under the 'good cause for a late claim' provisions – in which case any arrears may be paid for up to 52 weeks from the date your claim for backdating is treated as having been made (see p268).[192]

A decision of a review board may be subsequently reviewed by a local authority in certain circumstances (see p291).

There is no right of appeal from a review board's decision but, if the decision was wrong in law, you can apply for judicial review (see p297).

Correcting a decision

Both local authorities and review boards can correct any accidental errors which have occurred in their decisions.[193] An accidental error is a slip of the pen, a misprint, a mathematical error, or the omission of a word etc. Corrections may be made at any time and take effect as though they were part of the original decision, or record of a decision, being corrected. Every person affected must be informed of the correction. You cannot seek a review against the correction of a decision, but you can ask for a review of the decision itself.[194]

Setting aside a decision

Both local authorities and review boards also have the power to set aside their own decisions if the interests of justice warrant it.[195] 'Setting aside' means deleting the decision as though it had never been made in the first place. A new decision is then made.

The law allows a decision to be set aside if it appears just to do so because:[196]

- you, your representative, or some other person affected by the decision, were not sent, or did not receive, a document relating to the matters concerned in that decision, or the document arrived too late;
- in the case of a hearing before a review board, you, your representative, or some other person affected by the decision were not present;
- for some other reason, the interests of justice require it.

Any person affected by a decision may apply to have that decision set aside.[197] Applications must be in writing and must reach the local authority or review board concerned within 13 weeks of the notification of that decision being posted to the applicant.[198] The 13-week limit cannot be extended but does not include any period before the correction of (or refusal to correct) that decision, or the setting aside of a previous decision.[199] The local authority or review board must send copies of the application to any other persons affected by the decision and give them a reasonable opportunity to comment.[200]

The outcome of an application to have a decision set aside must be notified in writing to every person affected as soon as possible, and this must contain a statement explaining the reasons for meeting or rejecting that request.[201]

If your request to have a decision set aside is rejected, this cannot be challenged by means of a review,[202] but you may still request a review of the original decision itself. In applying the time limits for requesting a review, no account is taken of any period between the date when the notification of the decision, and the notification of the refusal to set it aside, were each posted to you.[203] If you have been denied a fair hearing before the review board and your request to have the board's decision set aside is turned down, you may be able to challenge this by way of a judicial review (see below).

Judicial review

Judicial review is a method of challenging a decision of any form of tribunal, government department or local authority.

Applications are to the High Court (in Scotland, the Court of Session), and should be made within three months.

In practice, it is not a procedure that can be used very much in social security cases except in HB and CTB cases against decisions of review boards. That is because there are two major restrictions on the power of the court to intervene. First, the court very seldom intervenes if there is an alternative right of appeal. Secondly, the court can only intervene to correct an error of law. For these purposes, error of law has the same meaning as for appeals to a Social Security Commissioner in income support (IS) cases (see p168).

Review boards quite often make errors of law (including the failure to make proper findings of fact and give adequate reasons for their decisions). If you consider that one has been made in your case, you should consult a solicitor. Legal aid is available in judicial review cases. CPAG's solicitor may be able to advise if you go through an advice agency.

Claims for damages

If a local authority has failed to carry out its obligations under the HB scheme or has failed to carry them out properly – in other words if it is in 'breach of statutory duty' – you may be able to sue for damages if you can show you have suffered financial loss as a result. An authority would be in breach of statutory duty if, for example, it had not determined a claim where it was under a duty to do so or if it had not paid HB to which you were entitled.

However, the Court of Appeal has held that a landlord cannot sue a local authority for failure to make direct payments (see p275) even if s/he has suffered financial loss as a result.[204] The Court said a landlord would, in these circumstances, simply have to follow the review procedure (see p293). The Court made other comments in this case which appear to indicate that *no one* (whether a claimant, landlord or anyone else) could ever sue for breach of statutory duty. Elsewhere in the judgement they appear to accept that such claims *can* sometimes be brought. You should argue that the case simply related to direct payments and that claims for damages for breach of other statutory duties can be brought. An example is where someone loses their home because the authority failed to make a payment on account of HB (see p274). You should get advice.

8. COMPLAINTS

Complaints

The review procedure enables you to challenge the way that a local authority has applied the law in your case. If you wish to challenge the manner in which your claim was dealt with rather than the actual decision itself, you should make use of the council's complaints procedure. Where there is no formal procedure, you should begin by writing to the supervisor of the person dealing with your claim, making it clear why you are dissatisfied. Include details of everything that has gone wrong, and make it clear what you expect the council to do about it – eg, sort out the claim within seven days, make a formal apology, compensate you for any loss. If you do not receive a satisfactory reply, you should take the matter up with someone more senior in the department and ultimately the principal officer.

Local authority offices are the responsibility of a senior officer (the relevant officer's name or title usually appears on its headed notepaper). In turn, those officers are responsible to councillors and you can write to one of your local councillors or the chair of the relevant council committee. Government departments also monitor local authorities so, if all else fails, you can write to the relevant minister – ie, the Secretary of State for Social Security.

The local government Ombudsman

If you have tried to sort out your complaint with the local authority but you are still not satisfied with the outcome, you can apply to the Commissioner for Local Administration (more commonly known as the local government Ombudsman). The Ombudsman can investigate any cases of maladministration by local authorities. The most common type of maladministration dealt with by the Ombudsman is delays in processing claims or applications for review. Failure to properly apply the procedure for dealing with claims or to give you proper notifications about your entitlement are also covered, though in most cases if there is a right of appeal against a decision the best remedy is to use that right.

You may apply to the Ombudsman by writing to the appropriate local office (see Appendix 2). The Ombudsman has extensive powers to look at documents held by the local authority on your claim. You may be interviewed to check any facts. Straightforward cases can be dealt with in about three months. The Ombudsman can recommend financial compensation if you have been unfairly treated or suffered a loss as a result of the maladministration. A complaint may also make the authority review its procedures, which could be of benefit to claimants other than you.

Good cause for a late claim

Good cause means 'some fact which having regard to all the circumstances (including the claimant's state of health and the information which he received and that which he might have obtained), would probably have caused a reasonable person of his age and experience to act (or fail to act) as the claimant did.'[205]

There is a general duty to find out your rights, but your age and experience are taken into account in deciding whether you acted reasonably. If you did not know your rights, you need to explain why.[206]

You are expected to make enquiries, for example, to the local authority, Benefits Agency,[207] a solicitor[208] or a citizens' advice bureau.[209] Relying on the advice of work colleagues, friends,[210] or even a doctor,[211] is not enough.

If you have made enquiries, you will have good cause of you were misled or insufficiently informed of your rights.[212] The enquiries need not necessarily have been in connection with that particular claim, and people have succeeded in proving good cause where they have simply misunderstood the system. Difficulties with the English language, illiteracy or unfamiliarity with technical documents should be taken into account.[213] Physical or mental ill-health may amount to good cause.[214] If you have made no enquiries you may have good cause if your ignorance was due to a mistaken belief, reasonably held.[215]

Council tax benefit

This chapter covers:

I. THE BASIC RULES

Council tax benefit (CTB) is paid by local authorities and not by the Benefits Agency, although it is a national scheme and the rules are mainly determined by DSS regulations.

There are two types of benefit: main CTB and alternative maximum CTB usually known as second adult rebate. Most people will only qualify for the former, but if you are eligible for both, you will be paid whichever is the higher.

Who can claim

To claim you must be liable to pay council tax on a property which you normally occupy as your home. If you have more than one home it must be your main home.

You can claim main CTB if:[1]

- your income is low enough. How low it has to be depends on your circumstances (see Chapter 19); *and*
- your savings and other capital are not worth more than £16,000 (see Chapter 20); *and*
- you are not a student.[2] There are certain, limited, exceptions – see p314; *and*

- you are not a 'person from abroad' (see p222 for what this means). NB, if you were not entitled to CTB while you were an asylum-seeker, you may be retrospectively entitled to CTB for that period if you are subsequently granted refugee status (see p225).

You can claim a second adult rebate if:

- with certain exceptions you are the only person liable for the council tax on your home (see below); *and*
- with certain exceptions no one living in your home pays you rent (see p307); *and*
- there are certain other adults living with you who are on low incomes; *and*
- you are not a 'person from abroad' (see p222 for what this means).

For second adult rebate it does not matter if you are a student and/or have capital of more than £16,000.

Also note that:

- CTB is non-taxable and is not dependent on you having paid national insurance contributions;
- you must be aged 18 or more to qualify for CTB;
- you may claim CTB regardless of whether or not you or your partner are working or on income support/income-based jobseeker's allowance;
- you can still claim CTB if you have already paid your council tax bill in advance;
- if you are in arrears with your council tax bill this does not affect your right to claim CTB. You may even be able to get your claim backdated for up to one year (see p268);
- if you are temporarily absent from home you can continue to get CTB. The rules are the same as for housing benefit (HB) (see p217).

Who you claim for

You claim for your 'family' (see Chapter 17).

2. LIABILITY TO PAY COUNCIL TAX

There is not space here to describe the rules relating to the council tax itself. For an explanation of the following issues consult the *Council Tax Handbook* by Martin Ward and Bob Prew (see Appendix 4).

- which properties are subject to council tax;

- who is liable to pay council tax;
- disability reductions;
- discounts;
- transitional reduction.

3. THE AMOUNT OF BENEFIT

The calculation of council tax benefit (CTB) and second adult rebate is explained below.

Main council tax benefit

The calculation of CTB is based on your net weekly liability for council tax – ie, your bill after any of the following reductions have been applied:[3]

- a disability reduction;
- a discount;
- transitional reduction.

Joint liability

If you are jointly liable for the council tax, the local authority calculate your share of the bill by dividing the total net liability by the number of liable persons (but ignoring any liable persons who are students who cannot claim CTB)[4] (see p314). This does not apply where you only share joint liability with your heterosexual partner, as one of you makes a joint claim for both on the total bill.[5] Where a couple are also jointly liable with one or more other residents, the couple can claim on a two-person share of the bill.

Example
Three residents are jointly liable for a net annual council tax bill of £600. They can each make a separate claim on £200 liability (an equal share). If two of the residents were a couple, however, either member of the couple could make a single claim on £400 liability (a two-person share), with the third resident making a separate claim on £200 liability (a one-person share).
If the third resident became a student and was therefore excluded from CTB, the couple could then claim on the full £600 liability.

Under the council tax rules, a person who is jointly and severally liable can be held responsible for the full amount of the tax due on the property while receiving CTB only on her/his 'share'.

Weekly council tax figure

Weekly net liability is assessed by dividing the annual charge by the number of days in the financial year (365 or 366) and then multiplying this by seven.[6]

Example

Net liability £490
Divide this by 365 (or 366, if appropriate) = £1.342466
Multiply this by 7 = £9.397262

DSS guidance recommends that the figures should not be rounded until the final annual amount of CTB is worked out, and that calculations should usually be done to six decimal places.[7] When notifying you of your CTB a rounded figure can be specified.[8]

Calculation of benefit

The steps below will help to calculate your CTB entitlement.

If you are on income support (IS)/income-based jobseeker's allowance (JSA):
- Work out your maximum CTB. This is your total liability minus any non-dependant deductions.
- If you are on IS/income based JSA, you are entitled to maximum CTB.

If you are not on IS/income-based JSA:
- Check that your capital is not too high (see Chapter 20).
- Work out your maximum CTB. This is your eligible rent minus any non-dependant deductions.
- Work out your applicable amount (see Chapter 18).
- Work out your income (see Chapter 19).
- **If your income is less than or equal to your applicable amount,** you are entitled to maximum CTB.
- **If your income is greater than your applicable amount,** work out the difference. The amount of CTB you are entitled to is maximum CTB **minus 20 per cent** of the difference between your income and applicable amount.

Unlike HB, there is no minimum payment rule.

If you were entitled to IS/income-based JSA but your entitlement ceases because you start work or increase your hours of or income from work, you may be entitled to an extended payment of CTB for the four weeks following the end of your entitlement to IS/income-based JSA (see p250).

Note: *The Government has announced its intention to limit the amount of CTB payable on higher banded property. From April 1998, it is proposed that CTB will not be paid in full on homes valued at more than £120,000 (in England). See CPAG's* Welfare Rights Bulletin *for further details.*

Non-dependant deductions

A non-dependant is someone who normally lives with you on a non-commercial basis[9] but who is not your partner or dependent child. Only heterosexual couples are recognised in social security law so a lesbian or gay partner counts as a non-dependant unless s/he is a joint tenant or owner. Non-dependants have no liability to pay the tax themselves and are assumed to contribute towards your council tax. In most cases, a deduction is made from your CTB if you have non-dependants regardless of whether they do contribute,[10] and you should consider asking them to reimburse you for at least the amount of the deduction.

The following people do not count as non-dependants:

- a child or young person living with you who is not a member of your household.[11]
- Someone who is jointly liable with you for the council tax. However, they will count as a non-dependant if:
  - they live with the person they are liable to pay rent to and either that person is a close relative or the agreement is not on a commercial basis; *or*
  - their liability to make payments in respect of their home is 'contrived' (see below).[12]
- Someone who pays rent to you or your partner.[13] However, if s/he is a close relative (see p27) or the arrangement is not a commercial one s/he will count as a non-dependant.[14] Their liability for rent must not be 'contrived' (see below). 'Commercial' does not necessarily mean profit-making but it does imply that you must at least break even.
- Someone who is employed by a charitable or voluntary body to live with, and provide care for you or your partner, if you have to pay for this service.[15]

Arrangements 'contrived' to take advantage of the council tax benefit scheme

If the local authority consider that a person's liability to pay rent or other housing costs was contrived to take advantage of the CTB scheme (ie, to avoid a non-dependant deduction) that person counts as a non-dependant.[16]

This applies where:

- it appears to the local authority that the liability to pay rent/housing costs was contrived to take advantage of the CTB scheme, unless they were otherwise liable to pay rent in the eight weeks prior to the agreement was made; *or*
- a joint occupier was a non-dependant in the previous eight weeks unless the local authority is satisfied that the change in arrangements was not made to take advantage of the CTB scheme.

Once it is established that you have one or more non-dependants, deductions are usually made for each non-dependant in your household. Only one deduction is made if the non-dependant is part of a couple, whether married or unmarried.[17] If you share liability for the council tax with others, the amount of the non-dependant deduction is shared equally between you, even if the other person is not claiming CTB. However, if the local authority thinks that the non-dependant only belongs to one resident, the whole deduction is made from that person's benefit.[18] If a couple share liability with a single person their CTB is reduced by two-thirds of the non-dependant deduction (ie, apportionment is made on the same basis as liability – see p302).

When no deduction is made[19]

The rules as to when a non-dependant deduction is not made are the same as for HB (see p253) except that:

- all non-dependants on IS/income-based JSA are ignored and not just those under 25; *and*
- no deduction is made for the following people with status discounts (for full details see CPAG's *Council Tax Handbook*):
  - people under 19 if child benefit is payable;
  - recent school and college-leavers under 20;
  - student nurses;
  - foreign language assistants;
  - apprentices;
  - people who are severely mentally impaired (see p306);
  - certain carers;
  - members of visiting armed forces, members of international headquarters and defence organisations and their dependants; *and*
  - foreign spouses or dependents of students;
- no non-dependant deduction is ever made for a full-time student – even if s/he works during the summer vacation.

A person counts as severely mentally impaired if a doctor has certified that s/he has a severe impairment of intelligence and social functioning which appears to be permanent.[20] S/he must also be entitled to a qualifying benefit.[21]

The amount of the deduction[22]

Circumstances of the non-dependant	*Deduction*
18 or over and in full-time work with a weekly gross income of:	
£250 or more	£4.00
£200-£249.99	£3.50
£116-£199.99	£3.00
up to £115.99	£1.50
Others aged 18 or over (for whom a deduction is made)	£1.50

Only one deduction is made for a couple (or members of a polygamous marriage). Where the individual circumstances of each partner are different, the highest deduction is made.[23] For the purpose of deciding which earnings band applies, their joint income counts even if only one of them is in full-time work.[24]

The definitions of full-time work and earnings and the kinds of income which are ignored are the same as for HB (see p254).

Income and capital of a non-dependant

As with HB, your main CTB can be assessed using the income and capital of a non-dependant, instead of your own, if it is felt you are trying to take advantage of the CTB scheme[25] (see p255).

Increasing the amount of your CTB

You can be awarded more than the normal amount of main CTB if your circumstances are exceptional.[26] The rules are the same as for HB (see p256). Your CTB can be increased up to the total amount of council tax on which you are eligible to claim (see p302). The limit is your apportioned share if you are jointly liable (see p302).

Second adult rebate

Second adult rebate is an alternative type of CTB which can be paid instead of, but not as well as, main CTB. Whenever you claim CTB the local authority must assess you for both types and award whichever is the greater.[27] Second adult rebate is designed to help you if you have certain other residents (referred to as 'second adults') in your home who do not share liability for council tax with you and who do not pay rent to you. In certain cases the presence in your home of a second adult means you have to pay the full council tax without discount, but if their income is low they may not be able to contribute towards the cost. Second adult rebate compensates you for this.

Who is eligible to claim a second adult rebate?

You will be able to claim a second adult rebate where:[28]

- you are liable to pay the council tax on the dwelling you normally occupy as your home; *and*
- there is at least one other resident in the dwelling who is classed as a second adult (see below for who counts); *and*
- there is no other resident of the dwelling (apart from someone with a status discount) who is liable to pay you rent in order to live there. The DSS believe that where any resident pays you rent, you cannot get a second adult rebate. If the local authority follows this advice you should argue that this is not what the Act says, and that a specific exception is allowed where the person paying rent has a status discount.[29]

Note that the whole of your income and capital are ignored when you claim second adult rebate. So you can get it even if you have a high income and/or assets worth more than £16,000.[30]

You cannot claim a second adult rebate if you live with another person(s) (including a partner) who is jointly liable for the council tax with you unless all, or all but one of you, have status discounts.[31]

Who counts as a 'second adult'?

A second adult is someone who lives with you on a non-commercial basis. It does not include anyone who:[32]

- is aged under 18 (they do not count as 'residents' and do not affect any possible discount);
- has a status discount (they are ignored for discount purposes and do not affect any possible discount);
- is your partner with whom you are jointly liable (they do affect discount entitlement but will be included in any claim for main CTB);
- is jointly liable to pay the council tax on the dwelling with you as a joint owner or tenant etc (they do affect discount entitlement but can claim main CTB for their own share of the bill – see p302).

In practice, residents classified as second adults will tend to be the same persons as those treated as non-dependants for main CTB purposes (see p304).

Council tax liability for a second adult rebate

The council tax figure used to work out your second adult rebate is:[33]

- the gross council tax liability for the dwelling as a whole; *less*
- any disability reduction; *and*
- transitional reduction.

Note that this is not the same figure as used for main CTB (see p302). However, the procedure for converting annual to weekly amounts is the same (see p303). Where you have received a discount it must be added back on to the net amount of council tax payable to arrive at the figure used in the second adult rebate calculation. This is only done for the purposes of the CTB calculation – you will still receive your discount in practice.

Assessment of second adult income

To obtain a second adult rebate, you must give the local authority details of the gross income of any second adults living with you. Where there is more than one second adult, their combined gross income is used.[34]

Gross income[35] includes the second adult's:

- earnings;
- non-earned income, including social security benefits;
- actual income from capital (as opposed to tariff income). The capital itself is ignored.

Gross income does not include:
- any income of a second adult on income support/income-based JSA;
- any attendance allowance;
- any disability living allowance;
- payments from the MacFarlane Trusts, the Eileen Trust, the Fund and the Independent Living Funds;
- the income of any person with a status discount, except where that person has a partner who is not ignored for discount purposes (in which case the gross income of both partners, less disregarded income, is taken into account).[36]

A basic problem with second adult rebate is that it involves means-testing someone who is not the claimant and who may not always wish to co-operate. If you have difficulty establishing the income of the second adults you may find that the local authority automatically assumes the highest income and that you are not entitled to CTB. If you cannot persuade any second adults to give details of their income to you, they may be prepared to tell the local authority directly. Failing this, you could try finding out the going rate for the type of work they do, or social security benefits they receive, and ask the local authority to make a reasonable estimate based on that.

How much second adult rebate can you get?

The amount of second adult rebate, as a percentage of pre-discounted council tax liability, is:[37]

Income of second adult(s)	*Second adult rebate*
2nd adult (or all 2nd adults) on IS/ income-based JSA	25%
2nd adult(s) total gross income:	
– up to £116	15%
– £116–£151.99	7.5%
– £152 or more	Nil

Note that the maximum CTB payable is always 25 per cent of liability, even in those cases where you would have received a 50 per cent discount, or would have been exempt altogether, were it not for the presence of two or more second adults in your home – eg, as in the case of a student nurse with two second adults on income support.

Second adult rebates and jointly liable claimants

In contrast to main CTB, where there is more than one resident liable for the council tax in your dwelling, any second adult rebate is always calculated on the (pre-discounted) liability for your dwelling as a whole. Any CTB arising is then split equally between all the jointly liable residents.[38] This does not need to happen where you are jointly liable with your heterosexual partner only since, in this case, one of you claims on behalf of both and receives all of the CTB.[39] Apart from this, every other jointly liable person must make their own separate claim in order to get their share of the CTB. For example, three eligible joint tenants would each be entitled to one-third of the total second adult rebate for the dwelling as a whole. If two of them were a couple, however, then they would be entitled to receive two-thirds, and the other single tenant, one-third, of the total CTB.

Extra benefit in exceptional circumstances

Where you are entitled to a second adult rebate of either 7.5 or 15 per cent, the local authority can increase your CTB up to the 25 per cent figure (or your share of it where you are jointly liable), if it considers your circumstances to be exceptional.[40] As with HB, it is for the local authority to decide what is meant by 'exceptional' in any case (see p256), but you have a right of review (see p314).

4. CLAIMS, PAYMENTS AND REVIEWS

Claims

The rules for claiming council tax benefit (CTB) are the same as for housing benefit (HB). See p265 for full details, substituting CTB where it says HB. (The footnotes to that chapter give references to both HB and CTB legislation.) Second adult rebate is a type of CTB so the normal rules apply for claiming.

The rules about advance claims for CTB are slightly different. You can claim up to eight weeks before you become liable for council tax and you are treated as having claimed on the day your liability begins.[41] If you make an unsuccessful claim for CTB but you are likely to become entitled within the next 13 weeks, your claim can be treated as made in the week before your entitlement begins.[42]

There is also a special rule when your local authority has not set its council tax rate by the beginning of the financial year. So long as you claim within four weeks of the council tax being agreed your claim is backdated to 1 April, or the date you first became entitled, if that is later.[43]

Late claims and backdating

The rules about late claims and backdated CTB are the same as for HB (see p268). A special case may arise for CTB where you are jointly liable for the council tax but did not claim because your name was not put on the bill. You could argue that you have good cause for a late claim because you did not realise you were liable as the council had failed (via the bill) to inform you of this.[44]

Decisions and notifications

You will receive separate notifications for HB and CTB. The information which is to be included in a written notification is the same except that those items specifically relating to rent are, of course, excluded in a CTB notification and, instead, it is required that it includes notice of your weekly council tax liability rounded to the nearest penny.[45] The notification should also include the following, where relevant:

- if you have been assessed for, and are entitled to, both main CTB and second adult rebate, the amount of benefit entitlement in each case and the fact you can only be paid the higher amount;[46]
- if you have been assessed for a second adult rebate, the gross income of any second adult(s) used to determine the rate of CTB, including

where any second adult is on income support/income-based jobseeker's allowance (JSA);[47]
- details of how any of the figures supplied on the notification have been rounded (ie, to the nearest penny).[48]

Payment

As with HB, your CTB is paid for a benefit period, which usually runs from the Monday after your date of claim. If you have only just become liable for the council tax and you claim in the same week in which your liability begins, you will be paid from the Monday of that week.[49] The rules about when your benefit period ends are the same as for HB (see p272).

Payment of CTB is normally made by means of a reduction to your annual council tax bill. Your weekly benefit is converted to a daily figure by dividing by 7 and then multiplying the answer by the number of days between your first day of entitlement and the following 31 March. If your circumstances change before 31 March so that you become entitled to less CTB, or if you are overpaid for some other reason, any overpaid CTB credited to your council tax account for any period after the date your benefit is actually reviewed (ie, up to the following 31 March) will be legally recoverable.[50]

If you are jointly liable for the council tax with one or more other residents, apart from your partner, remember that any CTB they receive will also be credited to the same bill as your own. You will need to take this into account when agreeing with them how any remaining balance of council tax liability should be shared out between you.

Where your CTB cannot be used to reduce your bill payment can be made direct to you.[51] This is normally only done once you have paid your final installment of council tax, and usually you must ask for the money. If you do not, your CTB is likely to be credited against your next year's council tax bill.[52]

However, if you are no longer liable for council tax in that authority's area, they should send you any outstanding CTB within 14 days if possible.[53] Payment is normally made to you as the claimant or to your appointee if you have one[54] (see p265).

Withholding of benefit[55]

The local authority can withhold all or part of your CTB:

- if there is a question about your entitlement to CTB (IS/income-based JSA) while it reviews your entitlement;
- if it thinks you may have been overpaid CTB, it can withhold payment of arrears.

Payments on death[56]

If a claimant dies, any outstanding CTB can be paid to the personal representative or, if there is none, to the next of kin aged 16 or over. A written application for this must be sent to the local authority within 12 months of the death.

Overpayments

An overpayment of CTB is called 'excess benefit'[57] but the rules about recovery are the same as for HB (see pp282-88).

As with all overpayments, the amount overpaid is the difference between what you were actually paid and what you should have received. However, there are two possible variations of what should have been paid – either a reduced amount of main CTB, or a second adult rebate if you are eligible for this and it would have been higher than the revised amount of main CTB. When assessing the amount overpaid the local authority should do both calculations, and can only recover the balance between the higher of the two figures and the amount which you, in fact, received. It is always worth checking that the second adult rebate calculation has been done and that the correct amount is being recovered.

You must always repay an overpayment which has arisen because you were paid CTB, but then your council tax liability was reduced because of a disability reduction, discount, transitional relief or charge-capping.[58] Unlike HB, recovery is always from the claimant or the person to whom benefit was paid (eg, an appointee) not from any other person, even if s/he caused the overpayment. However, the overpayment can be recovered by deductions from your partner's benefit if you were a couple at the time the overpayment was made, and still are when it is recovered.[59] If both HB and CTB have been overpaid they must be recovered separately. CTB overpayments cannot be recovered from HB.[60]

The rules on how the overpayment is recovered are also different from HB. The overpayment can be recovered by increasing your outstanding council tax liability.[61] If you wish, you can repay the overpayment instead.[62] This avoids you getting into arrears with your council tax. If the local authority cannot get the overpayment back by either of these methods, it can ask the Benefits Agency to make deductions from any other benefits which you receive[63] apart from guardian's allowance, child benefit and possibly incapacity benefit because they are not covered by the Social Security Act 1975.[64] If the overpayment was caused by your failure to tell the local authority relevant information, or, because you misrepresented your circumstances, the Benefits Agency will pay part of your benefit over to the local authority, so long as you receive enough benefit for deductions to be made.[65] Overpaid CTB can be recovered by court action but not until 21 days after you have been notified of the amount.[66]

Changes of circumstances

You must always notify the local authority of changes which affect your rights to, or the amount of, CTB.[67] The rules are the same as for HB (see p277) except that you do not need to notify any changes in rent for council tax purposes. Nor do you have to tell the local authority the amount of council tax you pay as they have this information already.[68]

If you are getting second adult rebate, you must write and tell the local authority of any changes in the number of adults living in your home and any changes to their gross income.[69]

The rules about when changes of circumstances take effect are slightly different to those for HB. Normally, a change affects your CTB from the Monday after it occurs.[70] However, the following changes affect your benefit from the date they occur:[71]

- a change in the amount of your council tax;
- changes to the CTB regulations;
- the fact that you have become part of a couple;
- the death of, or separation from, your partner.

If two or more changes occur in the same week and each takes effect from a different date under the above rules, they are all taken into account from the date of the first change.[72]

If you stop getting another social security benefit, the change in circumstances is deemed to occur on the day after your entitlement ends and your CTB is changed from the following Monday.[73]

If your applicable amount includes a personal allowance for a child (see p330) that allowance increases on the first Monday in September following the child's 11th and 16th birthdays. An allowance for childcare costs (see p362) is payable until the first Monday in September after the child's 11th birthday.

The rules for reassessing your CTB following a change of circumstances are the same as for HB (see p277), but remember that the local authority should recalculate both main CTB and second adult rebate and award whichever is currently the higher.

Reviews and complaints

The rules for CTB reviews are the same as those for HB (see pp291-95). The notes to Chapter 15 include CTB legislation. It is always worth applying for a review if you think the decision of the local authority is wrong. If you are applying for a review on both your CTB and your HB, one review board can deal with both claims if everyone agrees[74] (in Scotland, HB is administered by district councils and CTB by regional councils and this situation cannot arise). The local authority can also consider an outstanding review on community charge benefit at the same time as your HB and/or CTB.

If you are dissatisfied with the decision of a review board, judicial review may be possible (see p297). If you wish to complain about the way the local authority has dealt with your claim, see p298.

5. STUDENTS

The definition of full-time student is the same as for HB (see p258).

As with housing benefit (HB), most full-time students cannot get council tax benefit (CTB), but you can claim if:[75]

- you are on income support/income-based jobseeker's allowance;
- you are a pensioner who satisfies the conditions for one of the pensioner premiums;
- you are a lone parent who satisfies the conditions for the family premium (lone parent rate);
- you are a registered lone foster parent and a child has been placed with you by a local authority or voluntary agency;
- you and your partner are both full-time students and have one or more dependent children;
- you are under 19 and not following a course of higher education;
- you qualify for the disability premium or would do if you were not disqualified from incapacity benefit (see p10);
- you have been incapable of work for 28 weeks (see p10). Two or more periods when you are incapable are joined to form a single period if they are separated by less than eight weeks;
- you satisfy the conditions for a grant supplement in the form of a disabled student's allowance awarded because of deafness;
- you are a work trainee on a training allowance.[76]

If you are a student who can claim, you may be entitled to more CTB outside the 'period of study' (see p260), for example, during the summer vacation.

Overseas students

The rules on overseas students are the same as for HB. To qualify for CTB, overseas students must satisfy both the special rules which allow persons from abroad to claim (see p222) and the special rules for students (see p314). The footnotes covering these matters in Chapter 14 include references to CTB legislation.

Students and second adult rebate

Full-time students are not precluded from getting second adult rebate and should be assessed in the normal way (see p306).

6. PEOPLE IN HOSPITAL

You can continue to get council tax benefit (CTB) while in hospital, the rules are the same as for housing benefit (HB) (see p256). If you cease to be treated as residing in your home for council tax purposes because of a prolonged stay in hospital you cannot claim CTB. If this leaves your home unoccupied it will be exempt from council tax altogether. However, if your partner still lives in your former home s/he will now probably be treated as the liable person and can put in her/his own claim for CTB. Your CTB may also be adjusted if the local authority decides you are no longer part of a family and reassesses you as a single person (see p323).

PART FIVE

Common rules

Income support (IS), family credit (FC), disability working allowance (DWA), housing benefit (HB) and council tax benefit (CTB) are all means-tested benefits. The amount you get depends on the size of your family, how much capital you have and how your income compares with your needs (called your 'applicable amount'). The rules for all five benefits are the same or similar. This Part covers those rules which are common to all.

Since 7 October 1996, IS for people who have to register for work has been replaced by income-based jobseeker's allowance (JSA). The rules for this new benefit are set out in CPAG's Jobseeker's Allowance Handbook *(2nd edition published April 1997). Income support is now only for people who do not have to register for work (eg, single parents with dependent children). This Part deals with the common rules which apply to IS but not income-based JSA.*

CHAPTER SEVENTEEN

Who counts as your family

This chapter explains who is included in your benefit claim. It covers:

1. Introduction (below)
2. Claiming as a couple (p319)
3. Claiming for children (p325)

1. INTRODUCTION

What is a 'family'?

You claim income support (IS), family credit (FC), disability working allowance (DWA), housing benefit (HB), council tax benefit (CTB) for yourself, your partner and any dependent children who are members of your household. This is your 'family' for benefit purposes.[1] A partner can include a wife, husband or cohabitee (of the opposite sex). When your benefit is worked out, the needs of your partner and any children are usually added to yours and so are your partner's income and capital. There are special rules for the treatment of the income and capital of dependent children (see pp345 and 385).

If one member of your family is claiming IS/FC/DWA/HB/CTB, no other member can claim the same benefit for the same period.[2] However, partners can choose which of them should be the claimant, except for FC which the woman must usually claim,[3] and DWA which the disabled partner must claim.[4] (If both of you are disabled, you can choose which one of you should be the claimant.[5]) For details about how to claim see p122 (IS), p192 (FC), p206 (DWA), p265 (HB) and p310 (CTB).

Membership of the same household

The idea of sharing a household is central to whether you can include a child or a partner in your claim.

However, the term 'household' is not defined. Whether two people should be treated as members of the same household is very much a question of fact. Physical presence together will not in itself be conclusive. There must be a 'particular kind of tie' binding two people together in a domestic establishment (although this could, in appropriate circumstances, include a household within, for example, a hotel or boarding house[6]).

There will be some occasions when you and another person are regarded as members of the same household when you think you should not be. If this arises it will be important to try to show that, although you both live in the same house, you maintain separate **households**.

A separate household might exist if there are:

- independent arrangements for the storage and cooking of food;
- independent financial arrangements;
- separate eating arrangements;
- no evidence of family life;
- separate commitments for housing costs, even if the liability is to another person in the same premises.

You cannot be a member of more than one household at the same time.[7] If two people can be shown to be maintaining separate homes, they cannot be said to be sharing the same household.[8] Even if you have the right to occupy only part of a room, you may have your own household.[9]

Where a child lives for part of the week with each parent, the rules for each benefit allow only one parent to claim that benefit for that child, and s/he is treated as a member of her/his household for the whole week (see p325).

2. CLAIMING AS A COUPLE

You claim as a couple if you and your partner are both 16 or over, *and*:[10]

- married, and living in the same household (see above for definition); *or*
- not married but 'living together as husband and wife' in the same household.

Special rules apply if one or both partners are under 18 (see pp45, 331 and 345).

Being married to someone does not necessarily mean that you cannot be treated as part of a couple with someone else instead.[11] If you are lesbian or gay partners you do not count as a couple, and must claim as single people.

You count as polygamously married if you are married to more than one person and your marriages took place in a country which permits polygamy.[12] There are special rules if you are polygamously married.[13]

Living together as husband and wife

If it is decided that you are 'living together as husband and wife' (cohabiting), only one of you will be able to claim benefit. The amount of benefit for a couple is usually less than that for two single people, so it is important to dispute a decision that you are cohabiting if you believe you are not. However, in some cases you may have to *prove* that you are cohabiting – eg, where you want to claim FC, you have children and do not work yourself, but your partner does. You should, of course, be consistent about your circumstances for each benefit. If you are awarded IS, the local authority should not make a separate decision when considering your claim for HB/CTB.[14] However, if you have not been awarded IS, the local authority has a duty to give its own consideration to the cohabitation test, and may reach a different conclusion from that of the Benefits Agency.

The factors considered below are used as 'signposts' in determining whether or not you are cohabiting.[15] No one factor need in itself be conclusive, as it is your 'general relationship' as a whole which is of paramount importance[16] and, just as relationships between couples may often vary considerably, so each case will depend on all its own particular facts and circumstances.

Do you live in the same household?

In all cases you must spend the major part of your time in the same household (see p318 for a discussion of 'household'). If one of you has a separate address where you usually live, the cohabitation rule should not be applied. You cannot be a member of more than one household at the same time (see p319) so, if you are a member of one couple, you cannot also be treated as part of another.

Even if you *do* share a 'household', you may not be cohabiting. It is essential to look at *why* two people are in the same household.[17] For example, where a couple were living in the same household for reasons of 'care, companionship and mutual convenience' they were not 'living together as husband and wife'.[18]

Separated couples living under the same roof should not be treated as couples if they are maintaining separate households.[19] Where a relationship has only recently broken down, continuing financial support and shared responsibilities and liabilities may be particularly inconclusive, especially where there is evidence of active steps being taken to live apart. The way people live and their attitude of mind will be more significant.

Any 'mere hope' of a reconciliation will not be a 'reasonable expectation' where at least one partner has accepted that the relationship is at an end.[20]

Do you have a sexual relationship?

In practice, officers may not ask you about the existence of a sexual relationship, in which case they will only have the information if you volunteer it. If you do not have a sexual relationship, you should tell the officer yourself – and perhaps offer to show her/him the separate sleeping arrangements.

Having a sexual relationship is not sufficient by itself to prove you are cohabiting, and if you have never had a sexual relationship there will be a strong (but not necessarily conclusive) presumption that you are not cohabiting.[21]

A couple who abstain from a sexual relationship before marriage on grounds of principle (eg, religious reasons) should not be counted as cohabiting until they are formally married.[22]

Even if the Benefits Agency or local authority does not go into the question of whether or not there is a sexual relationship, any tribunal or review board has a duty to ask such questions in order to determine whether or not you are cohabiting.[23]

What are your financial arrangements?

If one partner is supported by the other or household expenses are shared, this may be treated as evidence of cohabitation. However, it is important to consider how they are shared. There is a difference between, on the one hand, payment of a fixed weekly contribution or the rigid sharing of bills 50/50 and, on the other hand, a free common fund attributable to income and expenditure. The former does not imply cohabitation, the latter might.

Is your relationship stable?

Marriage is expected to be stable and lasting. It follows that an occasional or brief association should not be regarded as cohabiting. However, the fact that a relationship is stable does not make it cohabitation – eg, you can have a stable landlord/lodger relationship but not be cohabiting.

Do you have children?

If you have had a child together, and live in the same household as the other parent, there is a strong (but not conclusive) presumption of cohabitation.

How do you appear in public?

Officers may check the electoral roll and claims for national insurance benefits to see if you present yourselves as a couple. Many couples retain their separate identity publicly as unmarried people. They should, however, be aware that they may be regarded as cohabiting.

Challenging a 'living together' decision

Sometimes benefit is stopped or adjusted because someone regularly stays overnight, even though you might have none of the long-term commitments generally associated with marriage. But couples with no sexual relationship who live together (eg, as landlord/lodger, tenant or housekeeper, or as flat-sharers) also sometimes fall foul of the rule. People who provide mutual support and share household expenses are not necessarily cohabiting – this is also the case where people of the same sex or friends of different sexes share a home.[24]

If you are at all unhappy with a decision that you are cohabiting, you should appeal (see p156) or apply for a review (see pp131 and 291), and carefully consider what evidence to put before the tribunal/review board in relation to each of the six questions above and any other matters that you consider relevant. Possibilities include evidence of the other person having another address[25] (eg, a rent book and other household bills), receipts for board and lodging, statements from friends and relatives or, where you have been married, evidence of a formal separation or divorce proceedings.

On an initial application for benefit it is not for you to prove that you are not cohabiting,[26] though you are required to provide the Benefits Agency with any information it reasonably requires to decide your claim.[27] Neither party has the burden of proof in this situation – a decision should simply be made on all the evidence available.[28] By contrast, if your benefit as a single person is stopped because it is alleged that you are cohabiting, the burden of proof is on the Benefits Agency to prove that you are cohabiting.[29]

If your benefit is withdrawn because you are cohabiting, you should re-apply immediately if your circumstances change. You should also apply immediately for any other benefits for which you might qualify – eg, HB/CTB, where the local authority may reach a different decision to that of the Benefits Agency (see p320). You should apply on the basis of low income for other benefits, which you previously qualified for automatically if you were on IS – eg, health benefits (see Chapter 26).

If you are still entitled to benefit, even though it is decided that you are cohabiting, you should be paid as a couple.

If your IS stops and you have diverted a maintenance order to the Benefits Agency (see p104), contact the magistrates' court immediately to get payments sent direct to you. If the Child Support Agency is collecting a child maintenance assessment for you (see p105), ask them to start paying the money to you.

If you have no money at all, you may be able to get a social fund crisis loan (see Part Seven).

Couples living apart

If you separate *permanently* you can claim as a single person immediately. However, you continue to be treated as a couple while you and your partner are *temporarily* apart.[30] Your former household need not have been in this country.[31] The following rules apply in determining whether you still count as a couple.

For FC/DWA

You no longer count as a couple if you or your partner:[32]

- are living apart and do not intend to resume living together (see p320); *or*
- have been in hospital for 52 weeks or more; *or*
- are a compulsory patient detained in hospital under the mental health provisions; *or*
- are detained in custody serving a sentence of 52 weeks or more.

For CTB

You continue to be eligible as a couple as long as you both remain liable for the council tax at your address.[33] Note that the rules for establishing a couple's liability for council tax are not the same as the rules for establishing their entitlement to CTB (see CPAG's *Council Tax Handbook*).

For IS/HB

You will count as a couple, even if you or your partner are living away from your family, if you:[34]

- intend to resume living together (see p320); *or*
- are likely to be separated for less than 52 weeks. However, you can still be treated as a couple if you are likely to be separated for more than 52 weeks provided it is not 'substantially' longer and there are exceptional circumstances such as a stay in hospital, or if there is no control over the length of the absence.

For IS

You will no longer count as a couple if any of the following apply to either of you:[35]

- you are in custody;
- you are on temporary release from prison;
- you are a compulsory patient detained in hospital under the mental health provisions;
- you are staying permanently in local authority residential accommodation, or a residential care or nursing home;
- the *claimant* is abroad and does not qualify for IS. However, where your *partner* is temporarily abroad you continue to be treated as a couple, but after four weeks (eight if s/he has taken a child abroad for medical treatment) the amount of IS you receive is that for a single claimant or single parent.[36] You can get benefit without signing on if you have children under 16.[37] Your partner's income and capital continue to be treated as yours for as long as the absence is held to be temporary.

If you are no longer treated as a couple for the purposes of calculating your IS, you may still be liable to maintain your partner (see p103).

You are still treated as a couple if you are temporarily living apart and the following applies: one of you is at home or in hospital, or in local authority residential accommodation or in a residential care or nursing home, and the other is:[38]

- resident in a nursing home, but not counted as a patient; *or*
- staying in a residential care home; *or*
- in a home for the rehabilitation of alcoholics or drug addicts; *or*
- in Polish resettlement accommodation; *or*
- on a government training course and has to live away from home (see below for your right to housing costs for more than one home); *or*
- in a probation or bail hostel.

Although your income and capital are calculated in the normal way for a couple, your applicable amount is calculated as if each of you were single claimants if this comes to more than your usual couple rate. If you have children, one of you is treated as a single parent. If you have housing costs (see p25), your applicable amount includes these as well as any costs of the temporary accommodation of the partner away from home. If you are both away from home, the costs of both sets of temporary accommodation and the family home are met.[39] If both homes are rented, see pp216-20 for when HB can be paid for more than one home at a time. If you own your home and your partner is staying in rented accommodation, you will get your housing costs met by IS and your partner will be able to claim HB.

Additional points

- Where questions of 'intention' are involved (eg, in deciding whether you or your partner intend to resume living with your family), the intention must be unqualified – ie, it must not depend on some factor over which you have no control (eg, where it depends on the right of entry to the UK being granted by the Home Office[40] or on the offer of a suitable job[41]).
- See pp29 and 218 if one of you lives away from home as a student or on a government training course and you have to pay for two homes.
- See p442 if your child is in hospital and you have to stay in lodgings to be nearby.
- See p92 if one or both of you are temporarily in local authority residential accommodation.

3. CLAIMING FOR CHILDREN

You do not have to be a *parent* to receive benefit for a child, but you must be 'responsible' for a child who is living in your household.[42] You claim for any child under 16; or under 19 if they are still in full-time 'relevant' education[43] (see p16 for what this means). Where the same benefit is involved, a child can only be the responsibility of one person in any week.[44] There is no provision allowing benefit to be split between parents where a child divides her/his time equally between the homes of two parents. See p327 for when a child no longer counts as your dependant.

'Responsibility' for a child

You claim IS, FC, DWA, HB or CTB for a child for whom you are 'responsible'. You will be treated as 'responsible' for a child if:

For FC/DWA/HB/CTB

- the child is 'normally living' with you.[45] This means that s/he spends more time with you than with anyone else.[46]

  Where it is unclear whose household the child lives in, or where s/he spends an equal amount of time with two parents in different homes

(this may not mean literally 3½ days with each parent[47]), you will be treated as having responsibility if:[48]
- you get child benefit for the child;
- no one gets child benefit, but you have applied for it;
- no one has applied for child benefit, or both of you have applied, but you appear to have the most responsibility;

For IS

- you get child benefit for the child.[49]

   Where no one gets child benefit you will be 'responsible' if you are the only one who has applied for it. In all other cases the person 'responsible' will be the person with whom the child *usually lives*.[50]

   Where a child for whom you are 'responsible' gets child benefit for another child, you will also be 'responsible' for that child.[51]

Note: For FC/DWA/HB/CTB, it is important to look at who gets child benefit only where it is unclear whose household the child *normally* lives in. For IS it is essential to look first at who gets child benefit, and only where this is not decisive is it relevant to look at where the child *usually* lives. This difference may mean that in some situations one parent may be able to claim IS for a child while the other parent can claim FC/DWA/HB/CTB for the same child at the same time.

Living in the same household[52]

If you are counted as responsible for a child, then that child is usually treated as a member of your household despite any temporary absence. (For the meaning of 'household', see p318.) However, s/he does not count as a member of your household if s/he:

IS/FC/DWA/HB/CTB

- is being fostered by you under a statutory provision. However, you can claim benefit for a child you are fostering privately;
- is living with you prior to adoption, and has been placed with you by social services or an adoption agency;

IS/HB/CTB

- is boarded out or has been placed with someone else prior to adoption;
- is in the care of, or being looked after by, the local authority and not living with you. You should receive IS for her/him for the days when s/he comes home – eg, for the weekend or a holiday.[53] Make sure you tell the Benefits Agency in good time so they can pay you the extra money. The local authority can also increase your applicable amount to

include the child for HB/CTB for all of that week whether the child returns for all or only part of it;[54]

IS/FC/DWA

- has been in hospital or a local authority home for more than 12 weeks, and you or other members of your household have not been in regular contact with her/him. For FC/DWA this means 12 weeks prior to the claim.[55] For IS the 12 weeks run from the date s/he went into the hospital or home, or from the date you claimed IS, if later.[56] However, if you were getting income-based JSA immediately before you claimed IS, the 12 weeks run from the date s/he went into the hospital or home;[57]
- has been in hospital or a local authority home for 52 weeks or more because of illness or disability (unless, for IS only, you are still in regular contact);[58]
- is in custody. (For FC/DWA, being in custody on remand does not count.) You should receive IS for any periods your child spends at home;[59]

IS only

- has been abroad for more than four weeks (the four weeks run from the day after s/he went abroad, or from the date you claimed IS, if later), or for more than eight weeks if the absence abroad is to get medical treatment for the child.[60] Note, however, that if you were getting income-based JSA immediately before you claimed IS, the four- or eight-week periods are calculated from the day after the child went abroad;[61]
- is living with you and away from her/his parental or usual home in order to attend school. The child is not treated as a member of your family, but remains a member of her/his parent's household.[62]

When you stop claiming for a child

For IS

You stop claiming for a child as soon as someone else starts receiving child benefit for her/him.

For FC/DWA/HB/CTB

You stop claiming as soon as the child starts 'normally living' elsewhere (see p325).

For IS/HB/CTB

You claim for a child until s/he is 16, or 19 if s/he is in relevant education (see p16). Children count as in relevant education until the 'terminal date' (see p18), or until they get a full-time job if that is earlier. 'Full-time' work for dependent children means at least 24 hours a week.[63]

A 16/17-year-old who has left school or college may continue to be counted as part of your 'family' for a few months after the terminal date. You will get benefit for them during the child benefit extension period (see p18 for details and dates) provided the following apply:[64]

- you were entitled to child benefit for that child immediately before the child benefit extension period started; *and*
- you have made a fresh claim for child benefit in writing for the child benefit extension period; *and*
- s/he has registered for work/Youth Training (YT) at the JobCentre or Careers Office; *and*
- s/he is not in full-time work.

If s/he loses the job or leaves YT before the end of the child benefit extension period, s/he becomes your dependant again and you can claim for her/him as long as the above conditions are satisfied.

Some 16/17-year-olds can get IS in their own right before they are 18 (see p57) and you will not be able to claim for them.[65]

For FC/DWA

A child counts as your dependant for the purposes of your FC/DWA claim where, at the date of the claim, s/he is actually undergoing full-time education. Children do not count as dependants once they have left school, even if you are still getting child benefit for them. They are also not counted as dependants if they become entitled to IS or income-based JSA in their own right[66] (or, in the case of income-based JSA, would be so entitled, had a member of their family not been entitled).

CHAPTER EIGHTEEN

Applicable amounts

This chapter covers:
1. Introduction (below)
2. Personal allowances (p330)
3. Premiums (p332)

1. INTRODUCTION

For income support (IS), housing benefit (HB) and council tax benefit (CTB) the 'applicable amount' is a figure representing your weekly needs for the purpose of calculating your benefit. For IS, your applicable amount is the amount you are expected to live on each week. For HB/CTB, it is the amount used to see how much help you need with your rent or council tax. This chapter explains how you work out your applicable amount for those benefits. For the way benefit payable is calculated, see p24 for IS, p247 for HB and p302 for CTB.

The applicable amount for family credit (FC) is always £77.15. For disability working allowance (DWA) it is £57.85 for single people (other than lone parents) and £77.15 for couples/lone parents. For the way FC/DWA are calculated, see pp190 and 204 respectively.

For IS, HB and CTB, your applicable amount is made up of:

• personal allowances: this is the amount the law says you need for living expenses (see p330);
• premiums: this is the amount given for certain extra needs you or your family may have (see p332);
• for IS only, housing costs: (see p25).

For IS, your applicable amount is different if you live in a residential care home, nursing home or local authority residential accommodation (see p84). Your applicable amount is reduced if you are:

• receiving an urgent cases payment (see p82);
• in hospital (see p94);

- a 16/17-year-old, in certain circumstances (see p54);
- a couple, one of whom is a person from abroad (see p66);
- without accommodation (see p99);
- a prisoner (see p98);
- appealing against a decision that you are not incapable of work under the 'all-work' test[1] (see p11, and CPAG's *Rights Guide to Non-Means-Tested Benefits* for more information on the 'all-work' test).

In addition, there are a number of other reasons why your benefit may otherwise be reduced, such as:

- you are subject to a benefit penalty for refusing to co-operate with the Child Support Agency (see p110);
- you are repaying an overpayment of benefit (see p151);
- you are repaying a social fund (SF) loan (see p451);
- the Benefits Agency is making direct payments on your behalf in respect of housing costs, water charges, fuel debts, council tax and community charge arrears, fines or child support maintenance (see pp141-46).

Some IS/HB claimants get an amount of transitional protection on top of their ordinary IS/HB (see pp46 and 257).

2. PERSONAL ALLOWANCES

The amount of your personal allowance for IS, HB and CTB depends on your age and whether you are claiming as a single person or a couple. You also get an allowance for each dependent child (but see pp345 and 385 for the rules on income and capital belonging to children).

If you are polygamously married (see pp319-20) you usually receive an extra amount for each additional partner in your household.[2] For IS, where any additional partner is under the age of 18, you will only receive an extra amount if they are responsible for a child (see p325) or would otherwise meet the special conditions for qualifying for JSA as a 16/17-year-old[3] (see CPAG's *Jobseeker's Allowance Handbook, 2nd edn*, 1997/98). For the treatment of additional partners in polygamous marriages for FC and DWA, see pp190 and 204.

Rates of personal allowances[4]

The rates for people aged 18 or over, and for dependent children, are the same for IS and HB/CTB. No CTB is payable for single people under 18 or for a couple where both are under 18 because they are not liable to pay the tax (see p301). Where one partner is 18 or over, they get the couple rate for over-18s.

Single claimant:

Aged under 18 (some IS cases (see p44) and all HB cases)	£38.90
Aged under 18 (other IS cases only (see p44))	£29.60
Other claimants aged under 25	£38.90
Aged 25 or over	£49.15

Single parents:

Aged under 18 (some IS cases (see p44) and all HB cases)	£38.90
Aged under 18 (other IS cases only (see p44))	£29.60
Aged 18 or over	£49.15

Couple:

Both aged under 18 (some IS cases (see p45) and all HB cases)		£58.70
Both aged under 18 (other IS cases only (see p45))	*either*	£38.90
	or	£29.60
One aged under 18 (some IS cases (see p45) and all HB and CTB cases)		£77.15
One aged under 18 (other IS cases only (see p45))	*either*	£49.15
	or	£38.90
Both aged 18 or over		£77.15
Polygamous marriages: Each additional qualifying partner living in the same household[5]		£28.00

Children:

Under 11	£16.90
11-15	£24.75
16-18	£29.60

For the purpose of calculating the personal allowances above, a child is not treated as being 11 or 16 until the first Monday in September following her/his 11th or 16th birthday.[6] However, the higher amount applies straightaway in respect of a child who reached 11 or 16 before 7 April 1997. In addition, £38.90, not £29.60, applies in respect of a child who reached 18 before that date (apart from this, there is no longer a special rate for 18-year-olds).[7]

3. PREMIUMS

Introduction

Premiums are added to your basic personal allowances and are intended to help with extra expenses caused by age, disability or the cost of children. The eight premiums and their rates are:

Family premium (couple rate)	£10.80	
Disabled child premium	£20.95	
(for each qualifying child)		
Severe disability premium		These can be paid
Single	£37.15	on top of any
Couple (both partners qualifying)	£74.30	other premiums
Carer's premium		
Single, or one partner qualifying	£13.35	
Both partners qualifying	£26.70	
Family (lone parent rate)		
IS	£15.75	
HB/CTB	£22.05	
Disability premium		
Single	£20.95	
Couple	£29.90	Only one of these
Pensioner premium		can be paid; if you
(i) if aged 60-74		qualify for more
Single	£19.65	than one you get
Couple	£29.65	whichever is the
(ii) if aged 75-79		highest.[8]
Single	£21.85	
Couple	£32.75	
Higher pensioner premium		
Single	£26.55	
Couple	£38.00	

Entitlement to some premiums depends on receipt of other benefits. Once you have qualified for a premium, if you or your partner cease to receive a qualifying benefit because of the overlapping benefit rules (ie, because you are receiving another benefit at the same or a higher rate), or because you or your partner are on an employment training course or getting a training allowance, you will continue to receive the relevant premium.[9] In addition, you or your partner (if any) must be getting the benefit for yourself (or for your partner), and not on behalf of someone else – eg, as an appointee.[10]

Sometimes, you may be able to get payment of a premium backdated (see pp127 and 335).

Family premium[11]

You are entitled to this if your family includes a child. As from April 1997, it is paid at two rates. The couple rate is paid if you are a member of a couple and the lone parent rate if you are a lone parent. In each case it is paid even if you are not the parent of the child and even if you do not receive a personal allowance for any child because they have capital over £3,000.

Only one family premium is payable regardless of the number of children you have. Where a child who is in the care of or being looked after by a local authority or who is in custody, comes home for part of a week, your IS includes a proportion of the premium, according to the number of days the child is with you;[12] for HB and CTB you may be paid the full premium if your child who is in care or being looked after by a local authority is part of the household for any part of the week: how often and for how long the child visits will be taken into account.[13]

The Government intends to phase out the lone parent rate in April 1998.

Disabled child premium[14]

You are entitled to a disabled child premium for each of the children in your family who gets disability living allowance or who is blind.

A child is treated as blind if s/he is registered as blind and for the first 28 weeks after s/he has been taken off the register on regaining her/his sight.[15] If disability living allowance stops because the child has gone into hospital, see p96. Where your child is in local authority care or in custody for part of the week, this premium will be affected in the same way as the family premium (see above). For how to qualify for disability living allowance, see CPAG's *Rights Guide to Non-Means-Tested Benefits*.

If the child has over £3,000 capital, you do not get this premium.[16]

Disability premium[17]

The way in which you can get a disability premium differs depending on whether you have a partner or not (see p319). In either case, the person who satisfies the qualifying conditions set out below has to be aged under 60. If you or your partner (if any) are aged 60 or over you may get the higher pensioner premium (see p336). A disability premium will be awarded if:

- You or your partner (if any) are getting a qualifying benefit. For the disability premium, these are attendance allowance (or an equivalent benefit paid to meet attendance needs because of an injury at work or a war injury[18]), disability living allowance, disability working allowance or mobility supplement, and also severe disablement allowance or incapacity benefit paid at the long-term rate if *you* are getting it. Note that if you are getting the special short-term rate of incapacity benefit because you are terminally ill (see below), this counts as a qualifying benefit.[19] Extra-statutory payments to compensate you or your partner (if any) for not getting these benefits also count.[20] See CPAG's *Rights Guide to Non-Means-Tested Benefits* for who can claim these benefits.

You must be getting the benefit in question for yourself, not on behalf of someone else – eg, as an appointee. The same applies if it is your partner who gets the benefit.[21]

Once you qualify for the premium, you, or your partner (if any), are treated as still getting a qualifying benefit you no longer in fact get, if you would have got it but for the overlapping benefit rules – eg, your severe disablement allowance stops because you start to get a widow's pension.[22]

- You, or your partner (if any), are registered as blind with a local authority. If you, or your partner, regain your sight you still qualify for 28 weeks after being taken off the register.[23]
- You, or your partner (if any), have an NHS invalid trike or private car allowance because of disability.[24]
- You, or your partner (if any), were getting incapacity benefit paid at the long-term rate (or at the short-term rate because of terminal illness) which stopped when retirement pension became payable, since when you have been continuously entitled to IS/HB/CTB.[25] If it is your partner who began receiving a retirement pension, s/he must still be alive (IS),[26] or still be a member of your family (HB/CTB).[27] In the case of IS only, you or your partner (if any), must have previously qualified for a disability premium.[28]
- You, or your partner, were getting attendance allowance or disability living allowance but payment of that benefit was suspended when one of you became a hospital inpatient.[29] In the case of IS only, you or your partner must have previously qualified for a disability premium.
- You are entitled to statutory sick pay (IS only), or (for IS/HB/CTB) an adjudication officer has decided that you are 'incapable of work' or you

are treated as incapable and you have been so entitled, incapable of work or treated as incapable of work for a continuous period of:[30]

- 196 days if you have been certified as 'terminally ill' – ie, it can reasonably be expected that you will die within six months in consequence of a progressive disease[31];
- 364 days in all other cases, provided you have claimed incapacity benefit.

Breaks in entitlement/incapacity of up to 56 days are included in these periods. See CPAG's *Rights Guide to Non-Means-Tested Benefits* for more details about statutory sick pay and 'incapacity for work'.

If you are a couple, you will get the disability premium at the couple rate (£29.90) provided that one of you meets one of the above qualifying conditions, except in the case of the condition concerning statutory sick pay and incapacity for work. In that case, you will not get the premium at all unless the person who qualifies is the claimant.[32] You may, therefore, need to swap who is the claimant (see pp123 and 265).

If you go on a Training for Work (TFW) or Youth Training (YT) course, or for any period you receive a training allowance, you will keep the disability premium even though you may cease to receive one of the 'qualifying benefits', or cease to be entitled to statutory sick pay or be incapable of work during the course, as long as you continue to be entitled to IS/HB/CTB. After the course, the premium continues if you remain entitled to statutory sick pay (for IS only), are still incapable of work, or getting a qualifying benefit.[33]

Backdating

- Your 'qualifying benefit' (see p334) may not be awarded until some time after you claim it. If you are already getting IS/HB/CTB you should ask for your claim to be reviewed and for your disability premium to be backdated either to the same day as your claim, or to when you first got IS, HB or CTB if that is later.[34]

Example
You apply for disability living allowance in May 1997. Disability living allowance is awarded in November 1997 backdated to May 1997. You request a review of your IS to include a disability premium in December 1997. You have been getting IS from July 1997. The increase in your IS will be backdated to July 1997.

- If as a result of getting a 'qualifying benefit' backdated you now qualify for IS, HB or CTB, you should make a new claim and ask for it to be backdated for up to three months (for IS) or 12 months (for HB/

CTB). However, for IS, backdating of up to three months is only possible if you have a specified reason for making a late claim (see p127). For HB/CTB, backdating is possible if you have 'good cause' for not claiming earlier (see pp268 and 310).

Similar considerations will apply to backdating the disabled child premium (p333), the higher pensioner premium (see below), the severe disability premium (p338) and the carer's premium (p346).

- If you consider you have been incapable of work for 364/196 days or more, but you have not previously been certified or assessed as incapable of work, you should claim incapacity benefit. You do not have to be awarded incapacity benefit, you only have to show that you have been incapable of work. A medical note is not necessary for any period after 13 April 1995, although one will still be helpful as you will have to persuade an adjudication officer that you have been incapable of work throughout. Even if you have not yet been incapable of work for 364/196 days, it is advisable to claim incapacity benefit as soon as possible so that the disability premium can be awarded to you as soon as you reach the qualifying period.
- For HB/CTB, if you are one of a couple and the person who is incapable of work is not the claimant, you can swap the claimant role and s/he can apply to backdate a new claim if s/he has 'good cause' (see pp268 and 310). In this way you can get the disability premium backdated for up to 12 months.[35]

Pensioner premium[36]

The pensioner premium is paid at two rates according to age:

- the lower rate if you are aged 60–74 inclusive;
- the enhanced rate if you are 75–79 inclusive.

The couple rate for either is paid even if only one partner fulfils the condition. If you or your partner are sick or disabled check to see if you could get the higher pensioner premium instead (see below).

Higher pensioner premium

You can get this if one of the following applies:[37]

- You or your partner are 80 or over.
- You were getting a disability premium as part of your IS, HB or CTB before you were 60 and you have continued to claim that benefit since reaching that age. You must have been getting a disability premium at some time during the eight weeks before you were 60, and have

received that benefit continuously since you reached 60.[38] But you can have a period off that benefit of up to eight weeks and still qualify. For HB/CTB if you were entitled to a higher pensioner premium for one benefit in the previous eight weeks you will get a higher pensioner premium with the other if you then qualify or requalify for that benefit.[39] However, previous entitlement to a premium while on HB/CTB will not help you qualify for the higher pensioner premium when you claim IS, and *vice versa*. In the case of couples, the person who was the claimant for that benefit before s/he was 60 must continue to claim after that, but it is not necessary for the claimant to have been the person who qualified for the disability premium.[40]

- You or your partner are aged 60–79 *and* either of you receive a qualifying benefit (as for the disability premium – see p334), are registered blind, or have an NHS trike or a private car allowance (see p334).
  - If your attendance or disability living allowance stops because you go into hospital – see p94 (IS), pp256 and 315 (HB/CTB).
  - If you, or your partner, stop getting incapacity benefit (or if in the past you stopped getting invalidity benefit) because you get retirement pension instead, you will still get a higher pensioner premium with your IS, HB or CTB, if you remain continuously entitled (apart from breaks of eight weeks or less) to the same benefit.[41] In the case of HB/CTB, if you were entitled to a higher pensioner premium for one of these benefits in the previous eight weeks, you will get a higher pensioner premium with the other if you then qualify or requalify for that benefit.[42] If it is your partner who had changed to a retirement pension, s/he must still be alive (IS), or still be a member of your family (HB/CTB).[43] In the case of IS, the higher pensioner premium or a disability premium must also have been 'applicable' to you or your partner.[44] So, if, up to the time your incapacity (or invalidity benefit) ceased, your applicable amount was calculated by a method that did not include premiums (eg, because you were in a hostel prior to 9 October 1989, or you lived in a residential care or nursing home before 31 March 1993), you will not be able to qualify in this way.[45]
  - If you are getting severe disablement allowance by the time you reach 65, you will be awarded it for life even if you no longer satisfy the incapacity or disability conditions.[46] You will therefore continue to qualify for the higher pensioner premium. This will also apply even if it ceases to be paid because you get retirement pension at a higher rate.[47]

338 Common rules 18: Applicable amounts

Severe disability premium[48]

You can get the severe disability premium if all of the following apply to you:

- You receive a qualifying benefit. For the severe disability premium this is either attendance allowance (or the equivalent war pension or industrial injury benefit), or the middle or higher rate care component of disability living allowance (or extra-statutory payments to compensate you for not receiving any of these[49]). If you are a couple (or polygamously married), whichever one of you is claiming IS/HB/CTB must be getting a qualifying benefit and your partner(s) must also either be getting a qualifying benefit or else s/he must be registered blind (or treated as blind).[50] However, in either case you are treated as getting the qualifying benefit while still in hospital (see pp94, 256 and 315). The qualifying benefit must be paid in respect of yourself/selves, as receipt of benefit for someone else (eg, a child) does not count.[51]
- No non-dependant aged 18 or over is 'residing with you' (see p339) – for example, a grown up son or daughter, or your parents. It does not matter whose house it is, yours or the non-dependant's.[52] For IS/HB, someone is only counted as living with you if you share accommodation apart from a bathroom, lavatory or a communal area such as a hall, passageway or a room in common use in sheltered accommodation. If s/he is separately liable to make payments for the accommodation to the landlord, s/he will not count as living with you.[53] This is not explicitly stated in the rules for CTB, although the same test may in practice be applied for consistency.
- No one gets invalid care allowance for looking after you, or, if you are a couple (or polygamously married), no one gets invalid care allowance for both (or all) of you. Only 'payments' of invalid care allowance count,[54] so no account is taken of any underlying entitlement to invalid care allowance where it is awarded but not paid because of the overlapping benefit rules, or of any extra-statutory payments to compensate for it not being paid. Similarly, no account will be taken of any backdated payments or arrears of invalid care allowance[55] (see Carers and the severe disability premium, p342).

Couples will get the couple rate if both (or, in a polygamous marriage, all) of you are getting a qualifying benefit and no one gets invalid care allowance for either one (or any) of you. Note that in this situation a person will be treated as getting attendance allowance (or the higher or middle rate care component of disability living allowance), even though it has stopped because s/he has been in hospital for more than four weeks. Similarly, a person will be treated as receiving invalid care allowance, even if the qualifying benefit of the person for whom s/he is caring has stopped because that person has been in hospital for more than four weeks.[56]

However, if your partner does not get a qualifying benefit but is registered blind (or treated as blind), or if invalid care allowance is paid for one of you, you will still get the single rate.

Non-dependants[57]

The following people who live with you will *not* be counted as non-dependants:

For IS/HB/CTB

- Anyone aged under 18.
- Your partner, but remember, s/he must be getting a qualifying benefit (or would be but for being in hospital, see above) or be registered or treated as blind (see p334).
- Anyone else who receives a qualifying benefit.[58]
- Anyone who is registered blind (or treated as blind).[59]
- Anyone staying in your home who normally lives elsewhere.
- Any person (and, for IS only, their partner) employed by a charitable or voluntary body as a resident carer for you or your partner if you pay a charge for that service (even if the charge is only nominal).

For IS only

- Any person (or their partner) who jointly occupies (see p341) your home and is either the co-owner with you or your partner, or jointly liable with you or your partner to make payments to a landlord in respect of occupying it. If this person is a close relative, however, s/he *will* count as a non-dependant *unless* the co-ownership or joint liability to make payments to a landlord existed either before 11 April 1988 or by the time you or your partner first moved in (but see transitional provisions below).
- Any person (or any member of their household) who is liable to pay you or your partner on a commercial basis (see p341) in respect of occupying the dwelling (eg, tenants or licensees), unless they are close relatives of you or your partner (but see transitional provisions below).
- Any person (or any member of their household) to whom you or your partner are liable to make such payments on a commercial basis, unless they are a close relative (see p341) of you or your partner (but see transitional provisions below).
- Transitional provisions. In the three situations above, the presence of close relatives will *not* prevent you from continuing to get the severe

disability premium if you fall within the scope of the transitional provisions which applied to claimants entitled to this premium before 21 October 1991. These were set out in the 22nd edition of the *National Welfare Benefits Handbook* (1992/93).

- If someone (other than those listed above) comes to live with you in order to look after you, or your partner, your severe disability premium will remain in payment for the first 12 weeks.[60] After that, you will lose the premium (or get a lower rate premium). The carer should then consider claiming invalid care allowance.

For HB only[61]

- Any person who jointly occupies your home and is either the co-owner with you or your partner, or liable with you or your partner to make payments in respect of occupying it. A joint occupier who was a non-dependant at any time within the previous eight weeks will count as a non-dependant if the local authority thinks that the change of arrangements was created to take advantage of the HB scheme.
- Any person who is liable to pay you or your partner on a commercial basis in respect of occupying the dwelling unless they are a close relative of you or your partner, or if the local authority thinks that the rent or other agreement has been created to take advantage of the HB scheme (but this cannot apply if the person was otherwise liable to pay rent for the accommodation at any time during the eight weeks before the agreement was made).
- Any person, or any member of their household, to whom you or your partner are liable to make payments in respect of your accommodation on a commercial basis unless they are a close relative of you or your partner.

For CTB only[62]

- Any person who is jointly and severally liable (see p302) with you to pay council tax. If s/he was a non-dependant at any time within the eight weeks before s/he became liable for council tax, s/he will count as a non-dependant if the local authority thinks that the change of arrangements was created to take advantage of the CTB scheme.
- Any person who is liable to pay you or your partner on a commercial basis in respect of occupying the dwelling unless they are a close relative of you or your partner, or if the local authority thinks that the liability to make payments in respect of the dwelling has been created to take advantage of the CTB scheme (but this cannot apply if the person was otherwise liable to pay rent for the accommodation at any time during the eight weeks before that liability arose).

Close relative means parent, parent-in-law, son, son-in-law, daughter, daughter-in-law, step-parent, step-son, step-daughter, brother, sister, or partners of any of these.[63]

Jointly occupies has a technical meaning. It is a legal relationship involving occupation by two or more persons (whether as owner-occupiers or as tenants or licensees), with one and the same legal right.[64] It will not exist if people merely have equal access to different parts of the premises (as had previously been decided by a commissioner[65]).

Commercial basis has no technical meaning, and there is no requirement that there need be any intention to make a profit.[66] It may be sufficient if a 'reasonable' charge is made, even if this does not fully cover the cost of the accommodation and meals being provided.[67] The reasonableness of the charge made should be judged solely against the cost of occupying the dwelling, disregarding the additional costs of providing food, clothing and care for the claimant.[68] A useful, but not conclusive, test to apply is to consider whether the same arrangement *might* have been entered into with a lodger rather than with the claimant.[69] It is not relevant to the question of whether the arrangement is on a commercial basis to consider either whether the non-dependant depends financially on the charge being paid or if s/he would take action against the claimant if s/he did not pay.[70] However, these last two matters are relevant to whether there is a *liability* (see below).

Liability means a legal or contractual liability (as distinct from a moral or ethical obligation), although this can always be inferred from the circumstances, there being no requirement that any arrangements need be evidenced in writing.[71] Any liability must arise from the costs of occupying the home. People with no contractual capacity (eg, people with very severe learning disabilities) cannot establish liability under English law. However, there will always be a presumption that capacity exists and the test of capacity may not be very stringent. In any case, a commissioner has urged a consistency of approach for England and Scotland where the law is different in that a liability can exist even where contractual capacity is not established.[72]

Note: The conditions of entitlement to the severe disability premium are considerably more stringent than they used to be. In particular, the rules about living with 'joint occupiers' and those now relating to payments on a commercial basis (see above), have been the subject of considerable legal dispute as a result of which the law has changed regularly since it was first introduced in 1988. However, even where a claimant has been a householder and has lived with close relatives, s/he may still be able to show that entitlement existed from 11 April 1988 to 30 September 1990 if there was a 'liability' (see above), and from 1

October 1990 to 10 November 1991 if the arrangements were 'on a commercial basis' (see p341).

If you think you could have qualified for the severe disability premium in an earlier period, you should get advice from a local advice agency and see if it might be possible to put in a late appeal (see p158). For further information see the 24th edition of the *National Welfare Benefits Handbook*, p354.

Carer's premium[73]

You qualify for this if you or your partner are getting, or are treated as getting, invalid care allowance.

* For how to qualify for invalid care allowance, see CPAG's *Rights Guide to Non-Means-Tested Benefits*. Note that if you are entitled to invalid care allowance by the time you reach the age of 65, you will continue to be entitled to it for life even if you stop providing care to a severely disabled person or if you start full-time work.[74]
* You are treated as getting invalid care allowance even if you do not receive it but:
  - you would get it but for the overlapping benefit rules (eg, you get long-term incapacity benefit instead), provided you claimed (or reclaimed) it on, or after, 1 October 1990, and the person you are claiming for continues to get attendance allowance or the care component (middle or higher rate) of disability living allowance.[75] The Benefits Agency may argue that you cannot benefit from this if you originally claimed invalid care allowance before 1 October 1990, but you should argue that that was not the intention of the rule;
  - you are awarded an extra-statutory payment to compensate you for non-payment of invalid care allowance.[76]
* If you stop getting, or being treated as getting, invalid care allowance, your entitlement to a carer's premium continues for a further eight weeks, even if you first claim IS/HB/CTB in this time.
* A double premium is awarded where both you and your partner satisfy the conditions for it.

Carers and the severe disability premium

Before claiming invalid care allowance, carers should consider how their claim may affect the disabled person's entitlement to the severe disability premium (see p338), particularly where the only financial advantage to the carer is the amount of the carer's premium which is considerably less than the severe disability premium.

Rules which came into force from 3 October 1994 provide that any backdated award of invalid care allowance will not affect a disabled person's entitlement to the severe disability premium.[77] There may therefore now be scope for careful planning to take advantage of these rules so that carers can be paid invalid care allowance or the carer's premium for the same period that the disabled person has already received the severe disability premium.

It is still possible that any award of invalid care allowance backdated to a period before 3 October 1994 may be reduced before it is paid, or else may result in the patient's award of the IS severe disability premium over the same period being treated as a recoverable overpayment under the rules intended to avoid duplication of payments[78] (see p146). HB/CTB overpayment rules are different (see pp200 and 312) and, arguably, may not apply in such circumstances. In any case, however, in the course of an appeal against a commissioner's decision which held that this could happen with IS,[79] the DSS conceded that this was wrong. You should therefore appeal if this happens to you.

CHAPTER NINETEEN

Income

This chapter explains the rules for working out your weekly income for income support (IS), family credit (FC), disability working allowance (DWA), housing benefit (HB) and council tax benefit (CTB). It contains:

1. Introduction (below)
2. Earnings of employed earners (p349)
3. Earnings from self-employment (p359)
4. Other income (p365)
5. Notional income (p380)

I. INTRODUCTION

Your entitlement to IS/FC/DWA/HB/CTB and the amount you receive depends on how much income you have. Note that if you get IS you do not need to work out your income again for HB/CTB purposes.[1]

The rules for working out your income are very similar for each benefit. Where there are differences these are indicated. Some of your income may be completely ignored, *or* partially ignored, *or* counted in full. Some income may be treated as capital (see p389), and some capital may be treated as income (see p376). There are some important differences in the rules on income for urgent cases payments under the income support scheme. These are set out at p82.

Note that, if you have to register for work, you will need to claim jobseeker's allowance rather than IS (see p317).

Whose income counts

Income of a partner

If you are a member of a couple (see p319), your partner's income is added to yours.[2]

If you receive a reduction of the normal personal allowance for a couple because your partner is under 18 and not eligible for IS (see p45), an amount of her/his income equivalent to the reduction is ignored.[3]

Similar rules apply to additional partners in polygamous marriages.[4]

Example

Kalid is 19. His partner, Kate, is 17 and is not able to claim IS. Kalid's personal allowance is £38.90 (the rate for a single person aged 18–24, see p00). If Kate was eligible for IS, their personal allowance would be £77.25. Up to £38.25 (£77.15 – £38.90) of any income that Kate has is ignored.

Income of a dependent child

If your child has over £3,000 capital, you do not get benefit for her/him[5] (although for IS/HB/CTB, either rate of the family premium may still be payable – see p332) and her/his income is not counted as yours. However, maintenance paid to, or for, a child does count as yours.[6]

If your child has capital of £3,000 or less, any of her/his income (subject to disregards) is usually treated as yours.[7]

With IS/HB/CTB, if that income comes to more than your child's personal allowance (plus any disabled child premium payable for her/him), the extra is ignored and not counted as yours.[8] In the case of FC/DWA, if your child's income (ignoring any maintenance payments) comes to more than the child credit (plus, for DWA, any disabled child allowance payable for your child) the whole of your child's income is ignored, but you do not get any credit/allowance for her/him.[9] However, in all cases, any maintenance that is not disregarded and which is paid to, or for, your child counts in full.[10]

Your child's earnings (as opposed to other forms of income) while s/he is *at school* do not normally count,[11] but if you are on IS/HB/CTB (not FC/DWA), and your child gets a *full-time* job *after leaving school* but while you are still claiming for her/him (eg, during the summer holiday), her/his earnings over £5 count as your income.[12] If the child qualifies for the disabled child premium (see p333) – or would, but for her/his being in a residential care or nursing home – and her/his earning capacity is not, as a result of the disability, less than 75 per cent of what it otherwise would be, £15 is ignored.[13] In either case, any income that exceeds her/his personal allowance and any disabled child premium is also ignored.[14] However, part-time earnings are still completely ignored. **School fees** paid by someone other than you or your partner are dealt with differently for each benefit.

Your entitlement to IS is not affected if someone is paying school fees directly to the school,[15] except that the payments for the child's living expenses at the school count as the child's income for the period that the child is there.[16] If your child comes home for part of the week, you receive benefit for the child for the days s/he is at home.[17] If your child spends a night with you s/he does not count as at school on that day.[18]

If your child goes away to school and this is paid for by the local education authority, the child is treated as having income equal to the amount of their IS for the days they are at school.[19] You are entitled to benefit for the child for the days they spend at home.

There are no special rules about school fees for FC/DWA. For HB/CTB, the local authority is advised that boarding school fees met by, for example, a child's grandparents should be ignored unless they are already broken down into separate amounts for education and maintenance. In that case, the education element is disregarded and the living expenses part, if it is taken into account as the child's income under the rules for payments made to someone else on your behalf (see p381), is treated as a charitable or voluntary payment and qualifies for the £20 disregard (see p373).[20] (See p345 for how a child's income is counted.) The education element of school fees paid by a former partner is also ignored, but the living expenses part, if taken into account as income under the rules for payments made to someone else on your behalf (see p381), counts as maintenance (see p368) and qualifies for the £15 disregard (see p369).[21]

Converting income into a weekly amount

IS, FC/DWA, HB and CTB are all calculated on a weekly basis so your income has to be converted into a weekly amount if necessary.

The following rules apply to income from employment[22] (except self-employment) – see p349. For other income, see p365.

- If the payment is for less than a week it is treated as the weekly amount.
- If the payment is for a month, multiply by 12 and divide by 52.
- For IS, FC and DWA, multiply a payment for three months by four and divide by 52.
- For IS, FC and DWA, divide a payment for a year by 52.
- For all benefits, multiply payments for other periods by seven and divide by the number of days in the period.

If you work on certain days but are paid monthly, it is necessary to decide whether the payment is for the days worked or for the whole month. This, generally, will depend on the terms of your contract of employment,[23] but may turn on the arrangements adopted by your employer for making payments to you.[24]

For IS, where your income fluctuates or your earnings vary because you do not work every week, your weekly income may be averaged over the cycle, if there is an identifiable one; or, if there is not, over five weeks, or over another period if this would be more accurate.[25] If the cycle involves periods when you do no work, those periods are included in the cycle, but not other absences – eg, holidays, sickness.

Example

Ahmed works a cycle of two weeks 'on' and one week 'off'. He works 20 hours a week in the weeks he works for which he is paid £60. In the third week he is paid a retainer of £30. He claims IS in the third week. His average weekly earnings will be £50 a week (£60 + £60 + £30 = £150 ÷ 3 = £50) which will be taken into account in calculating his IS entitlement.

For IS, there are a number of rules about the calculation of income for part-weeks. They are:

- Where income covering a period up to a week is paid before your first benefit week, and part of it is counted for that week; or, if, in any case, you are paid for a period of a week or more, and only part of it is counted in a particular benefit week: you multiply the whole payment by the number of days it covers in the benefit week, and then divide the result by the total number of days covered by the payment.[26]
- Where any payment of JSA, maternity allowance, incapacity benefit, or severe disablement allowance falls partly into the benefit week, only the amount paid for those days is taken into account. For any payment of IS, that amount is the weekly amount multiplied by the number of days in the part-week and divided by seven.[27]

For IS, where you have regularly received a certain kind of payment of income from one source, and in a particular benefit week you receive that payment and another of the same kind from the same source, only the one paid first is taken into account.[28]

This does not apply if the second payment was due to be taken into account in another week, but the overlapping week is the first in which it could practically be counted (see p348).

See p348 for definition of IS benefit week.

The period covered by income for IS

If you are an employed earner, or getting 'other income' and claiming IS, your income counts for a future period. There are special rules for deciding the length of this period and the date from which payments count. This rule does not apply to self-employed earnings (see p359).

- Where a payment of income is made in respect of an identifiable period, it will be taken into account for a period of equal length.[29] For example, a week's part-time earnings will be taken into account for a week.
- If the payment does not relate to a particular period, the amount of the payment will be divided by the amount of the weekly IS to which you would otherwise be entitled. If part of the payment should be disregarded, the amount of IS will be increased by the appropriate disregard. The result of this calculation is the number of weeks that you will not be entitled to IS.[30]

Example

You receive £700 net earnings for work which cannot be attributed to any specific period of time. You are a single parent aged 28 with one child aged 8, and your rent and your council tax are met by HB/CTB. Your IS is £64.70 (applicable amount of £81.80 less child benefit of £17.10). As a single parent you are entitled to a £15 earnings disregard.

£700 ÷ (£64.70 + £15 = £79.70) = 8 with £62.40 left over.

This means that you are not entitled to IS for eight weeks and the remaining £62.40 (less a £15 earnings disregard, leaving £47.40) is taken into account in calculating your benefit for the following week.

- Payments made on leaving a job are taken into account for a forward period (see p359).

The date from which a payment is counted

The date from which a payment counts depends on when it was due to be paid. If it was due to be paid before you claimed IS, it counts from the date on which it was due to be paid.[31] Otherwise it is treated as paid on the first day of the benefit week in which it is due, or on the first day of the first benefit week after that in which it is practical to take it into account.[32] Payments of IS, jobseeker's allowance, maternity allowance, incapacity benefit or severe disablement allowance are treated as paid on the day they are officially due.[33]

The benefit week for IS is the seven days running from the day of the week on which benefit is paid. It will often overlap two calendar weeks.[34]

The date that a payment is due may well be different from the date of actual payment. Earnings are due on the employee's normal pay day. If the contract of employment does not reveal the date of due payment, and there is no evidence pointing in another direction, the date the payment was received should be taken as the date it was due.[35] If your contract of employment is terminated without proper notice, outstanding wages, wages in hand, holiday pay and any pay in lieu of notice are due on the last day of employment and are treated as paid on that day, even if this does not happen.[36] If income due to you has not been paid you may be entitled to an urgent cases payment (see p82) or a crisis loan from the social fund (see p446). For the treatment of payments at the end of a job, see p354. If you receive compensation for, say, being dismissed in circumstances constituting sex discrimination, the relevant date is the date when the earnings in question were due to be paid, not when the compensation was awarded.[37]

2. EARNINGS OF EMPLOYED EARNERS

Calculating net earnings from employment

Both your 'gross' earnings and 'net' earnings need to be calculated so that a proper assessment can be made of your income from employment.

'Gross' earnings means the amount of earnings received from your employer less deductions for any expenses wholly, necessarily and exclusively incurred by you in order to carry out the duties of your employment.[38] In appropriate circumstances these could, for example, include tools or work equipment, special clothing or uniform,[39] telephone costs (including rental),[40] postage, fuel costs (including standing charges) and even secretarial expenses,[41] and the costs of running a car (including petrol, tax, insurance, repairs and maintenance and rental on a leased car).[42] It has also been held that an armed forces local overseas allowance (representing the additional cost of essential living expenses incurred from working overseas) also counts.[43] Where any expenditure serves a dual purpose for both business and private use it should be apportioned as appropriate to the circumstances (and any determination by the inland revenue – which commonly allows for 85 per cent business usage – should normally be followed).[44]

'Net' earnings mean your 'gross' earnings less any deductions made for income tax, class 1 national insurance contributions (but not class 3 voluntary contributions[45]) and half of any contribution you make towards a personal or occupational pension scheme.[46] For FC/DWA/HB/CTB, allowance is also made in certain cases for some childcare costs (see p362).

If your earnings are estimated the authorities estimate the amount of tax and national insurance you would expect to pay on those earnings, and deduct this plus half of any pension contribution you are paying.[47]

For HB/CTB, the local authority has the discretion to ignore changes in tax or national insurance contributions for up to 30 benefit weeks. This can be used, for example, where Budget changes are not reflected in your actual income until several months later. When the changes are eventually taken into account and your benefit entitlement is either increased or reduced accordingly, you are not treated as having been underpaid or overpaid benefit during the period of the delay.[48]

What counts as earnings

Earnings means 'any remuneration or profit derived from...employment'. As well as your wages, this includes:[49]

- Any bonus or commission (including tips).
- Holiday pay. But if it is not payable until more than four weeks after your job ends or is interrupted, it will be treated as capital.[50]
  Note: For IS, this rule does not apply if you are involved in, or returning to work after, a trade dispute (see p58). For more detail on payments at the end of a job, see p354.
- Except for IS, any sick pay.[51] For IS this is treated as other income and counted in full less any tax, class 1 national insurance contributions and half of any pension contributions.[52]
- For HB/CTB, any maternity pay.[53] For FC/DWA, any statutory maternity pay and maternity allowance is ignored altogether,[54] although any additional non-statutory contributions that may be made by an employer should be treated as earnings. For IS, any maternity pay is treated as other income and counted in full less any tax, class 1 national insurance contributions and half of any pension contributions.[55]
- Any payments made by your employer for expenses not 'wholly, exclusively and necessarily' incurred in carrying out your job, including any travel expenses to and from work, and any payments made to you for looking after members of your family.
- A retainer fee (eg, you may be paid during the school holidays if you work for the school meals service) or a guarantee payment.[56]
- For DWA, any payment made by your employer towards your council tax or community charge.[57]
- For IS/HB/CTB, payments in lieu of wages or in lieu of notice, but only insofar as they represent loss of income.[58]
- An award of compensation for unfair dismissal, or loss of earnings compensation for sex or race discrimination[59] and certain other awards of pay made by an industrial tribunal, and for IS/HB/CTB, certain payments made directly by your employer as compensation for loss of

employment (excluding, for IS only, any lump sum payment made under the Iron and Steel Re-adaptation Benefits Scheme).[60]

- Certain other payments from your employer – eg, arrears of wages (but see below for payments from an employer which do not count).

See pp354-57 for definitions of the last three.

The following are examples of payments not counted as earnings:

- Payments in kind – eg, petrol.[61] These are ignored[62] unless you are on IS and involved in a trade dispute (see p58), or unless there is any cause for applying the notional income rules (see p386).
- An advance of earnings or a loan from your employer. This is treated as capital[63] (although it will still be treated as earnings for IS if you or your partner are involved in a trade dispute, or have been back at work after a dispute for no longer than 15 days[64]).
- Payments towards expenses that are 'wholly, exclusively and necessarily' incurred, such as travelling expenses during the course of your work.[65] Such disregards from payments by your employer may be in addition to the allowances to be taken into account for expenses incurred by you in the assessment of your 'gross' earnings (see p349).
- If you are a local councillor, travelling expenses and subsistence payments are (and basic allowances may be[66]) ignored as expenses 'wholly, exclusively and necessarily' incurred in your work. However, allowances for attending meetings etc are counted as earnings.[67]
- Earnings payable abroad which cannot be brought into Britain – eg, because of exchange control regulations.[68] If your earnings are paid in another currency, any bank charges for converting them into sterling are deducted before taking them into account.[69]
- Any occupational pension.[70] This counts as other income and the net amount is taken into account in full.[71]

The value of any accommodation provided as part of your job will be ignored for IS.[72] For FC/DWA, if it is free, the authorities will take account of its value by adding £12 to the calculation of your weekly earnings. If your employer charges you less than £12 rent, the difference between that amount and £12 is added instead. If the accommodation is worth less to you – eg, it is provided but you never use it,[73] no amount will be added.

For CTB, and for HB where job-related accommodation is in addition to the normal home, argue that this is payment in kind[74] and should be disregarded.

How earnings are assessed

For IS, it is necessary to work out the period which payments cover. However, for FC/DWA/HB/CTB a past period is usually used to assess your 'normal weekly earnings'.

For FC

Unless you are employed as a director (see below), the normal rule is to average your weekly earnings over an 'assessment period' of:

- six consecutive weeks immediately preceding the week you claim (or the week before that if this information is not available) if you are paid weekly; *or*
- three consecutive fortnights immediately preceding the week you claim (or, if this information is not available, the three consecutive fortnights leading up to the week before you claim) if you are paid fortnightly; *or*
- three months or three four-week periods if you are paid monthly or four-weekly; *or*
- six consecutive pay periods if you are paid at another interval that is less than a month (eg, daily); *or*
- one year if your pay period is longer than a month.

In the last three cases, the periods in question must immediately precede the week of your claim.[75]

In all cases, it is the earnings which you *received* during the assessment period which count, even though some of these earnings may be for a period falling outside the assessment period – eg, an early payment of holiday pay.[76]

Any weeks/months in the assessment period are ignored and replaced by the next earliest 'normal' pay period if your earnings are reduced because you have been involved in a trade dispute[77] or if you have deliberately chosen to reduce the number of hours you work with the intention of becoming entitled to, or increasing your entitlement to, FC.[78]

Any pay period in which your earnings are 20 per cent or more above or below your average earnings are left out. If this applies to all the weeks/months in your assessment period, only those in which you received no pay or received pay for a longer period than usual (eg, two weeks' holiday pay in one week) are left out. If this still results in all the weeks/months in your assessment period being left out, your employer will be required to provide an estimate of your likely earnings for the period for which you are normally paid.[79]

Where your earnings vary widely you may find that the figure arrived at can be based on just one wage slip which could be up to 20 per cent above or below your real average earnings. Therefore it may sometimes be sensible to delay your claim in order to allow for the lowest possible rate of pay to be taken into account and thus maximise the amount of FC you will receive for the next 26 weeks.

If you are employed as a director of a company, different rules apply.[80] Your normal weekly earnings are worked out by looking at how much you received in the year immediately before the week of your claim. If you have been employed for less than a year, an estimate is made of what you are likely to earn in the first year, taking into account what you have already received. Any week when you do no work and do not get paid is ignored in calculating your weekly earnings.[81]

For DWA

The normal rule is to take your weekly earnings over an 'assessment period' of:

* five consecutive weeks in the last six weeks if you are paid weekly; *or*
* two months if you are paid monthly;

immediately before the week of your claim.[82]

As with FC, it is the earnings which are *received* during the assessment period which count, whether or not they were actually earned in respect of that period.[83]

However, any time in the assessment period during which your earnings were irregular or unusual does not count[84] – eg, any week in which you received, for instance, a one-off bonus or holiday pay, or in which large deductions were made from your wages.

If your earnings fluctuate, or in the five-week or two-month period before your claim do not represent your normal earnings (eg, because you are on unpaid maternity leave[85]), a different period can be used if this gives a more accurate picture of your normal weekly earnings.[86]

If there is a period of short-time working of not more than 13 weeks or a trade dispute at your place of work, your normal weekly earnings will be taken as those prior to the period of short-time working or dispute. Trade dispute includes a work-to-rule or overtime ban as well as a strike.[87]

For FC/DWA

A bonus or commission paid separately, or for a longer period than other earnings, and which is paid in the year prior to your claim, counts as earnings.[88] The net amount is divided by 52 before it is taken into account.[89]

If you have just started a job or have just returned to work after a break of more than, for FC four weeks, or, for DWA 13 weeks, or your hours have just changed, and the period since the start or resumption of your employment or the change in hours is less than your assessment period, your employer will be required to provide an estimate of your likely earnings for the period for which you are normally paid.[90] If your actual earnings turn out to be lower than the estimate, this will not result in your FC/DWA being reviewed and increased, so it is important that your employer does not overestimate your earnings.

For HB/CTB

Earnings as an employee are usually averaged out over:

- the previous five weeks if you are paid weekly; *or*
- two months if you are paid monthly.[91]

Where your earnings vary, or if there is likely to be or has recently been a change (eg, you usually do overtime but have not done so recently, or you are about to get a pay rise), the local authority may average them over a different period where this is likely to give a more accurate picture of what you are going to earn during the benefit period.[92]

If you are on strike, the local authority should not take into account your pre-strike earnings and average them out over the strike period.[93]

If you have only just started work and your earnings cannot be averaged over the normal period (ie, five weeks/two months), an estimate is made based on any earnings you have been paid so far if these are likely to reflect your future average wage. Where you have not yet been paid or your initial earnings do not represent what you will normally earn over the benefit period, your employer must provide an estimate of your average weekly earnings.[94] Where your earnings change during your benefit period, your new weekly average figure is estimated on the basis of what you are likely to earn over the remainder of the benefit period.[95]

Payments at the end of a job

Redundancy payments are normally treated as capital (see below).

Some redundancy schemes make periodic payments after leaving work; for IS/HB/CTB, these are treated as other income (see p365).[96]

Other payments can cause problems, and are dealt with separately for each benefit.

For IS

In most cases, when you finish a job you will need to claim income-based jobseeker's allowance rather than IS (see the *Jobseeker's Allowance*

Handbook, 2nd edn, 1997/98). However, if you do not need to register for work, you may need to claim IS.

If you retire from a full-time job (16 hours or more) and you are aged at least 60 (women) or 65 (men), any payments counted as earnings (eg, final wages, holiday pay, etc) that you receive are disregarded in full.[97] You are not treated as in full-time work for any period covered by those earnings after the end of your job.

In all other cases, only the following final payments that you receive when you leave a *full-time* job affect your right to IS:[98]

- holiday pay which counts as earnings (see p350);
- pay in lieu of notice;
- pay in lieu of wages;
- a compensation payment in respect of employment (ie, where you do not get pay in lieu of notice, or only get part of your pay in lieu of notice, and receive a lump sum instead – ie, *ex gratia*). This is divided by the maximum payable under the statutory redundancy scheme (uprated yearly). The result is the number of weeks the payment will cover up to a maximum of your notice period, whether statutory, contractual or customary.[99] If the amount is less than the statutory maximum for one week or if the calculation creates a fraction, these are treated as capital.[100] If the *ex gratia* payment is not compensation but a gift (eg, a 'golden handshake') it should be treated as capital, not income.

You are treated as in full-time work for the number of weeks covered by these payments after your employment ended.[101] These payments are taken into account consecutively and in the following order:

- any pay in lieu of wages or in lieu of notice; *then*
- payments of compensation for loss of employment; *then*
- holiday pay.[102]

The period for which you are treated as in full-time work starts on the earliest date that any of these payments are due to be paid.[103]

Example

Mary leaves her full-time job with a final week's wages, a week in hand and one week's holiday pay. All three amounts are due to be paid on 30 May. Only the holiday pay will be taken into account, starting from 30 May. Mary will not be entitled to IS for one week.

If you receive an award of compensation for unfair dismissal or certain other awards of pay from an industrial tribunal, these are taken into account as earnings in calculating the amount of your IS from when the award is made.

If your employment is interrupted (eg, you are laid off), any holiday pay that is paid to you affects your right to IS; all other payments are disregarded except that any retainer you are paid is taken into account as earnings in calculating the amount of your IS.[104] If you have been suspended, any payment you receive will be taken into account and affect your right to IS.

If you were working part-time (less than 16 hours a week) before you claimed IS, any payments you receive when the job ends or is interrupted, except any retainer, are ignored and do not affect your IS (unless you have been suspended).[105] If, however, you were claiming IS while you were in part-time work, any payments made to you when that job ends are taken into account as earnings in the normal way. Your wages, including any final wages, are counted first, then any pay in lieu of wages or notice, then any compensation paid by your employer for loss of employment (although this will be taken into account for a period of one week only[106]) and then any holiday pay.[107]

Once the period covered by payments at the end of a job has ended, any money remaining will be treated as capital.[108]

For FC/DWA

There are no special FC/DWA rules for payments received at the end of a job. However, if, for example, your partner has just lost her/his job and you apply for FC because you are working full time, any payments that s/he received at the end of the employment (and indeed the amount of previous wages) should not be included as part of your 'normal' weekly income, unless there is evidence that the job will resume while you are getting your current FC award.

For HB/CTB

If you retire from a full-time job (16 hours or more) and have reached the age of 65 (men) or 60 (women), any payments counted as earnings that you receive are disregarded.[109]

In all other cases, only the following final payments that you receive are taken into account as earnings:[110]

- holiday pay which counts as earnings (see p350);
- pay in lieu of notice;
- pay in lieu of wages;
- compensation for loss of employment, but only insofar as it represents loss of income (the detailed rules for IS do not apply);

- an award of compensation for unfair dismissal, or certain other awards of pay from an industrial tribunal;
- any statutory sick pay or statutory maternity pay;
- any retainer fee.

If your work is interrupted, your earnings are disregarded except for holiday pay which counts as earnings (see p350) and any retainer paid to you.

Where you were in part-time work (ie, less than 16 hours a week) before claiming HB/CTB, any earnings paid when your job ended or was interrupted are disregarded, *except* where that payment is a retainer.[111] This disregard does not apply to earnings paid when your job ends if you are already getting HB/CTB.

Disregarded earnings

For FC/DWA, your earnings, worked out in the way described above, are taken into account in full. (Though see provisions on deductions for certain childcare costs, p362.)

For IS and HB/CTB, some of your earnings are disregarded and do not affect your benefit. The amount of the 'disregard' depends on your circumstances. There are three levels.

£25 disregard

Lone parents on HB/CTB but not receiving IS have £25 of their earnings ignored.[112] This does not apply to IS.

£15 disregard

£15 of your earnings (including those of your partner, if any) is disregarded if:

- for IS, you qualify for the lone parent rate of the family premium (see p333). You are treated as qualifying for the premium if you would do so but for getting a pensioner premium or for being in a local authority home, or because you are a person in a residential care or nursing home with preserved rights (see p85);[113]
- you or your partner (if any) qualifies for a disability premium (see p333).[114] For IS, you are treated as qualifying for the premium if you would do so but for being in hospital, or a local authority home or because you are a person in a residential care or nursing home with preserved rights (see p85);
- for HB/CTB only, you or your partner (if any) qualifies for a severe disability premium (see p338);[115]

- you or your partner (if any) qualifies for the higher pensioner premium (see p336), you or your partner are over 60 and, immediately before reaching that age, you or your partner were in employment (part-time for IS) and you were entitled to a £15 disregard because of qualifying for a disability premium. For HB/CTB this includes where, in the case of a couple, you would have qualified for a disability premium but for the fact that a higher pensioner premium was payable. Since reaching 60, you or your partner must have continued in employment (part-time for IS), although breaks of up to eight* weeks when you were not getting IS (or HB/CTB where you claim either of these benefits) are ignored. For IS, you are treated as qualifying for the higher pensioner premium even if you are in hospital etc;[116]
- you are a member of a couple, your benefit would include a disability premium but for the fact that one of you qualifies for the higher pensioner premium or the enhanced rate of pensioner premium (see p336), one of you is under 60 and either of you are in employment. For IS, you are treated as qualifying for the higher or enhanced pensioner premium if you would do so, but for being in hospital, etc (see above);[117]
- you are a member of a couple, one of you is aged 75-79 and the other over 60, and immediately before that person reached 60 either of you were in part-time employment and you were entitled to a £15 disregard because of qualifying, or being treated as qualifying for an enhanced pensioner premium (see above). Since then either of you must have continued in part-time employment, although breaks of up to eight* weeks when you were not getting IS (or HB/CTB where you claim either of these benefits), are ignored;[118]
- you or your partner (if any) qualifies for a carer's premium (see p342). The disregard applies to the carer's earnings. For a couple, if the carer's earnings are less than £15, the remainder of the disregard can be used up on her/his partner's earnings as an auxiliary coastguard, etc (see below), or up to £5 (for HB/CTB up to £10) of it can be used up on her/his partner's earnings from another job;[119]
- you or your partner (if any) are an auxiliary coastguard, part-time firefighter or a part-time member of a lifeboat crew, or a member of the Territorial Army.[120] If you earn less than £15 for doing any of these services you can use up to £5 (for HB/CTB up to £10 if you have a partner) of the disregard on another job[121] or a partner's earnings from another job.[122]

*For IS, this is increased to 12 weeks if you stopped getting IS because you or your partner started full-time work (see p13 for the detailed rules on this). Any period when you were not entitled to IS because you or your partner went on a government training scheme is ignored. But it will count as a period that you were in receipt of IS if you qualify for the £15 disregard as a long-term claimant (see above).[123]

If you qualify under more than one category you still have a maximum of only £15 of your earnings disregarded.

Basic £10 or £5 disregard

If you do not qualify for a £25 or £15 disregard, £5 of your earnings is disregarded if you are single. If you claim as a member of a couple, £10 of your total earnings is disregarded – whether or not you are both working.[124]

3. EARNINGS FROM SELF-EMPLOYMENT

Calculating net earnings

Your 'net profit' over the period before your claim must be worked out. This consists of your self-employed earnings, including any Business Start-Up Allowance,[125] minus:[126]

- reasonable expenses (see below); *and*
- income tax and national insurance contributions; *and*
- half of any premium paid in respect of a personal pension scheme or a retirement annuity contract which is eligible for tax relief.[127] If you and your partner (if any) are aged under 60, you must supply certain information about the scheme or annuity contract to the relevant authority if requested.[128]

For FC/DWA, the Business Start-Up Allowance will not count if it ended before you claimed – so it may be worthwhile delaying your claim.[129] In calculating your earnings any capital grant to set up a business, or a loan of working capital, or the sale of capital assets is excluded,[130] and any capital (eg, a legacy) not generated by the business cannot be treated as earnings.[131]

For IS/HB/CTB, if you receive payments for fostering from a local authority or voluntary organisation, and for IS/FC/DWA/HB/CTB if you receive payments from a health authority or local authority or voluntary organisation for providing temporary respite care, these do not count as earnings[132] but are ignored.[133] For IS, if you receive payments for board and lodging charges these do not count as earnings[134] but as other income (see p345). For FC/DWA, these are treated as earnings if, after discounting all the disregards on pp365-80 (other than the boarder's allowance on p374), they form a *major part* of your total income.[135] Otherwise they are treated as other income, as for IS.

Reasonable expenses

Expenses must be reasonable and 'wholly and exclusively' incurred for the purposes of your business.[136] This will involve similar considerations to those that apply in the allowances permitted in the assessment of 'gross' earnings of employed earners (see p349). Where a car or telephone, for example, is used partly for business and partly for private purposes, the costs of it can be apportioned and the amount attributable to business use can be deducted.[137]

Reasonable expenses include:[138]

- repayments of capital on loans for replacing equipment and machinery;
- repayment of capital on loans for, and income spent on, the repair of a business asset except where this is covered by insurance;
- interest on a loan taken out for the purposes of the business;
- excess of VAT paid over VAT received.

Reasonable expenses do not include:[139]

- any capital expenditure;
- depreciation. However, there are conflicting decisions as to whether any decrease (or increase) in the valuation of stock (which can be taken into account for tax purposes) should be taken into account.[140] The most recent case holds that these should be taken into account;[141]
- money for setting up or expanding the business (eg, the cost of adapting the business premises);
- any loss incurred before the beginning of the current assessment period. If the business makes a loss, the net profit is nil. The losses of one business cannot be offset against the profit of any other business in which you are engaged, or against your earnings as an employee,[142] (although where two businesses or employments share expenses these may be apportioned and offset);[143]
- capital repayments on loans taken out for business purposes;
- business entertainment expenses;
- for HB/CTB only, debts (other than proven bad debts), but the expenses of recovering a debt can be deducted.

Working out your average

There are different rules for each benefit.

For IS

The weekly amount is the average of earnings:[144]

- over a period of any one year (normally the last year for which accounts are available);
- over a more appropriate period where you have recently taken up self-employment or there has been a change which will affect your business.[145]

If your earnings are royalties or copyright payments, the amount of earnings is divided by the weekly amount of IS which would be payable if you had not received this income plus the amount which would be disregarded from those earnings.[146] You will not be entitled to IS for the resulting number of weeks.

For FC/DWA

Your normal weekly earnings are worked out by looking at:[147]

- your profit and loss account (and your trading account and/or balance sheet if appropriate), if this covers a period of at least six but not more than 15 months, which ends within 12 months before the date of your claim; *or*
- if you do not provide such a profit and loss account, but do provide a statement of your earnings and expenses for the six calendar months up to and including the month before your claim, your earnings over that period of six months; *or*
- if you do not provide a profit and loss account or statement of earnings and expenses, the six calendar months up to and including the month preceding your claim; *or*
- a different past period, if this represents your normal weekly earnings more accurately.

Your weekly earnings are worked out by averaging the earnings you have received or can expect to receive over the assessment period or, where you have provided a profit and loss account, by averaging the earnings relevant to the period covered by that account.[148]

Any complete week(s) in the assessment period when you are not actually working (eg, because you are sick or on holiday) are ignored.[149]

If you have just started being self-employed (ie, for less than seven calendar months), for FC your normal weekly earnings are worked out over six calendar months, beginning with the month after the one in which you started the business. If you provided a statement of earnings and expenses for those months, up to and including the last month before the month in which you claim, the earnings of those months are taken; if you do not provide such a statement, the earnings up to and including the month before the one preceding your claim are taken. In either case, the amount you can expect to earn for the remainder of the six-month period is added. Any week where you do not work for the business is ignored.[150] For DWA an estimate will be made of your likely weekly earnings over the next 26 weeks from the date of your claim.[151] If your actual earnings turn out to be lower than the estimate this will not result in your FC/DWA being reviewed and increased.[152] However, if you were not *awarded* FC/DWA because your estimated earnings were too high, but by the time your appeal is heard you would be entitled on the basis of your actual earnings, the tribunal should have regard to your earnings up to the date of the social security appeal tribunal hearing in deciding what your income really was at the date of claim. In this case, the tribunal is deciding whether you are entitled to an award, not dealing with a change of circumstances affecting an existing award.[153]

For HB/CTB

The amount of your weekly earnings is averaged out over an 'appropriate' period (usually based on your last year's trading accounts) which must not be longer than a year.[154]

Childminders

Childminders, in practice, are always treated as self-employed. Your net profit is deemed to be one-third of your earnings less income tax, your national insurance contributions and half of certain pension contributions[155] (see p359). The rest of your earnings are completely ignored.

Disregarded earnings[156]

The rules are the same as for employed earners (see p349).

Childcare costs[157]

For FC/DWA/HB/CTB an allowance of up to £60 a week may be deducted from your earnings (from employment or self-employment) in respect of childcare costs if you are:

- a single parent working 16 hours a week or more; *or*
- a couple and both of you work 16 hours a week or more, or else one of you works 16 hours a week or more and the other is 'incapacitated' (see below).

This will only apply if you have a child under the age of 11 and you are paying charges for childcare (not counting charges in respect of compulsory education or charges paid by you to your partner for a child in your family) which is provided:

- by a registered childminder or other registered childcare provider (such as a nursery or after-school club catering for the under-eights); *or*
- by (for children between the ages of 8 and 11) a school on school premises or a local authority – eg, an out-of-hours or holiday play scheme. For FC/DWA it is the age of the child at the start of the claim which counts; *or*
- by a childcare scheme operating on Crown property; *or*
- in schools or establishments exempt from registration.

Note: A child is not treated as having reached the age of 11 until the day before the first Tuesday (for FC/DWA) or first Monday (for HB/CTB) in September *following* her/his actual 11th birthday. For HB and CTB, this rule applies from 7 April 1997. For FC and DWA, it applies from 7 October 1997 for children reaching the relevant age from that date on.[158]

You (or your partner) will be treated as 'incapacitated' if:

- you get short-term (higher rate) or long-term incapacity benefit; *or*
- you get severe disablement allowance; *or*
- you get attendance allowance, disability living allowance or constant attendance allowance (or an equivalent award under the war pensions or industrial injuries schemes), or else you would receive one of these benefits but for the fact that you (or your partner) are in hospital; *or*
- you have an invalid carriage or similar vehicle; *or*
- HB/CTB is payable and includes (or would include, but for a disqualification of up to six weeks for misconduct) a disability or higher pensioner premium (see Chapter 18) in respect of the incapacity; *or*
- for HB/CTB, you (but not your partner) have been treated as incapable of work for a continuous period of 196 days or more (disregarding any break of up to 56 days); *or*
- for HB/DWA, you have already been awarded an allowance for childcare costs in HB/CTB.

Calculating childcare costs

For FC/DWA[159]

Because childcare costs are likely to vary considerably between term-time and holiday periods, a formula is used to assess the costs that will be taken into account.

Where charges are paid other than monthly, the amount will be *either*:

- 1/52 of the aggregate of:
  - the average weekly charge in the four most recent complete weeks falling in term-time, multiplied by 39; *and*
  - the average weekly charge in the two most recent weeks falling out of term-time, multiplied by 13; *or*
- where your child does not yet attend school, the average weekly charge in the four most recent complete weeks.

Where charges are paid monthly:

- if the charge is for a fixed amount, that amount multiplied by 12 and divided by 52; *or*
- if the charge is variable, 1/52 of the aggregate of charges over the previous 12 months.

However, where there is no, or insufficient, information available in order to assess the childcare costs in any of these ways, an estimate will be made based on information provided by the care provider or, if that is not available, by you.

For HB/CTB[160]

The costs to be taken into account will be estimated over whatever period, not exceeding a year, that will give the best estimate of the average weekly charge over the 'benefit period' (see pp272 and 311), based on information to be provided by the childminder or care provider.

Additional points to note:

- These rules do *not* apply to IS.
- £60 is the maximum amount that can be deducted regardless of the number of children you are paying childcare for.
- If you are claiming FC or DWA only, the net gain to you of the £60 allowance will be a maximum of £42 (because of the 70 per cent taper used in the calculation of FC/DWA – see pp191 and 204). Similar considerations also apply to HB/CTB (see pp248 and 303 for the taper rules).
- The childcare costs calculation will apply both on your claim for FC or DWA and your claims for HB/CTB.
- Local authorities may not charge you for nursery services provided under the Children Act if you are on FC/DWA.[161] If your income, but for the childcare allowance, would be too high to qualify for FC/DWA, any charges a local authority makes could be used to enable you to qualify. You should then be able to keep your FC/DWA throughout

the 26-week period of the award even though, as soon as you are awarded it, the local authority will have to stop charging you. When your award expires, the local authority will be able to charge you again, and you can then claim again.

• A commissioner recently rejected the argument that the fact that no childcare costs could be taken into account for FC prior to 1 October 1994 unlawfully discriminated against women.[162]

4. OTHER INCOME

Most other types of income are taken into account less any tax due on them.[163] For HB/CTB, changes in tax and national insurance rates may be ignored for up to 30 weeks,[164] as for earnings (see p349).

Payments from Training for Work (TFW) and Youth Training (YT) schemes are for the most part taken into account.

All income is converted into a weekly amount (see p346). For IS, this amount is attributed to a forward period (see p347) and affects the benefit payable for that period.

For FC/DWA/HB/CTB, a past period is used where possible to assess normal weekly income, and this figure is used to calculate benefit.

For HB/CTB, an estimate of income is made by looking at an appropriate period (not exceeding one year). The period chosen must give an accurate assessment of your income.[165]

For FC/DWA, your income during the 26 weeks immediately before the week of your claim will be used, unless a different period immediately before your claim would produce a more accurate assessment.[166]

Benefits

Benefits that count in full:

• contribution-based JSA;
• incapacity benefit and severe disablement allowance;
• except for FC/DWA, maternity allowance;
• invalid care allowance;
• widows' benefits (including industrial death benefit);
• retirement pensions;
• industrial injuries benefits (except constant attendance allowance and exceptionally severe disablement allowance);
• except for FC/DWA, child benefit;
• for IS only, guardian's allowance;
• child's special allowance and war orphan's pension;

- for IS, FC/DWA or earnings top-up (ETU). For HB/CTB, any additional FC/DWA/ETU paid because you, or your partner, are working 30 hours or more a week is ignored (see pp190 and 204). Otherwise, FC/DWA/ETU are taken into account.[167]
- for IS only,[168] statutory sick pay and statutory maternity pay – less any class 1 national insurance contribution and half of any pension contribution and any tax. For HB/CTB, statutory sick pay and statutory maternity pay are treated as earnings (see p350) and you may, therefore, benefit from an earnings disregard (see p357). For FC/DWA, statutory sick pay is counted as earnings but statutory maternity pay is ignored (see p350).

Problems can arise where, for example, the Benefits Agency or local authority try to take into account a benefit you are not receiving, such as child benefit that has been delayed. In such a case, the benefit should not be treated as income possessed by you. For IS, you should get your full benefit and leave the Benefits Agency to deduct the difference from arrears of the delayed benefit when it is eventually awarded.[169]

For IS/FC/DWA/HB/CTB, arrears of all means-tested and some disability benefits should be treated as capital and ignored for 52 weeks (see p394).[170] This rule only applies to arrears of benefit which you actually receive. Therefore, for IS, it will only apply to arrears of benefit which are paid to you *after* the Benefits Agency have made any deductions because the award of the benefit was delayed.

Benefits that are ignored completely:

- attendance allowance (or constant attendance allowance, exceptionally severe disablement allowance or severe disablement occupational allowance paid because of an injury at work or a war injury) or any care component of disability living allowance. For IS only, it is taken into account in full up to a maximum of £48.50 a week if you went to live in a residential care or nursing home before 31 March 1993 and you are a person with preserved rights (see p85), or you are accommodated under The Polish Resettlement Act;[171]
- pensioner's Christmas bonus;[172]
- mobility allowance or either of the mobility components of disability living allowance;[173]
- mobility supplement under the War Pensions Scheme;[174]
- any extra-statutory payment made to you to compensate for non-payment of IS, income-based JSA, mobility allowance, mobility supplement, attendance allowance or disability living allowance;[175]
- for FC, disability working allowance.[176] For DWA, family credit;[177]

- social fund payments.[178] For FC/DWA, they are not specifically disregarded, but they should not count as part of your 'normal weekly' income. For IS/FC/DWA/HB/CTB, social fund payments are disregarded as capital indefinitely;[179]
- except for DWA, resettlement benefit paid to certain patients who are discharged from hospital and who had been in hospital for more than a year before 11 April 1988;[180]
- any transitional payment made to compensate you for loss of benefit due to the changes in benefit rules in April 1988;[181]
- HB, CCB, CTB and refunds on community charge/council tax liability;[182]
- IS and income-based JSA are ignored for FC/DWA and HB/CTB.[183] There are special HB/CTB rules for IS/income-based JSA claimants (see pp207 and 303);
- certain special war widows' payments,[184] including any special or supplementary payments (currently £52.80) to pre-1973 war widows;[185]
- for FC/DWA/HB/CTB, guardian's allowance;[186]
- for FC/DWA, child benefit;[187]
- for FC/DWA, maternity allowance and statutory maternity pay;[188]
- for FC/DWA, any payment of ETU (see p197);[189]
- for HB/CTB, any additional payment of FC, DWA or ETU made because you or your partner (if any) are working for 30 hours or more a week;[190]
- any increase for adult or child dependants who are not members of your family (see p318), where you are getting incapacity benefit, maternity allowance, widowed mother's allowance, retirement pension, industrial injuries benefits (including unemployability supplement), invalid care allowance or a service pension.[191]

For the treatment of payments of arrears of benefits, see p394. Also, for the treatment of payments of child maintenance bonuses, see p177, and back to work bonuses, p176.

Benefits that have £10 ignored:

- war disablement pension;
- war widow's pension;
- widow's pension payable to widows of members of the Royal Navy, Army or Royal Air Force;
- an extra-statutory payment made instead of the above pensions;
- similar payments made by another country;
- a pension from Germany or Austria paid to the victims of Nazi persecution.[192]

Only £10 in all can be ignored, even if you have more than one payment which attracts a £10 disregard.[193] However, the £10 disregard allowed on these war pensions is additional to the total disregard of any mobility supplement or attendance allowance (ie, constant attendance allowance, exceptionally severe disablement allowance and severe disablement occupational allowance) paid as part of a war disablement pension (see p366).

Local authorities are given a limited discretion to increase the £10 disregard on war disablement, war widows' pensions and the pension payable to widows of members of the Royal Navy, Army or Royal Air Force, when assessing income for HB/CTB.[194] Check your local authority's policy on this issue.

Maintenance payments

If you are claiming IS and receiving maintenance payments, or child support maintenance payments (see p114), from a former partner for yourself or any children, the rules on how this money is treated are considered on p113.

If you claim **FC/DWA** and regular amounts of maintenance payments, or child support maintenance payments, are being made at regular intervals (eg, weekly or monthly) before you claim, the normal weekly amount counts as income.[195] If any child support maintenance payments made are more than the amount due under a maintenance assessment, only the amount due under the assessment is taken into account. If maintenance payments are due to be paid regularly but are not being so, the average of the payments made in the 13 weeks up to the week of your claim counts as income. With child support maintenance payments not paid regularly, you take the average of the payments made over the last 13 weeks, or, if the maintenance assessed was notified to you within the last 13 weeks, over the period since the notification. However, if that average is more than the maintenance assessment, it is the assessment which is taken into account.[196] Payments are taken into account from the date they are received by you, not the date they are received into court or by the DSS (if appropriate).[197] Other payments of maintenance are treated as capital.[198] However, any payments made by the Secretary of State as compensation for a reduction in child support maintenance assessment are disregarded as income and (for 52 weeks) as capital.[199] Maintenance payments to or for a child in your family (see p325) should be treated as yours but only if the payments are actually made.

For **HB** and **CTB**, periodical payments should count as income and lump sums as capital. Maintenance paid to or for your dependent child counts as yours.[200]

If you are a single parent, or a couple with a child, for FC/DWA, HB and CTB, £15 of any maintenance payment made by your former partner, or your partner's former partner, or the parent of any child in your family is disregarded. If you receive maintenance from more than one person, only £15 of the total is disregarded.[201]

If you *pay* maintenance to a former partner or a child not living with you, your payments are not disregarded for the purpose of calculating your income for IS/FC/DWA/HB/CTB.[202]

Grants and covenants to students

The term grant includes bursaries, scholarships and exhibitions as well as grants or awards from education authorities.[203] An educational award which is paid by way of a loan does not count as a grant for IS,[204] but is nevertheless taken into account as 'other income' (see p365). You are treated as having the parental or partner's contribution to your grant whether or not it has been paid to you. However, if you are a single parent, a single foster parent or a disabled student, only the amount of any contribution that you actually receive counts for IS.[205] Grant income is taken into account for the academic year, excluding the summer vacation, unless the grant expressly covers a different period. In each case, it is divided equally over the weeks in the period.[206] In the case of a sandwich course, grant income is averaged out over the period of study excluding the periods of experience – ie, in industry or commerce.[207] Any grant income paid under the Education (Mandatory Awards) Regulations that is intended for the maintenance of a student's dependants or which is an allowance for mature students or single parents[208] is spread over 52 or 53 weeks.[209] (Benefit weeks and academic years sometimes run to 53 weeks, including part-weeks.) However, for other grants the normal rule (period of study or period for which grant payable) applies. So where a student on a sandwich course received a grant from the Department of Health, the element for his dependants was spread over the period of study only.[210]

The following grant income is ignored:[211]

- a fixed amount of £280 or whatever you get in your grant towards the cost of books and equipment;
- a fixed amount for travelling expenses. Where you are in receipt of a mandatory grant, and living away from your parents' home, this will usually be £149. If you are living at your parents' home it will usually be £231. There is no additional disregard even if your actual travelling expenses are higher;[212]
- any allowance for tuition and examination fees;

- any allowance to meet extra expenses because you are a disabled student;
- any allowance to meet the cost of attending a residential course away from your normal student accommodation during term-time;
- any allowance for the costs of your normal home (away from college) but, for IS, only if your rent is not met by HB;
- any amount for a partner or children abroad is ignored for IS and HB/CTB, but not FC/DWA.

These disregards apply only to the maintenance grant you receive during the academic year, and not to any element for dependants you may receive during the summer vacation.[213]

Covenant income

There has been no tax relief available on covenants since April 1988. Further details of these rules were set out in the 23rd edition of the *National Welfare Benefits Handbook* (1993/94).

General points about grant income

- If you receive any payments over and above your grant, covenant or top-up loan, to help you with certain expenses (see p369), and these payments are greater than the amounts for those expenses disregarded from your grant or covenant income, the excess amount is ignored.[214]
- In the case of a couple, the amount of any contribution that one member has been assessed to pay to her/his partner who is a student does not count as the non-student's income for IS/FC/DWA/HB/CTB.[215]
- For HB only, if your eligible rent is subject to a flat-rate deduction (see p263), the same amount is disregarded from your income. If your income does not cover the deduction, the balance is ignored from your partner's income.[216]
- For IS only, if you either give up or are dismissed from your course before it finishes, your grant will be taken account of as if you were still a student[217] until you either repay the grant or the academic term or vacation in which you ceased to be a student ends, whichever is the earlier.[218]

Student loans[219] under the statutory scheme are treated as income. Weekly income is calculated by dividing the loan over the 52 (or 53) weeks of the academic year. In the final year of the course, or for a one-year course, the loan is divided by the number of weeks from the start of the academic year to the end of the course – ie, the last day of the last term.[220]

There is a £10 disregard on loan income, but it may overlap with other disregards on other income (see p373).[221]

If you give up your course before it finishes, your loan continues to be counted in the same way, but without any disregard.[222]

If you fail to take responsible steps to get a loan to which you are entitled, the maximum amount payable to you is counted as weekly income, calculated as if you actually received it.[223] This does not apply if you have given up your course early (see above), since you are no longer a 'student'.

Career development loans paid under section 2 of the Employment and Training Act 1973 are taken account of as income.[224] For IS, the weekly income is calculated by dividing the loan by the number of weeks of education and training which the loan was paid for.[225] However, for IS/FC/DWA/HB/CTB, this income is ignored – except where it was paid for and is used to meet the cost of food, clothing and footwear, household fuel, rent, mortgage interest charges, certain other accommodation charges, council tax and water charges.[226]

For IS only, any grant income, covenant income, student loan or career development loan which you have left over at the end of your course is ignored.[227]

Access Fund payments[228] made to students by educational establishments to prevent hardship will be treated as voluntary or charitable payments (see below).

Loans to students from overseas are neither grants nor awards, but should be taken into account as income.[229]

Adoption, fostering and residence order (in Scotland custody) payments

An **adoption allowance** counts in full for IS and HB/CTB up to the amount of the adopted child's personal allowance and disabled child premium, if any. Above that level it is ignored completely.[230]

For FC/DWA, anything above the level of the child's credit/allowance is ignored.[231]

If the child has capital over £3,000, you are not entitled to any benefit for the child (see p385) and the entire adoption allowance is ignored.[232]

The way that a **fostering allowance** is treated depends on whether the arrangement is an official or a private one. If a child is placed or boarded out with you by the local authority or a voluntary organisation under legal provisions, any fostering allowances you receive are ignored altogether.[233]

If the fostering arrangement is a private one, any money you receive from the child's parents is counted as maintenance (see p368). If the money you receive is not from the child's parents, you should probably be treated as a childminder (see p362).

If you are paid a **residence order allowance** (in Scotland, custody allowance) by the local authority, this is treated in the same way as an adoption allowance[234] (see above). Arrears of residence order (in Scotland, custody) allowances are treated as capital for IS.[235] Any payments made by the natural parents count as maintenance (see p368).

If the local authority makes a lump-sum payment to enable you to make adaptations to your home for a disabled child, this is treated as capital and ignored (see p391).[236]

Charitable and voluntary payments

Payments from the Macfarlane and similar trusts

Any payments, including payments in kind, from the Macfarlane Trust, the Macfarlane (Special Payments) Trust, the Macfarlane (Special Payments) (No. 2) Trust, the Fund, the Eileen Trust (see Appendix 1) or either of the Independent Living Funds (see Appendix 1) are disregarded in full.[237]

The Macfarlane Trusts make payments to haemophiliacs. The Fund was set up on 24 April 1992 for people who are not haemophiliacs who have contracted HIV through blood or tissue transfusions.

If you are, or were, a haemophiliac, or have received a payment from the Fund or the Eileen Trust, the following payments from money that originally came from any of the three Macfarlane Trusts, the Fund or the Eileen Trust are also disregarded in full:[238]

- any payment made by you, or on your behalf, to, or for the benefit of:
  - your partner, or former partner from whom you are not estranged or divorced;
  - any child (see p325) who is a member of your family, or who was but is now a member of another family; or
- if you have no partner or former partner (other than one from whom you are estranged or divorced), or children, any payment made by you (or from your estate in the event of your death) to:
  - your parent or step-parent; or
  - your guardian if you have no parent or step-parent and were a child (see p325) or student at the date of the payment (or at the date of your death).

In the case of a payment to a parent, step-parent or guardian, this is only disregarded until two years after your death;

- any payment made by your partner, or former partner from whom you are not estranged or divorced, or on her/his behalf, to, or for the benefit of:
  - you;
  - any child who is a member of your family, or who was and is now a member of another family.

Any income or capital that derives from any such payment is also disregarded.

Other payments

Most other charitable or voluntary payments that are made irregularly and are intended to be made irregularly are treated as capital and are unlikely to affect your claim unless they take your capital above the limit.[239] However, if you are on IS it will count as income:

- if you are involved in a trade dispute and for the first 15 days following your return to work after a dispute[240] (see p58); *or*
- where payments made to a child's boarding school are treated as the child's notional income[241] (see p345).

Charitable or voluntary payments made, or due to be made regularly, are completely ignored if:[242]

- for IS/HB/CTB, they are intended, and used, for anything *except* food, ordinary clothing or footwear, household fuel, council tax, water rates and rent (less any non-dependant deductions) for which HB is payable; and, for IS only, housing costs met by IS and residential care or nursing home accommodation charges for people with preserved rights (see p85) met by IS or by a local authority. Where you do not have a preserved right (see p85) and the local authority has placed you in a residential care or nursing home that is more expensive than normal for a person of your needs because you preferred that home, a charitable or voluntary payment towards the *extra* cost will be ignored for IS;[243]
- for FC/DWA, they are intended, and used, for anything *except* food, ordinary clothing or footwear, household fuel, council tax, community charge (but not standard community charge) and any housing costs.

    School uniform and sportswear are examples of clothing and footwear that is not ordinary.

If not ignored altogether, charitable or voluntary payments have a £20 disregard. However, note that there is an overall limit of £20 for these sorts of payments and some other sorts of income which attract a disregard, such as student loans (see p371).[244]

For IS, these rules do not apply where you are involved in a trade dispute, and for the first 15 days following your return to work after a trade dispute. For IS/FC/DWA/HB/CTB, payments from a former partner, or the parent of your child are dealt with as maintenance (see p368).

- See also, payments made to someone else on your behalf, p381, and payments disregarded under miscellaneous income, p377.

Concessionary coal or cash in lieu

Coal that is provided free by British Coal to a former employee or widow is ignored as income in kind (for IS, if you or your partner are involved in a trade dispute, see p58).[245] Cash in lieu of coal is not a voluntary payment[246] but counts in full as income, or as earnings if paid to a current employee.[247]

Income from tenants and lodgers

Lettings without board

If you let out room(s) in your home to tenants/sub-tenants/licensees under a formal contractual arrangement, £4 of your weekly charge for each tenant/sub-tenant/licensee (and her/his family) is ignored, and an extra £9.25 if the charge covers heating costs.[248] The balance counts as income.

If someone shares your home under an informal arrangement, any payment made by them to you for their living and accommodation costs is ignored,[249] but a non-dependant deduction may be made (see p36).

Boarders

If you have a boarder(s) on a commercial basis in your own home, and the boarder or any member of her/his family is not a close relative of yours, the first £20 of the weekly charge is ignored and half of any balance remaining is then taken into account as your income.[250] (With HB/CTB, there is no specific reference to non-commercial arrangements or close relatives, but the rules on contrived tenancies could possibly apply – see p220.) This applies for each boarder you have. The charge must normally include at least some meals.[251]

Tenants in other properties

If you have a freehold interest in a property other than your home and you let it out, the rent is treated as capital.[252] This rule will also apply if you have a leasehold interest in another property which you are subletting. There is disagreement between commissioners as to whether it is the gross rent which should be taken into account, or only the sum left after deducting expenses.[253]

Income from capital

In general, actual income generated from capital (eg, interest on savings) is ignored as income[254] but counts as *capital*[255] from the date you are due to receive it. However, income derived from the following categories of capital is treated as *income*[256] (though the capital itself is disregarded – see p389):

- your home;
- your former home if you are estranged or divorced;
- property which you have acquired for occupation as your home but which you have not yet been able to move into;
- property which you intend to occupy as your home but which needs essential repairs or alterations;
- property occupied wholly or partly by a partner or relative of any member of your family who is 60 or over or incapacitated;
- property occupied by your former partner, but not if you are estranged or divorced – unless (for HB/CTB) s/he is a single parent;
- property up for sale;
- property which you are taking legal steps to obtain to occupy as your home;
- your business assets;
- a trust of personal injury compensation.

Income from any of the above categories (other than your current home, business assets or a personal injuries trust) is ignored up to the amount of the total mortgage repayments (ie, capital and interest, and any payments that are a condition of the mortgage such as insurance or an endowment policy[257]), council tax and water rates paid in respect of the property for the same period over which the income is received.[258]

Tariff income from capital over £3,000[259]

If your capital is over £3,000, you are treated as having an assumed income from it, called your tariff income. You are assumed to have an income of £1 for every £250, or part of £250, by which your capital exceeds £3,000 but does not exceed £8,000 (IS/FC) or £16,000 (DWA/HB/CTB). **Note:** For IS/HB, if you are in residential care or similar accommodation (see p84), tariff income applies between £10,000 and £16,000.

If you are underpaid because of a reduction in your capital affecting your tariff income, you should ask for a review (see p131 for IS, p291 for HB and p294 for CTB). You should report any increase in your capital to the Benefits Agency for IS,[260] and to the local authority for HB/CTB, except where the increase does not stop you getting some IS.[261] If there is a change in your capital which increases the amount of your tariff income and as a result of which you are overpaid, see p146 for IS, and p280 for HB and p312 for CTB on recovery of overpayments. For FC/DWA, any increase or reduction in the amount of your capital during the period of your award will not affect your entitlement (see pp196 and 209) and you will not need to notify the Benefits Agency unless or until you renew your claim.

Capital which counts as income

The following will count as income:

- Instalments of capital outstanding when you claim benefit if they would bring you over whichever capital limit is applicable. For IS, the instalments to be counted are any outstanding either when your benefit claim is decided, or when you are first due to be paid benefit, whichever is earlier, or at the date of any subsequent review.[262] For FC/DWA it is any instalments outstanding at the date of your claim.[263] For HB/CTB it is any instalments outstanding when your claim is made or treated as made, or when your benefit is reviewed.[264] Any balance over the capital limit will be counted as income, by spreading it over the number of weeks between each instalment.[265] Note that for IS, there are two capital limits of £8,000 and £16,000 (see pp384-85). If instalments are outstanding in this way on your child's capital, a similar rule applies. If the total of these instalments and your child's existing savings come to more than £3,000, the outstanding instalments should count as your child's income,[266] and be spread over the period between each instalment.[267]
- Any payment from an annuity[268] (see p378 for when this is disregarded).
- Any career development loan paid under section 2 of the Employment and Training Act 1973[269] (see p371 for how such loans are treated).
- For IS, a tax refund if you or your partner have returned to work after a trade dispute[270] (see p58).
- For IS, a payment from a social services department under section 17 of the Children Act 1989 or, in Scotland, a payment from a social work department under sections 12, 24 and 26 of the Social Work (Scotland) Act 1968 (see Appendix 1), or payments from social services to young people who have previously been in care or been looked after by them,

if you or your partner are involved in or have returned to work after a trade dispute (see p58).[271]

- For HB/CTB, a local authority will sometimes treat withdrawals from a capital sum as income.[272] This is most likely where a sum was intended to help cover living expenses over a particular period – eg, a bank loan taken out by a mature student. If this is not the intended use of any capital sum, you should dispute the decision. Even where the sum is intended for living expenses, you should argue that unless it is actually paid in instalments it should be treated as capital.[273]

  Any payments of capital, or any irregular withdrawals from a capital sum, which are clearly for one-off items of expenditure and not regular living expenses, should be treated as capital. Further, whatever the intention behind the sum, if no withdrawals are in fact made, it should be treated as capital.[274]

- Some lump sums from liable relatives (see p113).

Capital which is counted as income cannot also be treated as producing a tariff income (see p375).[275]

Income tax refunds

PAYE income tax refunds are not payable to unemployed people receiving unemployment benefit or IS until the end of the tax year, or until they obtain a job, whichever comes first. Strikers can only get a tax refund on return to work. Other people who are not entitled to unemployment benefit or IS can still get tax refunds when they fall due.

- PAYE refunds (employed earners) and tax refunds under schedule D (self-employed) are treated as capital.[276]
- For IS only, if you or your partner have returned to work after a trade dispute (see p58), tax refunds will be treated as income and are taken into account in full.[277]

For treatment of income tax refunds on mortgage interest or loans for repairs and improvements, see below.

Miscellaneous income

Count in full:

- An occupational pension, income from a personal pension or retirement annuity contract (except any discretionary payment from a hardship fund and, for IS, half of a pension or retirement annuity contract in some residential care situations where at least half of it is for your spouse).[278]

- Payments from an annuity. *Except* that in the case of 'home income plans', income from the annuity equal to the interest payable on the loan with which the annuity was bought is ignored if the following conditions are met:
  - you used at least 90 per cent of the loan made to you to buy the annuity; *and*
  - the annuity will end when you and your partner die; *and*
  - you or your partner are responsible for paying the interest on the loan; *and*
  - you, or both your partner and yourself, were at least 65 at the time the loan was made; *and*
  - the loan is secured on a property which you or your partner owns or has an interest in, and the property on which the loan is secured is your home, or that of your partner.

If the interest on the loan is payable after income tax has been deducted, it is an amount equal to the net interest payment that will be disregarded, otherwise it is the gross amount of the interest payment.[279]

The following are ignored:

- For IS only, payments you receive under a mortgage protection policy which you took out, and which you use, to pay the housing costs which are not being met by the Benefits Agency in your IS[280] (for restrictions on housing costs see p38). However, if the amount you receive exceeds the total of:
  - the interest you pay on a qualifying loan which is not met by the Benefits Agency;
  - capital repayments on a qualifying loan; *and*
  - any premiums you pay on the policy in question and any building insurance policy;

  then the excess is counted as your income.

- For IS only, and as long as you have not already used insurance payments for the same purpose, *any* money *you* receive which is given, and which *you* use to make:[281]
  - payments under a secured loan which do not qualify under the housing costs rules;
  - interest payments which are not met under the housing costs rules, even though some interest payments under the loan in question are met;
  - capital repayments on a qualifying loan;
  - payments of premiums on an insurance policy which you took out to insure against the risk of not being able to make the payments in

the above three categories, and premiums on a building insurance policy;
- any rent that is not covered by HB (see Chapter 12);
- the part of your accommodation charge that is above the maximum payable by IS if you live in a nursing home or residential care home and you are a person with preserved rights (see p85) or above that payable by a local authority.
• For FC/DWA, compensation for a reduced child support maintenance assessment.[282]
• For HB/CTB, payments you receive under a mortgage protection policy are ignored up to the level of your repayments.[283]
• Educational maintenance allowances[284] (see Appendix 1).
• Any payment to cover expenses if you are working as a volunteer.[285]
• Payments in kind (for IS, if you or your partner are involved in a trade dispute, see p58).[286]
• For FC/DWA, a Jobmatch allowance paid under the Employment and Training Act 1973 if the payments are before your award begins.[287]
• A payment (other than a training allowance) to a disabled person under the Employment and Training Act 1973 or the Disabled Persons (Employment) Act 1944 to assist them to obtain or retain employment.[288]
• If you are participating in arrangements for training under section 2 of the Employment and Training Act 1973 or, in Scotland, section 2 of the Enterprise and New Towns (Scotland) Act 1990 (or an employment rehabilitation course under the 1973 Act), certain travel expenses, living away from home expenses and training premiums.[289]
• Any payments, other than for loss of earnings or of a benefit, made to jurors or witnesses for attending at court.[290]
• A payment from a social services department under sections 17 or 24 of the Children Act 1989, or, in Scotland, a payment from a social work department under sections 12, 24 or 26 of the Social Work (Scotland) Act 1968 (see Appendix 1), and payments from social services to young people who have been in care or been looked after by them.[291] For IS, such payments are not ignored if you or your partner are involved in or have returned to work after a trade dispute (see p58).
• Any payments made under the Community Care (Direct Payments) Act 1996 or under section 12B of the Social Work (Scotland) Act 1968.[292]
• Any payment you receive from a health authority, local council or voluntary organisation for looking after a person temporarily in your care.[293]
• Victoria Cross or George Cross payments or similar awards.[294]

- Income paid outside the UK which cannot be transferred here.[295]
- If income is paid in another currency, any bank charges for converting the payment into sterling.[296]
- Fares to hospital.[297]
- Payments instead of milk tokens and vitamins.[298]
- Payments to assist prison visits.[299]
- For HB/CTB, if you make a parental contribution to a student's grant, an equal amount of any 'unearned' income you have for the period the grant is paid, is ignored.[300] If your 'unearned' income does not cover the contribution the balance can be disregarded from your earnings.[301] If you are a parent of a student under 25 who does not get a grant (or who only gets a smaller discretionary award) and you contribute to her/his living expenses, the amount of your 'unearned' income that is ignored is the amount equal to your contribution up to a maximum of £38.90 (less the weekly amount of any discretionary award the student has).[302] This is only ignored during the student's term. Again, any balance can be disregarded from your earnings.[303]

5. NOTIONAL INCOME

In certain circumstances you will be treated as having income although you do not possess it, or have used it up.

Deprivation of income in order to claim or increase benefit

If you deliberately get rid of income in order to claim or increase your benefit, you are treated as though you are still in receipt of the income.[304] The basic issues involved are the same as those for the deprivation of capital (see p397). A deliberate decision to 'de-retire' and give up your retirement pension (in the expectation of achieving an overall increase in benefit in the future) can come within this rule.[305] For an explanation of de-retirement, see CPAG's *Rights Guide to Non-Means-Tested Benefits*.

Failing to apply for income[306]

If you fail to apply for income to which you are entitled without having to fulfil further conditions, you will be deemed to have received it from the date you could have obtained it.

This does not include income from a discretionary trust or a trust set up from money paid as a result of a personal injury or, where you are under 60, income from a personal pension scheme or retirement annuity.

However, if you are 60 or over, you will be treated as receiving income in certain circumstances if you fail to purchase an annuity.[307] For IS only, the lone parent element of child benefit, JSA, FC, DWA and ETU are also exempted.

Previously, DSS guidance for HB/CTB said that FC (and presumably other benefits as well) should not count as notional income if you might be entitled but had not applied for it, although local authorities should notify the Family Credit Unit where it appeared to them a successful claim could be made. It also said that if you applied for FC/DWA but had not yet been paid, it did not count as income or notional income and should be ignored until you actually received it. Current guidance does not deal with these points, but you should argue that the same still applies.

Income due to you that has not been paid

This applies to IS only.[308] You will be treated as possessing any income owing to you. Examples could be wages legally due but not paid, or an occupational pension payment that is due but has not been received. However, this does not apply where an occupational pension has not been paid, or fully paid, because the pension scheme has insufficient funds.[309] The rule also does not apply if any social security benefit has been delayed, or you are waiting for a late payment of a pension under the Job Release Scheme, a government training allowance or a benefit from a European Union country. Nor does it apply in the case of money due to you from a discretionary trust, or a trust set up from money paid as a result of a personal injury.

If this rule is applied, an urgent cases payment should be considered (see p82).[310]

Unpaid wages

This applies to IS only. If you have wages due to you, but you do not yet know the exact amount or you have no proof of what they will be, you are treated as having a wage similar to that normally paid for that type of work in that area.[311] If your wages cannot be estimated you might qualify for an interim payment[312] (see p136).

Income payments made to someone else on your behalf[313]

If money is paid to someone on your behalf (eg, the landlord for your rent) this can count as notional income. The rules are the same as for notional capital (see p397). For IS, payments of income in kind are ignored, unless you or your partner are involved in a trade dispute (but even then they are ignored if they are from the Macfarlane Trusts, the Fund, the Eileen Trust or either of the Independent Living Funds, see Appendix 1).[314]

Income payments paid to you for someone else[315]

If you or a member of your family get a payment for somebody not in the 'family' (see p318) (eg, a relative living with you) it will count as your income if you keep any of it yourself or spend it on your family. This does not apply if the payment is from the Macfarlane Trusts, the Fund, the Eileen Trust or either of the Independent Living Funds. Note that the same exception for payments in kind applies for IS as for income payments made to someone else on your behalf.

Cheap or unpaid labour

If you are helping another person or an organisation by doing work of a kind which would normally command a wage, or a higher wage, you are deemed to receive a wage similar to that normally paid for that kind of job in that area.[316] The burden of proving that the kind of work you do is something for which an employer would pay, and what the comparable wages are, lies with the adjudication officer.[317]

The rule does not apply if:

either you can show that the person ('person' in this context includes a limited company[318]) cannot, in fact, afford to pay, or pay more;

or you work for a charitable or voluntary organisation or as a volunteer, and it is accepted that it is reasonable for you to give your services free of charge.[319] A 'volunteer' in this context is someone who, without any legal obligation, performs a service for another person without expecting payment.[320]

It has been held that even if you are caring for a sick or disabled relative or another person, it may be reasonable for them to pay you from their benefits, unless you can bring yourself within these exceptions.[321] It may, for example, be more reasonable for a close relative to provide services free of charge out of a sense of family duty,[322] particularly if a charge would otherwise break up a relationship.[323] Whether it is reasonable to provide care free of charge will depend on the basis on which the arrangement is made, the expectations of the family members concerned, the housing arrangements and the reasons (if appropriate) why a carer gave up any paid work. The risk of a carer losing entitlement to invalid care allowance if a charge were made should also be considered[324] as should the likelihood that a relative being looked after would no longer be able to contribute to the household expenses.[325] If there is no realistic alternative to the carer providing services free to a relative who simply will not pay, this may also make it reasonable not to charge.[326] Sometimes it may also be reasonable to do a job for free out of a sense of community duty, particularly if the job would otherwise have remained undone, and there would be no financial profit to an employer.[327]

Reducing the number of hours you work

For FC only, if you deliberately choose to reduce the number of hours you work in order to be able to claim or increase your entitlement to FC, any period of reduced hours will be ignored when assessing your normal weekly earnings.[328]

CHAPTER TWENTY

Capital

This chapter covers:

1. INTRODUCTION

The capital limit

This chapter explains how capital affects your entitlement to income support (IS), family credit (FC), disability working allowance (DWA), housing benefit (HB) and council tax benefit (CTB). If you get IS, you do not need to work out your capital again for HB/CTB purposes because you receive your maximum HB (see p248) or CTB (see p303),[1] less any deductions for non-dependants.

If you have over £8,000 (IS and FC)[2] or £16,000 (DWA, HB and CTB)[3] you are not entitled to benefit (but for CTB, see p306 for second adult rebate). Some capital is disregarded (see p390), but you may also be treated as having some capital which you do not actually possess (see p397). If you have up to £3,000 it is ignored and does not affect your weekly benefit at all. If you have between £3,000.01 and £8,000 (IS and FC)/£16,000 (DWA, HB and CTB) you may be entitled to benefit but some income will be assumed.[4] This is known as tariff income (see p375).

There are some important differences in the rules on capital for urgent cases payments under the income support scheme (see pp46-49).

Residential care

There are higher capital limits for people in residential or similar accommodation.

For IS[5] the higher limits apply if you live permanently in:

- residential care or a nursing home and in either case you are given board and personal care because of:
  - old age;
  - disablement;
  - past or present dependence on alcohol or drugs;
  - past or present mental disorder;
- residential accommodation. For what is meant by residential accommodation see p92, but note that for the higher capital rules the exceptions for people under 18 or for people not receiving board do not apply;
- Abbeyfield Society homes; *or*
- a home provided under the Polish Resettlement Act in which you are receiving personal care.

Note that you are treated as living permanently in one of these homes for periods of absence of up to 13 weeks. However, if you are over pensionable age or (in some cases) were getting supplementary benefit as a residential care home boarder before 27 July 1987, it can be up to 52 weeks.

For HB[6] the higher limits apply, broadly speaking, if you live permanently in one of the limited categories of accommodation referred to on p233. Sometimes temporary absences are again ignored.

For both IS and HB, tariff income starts at £10,000 (instead of £3000) and the upper limit is £16,000 (for HB that is the limit for other claimants too).

Whose capital counts

Your partner's capital is added to yours.[7] Your child's capital does not count as belonging to you,[8] but if it is over £3,000 you will not get benefit for that child[9] (although, for IS/HB/CTB, both rates of the family premium are still payable – see p333), in which case any income of the child will not be counted as yours either.[10] However, maintenance paid to, or for, a child does count as yours.[11] The rules used to work out your child's capital also apply to you.[12]

2. WHAT COUNTS AS CAPITAL

The term 'capital' is not defined. In general, it means lump-sum or one-off payments rather than a series of payments.[13] It includes, for example, savings, property and redundancy payments. It also includes any payments of child maintenance bonus[14] (see p177) or back to work bonus[15] (see p176).

Capital payments can normally be distinguished from income because they are not payable in respect of any specified period or periods, and they do not form nor are intended to form part of a regular series of payments[16] (although capital can be paid by instalments).

However, some capital is treated as income (see p376), and some income is treated as capital (see p389).

Savings

Your savings generally count as capital – eg, cash you have at home, premium bonds, stocks and shares, unit trusts, and money in a bank account or building society.

Your savings from past earnings can only be treated as capital when all relevant debts, including tax liabilities, have been deducted.[17] Savings from other past income (including social security benefits) will be treated as capital (see p394). There is no provision for disregarding money put aside to pay bills.[18] If you have savings just below the capital limit, it may be best to pay bills for gas, electricity, telephone etc by monthly standing order, or by use of a budget account, to prevent your capital going above the limit.

Fixed-term investments

Capital held in fixed-term investments counts. However, if in reality it is presently unobtainable, it may have little or no value (but see p405 for jointly held capital). If you can convert the investment into a realisable form, sell your interest, or raise a loan through a reputable bank using the asset as security, its value counts. If it takes time to produce evidence about the nature and value of the investment, you may be able to get an interim payment for IS, FC or DWA (see p136) or HB[19] (see p274) or a crisis loan from the social fund (see p446).

Property and land

Any property or land which you own counts as capital. Many types of property are disregarded (see p390). See also proprietary estoppel – p388.

Loans

A loan usually counts as money you possess. However, a loan granted on condition that you only use the interest but do not touch the capital should not be counted as part of your capital because the capital element has never been at your disposal.[20] Where you have been paid money to be used for a particular purpose on condition that the money must be returned if not used in that way, it should not be treated as part of your capital.[21] Where you have bought a property on behalf of someone else who is paying the mortgage,[22] or where you are holding money in your bank account on behalf of another person which is to be returned to them at a future date,[23] the capital should not count as yours.

For HB/CTB some loans might be treated as income even though paid as a lump sum (see p377).

Trusts

A trust is a way of owning an asset. In theory, the asset is split into two notional parts: the legal title owned by the trustee, and the beneficial interest owned by the beneficiary. A trustee can never have use of the asset, only the responsibility of looking after it. An adult beneficiary, on the other hand, can ask for the asset at any time. Anything can be held on trust – eg, money, houses, shares etc.

If you are the adult beneficiary of:

• a non-discretionary trust – You can obtain the asset from the trustee at any time. You effectively own the asset, and so its market value will count as your capital;
• a discretionary trust – You cannot insist on receiving payments from the trust. Payments are at the discretion of the trustee within the terms of the trust. Any payments made will be treated in full as income or capital depending on the nature of the payment. The trust asset itself would not normally count as your capital because you cannot demand payment (of either capital or income);
• a trust which gives you the right to receive payments in the future (eg, on reaching 25) – this is a right that has a present capital value, unless disregarded (see p394).

If you have a life interest only in an asset, the value of your right to receive income is disregarded[24] (see p394), but not the income itself if you get any.

If the beneficiary is under 18, even with a non-discretionary trust, s/he has no right to payment until s/he is 18 (or later if that is what the trust stipulates). Her/his interest may nevertheless have a present value.[25]

If you hold an asset as a trustee, it is not part of your capital. You are only a trustee either if someone gives you an asset on the express condition that you hold it for someone else (or use it for their benefit), or if you have expressed the clearest intention that your own asset is for someone else's benefit, and renounced its use for yourself[26] (assets other than money may need to be transferred in a particular way to the trust).

It is not enough to only *intend* to give someone an asset. However, in the case of property and land, proprietary estoppel may apply. This means that if you lead someone to believe that you are transferring your interest in some property to them, but fail to do so (eg, it is never properly conveyed), and they act on the belief that they have ownership (eg, they improve or repair it, or take on a mortgage), it would then be unfair on them were they to lose out if you insisted that you were still the owner.[27] In this case, you can argue the capital asset has been transferred to them, and you are like a trustee. Thus you can insist that it is not your capital asset, but theirs, when claiming benefit.

If money (or another asset) is given to you to be used for a special purpose, it may be possible to argue that it should not count as your capital. This is called a purpose trust[28] (see also p387).

Trust funds from personal injury compensation

Where a trust fund has been set up out of money paid because of a personal injury, the value of the trust fund is ignored.[29] Although the regulations refer to 'personal injury to the claimant' only, in practice the capital value of the trust fund is ignored regardless of whether the money was paid in respect of you, your partner (if any), or your children.

It is not necessary for the trust to be set up by a formal deed. For these purposes, personal injuries compensation held by the Court of Protection (because the injured person is incapable of managing her/his own affairs) and administered by that Court and/or the Public Trustee will count as a trust.[30] The important point is that the person who is awarded the compensation should not be able to have any direct access to it.

In this context, 'personal injury' includes not only accidental and criminal injuries, but also any disease and injury suffered as a result of a disease. Thus, a trust fund for a child who had both legs amputated following meningitis and septicaemia could be disregarded for the purposes of the parent's claim.[31]

Any payments actually made to you from these trusts may count in full as income or capital depending on the nature of the payment.[32] However, trustees may have a discretion to use such funds to purchase items that would normally be disregarded as capital such as personal possessions (see p392) – eg, a wheelchair, car, new furniture – or to arrange payments that would normally be disregarded as income – eg, for IS/HB/CTB, ineligible housing costs. Similarly, they may have discretion to clear debts or pay for a holiday, leisure items or educational or medical needs. See p372 for the treatment of voluntary payments and pp381-82 and 402 for the treatment of payments made to third parties. Note that the notional income and capital rules (see pp380 and 397) cannot apply to personal injury trusts.

If there is no trust, or until one can be set up, the whole of the compensation payment counts as capital, even if the money is held by your solicitor.[33]

Infant funds in court[34]

Where damages are awarded to minors (ie, under the age of 18) in respect of personal injury or compensation for the death of one or both parents, the money may be paid into a special fund to be administered by, and at the discretion of, the court. This will be disregarded as capital, and any payments actually made from the fund will be treated in the same way as payments from trust funds (see p387).

Income treated as capital

Certain payments which appear to be income are nevertheless treated as capital. These are:[35]

- an advance of earnings or loan from your employer;*
- holiday pay which is not payable until more than four weeks after your employment ends or is interrupted;*
- income tax refunds;*
- income from capital (eg, interest on a building society account) and income from rents on properties let to tenants (see pp374 and 394); however, income from disregarded property listed on p390 (eg, a home you are trying to move into or sell, or which is occupied by elderly relatives) and income from business assets or personal injury trusts counts as income not capital;
- for IS/HB/CTB, a lump sum or 'bounty' paid to you not more than once a year as a part-time firefighter or part-time member of a lifeboat crew, or as an auxiliary coastguard or member of the Territorial Army – for FC/DWA this will normally count as earnings;[36]
- irregular (one-off) charitable payments;*
- for IS only, the part, or the whole, of a compensation payment for loss of employment that is treated as capital under the IS rules (see p356);
- for IS only, a discharge grant paid on release from prison;

- for IS only, arrears of residence order (in Scotland, custody) payments from a local authority (see p372);
- for FC/DWA only, irregular maintenance payments (see p368).[37]

*Except, for IS, in the case of people involved in, or returning to work after, a trade dispute (see p58).

Any income treated as capital is disregarded as income.[38]

3. DISREGARDED CAPITAL

Your home

If you own the home you normally live in, its value is ignored.[39] Your home includes any garage, garden, outbuildings and land, together with any premises that you do not occupy as your home but which it is impractical or unreasonable to sell separately – eg, croft land.[40] If you own more than one property, only the value of the one normally occupied is disregarded under this rule.[41]

The value of property can be disregarded even if you do not live in it, in the following circumstances.

- **If you have left your former home following a marriage or relationship breakdown**, the value of the property is ignored for six months from the date you left. It is also disregarded for longer if any of the steps below are taken. For HB/CTB, if it is occupied by your former partner who is a single parent its value is ignored as long as s/he lives there.[42]
- **If you have sought legal advice or have started legal proceedings in order to occupy property** as your home, its value is ignored for six months from the date you first took either of these steps.[43] The six months can be extended, if it is reasonable to do so, where you need longer to move into the property.
- **If you are taking reasonable steps to dispose of any property**, its value is ignored for six months from the date you *first* took such steps.[44] The definition of 'property' here includes land on its own, without any buildings on it.[45] Putting the property in the hands of an estate agent or getting in touch with a prospective purchaser should constitute 'reasonable steps'.[46] The test for what constitutes 'reasonable steps' is an objective one.[47] If you need longer to dispose of the property, the disregard can continue if it is reasonable – eg, where a husband or wife attempts to realise their share in a former matrimonial home but the court orders that it should not be sold until the youngest child reaches a certain age.

- **If you are carrying out essential repairs or alterations** which are needed so that you can occupy a property as your home, for IS/FC/DWA/HB/CTB the value of the property is ignored for six months from the date you first began to carry them out.[48] If you cannot move into the property within that period because the work is not finished, its value can be disregarded for as long as is reasonable.
- **If you sell your home** and intend to use the money from the sale to buy another home, the capital is ignored for six months from the date of the sale.[49] This also applies even if you do not actually own the home but, for a price, you surrender your tenancy rights to a landlord.[50] If you need longer to complete a purchase, the authorities can continue to ignore the capital if it is reasonable to do so. You do not have to have decided within the six months to buy a *particular* property. It is sufficient if you intend to use the proceeds to buy *some* other home.[51] If you intend to use only part of the proceeds of sale to buy another home, only that part is disregarded even if, for example, you have put the rest of the money aside to renovate your new home.[52]
- **If you have acquired a house or flat for occupation** as your home but have not yet moved in, its value is ignored if you intend to live there within six months.[53] If you cannot move in by then the value of the property can be ignored for as long as seems reasonable.
- **If your home is damaged or you lose it altogether**, any payment, including compensation, which you intend to use for its repair, or for acquiring another home, is ignored for a period of six months, or longer if it is reasonable to do so.[54]
- **If you have taken out a loan or been given money for the express purpose of essential repairs and improvements** to your home, it is ignored for six months, or longer if it is reasonable to do so.[55] If it is a condition of the loan that the loan must be returned if the improvements are not carried out, you should argue that it should be ignored altogether.[56]
- **If you have deposited money with a housing association as a condition of occupying your home**, this is ignored indefinitely.[57] If money which was deposited for this purpose is now to be used to buy another home, this is ignored for six months, or longer if reasonable, in order to allow you to complete the purchase.[58]
- **Grants made to local authority tenants to buy a home or do repairs/alterations** to it can be ignored for up to 26 weeks, or longer if reasonable, to allow completion of the purchase or the repairs/alterations.[59]

When considering whether to increase the period of any disregard, all the circumstances should be considered – particularly your and your family's personal circumstances, any efforts made by you to use or dispose of the home (if relevant) and the general state of the market (if relevant).

It is possible for property to be ignored under more than one of the above paragraphs in succession.

Some income generated from property which is disregarded is ignored (see p375).

The home of a partner or relative

The value of a house will also be ignored if it is occupied wholly or partly as their home by:[60]

* *either* your partner[61] – ie, your husband/wife, provided you are both still treated as living in the same household (see p318) or your cohabitee, provided you are still treated as living together as husband and wife (see p320);
  or a relative of yours, or any member of your family; who in either case, is aged 60 or over or is incapacitated (see below);
* your former partner from whom you are not estranged or divorced. This means your husband/wife where you are not still treated as living in the same household or your former cohabitee where you are not still treated as living together as husband and wife;
* for HB/CTB only, your former partner from whom you are estranged or divorced if s/he is a lone parent.[62]

'Incapacitated' is not defined, but guidance for IS/FC/DWA/HB/CTB suggests it refers to someone who is getting an incapacity or disability benefit, or who is sufficiently incapacitated to qualify for one of those benefits.[63] However, you should argue for a broader interpretation, if necessary. For FC/DWA, the relative must have been incapacitated throughout the 13 weeks before you claim.[64]

Relative includes: a parent, son, daughter, step-parent/son/daughter, or parent/son/daughter-in-law; brother or sister; or a partner of any of these people; or a grandparent or grandchild, uncle, aunt, nephew or niece.[65] It also includes half-brothers and sisters and adopted children.[66]

Personal possessions

All personal possessions, including items such as jewellery, furniture or a car, are ignored unless you have bought them in order to be able to claim or get more benefit[67] (in which case the sale value, rather than the purchase price, is counted as actual capital, and the difference is treated as notional capital[68] - see p397).

Compensation for damage to, or the loss of, any personal possessions, which is to be used for their repair or replacement is ignored for six months, or longer if reasonable.[69]

Business assets

If you are self-employed, your business assets are ignored for as long as you continue to work in that business. For IS/FC/DWA, as little as half an hour's work a week may be sufficient.[70] If you cannot work because of physical or mental illness, but intend to work in the business when you are able, the disregard operates for 26 weeks, or for longer if reasonable in the circumstances.[71] If you stop working in the business, you are allowed a reasonable time to sell these assets without their value affecting your benefit. For FC/DWA, if you have sold a business asset but intend to reinvest the proceeds in that business within 13 weeks (or longer if reasonable) the money is ignored.[72] It will sometimes be difficult to distinguish between personal and business assets. The test is whether the assets are 'part of the fund employed and risked in the business'.[73] Note that letting out a single house does not constitute a business.[74]

Tax rebates

Tax rebates for the tax relief on interest on a mortgage or loan obtained for buying your home or carrying out repairs or improvements are ignored.[75]

Personal pension schemes and retirement annuity contracts

The value of a fund held under a personal pension scheme or retirement annuity is ignored.[76]

Insurance policy and annuity surrender values

The surrender value of any life assurance or endowment policy is ignored. Note that the life assurance aspect need not be the sole or even the main aspect of the policy.[77] The surrender value of any annuity is also ignored.[78] Any payment under the annuity counts as income[79] (but see p378 for when this is ignored).

Personal injuries trust funds

The value of a trust fund set up out of money paid because of personal injury is ignored (see p388).

Future interests in property

A future interest in most kinds of property is ignored. A future interest is one which will only revert to you, or become yours for the first time, when some future event occurs.[80]

However, this does not include a freehold or leasehold interest in property which has been let *by you* to tenants. If you did not let the property to the tenant (eg, because the tenancy was entered into before you bought the property), then your interest in the property should be ignored as a future interest in the normal way. In addition, a commissioner has recently suggested that if you grant someone an '*irrevocable* licence' to occupy property, your interest in that property is a future one and should be ignored.[81]

An example of a future interest is where someone else has a life interest in a fund and you are only entitled after that person has died.

The right to receive a payment in the future

If you know you will receive a payment in the future, you could sell your right to that payment at any time so it has a market value and therefore constitutes an actual capital resource. The value of this will be ignored where it is a right to receive:

- income under a life interest or, in Scotland, a liferent.[82] When the income is actually paid, it will count in full (see p375);
- any earnings or income which are ignored because they are frozen abroad[83] (see pp351 and 380);
- any outstanding instalments where capital is being paid by instalments[84] (see p376);
- an occupational or a personal pension;[85]
- any rent if you are not the freeholder or leaseholder;[86]
- any payment under an annuity (see p378);[87]
- any payment under a trust fund that is disregarded[88] (see p387).

Benefits and other payments

Arrears of certain benefits are ignored for 52 weeks after they are paid.[89] These are mobility allowance, attendance allowance (or an equivalent benefit paid because of a war or work injury), mobility supplement, disability living allowance, DWA, income-based jobseeker's allowance, IS, supplementary benefit, FC, earnings top-up, family income supplement, HB/CTB, or concessionary payments made instead of any of these, certain war widows' payments,[90] and refunds on community charge and council tax liability.[91]

Compensation for loss of housing benefit supplement, HB or supplementary benefit (if you did not become entitled to IS instead) at the changeover to IS in April 1988 is completely ignored, as is community charge benefit (CCB) and HB for CTB, and CTB and CCB for HB.[92]

For IS, any backdated payments of IS/HB/CTB made once the Home Office has accepted you are a refugee (see p76) are ignored for 52 weeks from the date of receipt.[93] The same rule also applies in relation to backdated payments of IS and HB (for HB)[94] and IS and CTB (for CTB)[95]. For special capital rules and urgent cases, see pp48-49.

For FC, DWA, HB and CTB only, any child maintenance bonus (see p177) or back to work bonus (see p176) is ignored for 52 weeks from the date you receive it.[96]

The following payments are ignored for 52 weeks from receipt:

- fares to hospital;[97]
- payments in place of milk tokens or vitamins;[98]
- payments to assist prison visits;[99]
- for FC/DWA only, payments made by the Secretary of State as compensation for a reduction in your child support maintenance assessment.[100]

Social fund payments are ignored indefinitely.[101]

A payment to a disabled person under the Disabled Persons (Employment) Act 1944 or the Employment and Training Act 1973 (other than a training allowance or training bonus) to assist with employment, or a local authority payment to assist blind homeworkers is ignored.[102]

Any payments made to holders of the Victoria or George Cross are ignored.[103]

Payments by social services

A payment under section 17 of the Children Act 1989 from a social services department or, in Scotland, a payment from a social work department under section 12 of the Social Work (Scotland) Act 1968 (see Appendix 1), is ignored. 'Section 24' (or, in Scotland, 'section 24 or 26') payments made by local authorities to young people who have previously been in care or been looked after by social services are also ignored. But if you or your partner are involved in a trade dispute or it is paid during the first 15 days following your return to work after the dispute, it counts as income for IS.[104]

Charitable payments

Any payment in kind by a charity is ignored.[105] All payments from the Macfarlane Trusts, the Fund, the Eileen Trust and either of the Independent Living Funds (see Appendix 1) are ignored.[106] Payments from the Macfarlane Trusts, the Fund or the Eileen Trust do not have to be declared for HB/CTB at all, or to the Benefits Agency, if they are kept separately from the claimant's other capital and income.[107] Certain payments from money that originally came from any of the three Macfarlane Trusts, the Fund or the Eileen Trust are also ignored – the rules are the same as for income (see p372).

Payments to jurors and witnesses

Any payments made to jurors or witnesses for attending at court are ignored, except for payments for loss of earnings or of benefit.[108]

Training bonus

A training bonus of up to £200 is ignored,[109] but only for a year for HB/CTB, FC and DWA. For IS only, this disregard does not apply to trainees in Scotland.

Payments in other currencies

Any payment in a currency other than sterling is taken into account after disregarding banking charges or commission payable on conversion to sterling.[110]

Capital treated as income

Some payments which appear to be capital are treated as income. See p376 for the detailed rules.

Any capital treated as income is ignored as capital.[111]

4. NOTIONAL CAPITAL

In certain circumstances, you are treated as having capital which you do not, in fact, possess. This is called 'notional capital' and it counts in the same way as capital you actually do possess.[112] There is a similar rule for notional income (see p380).

Deprivation of capital in order to claim or increase benefit

If you deliberately get rid of capital in order to claim or increase your benefit, you are treated as still possessing it.[113] You are likely to be affected by this rule if, at the time of using up your money, you know that you may qualify for benefit (or more benefit) as a result, or qualify more quickly. It should not be used if you know nothing about the effect of using up your capital (eg, you do not know about the capital limit for claiming benefit),[114] or if you have been using up your capital at a rate which is reasonable in the circumstances. Knowledge of capital limits can be inferred from a reasonable familiarity with the benefit system as a claimant,[115] but if you fail to make enquiries about the capital limit, this does not constitute an intention to secure benefit. This is because you cannot form the required intention if you do not know about the capital rules.[116] Even if you do know about the capital limits, it still has to be shown that you intended to obtain, retain or increase your benefit.[117] For example, where a claimant, facing repossession of his home, transferred ownership to his daughter (who, he feared, would otherwise be made homeless), in spite of having been warned by Benefits Agency staff that he would be disqualified from benefit if he did so, it was held that, under the circumstances, he could not be said to have disposed of the property with the intention of gaining benefit.[118] The longer the period that has elapsed since the disposal of the capital, the less likely it will be that it was for the purpose of obtaining benefit.[119]

A person who uses up her/his resources may have more than one motive for doing so. Even where qualifying for benefit as a result is only a subsidiary motive for your actions, and the predominant motive is something quite different (eg, ensuring your home is in good condition by spending capital to do necessary repairs and improvements) you are still counted as having deprived yourself of a resource in order to gain benefit.[120] Local authorities tend to apply this test less stringently in the case of HB and CTB. Examples of the kinds of expenditure that could be caught by the rule are an expensive holiday and putting money in trust. (For IS/FC/DWA, putting money in trust for yourself does not constitute deprivation if the capital being put in trust came from compensation paid for any personal injury.[121]) But the essential test is not the kind of item that the money has been spent on but the *intention* behind the expenditure.

If you pay off a debt which you are required by law to repay immediately, you will not be counted as having deprived yourself of money in order to gain benefit.[122] However, even if you pay off a debt which you are not required by law to repay immediately, it is still for the Benefits Agency (for IS/FC/DWA) or the local authority (for HB/CTB) to prove that you did so in order to get benefit.[123]

In practice, arguing successfully that you have not deprived yourself of capital to get or increase benefit may boil down to whether you can show that you would have spent the money in the way you did (eg, to pay off debts or reduce your mortgage), regardless of the effect on your benefit entitlement. Where this is unclear, the burden of proving that you did it in order to get benefit lies with the Benefits Agency (IS/FC/DWA) or local authority (HB/CTB). In one case a man lost over £60,000 speculating on the stock market. Due to his wife's serious illness which affected his own health and judgement, he did not act to avoid losses when the stock market crashed. It was held that the adjudication officer had not discharged the burden of proving that this had been done for the purpose of obtaining IS.[124]

For IS, FC and DWA, you can only be treated as having notional capital under this rule if the capital of which you have deprived yourself is *actual* capital.[125] So if you are counted as owning half a joint bank account under the rule about jointly held capital (see p405), but your real share is only a quarter, you should not be caught by the deprivation rule in relation to the other quarter. It is also arguable that the deprivation rule should not apply even to the quarter you actually hold.[126] There is no express rule spelt out in HB/CTB law that for the notional capital rule to apply you must have deprived yourself of actual capital, but you should argue that the same principle applies.

Note that where a disposal of capital is not effective (eg, where there is a disposal between the serving of a bankruptcy notice and the appointment of a trustee in bankruptcy) the notional capital rules will not apply (but the actual capital rules will apply if you still own the asset in question).[127]

If you are treated as possessing notional capital, it is calculated in the same way as if it were actual capital[128] and the same disregards usually apply. The only possible exception is that you may not be able to rely on the disregard for the 26 weeks (or longer) you would otherwise be allowed to take steps to dispose of a property, even if the new owner is trying to sell it. However, there is conflicting commissioner case law on this.[129]

Other points on deprivation of capital

- Any deprivation must be found to have been for the purposes of claiming or increasing your entitlement to *that* benefit.

Deprivation for the purposes of obtaining supplementary benefit cannot be said to have been deprivation for the purposes of obtaining IS,[130] because IS did not exist at that time. It should also, therefore, be argued that there could have been no deprivation for the purposes of obtaining FC prior to April 1988, DWA prior to April 1992, and CTB prior to April 1993, as those benefits did not come into existence until those dates.

Where an intentional deprivation has been found for the purposes of obtaining IS, for example, it does not necessarily follow that there has also been any intention to gain HB/CTB. Where your circumstances change – eg, you start work and claim FC – any finding of intentional deprivation for IS will not necessarily be relevant to your claim for FC.

- Each adjudicating authority must reach its own decision on each benefit. Even decisions on deprivation for HB must be made independently of decisions for CTB.[131] This may result in different conclusions being drawn on any disposal for each benefit. And even where intent is found in two different benefits, there may be different views about the amount of capital that has been intentionally disposed of.[132]

However, where you are held to have deprived yourself of capital for the purposes of claiming HB/CTB, and you then submit a successful claim for IS, the notional capital rules for HB/CTB should be put in abeyance for as long as IS remains in payment.[133]

The diminishing notional capital rule

This rule provides a calculation for working out how your notional capital may be treated as *spent*.[134] Prior to 1 October 1990 there was a different rule (see p401). The rule starts to operate from the first week (or, for IS/CTB only, part-week) after the week in which it is first decided that the notional capital will be taken into account. The rule provides that:

- **where your benefit has been refused altogether** because of your notional capital, the amount of your notional capital will be reduced by the weekly total of any of the following benefits (or the additional amounts of the benefits, unless it is IS) that you would have been entitled to but for the notional capital rule:

  for IS   –   IS/HB/CCB/CTB
  for FC   –   FC/HB/CCB/CTB

```
for DWA  –   DWA/HB/CCB/CTB
for HB   –   IS/FC/DWA/HB/CCB/CTB
for CTB  –   IS/FC/DWA/HB/CTB
```

In order to ensure that account is taken of as many other benefits as possible, it is important (where you are not already doing so) to make a claim for any of the other benefits (where appropriate) as soon as the notional capital rule has been applied. Any notice you are then given of any amounts of benefits you have 'lost' can then be supplied as evidence of the total weekly aggregate that should be taken into account;

- **where your IS/FC/DWA/HB/CTB is reduced because of tariff income from your notional capital**, that capital is diminished by the amount of that reduction each week (or part-week). For example, if your notional capital is £3,750, giving a tariff income of £3 a week, the reduction is £3 a week until it reaches £3,500, when it will be £2 and so on. Account should be taken of any anticipated reduction in your tariff income band during any assessment period;[135]

   For FC/DWA/HB/CTB, the amount of your notional capital will also be reduced by the weekly aggregate of the following benefits (or any additional amounts of these benefits, unless it is IS) which you would have been entitled to but for the notional capital rule:

```
for FC   –   HB/CCB/CTB
for DWA  –   HB/CCB/CTB
for HB   –   IS/FC/DWA/CCB/CTB
for CTB  –   IS/FC/DWA/HB;
```

- **the reduction in your notional capital is calculated on a weekly basis**. However, where your benefit has been stopped altogether because of the notional capital rule, the amount is fixed for a period of 26 weeks. Even if the amount you would have been entitled to increases during this period, there will be no change in the amount by which the capital is reduced (except for HB/CTB where guidance[136] states that in circumstances not related to capital – eg, you have married or a baby has been born – a new assessment can be made). The aggregate of your benefit entitlement can, however, be recalculated from the end of this 26-week period when you reclaim benefit, and will be increased if it is more than it was before, but it will stay the same as in the earlier assessment if it is unchanged or less. You do not have to reclaim at the end of every 26-week period but there can be no recalculation unless and until you do. However, you cannot renew a claim until at least 26 weeks (IS/HB/CTB), 22 weeks (FC) or 20 weeks (DWA) have passed since the last assessment. Once the amount of reduction has been recalculated in this way, it is again fixed for the same period. For IS, you should ask the Benefits Agency for a forecast of when your notional capital will reduce to a point where a further claim might succeed, but the onus will be on you to reclaim when it is to your advantage to do so[137] – ie, when you may qualify for an increased assessment, or because you have requalified for benefit. Timing will be important. If you delay you may lose out as new assessments cannot take effect before you reclaim. However, if you reclaim too soon you will have to wait until the fixed periods have lapsed before you can apply for a fresh determination;

- **where you have both actual and notional capital**, you may have to draw on your actual capital to meet your living expenses, which may include (and will probably exceed) amounts equivalent to benefits you have 'lost'. There is no reason why this should affect the amount by which your notional capital is diminished, even if this effectively results in double-counting. Any reduction in your actual capital should be taken into account in calculating any tariff income arising from your combined actual and notional capital, unless, of course, you have spent it at such a rate and in such a way that it raises questions of intent, when you may find that the notional capital rules are applied all over again.

Note, however, that it has been decided that these rules on how your capital was *spent* only apply from 1 October 1990. Prior to that date, any reasonable living and other expenditure was counted, which was far more generous.[138] Any notional capital you have been held to possess until 30 September 1990 will be reduced under the earlier rules, and any notional capital carried forward to 1 October 1990 and onwards will be reduced under the current rules.[139] Note that the current rules apply to deprivation of capital only; the earlier rules still apply to other forms of notional capital (see below).

For IS or FC, where the current more restrictive rules have been applied to you for any period before 1 October 1990, you should consider submitting a late appeal (see p158) to take advantage of the more generous treatment. For HB, the position on how the rules should have applied in earlier periods is less clear, although you should argue that as the law was essentially the same, the more generous rules should apply.

Failing to apply for capital[140]

Under this rule you are treated as having capital you could get if you applied for it. Examples of failure to apply could be where money is held in court which would be released on application, or even an unclaimed premium bond win! For IS, HB and CTB, you are only treated as having such capital from the date you could obtain it. Although the FC/DWA rules do not make the same point, you should argue that the same applies.

This rule does not apply if you fail to apply for:

- capital from a discretionary trust; *or*
- capital from a trust set up from money paid as a result of a personal injury; *or*
- capital from a personal pension scheme or retirement annuity contract; *or*
- a loan which you could only get if you gave your home or other disregarded capital (see p390) as security.

Capital payments made to a 'third party' on your behalf

If someone else pays an amount to a 'third party' – eg, the electricity board or a building society – for you or a member of your family (if any), this may count as your capital.[141] It counts if the payment is to cover you or your family's food, household fuel, council tax or ordinary clothing or footwear. (School uniforms and sports wear are not ordinary clothing;[142] nor are, for example, special shoes because of a disability.[143])

It also counts if it is to cover:

- **for IS, HB and CTB**, rent for which HB is payable (less any non-dependant deductions) or water charges;
- **for IS alone**, housing costs met by IS or a residential care or nursing home accommodation charge for a person with preserved rights (see p85) met by IS;
- **for FC/DWA**, any housing costs (or any outstanding community charge, but not any standard community charge).

If the payment is for other kinds of expenses – eg, children's school fees (see p345-46), a TV licence, accommodation charges above the IS limit, or (except for FC/DWA) mortgage capital repayments – it does not count. Also remember that payments from the Macfarlane Trusts, the Fund, the Eileen Trust or either of the Independent Living Funds do not count, whatever they are for.

Payments made for the food etc, of any member of the family, count as the capital of the member of the family in respect of whom they are paid. Since a child's capital is not counted as belonging to the claimant, a payment to, for example, a clothes shop for your child, should count as the child's notional capital and not yours.

For IS only, payments *derived* from certain social security benefits (including war disablement pensions and war widows' pensions) and paid to a third party count:

- as yours, if you are entitled to the benefit; *and*
- as a member of your family's, if it is the family member who is entitled to the benefit.[144]

For IS, there are different rules if you could be liable to pay maintenance as a liable relative (see p113).

Capital payments paid to you for a 'third party'[145]

If you or a member of your family get a payment for someone not in your family – eg, a relative who does not have a bank account – it only counts as yours if it is kept or used by you. Payments from the Macfarlane Trusts, the Fund, the Eileen Trust or either of the Independent Living Funds do not count at all.

Companies run by sole traders or a few partners

This applies if, as a sole trader or a small partnership, you have registered your business as a limited company. For IS/FC/DWA the value of your shareholding is ignored but you will be treated as possessing a proportionate share of the capital of the company.[146] This does not apply while you are working for the company.[147] Even if you work for the company for, say, only half an hour a week, this will suffice.[148] DSS guidance for FC/DWA indicates that it is not necessary for the work to be paid.[149]

For HB/CTB, the local authority has a discretion whether to apply the same rules as for IS/FC/DWA, but if it decides to it must apply them all.[150]

5. HOW CAPITAL IS VALUED

Market value

Apart from national savings certificates (see below), your capital is valued at its current market or surrender value.[151] This means the amount of money you could raise by selling it or raising a loan against it, etc. The test is the price that would be paid by a willing buyer to a willing seller on a particular date.[152] So if an asset is difficult, or impossible, to realise, its market value should be very heavily discounted or even nil.[153]

In the case of a house, an estate agent's figure for a quick sale is a more appropriate valuation than the District Valuer's figure for a sale within three months.[154]

Appeal if you disagree with the valuation of your capital (see p156).

Expenses of sale

If there would be expenses involved in selling your capital, 10 per cent is deducted from its value for the cost of sale.[155]

Debts

Deductions are made from the 'gross' value of your capital for any debt or mortgage secured on it.[156] If a creditor (eg, a bank), holds the land certificate to your property as security for a loan and has registered notice of deposit of the land certificate at the Land Registry, this counts as a debt secured on your property.[157] Where a single mortgage is secured on a house and land and the value of the house is disregarded for benefit purposes, the whole of the mortgage can be deducted when calculating the value of the land.[158]

If you have debts which are not secured against your capital (eg, tax liabilities), these cannot be offset against the value of your capital.[159] However, once you have paid off your debts, your capital may well be reduced. You can be penalised if you deliberately get rid of capital in order to get benefit (see p397).

National savings

For IS, a certificate bought from an issue which ceased before the 1 July before your claim is decided, or your benefit is first payable (whichever is earlier), or the date of any subsequent review, has the value it would have had on that 1 July if purchased on the last day of the issue. For FC/DWA, it is the 1 July before the date of your claim; for HB/CTB, it is the

1 July before your claim is made or treated as made or when your benefit is reviewed. In any other case, the value is the purchase price.[160] DSS guidance contains a convenient valuation table for each issue.[161]

Capital that is jointly owned with someone other than your partner

This is treated as being shared equally between you regardless of your actual shares.[162] For example, if you own 70 per cent of an asset, and your brother 30 per cent, each of you are treated as having a 50 per cent share. The value of the remaining 20 per cent that you actually own does not count as your capital. Similarly, if you actually own only 10 per cent of an asset and one other person owns the other 90 per cent, you are nevertheless treated as owning a 50 per cent share. The value of this 50 per cent share is then calculated by taking the net value of the whole property and dividing this figure by two.

If you are caught by this rule you should consider, where possible, selling your share as, once sold, only the proceeds of your actual share can be treated as capital (the notional capital rule should not apply here – see p397). In the meantime, you may be able to apply for a crisis loan from the social fund (see p446).

It is arguable that the method of valuing your capital by simply dividing the set value of the whole asset by the number of co-owners is unlawful. It could prevent you from ever being entitled to benefit – you could be treated as owning capital over the limit, even though the capital you *actually* own may be worth much less at the moment – eg, because it cannot be sold on its own and your co-owner will not agree to selling the whole property.

Treatment of assets following the breakdown of a relationship

When partners separate, assets such as their former home or a building society account may be in joint or sole names. For example, if a building society account is in joint names, under the rule about jointly owned capital, you and your former partner are treated as having a 50 per cent share each (see above). But if your former partner is claiming sole ownership of the account, DSS guidance for FC/DWA says that your interest in the account should count as having a nil value until the question of ownership is settled.[163] Arguably, the same should apply to IS. The guidance deals only with a marriage breakdown, but there is no reason why the same should not apply if you were not married. If your former partner puts a stop on the account, in effect freezing it, the account should be disregarded until its ownership is resolved.

On the other hand, a former partner may have a right to some or all of an asset that is in your sole name – eg, s/he may have deposited most of the money in a building society account in your name. If this is established, then the partner in whose name the account is held may well, depending on the circumstances, be treated as not entitled to the whole of the account but as holding part of it as trustee for her/his former partner.[164] In that event, the rule about jointly owned capital will have the effect of treating you as owning half of the amount in the account. However, the point made in the DSS guidance referred to above (p405) should logically apply equally here, so you should not be treated as owning half the capital (or indeed any of it) unless or until it is established that you do own at least some share of it.

Shares

Shares are valued at their current market value less 10 per cent for the cost of sale[165] and after deducting any lien held by brokers for sums owed for the cost of acquisition and commission. Market value should be calculated in accordance with Inland Revenue guidance which is based on the bid price plus a quarter of the difference between this and the offer price (rather than *Financial Times* figures which rely on the mean between the bid and offer prices).[166] Fluctuations in price between routine reviews of your case are normally ignored. Where a claimant has a minority holding of shares in a company, the value of the shares should be based on what the claimant could realise on them, and not by valuing the entire share capital of the company and attributing to the claimant an amount calculated according to the proportion of shares held.[167] Although there may be some practical difficulties in selling shares held by children, there are no obstacles to sale that cannot be overcome by courts, if necessary. They would, therefore, still have a value, even though allowance would have to be made for some inducement to overcome the reluctance of stockbrokers, registrars and potential purchasers in contracting with minors for an immediate sale.[168]

Unit trusts

These are valued on the basis of the 'bid' price quoted in newspapers. No deduction is allowed for the cost of sale because this is already included in the 'bid' price.[169]

The right to receive a payment in the future

The value of any such right that is not ignored (see p394) is its market value: what a willing buyer will pay to a willing seller.[170] For something which is not yet realisable this may be very small.

Overseas assets

If you have assets abroad, and there are no exchange controls or other prohibitions that would prevent you transferring your capital to this country, your assets are valued at their current market or surrender value in that country.[171] If there are problems getting benefit because it is difficult to get the assets valued, you may be able to get an interim payment of IS, FC or DWA (see p136), or a 'payment on account' of HB (see p274).

If you are not allowed to transfer the full value of your capital to this country, you are treated as having capital equal to the amount that a willing buyer in this country would give for those assets.[172] It seems likely that the price such a person (if there is one) would be willing to pay may bear little relation to the actual value of the assets.

The same deductions of 10 per cent if there are expenses of sale, and for any debts or mortgage secured on the assets abroad, are made. If the capital is realised in a currency other than sterling, charges payable for converting the payment into sterling are also deducted.[173]

PART SIX

The regulated social fund

CHAPTER TWENTY-ONE

The regulated social fund

This chapter covers:
1. Maternity expenses payments (below)
2. Funeral expenses payments (p413)
3. Cold weather payments (p418)
4. Reviews and appeals (p420)

The social fund is a government fund which makes payments to people in need. Eligibility depends on receipt of certain means-tested benefits. There are two types of payments available from the social fund:

• Discretionary grants and loans to meet a variety of needs. These are covered in Part Seven – see p422.
• Grants available by right for maternity expenses, funeral expenses and periods of cold weather. Unlike the discretionary payments, you are *legally entitled* to these grants if you satisfy the eligibility conditions, which are laid down in regulations.

Note: Considerable changes have been proposed to the regulated social fund, in particular to the rules covering funeral expenses payments. The description of the provisions assumes the proposals will be implemented in full. Check CPAG's *Welfare Rights Bulletin* for any changes.

I. MATERNITY EXPENSES PAYMENTS

The basic rules[1]

You are entitled to a payment for help with maternity expenses if:

• you or your partner (see note below) have been awarded a qualifying benefit: income support (IS), income-based jobseeker's allowance (JSA) (including hardship payments of JSA), family credit (FC) or disability working allowance (DWA) for the day you claim a maternity expenses payment; *and*
• you do not have too much capital (see p411 – Amount); *and*

- you or a member of your family (see note below) are expecting a child within the next 11 weeks or have recently given birth or have adopted a child or are having a child by a surrogate mother (see p412); *and*
- you claim within the time limits (see p412).

Notes:

- 'Family' and 'partner' are defined in virtually the same way as for IS (see p318).
- You cannot claim FC until your first child is born. Even if your FC claim has not been decided, you should claim a maternity expenses payment within the time limits (see below). You will be paid when your FC is awarded.
- If you are under 19 and not able to claim IS, income-based JSA, FC or DWA in your own right, an adult getting one of these benefits can claim a maternity expenses payment for you if you count as a member of her/his family (see p328).
- If you or your partner are involved in a trade dispute (see p58 for meaning), and either one of you is getting IS or income-based JSA, you will qualify for a payment if the dispute has been going on for six weeks or more at the date of claim. If either of you is getting FC or DWA, you will qualify for a payment if the claim for FC or DWA was made before the beginning of the dispute.[2]

Amount

The maternity expenses payment is £100 for each child.[3] If this is insufficient to meet your needs, you could apply to the discretionary social fund for the extra amount you need (see Part Seven). DSS guidance[4] says that discretionary payments cannot be made for any maternity expenses (see p430). This has been challenged, so far unsuccessfully, but the case may be appealed.[5]

The £100 is reduced by the amount of any capital you and your partner have in excess of £500 (£1,000 if you or your partner is 60 or over).[6] Capital is calculated in the same way as for IS or income-based JSA,[7] except that lump-sum widow's payment (£1,000) is ignored for 12 months from the date of your husband's death.[8]

Stillbirths

You are entitled to a payment for a stillborn child if your pregnancy has lasted 24 weeks.[9]

Adopted babies

You are entitled to a payment for a baby adopted by you or your partner if the baby is no more than 12 months old at the date of claim.[10] You will receive a payment even if one has already been made to the natural mother or a member of her family.[11]

Babies by a surrogate mother

You are entitled to a payment where you are granted an order allowing you or your partner to have a child by a surrogate mother.[12] You will receive a payment even if one has already been made to the natural mother or a member of her family.[13]

Time limits

You can claim at any time from the 11th week before your expected week of confinement (your 29th week of pregnancy) until three months after your actual date of confinement. If you adopt a baby, you can claim up to three months following the date of the adoption order. If you are granted an order allowing you to have a baby by a surrogate mother you can claim up to three months after the order.[14]

There is no provision for making payments if you claim outside the time limits. But if you claim and are refused because you are not getting a qualifying benefit (see p410) as long as you:

- have already made a claim for a qualifying benefit; *and*
- are awarded the qualifying benefit; *and*
- make a second claim for the maternity expenses payment within three months of being awarded the qualifying benefit

your claim is treated as made on the same day as the original claim, or the date on which the qualifying benefit is awarded, whichever is later.[15]

Claiming and getting paid

You should claim on form SF100 which you can get from your local Benefits Agency. The date of claim is the date the form is received by the Benefits Agency.[16] If you make a written claim in some other way, you must be sent the appropriate form to complete. If you return it within one month the date of claim will be the date the Benefits Agency received your initial application.[17]

If you claim before confinement, you will need to submit a maternity certificate (form MAT B1) or note from your doctor or midwife. If you claim after the child is born, you will usually be asked for a maternity, birth or adoption certificate.

The rules for getting paid and the recovery of overpayments are the same as for IS (see pp135 and 148).

2. FUNERAL EXPENSES PAYMENTS

The basic rules[18]

You are entitled to a funeral expenses payment if you satisfy all the following rules:

- You or your partner (see notes on p415) have been awarded a qualifying benefit: IS, income-based JSA, FC, DWA, housing benefit (HB) or council tax benefit (CTB – see notes below) for the day you claim a funeral expenses payment.[19]
- You do not have too much capital (see p417).
- You (or your partner) accept responsibility for paying the costs of the funeral *and* you are a person the Benefits Agency accept as the responsible person (see below).[20]
- The funeral (ie, burial or cremation) takes place in the UK.[21]
- The deceased was ordinarily resident (see p185) in the UK at the time of death.[22]
- You claim within the time limits.

Who can be a responsible person?

You can be the responsible person if:[23]

- you were the partner (see p415) of the deceased when s/he died;[24]
- where the deceased is a child, you were the person (or partner) responsible for the child at the date of death unless there is an absent parent (see p415) who was not (and whose partner was not) getting a qualifying benefit at the date of death;
- in the case of a stillborn child, you are the parent of that child unless there is a person who would have been an absent parent of that child who was not (and whose partner was not) getting a qualifying benefit at the date of death.[25]

(We understand that where there is an absent parent who is estranged from the child (and possibly, by implication, at odds with the caring parent) this will not exclude the caring parent from getting a payment.)

If you are:[26]

- an immediate family member (ie, parent, son or daughter); *or*

- a close relative; *or*
- a close friend of the deceased; *and*

it is reasonable for you to accept responsibility, you can be treated as the responsible person. The nature and extent of your contact with the deceased determines whether it is reasonable for you to accept responsibility for meeting the expenses of a funeral.

However, you may be excluded from entitlement to a funeral expenses payment in certain circumstances by either an immediate family member (see below) or a close relative (see p415).

You are excluded from entitlement if:

- the deceased had a partner at the date of death unless that partner died before the funeral without having made a claim for a funeral expenses payment;[27]
- where the deceased is a child (including a stillborn child), there is a person responsible for the child or a parent;[28]
- there is an immediate family member of the deceased if neither s/he nor her/his partner are getting a qualifying benefit and s/he was not estranged from the deceased at the time of death.[29] But this does not apply where the immediate family member is:[30]
  - a person under 19 who is doing a full-time course of advanced education (see p19);
  - a person who is 19 or over, but under pension age and a full-time student (see p19);
  - a member of a religious order and maintained by it;
  - a person who is held in prison, remand centre or youth custody, and before being taken into custody, s/he or her/his partner were getting a qualifying benefit (see p413);
  - a patient who is cared for free of charge in hospital or similar institution, or accommodation maintained and run by the Defence Council and before becoming a patient s/he or her/his partner were getting a qualifying benefit (see p413).

Nor does it apply where the immediate family member was a child at the date of death.

You will also be excluded if there is a close relative, including an immediate family member, who was:

- in closer contact with the deceased than the responsible person; *or*
- in equally close contact with the deceased *and either*:
  - s/he (or her/his partner) was not getting a qualifying benefit; *or*
  - s/he has more than £500 capital (or more than £1,000 if both s/he and her/his partner are aged 60 or over), and s/he has more capital than you do.

However, this does not apply if that close relative was a child at the date of death.[32]

Example 1
James, who is in receipt of IS, applies for a funeral payment when his close friend Yuri dies. He is able to get a funeral expenses payment because although Yuri has one surviving relative, a brother who is also receiving IS, the brother has, in recent times, had less contact with Yuri than James.

Example 2
John, a widower, died in June. His sister, Jane, looked after him during his severe illness before he died. Jane was very close to her brother but was refused a payment because her brother's son is working and not receiving a qualifying benefit, even though the son had infrequent contact with his father.

Notes:
- 'Child' has the same meaning as for IS and income-based JSA.[33]
- 'Absent parent' means the parent who is not living in the same household as the child at the time of the child's death and who is not the parent responsible for that child (and in the case of a stillborn child would not have been part of the same household as the child had it lived).[34]
- 'Partner' is defined in virtually the same way as for IS[35] (see p319 and 'member of the same household' below).
- 'Close relative' means parent, parent-in-law or step-parent, son, son-in-law, stepson or stepson-in-law, daughter, daughter-in-law, stepdaughter or stepdaughter-in-law, brother or brother-in-law, sister or sister-in-law.[36]
- 'Immediate family member' is a parent, son or daughter.[35]
- An award of CTB includes a second adult rebate.
- 'Member of the same household' includes:
  - a married couple living in the same residential accommodation, residential care or nursing home (see pp84-92 for meanings); *or*
  - a couple living together as husband and wife immediately before one or both moved into the same residential accommodation (see above),
  and the surviving partner was living in the home at the date of the death of the deceased.[38]
- Involvement in a trade dispute has no effect on a claim for a funeral expenses payment.

Amount

You can get a payment sufficient to meet certain funeral expenses, unless they have already been paid for under a pre-paid funeral plan or similar arrangement.[39] The expenses covered by the payment include the cost of:[40]

- buying a new burial plot, exclusive rights to burial in that plot and the burial;
- cremation, including medical references, certificates and doctor's fees for the removal of a heart pacemaker. (If the pacemaker is not removed by a doctor, then you will only get £20);
- any documentation necessary to obtain access to the assets of the deceased;
- transport, for the portion of journeys which are more than 50 miles in the following circumstances:
  - whether or not the deceased died at home, transport of the body to a funeral director's premises or to a place of rest;
  - where necessary, transport of the coffin and bearers by hearse and another vehicle from the funeral director's premises or place of rest to the funeral.

Only the reasonable costs can be met, and in the second case the cost of this transport *plus* burial in an existing grave must not be more than the cost of a burial and purchase of a new plot;

- the reasonable expenses of one return journey within the UK for the responsible person to arrange *or* attend the funeral.

The costs allowed for burial, cremation and transport do not include any extra requirements arising from the religious faith of the deceased.[41]

In addition, you can claim up to £600 additional funeral expenses.[42] If you have already met the cost of some of these from a pre-paid funeral plan or similar arrangement you can only get an additional payment of £100.[43]

You could try applying to the discretionary social fund for help with funeral expenses other than the above. DSS guidance[44] says that discretionary payments cannot be awarded for any funeral expenses. The principle that payments from the discretionary fund cannot be used to top up payments from the regulated social fund has been challenged but so far unsuccessfully (see p430). You may also be able to argue that some items you need are *not* funeral expenses – eg, a headstone – and get a discretionary payment for these.

Apart from any payments made to you from the Macfarlane Trust, the Macfarlane (Special Payments) Trust, the Macfarlane (Special Payments)

(No.2) Trust, the Fund, and the Eileen Trust (see Appendix 1), all of which are ignored,[45] the following amounts are deducted from an award of a funeral expenses payment:[46]

- any capital you or your partner have in excess of £500 (£1,000 if you or your partner are aged 60 or over).[47] Capital is calculated as for IS or income-based JSA[48] except that lump-sum widow's payment (£1,000) is ignored for 12 months from the date of your husband's death.[49] Any money you have been given or borrowed on the express condition that it be used to meet the costs of the funeral is ignored.[50] However, if you have used any of your own capital (apart from disregarded capital) to pay for the funeral expenses listed above you are treated as though you still possessed it;[51]
- the value of the deceased person's assets which are or will be available to you without a grant of probate or letters of administration (the assets which existed at the time of death can count even if you have used them for other purposes[52]);
- any payment legally due to you, or a member of your family, from an insurance policy, occupational pension scheme, burial club or similar source on the death of the deceased;
- any contribution from a charity or a relative of your family (see p318) or the deceased's family, after offsetting any funeral expenses other than those specified above;
- a funeral grant paid by the government to a war disablement pensioner;
- arrears of attendance allowance (and probably other benefits) in respect of the deceased, paid to the claimant as next-of-kin;[53]
- any amount payable from a pre-paid funeral plan or similar arrangement to meet the deceased's funeral expenses where the plan was not fully paid for before the person's death.[54]

Time limits

You must claim within three months of the funeral.[55]

There is no provision for making payments outside the time limits. But if you claim and are refused because you are not getting a qualifying benefit (see p413), as long as you:

- have already made a claim for a qualifying benefit; *and*
- make a second claim for the funeral expenses within three months of being awarded the qualifying benefit

your claim is treated as made on the same day as the original claim, or the date the qualifying benefit was awarded, whichever is the later.[56]

Claiming and getting paid

You should claim on form SF200 which you can get from your local Benefits Agency. When completing the questions about your contact with the deceased in the form, bear in mind the rules about close relatives and contact (see p414).

The current claims pack includes a form SF216 plus notes, but when the proposed rules for funeral expenses payments are introduced, this form will be abolished.

The date of claim is the date the form is received by the Benefits Agency. If you make a written claim in some other way, you should be sent the form to complete. If you return it within a month, the date of claim will be the date the Benefits Agency received your first claim.[57] The Benefits Agency can treat an initial claim by letter as sufficient and will then not ask you to complete a form as well.

The Benefits Agency will usually pay you by giro, made out to the funeral director, unless the bill has already been paid.[58] You qualify for a payment even if you have already met all the costs.[59] The rules for getting paid and the recovery of overpayments are as for IS (see pp135 and 148).

If a funeral payment has already been made to cover the particular funeral expenses, you cannot get a second payment.

Recovery from the deceased's estate

The Secretary of State is entitled to recover funeral expenses payments from the deceased's estate and will normally seek to do so.[60] Funeral expenses are legally a first charge on the estate although there may, of course, be insufficient assets to meet full repayment.[61] Personal possessions left to relatives and the value of a house occupied by a surviving partner should not count as the deceased's estate.

3. COLD WEATHER PAYMENTS

The basic rules

You are entitled to a cold weather payment if:

- a 'period of cold weather' has been forecast or recorded for the area in which your normal home is situated (see below);[62] *and*
- you have been awarded IS or income-based JSA for at least one day during the period of cold weather; *and*

- *either* your IS or income-based JSA includes one or more of the following premiums: pensioner; disability; higher pensioner; severe disability; disabled child (see p332);
- *or* you have a child under five.[63] The exclusion of claimants with children over five may be challengeable.

Notes:

- The amount of capital you have does not affect the payment.
- You are not entitled to a payment if you live in residential or nursing care and do not have preserved rights (see p85).[64]

A 'period of cold weather'

This is a period of seven consecutive days during which the average of the mean daily temperature forecast or recorded for that period is equal to or below 0° Celsius. The 'mean daily temperature' is the average of the maximum and minimum temperatures recorded for that day.[65] The regulations divide the country into 70 areas, each covered by a weather station at which temperatures are forecast or recorded.[66] The area your home is in is determined by your postcode.

The amount of the payment

The sum of £8.50 is paid for each week of cold weather.[67]

Claiming and getting paid

You do *not* need to make a claim for a cold weather payment. The Benefits Agency should automatically send you a giro if you qualify.[68] Your district Benefits Agency should publicise when there are periods of cold weather in your area by placing advertisements in local newspapers, by radio broadcasts, and by distributing posters and leaflets – eg, to doctors' surgeries and local advice centres.[69] If you do not receive a giro and you think you are entitled, contact your local Benefits Agency. If you do not receive a payment or are told you are not entitled, submit a written claim and ask for a written decision. You can then appeal against an unfavourable decision.[70]

The rules for getting paid and the recovery of overpayments are the same as for IS.

4. REVIEWS AND APPEALS

The rules relating to reviews and appeals are the same as for IS – see pp131 and 156. Decisions are made by adjudication officers and you can appeal against the refusal of a payment (see above).

PART SEVEN

The discretionary social fund

CHAPTER TWENTY-TWO

General principles

This chapter covers:

1. INTRODUCTION

In addition to the grants available by right for maternity expenses, funeral expenses and periods of cold weather described in Part Six, the social fund (SF) also provides discretionary grants and loans to meet a variety of other needs. This part of the SF is very different in character to all other social security provision:

- It is strictly **budget-limited**. Each district office of the Benefits Agency is given an annual budget which it must not exceed.
- Payments are **discretionary**. There is no legal entitlement to a payment. The rules are only concerned with eligibility and how discretion is to be exercised.
- Many payments are in the form of **loans**. These have to be repaid to the Benefits Agency, usually by deductions from weekly benefit.
- Decisions are made by **social fund officers**.
- There is **no right of appeal** to an independent tribunal. Instead there is a system of internal review and further review by quasi-independent **social fund inspectors**.

Despite the unpopularity and inherent problems of the discretionary SF, its wide scope makes it an important and valuable, though unpredictable source of help and you should *always apply* if you have a need which can be met by the fund.

Decisions are governed by law, guidance and district budgets.

2. THE LAW

Primary legislation

The social fund (SF) exists by Act of Parliament.[1] The Act empowers social fund officers (SFOs) to make discretionary payments from the fund. In deciding whether to make a payment, the Act requires SFOs to take into account all the circumstances of each case and, in particular:[2]

- the nature, extent and urgency of the need;
- the existence of resources which could meet the need;
- whether any other person or body could meet the need;
- whether a loan is likely to be repaid;
- the amount of the Benefits Agency district office budget (see p425);
- SF directions and guidance (see below).

The Act also empowers the Secretary of State to issue directions to SFOs which are legally binding.[3]

The directions

The directions establish three types of discretionary payment available from the SF:

- community care grants (CCGs) (see p434);
- budgeting loans (see p444);
- crisis loans (see p446).

The directions set out the eligibility conditions for each type of payment. They also exclude payments for certain expenses (see p428) and cover reviews (see pp457 and 461) and control of budgets.

The regulations[4]

These deal with procedures. They cover:

- applications for grants and loans;
- applications for reviews;
- the acceptance and recovery of loans.

The Act, directions and regulations are included in CPAG's *Income Related Benefits: The Legislation* and *The Social Fund: Law and Practice* (see Appendix 4).

3. GUIDANCE

National guidance

The Secretary of State issues guidance on how to interpret the directions and administer the social fund (SF). The guidance and directions are published in a *SF Guide* (see Appendix 4). The guidance suggests the circumstances in which a payment should be made and for what items and services. It also sets out which types of need should normally be given high, medium or low priority.

Social fund officers (SFOs) must take account of the guidance,[5] but it is *not* legally binding. The guidance repeatedly reminds SFOs that they must exercise discretion according to the individual circumstances of each case.[6] The absence of guidance on a particular situation does not mean that help should be refused.[7] The guidance on priorities is not exhaustive[8] and stresses that ' ... the overriding concern in determining priority is the assessment of **individual** need.[9] Despite this, SFOs tend to use the *SF Guide* as a rulebook!

Local guidance

In addition to the national guidance, local guidance is issued by SF managers in Benefits Agency district offices.[10] Copies should be available from your local office and is public information.

The main purpose of local guidance is to specify which levels of priority (ie, high, medium or low), determined in accordance with the national guidance, can be met from the district budget.[11] It must be reviewed at least every month.[12] The guidance may also include details of the district budget and a monthly expenditure profile, ie, planned expenditure (see p425).

SFOs must take account of the local guidance but it is not legally binding and must not conflict with the directions or national guidance by, for example, excluding groups of claimants from payments.[13] In practice, however, SFOs tend to only award payments to meet rigidly defined high priority needs which may not be explicitly listed in the local guidance.

Social fund inspectors' decisions

Social fund inspector (SFI) decisions can be useful guidance because they indicate how discretion can be exercised by SFOs. However, they apply only to the case under review and do not create precedents. The SFI Office issues a regular journal which includes a digest of SFI decisions.

Advice notes

These were issued to SFIs by the legal adviser to the Social Fund Commissioner from 1993 to 1995. They are not binding but can be useful on difficult problems of interpretation. They are included in *The Social Fund: Law & Practice* with commentary by Trevor Buck.

4. THE BUDGET

The Government sets the total budget for the discretionary social fund (SF) each year. Each Benefits Agency district office is then allocated a fixed sum for grants and another for loans.[14]

The district SF manager is responsible for planning and monitoring expenditure on a monthly basis.[15] Any under- or overspend in a particular month should lead to a revision of planned monthly expenditure for the rest of the year. However, there is no monthly limit on expenditure and it would be unlawful to refuse a payment solely because planned expenditure for a particular month had been exceeded.[16]

The only limit on district expenditure is the total budget allocated for the year. The directions prohibit social fund officers (SFOs) from spending more than their annual district budget.[17] It is possible, however, for the Secretary of State to allocate additional funds to a district in the course of the year,[18] and there is nothing to stop a district manager asking for more funds if the budget is likely to be overspent. However, many appear to be unaware that this action is open to them and are usually reluctant to do anything which could be interpreted as an inability to manage the budget (see p427 – Tactics).

SFOs must have regard to the budget when deciding whether to make a payment and how much to award.[19] However, the budget is only one factor they must take into account when making decisions. Refusal of an application on budgetary grounds alone is unlawful, unless the budget is exhausted. You should consider asking for a review if your application is refused because of the budget (see p457).

The directions require SFOs to manage the budget so as to give priority to 'high-priority needs' throughout the year.[20] There is no legal definition of what constitutes a high-priority need but SFOs are advised to take account of guidance (see p424) and try to treat applications consistently throughout the year.[21] If you are refused a payment on the grounds of insufficient priority and you are considering requesting a review see p457.

5. HOW DECISIONS ARE MADE

The theory

The legal demands placed on social fund officers (SFOs) when making decisions are onerous and in some respects, contradictory. They must:

- carefully consider all the circumstances of each case including the nature, extent and urgency of the need and the other matters set out on p423, and use their discretion to decide whether to award a payment;
- follow the directions (see p423);
- take account of national and local guidance (see p424), without being rigidly bound by either;
- have regard to the budget (see p425);
- decide on the priority of the application and give priority to high-priority needs (see above).

They are also expected to:

- exercise discretion flexibly but consistently;[22]
- ensure their decisions are not in any way affected by bias or prejudice on such grounds as race, colour, religion, gender or sexual orientation;[23]
- liaise with local social services departments, the probation service and other local organisations about the operation of the fund and priorities as well as individual applications, subject to normal confidentiality rules.[24]

The practice

Not surprisingly, the practice rarely matches the theory. Many people would argue that there is a basic conflict between meeting need and having regard to the budget; or between exercising discretion on an individual basis and taking account of the guidance. Also, most SFOs have neither the training nor the time to achieve the standard of decision-making imposed by all the above requirements.

In practice, SFOs tend to use the *SF Guide* as a 'rule book' and only make payments to meet rigidly defined 'high priority needs' in order to stay within budget. Other applications are routinely rejected, regardless of the circumstances of the applicants.

The social fund has been likened to a lottery by many critics because your chances of success can depend on when you apply (ie, the state of the budget at that time) and where you live (there is little national consistency in decision-making).

6. TACTICS

- Do not be put off from applying for any payment you need. The social fund (SF) can pay for anything other than excluded items (see p428) as long as you satisfy the basic eligibility rules.
- Refer to the national guidance on priorities, if it helps your case. The high priority category for community care grants (CCGs) is wide in scope (see p436).
- Get a copy of your district office's local guidance and refer to it in your application if it helps your case.
- Always ask for a grant, rather than a loan, if you satisfy the conditions on p434. However any application is to the SF as a whole and the SFO should consider whether you are eligible for a grant even if you ask for a loan.
- Tips on completing the application forms are on p454.
- If you are unhappy about a decision, *you should consider asking for a review and, if necessary, a further review by the social fund inspectors* (SFIs)(see p461). This could apply if you have been refused a payment, been given less than you asked for, or been offered a loan rather than a grant. Social fund officer (SFO) decisions are often overturned by SFIs – in particular a loan award may be replaced by a CCG. *A decision may, however, not be made in your favour,* see p457.
- A local campaign could be persuasive in highlighting the need for the district budget to be increased, but the request for an increase to the budget allocation would probably have to be made by an organisation outside the Benefits Agency via the local MP. A campaign could also highlight the extent to which there has been any local underspend.

7. EXCLUDED ITEMS

Help with the items listed below is excluded by the directions.[25] If you request a payment for an excluded item you will be refused.

The general list of exclusions

- A need which occurs outside the UK.
- An educational or training need, including clothing and tools.
- 'Distinctive' school uniform, sports clothes or equipment (see Appendix 1 for local authority grants).
- Travelling expenses to and from school (but see Appendix 1).
- School meals and meals taken during the holidays by children entitled to free school meals (but see Appendix 1).
- Expenses in connection with court proceedings (including a community service order) – eg, legal fees, court fees, fines, costs, damages and travelling expenses. You can get a crisis loan, however, for emergency travelling expenses (see p450).
- Removal charges where you are permanently rehoused following a compulsory purchase order, a redevelopment or closing order, or where there is a compulsory exchange of tenancies or you are permanently rehoused as homeless under the Housing Acts. In all these circumstances your local authority may help you.
- The cost of domestic assistance or respite care. This would include the cost of home care or short breaks in residential care.[26]
- Repairs to property owned by public sector housing bodies including Councils, most housing associations, housing co-operatives and housing trusts.[27]
- Medical, surgical, optical, aural or dental items or services. A medical item does not include an ordinary everyday item needed because of a medical condition – eg, cotton sheets and non-allergic bedding when a person is allergic to synthetics, built-up shoes, special beds, incontinence pads and even wheelchairs.[28] Social fund officers, however, are told to find out whether help is available from the NHS or other relevant agencies.[29]
- Work-related expenses. The guidance says this includes fares when seeking work and the cost of work clothes.[30] You may be able to get help with fares to interviews from the Employment Service.
- Debts to government departments. These could include national insurance arrears, income tax liabilities and customs charges.[31] Debts to other organisations or people, however, are not excluded, even if they are incurred in respect of an excluded item.[32]
- Investments.

- Council tax, council water charges, arrears of community charge, collective community charge contributions and community water charges.
- Most housing costs, including:[33]
  - repairs and improvements to your home, including garage, garden and outbuildings, (**NB** repairs and improvements are no longer defined with reference to the income support (IS) regulations);
  - deposits to secure accommodation;
  - mortgage payments, rent, service charges, water and sewerage rates and any other accommodation charges.

Note on housing related expenses

You can get a payment for the following housing costs:
- a community care grant (CCG) or loan for minor repairs and improvements (the type of work, rather than the cost should determine whether a repair is major or minor[34]);
- a CCG for overnight accommodation as part of a travel expenses payment (see p442);
- a loan for rent in advance where the landlord is not a local authority;
- a loan for housing costs not met by housing benefit (HB), IS or income-based jobseeker's allowance (JSA) (see pp228 and 26) are not eligible for direct deductions from IS or income-based JSA (see p141) – eg, emptying cesspits or septic tanks;
- a crisis loan for board and lodging or hostel charges *or* a budgeting loan for such charges in advance (excluding meals, services, deposits).

Additional items excluded from community care grants[35]

- Telephone costs, including installation, call and rental charges (see Appendix 1 if you are chronically sick or disabled and need a telephone).
- Any expenses which the local authority has a *statutory duty* to meet (discretionary powers do not trigger the exclusion, nor should statutory duties not accepted by the local authority).
- The cost of any fuel and standing charges.
- Any daily living expenses such as food and groceries except where incurred in caring for a prisoner on temporary release or where the maximum amount for a crisis loan has already been awarded (see p449).
- Any item worth less than £30, or several items which together are worth less than £30.[36]

Additional items excluded from budgeting loans[37]

- The cost of 'mains' fuel and standing charges. This exclusion does not apply to help with liquid gas, paraffin and coal.
- Any item worth less than £30, or several items which together are worth less than £30.[38]

Additional items excluded from crisis loans[39]

- Telephone costs including installation, call and rental charges (see Appendix 1 if you are chronically sick or disabled and need a telephone).
- Mobility needs (this does not include travel expenses).
- Holidays.
- Television or radio, TV licence, aerial, TV rental.
- Garaging, parking, purchase and running costs of any motor vehicle – except where payment is being considered for emergency travel expenses.

Help with maternity and funeral expenses

The regulated SF covers maternity and funeral expenses (see p410). The discretionary SF covers 'other needs'.[40] According to the *SF Guide*, this means that any maternity or funeral expense not covered by a regulated grant, cannot be met by the discretionary SF.[41] It was argued unsuccessfully in a legal challenge that items not paid for by a regulated grant could be met by the discretionary SF[42] – the decision may be appealed. The *SF Guide* concedes, however, that there is no definition of 'maternity' and 'funeral' expenses[43] and that items such as clothing for a pregnant mother or a growing (as opposed to newborn) baby may not be maternity expenses,[44] while items such as a headstone or clothing to attend a funeral may not be funeral (ie, burial or cremation) expenses.[45]

8. JOBSEEKER'S ALLOWANCE AND CRISIS LOANS

Special rules apply to some claimants of income-based jobseeker's allowance (JSA) who need to claim a crisis loan. You will get limited help if:[46]

- you claim income-based JSA but are disallowed benefit because you fail the main labour market conditions for qualifying – ie, availability for, and actively seeking, work and having a current jobseeker's agreement; *or*

- you have claimed income-based JSA but your benefit stops because you are sanctioned. This may happen if, for example, you refuse to carry out a reasonable jobseeker's direction, lose your last job because of misconduct, have left your last job voluntarily without a good reason or have failed to take up a job without a good reason.

(For full details of the labour market conditions and when sanctions apply, see CPAG's *Jobseeker's Allowance Handbook*.)

Crisis loans during the first 14 days

If you are not paid JSA for the above reasons, you are entitled to a crisis loan only in limited circumstances during the first 14 days following the decision to disallow benefit or apply a sanction.[47] You are entitled to a crisis loan for:[48]

- expenses, including living expenses (see below) arising from a disaster;
- the cost of items needed for cooking or space heating (including fireguards). This could include cooking utensils as well as a cooker.

Example
According to the guidance to social fund officers (SFOs),[49] if a decision to apply a two-week sanction was taken on 3 December 1996 and JSA was therefore not payable from 20 November to 3 December - payment of JSA is in arrears - the period when you are actually without any income-based JSA is 4 December to 17 December. It is during this second two-week period that you may get a crisis loan only if it is for expenses arising from a disaster, and for items needed for cooking and space heating.

How your loan for living expenses is calculated

The maximum you are paid is:[50]

- if you are the claimant for income-based JSA and you have been disallowed or sanctioned and you make the application for the crisis loan, and you are not getting a hardship payment of JSA – 75 per cent of the appropriate income-based JSA personal allowance for you and your partner (if any) *plus* £16.90 for each child (if any); *or*
- if you are the claimant and you receive a hardship payment of JSA – 75 per cent of the full rate appropriate income-based JSA personal allowance for you and your partner (if any) *plus* £16.90 for each child (if any), *or* an amount equal to the hardship rate of JSA for you and your family, whichever is the lower; *or*

- if you are the partner of the claimant for income-based JSA who has been disallowed or sanctioned and you apply for a crisis loan – 75 per cent of the appropriate personal allowance payable to you as the partner *only*.

The loan must, in all cases, not be more than £1,000 *minus* any outstanding SF loan you have.

Notes:

- A partner who claims is subject to the normal rules for getting crisis loans (see p446) and can therefore get living expenses that do not arise as a result of a disaster. S/he is only likely to make a claim during the first 14 days after her/his partner is disallowed/sanctioned and that partner cannot qualify in her/his own right for a loan.
- A claimant with a hardship payment of JSA is subject to the normal rules for getting crisis loans (see p446) but the maximum payment for living expenses is calculated differently (see above).
- A claimant who is disallowed/sanctioned and is not getting a hardship payment can qualify for a crisis loan at any time, but during the first 14 days after being disallowed/sanctioned can only qualify for crisis loans on limited grounds. The amount payable if s/he qualifies is the same whether during the 14-day period or afterwards.

Crisis loans after the first 14 days

You are able to get crisis loans under the normal rules (p446). Where a claimant has a hardship payment the maximum payment for living expenses is calculated differently (see above).

9. PEOPLE INVOLVED IN TRADE DISPUTES

There are special rules affecting people involved in trade disputes (see p58 for meaning).

Community care grants

If you or your partner are involved in a trade dispute (see p58 for what this means) you are not eligible for a grant other than for travelling expenses to visit somebody who is ill and then only in the following circumstances.[51]

- **You are involved in a trade dispute and are visiting:**
  - your partner in hospital or a similar institution;

- a dependant in hospital or similar institution, but only if you have no partner living with you who could get a grant, or your partner is also in hospital or a similar institution;
- a close relative or member of your household who is critically ill (whether or not in hospital or a similar institution).
- **You are not involved in a trade dispute but you are the partner or dependant of somebody who is, and you are visiting:**
  - a close relative or member of your household who is a patient in a hospital or similar institution or who is critically ill (whether or not in hospital or a similar institution).

To get a community care grant you must be receiving income support or income-based jobseeker's allowance or would be but for the trade dispute. For how your travelling expenses will be calculated, see p442.

Budgeting loans

You are not eligible for a budgeting loan if you or your partner are involved in a trade dispute[52] (see p58 for what this means).

Crisis loans

If you or your partner are involved in a trade dispute (see p58 for what this means), you are only entitled to a crisis loan for:[53]

- expenses arising from a disaster (see p448);
- the cost of items needed for cooking or space heating (including fireguards). This could include cooking utensils as well as a cooker.

CHAPTER TWENTY-THREE

Community care grants

This chapter covers:
1. Introduction (below)
2. Moving out of institutional or residential care (p437)
3. Staying out of institutional or residential care (p439)
4. Easing exceptional pressures on families (p440)
5. Travelling expenses (p442)

1. INTRODUCTION

Community care grants (CCGs) are intended to promote community care by helping people to move out of, or stay out of, institutional or residential care and by assisting families under exceptional pressure.

There is no legal entitlement to a CCG. Payments are discretionary. However, you can ask for a review if you are not paid what you ask for (see p457). Unlike loans, CCGs are not repayable.[1]

The basic rules

You must satisfy all the following rules in order to be considered for a CCG. The rules are laid down in legally binding directions. None of the words used are legally defined. 'Partner' and 'family' are not, therefore, restricted to their meanings for the purposes of income support (IS) or income-based jobseeker's allowance (JSA).

- You must be in receipt of a qualifying benefit, either IS or income-based JSA, when your application for a CCG is treated as made (see p453).[2] The only exception to this rule is if you are due to leave institutional or residential care (see p437) within six weeks of your application for a CCG and you are likely to get a qualifying benefit when you leave.[3] You will not be treated as receiving income-based JSA if you make your application on one of the three waiting days for

JSA (see p50). This rule does not apply if you are applying for a grant in order to move out of institutional or residential care.[4]

You are treated as receiving income-based JSA if you get a hardship payment of JSA.[5] (For when you can get a hardship payment, see CPAG's *Jobseeker's Allowance Handbook*.)

You should be treated as 'in receipt of' benefit if you receive a backdated award covering the date of your CCG application.[6] You are only 'in receipt of' a qualifying benefit if you are claiming the benefit.[7] Arguably, this is a very restrictive way to interpret the directions of a discretionary safety net scheme and could be challenged.

- You must not have too much capital. Any CCG awarded is reduced by the amount of capital you have in excess of £500 (£1,000 if you or your partner is 60 or over).[8] Capital is calculated as for IS, if you get IS (see p384).[9] If you get income-based JSA then the capital rules for income-based JSA apply (see CPAG's *Jobseekers Allowance Handbook*). These are virtually the same, but not quite. Payments made from the family fund to the claimant, partner or child are ignored whether you get IS or income-based JSA.[10] Any back-to-work bonus you have received counts as capital.[11] Capital held by your children should be disregarded.[12] **Note:** Although a limited amount of capital means you are eligible to be considered for a CCG, the fact that you have capital can affect the amount of an award. When deciding whether or not to make an award, all income and capital resources can be taken into account, apart from the mobility component of disability living allowance.[13]
- You or your partner must not be involved in a trade dispute unless your claim is for travelling expenses to visit a sick person (see p432). For what counts as being involved in a trade dispute, see p58.
- You cannot get a CCG for an excluded item (see p428).
- You must be awarded a CCG of at least £30, unless your award is for daily living expenses or travelling expenses,[14] but see p429 (excluded items).
- You must need a CCG for one or more of the following purposes:[15]
  - to help you, or a member of your family, or other person for whom you or a member of your family will be providing care, to re-establish yourselves in the community following a stay in institutional or residential care (see p437);
  - to help you, or a member of your family, or other person for whom you or a member of your family will be providing care, to remain in the community rather than enter institutional or residential care (see p439);
  - to ease exceptional pressures on you and your family (see p440);

- to allow you, or your partner, to care for a prisoner or young offender on temporary release (see p98);
- to help you, or one or more members of your family, with travel expenses within the UK in certain circumstances (see p442).

The guidance and priorities

The Secretary of State and district office managers issue guidance to social fund officers (SFOs) to help them decide which applicants should get a CCG.

The guidance is *not legally binding* and SFOs must exercise discretion in each individual case, taking into account the nature, extent and urgency of the need (see p423). They are told to use their discretion sensitively and with imagination to promote the objectives of community care; to avoid a rigid interpretation of the guidance; and to consider circumstances not covered by the guidance.[16] In practice, however, SFOs tend to use the *SF Guide* as a rule book and only award CCGs to meet those needs specifically identified.

The *SF Guide* suggests needs are prioritised as follows:[17]

- High priority should normally be given if a CCG will have a significant and substantial impact in resolving or improving the circumstances of the applicant and be very important in fulfilling the purpose of CCGs (see p434).
- Medium priority should normally be given if a CCG will have a substantial impact in resolving or improving the circumstances of the applicant but is less important in fulfilling the purpose of CCGs.
- Low priority should normally be given if the need in question is indirectly limited to the circumstances of the applicant or will be of minor importance in fulfilling the purpose of CCGs.

Examples given of circumstances which may affect priority include:[18]

- mental or physical disability and illness and general frailty;
- physical or social abuse or neglect;
- a long period of sleeping rough;
- unstable family circumstances and broken homes;
- behavioural problems—eg, due to drug or alcohol misuse.

Social fund officers are reminded that the above guidance is not exhaustive.[19] They might, for example, identify circumstances which would give an application higher priority than normally given to the need in question.

The *SF Guide* suggests higher priority is given to a new type of expense (particularly if unforeseeable) than to items which need replacing in the normal course of events – eg, a broken cooker.[20] Nothing in the law justifies this distinction, however, and it has been criticised by the legal adviser to the Social Fund Commissioner.[21] Moreover, the guidance implies that the claimant *should* meet the cost of replacing items (with or without the help of a loan) from weekly IS/income-based JSA. This suggests the assumption that the benefit rates cover these needs but nowhere is there a list of needs which IS or income-based JSA should meet.[22]

Local guidance will state which level of priority (usually high only) can be met by the budget. Unfortunately, the vagueness of the above definition of high priority needs gives district offices considerable leeway to interpret 'high priority' as they want.

The important thing to remember, however, is that the only legal requirement for eligibility for a CCG is that you satisfy the basic rules set out on pp434-36. Always give *your* reasons why your needs are high priority and how a CCG will help your circumstances and promote community care.

Items and amounts

You can ask for a payment for any item or service which is not excluded by law (see p428).

The *SF Guide* states that the amount you request should normally be allowed unless it is unreasonable.[23]

Local offices often refer to well known catalogue shop prices as a guide as to what is reasonable. There is no legal maximum award. The minimum that can be awarded in most cases is £30 (see p429).[24]

If you have borrowed money to obtain an item or service, even if help for that item is excluded by the directions, you can apply for a CCG to repay the debt.[25]

If you are caring for a prisoner or young offender on temporary release, the *SF Guide* suggests it is normally reasonable to award one-seventh of your IS or income-based JSA for each day (if the prisoner is your partner, one-seventh of the difference between the couple rate and your personal allowance).[26]

2. MOVING OUT OF INSTITUTIONAL OR RESIDENTIAL CARE

A CCG can be paid to help you, or a member of your family, or other person for whom you or a member of your family will be providing care, to re-establish yourselves in the community following a stay in institutional or residential care.[27] The social fund (SF) directions do not define the meaning of 'family' (see p441), 're-establish', 'the community', 'stay' or 'institutional and residential care' but they have been interpreted in caselaw (see below). The *SF Guide* particularly mentions people leaving hospital, prison or detention, care and nursing homes and local authority care (young people).[28]

Re-establishment in the community

The term 're-establish' (rather than 'establish') would appear to exclude those moving into the community for the first time. A High Court decision ruled that a refugee coming to the UK for the first time following a stay in a refugee camp in Somalia could not be re-establishing herself in the community. 'The community' was restricted to Great Britain.[29] Refugees who spend time in care in the UK, however, may qualify.[30] Another case said you must be actually or imminently in the community to qualify.[31]

A 'stay in' care

The *SF Guide* suggests that a 'stay in' care should normally mean at least three months, or a pattern of frequent or regular admission.[32] However, the High Court has ruled that undue importance should not be attached to the reference to three months.[33]

'Institutional or residential care'

The *SF Guide* says this means accommodation where a resident receives 'a significant and substantial amount of care, supervision or protection because s/he is unable to live independently in the community or might be a danger to others in the community'.[34] Examples given are hospitals, residential care homes, nursing homes, group homes, hostels, supported lodgings and prison.[35] The High Court has ruled that only accommodation in an institution specifically set up to provide care for those unable to live independently is 'institutional or residential care'.[36] Nevertheless social fund officers are advised that if you receive a high level of care you may be able to be treated as being in institutional or residential care.[37]

If you cannot establish that your previous accommodation was institutional or residential care, you might still qualify for a grant under section 3 (Staying out of care – see p439).

What to claim for

You can claim for help with any expenses which are necessary to help re-establish yourself or your family in the community. Examples include:

- Furniture, cookers, beds, bedding, kitchen, cleaning and household equipment, floor-covering, curtains and connection charges, when setting up home.
- Moving expenses including fares, connection charges and storage charges.
- Clothing and footwear.
- Items (including wheelchairs[38] or extra clothing etc) needed due to a disability.

3. STAYING OUT OF INSTITUTIONAL OR RESIDENTIAL CARE

A community care grant (CCG) can be paid to help you, or a member of your family, or other person for whom you or a member of your family will be providing care, to remain in the community, rather than enter institutional or residential care – eg, children.[39] None of these terms are defined in the social fund (SF) directions. See p438 above for the meaning of 'institutional or residential care'.

The legal test is whether a CCG will help somebody remain in the community rather than enter care. There is no requirement that a CCG must be able to 'prevent' entry into care. The threat of care does not have to be immediate,[40] but where it is, then the application for a CCG may have higher priority.[41] Social fund officers are told to consider whether a CCG 'would improve the applicant's independent life in the community and therefore lessen the risk of admission into care' or delay such an admission.[42] Actual or potential risk to physical or mental health because of the lack of such items as basic furniture and cooking facilities, protective clothing, bedding and heating can be used to argue for a CCG on the basis that an award will lessen the risk of entry into hospital or other care. Special needs such as an orthopaedic mattress or a firm upright armchair could be covered on the same basis.

What to claim for

You can claim for help with any expenses which will help you remain in the community by lessening the risk of you ending up in care – eg, hospital. Examples include:

- Minor repairs, redecoration and refurbishment, a survey fee which cannot be included in a mortgage/loan met by income support/income-based jobseeker's allowance,[43] heaters, fuel reconnection charges, installation of a pre-payment meter, bedding, a washing machine to improve your living conditions.
- Moving expenses, furniture and household equipment if a move to more suitable accommodation will help you to remain in the community, or if you are moving to help look after a vulnerable person.
- Items (including wheelchairs[44] or extra clothing etc) needed due to a disability.
- Expenses of setting up home where, eg, you have been living rough or in temporary accommodation (the *SF Guide* particularly mentions people undergoing a planned programme of resettlement[45]).

4. EASING EXCEPTIONAL PRESSURES ON FAMILIES

You can get a community care grant (CCG) to ease exceptional pressures on you and your family.[46] The scope for applications is very wide.

When making your application, always fully explain all the pressures your family is experiencing and how a CCG will ease those pressures and help you to continue living independently in the community.

If your application is refused on the grounds of insufficient priority, consider asking for a review (see p457).

'Exceptional pressures'

The term 'exceptional pressures' is not defined in the social fund (SF) directions and should be given its normal, everyday meaning. The following points may be of relevance:

- Comparisons with 'normal' families by SFOs are usually based on generalised assumptions. The level of pressure should be considered in terms of its effect on the individual family in question.[47] Clearly though, 'exceptional' means something greater than the normal range of pressures experienced by all families.
- The cumulative impact of different pressures should be considered. (You should always, therefore, list all the different pressures which are affecting your family.)
- Whether the pressures were foreseeable or are common is irrelevant.

- The breakdown of a relationship, particularly involving domestic violence is a common source of exceptional stress.
- Low income, single parenthood and poor or overcrowded living conditions can bring exceptional pressures.
- Pressures that arise from a sudden event (eg, a disaster) can be exceptional and traumatic. Pressures which have existed for a long time do not necessarily become easier to handle.
- There does not have to be any risk of a person going into care for exceptional pressures to exist.
- Mental stress, anxiety, depression, disability and illness are all sources and symptoms of exceptional pressures. The fact that an applicant does not appear stressed at an interview does not mean that exceptional pressures do not exist.
- Exceptional pressures experienced by children are entirely valid – eg, shame, discomfort, health risks from lack of clothes or facilities in the home.
- The *SF Guide* suggests higher priority should be given to a new type of expense[48] but this approach should be challenged (see p457).

'Family'

The law refers to 'easing exceptional pressures on a person and his family'. This implies that people not living in a family are excluded. This interpretation was endorsed in a High Court case.[49]

The word 'family' is not defined. The *SF Guide* says it should be given a flexible interpretation.[50] It could encompass:

- a couple with or without children;
- a household with grown-up children;
- adult brothers and sisters or relatives living together;
- a parent living with children for part of the week only;
- a pregnant woman – most likely to be accepted if the foetus is at least 24 weeks.[51]

What to claim for

You can claim for any non-excluded items which will help ease the exceptional pressures your family is facing. Examples include:

- Items which will improve your family's living conditions or physical or mental health.
- Maternity and funeral expenses that are arguably not strictly maternity or funeral expenses payment – but see p430.

- Moving and setting-up home expenses if you move to more suitable accommodation or following the breakdown of a relationship.
- Minor structural repairs.
- Repairs or replacement of items damaged by behavioural problems.
- Items (including wheelchairs[52] or extra clothing, etc.) needed because of a disability.

5. TRAVELLING EXPENSES

A community care grant (CCG) can be paid to assist you and/or a member of your family with travel expenses in the UK (including overnight accommodation charges) to:[53]

- visit someone who is ill (in hospital or elsewhere); *or*
- attend a relative's funeral; *or*
- ease a domestic crisis (not defined); *or*
- visit a child who is with the other parent pending a court decision on which parent the child is to live with; *or*
- move to suitable accommodation.

The amount of the payment

The *SF Guide* suggests that grants for travelling expenses should be calculated as follows:[54]

- the cost of 'standard' rate public transport (excluding air fares); *or*
- the cost of petrol, either up to the cost of public transport if available or in full if public transport is not available or you are unable to use it; *or*
- taxi fares, if public transport is unavailable or you or your partner cannot use public transport and have no access to private transport;
- the cost of an escort's fare if you cannot travel alone;
- the reasonable cost of necessary overnight accommodation.

According to guidance a CCG for hospital fares may be reduced by the amount of any income support or income-based jobseeker's allowance personal allowance you are receiving for a hospital patient which exceeds the hospital personal allowance (see p94).[55] CCGs for travel expenses can be paid in advance or by instalment if you are making regular visits.[56]

Loans

This chapter covers:

Budgeting loans are intended to help people who have been receiving a qualifying benefit (income support (IS) or income-based jobseeker's allowance (JSA)) for at least 26 weeks, to meet one-off expenses. Crisis loans are not restricted to those receiving a qualifying benefit, but are only available to deal with special problems. Special rules apply if people are involved in a trade dispute (see p432), or are excluded from income-based or contributory JSA because they fail the 'labour market' conditions of entitlement or JSA stops because they are sanctioned (see p430).

There is no legal entitlement to a loan. Payments are discretionary. You can, however, ask for a review if you are refused a loan or awarded less than you asked for (see p457).

Loans are obviously far less attractive than grants because they must be repaid although they are, at least, interest-free.[1] Another problem with loans is that they cannot exceed what the Benefits Agency thinks you can afford to repay.

It is always better, therefore, to ask for a grant if you are eligible to do so (see Chapter 23). There is nothing to stop you asking for a grant and a loan for the same item at the same time (see p427). Legally, your application is to the SF as a whole and should be automatically considered for a grant and a loan.[2] If you are awarded a loan, you can accept it and request a review to get it changed to a grant (see p458).

1. BUDGETING LOANS

The basic rules

The rules are laid down in directions which are legally binding. None of the words used are defined in the directions. You must satisfy all the following rules in order to be eligible for a budgeting loan:

- you must be in receipt of income support (IS) or income-based jobseeker's allowance (JSA) when your application for a budgeting loan is decided by the Benefits Agency.[3] Note that if you are claiming income-based JSA there are three waiting days when you are not entitled to benefit,[4] although this does not apply if:[5]
  - you were entitled to IS, incapacity benefit or invalid care allowance 12 weeks or less before your entitlement to income-based JSA started; *or*
  - you are under 18 and have been entitled to a severe hardship payment; *or*
  - you are claiming income-based JSA and this jobseeking period is linked to an earlier jobseeking period[6] (see CPAG's *Jobseeker's Allowance Handbook*); *and*
- you, or your partner, between you must have been receiving IS or income-based JSA throughout the 26 weeks before the date on which your application is decided.[7] One break of 14 days or less when IS/JSA was not being paid can be included in the 26 weeks.[8] A period covered by benefit paid in arrears counts towards the 26 weeks.[9] If you received benefit while in Northern Ireland, that also counts.[10] The *SF Guide* says that you can have had more than one partner during the 26 weeks;[11] *and*
- you must not have too much capital. The rules are the same as for CCGs (see p435 for details); *and*
- you, or your partner, must not be involved in a trade dispute (see p432); *and*
- the loan must be to assist you to meet important intermittent expenses for which it may be difficult to budget;[12] *and*
- the loan must not be for an excluded item (see p428); *and*

- the loan must be at least £30. But if the item for which you need the loan is worth less than £30, or the value of several items is worth in total less than £30, then you get nothing at all. The maximum you can get is £1,000 less any outstanding SF loan(s) you have;[13] *and*
- the loan must not exceed an amount which you are likely to be able to repay[14] (see p451).

The guidance and priorities

The Secretary of State and district office managers issue guidance to social fund officers (SFOs) to help them decide who should get a budgeting loan.

The guidance is not legally binding and SFOs must exercise discretion in each individual case, taking into account the nature, extent and urgency of the need (see p423). They are told to avoid a rigid interpretation of the guidance and consider circumstances not covered by the guidance.[15] In practice, however, SFOs tend to use the *SF Guide* as a rulebook and only award loans to meet rigidly defined 'high priority' needs.

The *SF Guide* gives the following examples of high, medium and low priority needs:[16]

- **High priority**: Essential furniture and household equipment; bed-clothes; essential removal charges; fuel meter installation and reconnection charges; non-mains fuel costs; essential minor repairs and maintenance for owner-occupiers, which could not be met by IS, or a home loan or grant.
- **Medium priority**: Non-essential furniture and household equipment; clothing; debts; redecoration.
- **Low priority**: Leisure items; removal charges and rent in advance if a move is not essential.

Social fund officers are reminded that the examples are not exhaustive and that they should identify circumstances which might give an application higher priority than normally given to the need in question.[17] Local guidance will state which level of priority (usually only high) can be met by the budget.

If you are applying for a high priority need as defined above, point this out in your application. Otherwise, do not be put off from applying by the guidance. Always give *your* reasons why your needs are high priority and consider requesting a review if your application is refused. You should also make sure the items you need the loan for are worth £30 or more! (See above – the basic rules.)

The amount of the loan

The amount awarded must be between £30 and £1,000 but see p430.[18]

There is no guidance on how much should be paid for specific items or services. SFOs are told to accept your estimate of the cost if it is 'within the broad range of prices considered reasonable for an item of serviceable quality'.[19] Local offices often refer to well known catalogue shop prices as a guide as to what is reasonable. Ask for a review if you are unhappy about the amount awarded to you (but see p457).

You cannot be awarded more than you can afford to repay.[20] The amount you can afford to repay is usually calculated by multiplying your weekly repayment rate by 78 (see p451). If you already have one or more loans, you may also find you are offered less than you ask for.

2. CRISIS LOANS

The basic rules

The rules are laid down in directions which are legally binding. None of the words used are defined in the directions. You must satisfy all the following rules in order to be eligible for a crisis loan:

- you must be 16 or over;[21] *and*
- you must not be an 'excluded person' (see p447);[22] *and*
- the loan must not be for an excluded item (see p428); *and*
- the loan must not exceed an amount which you are likely to be able to repay.[23] There are maximum awards (see p450), but no minimum amount is laid down in law (but for how a loan for living expenses is calculated, see p450);[24] *and*
- you must be without sufficient resources to meet the immediate short-term needs of yourself and/or your family[25] (see p448); *and*
- the loan must be for expenses in an emergency, or as a consequence of a disaster, and be the only means by which serious damage or serious risk to the health or safety of yourself or a member of your family may be prevented[26] (see p448); *or* the loan must be for rent in advance payable to a non-local authority landlord and a CCG is being awarded following a stay in institutional or residential care[27] (see p437).

Making an application

It is common for Benefits Agency counter staff to advise potential applicants (eg, homeless or young people without money) that they will not be given a crisis loan. Do not be put off. Always insist on completing an application form and being given a written decision. You should be given a 'self-completion' application form if you ask for one. Ask for a review if your application is refused.

Excluded persons

The following people are excluded by the directions from getting a crisis loan, in all circumstances.[28]

- People in hospital, nursing homes or residential care homes (private or local authority), *unless* their discharge is planned to take place within the next two weeks.
- Prisoners and people lawfully detained, including those on temporary release.
- Members of religious orders who are fully maintained by the order.
- People in 'full-time relevant education' who are not entitled to income support (IS) (see p16).

The following people are excluded by the directions from getting a crisis loan except in very limited circumstances:

- Full-time students not on IS or income-based JSA can only claim a crisis loan for expenses arising out of a disaster.[29]
- 'Persons from abroad' for the purposes of IS and income-based JSA who are not entitled to these benefits either at the ordinary or the urgent cases rate (see p64) can only claim a crisis loan for expenses arising out of a disaster.[30] Many asylum-seekers are now in this position as most are no longer entitled to benefit (see p77). To get a crisis loan, they would have to show that their situation constitutes a disaster and that they are likely to be able to repay the loan. Social fund officers are told to give particular attention to the statutory needs of asylum-seekers and refugees.[31]
  Note: If you are an overstayer, subject to a deportation order, or an illegal entrant, you should not apply for a crisis loan before getting advice about regularising your status here.
- People involved in a trade dispute (see p58 for details).
- People who are disallowed income-based JSA because they fail one or more of the labour market conditions for getting income-based JSA, or who have been sanctioned and therefore do not receive income-based JSA.[32] Different rules apply to applications by partners (see p430 for details about JSA and crisis loans). A person who gets a hardship payment of income-based JSA in these circumstances, can qualify for a crisis loan in the ordinary way.[33]

Emergencies and disasters

Most crisis loans can only be awarded in an emergency or following a disaster (see The basic rules, p446). Neither of these terms is defined in the directions. You should always explain why a particular situation constitutes an emergency or disaster for you or your family.

Serious damage/risk to health or safety

A crisis loan has to be the only means of preventing serious damage or risk to health or safety. You will have to show there are no other resources or ways of meeting your need. This is often interpreted very strictly by SFOs. If an SFO suggests other means which are impractical or unavailable to you, ask for a review.

The potential serious risk to your health or safety might be obvious – eg, you have no money for food or other essentials. Any supporting evidence you can get from your doctor, social worker, etc. will help your case.

Resources

You must be without sufficient resources to meet the immediate short-term needs of yourself and/or your family. 'Resources' are not defined in the SF directions. The *SF Guide* says all resources which '...are actually available to the applicant or could be obtained in time to meet the need' should be taken into account.[34] Resources available on credit should only be taken into account if the applicant is not on IS or income-based JSA and can afford the required repayments.[35]

The *SF Guide* says the following resources should be disregarded:[36]

- other SF payments, housing benefit, disability living allowance (mobility component);
- the value of your home, premises acquired for occupation within the next six months, and premises occupied by a relative or your ex-partner;
- the value of any reversionary interest (see p344, 25th edition, *National Welfare Benefits Handbook*);
- your business assets;
- any sum paid to you because of damage to, or loss of, your home or personal possessions and intended for their repair or replacement;
- any sum acquired on the express condition that it is used for essential repairs or improvements to your home;
- any personal possessions, except those acquired for the purpose of qualifying for a crisis loan;

- any payments from the Independent Living Funds, and the Macfarlane Trusts (see Appendix 1).

SFOs are told not to routinely refer applicants to employers, relatives or close friends 'unless there is reason to believe their help will be forthcoming'.[37] They are reminded that social services do not normally meet financial needs.[38] Emergency payments for children should be disregarded unless they meet the need for which the crisis loan is requested.[39]

The *SF Guide* suggests it may be reasonable to disregard other resources at least for a temporary period.[40] You could argue that money set aside to meet forthcoming bills (eg, council tax, fuel bills) is not available.

Guidance on crisis loan situations

The Secretary of State and district office managers issue guidance to SFOs to help them decide who should get a crisis loan.

The guidance is *not legally binding*. SFOs must consider each application on its merits, taking into account the nature, extent and urgency of the need in each case (see p423). The guidance says that if a crisis loan is appropriate, it would be rare to refuse it on the grounds of insufficient priority.[41] If you are refused a crisis loan, ask for a review (see p457).

The *SF Guide* gives a few examples of situations where a crisis loan may be appropriate. Remember, however, you are eligible for a loan in *any* situation as long as you satisfy the basic rules set out on p446.

Living expenses for a short period

The *SF Guide* suggests a crisis loan could be awarded to meet day-to-day living expenses in the following situations:

- You are waiting for your first benefit payment or wages (and your employer will not give you an advance).[42]
- You are suffering hardship because your employer has imposed a compulsory unpaid holiday.[43]
- You have lost money or you have lost a giro and replacement is delayed (see p136 on lost giros).[44]
- You cannot get IS or income-based JSA because your capital is over £8,000 but you cannot realise your assets immediately.[45]
- You are homeless and need living expenses. The *SF Guide* stresses the risk to physical and mental health brought about by sleeping rough and prolonged homelessness.[46]

The guidance suggests a crisis loan should only cover living expenses for more than 14 days in exceptional circumstances – eg, a continuing crisis; loss of money which would normally cover you until your next income is due; or no money because of misfortune or mismanagement.[47]

Other situations

- Emergency travelling expenses if you are stranded away from home or emergency fares to hospital.[48]
- Fuel reconnection charges.[49]
- Rent in advance payable to a non-local authority landlord if you are also awarded a CCG on leaving care – the rules about serious risk to health and safety do not apply in this situation.[50]
- Disasters – eg, fire or flood[51] (see p448).

The amount of the loan

There is no legal minimum. There is a general legal maximum of £1,000 less any outstanding SF loan(s) you have.[52] You also cannot be awarded more than you can afford to repay,[53] usually calculated by multiplying your weekly repayment rate by 78 (see p451). If you already have one or more loans you may also find you are offered less than you asked for.

There are also more specific legal maximums for items, services and living expenses.

Items and services:[54] The maximum you can get is the reasonable cost of purchase (including delivery and installation) or the cost of repair, if cheaper.

Living expenses:[55] The maximum you can get is 75 per cent of the appropriate IS/JSA personal allowance for you *and* any partner (see p318), plus £16.90 for each child. If you have been disallowed income-based JSA or it is not paid because of a sanction, see p430. You can get a loan for living expenses according to the normal rules if:

- your JSA claim has been referred to a JSA adjudication officer either for a decision as to whether your JSA should be disallowed, or whether a sanction should be applied;[56]
- you are getting a hardship payment of JSA[57] (see p431 for how the loan is calculated).

If you are unhappy about the amount offered, you can ask for a review, but see p457.

3. REPAYMENTS

All loans must be repaid to the Benefits Agency. The rate of repayment, the repayment period and the method of recovery are technically decided by the Secretary of State and not by SFOs.[58] In practice, decisions are made on his behalf by SFOs. Guidance, which is *not legally binding*, is issued in a *Social Fund Decision and Review Guide* (see Appendix 4).

Unlike SFO decisions (eg, the amount of loan awarded), which can be challenged by review, Secretary of State decisions are not subject to review. You can request that a Secretary of State's decision is reconsidered, however, by 'making a complaint' (see p452).

The rate and period of repayment

There is no law specifying repayment rates or periods. The guidance says loans should normally be recovered over a period of 78 weeks,[59] or exceptionally 104 weeks,[60] at the weekly rate of:

- 15 per cent of your income support (IS)/income-based jobseeker's allowance (JSA) applicable amount, excluding housing costs (see p25) if you have no 'continuing commitments';[61]
- 10 per cent if you have 'continuing commitments' of up to £7.37 a week;[62]
- 5 per cent if you have higher 'continuing commitments'.[63]

Recovery of a loan should be deferred until any existing loans are repaid.[64]

You should argue that if you are getting the hardship rate of JSA, you should not be required to repay until income-based JSA is restored to its normal rate, or that recovery should be at the 5 per cent rate.

Recovery of loans

Methods of recovery

Loans are nearly always recovered by direct deductions from benefit, although you can make a direct payment at any time to partially or wholly pay off the debt. Deductions can only be made from the following benefits:[65]

- IS;
- family credit;
- JSA (contributory or income-based);
- incapacity benefit;
- severe disablement allowance;

- invalid care allowance;
- disability working allowance;
- disablement benefit, reduced earnings allowance and industrial death benefit;
- widows' benefits (excluding the lump-sum widow's payment);
- retirement pensions (all types);
- maternity allowance.

No recovery can be made from the back-to-work bonus paid with either IS or income-based JSA.[66]

Increases of benefit for age and dependants, and additional benefit under SERPS are also subject to deduction.

Deductions from benefit can be made even where an order for bankruptcy or sequestration has been made.[67]

From whom recoverable

A loan can be legally recovered from:

- you (the applicant) or the person who the loan was for;[68]
- your partner, if you are living together as a married or unmarried couple as defined for IS purposes (see p319);[69]
- a 'liable relative' (see p113) or a 'person who has given a sponsorship undertaking' (see p82).[70] If you claim IS or income-based JSA, a crisis loan will be recovered from you. If you cannot claim IS/JSA a crisis loan can be recovered from your liable relative or sponsor.[71]

There is no right of review or appeal against a decision about the rate of repayment of a loan.

Making a complaint

If you are unhappy about the repayment terms when a loan is offered, you should write to the Benefits Agency and explain why. This is technically known as 'making a complaint'.[72] You should do this before accepting the offer of a loan. If loan repayments are causing you hardship, you can write to the Benefits Agency at any time, outlining your commitments, and ask for rescheduling – ie, lower repayments over a longer period.[73]

CHAPTER TWENTY-FIVE

Applications, payments and reviews

This chapter covers:
1. Applications (below)
2. Decisions and payments (p456)
3. Internal reviews (p457)
4. Social fund inspector reviews (p461)

I. APPLICATIONS

Making an application

Applications for a social fund (SF) payment must be made in writing, either on a standard application form obtainable from the Benefits Agency or in some other way which is acceptable to the Secretary of State – eg, a letter with all the necessary details.[1] If your application is incomplete, the Benefits Agency can ask you to provide additional information either in writing, or by calling in at your local office.[2]

An application can be made on your behalf by somebody else, as long as you give your written consent (this is not necessary if an appointee is acting for you – see p123).[3] Social fund officers (SFOs) are advised that for budgeting loans the application must be made by whichever one of a couple is the claimant for income support (IS)/income-based jobseeker's allowance (JSA), unless the application is being made by a third party. Only the person who claims IS/income-based JSA counts as being 'in receipt' of a qualifying benefit.[4] This seems to be an unnecessarily rigid interpretation of the law given the safety net nature of the social fund.

Your application is treated as having been made on the day it is received at a Benefits Agency office.[5] If your application was incomplete and you comply with a request for additional information, your application will be treated as made on the day it was originally received.[6]

Each application is made to the fund as a whole and should be considered for a community care grant (CCG), budgeting or crisis loan as appropriate.[7]

Where to apply

You should normally apply to the Benefits Agency office which covers the area in which you live.[8] If you are applying for a crisis loan, however, you can apply to the office where your need arises.[9] In an emergency, social services or other agencies can contact the Benefits Agency 'out of hours' service on your behalf (see p139).

If you are moving out of care and claiming a CCG, you should apply to the office which covers the area you are moving to unless you are only claiming removal expenses and/or fares.[10]

Evidence and information

Your application should normally be decided on the information you give on your application form, unless this is incomplete.[11] Exceptionally, you may be asked for corroborating evidence such as an estimate or a medical note.[12] If you have to pay for this, you can be given an SF award to cover the cost.[13] Evidence from a third party should be made known to you on request, although its source may remain confidential.[14] Third party evidence can be used *without* that person's consent.[15]

Community care grants and budgeting loans

You should apply on form SF300, which is in an application pack available from the Benefits Agency and advice centres. The form is for both CCGs and budgeting loans.

Tips on completing the application form:

- In part 3 of the form, you are asked whether you want a grant or loan. Always ask for a grant if you satisfy the eligibility rules (see p434). You can ask for a grant and a loan. *Legally, your application is to the fund as a whole* and each application should automatically be considered for a grant and loan.[16]
- You should complete part 6 of the form with full details of what you need. Be as specific as possible (do not just write 'furniture' or 'clothes' – list each item needed). Write down the actual cost or a reasonable estimate for each item. It is not usually necessary to supply written estimates from a supplier (unless you are asking for removal expenses, when two written estimates are usually required).
- Part 6 also asks why the items are needed. Part 7 asks more specific questions about why you need help. It is important to establish that

you satisfy the rules of eligibility for a CCG or budgeting loan (see Chapters 23 and 24), including the purposes for which a CCG can be awarded. It is also important to show why your application should be given high priority. Refer to the local or national guidance if it helps your case (you can obtain a copy of the local guidance from your local Benefits Agency office). Use the space in Part 10 of the form and continue in a letter, if necessary.

- Submit any supporting evidence with your application – eg, a letter from your doctor or social worker.

Crisis loans

You apply for a crisis loan on a form at the Benefits Agency or by submitting a self-completion form SF401 available from the Benefits Agency or advice centres. It is common for Benefits Agency counter staff to 'advise' potential applicants that they will not be given a loan. Do not be put off. Always insist on completing an application form and receiving a written decision. Make sure the form fully records your needs and circumstances. You will usually be interviewed in connection with your application. Crisis loan decisions should be based on your circumstances at the date of decision and SFOs should never deliberately delay a decision until the need has passed.

Repeat applications

If you have been awarded or refused a payment for an item or service, you cannot get a payment for the same item or service within 26 weeks of a previous application unless:[17]

- there has been a relevant change of circumstances; *or*
- you are applying for a budgeting loan for which you were ineligible when you made your first application because neither you nor your partner had been on IS or income-based JSA, or a combination of both benefits for 26 weeks.

You should note the following points:

- Applications by different partners are not caught by the above rule. The second application must be made by the same person who made the first application for the rule to apply.[18]
- The rule does not apply if your first application was incomplete; *or* you withdrew it before a decision was made; *or* you declined or did not respond to a loan offer.[19]
- Only payments for the 'same item or service' are excluded. An application for bedding may be different to an application for sheets,

pillow cases and eiderdown. An application for a bed for one child is different to an application for a bed for another child.[20]

- Where there are a number of repeat applications for the same item or service, the 26 weeks should run from the date of the first application.[21]
- The Act refers to 'any relevant change of circumstances'[22] (which could include changes in the budget) whereas the SF direction refers to 'a relevant change in the applicant's circumstances'.[23] It can be argued that the direction wrongly restricts the powers laid down in the primary legislation.

If you think the rule about repeat applications has been wrongly applied, you are entitled to request a review (see p457).[24]

2. DECISIONS AND PAYMENTS

Decisions

You should receive a written decision on your application. If a payment is wholly or partly refused, the decision should explain why and state that you have the right to request a review. The reasons given are usually very general and sketchy – eg, your application is not high enough priority or is not for one of the purposes for which a payment can be made. If you are not satisfied you should consider asking for a review, see p457.

There are no legal time limits within which the Benefits Agency must make decisions. The *SF Guide*, however, says that 'all decisions should normally be made within 28 days of the date of the application.'[25] Decisions on urgent applications (eg, crisis loans) should be made within one working day.[26]

If there are unreasonable delays in getting a decision, you should complain to the social fund manager in your district office. If this does not help, you should ask your MP to take up your case with the manager, the Secretary of State or the Ombudsman. The Benefits Agency has published a *Customer Charter* for claimants. This gives target times for processing crisis loans (the day the need arises or the application is made) and community care grants (an average of seven days). There are no targets for dealing with budgeting loans.

Payments

You should normally be paid by giro made out to you.[27] The Benefits Agency can, however, choose to pay a supplier directly.[28] Payment can also be made in the form of travel warrants, food vouchers or cash, and in instalments. You can ask for a review of any decision to pay a supplier rather than you, or to pay in instalments.[29]

3. INTERNAL REVIEWS

Introduction

There is no right of appeal to an independent body against decisions regarding the discretionary social fund (SF). There is instead a review system, which is divided into two distinct stages.

First, you ask for a review of a decision and your case is reconsidered by the office which made the decision. Internal reviews are carried out by reviewing officers (ROs) who are SFOs or specially appointed social fund review officers.[30]

Second, if you are dissatisfied with the outcome, you can ask for a further review by an social fund inspector (SFI) based in an office in Birmingham, who reconsiders the case independently.[31]

You should always consider asking for a review if you are unhappy about a decision. If the decision is not changed following an internal review, you should always consider requesting a further review by an SFI who will reconsider your application more thoroughly and independently.

You should note that a review decision may be unfavourable to you and result in the award of a loan rather than a community care grant (CCG), or a smaller loan than the one originally awarded. The Benefits Agency can always recover a loan but there is no power to recover a CCG that has actually been paid to you. If you want to get a CCG award reviewed, wait until it has been paid and then request the review. But check the time limits for requesting a review (see p458). You should get advice if you are not sure whether to ask for a review. In general, but not always, decisions by SFIs appear to give greater weight to the urgency of the need.

The law regarding reviews is set out in legislation and the SF directions.

Decisions subject to review

All SFO decisions are subject to review, including:[32]

- the refusal of a grant or loan;
- the amount awarded;
- payment to a third party or by instalments;
- refusal to determine a repeat application.

Decisions about the repayment of loans are made by the Secretary of State and not subject to review, but can still be challenged (see p452).

Applying for a review

The basic rules

You must apply for a review of a decision by writing to the Benefits Agency **within 28 days** of the date the decision was issued to you.[33] Your application must include your grounds for requesting a review (see below – Tactics).[34] If somebody is making an application on your behalf, it must be accompanied by your written authority (unless the person is your appointee).[35]

Late applications can be accepted for 'special reasons'.[36] 'Special reasons' are not defined. They could include reasons why the application is late (eg, ill-health, domestic crises, wrong advice) or any other reasons (eg, you will suffer hardship without a review). The restrictive definition given to the phrase 'special reasons' for appeals (see Chapter 8) does not apply to the SF. If the Benefits Agency do not accept there are special reasons, get advice. You may have to threaten judicial review if their refusal is unreasonable (see p172).

If your application is out of time, you can also ask the reviewing officer to use her/his powers to conduct a review at any time without an application (see p411).

The Benefits Agency can ask you to submit further information in connection with your application if reasonably required.[37]

You can withdraw your application in writing at any time.[38]

Tactics

Your application must be in writing. Keep a copy if possible. Quote your national insurance number if possible. If you do not have a national insurance number your application can be dealt with clerically. Begin by stating that you are requesting a review and clearly identify the decision you are unhappy about.

- If your application is late, give your 'special reasons' why it should be considered out of time (see p458). Alternatively, you could ask the RO to conduct a review without an application (see below).
- Explain, as fully as possible, why you disagree with the SFO's decision.
- CCGs are often refused on the grounds that your application was not for one of the purposes for which a grant can be given. You can challenge such decisions by explaining how your application *is* for one of the purposes for which a CCG can be given – ie, moving out of care, staying out of care or easing exceptional pressures (see p435).
- CCGs and loans are often refused on the grounds of 'insufficient priority' (see Chapter 22). You can challenge such decisions by stating you are not satisfied your particular needs and circumstances have been properly looked at. You should then explain why your application should be high priority.
- If you are unhappy about the amount you have been awarded, you should state that you are not satisfied that the SFO has assessed your needs properly. Explain why you need the amount you asked for, giving any further evidence or information which was not in your original application.
- If you are awarded a loan rather than a CCG, you can refuse or accept the loan and also ask for a review explaining why you think you should be awarded a CCG.
- Bear in mind that however good your case a decision on review may be unfavourable – see p457.

Review without an application

An RO *must* review a decision which appears:[39]

- to have been based on a mistake about the law or directions; *or*
- to have been made in ignorance of a material fact or based on a mistake about a material fact; *or*
- where there has been a relevant change of circumstances since the decision was given.

A relevant change in circumstances is not restricted to changes in *your* circumstances or those of your family. It could include, for example, any additional allocations to a district office budget during the year (see p425).

An RO *may* also review a decision at any time '... in such other circumstances as he thinks fit'.[40] This is a wide discretionary power, not subject to any time limits or particular grounds for review.[41] You can ask an RO to initiate a review under the above powers at any time – eg, if you are out of time to apply for a review.

Deciding reviews

The theory

When carrying out a review, ROs must take into account all the factors listed on pp423 and 426 (eg, the nature, extent and urgency of the need, the SF directions and guidance and the budget).[42] In addition, they must consider:

- *first*, whether the original decision was legally correct (sustainable on the evidence, based on all relevant considerations and correct interpretation of the law), reasonable, procedurally correct and unbiased;[43]
- *second*, all the circumstances including any new evidence and relevant changes in circumstances since the decision was made.[44]

The practice

Not surprisingly, reviews are rarely conducted with the thoroughness demanded by the legal requirements. In practice, budget considerations and the guidance on priorities tend to be the major determinants of review decisions. Also there is a tendency for ROs only to change original decisions in the light of new evidence.

Review procedure

Interview

If a decision is not wholly revised in your favour, you must be given the opportunity to attend an interview.[45] You have the legal right to be accompanied by a friend or representative.[46] At the interview, you must be given an explanation of the reasons for the review decision and an opportunity to put your case, including any additional evidence you have.[47]

The interview should take place in a private room and can be held in your home if, for example, you are severely disabled or ill.[48] The RO must make an accurate written record of your representations, to be agreed and signed by you.[49]

Tactics

- Always ask to be interviewed in a private room and complain if one is not offered.
- Do not sign the written record unless you agree with it and everything you want to say has been recorded. It is particularly important to include any new evidence or information you have.

- If you do not wish to attend an interview, tell the Benefits Agency, making it clear you still want the review to go ahead. Unless you withdraw your review application in writing, the Benefits Agency must proceed with the review and issue you with a review decision.
- Always insist on an interpreter if you are not familiar with English.

Decisions

Review decisions must be notified to you in writing and inform you of your right to request a further review by an SFI if you do not agree with the decision.[50]

4. SOCIAL FUND INSPECTOR REVIEWS

Introduction

If you are dissatisfied with a review decision, you have a right to request a further review by a social fund inspector (SFI).[51] *You should always consider asking for a further review, if necessary, as your chances of success are higher than with the internal review, but see p457.*

SFIs are based in an office in Birmingham (see Appendix 2) and conduct their reviews independently of the Benefits Agency. They tend to produce a much higher standard of decision-making than review officers, and are generally better trained and have more time. They also tend to be less influenced by guidance and district budgets.

The law regarding SFI reviews is set out in legislation and SFI directions.

Applying for a further review

The basic rules

You must apply for a further review in writing within 28 days of the date the review decision was issued to you.[52] Your application must include your grounds for requesting a further review (see below – Tactics).[53] If somebody is applying on your behalf, you must send your written authority[54] (unless the person is your appointee). You should specifically authorise the person to make an application for further review by an SFI on your behalf. You will need to do this even if you supplied written authority when you first applied for an internal review.

Late applications can be accepted for 'special reasons'[55] (see p458). You must send your application to your local Benefits Agency office and not directly to the SFI office in Birmingham. The local office will send your application together with all relevant papers to Birmingham. Decisions about late or incomplete applications must be made by the SFI and not the local office. The SFI will write to you direct for further information or evidence.

Tactics

- Your application must be in writing to your local Benefits Agency office. Begin by stating you are requesting a further review by an SFI, identify clearly the decision you are unhappy about and quote your national insurance number. If your application is late, explain in full why this is the case.
- Your grounds for review are likely to be similar to the grounds for the initial review (see p457). Explain as fully as possible why you are unhappy with the review decision.
- It is a good idea to contact the SFI office a few days after submitting your application to make sure they have received it. Local Benefits Agency offices are told to send applications on to Birmingham by courier on the day they are received whenever possible.[56] Complain to the SF manager and, if necessary, your MP, if there are delays.
- If your case is urgent, state this and explain why. There is a special express procedure if you are seeking a review of a crisis loan decision; you can ask the local office to fax the decision and papers to the SFI office rather than rely on a courier.[57] You could also ask the local office to consider reviewing a decision where it is urgent but the request is for a CCG or BL.

Deciding SFI reviews

The law

When conducting a review, SFIs are legally bound to take into account the same matters as apply to internal reviews (see p457), including any new evidence and relevant changes of circumstances since the review decision (eg, the current state of the district office budget or any change in your circumstances).[58] Moreover, the High Court has ruled that it must be clear from the SFI's decision that s/he has taken the Secretary of State's guidance into account.[59] In another case, the Court ruled that the SFI must apply the law at the time of the SFI decision, not the law at the time of the original SFO decision.[60]

The procedure

Reviews are almost always conducted on the basis of written information. You have no right to an oral hearing although an SFI can interview you, if necessary, 'at a mutually convenient location'.[61]

You will be sent copies of all the papers which the SFI has about your case before the review takes place. You should look through the papers and send any written comments you have to the SFI on the form provided.

Social fund inspector decisions

SFIs can:[62]

* confirm the decision of the local office; *or*
* substitute their own decision; *or*
* refer the case back to a social fund review officer for redetermination.

You will receive a detailed written decision from the SFI. There are long delays (often several weeks) with SFI reviews and you could complain to your MP about these. Crisis loan reviews should be done urgently (see above). If you are unhappy about an SFI decision, get advice. There is no right of appeal, but you can ask an SFI to reconsider her/his decision – eg, because it is unreasonable or wrong in law.[63] You can also apply for a judicial review of the decision in the High Court.

If a case is referred back for another internal review, the SFI should identify the factors which need further consideration. The social fund review officer must re-determine the case and send you a new decision, with a full explanation of how this was reached, taking into account the SFI's comments.[64] The case in which this was established is due to be heard by the House of Lords. If you are dissatisfied with the new decision, you have the right to request another review by an SFI.

Further SFI reviews

The rules and procedure are identical to initial SFI reviews (see p457).

PART EIGHT

Health service benefits

CHAPTER TWENTY-SIX

Health service benefits

This chapter covers:

1. INTRODUCTION

Although the National Health Service (NHS) generally provides free health care, there are charges for some goods and services. Some people are **exempt from charges**, including anyone getting income support (IS), income-based jobseeker's allowance (JSA), family credit (FC) or disability working allowance (DWA).

You can also get a **full or partial reduction** of charges on the grounds of 'low income' if you have less than £8,000 capital. The low-income calculation is explained below. It is only relevant if you cannot gain exemption from charges on other grounds.

You can claim a **refund** if you have already paid charges, but think you would have qualified for an exemption or reduction.

2. HOW LOW INCOME IS WORKED OUT

The Benefits Agency decides if your income is 'low' by comparing your 'requirements' with your 'resources'. If your 'resources' are less than, or the same as, your 'requirements' you do not have to pay NHS charges. If they are more than your 'requirements' you may still qualify for partial help with dental costs, sight tests, glasses, wigs and fabric supports and fares to hospital. You cannot get partial help with prescriptions (you may be better off using a pre-payment certificate – see p471).

'Requirements' and 'resources' are calculated as at the date on which you claim help with charges, or the date you paid them if you are claiming a refund.[1]

Requirements[2]

Your requirements are based on your IS/income-based JSA applicable amounts (see p329) but there are important differences.

To calculate your requirements, add up the following items:

* your IS personal allowance(s) (see p330). The reductions which apply to IS (eg, because of involvement in a trade dispute) do not apply. Nor do the special rules for people from abroad or members of religious orders, whose requirements are calculated in the usual way. 16/17-year-olds are assumed to have the requirements of 18-year-olds if they are in full-time work or training, or are eligible for the disability premium. Couples under 18 who have children, are eligible for a disability premium or have housing costs, or where one is on youth training or in full-time work, are assumed to have the requirements of a couple over 18.

The children's allowance is based on actual age at the date of claim

* your IS premiums (see p332). Disability premiums can be added to your requirements if you, or your partner, have been getting incapacity benefit, statutory sick pay or you were incapable of work for 28 weeks, not 52 as for IS. If you jointly own your own home or share liability for rent with a close relative such that you would *not* get SDP included in IS, you nevertheless include this premium in your requirements. The Higher Pensioner premium is added to the requirements of anyone aged 60 or over;
* your rent *less* any housing benefit;
* your council tax *less* any council tax benefit;
* your housing costs, as for IS (see p25), but with the following differences:
  - you can include *all* interest and capital payments on house purchase loans and other loans secured on your home (with no waiting periods). You can also include all payments on loans (whether secured or not) where these are made for adapting the home to take account of the special needs of a disabled person;
  - you can also include endowment policy payments if they are in connection with the purchase of your home;

– the rules for non-dependant deductions (see p32) and housing costs payable when you are temporarily away from your home (including in a residential care home/nursing home – see p84) are modified.

If you are permanently in a residential or nursing home, your requirements are your accommodation charge plus £14.10 personal allowance.

Standard deductions are made for fuel or the actual cost of fuel but only where this is shown in the rent – you then declare the net rent.

Resources

Your resources are based on IS (see p344), but with some differences.[3]

Maintenance payments

Maintenance payments (including child support payments) are treated as follows:

• If you are due to receive regular payments, your normal weekly income will be:
  – the weekly amount of those payments if they are made regularly; *or*
  – the average weekly amount you have actually received in the 13 weeks immediately before you claimed, if the payments were not made regularly.
• Payments which are not part of a regular series (ie, lump sums), are treated as capital.

Earnings

In the case of employees the rules for deciding the *period* for which income is paid (see p347) and *when* income is treated as paid (see p348) do not apply. If you receive a payment of income it is likely that it will be counted as income in the week in which it is paid.

If you are affected by a trade dispute, your earnings are taken to be those you would have received had there been no dispute.[4] None of the modifications to treatment of income under IS which apply to people affected by a trade dispute apply.

The calculation of the earnings of the self-employed is usually based on the net profit over a longer period, with reference to accounts if available.

Disregards

• If you are one of a couple not entitled to a £15 disregard (see p357) you will have £10 of your earnings disregarded. If one partner's earnings are less than £10, the remainder of the disregard can be used on any earnings of the other partner.

- There is a £15 earnings disregard if you are entitled to the HPP (see p467).
- Payments you receive from an insurance policy to pay for housing costs not met under the IS regulations are normally taken into account as income. Most of the housing costs not eligible for IS are added into the calculation on the requirements side. However payments from an insurance policy on your home which you use to repay unsecured loans to do repairs and improvements or to pay any premiums on those loans do not count.
- There is no provision for dealing with the situation in which you receive two payments of earnings or income of the same kind from the same source in the same week. Your actual income or earnings for one week should be counted when calculating your resources.
- The £10 disregard from student loans only applies to student claimants who are eligible for a disability premium or who are deaf (in certain circumstances), and to non-student claimants with a student partner.

Applications for low-income certificates

The forms to apply for help with NHS costs are being changed. They are currently called AG1, AG2 and AG3, but will become HC1, HC2 and HC3. At present either form can be used.

To apply for a reduction of the charges on the grounds of low income, you need to complete form AG1(HC1), obtainable from doctors' surgeries, dentists, opticians, hospitals, advice agencies or the Benefits Agency. If your income is low enough to qualify for free services you get certificate AG2(HC2). If your income is higher, you may still qualify for partial reduction of the charges, in which case you get certificate AG3(HC3). If you are applying because you are entitled to IS or income-based JSA of less than 10p you should send in your DSS award letter which will then entitle you to free NHS prescriptions, etc. (Note: a person awarded benefit of less than 10p is not paid IS/income-based JSA.) If you do not have the letter apply on form AG1(HC1). Another person can apply on your behalf if you are unable to act.[5]

Certificates are normally valid for six months but for some applicants the certificates will last for up to 12 or 13 months from the date of the claim.[6] If your circumstances change, you can ask for a fresh assessment. You should make a repeat claim on form AG1(HC1) shortly before the expiry date. There is no right of appeal against a decision, but if you feel a mistake has been made, you can ask for your case to be reconsidered.

3. PRESCRIPTIONS

Free prescriptions

You qualify for free prescriptions if:[7]

- you receive IS, income-based JSA, FC or DWA, or you are a member of the family of someone who does (see p318); *or*
- you are entitled to IS or income-based JSA of less than 10p (see p469); *or*
- your income is low enough (see p466); *or*
- you are under 16, or under 19 and in full-time education; *or*
- you are aged 60 or over;[8] *or*
- you are pregnant; *or*
- you have given birth within the last 12 months (even if the child was stillborn or has since died); *or*
- you are a war disablement pensioner and you need the prescription for your war disability (in which case you claim from your War Pensions Office); *or*
- you suffer from one or more of the following conditions:
  - a continuing physical disability which prevents you leaving your home except with the help of another person;
  - epilepsy requiring continuous anti-convulsive therapy;
  - a permanent fistula, including a caecostomy, ileostomy, laryngostomy or colostomy, needing continuous surgical dressing or an appliance;
  - diabetes mellitus, except where treatment is by diet alone;
  - myxoedema;
  - hypoparathyroidism;
  - diabetes insipidus and other forms of hypopituitarism;
  - forms of hypoadrenalism (including Addison's disease) for which specific substitution therapy is essential;
  - myasthenia gravis.

Claims

You claim by ticking a box on the back of the prescription.

If you are pregnant, you should obtain a form from your doctor, midwife or health visitor (or, in Scotland, the Primary Care Division of the Health Board) and send it to the Family Health Services Authority (in Scotland, the Health Board). You will be sent an exemption certificate which lasts until a year after it is expected you will give birth.

If you are claiming on the ground that you have given birth within the last year (and do not already have an **exemption certificate**) or you are suffering from one of the conditions listed above, you should complete the form in DSS leaflet P11 which you can obtain from your doctor's surgery, a chemist or a Benefits Agency office.

If you are claiming on the grounds of low income, see p466.

Refunds[9]

If you think you may be entitled to free prescriptions but do not have an exemption or low-income certificate, ask the chemist for a special receipt – form FP57 (in Scotland, EC57) – when you pay the charge. The form explains how to claim a refund. You must apply within three months. This period can be extended for as long as you can show good cause.[10]

Pre-payment certificates[11]

If you need a lot of prescriptions, but are not entitled to them free, you can reduce the cost by buying a pre-payment certificate for four months or a year. It saves money if you need more than five prescription items in four months or 14 items in a year. You apply for a certificate on form FP95 (EC95 in Scotland) which you can get at the Benefits Agency, post office or chemist. A refund can be given if you buy a pre-payment certificate and then, within a month, qualify for free prescriptions. If you die within a month, your survivor can also claim a refund.

4. DENTAL TREATMENT AND DENTURES

Free NHS dental treatment and dentures

You qualify for free treatment (including check-ups) and appliances including dentures and bridges)[12] if:

- you receive IS, income-based JSA, FC or DWA, or you are a member of the family of someone who does (see p318); *or*
- you are entitled to IS or income-based JSA of less than 10p (see p469); *or*
- your income is low enough (see p466); *or*
- you are under:
  - 16 (for treatment, dentures or bridges),
  - 18 (for treatment),
  - 19 (for treatment, dentures or bridges if you are still in full-time education); *or*
- you are pregnant and were pregnant when the dentist accepted you for treatment or you have given birth within the last 12 months (even if the child was stillborn or has since died); *or*

- you are a war disablement pensioner and need the treatment or appliances because of your war disability (in which case you claim a refund from the War Pensions Directorate).

Claims

You claim by ticking a box on a form provided by the dentist, so tell the receptionist that you think you qualify for free treatment *before* you have it.

A woman who is pregnant or has a child under the age of one may be asked to show her Family Health Services Authority Exemption Certificate, so it is best to get one before you go for the treatment (see p470).

If you are claiming on the grounds of low income, see p466.

Reduced charges

If you do not qualify for *free* treatment, you may qualify for *partial* help with charges for dental treatment and appliances **on low-income grounds**. Your resources must not exceed your requirements (see pp466-69) by more than one-third of the charge, and you must have less than £8,000 capital. You will be entitled to the difference between the charge for one course of treatment, including any appliances, and three times the amount by which your resources exceed your requirements.[13] To qualify you need certificate AG3(HC3) (see p469). If you paid the full charge when you need not have done, you can obtain a refund (see below).

Refunds[14]

If you paid a charge when you could have had appliances or treatment free or at reduced cost you can obtain a refund. You should get a receipt for the items or treatment you have paid for. You must apply, within three months of paying the charge, using form AG5(HC5) (and AG1(HC1) if do not have a current AG2(HC2) or AG3(HC3) certificate). This period will be extended for as long as you can show good cause.

5. SIGHT TESTS AND GLASSES

Free sight tests and vouchers for glasses

There is no set charge for sight tests so it may be worth shopping around for them. Some opticians do not charge at all.

You qualify for a free NHS test if:[15]

- you receive IS, income-based JSA, FC or DWA, or you are a member of the family of someone who does (see p318); *or*
- your income is low enough (see p466); *or*
- you are under 16 or under 19 and in full-time education; *or*
- you are registered blind or partially sighted; *or*
- you have been prescribed complex lenses; *or*
- you have been diagnosed as suffering from diabetes or glaucoma; *or*
- you are aged 40 or over and are the parent, brother, sister or child of someone suffering from glaucoma; *or*
- you are a war disablement pensioner and require the sight test because of your war disability (in which case you claim from your War Pensions Office); *or*
- you are a patient of the Hospital Eye Service.

Claims

To claim, tell the optician before you have the test. You need certificate AG2(HC2) (see p469). If you do not have an AG2(HC2) before the test, you must apply for one within two weeks of the test and then apply for a refund (see p475).

Reduced-cost sight tests

If you do not qualify for a *free* eye test, you may be entitled to *partial* help with the cost of a private sight test **on low-income grounds.**[16] You pay the smaller of the actual sight test charge or what your certificate says you can pay. To qualify, you need certificate AG3(HC3) (see p469). If you do not have an AG3(HC3) before the test, you must apply for one within two weeks of the test and then apply for a refund (see p475).

'Full-value' vouchers for glasses and contact lenses

If your sight test shows you need glasses, you are given a prescription by the optician which is valid for two years.

You will qualify for a 'full-value' voucher to meet the cost of glasses or contact lenses if:[17]

- you receive IS, income-based JSA, FC or DWA; *or*

- you are a member of the family of someone who does (see p318); *or*
- you are entitled to IS or income-based JSA of less than 10p (see p469); *or*
- your income is low enough (see p466); *or*
- you are under 16 or under 19 and in full-time education; *or*
- you are a Hospital Eye Service patient needing frequent changes of glasses or contact lenses; *or*
- you have been prescribed complex lenses.

Certain war pensioners can obtain refunds of charges for glasses or contact lenses, even though they do not qualify for vouchers (see below). If you qualify for a voucher, the optician will give you one if:[18]

- you require glasses or contact lenses for the first time; *or*
- your new prescription differs from your old one; *or*
- your old glasses have worn out through fair wear and tear; *or*
- you are under 16 and have lost or damaged your old glasses or contact lenses and the cost of repair or replacement is not covered by insurance or warranty; *or*
- you are ill and, as a result of your illness, have lost or damaged your glasses or contact lenses and the cost of repair or replacement is not covered by insurance or warranty *and*:
  - you receive IS, income-based JSA, FC or DWA, or you are a member of the family of someone who does (see p318); *or*
  - your income is low enough (see p466); *or*
  - you have been prescribed complex lenses.

The voucher is valid for six months.[19] Its value depends on the type of lenses you need. (A Benefits Agency booklet called *NHS sight tests and vouchers for glasses* (G11) lists the different value vouchers available.) It does not, therefore, automatically cover the full cost of your glasses. It is supposed to enable you to buy glasses or contact lenses (or have your existing ones repaired) without having to pay anything yourself (except in the case of complex lenses when you are expected to contribute to the cost unless you would qualify for a voucher on other grounds), but you may have to shop around to find a cheap enough pair. If you cannot find a cheap enough pair, or if you choose to buy a more expensive pair, you will have to make up the difference yourself.

You must have the voucher *before* you buy the glasses or contact lenses. The circumstances in which refunds can be made are very limited (see p475).

Reduced-value vouchers

If you do not qualify for a full-value voucher, you may qualify for a lesser-value voucher on low-income grounds. It will be worth a full-value one less three times the amount by which your resources exceed your requirements (see p466). To qualify, you need certificate AG3(HC3) (see p469) before you pay for the glasses or contact lenses.

Refunds

Sight tests

Refunds can only be made if you are entitled to free or reduced-cost sight tests and apply for certificate AG2(HC2) or AG3(HC3) within two weeks of having the test (see p469). You will get a refund if you then send the certificate with a receipt from the optician to the Family Health Services Authority within three months of having the test.

Glasses and contact lenses

Refunds will only be made if the glasses or contact lenses were prescribed through the Hospital Eye Service *and* you would have had a voucher on the grounds of low income if you had had certificate AG2(HC2) or AG3(HC3), or you are getting IS, income-based JSA, FC or DWA. Ask the hospital or Benefits Agency for form AG5(HC5) (and form AG1(HC1) if you want to claim and you do not hold a current AG2(HC2) or AG3(HC3) certificate). You must submit your claim within one month of the date of the receipt.

War pensioners

If you can only qualify for a free sight test, free glasses or contact lenses because you are a war pensioner, you must pay the charges and then claim a refund from Treatment Group, War Pensions Directorate, DSS, Norcross, Blackpool FY5 3TA.

Home visits

If you have certificate AG2(HC2) and you want to have your eyes tested at home, you can be visited free of charge. If you have certificate AG3(HC3), you can use it to reduce the cost of the visit.

6. WIGS AND FABRIC SUPPORTS[20]

Free wigs and fabric supports

You qualify for free NHS wigs and fabric supports if:

- you receive IS, income-based JSA, FC or DWA, or you are a member of the family of someone who does (see p318); *or*
- you are entitled to IS or income-based JSA of less than 10p (see p469); *or*
- your income is low enough (see p466); *or*
- you are under 16 or under 19 and in full-time education; *or*
- you are a hospital in-patient when the wig or fabric support is supplied; *or*
- you are a war disablement pensioner and need the wig or fabric support for your war injury.

Claims

You claim when you go to the hospital to have the wig or fabric support fitted. You may have to show some proof that you are entitled to free provision. You need certificate AG2(HC2) (see p469).

Refunds

The rules are the same as for dental treatment (see p472).

Reduced charges

The rules are the same as for dental treatment (see p472). To qualify, you need certificate AG3(HC3) (see p469).

7. FARES TO HOSPITAL[21]

Who can get full help

You qualify if you are attending an NHS hospital for treatment, or a disablement services centre *and*:

- you receive IS, income-based JSA, FC or DWA, or you are a member of the family of someone who does (see p318); *or*
- you are entitled to IS or income-based JSA of less than 10p (see p469); *or*
- your income is low enough (see p466); *or*

- you are a patient at a sexually transmitted disease clinic more than 15 miles from your home; *or*
- you are a war disablement pensioner and the treatment is for your war injury.

You also get help travelling to a mainland hospital if you live in the Highlands and Islands of Scotland or the Isles of Scilly.

Claims

Payment is made at the hospital each time you visit.

You usually have to get yourself to hospital, but once you are there you are paid the cost of the return trip. If you receive a qualifying benefit, you will need to show proof of this. However, you can ask the hospital to send you the money in advance. If you cannot get this in time you may be able to get a crisis loan from your local Benefits Agency office (see p450). You will need certificate AG2(HC2) (see p469).

What costs can be paid

You are expected to use the cheapest form of transport available. You can claim for:

- normal public transport fares;
- estimated petrol costs;
- a reasonable contribution to a local voluntary car scheme;
- taxi fares, but only if there is no alternative for all or part of the journey, or you cannot use public transport because of a disability.

The travelling costs of a companion will also be paid if it is necessary for you to be accompanied on medical grounds.

Refunds

The rules are the same as for dental treatment (see p472).

Partial help

If your resources exceed your requirements and you have savings of less than £8,000, you will get the difference between your excess income and your weekly fares. To qualify, you need certificate AG3(HC3) (see p469).

Visiting patients

If you are receiving IS or income-based JSA and are visiting a close relative or partner, you may be entitled to help from the social fund (see p442).

If you are visiting a war pensioner who is being treated for her/his war injury, you may also be entitled to help.

8. FREE MILK AND VITAMINS[22]

Free milk tokens

The following people qualify for free milk tokens:

- Disabled children aged 5 to 16 who cannot go to school because of their disability (claim on form FW20 available from your Benefits Agency office).
- Expectant mothers who are receiving IS or income-based JSA (or who are a member of the family of someone who is – see p318). You do not have to wait for the Certificate of Expected Date of Confinement. A note from your doctor or midwife will entitle you to free milk tokens at once.
- Children under 5 whose family receives IS or income-based JSA.

The milk tokens for each person entitled can be exchanged for 7 x 568 millilitres/8 half litres of liquid cow's milk a week. If they are for a child under one they can be exchanged for 900 grammes of dried milk or to buy milk for the mother if she is breastfeeding. You can use milk tokens at a clinic to get dried milk or they can be exchanged for fresh milk from suppliers who are then reimbursed by the Secretary of State. Tokens cannot be used to purchase soya milk. Suppliers can accept milk tokens as part-payment if the milk you buy is more expensive than the basic-cost milk.[23] If you cannot find a supplier who will accept your tokens you can apply to the Benefits Agency to cash them.[24]

If you lose your milk tokens or they are stolen or accidentally destroyed, the Benefits Agency will replace them.[25]

If you do not receive milk tokens to which you are entitled, they should be replaced by the Benefits Agency if this was due to '... some act or omission on [its] part'.[26]

If you are absent from home, with the result that you miss some of the milk covered by your token, your supplier can give you a refund for the pints you have missed. You have to ask the supplier to do this during the period within which the token is valid.[27]

Free milk for children in day-care

Children under 5 with a registered childminder, a registered day nursery, or a local authority or day nursery which is not required to register, can get 189 millilitres of milk or dried milk free each day they are looked after for two hours or more.[28] This entitlement is in addition to any entitlement outlined above. The childminder or organiser of the nursery applies to the Benefits Agency. Children under one are allowed the equivalent amount of dried milk instead.

Reduced-cost milk

Anyone attending a maternity or childcare clinic can buy dried milk at a reduced price.

Families on family credit (FC) with children under one can get dried milk at an even lower price from maternity and child health clinics.[29] You are allowed to buy up to 900 grammes of dried milk a week for each child under one. You need evidence that you get FC and of your child's age. If you do not have this evidence through 'some act or omission' on the part of the Secretary of State, you can get a refund.[30]

Free vitamins

The following qualify for free vitamins:[31]

* Expectant mothers or those breastfeeding a child under one who are receiving IS or income-based JSA (or who are a member of the family of someone who is – see p318).
* Children under 5 whose family receives IS or income-based JSA.

Entitlement gives 20 millilitres of vitamin drops every 13 weeks for children and expectant mothers. Breastfeeding mothers can have the same or 90 tablets instead. Vitamins are available from child health and maternity clinics.

If you are not entitled to free vitamins, you can buy them cheaply if you are attending a maternity or childcare clinic.

Other benefits and sources of help

This appendix briefly covers other benefits and sources of help for people on low incomes. It does not cover non-means-tested social security benefits and other schemes. For details of these, see CPAG's *Rights Guide to Non-Means-Tested Benefits* and the *Disability Rights Handbook* (see Appendix 4).

1. Education benefits

Free school meals

Children of families receiving income support (IS) or income-based jobseeker's allowance (JSA) are entitled to free school meals as are 16/18-year-olds receiving these benefits in their own right.

Clothing grants

Education authorities can give grants for school uniforms and other school clothes. Each authority can determine its own eligibility rules.

School transport

Education authorities must provide free transport to school for pupils living more than three miles away (two miles if aged under 8 or under 11 in Northern Ireland).

Education grants

Some grants are mandatory, others discretionary. Contact your education authority for details.

2. Housing grants

Local authority grants

Various types of grant are available to help with the cost of improving your home. These include housing renovation grants, disabled facilities grants and minor works grants. Some grants are mandatory, most are discretionary and all are subject to a means test. Contact your local authority for details.

Home insulation grants

These are available under the Government's Home Energy Efficiency Scheme for loft insulation and draught-proofing. For details, contact the EAGA Ltd, Freepost, PO Box 130, Newcastle-upon-Tyne NE99 2RP (tel: 0800 181 667; Minicom: 0191 233 1054).

3. Social services

Local authority social services departments have statutory duties to provide a range of practical and financial help to families, children, young people and people with disabilities. These include:

* help and support for children in need, including financial assistance under section 17 of the Children Act 1989;
* home care, meals, telephones, aids, adaptations, travel concessions for people with disabilities (reasonable charges can be made for these services);
* provision and funding of residential or nursing care (see p93) and residential accommodation for people who are destitute and whose health is at risk (see p81).

Contact your local authority social services department for details.

4. The Independent Living (1993) Fund

The fund gives grants to help severely disabled people aged 16-65 inclusive pay for care services in their own home. To qualify, you must be receiving the highest rate care component of disability living allowance and have less than £8,000 capital. You must be receiving at least £200 worth of services a week from social services and need additional care up to a total value of £500 a week. For more details, contact your local authority social services department, or the Independent Living Fund, PO Box 183, Nottingham NG8 3RD (tel 0115 9428191/2).

5. The Family Fund

The Family Fund gives grants and other help to families with children who have severe disabilities. It commonly helps with things like holidays, furniture, equipment and transport needs. For details, contact the Family Fund, PO Box 50, York YO1 1UY.

6. The Macfarlane and Eileen Trusts and the Fund

The Macfarlane Trust gives grants to people who have haemophilia and have been infected with HIV through treatment for their haemophilia. It also administers the Eileen Trust which helps people infected with HIV through NHS blood transfusions, or transplants etc.

For further information, contact the Macfarlane Trust, PO Box 627, London SW1H 0QG (tel: 0171 233 0342).

7. Charities

There are hundreds of charities which provide a variety of help to people on low incomes. Your local authority social services department may know about appropriate charities or you can consult the *Charities Digest*, in your local library.

Useful addresses

The President of the Independent Tribunal Service and regional chairpersons

The President
HH Judge K Bassingthwaighte
The President's Office
4th Floor, Whittington House
19-30 Alfred Place
London WC1E 7LW
Tel: 0171 814 6500

The President (Northern Ireland)
Mr CG MacLynn
6th Floor, Cleaver House
3 Donegal Square North
Belfast BT1 5GA
Tel: 01232 539900

Social Security Appeal Tribunals

National Chairperson
Mr R Huggins
The President's Office
4th Floor, Whittington House
19-30 Alfred Place
London WC1E 7LW
Tel: 0171 814 6500

Regional Chairpersons

North East
Mr JW Tinnion
3rd Floor, York House
York Place
Leeds LS1 2ED
Tel: 0113 245 1246

Midlands
Mr IG Harrison
3rd Floor, Auchinleck House
Broad Street
Birmingham B15 1DL
Tel: 0121 643 6464

South East
Mr RG Smithson
Whittington House
19-30 Alfred Place
London WC1E 7LW
Tel: 0171 957 9200

North West
Mr RS Sim
36 Dale Street
Liverpool L2 5UZ
Tel: 0151 236 4334

Wales and South West
Mr CB Stephens
Oxford House
Hills Street, The Hayes
Cardiff CF1 2DR
Tel: 01222 378071

Scotland
Mrs LT Parker
Wellington House
134-36 Wellington Street
Glasgow G2 2XL
Tel: 0141 353 1441

Child Support Appeal Tribunals
Independent Tribunal Service
8th Floor
Anchorage 2
Anchorage Quay
Salford Quays M5 2YN
Tel: 0345 626311

Disability Appeal Tribunals
DATs Central Office
PO Box 168
Nottingham NG1 5JX
Tel: 0345 247246

**Offices of the Social Security
  Commissioners**
England and Wales
Harp House
83 Farringdon Street
London EC4A 4DH
Tel: 0171 353 5145

Scotland
23 Melville Street
Edinburgh EH3 7PW
Tel: 0131 225 2201

Northern Ireland
Lancashire House
5 Linenhall Street
Belfast BT2 8AA
Tel: 01232 332344

Benefits Agency Chief Executive
Mr P Mathison
Quarry House
Quarry Hill
Leeds LS2 7UA
Tel: 0113 232 4000

**Severe Hardship Claims Unit
  (16/17-year-olds)**
174 Pitt Street
Glasgow G2 4DZ
Tel: 0141 225 4259

DSS Solicitor
New Court
48 Carey Street
London WC2A 2LS
Tel: 0171 962 8000

**Disability Working Allowance
  Unit**
Diadem House
2 The Pavilion
Preston PR2 2GN
Tel 01772 883300

Family Credit Unit
Government Buildings
Warbreck Hill Road
Blackpool FY2 OAX
Tel: 01253 500050

Independent Review Service for the Social Fund
4th Floor, Centre City Podium
5 Hill Street
Birmingham B5 4UB
Tel: 0121 606 2100

Central Adjudication Services
Quarry House, Quarry Hill
Leeds LS2 7UA
Tel: 0113 2324000

Health Benefits Division
Sandyford House
Newcastle-upon-Tyne NE2 1DB

Health Service Ombudsman
Millbank Tower
London SW1P 4QP
Tel: 0171 217 4051

Local Government Ombudsman

England
21 Queen Anne's Gate
London SW1H 9BU
Tel: 0171 915 3210

Scotland
23 Walker Street
Edinburgh EH3 7HX
Tel: 0131 225 5300

Wales
Derwen House
Court Road
Bridgend CF31 1BN
Tel: 01656 661325

Northern Ireland
Progressive House
33 Wellington Place
Belfast BT1 6HN
Tel: 01232 233821

The Parliamentary Ombudsman
Office of the Parliamentary
Commissioner
Church House
Great Smith Street
London SW1P 3BW
Tel: 0171 276 2130

Getting information and advice

Independent advice and representation

It is often difficult for unsupported individuals to get a positive response from the Benefits Agency. You may be taken more seriously if it is clear you have taken advice about your entitlement or have an adviser assisting you.

If you want advice or help with a benefit problem the following agencies may be able to assist.

- Citizens Advice Bureaux (CABx) and other local advice centres provide information and advice about benefits and may be able to represent you.
- Law Centres can often help in a similar way to CABx/advice centres.
- Local authority welfare rights workers provide a service in many areas and some arrange advice sessions and take-up campaigns locally.
- Local organisations for particular groups of claimants may offer help. For instance, there are Unemployed Centres, pensioners groups, centres for people with disabilities etc.
- Claimants Unions give advice in some areas. For details of your nearest group contact the Plymouth Claimants Union, PO Box 21, Plymouth PL1 1QS or The Swindon Unemployed Movement, Room 20, Pinehurst People's Centre, Beech Avenue, Pinehurst, Swindon, Wiltshire.
- Some social workers and probation officers (but not all) help with benefit problems, especially if they are already working with you on another problem.
- Solicitors can give free legal advice under the green form scheme (pink form in Scotland). This does not cover the cost of representation at an appeal hearing but can cover the cost of preparing written submissions and obtaining evidence such as medical reports. However, solicitors do not always have a good working knowledge of the benefit rules and you may need to shop around until you find one who does.
- Refugee Council, 3 Bondway, London SW8 1SJ.

• Joint Council for the Welfare of Immigrants (JCWI), 115 Old Street, London EC1V 9JR.

If you cannot find any of these agencies in the telephone book your local library should have details.

Unfortunately, CPAG is unable to deal with enquiries directly from members of the public but if you are an adviser you can phone the advice line, which is usually open from 2.00 to 4.00 pm on Monday to Thursday – 0171 253 6569. This is a special phone line; do not ring the main CPAG number. Alternatively, you can write to us at Citizens' Rights Office, CPAG, 4th Floor, 1-5 Bath Street, London EC1V 9PY. We can also take up a limited number of complex cases including appeals to the Social Security Commissioners or courts if referred by an adviser.

Advice from the Benefits Agency

You can obtain free telephone advice on benefits on the following numbers. These are for general advice and not specific queries on individual claims.

Enquiry line for people with disabilities 0800 882 200
   (Minicom 0800 243 355)
Disability Working Allowance Helpline 01772 883 300
   (this is not a freephone line)
Family Credit Helpline 01253 500 050 (this is not a freephone line)
Northern Ireland Benefit Enquiry Line 0800 616 757

If English is not your first language, ask your local Benefits Agency office to arrange for advice in your own language.

Books, leaflets and periodicals

Many of the books listed here will be in your main public library. Stationery Office books are available from Stationery Office bookshops and also from many others. They may be ordered by post, telephone or fax from: The Publications Centre, PO Box 276, London SW8 5DT (tel: 0171 873 9090; fax: 0171 873 8200. General enquiries tel: 0171 873 0011; fax: 0171 873 8247).

1. Textbooks

Claim in Time by M Partington (Legal Action Group, 3rd edn, 1994). Detailed study of the rules on the time limits for claiming benefits. Available from Legal Action Group, 242 Pentonville Road, London N1 9UN.

2. Caselaw and legislation

Social Security Case Law – Digest of Commissioners' Decisions by D Neligan (Stationery Office, looseleaf in two volumes). Summaries of commissioners' decisions grouped together by subject.

The Law Relating to Child Support (Stationery Office, looseleaf in one volume).

The Law Relating to Social Security (Stationery Office, looseleaf in 11 volumes). All the legislation but without any comment. Known as the 'Blue Book'. Volumes 6, 7, 8 and 11 deal with means-tested benefits.

Child Support: The Legislation by E Jacobs and G Douglas (Sweet & Maxwell), 3rd edn, £36 incl p&p from CPAG Ltd, 1-5 Bath Street, London EC1V 9PY – if you are a CPAG member. Contains the primary legislation with a detailed commentary.

CPAG's Income Related Benefits: The Legislation (Mesher) updated by P Wood (Sweet & Maxwell, 1997/98 edn available from August/September, £45.95 with December supplement, incl p&p from CPAG Ltd, 1-5 Bath Street, London EC1V 9PY – if you are a CPAG member). Contains the most useful legislation with a detailed commentary. If ordered from CPAG before 31 July 1997, the price is reduced to £42.50.

CPAG's Housing Benefit and Council Tax Benefit Legislation by L Findlay, R Poynter and M Ward (CPAG Ltd, 1997/98 edn available late 1997, £43.95 (incl Supplement) incl p&p from CPAG Ltd, 1-5 Bath Street, London EC1V 9PY). Contains the main legislation with a detailed commentary. If the main work and supplement are both ordered from CPAG before 31 July 1997, the total price is reduced to £39.95. The reduced price of just the main volume if ordered on the same conditions is £32.

Medical and Disability Appeal Tribunals: The Legislation by M Rowland (Sweet & Maxwell), 3rd edn, 1997, available from late 1997, approx £36 incl p&p from CPAG Ltd, 1-5 Bath Street, London EC1V 9PY – if you are a CPAG member. Reduced to £33 if ordered from CPAG before 31 July 1997.

3. Official guidance

*Since the HMSO became the Stationery Office, certain Departmental guides have not been updated and appear to be no longer available to the public.

Adjudication Officers' Guide (Stationery Office, looseleaf in 13 volumes). Volumes 4-8 deal with means-tested benefits. Supplementary guidance notes are issued internally – eg, Memo AOG Vol 3/77.

Benefits Agency Guide, *IS for 16/17-year-olds*, Stationery Office, amended February 1996.

Charging for Residential Accommodation Guide (Department of Health in one volume).

Child Support Adjudication Guide (Stationery Office, looseleaf in one volume).

Child Support Guide (Child Support Agency, looseleaf in eight volumes). Replaced the *Child Support Manual* during 1996.

Field Officers' Guide (Child Support Agency, looseleaf in one volume).

Housing Benefit and Council Tax Benefit Guidance Manual (Stationery Office, looseleaf in one volume).

Income Support Guide (Stationery Office, looseleaf in eight volumes). Procedural guide issued to Benefits Agency staff.

The Social Fund Guide (Stationery Office, looseleaf in two volumes).

The Social Fund Cold Weather Payments Handbook (Stationery Office, looseleaf in one volume).

**The Social Fund Customer and Application Details Guide*, (Stationery Office, looseleaf in one volume).

**The Social Fund Decision and Review Guide*, (Stationery Office, looseleaf in one volume).

The Social Fund Maternity and Funeral Payments Guide (Stationery Office, looseleaf in one volume).

4. Tribunal handbooks

Social Security Appeal Tribunals: A Guide to Procedure (Stationery Office).

5. Leaflets

The Benefits Agency publishes many leaflets which cover particular benefits or particular groups of claimants or contributors. They have been greatly improved in recent years and the bigger ones extend to 48-page booklets. They are free from your local Benefits Agency office or on Freephone 0800 666 555. If you want to order larger numbers of leaflets, or receive information about new leaflets, you can join the Benefits Agency Publicity Register by writing to the Benefits Agency, 3rd Floor South, 1 Trevelyan Square, Leeds LS1 6EB or by phoning 0645 540 000 (local rate). Free leaflets on HB/CTB are available from the relevant department of your local council.

6. Periodicals

The *Welfare Rights Bulletin* is published every two months by CPAG. It covers developments in social security law and updates this *Handbook* between editions. The annual subscription is £21 but it is sent automatically to CPAG Rights and Comprehensive Members.

7. Other publications – general

Rights Guide to Non-Means-Tested Benefits, £8.95 (£3 for claimants).
Jobseeker's Allowance Handbook, £6.95 (£2.50 for claimants).
Child Support Handbook, £9.95 (£3.30 for claimants).
Council Tax Handbook, £9.95.

Debt Advice Handbook, £10.95.
A Guide to Money Advice in Scotland, £14.95.
Migration and Social Security Handbook, £10.95.
Fuel Rights Handbook, £8.95.
Guide to Housing Benefit and Council Tax Benefit, £15.95.
Rights Guide for Home Owners, £8.95.
Disability Rights Handbook, £10.50.
Benefits: CHAR's Guide (for single homeless), £9.50
Youthaid's Guide to Training and Benefits for Young People, £6.95.
Unemployment and Training Rights Handbook (Unemployment Unit, £9.95).
Immigration and Nationality Law Handbook (Joint Council for the Welfare of Immigrants (JCWI), £12.99).

Most of these are available from CPAG Ltd, 4th Floor, 1-5 Bath Street, London EC1V 9PY. Prices include p&p.

Abbreviations used in the notes

AC   Appeal Cases
All ER   All England Reports
Art(s)   Article(s)
CA   Court of Appeal
CAO   Chief Adjudication Officer
CMLR   Common Market Law Reports
CSBO   Chief Supplementary Benefit Officer
DC   Divisional Court
ECJ   European Court of Justice
ECR   European Court Reports
FLR   Family Law Reports
HBRB   Housing Benefit Review Board
HC   High Court
HLR   Housing Law Reports

IRS   Independent Review Service for the Social Fund
NAB   National Assistance Board
para(s)   paragraph(s)
QBD   Queen's Bench Division
r   rule
reg(s)   regulation(s)
RSC   Rules of the Supreme Court
s(s)   Section(s)
SBAT   Supplementary Benefit Appeal Tribunal
SBC   Supplementary Benefits Commission
Sch(s)   Schedule(s)
SCLR   Scottish Civil Law Reports
WLR   Weekly Law Reports

Acts of Parliament

AIA 1996   Asylum and Immigration Act 1996
CA 1989   Children Act 1989
CSA 1991   Child Support Act 1991

HSS&SSA Act 1983   Health and Social Services and Social Security Adjudication Act 1983
JSA 1995   Jobseekers Act 1995
LAA 1988   Legal Aid Act 1988
NAA 1948   National Assistance Act 1948

NHSA 1977	National Health Service Act 1977	RHA 1984	Registered Homes Act 1984
NHSCCA 1990	National Health Service and Community Care Act 1990	SSAA 1992	Social Security Administration Act 1992
NHS(S)A 1978	National Health Service (Scotland) Act 1978	SSCBA 1992	Social Security Contributions and Benefits Act 1992

European law

Secondary legislation is made under the Treaty of Rome 1957, the Single European Act and the Maastricht Treaty in the form of Regulations (EEC Reg) and Directives (EEC Dir).

Regulations

Each set of regulations has a statutory instrument (SI) number and a date. You ask for them by giving their date and number.

CB Regs	The Child Benefit (General) Regulations 1976 No.965
CC(DIS) Regs	The Community Charge (Deductions from Income Support) Regulations 1990 No.107
CS(AIAMA) Regs	The Child Support (Arrears, Interest and Adjustment of Maintenance Assessments) Regulations 1992 No.1816
CS(C&E) Regs	The Child Support (Collection and Enforcement) Regulations 1992 No.1989
CS(CEOFM) Regs	The Child Support (Collection and Enforcement of Other Forms of Maintenance) Regulations 1992 No.2643
CS(IED) Regs	The Child Support (Information, Evidence and Disclosure) Regulations 1992 No.1812
CS(MA) Regs	The Child Support (Miscellaneous Amendments) Regulations 1996 No.1945
CS(MAP) Regs	The Child Support (Maintenance Assessment Procedure) Regulations 1992 No.1813
CS(MASC) Regs	The Child Support (Maintenance Assessments and Special Cases) Regulations 1992 No.1815

CSAT(P) Regs	The Child Support Appeal Tribunals (Procedure) Regulations 1992 No.2641
CT(DIS) Regs	The Council Tax (Deductions from Income Support) Regulations 1993 No.494
CTB Regs	The Council Tax Benefit (General) Regulations 1992 No.1814
DWA Regs	The Disability Working Allowance (General) Regulations 1991 No.2887
DWA&IS Regs	The Disability Working Allowance and Income Support (General) Amendment Regulations 1995 No.482
F(DIS) Regs	The Fines (Deductions from Income Support) Regulations 1992 No.2182
FC Regs	The Family Credit (General) Regulations 1987 No.1973
HB Regs	The Housing Benefit (General) Regulations 1987 No.1971
HB(Amdt) Regs	The Housing Benefit (General) Amendment Regulations 1995 No.1644
HB(Amdt) Regs 1996	The Housing Benefit (General) Amendment Regulations 1996 No.965
I(EEA)O	Immigration (European Economic Area) Order 1994 No.1895
IRB&JSA(PA) Amdt Regs	The Income-related Benefits & Jobseeker's Allowance (Personal Allowances for Children and Young Persons) (Amendment) Regulations 1996 No.2545
IRBS(Amdt 2) Regs	The Income-related Benefits Schemes (Miscellaneous Amendments) (No.2) Regulations 1995 No.1339
IRBS(MA) Regs	The Income-related Benefits Schemes (Miscellaneous Amendments) (No.3) Regulations 1994 No.1807
IS Regs	The Income Support (General) Regulations 1987 No.1967
IS(AT) Regs	The Income Support (General) Amendment and Transitional Regulations 1995 No.2287
IS(JSACA) Regs	The Income Support (General) (Jobseeker's Allowance Consequential Amendments) Regulations 1996 No.206
IS(LR) Regs	The Income Support (Liable Relatives) Regulations 1990 No.1777
JSA Regs	The Jobseeker's Allowance Regulations 1996 No.207
NA(AR) Regs	The National Assistance (Assessment and Resources) Regulations 1992 No.2977

NHS(CDA) Regs	The National Health Service (Charges for Drugs and Appliances) Regulations 1980 No.1503
NHS(GOS) Regs	The National Health Service (General Ophthalmic Services) Regulations 1986 No.975
NHS(OCP) Regs	The National Health Service (Optical Charges and Payments) Regulations 1989 No.396
NHS(TERC) Regs	The National Health Service (Travelling Expenses and Remission of Charges) Regulations 1988 No.551
RA(RPORE) Regs	The Residential Accommodation (Relevant Premises, Ordinary Residence and Exemptions) Regulations 1993 No.477
RCH Regs	The Residential Care Homes Regulations 1984 No.1345
RO(AF)O	The Rent Officers (Additional Functions) Order 1995 No.1642
SF(App) Regs	The Social Fund (Applications) Regulations 1988 No.524
SF(AR) Regs	The Social Fund (Application for Review) Regulations 1988 No.34
SF(Misc) Regs	The Social Fund (Miscellaneous Provisions) Regulations 1990 No.1788
SF(RDB) Regs	The Social Fund (Recovery by Deductions from Benefits) Regulations 1988 No.35
SFCWP Regs	The Social Fund Cold Weather Payments (General) Regulations 1988 No.1724
SFM&FE Regs	The Social Fund Maternity and Funeral Expenses (General) Regulations 1987 No.481
SS(AA) Regs	The Social Security (Attendance Allowance) Regulations 1991 No.2740
SS(Adj) Regs	The Social Security (Adjudication) Regulations 1995 No.1801
SS(BWB) Regs	The Social Security (Back to Work Bonus) Regulations 1996 No.193
SS(BWB) (No.2) Regs	The Social Security (Back to Work Bonus) (No.2) Regulations 1996 No.2570
SS(CMB) Regs	The Social Security (Child Maintenance Bonus) Regulations 1996 No.3195
SS(C&P) Regs	The Social Security (Claims and Payments) Regulations 1987 No.1968
SS(Cr) Regs	The Social Security (Credits) Regulations 1975 No.556

SS(DLA) Regs	The Social Security (Disability Living Allowance) Regulations 1991 No.2890
SS(ICA) Regs	The Social Security (Invalid Care Allowance) Regulations 1976 No.409
SS(ICB) Trans Regs	The Social Security (Incapacity Benefit) (Transitional) Regulations 1995 No.310
SS(HIP) Regs	The Social Security (Hospital In-Patients) Regulations 1975 No.555
SS(PAOR) Regs	The Social Security (Payments on account, Overpayments and Recovery) Regulations 1988 No.664
SS(PFA)MA Regs	The Social Security (Persons from Abroad) Miscellaneous Amendments Regulations 1996 No.30
SS(SDA) Regs	The Social Security (Severe Disablement Allowance) Regulations 1984 No.1303
SSCP Regs	The Social Security Commissioners Procedure Regulations 1987 No.214
WF Regs	The Welfare Foods Regulations 1996 No.1434

Other information

See Appendix 4 for fuller details of the following publications.

Advice Notes	Social Fund Inspectors' Advice Notes.
AOG	The *Adjudication Officers' Guide*.
BA Handbook	*IS for 16/17-years-olds*.
CSAG	The *Child Support Adjudication Guide*.
CSRCG	The *Child Support Requirement to Co-operate Guide*.
CWPH	The *Social Fund Cold Weather Payments Handbook*.
GM	The *Housing Benefit and Council Tax Benefit Guidance Manual*.
HC Handbook	*IS for Homeless Customers, Hostels, Residential Care and Nursing Homes*.
IS Guide	This is a largely procedural guide to the implementation of income support, which is issued to adjudication officers/DSS staff.
SF Dir/SFI Dir	Direction(s) on the discretionary social fund. They are printed in the *Social Fund Guide* and Mesher Wood.
SFCADG	The *Social Fund Customer and Application Details Guide*.

SFDRG	The *Social Fund Decision and Review Guide*.
SFG	The *Social Fund Guide*.
SFROG	The *Social Fund Review Officers' Guide*.

References like CIS/142/1990 and R(SB) 3/89 are references to commissioners' decisions (see p167).

Notes

References are to the statutes and regulations as amended up to 18 March 1997. All regulations are (General) Regulations unless otherwise stated. There is a full list of abbreviations in Appendix 5.

PART TWO: INCOME SUPPORT

Chapter 2: The basic rules of entitlement
(pp 8-23)

1 s124 SCCBA 1992
2 Reg 22A IS Regs; reg 19(5) DWA&IS Regs
3 para 18339 AOG
4 Sch 2 para 12(5) IS Regs
5 Reg 5 IS Regs
6 Reg 5(7) IS Regs
7 R(IS) 5/95
8 R(IS) 1/93
9 CIS/434/1994
10 Reg 5(2)(b)(i) and (3B) IS Regs
11 Reg 5(2)(b)(ii) IS Regs
12 Reg 5(2)(a) IS Regs; CIS/267/1993
13 Reg 5(3) IS Regs
14 Reg 5(5) IS Regs
15 Reg 5(4) IS Regs
16 Reg 6 IS Regs
17 CIS/649/1992
18 CIS/514/1990; *Smith v CAO*, (CA) (unreported)
19 s124(1)(d) SSCBA 1992
20 Reg 12 IS Regs; s142 SSCBA 1992 and reg 5(2) CB Regs
21 Regs 4ZA and 13(2) (a) – (e) IS Regs
22 R(IS) 9/94

23 CIS/11766/1996
24 R(IS) 9/94
25 R(SB) 2/87
26 CIS/11441/1995
27 R(IS) 9/94
28 Reg 7(4), (5) and (6) CB Regs
29 Reg 12 IS Regs; reg 7 CB Regs
30 Regs 4ZA and 61 IS Regs, definition of 'student'
31 Reg 61, definitions of 'student' and 'course of advanced education'
32 Reg 61 IS Regs definition of 'full-time course of advanced education', and 'full-time course of study'
33 Para 35045 AOG
34 R(SB) 40/83; R(SB) 41/83
35 CIS/152/1994
36 See note 32
37 Regs 4ZA and 61 and Sch 1B IS Regs
38 Sch 1B paras 10, 11 and 12 IS Regs
39 C7/89(IS) (N Ireland); CIS/368/1992
40 *Driver v the CAO*, CA, 6 December 1996 (unreported)
41 CIS/576/1994 (The Government has appealed to the Court

of Appeal (*CAO v Webber*). The case is due to be heard in June 1997.)
42 CIS/152/1994
43 Reg 4(1) and (2)(a) and (b) IS Regs
44 Reg 4(2)(c) IS Regs
45 Sch 7 paras 11 and 11A IS Regs

Chapter 3: How your benefit is calculated
(pp 24-49)

2. Housing costs
(pp 25-44)

1 Sch 3 para 1 IS Regs
2 Sch 3 paras 15-17 IS Regs
3 Sch 3 para 4(1) IS Regs
4 Sch 3 para 2 IS Regs
5 CSB/213/1987
6 Sch 3 para 5(5) IS Regs; CIS/743/1993
7 Reg 2(1) IS Regs; reg 2(1) HB Regs; R(SB) 22/87
8 CIS/636/1992 (confirmed by the Court of Appeal in *Brain v CAO*, 2 December 1993)
9 Sch 3 para 2(2) IS Regs
10 Sch 3 para 3(1) IS Regs
11 s137(1) SSCBA 1992, definition of 'dwelling';

reg 2(1) IS Regs, definition of 'dwelling occupied as the home'
12 CIS/297/1994
13 Sch 3 para 3(7) IS Regs
14 Sch 3 para 3(10) IS Regs
15 Sch 3 para 3(11) IS Regs
16 Sch 3 para 3(8) and (9) IS Regs
17 *R v Penwith District Council ex parte Burt*
18 Sch 3 para 3(6) IS Regs
19 CIS/543/1993
20 CIS/339/1993
21 Sch 3 para 3(5) IS Regs
22 CIS/719/1994
23 Sch 3 para 3(6)(b) IS Regs
24 Sch 3 para 3(3) IS Regs
25 Sch 3 para 3(11)(c)(viii) IS Regs
26 Sch 3 para 3(4) and regs 2 and 61 IS Regs
27 Sch 3 para 15 IS Regs
28 R(IS) 11/94
29 R(IS) 7/93
30 R(IS) 6/94
31 CIS/465/1994
32 Sch 3 para 5 IS Regs
33 Sch 3 para 4 IS Regs
34 Sch 3 para 4(4) IS Regs
35 paras 28481 and 28486-87, AOG, definition of 'relevant period'
36 Sch 3 para 4(6)(a) IS Regs
37 Sch 3 para 4(6)(b) IS Regs
38 Sch 3 para 4(8) IS Regs
39 R(IS) 8/94
40 Sch 3 para 4(11) IS Regs
41 Sch 3 paras 1(3) and (4) and 4(9) IS Regs
42 Sch 3 para 4(10) IS Regs
43 CIS/11293/1995

44 Sch 3 para 10 IS Regs; R(SB) 46/83
45 Sch 3 para 12 IS Regs
46 Sch 3 para 16 IS Regs
47 CIS/6010/1995
48 R(IS) 5/96
49 Sch 3 para 17 IS Regs
50 Sch 3 para 17(4) IS Regs
51 R(IS) 3/91; R(IS) 4/91; CIS/1460/1995
52 R(IS) 4/92; R(IS) 19/93
53 CIS/4/1988
54 Sch 3 para 17(2) IS Regs
55 Sch 3 para 18 IS Regs
56 Reg 3(4) and (5) IS Regs
57 Reg 3 IS Regs
58 CSB/1163/1988
59 Sch 3 para 18(6) and (7) IS Regs
60 Sch 3 para 11(4) and (5) IS Regs
61 Sch 3 para 11(6) IS Regs
62 Sch 3 para 13 IS Regs
63 R(IS) 12/91
64 Sch 3 para 13(2) IS Regs
65 Sch 3 para 13(4) and (5) IS Regs
66 R(SB) 7/89
67 R(SB) 6/89; R(SB) 7/89
68 R(IS) 10/93
69 CIS/347/1992
70 CSB/617/1988. This case has been reported as R(SB) 4/89, but the reported version omits the relevant paragraphs
71 R(SB) 7/89
72 Sch 3 para 13(6) and (7) IS Regs; Secretary of State for Social Security v Julien, reported as appendix to R(IS) 13/92
73 R(SB) 7/89

74 R(IS) 9/91
75 Sch 10 para 26 IS Regs
76 Sch 9 para 22 IS Regs
77 Sch 3 paras 6 and 8 IS Regs
78 Sch 3 para 9 IS Regs
79 Sch 3 paras 1(2) and 6 IS Regs
80 Sch 3 paras 1(2) and 8 IS Regs
81 Sch 3 para 8(2) and (3) IS Regs
82 Sch 3 para 11(2) IS Regs
83 Sch 3 para 14 IS Regs
84 Reg 32 IS(JSACA) Regs
85 Sch 3 paras 14(4), (5), (5A) and (5B) IS Regs
86 Reg 3 IS(AT) Regs
87 Sch 3 para 7 IS Regs

3. Rates of benefit paid to 16/17-year-olds
(pp44-46)
88 Sch 2 para 1(1)(a), (b) and (c) and (2)(a), (b) and (c) IS Regs
89 Sch 2 paras 1(1)(b) and (c), (2)(b) and (c), and 1A IS Regs
90 Sch 2 para 1(3) IS Regs

5. Urgent cases payments
(pp46-49)
91 Reg 70(2) IS Regs
92 Reg 70(4) IS Regs
93 Reg 71(1)(a) IS Regs
94 Reg 71(1)(b) and (c) IS Regs
95 Reg 71(1)(a) and (b) IS Regs
96 Reg 72(1) IS Regs
97 Reg 72(1)(c) IS Regs
98 Reg 72(2) IS Regs

Chapter 4: Jobseeker's allowance
(pp 50-56)

1 Reg 47(1) and (2) JSA Regs
2 Sch 1, para 4 JSA 1995; reg 46 JSA Regs
3 ss 1-3 JSA 1995
4 s6 JSA 1995; reg 5 JSA Regs
5 Reg 8 JSA Regs
6 Reg 10 JSA Regs
7 s6(5) and (7) JSA 1995; reg 16 JSA Regs
8 Reg 14 JSA Regs
9 Reg 15 JSA Regs
10 Reg 18 JSA Regs
11 Reg 18(3) JSA Regs
12 Reg 19 JSA Regs
13 s9 JSA 1995
14 s9(1) JSA 1995; reg 31 JSA Regs
15 s19 JSA 1995
16 Reg 140 JSA Regs
17 Reg 145(1) JSA Regs
18 s124(1)(f) SSCBA 1992; ss2(1)(d) and 3(1)(b) JSA 1995

Chapter 5: Special rules for special groups
(pp 57-100)

I. 16/17-year-olds
(pp 57-58)

1 s124(1)(a) SSCBA 1992
2 s124(1)(e) SSCBA 1992
3 s124(1)(d) SSCBA 1992
4 Reg 61(1)(c) JSA Regs

2. People involved in a trade dispute
(pp 58-63)

5 s14 JSA 1995
6 ss126 and 127 SSCBA 1992 and Sch 1B para 20 IS Regs
7 s35(1) JSA 1995
8 s14(1) and (2) JSA 1995
9 s14(4) and (5) JSA 1995
10 R(U) 4/62; R(U) 1/70
11 s126(1)(b) and (2) SSCBA 1992
12 s14(1) JSA 1995; paras 37210 and 37245 AOG
13 s14(3) JSA 1995
14 Regs 55 and 56(1)(b) and (3)(a) SS(Adj) Regs
15 Reg 5(4) IS Regs
16 s124(1)(c) SSCBA 1992
17 paras 37677 and 37678 AOG
18 para 37676 AOG
19 s126(3) SSCBA 1992
20 Sch 3 para 2(2) IS Regs
21 Sch 9 para 34 IS Regs
22 s126(5)(b) SSCBA 1992 and Sch 9 para 34 IS Regs
23 s126(5)(a)(ii) SSCBA 1992; reg 41(4) IS Regs
24 Sch 9 para 28 and Sch 10 para 17 IS Regs
25 Reg 48(9) and (10)(a) and (c), Sch 9 paras 15 and 39 and Sch 10 para 22 IS Regs
26 Sch 9 para 21 and reg 42(4) IS Regs
27 Reg 35(1)(d) IS Regs
28 Reg 48(6) IS Regs
29 s126(5)(a)(i) SSCBA 1992
30 s127 SSCBA 1992
31 Reg 6(e) IS Regs
32 s127(b) SSCBA 1992
33 para 37790 AOG
34 Reg 26(4) SS(C&P) Regs
35 s127(c) SSCBA 1992; reg 20 SS(PAOR) Regs
36 Reg 26 SS(PAOR) Regs
37 Reg 19(3), (4) and (5) SS(PAOR) Regs
38 Reg 18(2) SS(PAOR) Regs
39 Reg 22(2) SS(PAOR) Regs
40 Reg 22(3) SS(PAOR) Regs
41 Reg 22(4) SS(PAOR) Regs
42 Reg 20(1) and (2) SS(PAOR) Regs
43 Reg 22(5)(a) SS(PAOR) Regs
44 Reg 22(6) SS(PAOR) Regs
45 Reg 21(1) SS(PAOR) Regs
46 Reg 25 SS(PAOR) Regs
47 Reg 28 SS(PAOR) Regs
48 Reg 29 SS(PAOR) Regs
49 Regs 27 and 29 SS(PAOR) Regs
50 Reg 27(5) SS(PAOR) Regs
51 SF Dir 26
52 SF Dir 17
53 SF Dir 8(c)

3. People from abroad
(pp 63-83)

54 Reg 21(3) and Sch 7 para 17 IS Regs
55 Reg 21(3) IS Regs
56 s7(1) Immigration Act 1988
57 Reg 21(3)(a) IS Regs
58 s124 SSCBA 1992; reg 21(3)(3F) IS Regs
59 Reg 21(3) and Sch 7 para 17 IS Regs
60 Sch 7 para 17(c)(i) IS Regs
61 Sch 7 para 17(c)(i) IS Regs
62 Sch 7 para 17 IS Regs; para 28831 AOG
63 Sch 7 para 17(b) and (c)(ii) and (iii) IS Regs
64 Reg 21(3)(a) IS Regs
65 Sch 7 para 11 IS Regs
66 Reg 16 IS Regs
67 Reg 21(3) IS Regs; Reg

85 JSA Regs
68 Reg 21(3)(3F) IS Regs;
Reg 85 (4) and (4A)
JSA Regs
69 Reg 4(2) IRBS(MA)
Regs
70 EEC Reg 1408/71; *Di
Paolo v Office National de
l'Emploi*, Case 76/76
[1977] ECR 315; R(U)
8/88
71 CIS/1067/1995; CIS/
2326/1995
72 paras 20747-48 AOG
73 CIS/1067/1995; CIS/
2326/1995
74 CIS/2778/1995; *Re F
(child abduction)* [1992] 1
FLR 548
75 CIS/1067/1995, para 28;
CIS/2326/1995, para 24
76 CIS/1067/1995, para 29
77 CIS/2326/1995, para 28
78 CIS/1067/1995, para 15
79 CIS/2326/1995; CIS/
11481/1995
80 *R v Secretary of State ex
parte Sarwar, Getachew and
Urbanek* (CA), October
1996
81 CIS/2326/1995: Nessa -
to be appealed
82 CIS/7201/1995:
Swaddling - reference to
ECJ
83 Arts 48 and 52-60
Treaty of Rome;
I(EEA)O
84 s124 SSCBA 1992; reg
21(3)(a) IS Regs;
s1(2)(i) JSA 1995 and
reg 85 JSA Regs
85 Reg 21(3) IS Regs
86 Art 10 EEC Reg 1612/
68; Art 1 EEC Reg
1251/70; Art 1 EEC
Dirs 68/360 and 73/148
87 *R v Immigration Appeal
Tribunal and Surinder*

*Singh ex parte Secretary of
State for the Home
Department* (ECJ) Case
370/90 [1992] 3 All ER
798
88 *Levin* Case 53/81 [1982]
ECR 1035; EEC Reg
1251/70
89 *Levin, kempf* Case 139/
85 [1986] ECR 1741;
Raulin Case 357/89
[1992] ECR 1027
90 *Scrivner* Case 122/84
[1985] ECR 1027; Art
7 I(EEA)O; CIS/4521/
1995
91 *Lair* Case 39/86 [1988]
ECR 3161; Raulin; Art
7(2) EEC Reg 1612/68
92 *Raulin*, Art 7(2) EEC
Reg 1612/68
93 CIS/4521/1995, para 13
94 para 22680 AOG
95 *Lair*, Art 7(1) EEC Reg
1612/68
96 Art 2(b) EEC Reg
1251/70
97 Art 2(a) EEC Reg
1251/70
98 para 22680 AOG
99 *Lebon* Case 316/85
[1989] ECR 2811; CIS/
4521/1995
100 *Lair, Raulin*; CIS/4521/
1995, para 14
101 Art 1 EEC Dir 68/360
102 CIS/4521/1995
103 Art 1 EEC Dir 73/148
104 Art 1 EEC Dir 73/148;
Luisi [1984] 1 ECR 377
105 *Royer* [1976] ECR 497;
Echternach [1989] ECR
723; *Raulin*
106 *R v Secretary of State ex
parte Vitale and Do
Amaral, The Times*, 18
April 1995 and 26
January 1996
107 Art 15 I(EEA)O

108 *Lubbersen* [1984] 3
CMLR 77; *Roux* Case
363/89 [1993] 3 CMLR
109 *Antonissen*, Case 292/88
[1991] ECR 1-745
110 EEC Dirs 90/364, 90/
365 and 93/96
111 Reg 21(3)(h) and Sch 7
para 17 IS Regs; reg
85(4)(h) JSA Regs
112 *CAO v Remilien and
Wolke*, (QBD & CA) 18
June 1996
113 Reg 21ZA(1) IS Regs;
reg 85(4) JSA Regs
114 Reg 21(3) IS Regs; reg
85(4) JSA Regs
115 Reg 21ZA(2) and (4) IS
Regs; reg 4(3C) and
19(1A) SS(C&P) Regs
116 s124(1)(f) SSCBA 1992
117 Reg 21(3) IS Regs; reg
85(4) JSA Regs
118 Regs 21(3)(j) and
70(3A)(a) and (aa) IS
Regs; reg 85(4) JSA
Regs; Immigration
Rules
119 Reg 147(3) JSA Regs
120 s124(1)(f) SSCBA 1992
121 SS(PFA)MA Regs
122 *R v Secretary of State for
Social Security ex parte* Re
B and JCWI
123 s11 and Sch 1 AIA
1996
124 Regs 21(3)(j) and
70(3)(b) IS Regs
125 Reg 70(3)(b) and
(3A)(a) IS Regs
126 para 36040 AOG
127 Reg 70(3A)(b)(i) IS
Regs
128 Reg 70(3A)(b)(ii) IS
Regs
129 Reg 70(3A)(aa) IS Regs
130 Reg 70(3A)(b)(i) IS
Regs
131 Reg 12(1) SS(PFA)MA

Regs; Sch 1 para 6(2)(a)
AIA 1996

132 Reg 70(3A)(b)(ii) IS
Regs

133 para 36061 AOG

134 Sch 1 para 5 AIA 1996

135 *R v Secretary of State ex
parte Ms T* (HC) 1
November 1996

136 Sch 1 para 6(1)(b) AIA
1996

137 para 36078 AOG

138 paras 5204-05 SFG

139 s17(6) CA 1989

140 *R v Hammersmith and
Fulham London Borough
and others,* CA, *The
Times,* 19 February 1997

141 Reg 21(3)(i) IS Regs

142 Reg 21(3)(i) IS Regs

143 Reg 70(3)(c) IS Regs

144 Reg 12(2) SS(PFA)MA
Regs

145 ss105 and 106 SSAA
1992

146 ss78(6)(c), 105 and 106
SSAA 1992

147 Reg 70(3)(a) IS Regs

148 Reg 70(3)(b) IS Regs

149 Reg 70(3)(c) IS Regs

4. Residential and nursing care
(pp 84-94)

150 NHSCCA 1990

151 Reg 19(1ZB)-(1ZQ) IS
Regs

152 Reg 19 IS Regs

153 Reg 19(1ZB)(a)(iii) IS
Regs

154 Reg 19(1ZF) IS Regs

155 Reg 40 and Sch 9 para
9 IS Regs

156 Sch 4 para 13 IS Regs

157 Sch 4 para 1(1)(a) IS
Regs

158 Sch 4 para 2(2) IS Regs

159 Sch 4 para 2(1) IS Regs

160 Sch 4 para 3 IS Regs

161 Sch 4 para 5 IS Regs

162 Sch 4 paras 6 and 7 IS
Regs

163 Sch 4 para 9 IS Regs

164 Sch 4 para 10 IS Regs

165 Sch 4 paras 9(b) and
10(4) IS Regs

166 CIS/263/1991

167 s55 RHA 1984

168 Reg 1(2) RCH Regs

169 CSB/1171/1986

170 s20(1) RHA 1984

171 Sch 4 para 6(2) IS Regs

172 Sch 4 para 12(1) and
(2) IS Regs

173 Sch 4 para 12(1) and
(2) IS Regs

174 Sch 4 para 12(3) and
(4) IS Regs

175 Sch 9 para 30(d) IS
Regs

176 s26A NAA 1948;
RA(RPORE) Regs

177 Sch 4 paras 14-17 IS
Regs

178 Sch 7 para 16 IS Regs

179 CIS/5415/1995; CSIS/
833/1995

180 Sch 3 para 4(1)(b) IS
Regs; reg 7(1)(e) HB
Regs

181 Sch 2 para 2A IS Regs

182 Sch 3C IS Regs

183 Reg 17(1)(bb) and Sch
2 para 2A(3) IS Regs

184 Regs 17(1)(bb) and
19(3) and Sch 2 para
2A(3) IS Regs

185 Sch 2 para 2A(4) IS
Regs

186 Sch 2 para 2A(4A) IS
Regs

187 Regs 7 and 8 SS(AA)
Regs; regs 9 and 10
SS(DLA) Regs

188 Sch 9 para 15A IS Regs

189 Sch 9 para 30A IS Regs

190 Reg 21(3)-(4) IS Regs

191 Reg 21(3A) IS Regs

192 Sch 7 paras 10A-C and
13 IS Regs

193 Part III NAA 1948

194 s22(1) NAA 1948

195 NA(AR) Regs

196 s22 HSS&SSA Act
1983

197 s22(5A) NAA 1948

5. People in hospital
(pp 94-98)

198 Reg 21(3) IS Regs; reg
2(2) SS(HIP) Regs;
NHSA 1977; NHS(S)A
1978; NHSCCA 1990

199 Reg 2(2) SS(HIP) Regs;
s65 NHSA 1977 (s58
NHS(S)A 1978); Sch 2
para 14 NHSCCA 1990

200 *Botchett v CAO* (CA),
The Times, 8 May 1996;
paras 29332-33 and
29341-54 AOG

201 Sch 3 paras 1(1) and
3(11) IS Regs

202 Sch 2 para 13(3A) IS
Regs

203 s70(1) and (2) SSCBA
1992; Sch 2 para 14ZA
IS Regs

204 Sch 7 para 1(a) IS Regs

205 Sch 7 para 2(b) IS Regs

206 Sch 7 para 2(a) IS Regs

207 Sch 2 para 13(3A) IS
Regs

208 s70(2) SSCBA 1992;
Sch 2 para 14ZA IS
Regs

209 Sch 7 para 1(b) IS Regs

210 Reg 16(2)(b) IS Regs

211 Sch 2 para 15(5) IS
Regs

212 s70 SSCBA 1992; Sch 2
para 14ZA IS Regs

213 Sch 7 para 1(c) and Sch
2 para 12(1)(c)(ii) IS
Regs

214 Reg 16(2)(b) IS Regs

215 Sch 7 para 2 IS Regs

216 Reg 16(2) and Sch 7 para 1(b) IS Regs
217 Reg 16(2) and Sch 7 para 1(a) IS Regs
218 Sch 7 para 3(a) IS Regs
219 Sch 2 para 14(b) IS Regs
220 Sch 7 para 3(b) IS Regs
221 Sch 7 para 18(a)(i) and (ii) IS Regs
222 Sch 7 para 18(a)(iii) and (iv) IS Regs
223 Sch 2 para 2A(4A) IS Regs
224 Sch 7 para 13 IS Regs
225 Sch 7 para 18(b) and (c) IS Regs
226 Sch 7 para 13 IS Regs
227 Sch 7 para 2A IS Regs
228 Sch 7 para 7(1) SS(C&P) Regs; paras 29386-87 AOG
229 Reg 21(2) IS Regs
230 Sch 7 para 7(3)(d) SS(C&P) Regs
231 Sch 7 para 7(2) SS(C&P) Regs; R(S) 4/84, CS/249/1989, CIS/571/1994 and CIS/192/1991
232 para 29382 AOG

6. Prisoners
(pp 98-99)
233 Sch 7 para 8 IS Regs
234 Reg 16(3)(b) IS Regs
235 Reg 16(5)(f) IS Regs
236 Reg 21(3) IS Regs
237 para 29526 AOG; R(IS) 17/93
238 Reg 16(1) and (2) IS Regs
239 Reg 48(7) IS Regs

7. People without accommodation
(pp 99-100)
240 Sch 7 para 6 IS Regs
241 para 42 HC Handbook

242 para 29503 AOG
243 para 15 HC Handbook
244 *R v Hammersmith and Fulham London Borough and others*, CA, *The Times*, 19 February 1997

Chapter 6: Maintenance payments
(pp 101-121)

2. Liability to maintain
(pp 103-105)
1 s105(3) SSAA 1992
2 *Residual Liable Relative and Proceedings Guide*, paras 1630-1642
3 s108 SSAA 1992
4 s108(5) SSAA 1992; reg 3 IS(LR) Regs
5 s106(4)(a) SSAA 1992
6 s30(1) CSA 1991; CS(CEOFM) Regs
7 s106 SSAA 1992
8 ss8(3) and 9 CSA 1991
9 *NAB v Parkes* [1955] 2 QBD 506
10 *NAB v Parkes* [1955] 2 QBD 506; *Hulley v Thompson* [1981] 1 WLR 159
11 s106(2) SSAA 1992
12 s105(1) SSAA 1992

3. The child support scheme
(pp 105-113)
13 s6(1) CSA 1991; reg 34 CS(MAP) Regs
14 s2 CSA 1991
15 s6(8) CSA 1991
16 s6(1) and (11) CSA 1991
17 s6(9) CSA 1991; regs 2 and 3 CS(IED) Regs
18 App 1 CSRCG
19 para 2553 CSAG
20 s46 CSA 1991
21 Reg 35 (1) and (2)

CS(MAP) Regs
22 Reg 35(3) CS(MAP) Regs
23 Reg 25(2) CS(MA) Regs
24 s46(10) CSA 1991
25 R(SB) 33/85
26 s46(3) and (4) CSA 1991
27 s2 CSA 1991; para 2556 CSAG; CCS/1037/1995
28 Reg 35A CS(MAP) Regs
29 s46(7) CSA 1991
30 Reg 3 CSAT(P) Regs
31 s6(8) CSA 1991
32 Reg 40 CS(MAP) Regs
33 Reg 39 CS(MAP) Regs
34 Reg 36(8) CS(MAP) Regs
35 Reg 47(1) CS(MAP) Regs
36 Reg 36(2) CS(MAP) Regs
37 Reg 36(4) CS(MAP) Regs
38 Reg 37 CS(MAP) Regs
39 Reg 36(7) CS(MAP) Regs
40 Reg 47(2) CS(MAP) Regs
41 Reg 25(3) and (4) CS(MA) Regs
42 Reg 41 CS(MAP) Regs
43 Reg 38(2) and (3) CS(MAP) Regs
44 Reg 48 CS(MAP) Regs
45 Reg 48 CS(MAP) Regs
46 Reg 40 CS(MAP) Regs
47 Regs 43 and 44 CS(MAP) Regs
48 Reg 49 CS(MAP) Regs
49 Reg 46 CS(MAP) Regs
50 Reg 47(4) and (5) CS(MAP) Regs
51 Reg 25(4) CS(MA) Regs
52 Reg 42 CS(MAP) Regs

53 s43 CSA 1991; Reg 13 CS(MASC) Regs
54 Reg 28 CS(MASC) Regs
55 s43 and Sch 1 para 5(4) CSA 1991; reg 28 and Sch 4 CS(MASC) Regs; Sch 9 para 7A SS(C&P) Regs
56 Reg 28(5) and Sch 5 CS(MASC) Regs

4. The effect of maintenance on Income Support
(pp 113-121)
57 Reg 54 IS Regs
58 Reg 60B IS Regs
59 Regs 60C and 60D(b) IS Regs
60 s29(3) CSA 1991; reg 2 CS(C&E) Regs
61 s74(1) SSAA 1992; reg 7 SS(PAOR) Regs
62 s41(2) CSA 1991; reg 8 CS(AIAMA) Regs
63 Reg 60D(a) IS Regs
64 Regs 54-60 IS Regs
65 Reg 54 IS Regs, definition of 'periodical payment'; *Bolstridge v CAO*
66 Regs 54, definition of 'payment' and 55 and Sch 9 IS Regs
67 Reg 58 IS Regs
68 Reg 54 (h) IS Regs, definition of 'payment'
69 Reg 58(4) IS Regs
70 Reg 59(1) IS Regs
71 s74(1) SSAA 1992; reg 7(1) SS(PAOR) Regs
72 Reg 54 IS Regs, definition of 'periodical payment'
73 *Regina v West London SBAT ex parte Taylor* [1975] 1 WLR 1048 (DC); *McCorquodale v*

CAO (CA) reported as an appendix to R(SB) 1/88
74 Regs 54, definition of 'payment', 55 and 60(1) IS Regs
75 Reg 60(2) IS Regs
76 CSB/1160/1986; R(SB) 1/89
77 R(SB) 1/89
78 Reg 57(1) IS Regs
79 Reg 57(2) IS Regs
80 Reg 57(3) IS Regs
81 Regs 57(4) and 59(2) IS Regs

Chapter 7: Claims, reviews and getting paid
(pp 122-155)

I. Claims
(pp 122-129)
1 Reg 4(3C) SS(C&P) Regs
2 Reg 4(3) SS(C&P) Regs
3 Reg 4(4) SS(C&P) Regs
4 Reg 33 SS(C&P) Regs
5 R(SB) 5/90
6 CIS/642/1994
7 CIS/379/1992
8 Reg 4(1) SS(C&P) Regs
9 Reg 4(5) SS(C&P) Regs
10 Reg 4(7) SS(C&P) Regs
11 Reg 5(2) SS(C&P) Regs
12 Reg 7(1) SS(C&P) Regs
13 R(SB) 29/83
14 Reg 56 SS(Adj) Regs
15 R(IS) 4/93
16 Reg 32(1) SS(C&P) Regs
17 Reg 6(1) SS(C&P) Regs
18 R(SB) 8/89
19 CIS/759/1992
20 Reg 13(1) SS(C&P) Regs
21 Reg 19(1) and Sch 4 para 6 SS(C&P) Regs
22 Reg 6(28) SS(C&P) Regs

23 R(SB) 9/84
24 Reg 19(8) SS(C&P) Regs
25 Reg 19(6) and (7) SS(C&P) Regs
26 Reg 19(4) and (5) SS(C&P) Regs
27 Reg 19(4) SS(C&P) Regs
28 s68 SSAA 1992
29 R(SB) 17/83; R(IS) 5/91; CIS/812/1992
30 R(P) 2/85

2. Decisions and reviews
(pp 129-135)
31 ss20 and 21 SSAA 1992
32 Reg 56 SS(Adj) Regs
33 Reg 9(1) and sch 1 SS(C&P) Regs
34 Reg 55(1), (3) and (4) SS(Adj) Regs
35 Reg 55(7) SS(Adj) Regs
36 Reg 55(5) SS(Adj) Regs
37 s21(1) SSAA 1992
38 R(I) 50/56
39 *CAO v Eggleton & Others* (CA) March 1993
40 Reg 17(4) SS(C&P) Regs; CSIS/137/1994 (T)
41 s25(1) SSAA 1992
42 CIS/767/1994
43 *CAO v McKiernon* (CA) 8 July 1993
44 R(S) 4/86
45 CSIS/137/1994 (T); CIS/856/1994
46 Regs 63(5) and 64 SS(Adj) Regs
47 Sch 7 para 7 SS(C&P) Regs
48 CIS/714/1991
49 s36 SSAA 1992; R(IS) 15/93
50 Reg 63(1) SS(Adj) Regs
51 Reg 57(3) SS(Adj) Regs

52 Reg 57(2) SS(Adj) Regs
53 *Saker v Secretary of State for Social Services,* R(I) 2/88
54 Reg 63(1A) SS(Adj) Regs
55 R(IS) 11/92
56 s69 SSAA 1992; reg 58 SS(Adj) Regs; *CAO and Another-v-Bate* (HL) [1996] 2 ALL ER 790 (HL)
57 CDLA/577/1994
58 CIS/566/1991; CIS/788/1991

3. Payments of benefit
(pp135-146)
59 Reg 20 SS(C&P) Regs
60 Reg 21 SS(C&P) Regs
61 para 5039 IS Guide (payments volume)
62 Reg 38(1) SS(C&P) Regs
63 Reg 38(2A) SS(C&P) Regs
64 Sch 7 para 5 SS(C&P) Regs
65 Reg 28 SS(C&P) Regs
66 Reg 26(1) and Sch 7 SS(C&P) Regs
67 Sch 7 para 1 SS(C&P) Regs
68 Sch 7 para 6(1) SS(C&P) Regs
69 Sch 7 para 3(2) SS(C&P) Regs
70 Sch 7 para 3(1) SS(C&P) Regs
71 Reg 2 SS(PAOR) Regs
72 Regs 3 and 4 SS(PAOR) Regs
73 Reg 37(1)(a) SS(C&P) Regs
74 Reg 37(1)(b) SS(C&P) Regs
75 Reg 37(1)(c) SS(C&P) Regs
76 Reg 37B SS(C&P) Regs

77 *In R v Secretary of State ex parte Sutherland* (QBD) 7 November 1996, the court found Reg 37A SS(C&P) Regs to be *ultra vires*
78 *R v Secretary of State for Social Security ex parte Mulgrew* (unreported case)
79 Regs 37AA SS(C&P) Regs
80 Reg 37AB SS(C&P) Regs
81 *Walsh v DSS,* Bromley County Court, 12 February 1990. Not reported – see *Welfare Rights Bulletin* 96
82 R(IS) 7/91
83 *Hansard,* 4 May 1993
84 Reg 33 SS(C&P) Regs
85 Reg 34 SS(C&P) Regs
86 Reg 34A and Sch 9A para 2 SS(C&P) Regs
87 Sch 9A paras 8 and 9 SS(C&P) Regs
88 Sch 9A para 3 SS(C&P) Regs
89 Sch 9A paras 3 and 5 SS(C&P) Regs
90 Sch 9A para 6 SS(C&P) Regs
91 *Pazio v Secretary of State for Social Security* (Birmingham County Court, 1996). The case is being appealed to the Court of Appeal and is due to be heard in Spring 1997.
92 Sch 9A para 3 SS(C&P) Regs
93 Reg 35 and Sch 9 SS(C&P) Regs
94 Sch 9 para 2 SS(C&P) Regs
95 Sch 9 para 5 SS(C&P) Regs

96 Sch 9 para 5 (1)(c)(i) SS(C&P) Regs
97 Sch 9 para 5(1)(c)(ii) SS(C&P) Regs
98 Sch 9 para 5(6) SS(C&P) Regs; CIS/220/1994, to be reported as R(IS) 14/95
99 Sch 9 para 5(7) SS(C&P) Regs
100 Sch 9 para 3 SS(C&P) Regs
101 Sch 9 para 3(5) SS(C&P) Regs
102 Sch 9 para 1 SS(C&P) Regs
103 Sch 9 para 3(4) SS(C&P) Regs
104 Sch 9 para 4 SS(C&P) Regs
105 Sch 9 paras 1 and 7 SS(C&P) Regs
106 Sch 9 para 7(1) SS(C&P) Regs
107 Sch 9 para 7(2) SS(C&P) Regs
108 Sch 9 para 7(7) SS(C&P) Regs
109 Sch 9 para 6 SS(C&P) Regs
110 Sch 9 para 6(1) SS(C&P) Regs
111 Sch 9 para 6(4) SS(C&P) Regs
112 CC(DIS) Regs; CT(DIS) Regs
113 Sch 9 para 4A SS(C&P) Regs
114 Regs 1-7 F(DIS) Regs
115 s43 CSA 1991
116 Sch 9 SS(C&P) Regs
117 Sch 9 para 3(2A) SS(C&P) Regs
118 Sch 9 para 8(1) SS(C&P) Regs
119 Sch 9 paras 5(5), 6(6), 7(8) and 8(2) and (3) SS(C&P) Regs

120 Sch 9 paras 1 and 2(2) SS(C&P) Regs
121 Reg 2 CC(DIS) Regs; regs 2-3 CT(DIS) Regs
122 Sch 9 para 9 SS(C&P) Regs
123 Regs 15 and 16 SS(PAOR) Regs; reg 3 SF(RDB) Regs
124 Reg 4 CC(DIS) Regs; reg 8 CT(DIS) Regs
125 s74 SSAA 1992

4. Overpayments and fraud
(pp146-154)
126 R(SB) 3/91
127 Sch 9A para 11 SS(C&P) Regs
128 *R v Secretary of State for Social Security ex parte Golding* (CA)
129 s71 SSAA 1992
130 s71(5) SSAA 1992
131 CSSB/621/1988 and CSB/316/1989
132 CIS/451/1995, following this case, s71 SSAA 1992 was amended
133 CSB/688/1982
134 R(SB) 21/82; R(SB) 28/83; R(SB) 54/83; CA/303/1992
135 Reg 32(1) SS(C&P) Regs
136 CSB/688/1982; R(SB) 12/84; R(SB) 20/84; R(SB) 40/84
137 R(SB) 18/85
138 CWSB/2/1985
139 CSB/347/1983
140 R(SB) 33/85
141 R(SB) 54/83
142 CSB/393/1985
143 *Page v CAO* (CA), *The Times,* 4 July 1991
144 *Jones/Sharples v CAO,* [1994] 1 All ER 225; R(SB) 9/85

145 R(SB) 3/90
146 CIS/222/1991
147 *Sheriff v CAO, The Times,* 10 May 1995
148 *Jones/Sharples v CAO,* [1994] 1 All ER 225; *Franklin v CAO, The Times,* 29 December 1995; CIS/674/1994; CIS/583/1994
149 CIS/674/1994
150 CIS/53/1994
151 CIS/159/1990
152 R(SB) 20/84; R(SB) 24/87
153 Reg 13 SS(PAOR) Regs
154 *Commock v CAO* reported as appendix to R(SB) 6/90; CSIS/8/1995
155 R(IS) 5/92
156 Regs 15 and 16(3) SS(PAOR) Regs
157 Reg 14 SS(PAOR) Regs
158 Reg 15 SS(PAOR) Regs
159 s74(2)(b) SSAA 1992
160 Reg 16(3) SS(PAOR) Regs
161 Reg 16(4), (5) and (6) SS(PAOR) Regs
162 Reg 16(6) SS(PAOR) Regs
163 Reg 17 SS(PAOR) Regs
164 CIS/332/1993
165 *Secretary of State for Social Services v Solly* [1974] 3 All ER 922; R(SB) 21/82

Chapter 8: Appeals
(pp156-173)

1. Appealing to social security appeal tribunals
(pp156-165)
1 R(SB) 29/83; R(SB) 12/89; CIS/807/1992
2 Reg 55(7) SS(Adj) Regs
3 Reg 3(5A) SS(Adj) Regs

4 Reg 3(5) SS(Adj) Regs
5 Reg 3 and Sch 2 SS(Adj) Regs; CIS/550/1993
6 Reg 3(6C) SS(Adj) Regs
7 Reg 3(6) and (6B) SS(Adj) Regs
8 Reg 3(6A) SS(Adj) Regs
9 Reg 3(3) and (3A) SS(Adj) Regs
10 Reg 3(3E) SS(Adj) Regs
11 Reg 3(5) SS(Adj) Regs
12 Reg 3(3B) and (3C) SS(Adj) Regs
13 Reg 3(3D) SS(Adj) Regs
14 Reg 3(8) and (9) SS(Adj) Regs
15 R(SB) 24/82
16 s29 SSAA 1992
17 Reg 22(1) SS(Adj) Regs
18 Reg 22(1A) SS(Adj) Regs
19 Reg 2(1)(b) SS(Adj) Regs
20 para 38(1) *Social Security Appeal Tribunals: A guide to procedure,* HMSO
21 Reg 22(1c) SS(Adj) Regs
22 Reg 2(1)(aa) and (ab) SS(Adj) Regs
23 Regs 4(2A) and 7 SS(Adj) Regs
24 Reg 4(2B) SS(Adj) Regs
25 Reg 7 SS(Adj) Regs
26 Reg 7(3) SS(Adj) Regs
27 Reg 6(2) and (2A) SS(Adj) Regs
28 CIS/068/1991 (to be reported as R(IS) 5/94)
29 Reg 4(2) SS(Adj) Regs
30 Reg 4(3A) SS(Adj) Regs
31 Reg 5(1) SS(Adj) Regs
32 Reg 4(3) SS(Adj) Regs
33 CIS/566/1991;

CS/99/1993

34 Reg 4(4) SS(Adj) Regs

35 s41 SSAA 1992

36 Regs 22(2) and 23(1) SS(Adj) Regs

37 Sch 2 para 7 SSAA 1992

38 CIS/643A/1992

39 President's Circular No.1, 15 July 1996

40 Reg 22(3) SS(Adj) Regs

41 CSIS/118/1990; CSIS/110/1991

42 Reg 23(3) SS(Adj) Regs

43 Reg 23(3A) SS(Adj) Regs

44 Reg 23(3D) SS(Adj) Regs

45 Reg 37 SS(C&P) Regs

46 Reg 10 SS(Adj) Regs

47 R(SB) 4/90

48 CSB/172/1990

49 CI/79/1990; CIS/373/1994

50 Reg 9 SS(Adj) Regs

2. How to prepare an appeal
(pp 166-168)

51 R(SB) 33/85; R(SB) 12/89

52 R(SB) 10/86

53 R(IS) 6/91

54 R(SB) 1/81

55 R(SB) 6/82

56 s36 SSAA 1992; R(SB) 1/82; R(FIS) 1/82

57 s123(2) SSCBA 1992

58 s39(2) SSAA 1992

59 s23 SSAA 1992

60 R(I) 12/75

3. Appealing to the social security commissioner
(pp 168-171)

61 s23 SSAA 1992

62 R(A) 1/72; R(SB) 11/83

63 R(IS) 4/93

64 s23(9) SSAA 1992

65 Reg 24(1) SS(Adj) Regs; reg 3(1) SSCP Regs

66 Regs 3(3), 24 and Sch 2, para 7 SS(Adj) Regs

67 Reg 3(1) and (3) SSCP Regs; CIS/550/1993

68 Reg 3(2) and (5) SSCP Regs; CIS/500/1993

69 Reg 7(1) SSCP Regs

70 Reg 5(2) SSCP Regs

71 Regs 10, 11 and 12 SSCP Regs

72 Reg 27(3) and (4) SSCP Regs

73 Reg 15 SSCP Regs

74 s57 SSAA 1992

75 Reg 17(4) SSCP Regs

76 Reg 22(2) SSCP Regs

77 s23(7)(b) SSAA 1992

78 s23(7)(a) SSAA 1992

79 *Innes v CAO* (CA) (unreported) 19 November 1986

80 Regs 24 and 25 SSCP Regs

4. Appealing to the courts
(pp 171-173)

81 s24 SSAA 1992

82 Regs 27(2) and 31(1) SSCP Regs

83 *White v CAO* [1986] 2 All ER 905 (CA), also reported as an Appendix to R(S) 8/85

84 s24(2)(b) SSAA 1992

85 RSC 0.59 r.21(2)

86 RSC 0.3 r.5 and 0.59 r.14(2)

87 RSC 0.59 r.14(2), (2A), (2B)

88 RSC 0.59 r.4(3) and

r.21(2)

89 *Bland v CSBO* [1983] 1 WLR 262 (CA), also reported as R(SB) 12/83

90 ss2(4)(a) and 15(1) LAA 1988

PART THREE: BACK TO WORK BENEFITS, FAMILY CREDIT AND DISABILITY WORKING ALLOWANCE

Chapter 9: Back to work benefits
(pp 176-183)

1 SS(BWB) (Amdt.2) Regs

2 Reg 1(2) SS(CMB) Regs

3 Reg 3 SS(CMB) Regs

4 Reg 3(2) and (3) SS(CMB) Regs

5 Reg 4 SS(CMB) Regs

6 Reg 4(2)-(5) SS(CMB) Regs

7 Reg 5 SS(CMB) Regs

8 Reg 1(5) SS(CMB) Regs

9 Regs 2(2) and 6 SS(CMB) Regs

10 Reg 5(5) SS(CMB) Regs

11 Reg 10(1) SS(CMB) Regs

12 Reg 9 SS(CMB) Regs

13 Reg 9(4) and (5) SS(CMB) Regs

14 Reg 10 SS(CMB) Regs

15 Reg 11(3) SS(CMB) Regs

16 Reg 11(4) SS(CMB) Regs

17 Reg 10(3)-(5) SS(CMB) Regs

18 Reg 11(1) and (2) SS(CMB) Regs

19 Reg 8(1) and (2)
SS(CMB) Regs
20 Reg 8(4) and (5)
SS(CMB) Regs
21 Reg 8(3) SS(CMB) Regs
22 Reg 13 SS(CMB) Regs
23 Reg 7 SS(CMB) Regs

Chapter 10: Family credit
(pp 184-198)

2. The basic rules
(pp 185-190)

1 s128(1) SSCBA 1992
2 Reg 3(1) FC Regs
3 R(P) 1/78; R(M) 1/85
4 *Shah v Barnet LBC*
[1983] All ER 226
5 Reg 9(1) FC Regs; CIS/
508/1992
6 R(FC) 2/93
7 Reg 3(2) FC Regs
8 para 50100 AOG
9 Reg 3(1)(aa) FC Regs
10 Reg 3(1A) FC Regs; reg
12 SS(PFA)MA Regs
11 ss128(1)(b) and
129(1)(a) SSCBA 1992
12 R(FIS) 6/83; R(FIS)
1/84; R(FIS) 1/86
13 *Kevin Smith v CAO*, 11
October 1994
(unreported)
14 CFC/33/1993
15 R(FIS) 1/83
16 Reg 4(3)(c) FC Regs;
reg 6(3)(c) DWA Regs
17 R(FIS) 1/86;
CDWA/1/1992
18 Reg 4(3)(a) FC Regs;
reg 6(3)(a) DWA Regs
19 Reg 4(3)(b) FC Regs;
reg 6(3)(b) DWA Regs
20 Reg 4 FC Regs; reg 6
DWA Regs
21 R(IS) 1/93
22 Reg 4(5) FC Regs; reg
6(5) DWA Regs

23 Reg 4(6)(b) FC Regs;
reg 6(6)(b) DWA Regs
24 Reg 4(6) FC Regs; reg
6(6) DWA Regs
25 R(FIS) 2/83
26 R(FIS) 6/83; R(FIS)
1/84
27 R(FIS) 6/83
28 R(FIS) 1/85; *R v Ebbw
Vale & Merthyr Tydfil
SBAT ex parte Lewis*
[1982] 1 WLR 420
29 R(FIS) 2/81; R(FIS)
2/82
30 R(FC) 1/92
31 Reg 4(4)(a) FC Regs;
reg 6(4)(a) DWA Regs
32 paras 50381-82 AOG
33 R(FIS) 6/85; para 50372
AOG
34 Reg 4(4)(b) FC Regs;
reg 6(4)(b) DWA Regs
35 Reg 4(4)(c)(ii)(bb) FC
Regs
36 Reg 4(4)(c)(i) FC Regs;
reg 6(4)(c)(i) DWA
Regs;
CIS/261/1990
37 Reg 4(4)(c)(ii)(aa) FC
Regs; reg 6(4)(c)(ii)
DWA Regs
38 Reg 4(4A) FC Regs
39 Reg 5(1A) IS Regs; reg
4(1) FC Regs
40 s128(1)(d) SSCBA 1992
41 Reg 52 FC Regs

3. The amount of benefit
(pp 190-192)

42 s128(1)(a) SSCBA 1992;
reg 47(1) FC Regs
43 Reg 46(1) FC Regs
44 Sch 4 FC Regs
45 Reg 46(4)-(6) FC Regs
46 Regs 5 and 6
IRB&JSA(PA) Amdt
Regs amending reg 46
of, and Sch 4 to, the

FC Regs
47 Reg 10(3) and (4)
IRB&JSA(PA) Amdt
Regs
48 Reg 46(1)(aa) and Sch 4
para 1A FC Regs
49 Reg 4A FC Regs
50 s128(2)(b) SSCBA
1992; reg 48 FC Regs
51 Reg 28 SS(C&P) Regs
52 Reg 27(2) SS(C&P)
Regs

4. Special rules for special groups
(p 192)

53 Reg 14(3) FC Regs
54 s128(3) SSCBA 1992

5. Claims and getting paid
(pp 192-197)

55 Reg 4(2) SS(C&P) Regs
56 Reg 6(1) SS(C&P) Regs
57 Reg 6(1)(aa) SS(C&P)
Regs
58 Reg 4(7) SS(C&P) Regs
59 Reg 6(27) SS(C&P)
Regs
60 Reg 19(7)(e) and (f)
SS(C&P) Regs
61 Reg 5 SS(C&P) Regs
62 Reg 19 and Sch 4 para
7 SS(C&P) Regs
63 Reg 16(1) and (3)
SS(C&P) Regs
64 Reg 16(1B) SS(C&P)
Regs
65 Reg 13(6) SS(C&P)
Regs
66 Reg 9 and Sch 1 Part 1
SS(C&P) Regs
67 CFC/25/1993; see also
'4th Report of the
Parliamentary
Commissioner for
Administration 1993/
94', Case No.
C-761/93

68 Reg 7(3) SS(C&P) Regs
69 s21(1) SSAA 1992
70 DSS Press Release 95/176, December 1995
71 Reg 20 SS(Adj) Regs
72 Reg 27(1A) SS(C&P) Regs
73 Reg 27(2) SS(C&P) Regs
74 Reg 27(1) SS(C&P) Regs
75 Reg 21 SS(C&P) Regs
76 s128(3) SSCBA 1992
77 s128(4) SSCBA 1992; reg 50 FC Regs
78 Reg 49A FC Regs
79 Reg 49 FC Regs
80 Reg 51 FC Regs
81 CFC/18/1989
82 Regs 15 and 16 SS(PAOR) Regs

6.   Challenging a family credit decision
(p197)
83 Reg 65 SS(Adj) Regs

Chapter 11: Disability working allowance
(pp199-212)
1 Reg 4 NHS(TERC) Regs
2 Reg 7B SS(Cr) Regs
3 s129(1) SSCBA 1992
4 Reg 5 DWA Regs
5 s129(1)(b) SSCBA 1992
6 s11(2) SSAA 1992; reg 4 DWA Regs
7 Reg 3 and Sch 1 DWA Regs
8 Sch 1 para 24 DWA Regs
9 s129(1), (2) and (4) SSCBA 1992; reg 7 DWA Regs
10 Reg 17 SS(ICB) Trans Regs; regs 7A and 7B DWA Regs
11 s129(2A) and (2B)

SSCBA 1992
12 s11(3) SSAA 1992
13 s129(1)(d) SSCBA 1992
14 Reg 57 DWA Regs
15 Reg 51(1A) DWA Regs
16 s129(5) SSCBA 1992; reg 53 DWA Regs
17 Reg 51 and Sch 5 DWA Regs
18 Regs 8 and 9 IRB&JSA(PA) Amdt Regs
19 Reg 10(3) and (4) IRB&JSA(PA) Amdt Regs
20 Reg 51(1)(bb) and Sch 5 para 2A DWA Regs
21 Reg 6A DWA Regs
22 Reg 16(3) and (4) DWA Regs
23 Reg 4(1) SS(C&P) Regs
24 Reg 4(3A) SS(C&P) Regs
25 Reg 4(7) SS(C&P) Regs
26 Reg 5 SS(C&P) Regs
27 Reg 9 and Sch 1 Part 1 SS(C&P) Regs
28 Reg 6(1) SS(C&P) Regs
29 Reg 6(1)(aa) SS(C&P) Regs
30 Reg 6(10) SS(C&P) Regs
31 Reg 6(27) SS(C&P) Regs
32 Reg 6(13) SS(C&P) Regs
33 Reg 6(12) SS(C&P) Regs
34 Reg 6(15) SS(C&P) Regs
35 Reg 6(14) SS(C&P) Regs
36 s30(13) SSAA 1992
37 Reg 6(11) SS(C&P) Regs
38 Reg 19(7)(f) SS(C&P) Regs
39 Reg 19(1) and Sch 4 para 11 SS(C&P) Regs

40 Reg 7(1) SS(C&P) Regs
41 Reg 7(3) SS(C&P) Regs
42 ss20 and 21 SSAA 1992
43 s11(2) SSAA 1992; reg 4 DWA Regs
44 s54 SSAA 1992
45 s54(2) SSAA 1992
46 Reg 20 SS(Adj) Regs
47 Reg 16(1) and (3) SS(C&P) Regs
48 Reg 16(1C) SS(C&P) Regs
49 Reg 16(1B) SS(C&P) Regs
50 s129(6) SSCBA 1992
51 Reg 21 SS(C&P) Regs
52 Reg 27(1A) and (2) SS(C&P) Regs
53 Reg 36 SS(C&P) Regs
54 s129(6) SSCBA 1992
55 Reg 55 DWA Regs
56 Reg 54 DWA Regs
57 Reg 56 DWA Regs
58 s71 SSAA 1992
59 s30(5) SSAA 1992
60 Reg 66(1) SS(Adj) Regs
61 Reg 66(2) SS(Adj) Regs
62 ss42 and 68(10) SSCBA 1992
63 s93 SSCBA 1992
64 Regs 12 and 19 SS(ICB) Trans Regs

PART FOUR: HOUSING BENEFIT AND COUNCIL TAX BENEFIT

Chapter 12: The basic rules
(pp214-246)

1.   Introduction
(pp214-227)
1 s130 SSCBA 1992
2 Reg 6(1)(c)(i) HB Regs
3 Reg 6(1)(c)(ii) HB Regs

4 s134(2) SSCBA 1992; reg 71(1) HB Regs

5 Reg 10(5) HB Regs

6 Reg 10(3) HB Regs

7 Reg 6(2) HB Regs

8 Reg 6(1)(d) HB Regs

9 s130(1) SSCBA 1992; reg 5 HB Regs

10 para A3.15 GM

11 Reg 5(5)(c) HB Regs

12 Reg 5(8) HB Regs

13 Reg 5(8B) HB Regs

14 *R v Penwith District Council ex parte Burt*, HB/CTB A8/95

15 Reg 5 (8A) HB Regs

16 Reg 5(3) and (9) HB Regs

17 Reg 5(1) HB Regs

18 Reg 5(5)(b) HB Regs

19 Reg 5(5)(a) HB Regs

20 Reg 5(7A) HB Regs

21 Reg 5(5)(d) HB Regs

22 Reg 5(7A) HB Regs

23 Reg 5(4) HB Regs

24 Reg 5(5)(d) HB Regs

25 Reg 5(6) HB Regs

26 Reg 5(5)(e) HB Regs

27 Reg 5(5)(e) HB Regs

28 Reg 48(A)(1) HB Regs

29 Reg 7A HB Regs

30 Reg 7(1)(a) HB Regs

31 para A3.31 GM

32 Reg 7(1)(b) HB Regs

33 *R v HBRB Sutton ex parte Keegan* [1992]

34 Reg 7(1)(c) HB Regs

35 Reg 7(1)(d) HB Regs

36 Reg 7(1)(e) HB Regs

37 Reg 8(2)(b) HB Regs

38 Reg 8(2ZA) HB Regs

39 Reg 10(2)(a) and (c) HB Regs

40 Reg 2(1) HB Regs

41 Reg 8(2) HB Regs

42 Reg 8(3) HB Regs

43 Reg 10(2)(e) HB Regs; Part A8 GM

44 Reg 10(2)(b) HB Regs

45 Reg 10(2)(d) HB Regs

46 HB/CTB A7/94

47 Reg 7A(5) HB Regs

48 Reg 7A(2) HB Regs

49 Reg 7A(3) HB Regs

50 Reg 7A(4)(a) HB Regs

51 Reg 7A(4)(b) HB Regs

52 Reg 7A(4)(c) HB Regs

53 Reg 7A(4)(d) HB Regs

54 Reg 7A(4)(e) HB Regs

55 HB/CTB A7/94

56 Command Paper Cm 2609, para 31

57 Reg 7A(4)(e) and (5) HB Regs

58 Reg 7A(4)(f) and (5) HB Regs

59 Reg 12(2) SS(PFA)MA Regs

60 Reg 7A(5) HB Regs

61 Reg 12(1) SS(PFA)MA Regs

62 Reg 7A(5A) HB Regs

63 Sch A1 para 2(4) HB Regs; Sch A1 para 2 (4) CTB Regs

64 Sch A1 para 2(5) HB Regs; Sch A1 para 2 (5) CTB Regs

65 Sch A1 para 2(1) HB Regs; Sch A1 para 2(1) CTB Regs

66 Sch A1 para 1(2) HB Regs; Sch A1 para 1 (2) CTB Regs

67 Sch A1 para 1(3) and 2(3) HB Regs; Sch A1 paras 1(3) and 6 CTB Regs

68 Sch A1 para 9 HB Regs; Sch A1 para 8 CTB Regs

69 Sch A1 para 5(1) HB Regs; Sch A1 para 4(1) CTB Regs

70 Sch A1 paras 4 and 5(2) HB Regs; Sch A1 para 4(2) and (4) CTB Regs

71 Sch A1 para 6 HB Regs; Sch A1 para 5 CTB Regs

72 Sch A1 para 5(3) HB Regs; Sch A1 para 4(3) CTB Regs

73 Sch A1 para 8(1) HB Regs; Sch A1 para 7(1) CTB Regs

74 Sch A1 para 8(5) HB Regs

75 Sch A1 para 8(4) HB Regs

76 Reg 7(1)(e) HB Regs

77 Reg 7(2) HB Regs

78 Reg 7(4)-(12) HB Regs

2. 'Eligible rent'
(pp 227-232)

79 Reg 10(1) HB Regs

80 Reg 2(4)(a) HB Regs

81 Reg 10(3)(a) and (6) HB Regs

82 Reg 10(4) HB Regs

83 Reg 8 (2A) HB Regs

84 Reg 10 (6A) HB Regs

85 Sch 1 para 5(1) HB Regs

86 Sch 1 para 5(1)(a) HB Regs

87 Sch 1 para 5(2) and (2A) HB Regs

88 Reg 10(3)(b) HB Regs

89 Sch 1 para 5(3) and Sch 6 para 9(c) HB Regs

90 para A4.76(iii) GM

91 Sch 1 paras 4 and 5(1)(b) HB Regs; para A4.81 GM

92 Sch 1 para 7 HB Regs

93 Sch 1 para 7 HB Regs

94 Reg 10(1)(e) HB Regs

95 Sch 1 para 1(a)(iii) HB Regs

96 Sch 1 para 1(a)(ii) HB Regs

97 Sch 1 para 1(b) HB Regs

98 Sch 1 para 1(a)(iv) HB

Regs

99 Sch 1 para 1(a)(iv) HB Regs
100 Sch 1 para 1(c) HB Regs; para A4.67 GM
101 Sch 1 para 1(f) HB Regs; para A4.69 GM
102 Sch 1 para 3 HB Regs
103 Sch 1 para 1 HB Regs
104 Reg 10(3)(c) and Sch 1 para 2(1A) HB Regs
105 Sch 1 para 2 HB Regs
106 Sch 1 para 1(a)(i) HB Regs
107 Sch 1 para 1A(1) HB Regs
108 Sch 1 para 1A(5) and (6) HB Regs

3. Rent restrictions
(pp 232-246)

109 Reg 12A HB Regs
110 Reg 12A(2)(b) and Sch 1A HB Regs
111 Reg 12A HB Regs
112 Sch 1A para 2 HB Regs
113 Sch 1 para 1 RO(AF)O
114 Sch 1 para 2 RO(AF)O
115 Sch 2 RO(AF)O
116 Art 2(1) RO(AF)O
117 Sch 1 para 3 RO(AF)O
118 Sch 1 para 8(2) RO(AF)O
119 Sch 1 para 4A
120 Sch 1 para 4 RO(AF)O
121 Sch 1 para (6) RO(AF)O
122 Sch 1 para 4(4) and 5(2) RO(AF)O
123 Sch 1 para (5)(1) RO(AF)O
124 Sch 1 para 8(2A) RO(AF)O
125 Sch 1 para 4(3)(b) RO(AF)O
126 Sch 1 para 4A RO(AF)O
127 Sch 1 para 8 RO(AF)O
128 Reg 10 HB(Amdt) Regs

1995

129 Reg 10(2) HB(Amdt) Regs
130 Reg 10(6) HB(Amdt) Regs
131 Reg 10(6) HB(Amdt) Regs
132 Reg 11(13) HB Regs
133 Reg 11(3) and (4) HB Regs
134 Reg 11(8A) HB Regs
135 Reg 2(1) HB Regs
136 Reg 11(3A) HB Regs
137 Reg 11(6) HB Regs
138 Reg 11(6A) and (6B) HB Regs
139 Reg 11(7) HB Regs
140 Reg 11(9) and (10) HB Regs
141 Reg 61(3) HB Regs
142 HB/CTB A7/96
143 Reg 61(4) HB Regs
144 Reg 10(6B) HB Regs
145 Reg 10(1) HB (Amdt) Regs
146 Reg 12A(1)(c) HB Regs
147 Reg 12A(3) HB Regs
148 Sch 1 para 8 RO(AO)O
149 Reg 79(5B) HB Regs
150 Reg 11(2) HB Regs (pre Jan 1996)
151 *R v Beverley BC HBRB ex parte Hare* [1995] QBD
152 Reg 11(6)(a) HB Regs (pre Jan 1996)
153 *R v East Devon DC HBRB ex parte Gibson and Gibson* [1993]
154 para A4.110 GM
155 *Macleod v HBRB for Banff and Buchan District* [1988] SCLR 165; *Malcolm v HBRB for Tweedale* [1991]
156 Reg 11(3) HB Regs (pre Jan 1996)
157 Reg 11(3) HB Regs (pre Jan 1996)

158 *R v East Devon DC HBRB ex parte Gibson and Gibson* [1993]
159 *R v Sefton MBC ex parte Cunningham*
160 *R v London Borough of Waltham Forest ex parte Holder and Samuel* [1996], para A4.108 GM
161 Reg 11(6)(b) HB Regs (pre Jan 1996)
162 *R v London Borough of Brent ex parte Connery*, QBD 23 October 1989
163 Reg 11(3A) HB Regs
164 Reg 11(4) and (5) HB Regs (pre Jan 1996)
165 Reg 12(b) HB Regs; para A4.115 GM
166 Reg 12 HB Regs

Chapter 13: The amount of benefit
(pp 247-257)

1. The basic calculation
(pp 247-250)

1 Reg 61 HB Regs
2 Sch 4 para 4 HB Regs; Sch 5 para 5 CTB Regs
3 Reg 64 HB Regs
4 Reg 2 HB Regs
5 Reg 69 HB Regs
6 Reg 69(2)(b) HB Regs
7 Reg 70(3) and Sch 1 para 6(2) HB Regs; para A5.49-53 GM
8 Reg 70(3)(a) and Sch 1 para 6(2)(a) HB Regs
9 Reg 70(3)(b) and Sch 1 para 6(2)(b) HB Regs

2. Extended payments of HB/CTB

10 Sch 5A para 1 and reg 62A(2) and (3) HB Regs; Sch 5A para 1

and reg 53A(2) and (3) CTB Regs

11 Reg 62A(1)(b) and Sch 5A para 3(3)(b) HB Regs; reg 53A(1)(b) and Sch 5A para 3(3)(b) CTB Regs

12 Reg 76(4) HB Regs

13 Sch 5A para 4 HB Regs

14 Sch 5A para 6 HB Regs

15 Sch 5A paras 4 and 5 CTB Regs.

16 Reg 62A(5) HB Regs; reg 53A(5) CTB Regs

17 Sch 5A para 11 HB Regs; Sch 5A para 7 CTB Regs

18 Sch 5A para 10 HB Regs

3. Deductions for non-dependants
(pp252-255)

19 Reg 3 HB Regs

20 Reg 3 (2) HB Regs

21 Reg 3(4) and Sch 1 para 7 HB Regs

22 Reg 63(6) HB Regs; reg 52(6) CTB Regs

23 Reg 63(7) HB Regs; reg 52(7) CTB Regs

24 Reg 63(1) HB Regs; reg 52(1) CTB Regs

25 Reg 63(8) HB Regs

26 Reg 63(1) and (2) HB Regs

27 Reg 4(1) HB Regs; reg 4(1) CTB Regs

28 Reg 4(4) HB Regs; reg 4(4) CTB Regs

29 Reg 4(1) and (2) HB Regs; reg 4(1) and (2) CTB Regs

30 Reg 4(5) HB Regs; reg 4(5) CTB Regs

31 paras A5.30-32 GM

32 para A5.16 GM

33 Reg 63(9) HB Regs

34 para A5.23 GM

35 Reg 63(3) HB Regs

36 Reg 63(4) HB Regs

37 Reg 63(5) HB Regs

38 Sch 4 para 19 HB Regs

39 Reg 20(1) HB Regs

40 Reg 20 HB Regs

4. Extra benefit in exceptional circumstances
(p256)

41 Reg 61(2) HB Regs

42 *R v Maidstone BC ex parte Bunce 1994.*

43 Reg 61(2) HB Regs

44 Reg 61(2) HB Regs

45 ss134(8) and 139(6) SSAA 1992

5. People in hospital
(pp256-257)

46 Reg 18(1)(a) HB Regs

47 Reg 18(1)(b) HB Regs

48 Reg 18(1)(c)(i) HB Regs

49 Reg 18(1)(c)(ii) HB Regs

50 Reg 18(1)(d)(i) HB Regs

51 Reg 18(1)(d)(ii) HB Regs

52 Reg 18(3) HB Regs

Chapter 14: Special rules for students

1 Reg 46 HB Regs; reg 38 CTB Regs

2 Reg 46 HB Regs; reg 38 CTB Regs

3 Reg 46 HB Regs; reg 38 CTB Regs

4 para C5.03 GM

5 HB/CTB A26/96

6 Reg 7 IRBS&SF(MA) Regs

7 Reg 46 HB Regs; reg 38 CTB Regs

8 Reg 46 HB Regs; reg 38 CTB Regs

9 Reg 48A(2) HB Regs; reg 40(3) CTB Regs

10 s131 SSCBA 1992; reg 6(1)(e) HB Regs

11 Reg 48(1) HB Regs

12 Reg 48(2) HB Regs

13 para C5.30 GM

14 Reg 50(1) HB Regs

15 Reg 50(2) HB Regs

16 Reg 50(3) HB Regs

17 Reg 52 HB Regs

18 Reg 50(1) HB Regs; para C5.37 GM

19 s131 SSCBA 1992; regs 6(1)(b) and 52 HB Regs

20 Reg 51(1) HB Regs

21 Reg 52 HB Regs

22 Reg 51(2) HB Regs

23 Reg 61(2) HB Regs

Chapter 15: Claims, payments and reviews
(pp265-299)

1. Claims
(pp265-269)

1 Reg 71(1) HB Regs; reg 61(1) CTB Regs

2 Reg 71(2) HB Regs; reg 61(2) CTB Regsò

3 Reg 71(3) and (5) HB Regs; reg 61(3) and (5) CTB Regs

4 Reg 71(6) HB Regs; reg 61(6) CTB Regs

5 Reg 71(4) HB Regs; reg 61(4) CTB Regs

6 Reg 72(1) HB Regs; reg 62(1) CTB Regs

7 Reg 72(2) HB Regs; reg 62(2) CTB Regs

8 para A2.09 GM

9 Reg 72(7)(b) and (8) HB Regs; reg 62(7)(b) and (8) CTB Regs

10 Reg 72(7)(a) and (8)

HB Regs; para A2.24 GM; reg 62(7)(a) and (8) CTB Regs

11 Reg 74(1) HB Regs; reg 64(1) CTB Regs

12 Reg 74(2) HB Regs; reg 64(2) CTB Regs

13 Reg 72(4)(a) and (b) HB Regs; reg 62(4)(a) and (b) CTB Regs

14 Reg 72(4)(a) and (b) HB Regs; reg 62(4)(a) and (b) CTB Regs

15 Reg 72(4)(c) HB Regs; reg 62(4)(c) CTB Regs

16 Reg 72(1) HB Regs; reg 62(1) CTB Regs

17 Reg 73(1) HB Regs; reg 63(1) CTB Regs

18 Reg 76(2)(b) HB Regs; reg 66(2)(b) CTB Regs

19 Reg 73(1) and (3) HB Regs; reg 63(1) and (3) CTB Regs

20 Reg 72(5)(c) HB Regs; reg 62(5)(d) CTB Regs

21 Reg 72(5)(a) HB Regs; reg 62(5)(a) CTB Regs

22 Reg 72(5)(b) HB Regs; reg 62(5)(b) CTB Regs

23 Reg 72(5)(bb) HB Regs; reg 62(5)(c) CTB Regs

24 Reg 65(1) HB Regs; reg 56(1) CTB Regs

25 Reg 72(15) HB Regs; paras A2.14-16 and B2.29 GM; reg 62(16) CTB Regs

26 Reg 72(15) HB Regs; reg 62(16) CTB Regs

27 *R v Aylesbury Vale DC ex parte England* [1996]

28 Reg 5(6) HB Regs

29 Reg 72(11) HB Regs; reg 62(12) CTB Regs

30 Reg 66 HB Regs; paras A6.07 and B4.7 GM; reg 57 CTB Regs

31 Sch 6 paras 9(g)-(h) and 10(a) HB Regs; Sch 6 paras 9(d)-(e) and 10(a) CTB Regs

32 Reg 72(12) and (13) HB Regs; reg 62(13) and (14) CTB Regs

33 Reg 72(14) HB Regs; para A6.12 GM; reg 62(15) CTB Regs

34 Reg 66(4) HB Regs; A6.10 GM

35 Reg 67(1)(a) and (2) HB Regs; reg 58(1)(a) and (2) CTB Regs

36 Reg 72(13) HB Regs; para A6.12 GM; reg 62(14) CTB Regs

37 Reg 72(12) and (13) HB Regs; para A6.13 GM

38 Reg 66(1)(b) HB Regs; reg 57(1)(b) CTB Regs

2. Decisions
(pp 270-272)

39 Regs 76(3), 77(1)(a) and 88(3) HB Regs; regs 66(3), 67(1)(a) and 77(3)(b) and (c) CTB Regs

40 Reg 76(2) HB Regs; reg 66(2) CTB Regs

41 Reg 2(1) HB Regs; reg 2(1) CTB Regs

42 Reg 77(4), 79(2) and 86(1) and (2) HB Regs; regs 67(2), 69(2) and 75(1) CTB Regs

43 Reg 77 and Sch 6 HB Regs; reg 67 and Sch 6 CTB Regs

44 Sch 6 para 6 HB Regs; Sch 6 para 6 CTB Regs

45 Sch 6 para 2 HB Regs; Sch 6 para 2 CTB Regs

46 Sch 6 para 3 HB Regs; Sch 6 para 3 CTB Regs

47 Sch 6 paras 9-13 HB

Regs; Sch 6 paras 9-13 CTB Regs

48 para C12.10 GM

3. Payment of benefit
(pp 272-277)

49 Reg 65(1) HB Regs; reg 56(1) CTB Regs

50 Reg 2(1) HB Regs; reg 2(1) CTB Regs

51 Reg 65(2) HB Regs

52 Reg 69(4)(a) HB Regs

53 Reg 69(2)(b), (5)(a), and (6) HB Regs

54 Reg 66 HB Regs; reg 57 CTB Regs

55 s134(1)(b) SSAA 1992

56 s134(1)(c) SSAA 1992; reg 92(1) HB Regs

57 Reg 88(1)(b) HB Regs; reg 77(1) and (3) CTB Regs

58 para A6.24 GM

59 Reg 90(1) and (4) HB Regs

60 Reg 88(2) HB Regs

61 Reg 90(3) HB Regs

62 Reg 90(4) HB Regs; para A6.30 GM

63 Reg 90(2A) and (2B) HB Regs

64 Reg 11 HB (Amdt) Regs 1996

65 Reg 90(2) HB Regs (pre Oct 1996)

66 Reg 88(3) HB Regs

67 Reg 91(1) HB Regs

68 para A6.34 GM and HB/CTB (93)37

69 Reg 91(1) HB Regs; *R v London Borough of Haringey ex parte Azad Ayub*

70 Reg 91(2) HB Regs

71 Reg 91(3) HB Regs

72 Reg 88(1) HB Regs; reg 77(1) CTB Regs

73 Reg 92(2) HB Regs; reg 78(2) CTB Regs

74 Reg 92(3) HB Regs; para A6.40 GM

75 Reg 96 HB Regs; reg 81 CTB Regs

76 *R v London Borough of Haringey ex parte Azad Ayub*

77 Reg 93(a) HB Regs; Sch 9 para 1(2) SS(C&P) Regs.

78 Reg 93(b) HB Regs

79 Reg 94(1) HB Regs

80 *R v London Borough of Haringey ex parte Azad Ayub*

81 Sch A1 para 8(4) HB Regs; Sch A1 para 7(4) CTB Regs

82 Reg 94(1A) HB Regs

83 Reg 95(1) HB Regs

84 Reg 95(3)(a) and (b) HB Regs

85 Reg 95(2) HB Regs

86 Reg 95(3) HB regs.

87 Reg 95(7) and (8) HB Regs

88 Reg 95(4) HB Regs; reg 80(1) CTB Regs

89 Reg 95(5) HB Regs; reg 80(2) CTB Regs

90 Reg 95(4A) HB Regs; reg 80(2A) CTB Regs

4. Changes in your circumstances
(pp277-280)

91 Reg 75(1) HB Regs; reg 65(1) CTB Regs

92 Sch 6 paras 9(i) and 10(a) HB Regs; Sch 6 paras 9(f) and 10(a) CTB Regs

93 Reg 75(1), (2)(e) and (3) HB Regs; paras A6.52 and B4.10 GM; reg 65(1), (2)(d), (3) and (4) CTB Regs

94 Regs 73(2) and 75 HB Regs; regs 63(2) and 65 CTB Regs

95 Reg 75(1) HB Regs; reg 65(1) CTB Regs

96 Reg 75(2) HB Regs; reg 65(2) CTB Regs

97 Reg 75(3) HB Regs; reg 65(3)CTB Regs

98 Regs 2(1), 73(2) and 75(1) HB Regs; regs 2, 63(2) and 65(1) CTB Regs

99 Reg 68 HB Regs; reg 59 CTB Regs

100 Reg 68(1) HB Regs; reg 59(1) CTB Regs

101 Reg 68(1) HB Regs; reg 59(1) CTB Regs

102 Reg 67(1)(b) and (2) HB Regs

103 Reg 67(1)(a) and (b) HB Regs; reg 58(1)(a) and (b) CTB Regs

104 Sch 2 para 2 HB Regs; Sch 1 para 2 CTB Regs

105 Reg 68(2) HB Regs

106 Regs 26 and 68(1) HB Regs; regs 18 and 59(1) CTB Regs

107 Reg 68(3) HB Regs; reg 59(4) CTB Regs

108 Reg 68(6) and (7) HB Regs

109 *R v Middlesborough BC ex parte Holmes*, 15 February 1995

110 HB/CTB A9/95

111 *Welfare Rights Bulletin 135* p9; Sch 5 para 8 HB Regs; Sch 5 para 8 CTB Regs

112 Reg 68(4) HB Regs; reg 59(7) CTB Regs

113 Reg 68(5) HB Regs

114 Reg 67(c) HB Regs; reg 58(c) CTB Regs

115 Reg 67(1)(a) and (b) HB Regs; reg 581(a) and (b) CTB Regs

116 Reg 67(2) HB Regs

117 Reg 79(1)(a) and (3)(a) HB Regs; reg 69(1)(a) and (3)(a) CTB Regs

5. Overpayments
(pp280-288)

118 Reg 98 HB Regs; reg 83 CTB Regs

119 s134(2) SSAA 1992

120 paras A7.4-A7.16 GM

121 Reg 99(2) and (3) HB Regs; paras A7.22-4 and B5.5 GM; reg 84(2) and (3) CTB Regs

122 Reg 99(2) HB Regs; reg 84(2) CTB Regs

123 *Warwick DC v Freeman*

124 *R v Liverpool City Council ex parte Griffiths* [1990]

125 Reg 77(1)(b) HB Regs; reg 67(1)(b) CTB Regs

126 Sch 6 paras 2, 3, 6 and 14 HB Regs; para A7.42 GM; Sch 6 paras 2, 3, 6 and 16 CTB Regs

127 Reg 77(4) and (5) HB Regs; reg 67(2) and (3) CTB Regs

128 para A7.42 GM

129 Reg 91(3) HB Regs

130 Reg 100 HB Regs; reg 85 CTB Regs

131 Regs 79(2) and 101-102 HB Regs; regs 69(2) and 86 CTB Regs

132 A7.49 GM

133 Reg 79(2) HB Regs; Reg 69(2) CTB Regs; *Welfare Rights Bulletin 120*, p9

134 Reg 83(2) HB Regs; reg 72(2) CTB Regs;

135 Reg 104(a) HB Regs; reg 90(a) CTB Regs

136 Reg 104(b) HB Regs; para A7.27 GM; reg 90(b) CTB Regs

137 Reg 103(1) HB Regs;

reg 89(1) CTB Regs

138 Reg 103(1)(a) and (b) HB Regs; paras A7.30-32 GM; reg 89(1)(a) and (b) CTB Regs

139 Reg 103(2) HB Regs; reg 89(2) CTB Regs

140 Reg 101 HB Regs; reg 86 CTB Regs

141 Regs 93(2) and 94(2) HB Regs

142 paras A7.52-54 GM

143 *R v London Borough of Haringey ex parte Azad Ayub*

144 Reg 91(3) HB Regs

145 Regs 102 and 105 HB Regs; regs 87(3) and 91 CTB Regs

146 Reg 105 HB Regs; reg 91 CTB Regs

147 Reg 88 CTB Regs; para A7.38 GM

148 *Warwick DC v Freeman*

149 paras A7.37-40 GM

150 para A7.41 GM

6. Fraud

(pp 289-291)

151 s112 SSAA 1992

152 s15 Theft Act 1968

153 HB/CTB F7/95

154 HB/CTB F3/95

155 s116 SSAA 1992

156 HB/CTB 93(20); para 17 National Service Level Agreement

7. Reviews

(pp 291-298)

157 Reg 79(1) and (1A) HB Regs; reg 69(1) and (1A) CTB Regs

158 Reg 79(6) HB Regs; reg 69(7) CTB Regs

159 Reg 79(2) HB Regs; reg 69(2) CTB Regs

160 Reg 79(2) HB Regs; reg 69(2) CTB Regs

161 Reg 78(3) and (4) HB Regs; reg 68(3) and (4) CTB Regs

162 Sch 6 para 3 HB Regs; Sch 6 para 3 CTB Regs

163 Reg 78(3), (4) and (5) HB Regs; reg 68(3), (4) and (5) CTB Regs

164 Reg 79(4) HB Regs; reg 69(4) CTB Regs

165 Reg 77(4) and (5) HB Regs; reg 67(2) and (3) CTB Regs

166 Reg 79(2) and Sch 6 paras 4 and 5 HB Regs; reg 69(2) and Sch 6 paras 4 and 5 CTB Regs

167 Reg 79(3)(b) HB Regs; reg 69(3)(b) CTB Regs

168 Reg 79(3)(c) and (5)(a) HB Regs; reg 69(3)(c) and (5)(a) CTB Regs

169 Reg 81(1) and (2) HB Regs; reg 70(1) and (2) CTB Regs

170 Reg 78(3)-(5) HB Regs; reg 68(3)-(5) CTB Regs

171 Reg 82(1) HB Regs; reg 71(1) CTB Regs

172 Reg 82(2) and (1A) HB Regs

173 Reg 82(3) HB Regs; regs 70(5) and 71(3) CTB Regs

174 Reg 82(5) HB Regs; reg 71(5) CTB Regs

175 Sch 7 HB Regs; Sch 7 CTB Regs

176 Reg 82(7) HB Regs; reg 71(7) CTB Regs

177 paras A6.66 and B6.18 GM

178 Reg 81(4) HB Regs; reg 70(4) CTB Regs

179 Reg 82(2)(a) HB Regs; reg 71(2)(a) CTB Regs

180 Reg 82(2)(c) HB Regs; reg 71(2)(c) CTB Regs

181 Reg 82(9) HB Regs; paras A6.68 and B6.22 GM; reg 71(9) CTB Regs

182 Reg 82(2)(c)(ii) HB Regs; reg 71(2)(c)(ii) CTB Regs

183 Reg 82(4) HB Regs; reg 71(4) CTB Regs

184 Reg 82(5) and (6) HB Regs; reg 71(5) and (6) CTB Regs

185 Reg 83(1) HB Regs; paras A6.70 and B6.24 GM; reg 72(1) CTB Regs

186 Reg 82(8) HB Regs; reg 71(8) CTB Regs

187 Reg 83(4) HB Regs; reg 72(4) CTB Regs

188 Reg 83(2) HB Regs; reg 72(2) CTB Regs

189 Reg 83(5) HB Regs; reg 72(5) CTB Regs

190 *R v HBRB of Sefton MBC ex parte Cunningham*, 22 May 1991, QBD

191 Reg 84 HB Regs; reg 73 CTB Regs

192 Regs 79(3)(c), (5) and 83(3) HB Regs; regs 69(3)(c) and (5) and 72(3) CTB Regs

193 Regs 85(1) and 87(1) HB Regs; regs 74(1) and 76(1) CTB Regs

194 Reg 87(3) HB Regs; reg 76(3) CTB Regs

195 Reg 86(1) HB Regs; paras A6.79-82 and B6.33-6 GM; reg 75(1) CTB Regs

196 Reg 86(1) HB Regs; reg 75(1) CTB Regs

197 Reg 86(1) HB Regs; reg 75(1) CTB Regs

198 Regs 78(2) and 86(2) HB Regs; regs 68(2)

and 75(2) CTB Regs

199 Reg 87(2) HB Regs; reg 76(2) CTB Regs

200 Reg 86(3) HB Regs; reg 75(3) CTB Regs

201 Reg 86(4) HB Regs; reg 75(4) CTB Regs

202 Reg 87(3) HB Regs; reg 76(3) CTB Regs

203 Regs 78(2) and 87(2) and (3) HB Regs; regs 68(2) and 76(2) and (3) CTB Regs

204 *LB Haringey v Cotter*

205 CS/371/1949

206 R(P) 1/79

207 R(SB) 6/83

208 CS/50/1950

209 R(U) 35/36

210 R(U) 5/56

211 R(S) 5/56

212 R(S) 14/54; R(G) 4/68; R(U) 9/74

213 (IS) 11/59; R(G) 1/75

214 R(S) 10/59; R(SB) 17/83

215 R(SB) 6/83

Chapter 16: Council tax benefit
(pp300-315)

1 s131(3)-(5) SSCBA 1992

2 s131(3)(b) SSCBA 1992; reg 40 CTB Regs

3 Reg 51(1)(a) and (2)(a) CTB Regs

4 Reg 51(3) CTB Regs

5 Reg 51(4) CTB Regs

6 Reg 51(1) CTB Regs

7 para B3.27 GM

8 Sch 6 paras 9-10 CTB Regs

9 Reg 3 CTB Regs

10 Regs 51(1) and 52 CTB Regs

11 Reg 3(2)(c) CTB Regs

12 Reg 3(2)(d) CTB Regs

13 Reg 3(2)(e) CTB Regs

14 Reg 3(3)(a) CTB Regs

15 Reg 3(2)(f) CTB Regs

16 Reg 3(3) CTB Regs

17 Reg 52(3) CTB Regs

18 Reg 52(5) CTB Regs

19 Reg 52(6)-(8) CTB Regs

20 Sch 1(2) Local Government Finance Act 1992

21 Reg 3 Council Tax (Discount Disregards) Order 1992 SI No. 548

22 Reg 52(1), (2) and (9) CTB Regs

23 Reg 52(3) CTB Regs

24 Reg 52(4) CTB Regs

25 Reg 12 CTB Regs

26 Reg 51(5) CTB Regs

27 s131(9) SSCBA 1992

28 s131(1)(b), (6) and (8)(c) SSCBA 1992

29 s131(7)(a) SSCBA 1992

30 Reg 54, Schs 2 and 5 para 45(1) CTB Regs

31 Reg 55(b) and (d) CTB Regs

32 s131(6) SSCBA 1992; reg 55 and Sch 2(1) CTB Regs

33 Reg 54 and Sch 2 para 1(2) CTB Regs

34 Reg 54 and Sch 2 para 1 CTB Regs

35 Reg 54 and Sch 2 para 2 CTB Regs

36 Reg 54 and Sch 2 para 3 CTB Regs

37 Reg 54 and Sch 2 para 1 CTB Regs

38 Reg 54(2) CTB Regs

39 Reg 54(3) CTB Regs

40 Reg 54(4) CTB Regs

41 Reg 62(10) CTB Regs

42 Reg 62(12) CTB Regs

43 Reg 62(11) CTB Regs

44 Reg 62(16) CTB Regs

45 Sch 6 paras 9(a) and 10(a) CTB Regs

46 Sch 6 paras 12(b), 14(b)

and 15 CTB Regs

47 Sch 6 para 13(c) and (f) CTB Regs

48 Sch 6 paras 9, 10, 13 and 15 CTB Regs

49 Reg 56(2) CTB Regs

50 Reg 84(5) CTB Regs

51 Reg 77(1)(b) and (3) CTB Regs

52 Reg 77(3)(a)(ii) CTB Regs

53 Reg 77(3)(b) CTB Regs

54 Reg 78 CTB Regs

55 Reg 80 CTB Regs

56 Reg 81 CTB Regs

57 Reg 83(1) CTB Regs

58 Reg 84(2) and (4) CTB Regs

59 Reg 86(2) CTB Regs

60 Reg 91 CTB Regs

61 Reg 87(2)(b) CTB Regs

62 Reg 87(2)(a) CTB Regs

63 Reg 87(3) CTB Regs

64 Reg 91(1)(a) CTB Regs

65 Reg 91 CTB Regs

66 Reg 88 CTB Regs

67 Reg 65(1) CTB Regs

68 Reg 65(2) CTB Regs

69 Reg 65(4) CTB Regs

70 Reg 59(1) CTB Regs

71 Reg 59(2)-(6) CTB Regs

72 Reg 59(7) CTB Regs

73 Reg 59(1) CTB Regs

74 Reg 70(4) CTB Regs

75 Reg 40(3) CTB Regs

76 Reg 38 CTB Regs

PART FIVE: COMMON RULES

Chapter 17: Who counts as your family
(pp318-328)

1 s137 SSCBA 1992

2 s134(2) SSCBA 1992

3 Reg 4(2) SS(C&P) Regs

4 s129(1) SSCBA 1992

5 Reg 4(3A) SS(C&P)

Regs

6 *Santos v Santos* [1972] 2 All ER 246; CIS/671/ 1992

7 R(SB) 8/85

8 R(SB) 4/83

9 CSB/463/1986

10 s137 SSCBA 1992

11 R(SB) 8/85

12 **IS** Reg 2(1) IS Regs
HB Reg 2(1) HB Regs
CTB Reg 2(1) CTB Regs

13 **IS** Regs 18 and 23 IS Regs
FC Reg 10 FC Regs
DWA Reg 12 DWA Regs
HB Regs 17 and 19 HB Regs
CTB Regs 9 and 11 CTB Regs

14 *R v HBRB of Penwith District Council ex parte Menear*, 24 HLR 120 (11 October 1991)

15 *Crake and Butterworth v SBC* [1982] 1 ALL ER 498

16 R(SB) 17/81; R(G) 3/71; CIS/87/1993

17 *Crake and Butterworth v SBC* quoted in R(SB) 35/85

18 R(SB) 35/85

19 para 15027 AOG

20 CIS/72/1994

21 CIS/87/1993

22 CSB/150/1985

23 CIS/87/1993

24 CSSB/145/1983

25 R(SB) 13/82

26 CIS/317/1994

27 Reg 7(1) SS(C&P) Regs

28 CIS/317/1994

29 R(I) 1/71

30 **IS** Reg 16(1) IS Regs
FC Reg 9 FC Regs
DWA Reg 11 DWA

Regs
HB Reg 15(1) HB Regs
CTB Reg 7(1) CTB Regs

31 CIS/508/1992

32 **FC** Reg 9 FC Regs
DWA Reg 11 DWA Regs

33 Reg 7(1) CTB Regs

34 **IS** Reg 16(1) and (2) IS Regs
HB Reg 15(1) and (2) HB Regs

35 Reg 16(3) IS Regs

36 Sch 7 paras 11 and 11A IS Regs

37 Sch 1 para 22 IS Regs

38 Sch 7 para 9 IS Regs

39 Sch 7 para 9 col (2) IS Regs

40 CIS/508/1992

41 CIS/484/1993

42 s137 SSCBA 1992

43 **IS** Reg 14 IS Regs
FC Reg 6 FC Regs
DWA Reg 8 DWA Regs
HB Reg 13 HB Regs
CTB Reg 5 CTB Regs

44 **All** s134(2) SSCBA 1992
IS Reg 15(4) IS Regs
FC Reg 7(3) FC Regs
DWA Reg 9(3) DWA Regs
HB Reg 14(3) HB Regs
CTB Reg 6(3) CTB Regs

45 **FC** Reg 7(1) FC Regs
DWA Reg 9(1) DWA Regs
HB Reg 14(1) HB Regs
CTB Reg 6(1) CTB Regs

46 CFC/1537/1995

47 CFC/1537/1995

48 **FC** Reg 7(2) FC Regs
DWA Reg 9(2) DWA Regs
HB Reg 14(2) HB Regs
CTB Reg 6(2) CTB Regs

49 Reg 15(1) IS Regs

50 Reg 15(2) IS Regs

51 Reg 15(1A) IS Regs

52 **IS** Reg 16 IS Regs
FC Reg 8 FC Regs
DWA Reg 10 DWA Regs
HB Reg 15 HB Regs
CTB Reg 7 CTB Regs

53 Regs 15(3) and 16(6) IS Regs

54 **HB** Reg 15(5) HB Regs
CTB Reg 7(4) CTB Regs

55 **FC** Reg 8(2)(a) FC Regs
DWA Reg 10(2)(a) DWA Regs

56 Reg 16(5)(b) IS Regs

57 Reg 16(5A) IS Regs

58 **IS** Reg 16(5)(b)(ii) IS Regs
FC Reg 46(6) FC Regs
DWA Reg 51(6) DWA Regs

59 Regs 15(3) and 16(6) IS Regs

60 Reg 16(5a) and (aa) IS Regs

61 Reg 16(5A) IS Regs

62 Reg 16(5)(a), IS Regs

63 Regs 1(2) (definition of 'remunerative work') and 7 CB Regs

64 **All** Reg 7D(1) CB Regs
IS Reg 15(1) IS Regs
HB Reg 13 HB Regs
CTB Reg 5 CTB Regs

65 s134(2) SSCBA 1992

66 **FC** Reg 6(2) FC Regs
DWA Reg 8(2) DWA Regs

Chapter 18: Applicable amounts

(pp 329-343)

1 Reg 22A IS Regs
2 IS Reg 18 IS Regs
   HB Reg 17 HB Regs
   CTB Reg 9 CTB Regs
3 Reg 18(2) IS Regs
4 **IS** Part I Sch 2 IS Regs
   HB Part I Sch 2 HB Regs
   CTB Part I Sch 1 CTB Regs
5 **IS** Reg 18(1)(b) IS Regs
   HB Reg 17(b) HB Regs
   CTB Reg 9(b) CTB Regs
   HB/CTB paras C4.05-06 GM
6 **IS** Sch 2 para 2 IS Regs
   HB Sch 2 para 2 HB Regs
   CTB Sch 1 para 2 CTB Regs
7 **IS/HB/CTB** Reg 10(1) and (2) IRB&JSA(PA) Amdt Regs
8 **IS** Sch 2 para 5 IS Regs
   HB Sch 2 para 5 HB Regs
   CTB Sch 1 para 5 CTB Regs
9 **IS** Sch 2 para 7 IS Regs
   HB Sch 2 para 7 HB Regs
   CTB Sch 1 para 7 CTB Regs
10 **IS** Sch 2 para 14B IS Regs
   HB Sch 2 para 14B HB Regs
   CTB Sch 1 para 18 CTB Regs
11 **IS** Sch 2 para 3 IS Regs
   HB Sch 2 para 3 HB Regs
   CTB Sch 1 para 3 CTB Regs
12 Regs 15(3) and 16(6) IS Regs
13 **HB** Reg 15(4)-(5) HB Regs
   CTB Reg 7(3)-(4) CTB Regs
14 **IS** Sch 2 paras 14 and 15(6) IS Regs
   HB Sch 2 paras 14 and 15(6) HB Regs
   CTB Sch 1 paras 15 and 19(7) CTB Regs
15 **IS** Sch 2 paras 12(1)(a)(iii) and (2) and 14(c) IS Regs
   HB Sch 2 paras 12(1)(a)(v) and (2) and 14(c) HB Regs
   CTB Sch 1 paras 13(1)(a)(v) and (2) and 15(c) CTB Regs
16 **IS** Sch 2 para 14(a) IS Regs
   HB Sch 2 para 14(a) HB Regs
   CTB Sch 1 para 15(a) CTB Regs
17 **IS** Sch 2 para 11 IS Regs
   HB Sch 2 para 11 HB Regs
   CTB Sch 1 para 12 CTB Regs
18 **IS** Reg 2(1) IS Regs
   HB Reg 2(1) HB Regs
   CTB Reg 2(1) CTB Regs
   All Definition of 'attendance allowance'
19 **IS** Sch 2 para 12(6) IS Regs
   HB Sch 2 para 12(7) HB Regs
   CTB Sch 1 para 13(6A) CTB Regs
20 **IS** Sch 2 para 14A IS Regs
   HB Sch 2 para 14A HB Regs
   CTB Sch 1 para 17 CTB Regs
21 **IS** Sch 2 para 14B IS Regs
   HB Sch 2 para 14B HB Regs
   CTB Sch 1 para 18 CTB Regs
   See also R(IS) 10/94
22 **IS** Sch 2 para 7(1)(a) IS Regs
   HB Sch 2 para 7(1)(a) HB Regs
   CTB Sch 1 para 7(1)(a) CTB Regs
23 **IS** Sch 2 para 12(1)(a)(iii) and (2) IS Regs
   HB Sch 2 para 12(1)(a)(v) and (2) HB Regs
   CTB Sch 1 para 13(1)(a)(v) and (2) CTB Regs
24 **IS** Sch 2 para 12(1)(a)(ii) IS Regs
   HB Sch 2 para 12(1)(a)(iv) HB Regs
   CTB Sch 1 para 13(1)(a)(iv) CTB Regs
25 **IS** Sch 2 para 12(1)(c)(i) IS Regs
   HB Sch 2 para 12(1)(a)(ii) HB Regs
   CTB Sch 1 para 13(1)(a)(ii) CTB Regs
26 Sch 2 para 12(1)(c)(i) IS Regs
27 **HB** Sch 2 para 12(1)(a)(ii) HB Regs
   CTB Sch 1 para 13(1)(a)(ii) CTB Regs
28 Sch 2 para 12(1)(c) IS Regs
29 **IS** Sch 2 para 12(1)(c)(ii) IS Regs

HB Sch 2 para
12(1)(a)(iii) HB Regs
CTB Sch 1 para
13(1)(a)(iii) CTB Regs
30 **IS** Sch 2 para 12(1)(b)
IS Regs
HB Sch 2 para 12(1)(b)
HB Regs
CTB Sch 1 para
13(1)(b) CTB Regs
31 s30B(4) SSCBA 1992
32 **IS** Sch 2 paras 11(b)
and 12 IS Regs
HB Sch 2 paras 11(b)
and 12 HB Regs
CTB Sch 1 paras 12(b)
and 13 CTB Regs
33 **IS** Sch 2 paras 7(1)(b)
and 12(5) IS Regs
HB Sch 2 paras 7(1)(b)
and 12(5) HB Regs
CTB Sch 1 paras
7(1)(b) and 13(5) CTB
Regs
34 **IS** Reg 63(1A) SS(Adj)
Regs
HB Reg 79 HB Regs
CTB Reg 69 CTB Regs
35 CSIS/66/1992;
CIS/706/1992
36 **IS** Sch 2 paras 9 and
9A IS Regs
HB Sch 2 paras 9 and
9A HB Regs
CTB Sch 1 paras 9 and
10 CTB Regs
37 **IS** Sch 2 para 10 IS
Regs
HB Sch 2 para 10 HB
Regs
CTB Sch 1 para 11
CTB Regs
38 **IS** Sch 2 para
10(1)(b)(ii) and (3) IS
Regs
HB Sch 2 para
10(1)(b)(ii) and (3) HB
Regs
CTB Sch 1 para

11(1)(b)(ii) and (3) CTB
Regs
39 **HB** Sch 2 para 10(3)(c)
HB Regs
CTB Sch 1 para
11(3)(c) CTB Regs
40 **IS** Sch 2 para
10(2)(b)(ii) IS Regs
HB Sch 2 para
10(2)(b)(ii) HB Regs
CTB Sch 1 para
11(2)(b)(ii) CTB Regs
41 **IS** Sch 2 para 12(1)(c)(i)
IS Regs
HB Sch 2 para
12(1)(a)(ii) HB Regs
CTB Sch 1 para
13(1)(a)(ii) CTB Regs
42 **HB** Sch 2 para 10(3)(c)
HB Regs
CTB Sch 1 para
11(3)(c) CTB Regs
43 **IS** Sch 2 para 12(1)(c)(i)
IS Regs
HB Sch 2 para
12(1)(a)(ii) HB Regs
CTB Sch 1 para
13(1)(a)(ii) CTB Regs
44 Sch 2 para 12(1)(c) IS
Regs
45 CIS/458/1992
46 s68(11) SSCBA 1992;
regs 5 and 20(3)
SS(SDA) Regs
47 **IS** Sch 2 para 7(1)(a) IS
Regs
HB Sch 2 para 7(1)(a)
HB Regs
CTB Sch 1 para 7(1)(a)
CTB Regs
48 **IS** Sch 2 para 13 IS
Regs
HB Sch 2 para 13 HB
Regs
CTB Sch 1 para 14
CTB Regs
49 **IS** Sch 2 para 14A IS
Regs
HB Sch 2 para 14A

HB Regs
CTB Sch 1 para 17
CTB Regs
50 **IS** Sch 2 para 13(2A) IS
Regs
HB Sch 2 para 13(2A)
HB Regs
CTB Sch 1 para 14(2A)
CTB Regs
51 **IS** Sch 2 para 14B IS
Regs
HB Sch 2 para 14B
HB Regs
CTB Sch 1 para 18
CTB Regs
See also R(IS) 10/94,
upheld in *Rider v CAO*
(CA), *The Times,* 30
January 1996
52 *Bate v CAO* [1996] 2
All ER 790 (HL)
53 **IS** Reg 3(4) and (5) IS
Regs
HB Reg 3(4) HB Regs
54 **IS** Sch 2 para
13(2)(a)(iii) and (b) IS
Regs
HB Sch 2 para
13(2)(a)(iii) and (b) HB
Regs
CTB Sch 1 para
14(2)(a)(iii) and (b)
CTB Regs
55 **IS** Sch 2 para 13(3ZA)
IS Regs
HB Sch 2 para 13(4)
HB Regs
CTB Sch 1 para 14(4)
CTB Regs
56 **IS** Sch 2 para 13(3A) IS
Regs
HB Sch 2 para 13(3A)
HB Regs
CTB Sch 1 para 14(3A)
CTB Regs
57 **IS** Reg 3 IS Regs
HB Reg 3 HB Regs
CTB Reg 3 CTB Regs
58 **IS** Sch 2 para 13(3)(a)

IS Regs
HB Sch 2 para 13(3)(a)
HB Regs
CTB Sch 1 para
14(3)(a) CTB Regs
59 **IS** Sch 2 para 13(3)(d)
IS Regs
HB Sch 2 para 13(3)(c)
HB Regs
CTB Sch 1 para
14(3)(c) CTB Regs
60 Sch 2 para 13(3)(c) and
(4) IS Regs
61 Regs 3 and 7(1) HB
Regs
62 Reg 3 CTB Regs
63 **IS** Reg 2(1) IS Regs
HB Reg 2(1) HB Regs
CTB Reg 2(1) CTB
Regs
All Definition of 'close
relative'
64 *Bate v CAO* [1996] 2
All ER 790 (HL)
65 CIS/180/1989
66 CIS/529/1994 (Tribunal
of Commissioners)
67 CSIS/43/1989
68 CIS/754/1991 and
CIS/529/1994 para 12
69 CIS/529/1994 para 8
70 CIS/529/1994 paras 10
and 11
71 CIS/754/1991
72 CIS/754/1991 referring
to CSIS/28/1992 and
CSIS/40/1992
73 **IS** Sch 2 para 14ZA IS
Regs
HB Sch 2 para 14ZA
HB Regs
CTB Sch 1 para 16
CTB Regs
74 s70(6) SSCBA 1992;
reg 11 SS(ICA) Regs
75 **IS** Sch 2 paras 7 and
14ZA(2) IS Regs
HB Sch 2 paras 7 and
14ZA(2) HB Regs

CTB Sch 1 paras 7 and
16(2) CTB Regs
76 **IS** Sch 2 para 14A IS
Regs
HB Sch 2 para 14A
HB Regs
CTB Sch 1 para 17
CTB Regs
77 **IS** Sch 2 para 13(3ZA)
IS Regs
HB Sch 2 para 13(4)
HB Regs
CTB Sch 1 para 14(4)
CTB Regs
78 s74 SSAA 1992
79 R(IS) 14/94; *Barber v
CAO*

Chapter 19: Income
(pp 344-383)

1. Introduction
(pp 344-349)

1 **HB** Sch 3 para 10 and
Sch 4 para 4 HB Regs
CTB Sch 3 para 10 and
Sch 4 para 4 CTB Regs
2 s136(1) SSCBA 1992
3 Reg 23(4) IS Regs
4 Reg 23(5) IS Regs
5 **IS** Reg 17(b) IS Regs
FC Reg 46(4) FC Regs
DWA Reg 51(4) DWA
Regs
HB Reg 16(b) HB
Regs
CTB Reg 8(b) CTB
Regs
6 **IS** Regs 25 and 44(5)
IS Regs
FC Reg 27(3) FC Regs
DWA Reg 30(3) DWA
Regs
HB Reg 36(2) HB
Regs
CTB Reg 27(2) CTB
Regs
7 s136(1) SSCBA 1992
8 **IS** Reg 44(4) IS Regs

HB Reg 36(1) HB
Regs
CTB Reg 27(1) CTB
Regs
9 **FC** Regs 27(2) and
46(5) FC Regs
DWA Regs 30(2) and
51(5) DWA Regs
10 **IS** Reg 25 IS Regs
FC Reg 27(2) FC Regs
DWA Reg 30(2) DWA
Regs
HB Reg 36(1) HB
Regs
CTB Reg 27(1) CTB
Regs
11 **IS** Sch 8 para 14 IS
Regs
FC Sch 1 para 2 FC
Regs
DWA Sch 2 para 2
DWA Regs
HB Sch 3 para 13 HB
Regs
CTB Sch 3 para 13
CTB Regs
12 **IS** Sch 8 para 15(b) IS
Regs
HB Sch 3 para 14(b)
HB Regs
CTB Sch 2 para 14(b)
CTB Regs
13 **IS** Sch 8 para 15(a) IS
Regs
HB Sch 3 para 14(a)
HB Regs
CTB Sch 3 para 14(a)
CTB Regs
14 **IS** Reg 44(4) IS Regs
HB Reg 36(1) HB
Regs
CTB Reg 27(1) CTB
Regs
15 Reg 42(4)(a)(ii) IS Regs
16 Reg 44(2)(a) IS Regs
17 Reg 44(2)(b) IS Regs
18 Reg 44(9) IS Regs
19 Reg 44(3) IS Regs; CIS/
164/1994

20 **HB** Reg 35(3)(a) and
Sch 4 para 13(1), (2)
and (5) HB Regs
CTB Reg 26(3)(a) and
Sch 4 para 13(1), (2)
and (5) CTB Regs
Both paras C3.107 and
C3.112 GM
21 **HB** Reg 35(3)(a) and
Sch 4 paras 13(3) and
47 HB Regs
CTB Reg 26(3)(a) and
Sch 4 paras 13(3) and
46 CTB Regs
Both paras C3.89,
C3.110 and C3.112 GM
22 **IS** Reg 32(1) IS Regs
FC Reg 18(1) FC Regs
DWA Reg 20(1) DWA
Regs
HB Reg 25 HB Regs
CTB Reg 17 CTB Regs
23 R(IS) 3/93
24 CIS/242/1989 (to be
reported as R(IS) 10/
95)
25 Reg 32(6) IS Regs
26 Reg 32(2) and (3) IS
Regs
27 Reg 32(4) IS Regs
28 Reg 32(5) and Sch 8
para 10 IS Regs
29 Reg 29(2)(a) IS Regs
30 Reg 29(2)(b) IS Regs
31 Reg 31(1)(a) IS Regs
32 Reg 31(1)(b) IS Regs
33 Reg 31(2) IS Regs
34 Reg 2(1) IS Regs
35 R(SB) 33/83
36 R(SB) 22/84;
R(SB) 11/85
37 CIS/590/1993

**2. Earnings of
employed earners**
(pp349-359)
38 *Parsons v Hogg* [1985] 2
All ER 897, CA,
appendix to R(FIS) 4/

85
39 R(FC) 1/90
40 CFC/26/1989
41 R(FIS) 4/85
42 R(IS) 13/91; R(IS)
16/93; CFC/26/1989
43 CCS/318/1995 (applying
the identical provisions
in child support law)
44 R(U) 2/72; R(FIS)
4/85; R(FC) 1/91; R(IS)
13/91
45 CIS/521/1990
46 **IS** Reg 36(3) IS Regs
FC Reg 20(3) FC Regs
DWA Reg 22(3) DWA
Regs
HB Reg 29(3) HB
Regs
CTB Reg 20(3) CTB
Regs
47 **FC** Regs 14(2) and
20(4) FC Regs
DWA Regs 16(7) and
22(4) DWA Regs
HB Regs 22(2) and
29(4) HB Regs
CTB Regs 14(2) and
20(4) CTB Regs
HB/CTB para C3.22
GM
48 **HB** Reg 26 HB Regs
CTB Reg 18 CTB Regs
HB/CTB paras C3.03-
04 GM
49 R(SB) 21/86
IS Reg 35(1) IS Regs
FC Reg 19(1) FC Regs
DWA Reg 21(1) DWA
Regs
HB Reg 28(1) HB
Regs
CTB Reg 19(1) CTB
Regs
50 **IS** Reg 48(3) IS Regs
FC Reg 31(2) FC Regs
DWA Reg 34(2) DWA
Regs
HB Reg 40(3) HB

Regs
CTB Reg 31(3) CTB
Regs
51 **FC** Reg 19(1)(g)-(h) FC
Regs
DWA Reg 21(1)(g)-(h)
DWA Regs
HB Reg 28(1)(i)-(j) HB
Regs
CTB Reg 19(1)(i)-(j)
CTB Regs
52 Regs 35(2)(b) and 40(4)
and Sch 9 paras 1, 4
and 4A IS Regs
53 **HB** Reg 28(1)(i)-(j) HB
Regs
CTB Reg 19(1)(i)-(j)
CTB Regs
54 **FC** Sch 2 paras 27 and
31 FC Regs
DWA Sch 3 paras 27
and 31 DWA Regs
55 Regs 35(2)(b) and 40(4)
and Sch 9 paras 1, 4
and 4A IS Regs
56 CIS/743/1992
57 Reg 21(1)(i) DWA Regs
58 **All** *R v NIC ex parte
Stratton* [1979] QBD
361
IS Reg 35(1)(c) IS Regs
HB Reg 28(1)(c) HB
Regs
CTB Reg 19(1)(c) CTB
Regs
59 CIS/590/1993
60 Reg 35(2)(e) IS Regs
61 **IS** Reg 35(2)(a) IS Regs
FC Reg 19(2)(a) FC
Regs
DWA Reg 21(2)(a)
DWA Regs
HB Reg 28(2)(a) HB
Regs
CTB Reg 19(2)(a) CTB
Regs
62 **IS** Sch 9 para 21 IS
Regs
FC Sch 2 para 20 FC

Regs
DWA Sch 3 para 20
DWA Regs
HB Sch 4 para 21 HB
Regs
CTB Sch 4 para 22
CTB Regs
63 **IS** Reg 48(5) IS Regs
FC Reg 31(5) FC Regs
DWA Reg 34(5) DWA
Regs
HB Reg 40(5) HB
Regs
CTB Reg 31(5) CTB
Regs
64 Reg 48(6) IS Regs
65 **IS** Reg 35(2)(c) IS Regs
FC Reg 19(2)(b) FC
Regs
DWA Reg 21(2)(b)
DWA Regs
HB Reg 28(2)(b) HB
Regs
CTB Reg 19(2)(b) CTB
Regs
66 CIS/77/1993;
CIS/89/1989
67 R(IS) 6/92
IS paras 29155-166
AOG
HB/CTB para C3.10
GM
68 **IS** Sch 8 para 11 IS
Regs
FC Sch 1 para 1 FC
Regs
DWA Sch 2 para 1
DWA Regs
HB Sch 3 para 11 HB
Regs
CTB Sch 3 para 11
CTB Regs
69 **IS** Sch 8 para 12 IS
Regs
FC Sch 1 para 3 FC
Regs
DWA Sch 2 para 3
DWA Regs
HB Sch 3 para 12 HB

Regs
CTB Sch 3 para 12
CTB Regs
70 **IS** Reg 35(2)(d) IS Regs
FC Reg 19(2)(c) FC
Regs
DWA Reg 21(2)(c)
DWA Regs
HB Reg 28(2)(c) HB
Regs
CTB Reg 19(2)(c) CTB
Regs
71 **IS** Reg 40(4) and Sch 9
para 1 IS Regs
FC Reg 24(5) and Sch
2 para 1 FC Regs
DWA Reg 27(4) and
Sch 3 para 1 DWA
Regs
HB Reg 33(4) and Sch
4 para 1 HB Regs
CTB Reg 24(5) and
Sch 4 para 1 CTB Regs
72 Reg 35(2)(a) IS Regs;
para 29126 AOG
73 **FC** Reg 19(3) FC Regs
DWA Reg 21(3) DWA
Regs
74 **HB** Reg 28(2)(a) HB
Regs
CTB Reg 19(2)(a) CTB
Regs
75 Reg 14(1) and (2) FC
Regs
76 Reg 14(1) FC Regs
77 Reg 14(3) FC Regs
78 Reg 14(2A) FC Regs
79 Reg 20(5) FC Regs
80 Reg 14A FC Regs
81 Regs 14(1), 14A, 17(b)
and 18(3) FC Regs
82 Reg 16(2)-(4) DWA
Regs
83 Reg 16(1) DWA Regs
84 Reg 19(a) DWA Regs
85 R(FIS) 1/87; R(FIS)
2/87
86 Reg 16(5) DWA Regs
87 s27(3)(b) SSCBA 1992;

reg 16(3), (4)(b) and
(9)(b) DWA Regs; R(U)
5/87
88 **FC** Regs 14(4) and 20A
FC Regs
DWA Regs 16(6) and
23 DWA Regs
89 **FC** Reg 20A FC Regs
DWA Reg 23 DWA
Regs
90 **FC** Reg 14(5) and (6)
FC Regs
DWA Reg 16(7) and (8)
DWA Regs
91 **HB** Reg 22(1)(a) HB
Regs
CTB Reg 14(1)(a) CTB
Regs
HB/CTB para C3.16
GM
92 **HB** Reg 22(1)(b) HB
Regs
CTB Reg 14(1)(b) CTB
Regs
HB/CTB para C3.17
GM
93 *R v HBRB of the London
Borough of Ealing ex parte
Saville* [1986] 18 HLR
349
94 **HB** Reg 22(2)(a)-(b)
HB Regs
CTB Reg 14(2)(a)-(b)
CTB Regs
HB/CTB para C3.19
GM
95 **HB** Reg 22(3) HB
Regs
CTB Reg 14(3) CTB
Regs
96 **IS** Regs 35(1)(b) and
40(1) IS Regs; para
29189 AOG
HB Regs 28(1)(b) and
33(1) HB Regs
CTB Regs 19(1)(b) and
24(1) CTB Regs
97 Sch 8 para 1(a)(i) IS
Regs

98 Sch 8 para 1(a)(ii) IS Regs

99 Reg 29(4B) and (4D)(b) IS Regs

100 Reg 48(11) IS Regs

101 Regs 5(5) and 29(3)(a) IS Regs

102 Reg 29(4) IS Regs

103 Reg 29(3)(b) IS Regs

104 Reg 5(5) and Sch 8 para 1(b) IS Regs

105 Sch 8 para 2 IS Regs

106 Regs 29(4C) and 32(7) IS Regs

107 Reg 29(4) and (4C) IS Regs

108 R(IS) 3/93; CIS/104/1989

109 **HB** Sch 3 para 1(a)(i) HB Regs
CTB Sch 3 para 1(a)(i) CTB Regs

110 **HB** Sch 3 para 1(a)(ii) HB Regs
CTB Sch 3 para 1(a)(ii) CTB Regs

111 **HB** Sch 3 para 2 HB Regs
CTB Sch 3 para 2 CTB Regs

112 **HB** Sch 3 para 4 HB Regs
CTB Sch 3 para 4 CTB Regs

113 Sch 8 para 5 IS Regs

114 **IS** Sch 8 para 4(2) IS Regs
HB Sch 3 para 3(2) HB Regs
CTB Sch 3 para 3(2) CTB Regs

115 **HB** Sch 3 para 3(2) HB Regs
CTB Sch 3 para 3(2) CTB Regs

116 **IS** Sch 8 para 4(4) IS Regs
HB Sch 3 para 3(4) HB Regs

CTB Sch 3 para 3(4) CTB Regs

117 **IS** Sch 8 para 4(3) and (5) IS Regs
HB Sch 3 para 3(3) and (5) HB Regs
CTB Sch 3 para 3(3) and (5) CTB Regs

118 **IS** Sch 8 para 4(6) IS Regs
HB Sch 3 para 3(6) HB Regs
CTB Sch 3 para 3(6) CTB Regs

119 **IS** Sch 8 paras 6A and 6B IS Regs
HB Sch 3 paras 4A and 4B HB Regs
CTB Sch 3 paras 4A and 4B CTB Regs

120 **IS** Sch 8 para 7(1) IS Regs
HB Sch 3 para 6(1) HB Regs
CTB Sch 3 para 6(1) CTB Regs

121 **IS** Sch 8 para 8 IS Regs
HB Sch 3 para 7 HB Regs
CTB Sch 3 para 7 CTB Regs

122 **IS** Sch 8 para 7(2) IS Regs
HB Sch 3 para 6(2)(b) HB Regs
CTB Sch 3 para 6(2)(b) CTB Regs

123 Reg 3A and Sch 8 para 4(7) IS Regs

124 **IS** Sch 8 paras 6 and 9 IS Regs
HB Sch 3 paras 5 and 8 HB Regs
CTB Sch 4 paras 5 and 8 CTB Regs

3. Earnings from self-employment

(pp 359-365)

125 **IS** Reg 37(1) IS Regs
FC Reg 21(1) FC Regs
DWA Reg 24(1) DWA Regs
HB Reg 30 HB Regs
CTB Reg 21 CTB Regs

126 **IS** Reg 38(3) IS Regs
FC Reg 22(3) FC Regs
DWA Reg 25(3) DWA Regs
HB Reg 31(3) HB Regs
CTB Reg 22(3) CTB Regs

127 **IS** Reg 2(1) IS Regs
FC Regs 2(1) and 22(12)-(13) FC Regs
DWA Regs 2(1) and 25(14)-(15) DWA Regs
HB Regs 2(1) and 31(11)-(12) HB Regs
CTB Regs 2(1) and 22(11)-(12) CTB Regs

128 **IS/FC/DWA** Reg 32(3) SS(C&P) Regs
HB Reg 73(4) HB Regs
CTB Reg 63(4) CTB Regs

129 **FC** Reg 21(1) FC Regs
DWA Reg 24(1) DWA Regs

130 CFC/24/1989; CFC/3/1992

131 CFC/4/1991 (*Kostanczwk v CAO*); CFC/23/1991

132 **IS** Reg 37(2) IS Regs
FC Reg 21(3) FC Regs
DWA Reg 24(3) DWA Regs
HB Reg 30(2) HB Regs
CTB Reg 21(2) CTB Regs

133 **IS** Sch 9 paras 26-27 IS Regs
FC Sch 2 para 24 FC Regs
DWA Sch 3 para 24

DWA Regs
HB Sch 4 paras 24-25
HB Regs
CTB Sch 4 paras 25-26
CTB Regs

134 Reg 37(2)(a) IS Regs

135 **FC** Reg 21(2) FC Regs
DWA Reg 24(2) DWA
Regs

136 **IS** Reg 38(3)(a), (4), (7)
and (8)(a) IS Regs
FC Reg 22(3)(a), (4),
(7) and (8)(a) FC Regs
DWA Reg 25(3)(a),
(4)(a), (5), (6), (9) and
(10)(a) DWA Regs
HB Reg 31(3)(a), (4),
(7) and (8)(a) HB Regs
CTB Reg 22(3)(a), (4),
(7) and (8)(a) CTB
Regs

137 R(IS) 13/91; R(FC)
1/91; CFC/26/1989

138 **IS** Reg 38(6) and (8)(b)
IS Regs
FC Reg 22(6) and
(8)(b) FC Regs
DWA Reg 25(8) and
(10)(b) DWA Regs
HB Reg 31(6) and
(8)(b) HB Regs
CTB Reg 22(6) and
(8)(b) CTB Regs

139 **IS** Reg 38(5) IS Regs
FC Reg 22(5) FC Regs
DWA Reg 25(7) DWA
Regs
HB Reg 31(5) HB Regs
CTB Reg 22(5) CTB
Regs

140 Compare CFC/19/1993
and CFC/41/1993 with
CFC/22/1989, CFC/19/
1992 and CFC/10/1993

141 CFC/41/1993 (to be
reported as R(FC)
1/96)

142 **IS** Reg 38(11) IS Regs
FC Reg 22(11) FC

Regs
DWA Reg 25(13) DWA
Regs
HB Reg 31(10) HB
Regs
CTB Reg 22(10) CTB
Regs; R(FC) 1/93

143 CFC/836/1995

144 Reg 30 IS Regs

145 CIS/166/1994

146 Reg 30(2) IS Regs

147 **FC** Reg 15(1) FC Regs
DWA Reg 17(1) DWA
Regs

148 **FC** Reg 18(2) FC Regs
DWA Reg 20(2) DWA
Regs

149 **FC** Reg 17 FC Regs
DWA Reg 19(b) DWA
Regs

150 Regs 15(2) and (4) and
17(a) FC Regs

151 Reg 17(3) DWA Regs

152 **FC** s128(3) SSCBA
1992
DWA s129(6) SSCBA
1992

153 CFC/24/1989;
CFC/14/1991

154 **HB** Regs 23(1) and
25(2) HB Regs
CTB Regs 15(1) and
17(2) CTB Regs

155 **IS** Reg 38(9) IS Regs
FC Reg 22(9) FC Regs
DWA Reg 25(11) DWA
Regs
HB Reg 31(9) HB Regs
CTB Reg 22(9) CTB
Regs

156 **IS** Reg 38(2) IS Regs
FC Reg 22(2) FC Regs
DWA Reg 25(2) DWA
Regs
HB Reg 31(2) HB Regs
CTB Reg 22(2) CTB
Regs

157 **FC** Regs 13(1)(c) and
13A FC Regs

DWA Regs 15(1)(c) and
15A DWA Regs
HB Regs 21(1)(c) and
21A HB Regs
CTB Regs 13(1)(c) and
13A CTB Regs

158 **FC** Reg 13A(2) FC
Regs
DWA Reg 15A(2)
DWA Regs
HB Reg 21A (2) HB
Regs
CTB Reg 13A(2) CTB
Regs
FC and DWA Reg
10(3) IRB and JSA(PA)
Regs

159 **FC** Reg 13A FC Regs
DWA Reg 15A DWA
Regs

160 **HB** Reg 21A HB Regs
CTB Reg 13A CTB
Regs

161 s29 CA 1989

162 CFC/19/1990

4. Other income

(pp 365-380)

163 **IS** Reg 40 and Sch 9
para 1 IS Regs
FC Reg 24 and Sch 2
para 1 FC Regs
DWA Reg 27 and Sch
3 para 1 DWA Regs
HB Reg 33 and Sch 4
para 1 HB Regs
CTB Reg 24 and Sch 4
para 1 CTB Regs

164 **HB** Reg 26 HB Regs
CTB Reg 18 CTB Regs

165 **HB** Reg 24 HB Regs
CTB Reg 16 CTB Regs

166 **FC** Reg 16(1) FC Regs
DWA Reg 18(1) DWA
Regs

167 **HB** Sch 4 paras 57, 58
and 60 HB Regs
CTB Sch 4 paras 56,
57 and 59 CTB Regs

168 Reg 35(2) and Sch 9
para 4 IS Regs
169 s74(2) SSAA 1992
170 **IS** Sch 10 para 7 IS
Regs
FC Sch 3 para 8 FC
Regs
DWA Sch 4 para 8
DWA Regs
HB Sch 5 para 8 HB
Regs
CTB Sch 5 para 8 CTB
Regs
171 **IS** Sch 9 para 9 IS Regs
FC Sch 2 paras 4 and 7
FC Regs
DWA Sch 3 paras 4
and 7 DWA Regs
HB Sch 4 paras 5 and
8 HB Regs
CTB Sch 4 paras 5 and
8 CTB Regs
172 **IS** Sch 9 para 33 IS
Regs
FC Sch 2 para 28 FC
Regs
DWA Sch 3 para 28
DWA Regs
HB Sch 4 para 31 HB
Regs
CTB Sch 4 para 32
CTB Regs
173 **IS** Sch 9 para 6 IS Regs
FC Sch 2 para 4 FC
Regs
DWA Sch 3 para 4
DWA Regs
HB Sch 4 para 5 HB
Regs
CTB Sch 4 para 5 CTB
Regs
174 **IS** Sch 9 para 8 IS Regs
FC Sch 2 para 6 FC
Regs
DWA Sch 3 para 6
DWA Regs
HB Sch 4 para 7 HB
Regs
CTB Sch 4 para 7 CTB

Regs
175 **IS** Sch 9 paras 7-8 IS
Regs
FC Sch 2 paras 5-6 FC
Regs
DWA Sch 3 paras 5-6
DWA Regs
HB Sch 4 paras 6-7
HB Regs
CTB Sch 4 paras 6-7
CTB Regs
176 Sch 2 para 4 FC Regs
177 Sch 3 para 46 DWA
Regs
178 **IS** Sch 9 para 31 IS
Regs
HB Sch 4 para 30 HB
Regs
CTB Sch 4 para 31
CTB Regs
179 **IS** Sch 10 para 18 IS
Regs
FC Sch 3 para 19 FC
Regs
DWA Sch 4 para 19
DWA Regs
HB Sch 5 para 19 HB
Regs
CTB Sch 5 para 19
CTB Regs
180 **IS** Sch 9 para 38 IS
Regs
FC Sch 2 para 33 FC
Regs
HB Sch 4 para 37 HB
Regs
CTB Sch 4 para 39
CTB Regs
181 **IS** Sch 9 paras 40-42 IS
Regs
FC Sch 2 paras 35-37
FC Regs
DWA Sch 2 paras 34-
36 DWA Regs
HB Sch 4 paras 35-36
and 48 HB Regs
CTB Sch 4 paras 37-38
and 47 CTB Regs
182 **IS** Sch 9 paras 5, 45-46

and 52 IS Regs
FC Sch 2 paras 3, 41-
42 and 49 FC Regs
DWA Sch 3 paras 3, 39
40 and 47 DWA Regs
HB Sch 4 paras 40-41
and 51 HB Regs
CTB Sch 4 paras 36,
41 and 50 CTB Regs
183 **FC** Sch 2 para 3 FC
Regs
DWA Sch 3 para 3
DWA Regs
HB Sch 4 para 4 HB
Regs
CTB Sch 4 para 4 CTB
Regs
184 **IS** Sch 9 para 47 IS
Regs
FC Sch 2 para 43 FC
Regs
DWA Sch 3 para 41
DWA Regs
HB Sch 4 para 43 HB
Regs
CTB Sch 4 para 42
CTB Regs
185 **IS** Sch 9 paras 54-56 IS
Regs
FC Sch 2 paras 52-54
FC Regs
DWA Sch 3 paras 50-
52 DWA Regs
HB Sch 4 paras 53-55
HB Regs
CTB Sch 4 paras 52-54
CTB Regs
186 **FC** Sch 2 para 50 FC
Regs
DWA Sch 3 para 48
DWA Regs
HB Sch 4 para 50 HB
Regs
CTB Sch 4 para 49
CTB Regs
187 **FC** Sch 2 para 15 FC
Regs
DWA Sch 3 para 15
DWA Regs

188 **FC** Sch 2 paras 27 and
31 FC Regs
DWA Sch 3 paras 27
and 31 DWA Regs
189 **FC** Sch 2 para 56 FC
Regs
DWA Sch 3 para 54
DWA Regs
190 **HB** Sch 4 paras 57, 58
and 60 HB Regs
CTB Sch 4 paras 56,
57 and 59 CTB Regs
191 **IS** Sch 9 para 53 IS
Regs
FC Sch 2 para 51 FC
Regs
DWA Sch 3 para 49
DWA Regs
HB Sch 4 para 52 HB
Regs
CTB Sch 4 para 51
CTB Regs
192 **IS** Sch 9 para 16 IS
Regs
FC Sch 2 para 14 FC
Regs
DWA Sch 3 para 14
DWA Regs
HB Sch 4 para 14 HB
Regs
CTB Sch 4 para 14
CTB Regs
193 **IS** Sch 9 para 36 IS
Regs
FC Sch 2 para 29 FC
Regs
DWA Sch 3 para 29
DWA Regs
HB Sch 4 para 33 HB
Regs
CTB Sch 4 para 34
CTB Regs
194 ss134(8) and 139(6)
SSAA 1992; regs 7 and
8 IRBS(Amdt 2) Regs
195 **FC** Reg 16(2)(a) and
(2A)(a) FC Regs
DWA Reg 18(2)(a) and
(2A)(a) DWA Regs

196 **FC** Reg 16(2)(b) and
(2A)(b) FC Regs
DWA Reg 18(2)(b) and
(2A)(b) DWA Regs
197 CFC/48/1993
198 **FC** Reg 31(6) FC Regs
DWA Reg 34(6) DWA
Regs
199 **FC** Sch 2 para 55 and
Sch 3 para 48 FC Regs
DWA Sch 3 para 53
and Sch 4 para 47
DWA Regs
200 s136(1) SSCBA 1992
201 **FC** Sch 2 paras 13(3)
and 47 FC Regs
DWA Sch 3 paras 12(3)
and 13 DWA Regs
HB Sch 4 paras 13(3)
and 47 HB Regs
CTB Sch 4 paras 13(3)
and 46 CTB Regs
202 CIS/683/1993
203 **IS** Reg 61 IS Regs
FC Reg 37 FC Regs
DWA Reg 41 DWA
Regs
HB Reg 46 HB Regs
CTB Reg 38 CTB Regs
All Definition of 'grant'
204 CIS/758/1992
205 **IS** Reg 61 IS Regs
FC Reg 37 FC Regs
DWA Reg 41 DWA
Regs
HB Reg 46 HB Regs
CTB Reg 38 CTB Regs
All Definition of 'grant
income'
206 **IS** Reg 62(3) IS Regs
FC Reg 38(3) FC Regs
DWA Reg 42(3) DWA
Regs
HB Reg 53(3) HB Regs
CTB Reg 42(4) CTB
Regs
207 **IS** Reg 62(4) IS Regs
FC Reg 38(4) FC Regs
DWA Reg 42(5) DWA

Regs
HB Reg 53(4) HB Regs
CTB Reg 42(5) CTB
Regs
208 CIS/33/1994
209 **IS** Reg 62(3A) IS Regs
FC Reg 38(3A) FC
Regs
DWA Reg 42(4) DWA
Regs
HB Reg 53(3)(b) HB
Regs
CTB Reg 42(4)(b) CTB
Regs
HB/CTB para C5.47
and Annex A GM
210 CIS/109/1991
211 **IS** Reg 62(2) IS Regs
FC Reg 38(2) FC Regs
DWA Reg 42(2) DWA
Regs
HB Reg 53(2) HB Regs
CTB Reg 42(2) CTB
Regs
212 CIS/497/1993
213 CIS/91/1994
214 **IS** Reg 66(1) IS Regs
FC Reg 42 FC Regs
DWA Reg 46 DWA
Regs
HB Reg 57 HB Regs
CTB Reg 46 CTB Regs
215 **IS** Reg 67 IS Regs
FC Reg 43 FC Regs
DWA Reg 48 DWA
Regs
HB Reg 58(1) HB Regs
CTB Reg 48 CTB Regs
216 Reg 58(2) HB Regs
217 Reg 32(6A) IS Regs
218 Reg 29(2B) IS Regs
219 **IS** Reg 66A IS Regs
FC Reg 42A FC Regs
DWA Reg 47 DWA
Regs
HB Reg 57A HB Regs
CTB Reg 47 CTB Regs
220 **IS** Reg 61 IS Regs
FC Reg 37 FC Regs

DWA Reg 41 DWA Regs
HB Reg 46 HB Regs
CTB Reg 38 CTB Regs
All Definition of 'last day of the course'

221 **IS** Sch 9 para 36 IS Regs
FC Sch 2 para 29 FC Regs
DWA Sch 3 para 29 DWA Regs
HB Sch 4 para 33 HB Regs
CTB Sch 4 para 34 CTB Regs

222 **IS** Reg 40(3A) IS Regs
FC Reg 24(4A) FC Regs
DWA Reg 27(5) DWA Regs
HB Reg 33(3A) HB Regs
CTB Reg 24(4) CTB Regs

223 **IS** Reg 66A(3) IS Regs
FC Reg 42A(3) FC Regs
DWA Reg 47(3) DWA Regs
HB Reg 57A(3) HB Regs
CTB Reg 47(3) CTB Regs

224 **IS** Reg 41(6) IS Regs
FC Reg 25(3) FC Regs
DWA Reg 28(3) DWA Regs
HB Reg 34(4) HB Regs
CTB Reg 25(4) CTB Regs

225 Reg 29(2A) IS Regs

226 **IS** Sch 9 para 59 IS Regs
FC Sch 2 para 58 FC Regs
DWA Sch 3 para 56 DWA Regs
HB Sch 4 para 63 HB

Regs
CTB Sch 4 para 63 CTB Regs

227 Sch 9 paras 60-61 IS Regs

228 Excluded from definition of 'grant' in:
IS Reg 61 IS Regs
FC Reg 37 FC Regs
DWA Reg 41 DWA Regs
HB Reg 46 HB Regs
CTB Reg 38 CTB Regs

229 CIS/758/1992

230 **IS** Sch 9 para 25(1)(a) and (2)(b) IS Regs
HB Sch 4 para 23(1)(a) and (2)(b) HB Regs
CTB Sch 4 para 24(1)(a) and (2)(b) CTB Regs

231 **FC** Sch 2 para 22(1)(a) and (2)(b) FC Regs
DWA Sch 3 para 22(1)(a) and (2)(b) DWA Regs

232 **IS** Sch 9 para 25(2)(a) IS Regs
FC Sch 2 para 22(2)(a) FC Regs
DWA Sch 3 para 22(2)(a) DWA Regs
HB Sch 4 para 23(2)(a) HB Regs
CTB Sch 4 para 24(2)(a) CTB Regs

233 **IS** Sch 9 para 26 IS Regs
FC Sch 2 para 23 FC Regs
DWA Sch 3 para 23 DWA Regs
HB Sch 4 para 24 HB Regs
CTB Sch 4 para 25 CTB Regs

234 **IS** Sch 9 para 25(1)(b) and (2) IS Regs
FC Sch 2 para 22(1)(b)

and (2) FC Regs
DWA Sch 3 para 22(1)(b) and (2) DWA Regs
HB Sch 4 para 23(1)(b) and (2) HB Regs
CTB Sch 4 para 24(1)(b) and (2) CTB Regs

235 Reg 48(8) IS Regs

236 **IS** Sch 10 para 8(b) IS Regs
FC Sch 3 para 9(b) FC Regs
DWA Sch 4 para 9(b) DWA Regs
HB Sch 5 para 9(b) HB Regs
CTB Sch 5 para 9(b) CTB Regs

237 **IS** Reg 48(10)(c) and Sch 10 para 22 IS Regs
FC Sch 2 para 34 FC Regs
DWA Sch 3 para 33 DWA Regs
HB Sch 4 para 34 HB Regs
CTB Sch 4 para 35 CTB Regs

238 **IS** Sch 9 para 39 IS Regs
FC Sch 2 para 34 FC Regs
DWA Sch 3 para 33 DWA Regs
HB Sch 4 para 34 HB Regs
CTB Sch 4 para 35 CTB Regs

239 **IS** Reg 48(9) IS Regs
FC Reg 31(3) FC Regs
DWA Reg 34(3) DWA Regs
HB/CTB There are no specific provisions for HB/CTB but such payments are obviously capital

240 Reg 48(10)(a) IS Regs

241 Reg 48(10)(b) IS Regs

242 **IS** Sch 9 para 15 IS
Regs
FC Sch 2 para 13 FC
Regs
DWA Sch 3 para 12
DWA Regs
HB Sch 4 para 13 HB
Regs
CTB Sch 4 para 13
CTB Regs

243 Sch 9 para 15A IS Regs

244 **IS** Sch 9 paras 15(4)
and 36 IS Regs
FC Sch 2 paras 13(4)
and 29 FC Regs
DWA Sch 3 paras 12(4)
and 29 DWA Regs
HB Sch 4 paras 13(4)
and 33 HB Regs
CTB Sch 4 paras 13(4)
and 34 CTB Regs

245 **IS** Sch 9 para 21 IS
Regs
FC Sch 2 para 20 FC
Regs
DWA Sch 3 para 20
DWA Regs
HB Sch 4 para 21 HB
Regs
CTB Sch 4 para 22
CTB Regs

246 *R v Doncaster MBC ex
parte Boulton* [1992] 25
HLR 195; R(IS) 4/94

247 **IS** para 31047 AOG
FC/DWA para 51166
AOG
HB/CTB para C3.90
GM

248 **IS** Sch 9 para 19 IS
Regs
FC Sch 2 para 19 FC
Regs
DWA Sch 3 para 19
DWA Regs
HB Sch 4 para 20 HB
Regs

CTB Sch 4 para 20
CTB Regs

249 **IS** Sch 9 para 18 IS
Regs
FC Sch 2 para 18 FC
Regs
DWA Sch 3 para 18
DWA Regs
HB Sch 4 para 19 HB
Regs
CTB Sch 4 para 19
CTB Regs

250 **IS** Sch 9 para 20 IS
Regs
FC Sch 2 para 40 FC
Regs
DWA Sch 3 para 38
DWA Regs
HB Sch 4 para 42 HB
Regs
CTB Sch 4 para 21
CTB Regs

251 All Definition of 'board
and lodging
accommodation'
IS Reg 2(1) IS Regs
HB Sch 4 para 42(2)
HB Regs
CTB Sch 4 para 21(2)
CTB Regs

252 **All** *CAO v Palfrey and
Others, The Times,* 17
February 1995
IS Reg 48(4) IS Regs
FC Reg 31(4) FC Regs
DWA Reg 34(4) DWA
Regs
HB Reg 40(4) HB Regs
CTB Reg 31(4) CTB
Regs

253 *See* CIS/25/1989;
CIS/563/1991;
CIS/85/1992 (*Palfrey*)

254 **IS** Sch 9 para 22(1) IS
Regs
FC Sch 2 para 16(1)
FC Regs
DWA Sch 3 para 16(1)
DWA Regs

HB Sch 4 para 15(1)
HB Regs
CTB Sch 4 para 15(1)
CTB Regs

255 **IS** Reg 48(4) IS Regs
FC Reg 31(4) FC Regs
DWA Reg 34(4) DWA
Regs
HB Reg 40(4) HB Regs
CTB Reg 31(4) CTB
Regs

256 **IS** Sch 9 para 22(1) IS
Regs
FC Sch 2 para 16(1)
FC Regs
DWA Sch 3 para 16(1)
DWA Regs
HB Sch 4 para 15(1)
HB Regs
CTB Sch 4 para 15(1)
CTB Regs

257 CFC/13/1993

258 **IS** Sch 9 para 22(2) IS
Regs
FC Sch 2 para 16(2)
FC Regs
DWA Sch 3 para 16(2)
DWA Regs
HB Sch 4 para 15(2)
HB Regs
CTB Sch 4 para 15(2)
CTB Regs

259 **IS** Reg 53 IS Regs
FC Reg 36 FC Regs
DWA Reg 40 DWA
Regs
HB Reg 45 HB Regs
CTB Reg 37 CTB Regs

260 Reg 32(1) SS(C&P)
Regs

261 **HB** Reg 75 HB Regs
CTB Reg 65 CTB Regs

262 Reg 41(1) IS Regs

263 **FC** Reg 25(1) FC Regs
DWA Reg 28(1) DWA
Regs

264 **HB** Reg 34(1) HB Regs
CTB Reg 25(1) CTB
Regs

265 **IS** Reg 29(2)(a) IS Regs
FC Reg 18 FC Regs
DWA Reg 20 DWA
Regs
HB Reg 25 HB Regs
CTB Reg 17 CTB Regs
266 **IS** Reg 44(1) and (5) IS
Regs
FC Reg 27(1) and (3)
FC Regs
DWA Reg 30(1) and (3)
DWA Regs
HB Reg 36(2) and (5)
HB Regs
CTB Reg 27(2) and (5)
CTB Regs
267 **IS** Reg 32(1) IS Regs
FC Reg 18(1) FC Regs
DWA Reg 20(1) DWA
Regs
HB Reg 25(1) HB Regs
CTB Reg 17(1) CTB
Regs
268 **IS** Reg 41(2) IS Regs
FC Reg 25(2) FC Regs
DWA Reg 28(2) DWA
Regs
HB Reg 34(2) HB Regs
CTB Reg 25(2) CTB
Regs
269 **IS** Reg 41(6) IS Regs
FC Reg 25(3) FC Regs
DWA Reg 28(3) DWA
Regs
HB Reg 34(4) HB Regs
CTB Reg 25(4) CTB
Regs
270 Regs 41(4) and 48(2) IS
Regs
271 Reg 41(3) IS Regs
272 *R v SBC ex parte Singer*
[1973] 1 **All** ER 931; *R
v Oxford County Council
ex parte Jack* [1984] 17
HLR 419; *R v West
Dorset DC ex parte
Poupard* [1988] 20 HLR
295; para C3.118 GM
273 paras C2.09(xix) and

3.118 GM
274 *R v West Dorset DC ex
parte Poupard* [1988] 20
HLR 295
275 **IS** Sch 10 para 20 IS
Regs
FC Sch 3 para 21 FC
Regs
DWA Sch 4 para 21
DWA Regs
HB Sch 5 para 21 HB
Regs
CTB Sch 5 para 21
CTB Regs
276 **IS** Reg 48(2) IS Regs
FC Reg 31(1) FC Regs
DWA Reg 34(1) DWA
Regs
HB Reg 40(2) HB Regs
CTB Reg 31(2) CTB
Regs
277 Regs 41(4) and 48(2) IS
Regs
278 **IS** Reg 40(4) and Sch 9
para 15B IS Regs
FC Reg 24(5) FC Regs
DWA Reg 27(4) DWA
Regs
HB Reg 33(4) HB Regs
CTB Reg 24(5) CTB
Regs
All Definition of
'occupational pension'
in reg 2(1) of each of
those regs
279 **IS** Reg 41(2) and Sch 9
para 17 IS Regs
FC Reg 25(2) and Sch
2 para 17 FC Regs
DWA Reg 28(2) and
Sch 3 para 17 DWA
Regs
HB Reg 34(2) and Sch
4 para 16 HB Regs
CTB Reg 25(2) and
Sch 4 para 16 CTB
Regs
280 Sch 9 para 29 IS Regs;
para 33240 AOG

281 Sch 9 para 30(a)-(d) IS
Regs
282 **FC** Sch 2 para 55 FC
Regs
DWA Sch 3 para 53
DWA Regs
283 **HB** Sch 4 para 28 HB
Regs
CTB Sch 4 para 29
CTB Regs
284 **IS** Sch 9 para 11 IS
Regs
FC Sch 2 para 9 FC
Regs
DWA Sch 3 para 9
DWA Regs
HB Sch 4 para 10 HB
Regs
CTB Sch 4 para 10
CTB Regs
285 **IS** Sch 9 para 2 IS Regs
FC Sch 2 para 2 FC
Regs
DWA Sch 3 para 2
DWA Regs
HB Sch 4 para 2 HB
Regs
CTB Sch 4 para 2 CTB
Regs
286 **IS** Sch 9 para 21 IS
Regs
FC Sch 2 para 20 FC
Regs
DWA Sch 3 para 20
DWA Regs
HB Sch 4 para 21 HB
Regs
CTB Sch 4 para 22
CTB Regs
287 **FC** Sch 2 para 12 FC
Regs
DWA Sch 3 para 11A
DWA Regs
288 **IS** Sch 9 paras 14 and
51 IS Regs
FC Sch 2 paras 12 and
48 FC Regs
DWA Sch 3 para 45
DWA Regs

HB Sch 4 paras 12 and
49 HB Regs
CTB Sch 4 paras 12
and 48 CTB Regs
289 **IS** Sch 9 para 13 IS
Regs
FC Sch 2 para 11 FC
Regs
DWA Sch 3 para 11
DWA Regs
HB Sch 4 para 11 HB
Regs
CTB Sch 4 para 11
CTB Regs
290 **IS** Sch 9 para 43 IS
Regs
FC Sch 2 para 38 FC
Regs
DWA Sch 3 para 37
DWA Regs
HB Sch 4 para 38 HB
Regs
CTB Sch 4 para 40
CTB Regs
291 **IS** Sch 9 para 28 IS
Regs
FC Sch 2 para 25 FC
Regs
DWA Sch 3 para 25
DWA Regs
HB Sch 4 para 26 HB
Regs
CTB Sch 4 para 27
CTB Regs
292 **IS** Sch 9 para 58 IS
Regs
FC Sch 2 para 57 FC
Regs
DWA Sch 3 para 55
DWA Regs
HB Sch 4 para 62 HB
Regs
CTB Sch 4 para 62
CTB Regs
293 **IS** Sch 9 para 27 IS
Regs
FC Sch 2 para 24 FC
Regs
DWA Sch 3 para 24

DWA Regs
HB Sch 4 para 25 HB
Regs
CTB Sch 4 para 26
CTB Regs
294 **IS** Sch 9 para 10 IS
Regs
FC Sch 2 para 8 FC
Regs
DWA Sch 3 para 8
DWA Regs
HB Sch 4 para 9 HB
Regs
CTB Sch 4 para 9 CTB
Regs
295 **IS** Sch 9 para 23 IS
Regs
FC Sch 2 para 21 FC
Regs
DWA Sch 3 para 21
DWA Regs
HB Sch 4 para 22 HB
Regs
CTB Sch 4 para 23
CTB Regs
296 **IS** Sch 9 para 24 IS
Regs
FC Sch 2 para 30 FC
Regs
DWA Sch 3 para 30
DWA Regs
HB Sch 4 para 32 HB
Regs
CTB Sch 4 para 33
CTB Regs
297 **IS** Sch 9 para 48 IS
Regs
FC Sch 2 para 44 FC
Regs
DWA Sch 3 para 42
DWA Regs
HB Sch 4 para 44 HB
Regs
CTB Sch 4 para 43
CTB Regs
298 **IS** Sch 9 para 49 IS
Regs
FC Sch 2 para 45 FC
Regs

DWA Sch 3 para 43
DWA Regs
HB Sch 4 para 45 HB
Regs
CTB Sch 4 para 44
CTB Regs
299 **IS** Sch 9 para 50 IS
Regs
FC Sch 2 para 46 FC
Regs
DWA Sch 3 para 44
DWA Regs
HB Sch 4 para 46 HB
Regs
CTB Sch 4 para 45
CTB Regs
300 **HB** Sch 4 para 17 HB
Regs
CTB Sch 4 para 17
CTB Regs
301 **HB** Sch 3 para 9 HB
Regs
CTB Sch 3 para 9 CTB
Regs
302 **HB** Sch 4 para 18 HB
Regs
CTB Sch 4 para 18
CTB Regs
303 **HB** Sch 3 para 9 HB
Regs
CTB Sch 3 para 9 CTB
Regs

5. Notional income
(pp 380-383)
304 **IS** Reg 42(1) IS Regs
FC Reg 26(1) FC Regs
DWA Reg 29(1) DWA
Regs
HB Reg 35(1) HB Regs
CTB Reg 26(1) CTB
Regs
305 CSIS/57/1992
306 **IS** Reg 42(2) IS Regs
FC Reg 26(2) FC Regs
DWA Reg 29(2) DWA
Regs
HB Reg 35(2) HB Regs
CTB Reg 26(2) CTB

Regs

307 **IS** Reg 42(2A) IS Regs
FC Reg 26(2A) FC
Regs
DWA Reg 29(2A)
DWA Regs
HB Reg 35(2A) HB
Regs
CTB Reg 26(2A) CTB
Regs
308 Reg 42(3) IS Regs
309 Reg 42(3A) and (3B) IS
Regs
310 Reg 70(2)(b) IS Regs
311 Reg 42(5) IS Regs
312 Reg 2 SS(PAOR) Regs
313 **IS** Reg 42(4)(a)(ii), (4A)
and (9) IS Regs
FC Reg 26(3)(a) FC
Regs
DWA Reg 29(3)(a)
DWA Regs
HB Reg 35(3)(a) and
(8) HB Regs
CTB Reg 26(3)(a) and
(8) CTB Regs
314 Reg 42(4) IS Regs
315 **IS** Reg 42(4)(b) IS Regs
FC Reg 26(3)(b) FC
Regs
DWA Reg 29(3)(b)
DWA Regs
HB Reg 35(3)(b) HB
Regs
CTB Reg 26(3)(b) CTB
Regs
316 **IS** Reg 42(6) IS Regs;
CIS/191/1991
FC Reg 26(4) FC Regs
DWA Reg 29(4) DWA
Regs
HB Reg 35(5) HB Regs
CTB Reg 26(5) CTB
Regs
317 R(SB) 13/86
318 R(SB) 13/86
319 **IS** Reg 42(6) IS Regs
FC Reg 26(4) FC Regs
DWA Reg 29(4) DWA

Regs
HB Reg 35(5) HB Regs
CTB Reg 26(5) CTB
Regs
320 R(IS) 12/92
321 *Sharrock v CAO* (CA) 26
March 1991; CIS/93/
1991
322 CIS/93/1991
323 CIS/422/1992
324 CIS/701/1994
325 CIS/422/1992
326 CIS/701/1994
327 CIS/147/1993
328 Reg 14(2A) FC Regs

Chapter 20: Capital
(pp 384-407)

1. Introduction
(pp 384-385)

1 **HB** Sch 5 para 5 HB
Regs
CTB Sch 5 para 5 CTB
Regs
2 **IS** Reg 45 IS Regs
FC Reg 28 FC Regs
3 **DWA** Reg 31 DWA
Regs
HB Reg 37 HB Regs
CTB Reg 28 CTB Regs
4 **IS** Reg 53 IS Regs
FC Reg 36 FC Regs
DWA Reg 40 DWA
Regs
HB Reg 45 HB Regs
CTB Reg 37 CTB Regs
5 Regs 45 and 53(1A),
(1B), (1C) and (4) IS
Regs
6 Regs 7(9) and 45(1A),
(1B), (1C), (4) and (5)
HB Regs
7 s136(1) SSCBA 1992
8 **IS** Reg 47 IS Regs
FC Reg 30 FC Regs
DWA Reg 33 DWA
Regs
HB Reg 39 HB Regs

CTB Reg 30 CTB Regs
9 **IS** Reg 17(1)(b) IS Regs
FC Reg 46(4) FC Regs
DWA Reg 51(4) DWA
Regs
HB Reg 16(b) HB
Regs
CTB Reg 8(b) CTB
Regs
10 **IS** Reg 44(5) IS Regs
FC Reg 27(3) FC Regs
DWA Reg 30(3) DWA
Regs
HB Reg 36(2) HB
Regs
CTB Reg 27(2) CTB
Regs
11 **IS** Regs 25 and 44(5)
IS Regs
FC Reg 27(3) FC Regs
DWA Reg 30(3) DWA
Regs
HB Reg 36(2) HB
Regs
CTB Reg 27(2) CTB
Regs
12 **IS** Reg 17(1)(b) IS Regs
FC Reg 46(4) FC Regs
DWA Reg 51(4) DWA
Regs
HB Reg 16(b) HB
Regs
CTB Reg 8(b) CTB
Regs

2. What counts as capital
(pp 386-390)

13 para C2.09 GM; para
34020 AOG
14 Reg 14 SS(CMB) Regs
15 Reg 22 SS(BWB) Regs
16 *R v SBC ex parte Singer*
[1973] 1 WLR 713
17 R(SB) 35/83
18 CIS/654/1991
19 **IS/FC/DWA** Reg 2
SS(PAOR) Regs
HB Reg 91(1) HB

Regs
20 R(SB) 12/86
21 R(SB) 53/83; R(SB) 1/85
22 R(SB) 49/83
23 R(SB) 23/85
24 **IS** Sch 10 para 13 IS Regs
FC Sch 3 para 14 FC Regs
DWA Sch 4 para 14 DWA Regs
HB Sch 5 para 14 HB Regs
CTB Sch 5 para 14 CTB Regs
25 *Peters v CAO* reported as an appendix to R(SB) 3/89
26 R(IS) 1/90
27 R(SB) 23/85
28 *Barclays Bank v Quistclose Investments Ltd* [1970] AC 567; R(SB) 49/83; CFC/21/1989
29 **IS** Sch 10 para 12 IS Regs
FC Sch 3 para 13 FC Regs
DWA Sch 4 para 13 DWA Regs
HB Sch 5 para 13 HB Regs
CTB Sch 5 para 13 CTB Regs
30 CIS/368/1994
31 R(SB) 2/89
32 **IS** Regs 40 and 46 IS Regs
FC Regs 24 and 29 FC Regs
DWA Regs 27 and 32 DWA Regs
HB Regs 33 and 38 HB Regs
CTB Regs 24 and 29 CTB Regs
All CIS/559/1991
33 *Thomas v CAO*

(appendix to R(SB) 17/87)
34 **IS** Sch 10 paras 44-45 IS Regs
FC Sch 3 paras 46-47 FC Regs
DWA Sch 4 paras 45-46 DWA Regs
HB Sch 5 paras 46-47 HB Regs
CTB Sch 5 paras 46-47 CTB Regs
35 **IS** Reg 48 IS Regs
FC Reg 31 FC Regs
DWA Reg 34 DWA Regs
HB Reg 40 HB Regs
CTB Reg 31 CTB Regs
36 paras 51162, 51172-2 AOG
37 **FC** Reg 31(6) FC Regs
DWA Reg 34(6) DWA Regs
38 **IS** Sch 9 para 32 IS Regs
FC Sch 2 para 26 FC Regs
DWA Sch 3 para 26 DWA Regs
HB Sch 4 para 29 HB Regs
CTB Sch 4 para 30 CTB Regs

3. **Disregarded capital**
(pp390-396)
39 **IS** Sch 10 para 1 IS Regs
FC Sch 3 para 1 FC Regs
DWA Sch 4 para 1 DWA Regs
HB Sch 5 para 1 HB Regs
CTB Sch 5 para 1 CTB Regs
40 **IS** Reg 2(1) IS Regs meaning of 'dwelling occupied as the home';

R(SB) 13/84; CIS/427/1991
FC Sch 3 para 1 FC Regs
DWA Sch 4 para 1 DWA Regs
HB Sch 5 para 1 HB Regs
CTB Sch 5 para 1 CTB Regs
41 **IS** Sch 10 para 1 IS Regs
FC Sch 3 para 1 FC Regs
DWA Sch 4 para 1 DWA Regs
HB Sch 5 para 1 HB Regs
CTB Sch 5 para 1 CTB Regs
42 **IS** Sch 10 para 25 IS Regs
FC Sch 3 para 26 FC Regs
DWA Sch 4 para 26 DWA Regs
HB Sch 5 para 24 HB Regs
CTB Sch 5 para 24 CTB Regs
43 **IS** Sch 10 para 27 IS Regs
FC Sch 3 para 28 FC Regs
DWA Sch 4 para 28 DWA Regs
HB Sch 5 para 26 HB Regs
CTB Sch 5 para 26 CTB Regs
44 **IS** Sch 10 para 26 IS Regs
FC Sch 3 para 27 FC Regs
DWA Sch 4 para 27 DWA Regs
HB Sch 5 para 25 HB Regs
CTB Sch 5 para 25

CTB Regs
All CIS/6908/1995 (to
be reported as R(IS) 4/
96); CIS/7319/1995
45 CIS/7319/1995, para
1995
46 R(SB) 32/83
47 CIS/7319/1995, para 22
48 IS Sch 10 para 28 IS
Regs
FC Sch 3 para 29 FC
Regs
DWA Sch 4 para 29
DWA Regs
HB Sch 5 para 27 HB
Regs
CTB Sch 5 para 27
CTB Regs
49 IS Sch 10 para 3 IS
Regs
FC Sch 3 para 3 FC
Regs
DWA Sch 4 para 3
DWA Regs
HB Sch 5 para 3 HB
Regs
CTB Sch 5 para 3 CTB
Regs
50 CIS/63/1993
51 CIS/685/1992
52 R(SB) 14/85
53 IS Sch 10 para 2 IS
Regs
FC Sch 3 para 2 FC
Regs
DWA Sch 4 para 2
DWA Regs
HB Sch 5 para 2 HB
Regs
CTB Sch 5 para 2 CTB
Regs
54 IS Sch 10 para 8(a) IS
Regs
FC Sch 3 para 9(a) FC
Regs
DWA Sch 4 para 9(a)
DWA Regs
HB Sch 5 para 9(a) HB
Regs

CTB Sch 5 para 9(a)
CTB Regs
55 IS Sch 10 para 8(b) IS
Regs
FC Sch 3 para 9(b) FC
Regs
DWA Sch 4 para 9(b)
DWA Regs
HB Sch 5 para 9(b)
HB Regs
CTB Sch 5 para 9(b)
CTB Regs
56 *Barclays Bank v Quistclose
Investments Ltd* [1970]
AC 567; CSB/975/1985
57 IS Sch 10 para 9(a) IS
Regs
FC Sch 3 para 10(a) FC
Regs
DWA Sch 4 para 10(a)
DWA Regs
HB Sch 5 para 10(a)
HB Regs
CTB Sch 5 para 10(a)
CTB Regs
58 IS Sch 10 para 9(b) IS
Regs
FC Sch 3 para 10(b)
FC Regs
DWA Sch 4 para 10(b)
DWA Regs
HB Sch 5 para 10(b)
HB Regs
CTB Sch 5 para 10(b)
CTB Regs
59 IS Sch 10 para 37 IS
Regs
FC Sch 3 para 39 FC
Regs
DWA Sch 4 para 38
DWA Regs
HB Sch 5 para 37 HB
Regs
CTB Sch 5 para 36
CTB Regs
60 IS Sch 10 para 4 IS
Regs
FC Sch 3 paras 4 and
30 FC Regs

DWA Sch 4 paras 4
and 30 DWA Regs
HB Sch 5 para 4 HB
Regs
CTB Sch 5 para 4 CTB
Regs
61 IS Reg 2(1) IS Regs
definition of 'partner'
FC Reg 2(1) FC Regs
definition of 'partner'
DWA Reg 2(1) DWA
Regs definition of
'partner'
HB Reg 2(1) HB Regs
definition of 'partner'
CTB Reg 2(1) CTB
Regs definition of
'partner'
All s137(1) SSCBA
1992 definition of
'married couple' and
'unmarried couple'
62 HB Sch 5 para 24 HB
Regs
CTB Sch 5 para 24
CTB Regs
63 para 34429 AOG
HB/CTB para C2.12.ii.a
and b GM
64 FC Sch 3 para 4 FC
Regs
DWA Sch 4 para 4
DWA Regs
65 IS Reg 2(1) IS Regs
definition of 'relative'
FC Reg 2(1) definition
of 'close relative' and
Sch 3 para 4 FC Regs
DWA Reg 2(1)
definition of 'close
relative' and Sch 4 para
4 DWA Regs
HB Reg 2(1) HB Regs
definition of 'relative'
CTB This is not
defined for CTB but
presumably the same
definition will apply
66 CSB/209/1986;

CSB/1149/1986; R(SB) 22/87

67 **IS** Sch 10 para 10 IS Regs
FC Sch 3 para 11 FC Regs
DWA Sch 4 para 11 DWA Regs
HB Sch 5 para 11 HB Regs
CTB Sch 5 para 11 CTB Regs

68 CIS/494/1990

69 **IS** Sch 10 para 8(a) IS Regs
FC Sch 3 para 9(a) FC Regs
DWA Sch 4 para 9(a) DWA Regs
HB Sch 5 para 9(a) HB Regs
CTB Sch 5 para 9(a) CTB Regs

70 **IS** para 34375 AOG
FC para 53271 AOG

71 **IS** Sch 10 para 6 IS Regs
FC Sch 3 para 6 FC Regs
DWA Sch 4 para 6 DWA Regs
HB Sch 5 para 7 HB Regs
CTB Sch 5 para 7 CTB Regs

72 **FC** Sch 3 para 7 FC Regs
DWA Sch 4 para 7 DWA Regs

73 R(SB) 4/85

74 CFC/15/1990

75 **IS** Sch 10 para 19 IS Regs
FC Sch 3 para 20 FC Regs
DWA Sch 4 para 20 DWA Regs
HB Sch 5 para 20 HB Regs

CTB Sch 5 para 20 CTB Regs

76 **IS** Sch 10 para 23A IS Regs
FC Sch 3 para 24A FC Regs
DWA Sch 4 para 24A DWA Regs
HB Sch 3 para 39A HB Regs
CTB Sch 5 para 30A CTB Regs

77 **IS** Sch 10 para 15 IS Regs
FC Sch 3 para 16 FC Regs
DWA Sch 4 para 16 DWA Regs
HB Sch 5 para 16 HB Regs
CTB Sch 5 para 16 CTB Regs
CIS/7330/1995

78 **IS** Sch 10 para 11 IS Regs
FC Sch 3 para 12 FC Regs
DWA Sch 4 para 12 DWA Regs
HB Sch 5 para 12 HB Regs
CTB Sch 5 para 12 CTB Regs

79 **IS** Reg 41(2) IS Regs
FC Reg 25(2) FC Regs
DWA Reg 28(2) DWA Regs
HB Reg 34(2) HB Regs
CTB Reg 25(2) CTB Regs

80 **IS** Sch 10 para 5 IS Regs
FC Sch 3 para 5 FC Regs
DWA Sch 4 para 5 DWA Regs
HB Sch 5 para 6 HB Regs

CTB Sch 5 para 6 CTB Regs

81 CIS/635/1994

82 **IS** Sch 10 para 13 IS Regs
FC Sch 3 para 14 FC Regs
DWA Sch 4 para 14 DWA Regs
HB Sch 5 para 14 HB Regs
CTB Sch 5 para 14 CTB Regs

83 **IS** Sch 10 para 14 IS Regs
FC Sch 3 para 15 FC Regs
DWA Sch 4 para 15 DWA Regs
HB Sch 5 para 15 HB Regs
CTB Sch 5 para 15 CTB Regs

84 **IS** Sch 10 para 16 IS Regs
FC Sch 3 para 17 FC Regs
DWA Sch 4 para 17 DWA Regs
HB Sch 5 para 17 HB Regs
CTB Sch 5 para 17 CTB Regs

85 **IS** Sch 10 para 23 IS Regs
FC Sch 3 para 24 FC Regs
DWA Sch 4 para 24 DWA Regs
HB Sch 5 para 30 HB Regs
CTB Sch 5 para 30 CTB Regs

86 **IS** Sch 10 para 24 IS Regs
FC Sch 3 para 25 FC Regs
DWA Sch 4 para 25 DWA Regs

HB Sch 5 para 31 HB
Regs
CTB Sch 5 para 31
CTB Regs
87 **IS** Sch 10 para 11 IS
Regs
FC Sch 3 para 12 FC
Regs
DWA Sch 4 para 12
DWA Regs
HB Sch 5 para 12 HB
Regs
CTB Sch 5 para 12
CTB Regs
88 **IS** Sch 10 para 12 IS
Regs
FC Sch 3 para 13 FC
Regs
DWA Sch 4 para 13
DWA Regs
HB Sch 5 para 13 HB
Regs
CTB Sch 5 para 13
CTB Regs
89 **IS** Sch 10 para 7 IS
Regs
FC Sch 3 para 8 FC
Regs
DWA Sch 4 para 8
DWA Regs
HB Sch 5 para 8 HB
Regs
CTB Sch 5 para 8 CTB
Regs
90 **IS** Sch 10 para 41 IS
Regs
FC Sch 3 para 43 FC
Regs
DWA Sch 4 para 42
DWA Regs
HB Sch 5 para 38 HB
Regs
CTB Sch 5 para 37
CTB Regs
91 **IS** Sch 10 para 36 IS
Regs
FC Sch 3 para 38 FC
Regs
DWA Sch 4 para 37

DWA Regs
HB Sch 5 para 36 HB
Regs
CTB Sch 5 para 35
CTB Regs
92 **IS** Sch 10 paras 31-33
IS Regs
FC Sch 3 paras 33-35
FC Regs
DWA Sch 4 paras 33-
35 DWA Regs
HB Sch 5 paras 28-29,
35, 42 and 45 HB Regs
CTB Sch 5 paras 28-
29, 34, 41 and 44 CTB
Regs
93 Sch 10 paras 47-49 IS
Regs
94 Sch 5 paras 50-51 HB
Regs
95 Sch 5 paras 50-51 CTB
Regs
96 **FC** Sch 3 paras 49 and
50 FC Regs
DWA Sch 4 paras 48
and 49 DWA Regs
HB Sch 5 paras 50 and
51 HB Regs
CTB Sch 5 paras 50
and 51 CTB Regs
97 **IS** Sch 10 para 38 IS
Regs
FC Sch 3 para 40 FC
Regs
DWA Sch 4 para 39
DWA Regs
HB Sch 5 para 39 HB
Regs
CTB Sch 5 para 38
CTB Regs
98 **IS** Sch 10 para 39 IS
Regs
FC Sch 3 para 41 FC
Regs
DWA Sch 4 para 40
DWA Regs
HB Sch 5 para 40 HB
Regs
CTB Sch 5 para 39

CTB Regs
99 **IS** Sch 10 para 40 IS
Regs
FC Sch 3 para 42 FC
Regs
DWA Sch 4 para 41
DWA Regs
HB Sch 5 para 41 HB
Regs
CTB Sch 5 para 40
CTB Regs
100 **FC** Sch 3 para 48 FC
Regs
DWA Sch 4 para 47
DWA Regs
101 **IS** Sch 10 para 18 IS
Regs
FC Sch 3 para 19 FC
Regs
DWA Sch 4 para 19
DWA Regs
HB Sch 5 para 19 HB
Regs
CTB Sch 5 para 19
CTB Regs
102 **IS** Sch 10 paras 42-43
IS Regs
FC Sch 3 paras 44-45
FC Regs
DWA Sch 4 paras 43-
44 DWA Regs
HB Sch 5 paras 43-44
HB Regs
CTB Sch 5 paras 42-43
CTB Regs
103 **IS** Sch 10 para 46 IS
Regs
FC Sch 3 para 49 FC
Regs
DWA Sch 4 para 48
DWA Regs
HB Sch 5 para 48 HB
Regs
CTB Sch 5 para 48
CTB Regs
104 **IS** Sch 10 para 17 IS
Regs
FC Sch 3 para 18 FC
Regs

DWA Sch 4 para 18
DWA Regs
HB Sch 5 para 18 HB
Regs
CTB Sch 5 para 18
CTB Regs

105 **IS** Sch 10 para 29 IS
Regs
FC Sch 3 para 31 FC
Regs
DWA Sch 4 para 31
DWA Regs
HB Sch 5 para 32 HB
Regs
CTB Sch 5 para 32
CTB Regs

106 **IS** Sch 10 para 22 IS
Regs
FC Sch 3 para 23 FC
Regs
DWA Sch 4 para 23
DWA Regs
HB Sch 5 para 23 HB
Regs
CTB Sch 5 para 23
CTB Regs

107 **IS** para 34454 AOG
FC/DWA para 53471
AOG
HB Reg 73(1) and (3)
HB Regs
CTB Reg 63(1) and (3)
CTB Regs

108 **IS** Sch 10 para 34 IS
Regs
FC Sch 3 para 36 FC
Regs
DWA Sch 4 para 36
DWA Regs
HB Sch 4 para 38 HB
regs
CTB Sch 4 para 40
CTB Regs

109 **IS** Sch 10 para 30 IS
Regs
FC Sch 3 para 32 FC
Regs
DWA Sch 4 para 32
DWA Regs

HB Sch 5 para 33 HB
Regs
CTB Sch 5 para 33
CTB Regs

110 **IS** Sch 10 para 21 IS
Regs
FC Sch 3 para 22 FC
Regs
DWA Sch 4 para 22
DWA Regs
HB Sch 5 para 22 HB
Regs
CTB Sch 5 para 22
CTB Regs

111 **IS** Sch 10 para 20 IS
Regs
FC Sch 3 para 21 FC
Regs
DWA Sch 4 para 21
DWA Regs
HB Sch 5 para 21 HB
Regs
CTB Sch 5 para 21
CTB Regs

4. Notional capital
(pp 397-403)

112 **IS** Reg 51(6) IS Regs
FC Reg 34(6) FC Regs
DWA Reg 37(6) DWA
Regs
HB Reg 43(6) HB Regs
CTB Reg 34(6) CTB
Regs

113 **IS** Reg 51(1) IS Regs
FC Reg 34(1) FC Regs
DWA Reg 37(1) DWA
Regs
HB Reg 43(1) HB Regs
CTB Reg 34(1) CTB
Regs

114 CIS/124/1990;
CSB/1198/1989
115 R(SB) 9/91
116 CIS/124/1990
117 CIS/40/1989
118 CIS/621/1991
119 CIS/264/1989
120 R(SB) 38/85

121 **IS** Reg 51(1) IS Regs
FC Reg 34(1) FC Regs
DWA Reg 37(1) DWA
Regs
122 R(SB) 12/91
123 CIS/2627/1995
124 CIS/236/1991
125 **IS** Reg 51(7) IS Regs
FC Reg 34(7) FC Regs
DWA Reg 37(7) DWA
Regs
126 CIS/240/1992
127 CIS/634/1992
128 **IS** Reg 51(6) IS Regs
FC Reg 34(6) FC Regs
DWA Reg 37(6) DWA
Regs
HB Reg 43(6) HB Regs
CTB Reg 34(6) CTB
Regs
129 CIS/30/1993, but other
commissioners have
taken a different view
(*see*, eg,
CIS/25/1990 and
CIS/81/1991)
130 R(IS) 14/93
131 para C2.69 GM
132 para C2.97 GM
133 para C2.92 GM
134 **IS** Reg 51A IS Regs
FC Reg 34A FC Regs
DWA Reg 38 DWA
Regs
HB Reg 43A HB Regs
CTB Reg 35 CTB Regs
135 s25(1)(c) SSAA 1992
HB Reg 66(2) HB Regs
CTB Reg 57(2) CTB
Regs
136 para C2.84 GM
137 R(IS) 9/92
138 R(IS) 1/91; R(IS) 9/92
139 R(IS) 9/92
140 **IS** Reg 51(2) IS Regs
FC Reg 34(2) FC Regs
DWA Reg 37(2) DWA
Regs
HB Reg 43(2) HB Regs

CTB Reg 34(2) CTB
Regs
141 IS Reg 51(3)(a)(ii) and
(8) IS Regs
FC Reg 34(3)(a) FC
Regs
DWA Reg 37(3)(a)
DWA Regs
HB Reg 43(3)(a) and
(7) HB Regs
CTB Reg 34(3)(a) and
(7) CTB Regs
142 IS Reg 51(8) IS Regs
FC Reg 34(3)(a) FC
Regs
DWA Reg 37(3)(a)
DWA Regs
HB Reg 43(7)(b) HB
Regs
CTB Reg 34(7) CTB
Regs
143 IS para 34866 AOG
144 Reg 51(3)(a)(i) IS Regs
145 IS Reg 51(3)(b) IS Regs
FC Reg 34(3)(b) FC
Regs
DWA Reg 37(3)(b)
DWA Regs
HB Reg 43(3)(b) HB
Regs
CTB Reg 34(3)(b) CTB
Regs
146 IS Reg 51(4) IS Regs
FC Reg 34(4) FC Regs
DWA Reg 37(4) DWA
Regs
147 IS Reg 51(5) IS Regs
FC Reg 34(5) FC Regs
DWA Reg 37(5) DWA
Regs
HB Reg 43(5) HB Regs
CTB Reg 34(5) CTB
Regs
148 IS para 34375 AOG; *see
also* R(IS) 13/93
FC/DWA para 53372
AOG
149 para 53373 AOG
150 HB Reg 43(4) HB Regs

CTB Reg 34(4) CTB
Regs

5. How capital is valued
(pp404-407)
151 IS Reg 49(a) IS Regs
FC Reg 32(a) FC Regs
DWA Reg 35(a) DWA
Regs
HB Reg 41(a) HB Regs
CTB Reg 32(a) CTB
Regs
152 R(SB) 57/83; R(SB)
6/84
153 R(SB) 18/83
154 R(SB) 6/84
155 IS Reg 49(a)(i) IS Regs
FC Reg 32(a)(i) FC
Regs
DWA Reg 35(a)(i)
DWA Regs
HB Reg 41(a)(i) HB
Regs
CTB Reg 32(a)(i) CTB
Regs
156 IS Reg 49(a)(ii) IS Regs
FC Reg 32(a)(ii) FC
Regs
DWA Reg 35(a)(ii)
DWA Regs
HB Reg 41(a)(ii) HB
Regs
CTB Reg 32(a)(ii) CTB
Regs
157 CIS/255/1989
158 R(SB) 27/84
159 R(SB) 2/83; R(SB)
31/83
160 IS Reg 49(b) IS Regs
FC Reg 32(b) FC Regs
DWA Reg 35(b) DWA
Regs
HB Reg 41(b) HB
Regs
CTB Reg 32(b) CTB
Regs
161 IS Part 34 Appendix 3
AOG

FC/DWA Part 53
Appendix 2 AOG
HB/CTB C2: Annex B
GM
162 IS Reg 52 IS Regs
FC Reg 35 FC Regs
DWA Reg 39 DWA
Regs
HB Reg 44 HB Regs
CTB Reg 36 CTB Regs
163 para 53056 AOG
HB/CTB para 2.42 GM
164 CIS/449/1990
165 IS Reg 49(a) IS Regs
FC Reg 32(a) FC Regs
DWA Reg 35(a) DWA
Regs
HB Reg 41(a) HB Regs
CTB Reg 32(a) CTB
Regs
166 CIS/598/1992
167 R(SB) 18/83; R(IS)
2/90
168 CIS/654/1993
169 IS para 34681 AOG
FC/DWA para 53132
AOG
HB/CTB para C2.34
GM
170 *Peters v CAO* (appendix
to R(SB) 3/89)
171 IS Reg 50(a) IS Regs
FC Reg 33(a) FC Regs
DWA Reg 36(a) DWA
Regs
HB Reg 42(a) HB Regs
CTB Reg 33(a) CTB
Regs
172 IS Reg 50(b) IS Regs
FC Reg 33(b) FC Regs
DWA Reg 36(b) DWA
Regs
HB Reg 42(b) HB
Regs
CTB Reg 33(b) CTB
Regs
173 IS Sch 10 para 21 IS
Regs
FC Sch 3 para 22 FC

Regs
DWA Sch 4 para 22
DWA Regs
HB Sch 5 para 22 HB
Regs
CTB Sch 5 para 22
CTB Regs

PART SIX: THE REGULATED SOCIAL FUND

Chapter 21: The regulated social fund
(pp410-420)

1 Reg 5(1) SFM&FE Regs
2 Reg 6 SFM&FE Regs
3 Reg 5(2) SFM&FE Regs
4 paras 3123-24 SFG
5 *R v SFI ex parte Harper* QBD, 7 February 1997
6 Reg 9(1) SFM&FE Regs
7 Reg 9(2) SFM&FE Regs
8 Reg 9(3)(b) SFM&FE Regs
9 Reg 3(1) SFM&FE Regs meaning of 'confinement'
10 Reg 5(1)(b)(ii) SFM&FE Regs
11 Reg 4(2) SFM&FE Regs
12 Reg 5(1)(b)(iii) SFM&FE Regs
13 Reg 4(2) SFM&FE Regs
14 Reg 19 and Sch 4 para 8 SS(C&P) Regs
15 Reg 6(24) and (25) SS(C&P) Regs
16 Reg 6(1)(a) SS(C&P) Regs
17 Regs 6(1) and 4(7) SS(C&P) Regs
18 Reg 7(1)-(7) SFM&FE

Regs
19 Reg 7(1)(a)(i) and (ii) SFM&FE Regs
20 Reg 7(1)(e) SFM&FE Regs
21 Reg 7(1)(b) SFM&FE Regs
22 Reg 7(1)(c) SFM&FE Regs
23 Reg 7(1)(e) SFM&FE Regs
24 Reg 7(1)(e)(i) SFM&FE Regs
25 Reg 7(1)(e)(ii) SFM&FE Regs
26 Reg 7(1)(e)(iii) and (iv) SFM&FE Regs
27 Reg 7(1)(e)(i) and (2) SFM&FE Regs
28 Reg 7(1)(e)(ii) SFM&FE Regs
29 Reg 7(3) SFM&FE Regs
30 Reg 7(3) and (4) SFM&FE Regs
31 Reg 7(6) SFM&FE Regs
32 Reg 7(7) SFM&FE Regs
33 Reg 3(1) SFM&FE Regs
34 Reg 3(1) SFM&FE Regs
35 Reg 3(1) SFM&FE Regs
36 Reg 3(1) SFM&FE Regs
37 Reg 3(1) SFM&FE Regs
38 Reg 3(1A) SFM&FE Regs
39 Reg 7A(1) and (5) SFM&FE Regs
40 Reg 7A(2) SFM&FE Regs
41 Reg 7A(4) SFM&FE Regs
42 Reg 7A(2)(g) SFM&FE Regs

43 Reg 7A(5)(b) SFM&FE Regs
44 paras 3136 SFG
45 Reg 8(2) SFM&FE Regs
46 Reg 8(1) SFM&FE Regs
47 Reg 9(1) SFM&FE Regs
48 Reg 9(2) SFM&FE Regs
49 Reg 9(3)(b) SFM&FE Regs
50 Reg 9(3)(a) SFM&FE Regs
51 Reg 9(3)(c) SFM&FE Regs
52 R(IS) 14/91
53 R(IS) 12/93
54 Reg 8(1)(e) SFM&FE Regs
55 Reg 19 and Sch 4 para 9 SS(C&P) Regs
56 Reg 6(24) and (25) SS(C&P) Regs
57 Regs 6(1) and 4(7) SS(C&P) Regs
58 Reg 35(2) SS(C&P) Regs
59 Reg 7(2) SFM&FE Regs
60 CIS/616/1990
61 s78(4) SSAA 1992; R(SB) 18/84
62 Reg 2(1)(a) SFCWP Regs
63 Reg 1A SFCWP Regs
64 Reg 1A(i) SFCWP Regs
65 Reg 1(2) SFCWP Regs
66 Sch 1 SFCWP Regs
67 Reg 3 SFCWP Regs
68 SFCWP Regs; para 104 CWPH
69 paras 500-511 CWPH
70 paras 603 and 701-04 CWPH

PART SEVEN: THE DISCRETIONARY SOCIAL FUND

Chapter 22: General principles
(pp422-433)

1 s167 SSAA 1992
2 s140(1) and (2) SSCBA 1992
3 s140(2)-(4) SSCBA 1992
4 SF(App) Regs; SF(AR) Regs; SF(RDB) Regs; SF(Misc) Regs
5 s140(2) SSCBA 1992
6 paras 1043, 3011, 3705, 4055 and 5011 SFG
7 paras 1045, 3702, 4351 and 5011 SFG
8 paras 3704 and 4355 SFG
9 para 2147 SFG
10 s64(3) SSAA 1992; SF Dir 41
11 SF Dir 41(b)
12 SF Dir 41(c)
13 s140(5) SSCBA 1992; para 2145 SFG
14 s168 SSAA 1992
15 SF Dir 41
16 para 2144 SFG
17 SF Dir 42
18 s168(3)(c) and (d) SSAA 1992
19 s140(1)(e) SSCBA 1992
20 SF Dir 40
21 paras 2122 and 2124 SFG
22 paras 2124-25 SFG
23 para 1027 SFG
24 paras 1080-1103 SFG
25 SF Dirs 12, 23 and 29
26 paras 4214-15 SFG
27 para 4216 SFG
28 CSB/1482/1985; para 4225 SFG; Advice Notes 7 and 13; *R v SFI ex parte Connick*, 8

June 1993 (unreported)
29 para 4226 SFG
30 para 4228 SFG
31 para 4229 SFG
32 Advice Note 1
33 SF Dirs 12(o), 23(2)(f) and 29(d)
34 paras 3139 and 4218 SFG
35 SF Dir 29
36 SF Dir 28(a)
37 SF Dir 12(n)
38 SF Dir 10
39 SF Dir 23
40 s138(1)(b) SSCBA 1992
41 paras 3124 and 4201 SFG
42 *R v SFI ex parte Harper*
43 paras 3125 and 4202 SFG
44 paras 3129-30 and 4206-07 SFG
45 paras 3136 and 4213 SFG
46 SF Dir 17(b), (c) and (d)
47 SF Dir 17(b) and (c)
48 SF Dir 17(e)
49 para 7068 SFG
50 SF Dirs 18 and 20
51 SF Dir 26
52 SF Dir 8(1)(b)
53 SF Dir 17

Chapter 23: Community care grants
(pp434-442)

1 SF Dir 6
2 SF Dir 25(1) and (2)(a)
3 SF Dir 25(2)(b)
4 SF Dir 25(3)
5 para 7002 SFG
6 Advice Note 5
7 Advice Note 11
8 SF Dir 27
9 SF Dir 27(2)
10 SF Dir 27(2)
11 SF Dir 27(3)
12 para 3752 SFG

13 s140(1)(b) SSCBA 1992; Advice Note 10
14 SF Dir 28(b)
15 SF Dir 4
16 para 3011 SFG
17 para 3709 SFG
18 para 3710 SFG
19 paras 3704, 3710 and 3713 SFG
20 paras 3707-08 SFG
21 Advice Note 16
22 para 3706 SFG; Advice Note 16
23 para 3800 SFG
24 SF Dir 28
25 Advice Note 1
26 para 3622 SFG
27 SF Dir 4(a)(i)
28 paras 3231-3311 SFG
29 *R v The SFI ex parte Fatima Ahmed Mohammed, The Times,* 25 November 1992
30 Advice Note 9
31 *R v Secretary of State for Social Security ex parte Healey, The Times,* 22 April 1991
32 para 3203 SFG
33 *R v The SFI ex parte Sherwin, The Times,* 23 February 1990
34 para 3201 SFG
35 para 3208 SFG
36 *R v The SFI ex parte Ibrahim,* 9 November 1993
37 para 3207 SFG
38 Advice Note 13
39 SF Dir 4(a)(ii)
40 para 3351 SFG
41 para 3351 SFG
42 paras 3353-54 SFG
43 para 3363 SFG
44 Advice Note 13
45 paras 3455-67 SFG
46 SF Dir 4(a)(iii)
47 para 3500 SFG
48 para 3502 SFG

49 *R v Secretary of State for Social Security ex parte Healey, The Times,* 22 April 1991
50 para 3503 SFG
51 Advice Note 12
52 Advice Note 13
53 SF Dir 4(b)
54 paras 3665-68 SFG
55 para 3652 SFG
56 paras 3670-72 SFG

Chapter 24: Loans
(pp443-452)

1 SF Dir 5
2 para 4000 SFG
3 SF Dir 8(1)(a)
4 SF Dir 8(3)
5 Reg 46(1) JSA Regs
6 Reg 48(1) JSA Regs
7 SF Dir 8(1)(c)
8 SF Dir 8(2)
9 para 4101 SFG
10 para 4102 SFG
11 para 4104 SFG
12 SF Dir 2
13 SF Dir 10
14 SF Dir 11
15 para 4055 SFG
16 paras 4356-58 SFG
17 paras 4355 and 4363 SFG
18 SF Dir 10
19 para 4603 SFG
20 SF Dir 11
21 SF Dir 14(a)
22 SF Dirs 15-17
23 SF Dir 22
24 SF Dir 21; para 5553 SFG
25 SF Dir 14(b)
26 SF Dir 3(a)
27 SF Dir 3(b)
28 SF Dir 15
29 SF Dir 16(a)
30 SF Dir 16(b)
31 para 5205 SFG
32 SF Dir 17(b) and (c)
33 paras 7054 and 7071

SFG
34 para 5051 SFG
35 para 5052 SFG
36 paras 5053-105 SFG
37 para 5107 SFG
38 para 5108 SFG
39 para 5053 SFG
40 para 5104 SFG
41 para 5502 SFG
42 paras 5420-22 SFG
43 para 5423 SFG
44 para 5416 SFG
45 paras 5424-25 SFG
46 paras 5429-33 SFG
47 paras 5417-19 SFG
48 paras 5413 and 5427 SFG
49 para 5428 SFG
50 SF Dir 3(b)
51 para 5409 SFG
52 SF Dirs 18, 20 and 21
53 SF Dir 22
54 SF Dir 21
55 SF Dir 18
56 paras 7062 and 7077 SFG
57 paras 7054 and 7071 SFG
58 s78(1) and (2) SSAA 1992
59 para 4003 SFDRG
60 para 4004 SFDRG
61 para 4013 SFDRG
62 para 4014 SFDRG
63 para 4015 SFDRG
64 para 4019 SFDRG
65 Reg 3 SF(RDB) Regs
66 Reg 3(a) and (c) SF(RDB) Regs
67 *Mulvey v Secretary of State,* 13 March 1977; *R v Secretary of State ex parte Taylor and Chapman, The Times,* 5 February 1996; s78(3A) and (3B) SSAA 1992
68 s78(3)(a) SSAA 1992
69 s78(3)(b) SSAA 1992
70 s78(3)(c) SSAA 1992

71 para 4054 SFDRG
72 para 11001 SFDRG
73 paras 4040 and 11029 SFDRG

Chapter 25: Applications, payments and reviews
(pp453-463)

1 Reg 2(1) and (2) SF(App) Regs
2 Reg 2(5) SF(App) Regs
3 Reg 2(4) SF(App) Regs
4 para 4104 SFG
5 Reg 3(a) SF(App) Regs
6 Reg 3(b) SF(App) Regs
7 para 1046 SFG
8 para 2100 SFG
9 para 2101 SFG
10 paras 2103-05 SFG
11 paras 3015, 4056 and 5012 SFG
12 paras 3017, 4060 and 5018 SFG
13 paras 3022, 4065 ad 5021 SFG
14 paras 3023-27, 4066-70 and 5022-26 SFG
15 paras 3027, 4070 and 5026 SFG
16 para 1046 SFG
17 s140(4)(a) SSCBA 1992; SF Dir 7
18 s140(4)(a) SSCBA 1992; Advice Note 8
19 paras 3100, 4150 and 5300 SFG
20 Advice Note 17
21 Advice Note 17
22 s140(4)(a) SSCBA 1992
23 SF Dir 7(b)
24 Advice Note 17
25 para 2062 SFG
26 para 2061 SFG
27 para 4003 SFCADG
28 s138(3) SSCBA 1992
29 para 7052 SFG
30 s66 SSAA 1992; SF Dir 31

31 s66 SSAA 1992; SFI Directions
32 s66(1)(a) SSAA 1992; para 8052 SFG
33 Reg 2(1) and (2)(a) SF(AR) Regs
34 Reg 2(4) SF(AR) Regs
35 Reg 2(6) SF(AR) Regs
36 Reg 2(3) SF(AR) Regs
37 Reg 2(5) SF(AR) Regs
38 SF Dir 37
39 SF Dir 31
40 s66(1)(b) SSAA 1992
41 *R v SFO ex parte Hewson* (HC), 22 June 1995
42 s66(6) SSAA 1992
43 SF Dir 39
44 SF Dir 32
45 SF Dir 33
46 SF Dir 33
47 SF Dir 34
48 para 8500 SFG
49 SF Dir 35
50 SF Dir 36; para 8600 SFG
51 s66(3) SSAA 1992
52 Reg 2(1) and (2)(b) SF(AR) Regs
53 Reg 2(4) SF(AR) Regs
54 Reg 2(6) SF(AR) Regs
55 Reg 2(3) SF(AR) Regs
56 para 5004 SFROG
57 paras 5006-07 SFROG
58 s66(6) and (7) SSAA 1992; SFI Dirs 1 and 2
59 *R v IRS ex parte Connell* (QBD) 3 November 1994
60 *R v SFI ex parte Ledicott* (QBD) reported 24 May 1995
61 para 9013 SFG
62 s66(4) SSAA 1992
63 s66(5) SSAA 1992
64 SF Dir 38; paras 8753-55 SFG

PART EIGHT: HEALTH SERVICE BENEFITS

Chapter 26: Health service benefits
(pp466-479)

1 Reg 6(2) NHS(TERC) Regs
2 Reg 6 and Sch 1 Part II NHS(TERC) Regs
3 Sch 1 para 1 and Table A NHS(TERC) Regs
4 Reg 6(5) NHS(TERC) Regs
5 Reg 7(1A) NHS(TERC) Regs
6 Reg 7(6) and Sch 1A NHS(TERC) Regs
7 Reg 4 NHS(TERC) Regs; regs 3-7 NHS(CDA) Regs
8 Reg 7 NHS(CDA) Regs; *R v Secretary of State for Health ex parte Cyril Richardson*, Case C-137/94
9 Reg 9 NHS(CDA) Regs
10 Reg 8(2) NHS(TERC) Regs
11 Reg 8 NHS(CDA) Regs
12 Regs 3 and 4 NHS(TERC) Regs
13 Reg 5(1), (2) and (3) NHS(TERC) Regs
14 Reg 8 NHS(TERC) Regs
15 Reg 13 NHS(GOS) Regs
16 Reg 3 NHS(OCP) Regs
17 Reg 8(2) NHS(OCP) Regs
18 Regs 9(4) and 16 NHS(OCP) Regs
19 Reg 12(1) NHS(OCP) Regs
20 Regs 3, 4 and 5 NHS(TERC) Regs

21 Regs 3, 4, 5 and 5A NHS(TERC) Regs
22 Regs 3-5 WF Regs
23 Reg 14(3) WF Regs
24 Reg 15 WF Regs
25 Reg 13(4) WF Regs
26 Reg 12 WF Regs
27 Reg 14(2) WF Regs
28 Reg 18 WF Regs
29 Reg 7 WF Regs
30 Reg 8 WF Regs
31 Reg 5 WF Regs

Index

How to use this index

Because the *Handbook* is divided into separate sections covering the different benefits, many entries in the index have several references, each to a different section. Where this occurs, we use the following abbreviations to show which benefit each reference relates to:

(IS)	Income support	(CCB)	Community charge benefit
(FC)	Family credit	(CTB)	Council tax benefit
(DWA)	Disability working allowance	(RSF)	Regulated social fund
(HB)	Housing benefit	(SF)	Social fund

References to common provisions appear first in the sequence. We list individual references in the order above, which reflects the order of the sections of the *Handbook*.

Entries against the bold headings direct you to the general information on the subject, or where the subject is covered most fully. Sub-entries are listed alphabetically and direct you to specific aspects of the subject.

Business Start-up Allowance 359

C

caecostomy
  free prescriptions 470
calculation
  council tax benefit 302
  disability working allowance 205
  family credit 191
  housing benefit 247-50
  income support 24-5
campsite fees
  (HB) 228
  (IS) 26
capital 384-407
  back to work bonus 177
  budgeting loans 444
  capital treated as income 376-7, 396
  child's 345, 376, 385, 403
    (DWA) 204
    (FC) 191
  community care grants 435
  council tax benefit 300, 306
  definition 386
  deprivation of capital 397-9
  diminishing capital rule 399-401
    (HB) 285
    (IS) 151
  disability working allowance 200
  disregards 390-7
  expenses of sale 404
  family credit 185
  fixed-term investments 386
  health service benefits 468
  housing benefit 214
  income treated as capital 375, 389-90
  instalments 376, 394
  jointly owned 405
  limit for claiming 384
  loans 387
  maintenance payments 118-20
  matrimonial assets 405-6
  non-dependant
    (CTB) 306
    (HB) 255
  notional capital 397-403
  overpayments arising from
    (HB) 282
    (IS) 151
  partner's 385
  property 386
  residential care
    (IS) 84

    (IS/HB) 385
  savings 386
  tariff income 375-6
  third party payments 402
  trade dispute
    (IS) 61
  treatment of capital for urgent cases
  payments 48
  trusts 387-8
  valuation 404-7
  withdrawals 377
capital mortgage payments
  (IS) 33
care
  claiming for young person in care
    (IS/HB/CTB) 326
  community care grants 434
  treatment of payments to young people
  leaving care 376, 379, 395-6
career development loans
  treated as income 371
carers
  (IS) 15
  claiming
    (FC/DWA) 187
  entitlement to IS 11
  hours of work 15
  housing costs waiting period
    (IS) 42
  not a non-dependant
    (CTB) 305
    (HB) 253
    (IS) 37
  treatment of wages 382
carer's premium
  (IS/HB/CTB) 332, 342-3
  and severe disability premium 342
  while partner cared for in hospital 96
  while person cared for in hospital 95
**certificates for free or partial remission of
health charges** 469
changing which partners claim
  (HB) 265
  (IS) 123
changing your claim
  (DWA) 206
  (FC) 193
  (HB) 266
  (IS) 124
charitable payments 372-4, 396
  deduction from funeral payments 417
  payment direct to mortgagor
    (IS) 33
  trade disputes
    (IS) 61

full-time work *(cont.)*
  (FC/DWA) 186-9
  (IS) 13, 355
  non-dependants
    (HB) 254
funeral expenses payments 413-18
  claim form 418
  time limits for claiming 417
funerals
  travel to relative's funeral - community
  care grant 442
furniture
  budgeting loans 445
  community care grant 440
  community care grants 439
further review
  (CTB) 314
  (HB) 293
  (SF) 461-3
future interest in property 394
future payments 394

G

garage
  (HB) 228
Gas
  see: fuel charges
gay couple
  claiming 319
    (CTB) 304
  (HB) 216, 265
  (IS) 122
George Cross payments 379
gifts
  from relative, deduction from funeral
  expenses payment 417
  lump sum maintenance payments
    (IS) 118-21
giro
  (HB) 273
  (IS) 135
  lost, stolen or missing
    (IS/FC/DWA/HB) 138
    (SF) 449
  replacement
    (IS) 135
  time limit for cashing
    (IS) 135
glasses 473-5
glaucoma
  free sight tests 473
good cause
  for late claim
    (CTB) 310

    (FC) 193
  (HB) 223, 268
  (IS) 127
grant, repairs 391
grant, student 369-71
  disregards 369-70
  parental contribution 369
ground rent
  (IS) 26
guardian's allowance 365

H

habitual residence test
  (HB) 223
  (IS) 9, 22, 63, 69-72
  definition 69-70
  EEA citizens 73
  persons from abroad
    (IS) 64
  refugees 76
halls of residence
  (HB) 262
hardship
  avoiding student rent deduction
    (HB) 264
  recovery of overpayment
    (HB) 284
  rent restrictions
    (HB) 240
hardship payments 54-5
health benefits 466-79
heating
  see: fuel charges
higher pensioner premium
  (IS/HB/CTB) 332, 336-7
  earnings disregards 358
  qualifying benefits
    (IS/HB/CTB) 334
  qualifying for DWA 202
  temporary absence from GB
    (IS) 22
hire purchase agreement
  (HB) 222
  (IS) 26
holiday pay 350
  on leaving work 350
    (FC/DWA) 356
    (HB/CTB) 356
    (IS) 355
  trade dispute 350
    (IS) 61
  treatment 389
  unpaid holidays 449

lay off
absence from work
(FC/DWA) 188
learning difficulties
definition for residential care
(IS) 87
leaseholders
rent/ground rent
(IS) 26
service charges
(IS) 26
treatment of income from subletting a
property 374
leaving a job
payments 354-7
(FC/DWA) 356
(HB/CTB) 356-7
(IS) 348, 350
redundancy payments 354
legal aid
appealing to the courts
(HB) 297
(IS/FC/DWA) 173
legal fees
excluded from SF help 428
lesbian couple
claims 319
(HB) 216, 265
(IS) 122
liability to pay housing costs
(IS) 26-7
liability to pay rent
(HB) 215
liable relatives
maintenance payments 113-14
payments for - effect on health benefits
468
recovery of SF loan 452
licensee
not a non-dependant
(IS) 37
payments, counted as rent 228
(HB) 214
life insurance 393
life interest 394
lifeboat crew
(IS) 15
treatment of payments 358, 389
urgent cases payments 48
liferent (Scotland) 394
loans
educational 370-1
end of trade dispute
(IS) 61-3
from employer 351, 387

repair/improvement loans 391
(IS) 34-5
secured on your home
(IS) 31
SF loans 443-52
local reference rent
(HB) 235
lodgers 374
lone parent:
see: single parent
lone parent premium
(IS/HB/CTB) 332, 333
long lease
exclusion from HB 221
lost payments
(DWA) 209
(FC) 195
(IS) 138
(SF) 449
low income
entitlement to health benefits 466-9
low-paid work 382
lump sum payments of maintenance
(IS) 118-21
health benefit entitlement 468

M
Macfarlane Trust
(CTB) 308
(IS) 61
(SF) 449
treatment of 372, 382, 396, 402
maintenance 101-21
absent parent required to pay 103
arrears of periodical payments 116-18
benefit penalty 110-12
calculating maintenance 103
child maintenance bonus 177-83
Child Support Agency 105
child support scheme 114-15
effect on benefits
(IS) 113-21
fear of violence 107
liability for maintenance 103-5
liable relatives 113-14
lump sums 118-21
periodical payments 116-18
required to apply 106
market rent (old scheme)
(HB) 244
market value (assessing capital) 404
maternity
(during) trade dispute
(SF) 63

maternity *(cont.)*
  free dental treatment 471
  free milk tokens 478
  free prescriptions 470
maternity allowance 365
  SF loan repayments 452
maternity expenses payment 410-13
  claim form 412-13
  time limits for claiming 412
maternity leave
  (FC/DWA) 188
  non-dependants
    (HB) 254
maternity pay 350
maximum amount of benefit
  (CTB) 303
  (DWA) 204
  (FC) 191
  (HB) 247
maximum rent
  (HB) 238
meals
  deductions from benefit
    (HB) 231-2
medical treatment
  excluded from SF help 428
  housing costs
    (IS) 28
  taking child abroad
    (IS) 23, 324, 327
mentally ill
  (IS) 97
  authorising someone to act on your behalf
    (HB) 265-6
    (IS) 123
  definition for residential care
    (IS) 87
mesne profits
  (HB) 228
meters, fuel, installations/resiting of
  budgeting loans 445
  community care grant 440
method of payment
  (CTB) 311
  (DWA) 209
  (FC) 195
  (HB) 273
  (IS) 135
  (SF) 457
milk tokens 478-9
  treatment 380, 395
minimum amount of benefit
  (CTB) 303
  (DWA) 209

  (FC) 192
  (HB) 247
  (IS) 135
MIRAS
  mortgage payments outside of scheme
    (IS) 33
misrepresentation
  (HB) 287
  (IS/FC/HB) 149-51
missing payments
  (DWA) 209
  (FC) 195
  (IS) 138
  (SF) 449
mobility allowance
  treatment as income 366
mobility supplement
  qualifying for premiums
    (IS/HB/CTB) 334
  treatment as income 366
mortgage payments
  (IS) 30-4
  arrears
    (IS) 141, 147
  capital repayments
    (IS) 33
  excessive costs
    (IS) 38-41
  increasing or taking out a second mortgage
    (IS) 31
  ineligible for HB 221
  interest payments
    (IS) 33-4, 378
  mortgage direct payments
    (IS) 140-1
  overpayments of mortgage direct 146-7
  reduced payment during first weeks of claim
    (IS) 41-3
  seperate room for boys and girls
    (IS) 33
  transitional protection
    (IS) 43-4
  valuation of land 404
mortgage protection policy
  (HB/CTB) 379
  (IS) 26, 41
  refusal to make mortgage payments
    (IS) 42
moving home
  budgeting loans 445
  community care grants 439, 442
  extended payment of HB/CTB 251
  liability for housing costs before moving in
    (IS) 28

Rights Guide to Non-Means-Tested Benefits 1997/98

20th edition

This companion volume to the *National Welfare Benefits Handbook* is fully revised and updated to give clear, practical guidance on non-means-tested benefits. It is fully indexed and cross-referenced to social security law, regulations and official guidance, and also to Court and Commissioners' decisions.

This edition includes:
- expanded coverage of disability living allowance and attendance allowance
- the latest on incapacity benefit, particularly appeals and challenging decisions
- new rules for backdating of claims and reviews
- developments on equal treatment for women and men
- maternity pay and benefits
- how the contributions system works, and changes in rules on the calculation of earnings
- statutory sick pay, pensions and benefits for widows
- industrial injuries and diseases
- benefits administration and new rules on appeals

There is some basic information on unemployment benefits, with full details of contribution-based JSA contained in the new *Jobseeker's Allowance Handbook*.

The *Rights Guide* is widely recognised as the authoritative guide to non-means-tested benefits and how to claim them.

April 1997   **0 946744 93 9**   **£8.95**

(£3.00 for individual benefit claimants—direct from CPAG)

One copy sent automatically to CPAG Rights and Comprehensive members.

Send a cheque/PO for £8.95 (incl p&p) to CPAG Ltd, 1-5 Bath St, London EC1V 9PY

Jobseeker's Allowance Handbook

2nd edition: Richard Poynter & Martin Barnes

This handbook is fully updated, restructured and expanded in its coverage of jobseeker's allowance. It replaces *Benefits Handbook* coverage of income support for unemployed claimants and *Rights Guide* information on unemployment benefit. It can be used as a 'stand-alone' guide, but is also designed to be an integrated part of the CPAG benefits package for 1997/98 along with the *National Welfare Benefits Handbook, Rights Guide* and *Welfare Rights Bulletin*.

The *Jobseeker's Allowance Handbook* explains the Act and latest regulations including:

- expanded coverage of 'labour market conditions' – availability and actively seeking work
- the Jobseeker's Agreement
- contributory and income-based JSA, including treatment of income and capital
- benefit sanctions
- hardship payments
- special groups – students, 16 and 17 year olds and people with disabilities
- fraud
- deductions from JSA
- new rules on backdating and claiming JSA
- the adjudication process and appeals

The *Jobseeker's Allowance Handbook* is fully indexed and cross referenced to law, regulations and official guidance – as well as to its companion volumes. It is authoritative, accessible and geared to the needs of both claimants and advisers.

April 1997   **0 946744 95 5**   **£6.95**

(£2.50 for individual benefit claimants – direct from CPAG)

Send a cheque/PO for £6.95 (incl p&p) to CPAG Ltd, 1-5 Bath St, London EC1V 9PY

Welfare Rights Bulletin

The *Bulletin* is essential reading for welfare rights advisers, lawyers and anyone needing to keep up-to-date with social security issues. One of its unique roles is to provide a bi-monthly update to the *National Welfare Benefits Handbook* and *Rights Guide*, as well as to CPAG's *Jobseeker's Allowance Handbook* and *Child Support Handbook*.

Contents will include the fullest coverage of:

- the jobseeker's allowance, HB changes, incapacity benefit, back to work benefits and pilot schemes, the DSS Change Programme, fraud measures, child support et al
- new regulations, guidance and procedure, with comment, analysis and practical advice
- Social Security Commissioners' decisions
- Court decisions, including the latest test cases
- reports on benefit law and service delivery issues – eg, Chief Adjudication Officer, Parliamentary and advisory committees, ombudsmen
- news from welfare rights workers – campaigns, issues and tactics

Like the CPAG benefit guides, the **Welfare Rights Bulletin** is the best value in the field – and compulsory reading for any adviser needing the very latest benefits information.

£21.00 for a full year's subscription (6 issues)

ISSN 0263 2098

Sent automatically to CPAG Rights and Comprehensive members, and Bulletin subscribers.

To subscribe, send a cheque/PO for £21 to CPAG, 1-5 Bath St, London EC1V 9PY – or write for details of Rights and Comprehensive membership

AS A RIGHTS MEMBER OF CPAG YOU RECEIVE AUTOMATICALLY:

- *National Welfare Benefits Handbook* and the *Rights Guide* – rushed to you hot off the press
- 6 issues of the *Bulletin* – keeping you up-to-date with benefit changes all year round
- CPAG's *Poverty* journal – the facts and figures, the people and policies in the fight against poverty
- special offers on other welfare rights publications

Send £46.00 (cheques/POs payable to CPAG) to:
CPAG, Dept RM, 1-5 Bath Street. London EC1V 9PY
(this is for new members only – if you are already a Rights member, please wait for your renewal form from CPAG)

Child Support Handbook 1997/98

5th edition: Emma Knights & Simon Cox

The new *Child Support Handbook* is essential for advisers as it incorporates the latest regulation changes, the new and completely rewritten CSA guidance manuals and extensive new case law

Changes covered in this edition include:

- full details of the new system of departure from the formula
- the increased benefit penalty
- new requirement to co-operate procedures
- substantial changes to appeals
- the new April maintenance bonus for income support claimants
- the role of the new Independent Case Examiner in dealing with complaints

It includes coverage of: what the key terms mean, who is affected and how to apply for maintenance; the powers of the CSA to pursue maintenance and seek information; the requirement to co-operate for parents with care on benefit, the good cause exemption, the right to refuse to co-operate and the benefit penalty; how the formula for calculating maintenance payment works; collection and enforcement.

There are practical examples, and tactical hints and arguments for use when seeking exemption, withdrawal of applications, review or appeal. Fully indexed and cross-referenced to legislation, case law and to its companion volumes, the CPAG benefit guides. The *Child Support Handbook* is the standard guide for claimants and other parents affected, solicitors, welfare rights advisers, CABx, social workers, women's' groups and children's charities.

'*A practical guide for parents and advisers*' – The Independent
'*It is hard to beat the CPAG guide … it is outstanding value for money. It is clearly written and easy to find your way around … invaluable for advisers*' – New Law Journal
'*Gives a thorough explanation of the system*' – Woman's Own

May 1997   **0 946744 94 7**   **£9.95**
(*£3.30 for individual claimants – direct from CPAG*)

Send a cheque/PO for £9.95 (incl p&p) to CPAG Ltd, 1-5 Bath St, London EC1V 9PY

CPAG COURSES

CPAG courses provide comprehensive rights training, and detailed coverage of up-to-the minute legislative changes. Our tutors are expert in their area of work and draw on the extensive training experience of the Citizens' Rights Office.

CPAG training ranges from Introductory level to courses for advisers with more knowledge of the issues involved. Our current programme includes: a large range of day courses, a series of post-election seminars and a programme of half-day lawyers courses; issues covered include: Benefit Agency Change Programme, Reviews and Appeals, Jobseekers and Back-to-Work Post-Election. Other courses: Jobseeker's Allowance, Income Support Housing Costs, Lobbying in Europe, Working with the Media, Benefits for Young People, Introduction to the Child Support Scheme, Habitual Residence Test, Disability Benefits, Dealing with Debt, Community Care, Immigration Law and Social Security, Disability Appeal Tribunals and Medical Appeal Tribunals, Housing Benefit Review Boards, Commissioners' Appeals, Parliamentary Procedure & Lobbying, EC Social Security Law, Training for Trainers and our week long Welfare Rights Advocacy Courses. **CPAG's Welfare Rights for Franchising Lawyers has been chosen by the Law Society as the approved course for all lawyers needing to qualify for legal aid work.**

Our courses can also be tailored to meet the needs of specific groups, including those not normally concerned with welfare rights. To assess your training needs, we are happy to discuss your requirements for 'in-house' training to meet the internal needs of your organisation. For further information, contact Judy Allen at the address given below.

FEES:	*Lawyers*	*Statutory Organisations*	*Voluntary Organisations*
One-day	£190	£130	£85
Two-day	£250	£190	£160
Three-day	£270	£230	£200
Week-long	£390	£310	£230

Most of CPAG's courses are Law Society accredited and carry continuing education points.

For a full programme please contact Judy Allen, Training Administrator, Child Poverty Action Group, 1–5 Bath Street, London EC1V 9PY Tel: (0171) 253 3406; Fax: (0171) 490 0561.

Migration and Social Security Handbook: a rights guide for people entering and leaving the UK

2nd edition

Formerly known as the Ethnic Minorities' Benefits Handbook, this guide is unique in bridging the gap between benefits and immigration advisers. Developments since the first edition (1993) mean that there has never been a greater need for this handbook.

This expanded edition has been extensively revised, re-written and re-structured to give advisers quick access to clear, reliable and up-to date information. There is detailed coverage of all significant changes affecting persons from abroad, including new rules for migrants and the latest on the habitual residence test. The rules relating to asylum seekers are explained, with practical examples and arguments that advisers can use.

The handbook gives comprehensive guidance to social security entitlements as they apply to anyone entering or leaving the UK, with particular emphasis on the provisions most likely to affect ethnic minority claimants. All new and recent benefit changes are covered, such as JSA and the 1996 changes to disability benefits and child benefit. For the increasing numbers of people living, working and claiming benefits in various EC countries, there are details about claiming benefits abroad and transporting benefits between the EC and the UK.

The **Handbook** presents:

* detailed guidance on immigration law, written for welfare rights and other advisers
* a guide to social security benefits, interweaving benefits and immigration issues throughout
* a guide to EC law as it affects social security and immigration.

Fully indexed and cross-referenced to relevant legislation and decisions.

For all advisers whose clients include: non-EC immigrants, members of ethnic minorities in the UK, EC citizens in the UK and UK citizens in other EC countries.

'At JCWI we have often noticed a large gap between immigration and benefits advice, yet our clients often quite rightly demand both. This book bridges that gap in one volume for the first time ... The real achievement of the book is the way in which immigration and benefits advice have been interwoven throughout' – Claude Moraes, Director, Joint Council for the Welfare of Immigrants.

Spring 1997   **0 946744 87 4**   **£10.95**

Send a cheque/PO for £10.95 (incl p&p) to CPAG Ltd, 1-5 Bath St, London EC1V 9PY

NOTES

NOTES

NOTES

NOTES

NOTES

NOTES

NOTES

NOTES

NOTES

NOTES

NOTES